ETHNIC CLEANSING AND THE INDIAN

Also by Gary Clayton Anderson

Kinsmen of Another Kind: Dakota-White Relations in the Upper Mississippi Valley, 1650–1862 (Lincoln, Nebr., 1984; St. Paul, 1997)

Little Crow, Spokesman for the Sioux (St. Paul, 1986)

(Edited with Alan R. Woolworth) *Through Dakota Eyes: Narrative Accounts of the Minnesota Indian War of 1862* (St. Paul, 1988)

Sitting Bull and the Paradox of Lakota Nationhood (New York, 1996)

The Indian Southwest, 1580–1830: Ethnogenesis and Cultural Reinvention (Norman, Okla., 1999)

Conquest of Texas: Ethnic Cleansing in the Promised Land, 1820–1875 (Norman, Okla., 2005)

Power and Promise: The Changing American West (New York, 2008)

Will Rogers and "His" America (Boston, 2011)

ETHNIC CLEANSING AND THE INDIAN

The Crime That Should Haunt America

Gary Clayton Anderson

University of Oklahoma Press : Norman

Library of Congress Cataloging-in-Publication Data

Anderson, Gary Clayton, 1948–
Ethnic cleansing and the Indian : The crime that should
haunt America/ Gary Clayton Anderson.
pages cm
Includes bibliographical references and index.
ISBN 978-0-8061-4421-4 (hardcover : alk. paper)
1. Indians of North America—Crimes against. 2. Indians, Treatment of—
North America—History. 3. Genocide—United States—History. 4. Forced
migrations—United States—History. 5. United States—Ethnic relations.
6. United States—Politics and government. I. Title.
E98.C87A63 2014
970.004'97—dc23   2013024354

The paper in this book meets the guidelines for permanence and durability
of the Committee on Production Guidelines for Book Longevity of the
Council on Library Resources, Inc. ∞

1 2 3 4 5 6 7 8 9 10

CONTENTS

ACKNOWLEDGMENTS

Many years ago, while my colleagues and I were at lunch at Texas A&M University, someone brought up the growing problems in what was then Yugoslavia. The dictator Marshal Josip Broz Tito had recently died, and the Europeanists at the table feared the growing instability in the country would eventually lead to ethnic violence. Within a few months, Serbians, Croatians, and Kosovars were fighting, starting what became one of the most vicious periods of refugee flight and murder that Europe had experienced since the Second World War. As a result of the conflict, "ethnic cleansing" entered the American vernacular. Although many of Yugoslavia's ethnically diverse people had lived side by side for years, nationalistic agendas soon led to a general belief that certain border regions should be wholly Croatian, wholly Serbian, or part of Kosovo.

As I sat and listened to my colleagues that day, the similarities with Texas history suddenly struck me. During the nineteenth century, Anglo-Texans forced many Hispanic families to flee South, even back into Mexico, and, perhaps worse, Anglo-Texans attacked Indian villages, the homes of the "first Texans," with the general hope that the Natives would flee somewhere to the west or into Indian Territory, which the federal government had supposedly set aside specifically for Indians. Out of many discussions with colleagues that followed came a book, *The Conquest of Texas: Ethnic Cleansing in the Promised Land, 1820–1875.* The book attracted considerable notice, was a finalist for the Pulitzer Prize, and was even reviewed in the *New York Review of Books* (September 2006) by Larry McMurtry, whose fiction does much to preserve the mythology of the early development of Texas.

Having taught a course entitled "American Indian History" for nearly forty years, I soon realized that the story of Texas was little different from those elsewhere in North America. Early Europeans forced the Powhatan Indians from the best lands in Virginia, the Pequots fled from ancestral river valleys in central Connecticut, and Indians to the west of them eventually faced a policy of "Indian Removal." These were crimes that I decided to document in the study that follows.

The reader is forewarned. As an Air Force captain in one of the graduate courses I taught in Germany (War Crimes, Ethnic Cleansing, and Genocide in the Modern World) said on the final day of class, "This course was fascinating but terribly depressing." And so it is: history is often first written by the victors, but ultimately the truth comes out, and it is often, as another historian once said, a grimmer but more interesting story.

Many fellow historians have helped mold this story. Among them were those colleagues in College Station, some of whom are no longer with us. But I still wish to thank that wonderful humanist Robert Calvert for his many thoughts and contributions to my thinking. Often sitting by his side were R. J. Q. Adams, Terry Anderson, Albert Broussard, Walter Buenger, Joseph Dawson, Chester Dunning, and Walter Kamphoefner. It has been so many years that some may not recall the discussions we had, but I do.

After I moved on to the University of Oklahoma, both graduate students and fellow faculty helped formulate a better sense of the definitions that became so crucial to understanding the crime that I have wrestled to define. Paul Gilje, Stephen Norwood, Ben Keppel, Robert Griswold, and Elyssa Faison have all listened to my ramblings, and I thank them for it. Graduate students David La Vere (University of North Carolina, Wilmington), Paul Kelton (University of Kansas), and Jeffrey Means (University of Wyoming) often TA'd in classes where the issues central to this book took shape. Paul ultimately convinced me that I was wrong initially in my views regarding Indian Removal.

Other colleagues at Oklahoma read parts of the manuscript that became this book. They include Raphael Folsom, who has a book coming out on the early history of northwestern Mexico; Garret Olberding and Norman Stillman, both of whom work in fields unrelated to American Indian history. Much closer in terms of research is Albert Hurtado, a consummate western historian (now professor emeritus) who I first met at the Bancroft Library in 1987, and who ultimately joined us at Oklahoma. I am deeply indebted to my colleague David Wrobel, who read several chapters, in particular the section on California, which was the most difficult to develop. Finally, I wish to thank the History Department at Oklahoma, as well as Dean of Arts and Sciences Paul Bell, who provided the financial support to bring in speakers Benedict Kiernan from Yale and Norman Naimark from Stanford, two of the finest scholars of genocide in the world. My private discussions with both gave me the confidence to proceed with the thesis and the book.

Most historians struggle to find a publisher willing to invest time and resources in a study that is on the drawing board. I have been extremely fortunate in having the people at the University of Oklahoma Press consistently support the book from its inception. Director Byron Price and managing editor Steven Baker have both become friends over our many years of discussing history and working together. No historian has a better editor-in-chief than Charles Rankin, who read every chapter, and offered comments, while the work was still in progress. Chuck also convinced Richard White, the Margaret Byrne Professor of History at Stanford, and Roger Nichols, Professor Emeritus of History at the University of Arizona, to serve as readers. Both of them, scholars of the first rank in the field of Native American history, willingly revealed themselves and offered extensive and valuable comments that benefited me enormously.

I can hardly forget to acknowledge a certain anthropologist who has willingly been at my side for some forty-two years of research and writing—my wonderful wife, Laura. And, yes, she has opinions about history—and, yes, I listen and benefit from them. No historian can claim better guidance and assistance than I can.

University of Oklahoma, 2013

ACKNOWLEDGMENTS

ETHNIC CLEANSING AND THE INDIAN

INTRODUCTION

Definitions of Genocide, Crimes against Humanity,
Ethnic Cleansing, and War Crimes in Modern World History

At the close of World War II American troops stumbled onto several sites of horrific atrocities in Germany—the concentration camps where millions had died at the hands of Nazi fanatics. The piles of human remains were so mind-numbing that General Dwight Eisenhower ordered cameramen to take motion pictures. The reels, to be played countless times in later years, brought to mind what British prime minister Winston Churchill had said earlier about the Nazi destruction of entire villages and peoples across Europe: "We are in the presence of a crime without a name."[1]

Not long after the war ended, the United Nations applied the term "genocide" to the events in Europe. The term was invented by Polish refugee Raphael Lemkin. In Articles 2 and 3 of the 1948 UN Convention, genocide is defined as the intentional killing of people because of their "national, ethnical, racial or religious" identity.[2] Following this powerful statement, however, the convention included a host of lesser crimes as acts of genocide, such as "causing serious bodily harm" to the group, "deliberately inflicting on the group conditions of life calculated to bring about its physical destruction," "imposing measures intended to prevent births," and even "forcibly transferring children" from one group to another. Those committing these crimes also were defined in a nebulous way. While "constitutionally responsible rulers" understandably remained at the top of the list, at the bottom the convention included "private individuals" who could be charged. As might be expected given the convention's broad, legally unmanageable definitions, some of which described nothing more than felonies, many countries at the time and for many years thereafter rejected the convention, including the two most powerful in the world, the United States and the Soviet Union. The convention quickly became a dead letter and has never been enforced under its original language.[3]

As world history has evolved since the passing of the convention, many events have transpired that give historians insight into what exactly constitutes genocide. Mass killings entered our political and legal landscapes again in the 1970s with the Cambodian upheaval, and the world became even more attuned to such mass atrocities when Yugoslavia dissolved and when violent killings erupted in Rwanda in the 1990s. Certainly these examples give us a much better sense of how we can describe the policies, and what terminology we can use, in order to make sense of what happened to American Indians. Indeed, it is now increasingly possible to place the issue squarely in the context of world historical events, such as those mentioned above. Looking at it from another viewpoint, how did "Anglo" or "settler" global expansion, as some scholars would term it, impact Native, "aboriginal," or "Indigenous" societies?[4]

Despite a host of studies of Indian–white relations in North America, very few have carefully placed the conflict into the broader themes of world history. Interpretations and teaching reflect two extremes. At one extreme the historian sanitizes the topic to the point of nearly dismissing it. This is certainly the case in modern textbooks. One of the most popular American history surveys fails even to mention the destruction of the Pequots in 1637, barely mentions the ravages of Nathaniel Bacon's forces against peaceful Indians in 1675–76, offers little about Indian roles in the struggle for the Ohio Valley during the French and Indian War and the American Revolution, and devotes just three pages to discussing the Plains Indian wars.[5] At the other extreme, which is generally rejected by most historians, the scholar fashions new labels for these events, derived from the United Nations convention itself but broadening the UN's definitions and suggesting that the Indians' demise was genocide. This leaves professors in university classes wringing their hands when lecturing on the wronged Indian, given that the conflicts with Indians hardly resemble the mass killings of millions that occurred in Europe.

These two extremes leave us in a muddle. Genocide will never become a widely accepted characterization for what happened in North America, because large numbers of Indians survived and because policies of mass murder on a scale similar to events in central Europe, Cambodia, or Rwanda were never implemented. Patrick Wolfe, a historian of genocide, reaches an interesting conclusion: "settler colonialism" of the sort that

surfaced in North America, Africa, and Australia was "inherently eliminatory" when it came to Native peoples, though "not invariably genocidal."
Indeed Wolfe argues that "assimilation" was in essence an "effective mode
of elimination" when applied to Native culture but avoided killing. It also
avoided "a disruptive affront" to the rule of law, so crucial to the cohesion
of Anglo-American settler society.[6] Some historians have concluded that
U.S. Indian policy amounted to "a new colonialism" rather than genocide. But that argument begs the obvious question of what was so "new"
about it, other than the obvious: Americans seemingly promoted the assimilation, or integration, of Indians rather than the blatant exploitation
of them.[7]

What good does it do to pass off such occurrences as "eliminatory" or
even as simply a result of "colonialism," however, when those events constituted a crime? If all the events that make up the history of Indian-white
relations in North America were committed today, many of the actions
entailed in those events would be punishable in the International Criminal
Court (ICC), which meets regularly in The Hague in the Netherlands.
Given new definitions called the Rome Statutes that lawyers crafted between 1998 and 2002, Europeans and later Americans who committed
general acts of dispossession against Indians—or even "eliminatory" acts—
would likely face the charge of "ethnic cleansing" as defined in Article 7,
which has the broad title "Crimes against Humanity." On some occasions
Article 8, "War Crimes," might also apply. Some historians might argue
that Article 6, "Genocide," might apply in certain isolated incidences, but
it is much more difficult to prove this crime. Indeed the ICC has yet to
convict anyone of genocide (only separate nations, such as Estonia, have
used the term in recent convictions of war criminals from World War II).[8]

My basic premise in this book is that the UN–World Court definitions
are universally accepted today and can even be applied to U.S. history.
Some historians might disagree, viewing the World Court and its decisions as far too prescriptive. But if these definitions do not apply, where
do we turn for an understanding of what happened to American Indians?
Previous historians who have attempted to describe the fate of Indians,
sometimes claiming genocide, have often stretched the definition to include what might otherwise be considered war crimes. But most earlier
historians had only the 1948 convention definition to work with, and
it must be admitted that despite its problems the 1948 definition is the
foundation for the evolution of the debate itself. The Rome Statutes rely
heavily upon its words, particularly Article 6.

Of course it would be foolish to "indict" anyone for the events be-ginning in 1492 and ending about 1920. The crimes committed against American Indians have long since passed the bar of "latches," the legal term meaning that they are too old to be prosecuted. My indictment is a moral one, not a legal one. But it is my argument that the best term for what happened to Indians throughout this four-hundred-year period is "ethnic cleansing," not "genocide," as it is defined today.

Even with the new power vested in the World Court by the Rome Statutes, it is important to understand that the definitions adhered to today involve an extraordinarily high level of evidence when indictments are handed down against a government, the rogue element of a government, or even individuals. For genocide (Article 6) to occur, prosecutors must first prove that a "policy" authorizing such an action had been adopted by a government or a governmental agency. This is a high legal bar to cross and requires clear evidence of collusion on the part of government. Convictions for crimes against humanity (Article 7) are much easier, as evidenced by the many convictions of the past decade. Any political leader or government that purposefully creates a circumstance in which masses of people perish—say from starvation, such as in the Soviet Union in the 1930s, '40s, or '50s—can be charged with crimes against humanity. Al-though governments might also be guilty of implementing a "policy" that leads to crimes against humanity—the definition that best fits the events described in this study—individuals may also be tried for such crimes. In-deed a number of individuals have been charged and convicted in recent years. War crimes (Article 8) are an exception. These charges are waged against military units: some are clothed with governmental authority but acting on their own volition, while others can be charged even if taking the form of paramilitary units.[9]

Given the raised bar regarding evidence, President Bill Clinton signed off on the new definitions offered by the Rome Statutes for the United States on December 31, 2000, and sanctioned the work of the ICC, which originally had only a temporary status to investigate war crimes in the former Yugoslavia.[10] This has since changed. The court is now permanent and even has a prosecutor from the United States sitting on it. While the United States Senate rejected the UN Convention of 1948, its rationale for doing so has since disappeared—some United States senators feared at the time that the definition might include the historic "eradication" of Ameri-can Indians or the infliction of "mental harm" on African Americans in the South.[11] Clinton recognized that it would be ludicrous to indict the United States for these past crimes under the new definitions.

Reading past the definition for genocide (Article 6) and deeper into the several pages of Article 7, "Crimes against Humanity," it becomes obvious that its sections most readily fit the acts committed against Indians. Crimes against humanity are defined as "acts when committed as part of a widespread or systematic attack directed against any civilian population." They include rape, torture, sexual slavery, deprivation of food and medicine, and most important for this discussion, what has become known today as "ethnic cleansing," as defined in section 2, paragraph d: "'Deportation or forcible transfer of population' means forced displacement of the persons concerned by expulsion or other coercive acts from the area in which they are lawfully present, without grounds permitted under international law."[12] The policy of "expulsion" can be implemented in a variety of ways besides "coercive acts." It includes, for example, using simple threats to force people to leave.

While the term "ethnic cleansing" is not used in the statute itself, historians and journalists commonly apply it when analyzing world events of both the past and the present. Although the concept of "cleansing" can be found in historical events dating back centuries, its modern origin seemingly came in the late 1980s, when Russian journalists used it to describe the forced deportation of Christian Armenians from Azerbaijan.[13] The term is also commonly applied to the expulsion of literally millions of Germans from Czechoslovakia, Poland, and other east European nations in the late 1940s and has been used effectively to define forced deportations in many other parts of the world in both the nineteenth and twentieth centuries.[14] Even though the term "ethnic cleansing" has been applied mainly to the history of nations other than the United States, no term better fits the policy of United States "Indian Removal." This policy of forced deportation was informally used not long after the settlement of New Mexico and Virginia in the early seventh century and was adopted in written form by the federal government in the first half of the nineteenth century.

The definition of "war crimes," now clearly outlined by the Rome Statutes under Article 8, follows the laws established under the various Geneva Conventions, the last of which met in August 1949. Generally, the roughly sixty subarticles of Article 8 make it a crime for a military organization to implement a "plan or policy" willfully to kill individuals, torture them, or take them hostage, to intentionally direct "attacks against the civilian population," to deny civilians or other captives a "fair and regular trial," to subject persons to "physical mutilation," to improperly utilize a "flag of truce," to commit "rape," and, finally, to "pillage a town or place, even when taken by assault." Crimes can occur with or without state sanction, but nations cannot be held accountable for the actions of rogue military commanders.[15]

It is presumptive in some respects to use modern terms to describe past historical realities, but terms such as "holocaust" and "genocide" have already been applied to the four-hundred-year history of conflict between Native peoples and Europeans and Americans. David E. Stannard's *American Holocaust* (1992) first offered a broad, sweeping analysis of the issue, including the European invasion of the Caribbean, Mexico, and North and South America and even the human destruction resulting from the slave trade. Stannard argues that the European "Holocaust" brought to the Americas produced a far greater destruction of Native peoples than the destruction of the Jews of Europe. Indians "died of exploitation and disease and malnutrition and neglect," resulting in a "Holocaust," according to Stannard.[16]

Sociologist Russell Thornton's "demographic" history of Native Americans is similar to Stannard's account. While noting that most Indian tribes "survived the horrendous history" that began with contact in 1492, Thornton still calls the event a "holocaust" but leaves the term largely undefined.[17]

Others have contributed more or less to the argument. Writer Ward Churchill's many works include *A Little Matter of Genocide* (1998), *Struggle for the Land* (2002), and *Kill the Indian, Save the Man* (2004). These biased studies generally claim that early European and later American policies toward Indians constituted "genocide."[18] Mainline historians have also entered the debate, including Lawrence M. Hauptman, who argues that the English attack on the Pequots in 1637 was "genocide." Historians Robert H. Jackson and Edward Castillo declare that Indian population losses during the transition in California from Mexican rule to American dominance, which were substantial, constituted a "virtual genocide"; a host of other historians have gone further, suggesting that California constituted the worst case of genocide in North America.[19] Even American founding fathers, such as George Washington, cannot escape the critique. As Barbara Alice Mann concludes in her study of Washington's "War" on Native America, although the term "genocide" did not exist in 1779, Washington and his soldiers meant the same thing when they called for "extirpation," "chastisement," or "extermination" of Indians.[20]

While these examples constitute only a few instances of the use of such terms, the provocative nature of interpreting American history in this way owes much to attempts to define the conflict that swirled around the disintegration of Yugoslavia in the early 1990s. Debate about the crimes committed in that region invariably led to comparisons with other groups, including American Indians, and attempts to incorporate them into a larger historical context. Yale historian Benedict Kiernan, a specialist in the history of Southeast Asia, is one of the world's leading authorities on Pakistan and Cambodia and the genocide that occurred there in the 1970s. He published *Blood and Soil* (2007), which mostly analyzes events in countries other than the United States. Even so, Kiernan devotes two chapters to early North America, one entitled "Genocide in the United States." He concludes: "Americans perpetrated their own genocidal massacres during the war of independence, when they fought Indians as well as the British, and later while expanding across the continent throughout the nineteenth century."[21]

Kiernan's study fits nicely into the new field of research called "genocide studies."[22] But most scholars in this field understand that the issues are often not black and white and that giving the term genocide an "elastic" meaning can lead to confusion. Thus Kiernan is careful with his dialogue, clearly aware that what happened in the United States does not equal the destruction of Jews, Cambodians, or even Tutsi Rwandans. He contends that the conflict in Ohio during the American Revolution included the "collective threat of genocide." In addressing one of the most blatant examples of American injustice—the policy of Indian Removal—Kiernan argues that it "was as convenient as genocide."[23]

In reality the question becomes this: are Jackson's and Castillo's "virtual genocide," Mann's attempted "expiration" or "extermination," and even Kiernan's "genocidal massacre," "collective threat of genocide," and events "as convenient as genocide" really genocide? And can the destruction of one Pequot village perpetrated by ninety Englishmen along with just under a hundred Indian allies (some seventy Mohegans and a handful of Narragansett guides) be considered an act to destroy an entire ethnic group, as defined by the United Nations in 1948 or more importantly by the reformed definitions utilized by the ICC today?[24] And what of

California? Mass murders committed by miners certainly occurred between 1850 and 1862 in two or three mountainous northwestern counties, but such acts hardly reach the level of genocide as it is commonly defined today. Some scholars have termed these kinds of language "hyphenated" genocide, in need of asterisks to differentiate the actions from true genocide. Indeed these attempts only devalue what actually happened to people who experienced organized, policy-driven genocide in central Europe, Cambodia, Rwanda, and even perhaps Darfur.[25]

Even so, state-sponsored violence against Indians did occur in the United States. Governors of states like Texas and California, for example, called for the "extermination" of Indians, using the "rhetoric of genocide," and groups of "rangers" attempted to implement such calls to action. But to what degree is rhetoric a crime? The ICC recently convicted two managers of the radio station in Rwanda for promoting the genocide of the Tutsis in 1994 by broadcasting the "rhetoric of genocide." The ICC initially charged both with "genocide" under Article 6, but convicted them instead of the lesser crimes against humanity. They received jail sentences of thirty and thirty-two years, respectively. Article 7, defining crimes against humanity, makes it a crime to "direct" a course of "conduct involving the multiple commission of acts . . . against any civilian population, pursuant to or in furtherance of a state or organizational policy to commit such acts."[26]

To what degree can it be asserted that the actions of nineteenth-century governors of Texas and California fit the current framework? Much would depend upon making a clear, unambiguous link between the governors and their willingness to "direct" ranger elements that committed violent acts against Native civilians. Furthermore, courts today generally have concluded that actions of the sort often conducted by rogues should be punished by the national governments that had sovereignty over them, as is occurring today in some African nations. Admittedly, this never happened in the United States. While officers of the federal army might be charged with war crimes in many instances—Bear River, Sand Creek, and Wounded Knee are examples—the army often acted as a buffer between contending settlers and Indians, especially in Texas and California.

Given the difficult nature of sovereignty in what became the United States, the jurisdictional questions involving federal and state responsibility, the tension between eastern settled regions and frontier territories, and the sheer complexities involving individual people and events, the best descriptor for all this would seem to be ethnic cleansing. The clear "intent" of national policy was to remove Indians, force them west, and later concentrate them on reservations. Ultimately, a policy of "diminishment" would force Indians to give up pretensions to communal land holdings and would augur cultural change by destroying or drastically shrinking the reservations themselves. Some scholars have attempted to call this "cultural genocide." Nevertheless, many Indian tribes (indeed the vast majority) survived, along with their culture, as demographer Russell Thornton has admitted. This weakens and perhaps makes impossible the argument for calling what happened in North America genocide of any sort.

This assessment should not negate the hefty debate that swirls around defining genocide. The standard examples for genocide, as Kiernan accurately depicts, are usually the killing of millions of people in central Europe in the 1940s and the destruction of almost 2 million Cambodians in the 1970s.[27] The horrific crimes in Rwanda in 1994, where estimates suggest that a million people of the Tutsi tribe perished, most of them by machetes, also clearly constitute genocide.[28] But as the number of dead declines, does genocide still occur?[29] Is there a set number below which we should call it something else? In other words, should we use similar terminology to equate the killing of at least a million people to the slaughter of 150 Lakota Indians at Wounded Knee, South Dakota, in 1890? Wounded Knee might constitute a crime, but was it "genocide"?

Recent scholarship in Australia makes a strong case for genocide with a more limited number of deaths. Australians massacred literally thousands of Native Tasmanians, who became extinct on their native island. Some 80,000 Aborigines were also killed in Queensland between 1820 and 1880, often just for sport. These actions nearly wiped out the entire Aboriginal population. While these numbers are surely inferior to those in central Europe or Cambodia, the "intent" of Australians was literally to kill all Aborigines, because they constituted a different "ethnic" group.[30] Even so, the "numbers game" that the debate in Australia engenders likely will never be resolved. It does, however, offer some interesting comparisons.

Returning to North America, the six most infamous attacks on Indians were the attack on the Pequots in 1637, the slaughter of at least three hundred northern California Indians in 1859, the decimation of a Shoshone village at Bear River in 1863, the killing of Cheyennes at Sand Creek in 1864, the destruction of a Piegan village in Montana in 1870, and the murder of Lakota Indians at Wounded Knee in 1890. The total death count is likely about eighteen hundred people. "Genocidal massacres," as these killings are often called, might better be viewed as war crimes, perpetrated by American soldiers or paramilitary groups who were completely out of control and should have been prosecuted for the crimes. "War crimes" is also a better term for these actions because a vast number of American politicians and intellectuals condemned the events as such at the time and tried to bring about prosecution in at least some cases.

The numbers game is of interest to Stanford historian Norman Naimark, who has studied ethnic conflict and genocide in central Europe, the Soviet Union, and Yugoslavia. He argues that the overall policy in the former Yugoslavia, where thousands of people died (seven thousand were penned up and slaughtered in one city alone), was not necessarily genocide but in fact ethnic cleansing. Naimark concludes:

> The intention of ethnic cleansing is to remove a people and often all traces of them from a concrete territory. The goal, in other words, is to get rid of the "alien" nationality, ethnic, or religious group and to seize control of the territory they had formerly inhabited. At one extreme of its spectrum ethnic cleansing is closer to forced deportation or what has been called "population transfer"; the idea is to get people to move, and the means are meant to be legal and semi-legal.[31]

Naimark's definition mirrors that of the Rome Statutes, where the crime of "deportations or forcible transfer of population" is defined as a crime against humanity, not as genocide.

As cold as it may seem, the numbers killed are not as important as whether a policy existed and what it "intended" to accomplish—indeed "intent" is crucial to conviction. When it comes to genocide, various motivations may explain why a government adopts a "final solution" for ridding itself of a particular ethnic or religious group. Usually it involves the dehumanization of the "other" coupled with hate, leading to a conclusion that killing the group is a desired goal. But with ethnic cleansing and even at times war crimes, the motives and the intent are different. Mostly they involve the need or implicit desire to acquire land or property or even to dominate a people through war to a point where they can be exploited.[32]

All of these examples lead us to several questions. What is the nature of the act? Is it genocide, ethnic cleansing, or simply a series of unrelated war crimes, sanctioned or unsanctioned by government? Such questions are answerable. For either genocide or ethnic cleansing to occur, a legitimate government must plan, organize, and implement the crime. For genocide alone to occur, it must be a concerted effort to kill large numbers of people or indeed to annihilate a given people—nearly all the people of a particular group in a given region—rather than a select few who might be rebelling against the established government. But other actions such as removal or diminishment of ancestral lands require a different description because they are not genocide. To apply the term "genocide" indiscriminately to actions of an isolated nature, even though colonial assemblies or the government of the United States supposedly held sovereignty over the land, does much to demean the meaning of the term and obscures rather than clarifies how we should view many (probably most) actions toward American Indians.

Given this discussion and the new definitions agreed to by most scholars in the broad field of genocide studies today, it is almost impossible to make the argument that American Indians consistently suffered genocide at the hands of Europeans or later government officials of the United States. Unlike the Jews of Europe (who mostly perished in five or six years) or the Cambodians under the Khmer Rouge (who died by the millions in just three years) the American Indians survived the nearly four centuries of contact with Europe. And Indians did strike back (so in fact did some Jews), defending their lands and way of life. It took the federal army over twenty years finally to subdue the northern Plains Indians and even longer to defeat the Apaches in the Southwest. The end results included incarceration for some, deportation for others (which became a standard policy of the American army after 1873), impotence for many Native men and sexual exploitation for many Native women, and ultimately concentration on a "reservation" for nearly all American Indians. But these events did not include a general destruction of Indians or their dispersal into death camps. As historians we must make these distinctions and unmuddle these waters.

"MORAL RESTRAINT" AND THE ISSUE OF LAND

Genocide did not occur in America, primarily because moral restraints prevented it. Put simply, many Europeans and later Americans considered it wrong to kill Indians. Most actually respected the commandment

"Thou Shalt Not Kill." As Lisa Ford, a historian of the new "settler" history, has argued, while early modern Christian theorists were not in agreement over the legal status of Indigenous peoples in the Americas, some contended that they "possessed all of the significant rights of European princes and should be treated accordingly."[33] This belief was generally codified into law in the sixteenth century by those European powers.

The acceptance of such moral restraints emerged slowly. European monarchs fought over claims to land in both the Old and the New World and readily embraced the "right of discovery" as well as the "right of conquest." European historian Anthony Pagden has argued: "As all European empires in America were empires of expansion, all, at one stage or another, had been based upon conquest and had been conceived and legitimized using the language of warfare."[34] The rights of discovery and conquest became so ingrained in American thought that kings, colonial officials, and even the Supreme Court of the United States in the twentieth century all sanctioned the doctrines.[35] As to benefits, the evolution of nation-states and strong monarchs in Europe brought order to chaos and also encouraged greater economic activity, often extending commerce well beyond national borders. Global trade required international laws and thus the means by which states dealt with other states—which included rules of war. And the invention of the printing press in the mid–fifteenth century further cemented state rule; emerging monarchies could make their will known through published decrees.[36]

While Spanish canonical law modestly recognized individual rights, it too acquiesced to some degree to granting rights to American Indians not long after the voyage of Christopher Columbus. By the early sixteenth century the Spanish Catholic Church concluded that Indians did not fall under the Inquisition, a brutal institution that persecuted individuals whom the church suspected of challenging its authority. Such an enlightened view saved many Native Americans from the fire: their crimes could not be proven because they simply did not know the law.[37] In deference to canonical law, European civil law evolved from the simple Roman Catholic concept that Natural Law was derived from human law (*lex humanus*). Those who observed the law were in effect "humans"; those who did not were not. The Laws of Burgos required Spanish conquerors to treat Indians fairly, to make sure that they had proper food and clothing, to warn them when war (in the Spanish view) became necessary—all clear moral restraints designed to prevent genocide. Nevertheless, according to Aristotle, those who did not observe the law were "irrational souls," perhaps capable of understanding but not capable of practical wisdom. As a consequence, they could be enslaved and forced to do useful work but not willfully killed.[38]

Christian monotheism also had a profound impact on this evolving notion of Natural Law. Christians expressed a belief in only one God, who looked after all human beings. Under Natural Law all people had rights, certainly the right to life. How then could one question the right of existence of Native Americans, who remained part of God's creation? The notion that Natural Law gave people the right to life led to important changes in regard to the way in which the English viewed land. Peasant revolts in England challenged aristocratic rights to land.[39] The adoption of the Habeas Corpus Act of 1679 and the English Constitution a decade later protected mostly commoners from torture, imprisonment, and death at the hands of aristocratic lords. Views regarding the use of paper "titles" to lands emerged as well, with such titles becoming a natural right. English common law and courts (which were exported to Ireland) slowly institutionalized the concept of a "fee" or paying money for land in exchange for a complete title. It also affected the process of peasant tribute or service. The obligation could be dealt with by paying "quitrents," a simple tax (usually a small amount).[40]

Views regarding land title—which would have a significant impact on early American settlement—changed during the sixteenth century when successive English kings Henry VII and VIII confiscated lands from the Catholic Church in England, Scotland, and Ireland and offered them for sale. The Crown wanted immediate revenues and sold the lands with a fee-simple title. From 1550 to 1630 roughly twenty thousand new landholders were created in the British Isles, forming the backbone of a new class: the gentry. The lords, who consisted of a mere one thousand families, quickly embraced this new class when they discovered their own vulnerability to the peasantry during the English Civil War. This land policy created a "gentry mentality" in England, a general belief that it was no longer impossible for nonaristocratic people to acquire title to land. Indeed, the English gentry controlled about 50 percent of all English land by 1700, holding paper titles issued by both aristocrats and kings.[41]

Although it was a positive development, the gentry mentality seemed a perfect fit for yet another Crown goal—the religious conquest of Ireland. Queen Elizabeth I, in particular, recruited Protestant settlers (some the sons and daughters of the gentry) to go to Ireland and take up lands that the Crown had confiscated from Catholics and given out in fee simple. Perhaps as many as 100,000 Protestant Scots invaded Ulster alone, becoming the spearhead of the policy of "ethnic cleansing": removing Irish Catholics from lands that were given to Protestants.[42] With a surging population, sometimes forced from homes by the first industrial depressions, many English and some Scots-Irish signed on to go to new lands (estimates suggest as many as 250,000 Scots-Irish emigrated in the eighteenth century alone). Many went to America as both free people and indentured servants, in the hope that they eventually would gain fee titles to lands, much like the new settlers of Ulster.[43]

But how could such newly arriving settlers benefit from the evolving land policies of England? If Native titles to lands were recognized, those lands could then be bought legally in a fee-simple fashion. Evolving European laws regarding lands soon came together in the New World to create an enticing and rare opportunity for the English to acquire land and at the same time to force the recognition of Indians as free human beings who held vast acreage of land that might be purchased. Such "legal" purchases could not be made with Indians who had been annihilated. But to what degree did the English see such opportunity as simply a means of manipulation—what Ford has called taking advantage of the "figurative possession" of lands claimed by monarchs? Obviously, many settlers saw obtaining titles from Indians—what Ford calls the "messy work of settlement"—as a method of convenience, but generally the Crown remained too busy to challenge them.[44]

In a sense, both Catholics in Spanish dominions and Protestants who settled along the Atlantic Coast and eventually in the American West sought order through law, which in turn created political and social stability and moral restraints against killing Indians. This did not negate in any way the concept of the "right of conquest," but it softened the consequences. As Europeans embarked for the New World, they carried with them a variety of views regarding these new lands and their occupants. They could be conquered, forming parts of colonial enterprises, just as Spaniards had reconquered land from the Moors in Spain; but increasingly even that conquest faced moral scrutiny by colonial authorities. It was best to buy lands, by whatever means possible. Such a policy dominated land acquisition from Indians in America for four centuries.

The justification for such purchases, and often their unscrupulous nature, came from a pervasive European belief in "agrarian imperialism."

Settlers in the New World took from their religion the general belief that farming was a virtuous enterprise and that only those who produced from the land should inherit the earth. Even as late as the 1930s, in Adolf Hitler's Germany, the metaphor *völkische Flurbereinigung* was commonly used to justify agricultural imperialism. It meant simply that alien ethnic elements needed to be cleansed from the soil so that virtuous Germanic people could use it.[45] Agricultural imperialism is often connected to ethnic cleansing and genocide. The foundation for the argument is the simple belief that people of the "other" (ethnically different groups) do not use the soil efficiently, so they have no right to it.[46] And no greater force was exerted on Indians in American history than forcing them to move off productive lands, which, as the story unfolds, the Indians supposedly failed to utilize.

Recent historians have identified two elements that help explain this event. First, the act of dispossession, it has been argued, constituted Europe's explicit goal of eventually dominating the world—the establishment of "colonial sovereignty" in many parts of the globe, including the Americas, Africa, Asia, and even Australia. Colonies were extensions of national polities that inserted themselves into a supposedly "virgin" region and then sent "migrants" to exploit whatever resources were considered useful. Second, as historian Lorenzo Veracini has argued, once those migrants settled in, they tended to "become founders of political orders and carry their sovereignty with them."[47] This led to jurisdictional disputes between the sovereign and colonial authorities and more importantly between colonial authorities and settlers, who had moved into the interior and refused to obey an exogenous authority.

Ford has called this process "Settler Sovereignty": settlers in the interior of the North American colonies slowly began to formulate their own court system and their own laws. This, it seemed, became necessary in order to validate their existence, to "shore up the legitimacy of settlement."[48] They even created their own paramilitary units, often called "militias" or more frequently "rangers," that played major roles in forcefully ejecting Indians from their lands. At least some American political leaders, including those from the colonial era and during the rise of the new American republic, referred to such Anglo frontiersmen as "semi-savages," "lawless banditti," and "worthless fellows." Even George Washington called the frontier settlers "a parcel of banditti who will bid defiance to all authority."[49]

The origin of the notion of settler sovereignty is easily discovered in the growing enlightened philosophy of seventeenth- and eighteenth-century

European thought. The Dutch writer Hugo Grotius discussed the evolving "agrarian imperialism" of the age in the 1640s. He started by defining individual "Natural Right," which included property. "After it was established," he argued, "one man was prohibited by the law of nature from seizing the property of another against his will." Grotius, like others to follow, also believed that individuals entered into a government, which in turn had responsibilities under the "Law of Nations." In his chapters on the "Lawfulness of War," he determined what constituted "Just" and "Un-just" war. Obviously, unjust war included conflict with the motive of acquiring land or property. Of course, if we are confronted with war, "the law of nature indeed authorises our making such acquisitions in a just war."[50] In other words, Grotius sanctioned the right of conquest, as long as it occurred during a just war.

The principles that Grotius established, particularly in regard to the morality of nations making war, became standard practice in Europe and later were utilized to some degree by competing armies in the Americas, where Europeans fought Europeans—one exception being the struggles in the American South during the American Revolution. Grotius discussed everything relative to the state and the prosecution of war: honoring flags of truce; championing the immediate release of prisoners of war who had voluntarily surrendered, or giving them a proper trial if they were involved in war crimes; the need to prevent the pillaging of villages; the "right" to kill enemies in a just war; and, finally, the need to recognize the neutrality of women and children. Gustavus Adolphus carried a copy of Grotius's work with him into battle during the Thirty Years' War, and it graced the shelves of libraries of wealthy families in Pennsylvania, Massachusetts, and Virginia.[51]

Grotius wrote before much was known about the New World or its Native inhabitants. Even so, he offered many new ideas about land ownership, including the notion that those who did not cultivate the land could be displaced—"agrarian imperialism." His conclusion ultimately set the stage for what became the basic argument in the New World: "cultivation," rather than hunting or gathering, defined the right of ownership. Conversely, that right rested solely on the premise that people had no right to lands that they did not take a personal interest in developing. The argument vindicated "squatter sovereignty" in the United States, a commonly argued "natural right" particularly in nineteenth-century America.[52]

This debate over ownership had festered in England for several centuries, emerging as the peasantry resisted aristocratic oppression. As early as 1680 John Locke reconfirmed Grotius's argument in relation to the New World by arguing that the Laws of Nature protected Indians from extermination; but Indians hunted and gathered, he assumed, so they owned just the fruits of those labors. Property rights came only with improvement of the sort that involved agriculture. As Ford has argued, "Seventeenth and Eighteenth-century English Atlantic Charters gathered together Catholic, natural law, and proto-Lockean theory into spectacularly broad and untenable claims to sovereignty, jurisdiction, and property over North America."[53] While such claims never rejected the humanity of Indians, they did question their ownership of land.

These arguments had an impact on the next theorist to enter the field— Emer de Vattel. He touched on the nature of land possession and war in three volumes penned in the 1760s.[54] Vattel stressed the right of the state to self-preservation but reaffirmed the collective need of both individuals and states to observe the Laws of Nature. Yet he opened new ground in his analysis of people "in a state of nature." He believed in "equality," stating that "a dwarf is as much a man as a giant," but also provided the caveat that "all men and all states have a perfect right to those things that are necessary for their preservation." This included land—"every nation is then obligated by the law of nature to cultivate the land that has fallen to its share."[55] Vattel applied this axiom to the New World.

Vattel contended that when a country's population reached a point where it could no longer cultivate sufficient land to feed itself, it had a right to look elsewhere for land—for self-preservation. The best place to obtain it was "from wandering tribes of men [who] . . . possessed it [land] in common." It thus became "necessary that those tribes should fix themselves somewhere, and appropriate to themselves portions of land" to cultivate, in order to "derive their subsistence" and sustain their claim to land. Turning to North America and its European colonies, Vattel argued that the "wandering tribes" of this land "cannot exclusively appropriate to themselves more land than they have occasion for, or more than they are able to settle and cultivate." While the right of property was sacred, he believed, the possession of "immense regions" by tribal societies "cannot be accounted a true and legal possession."[56]

The entitlement of settlers to land increased as the United States expanded its sovereignty westward. But with this movement came a great jurisdictional divide: enforcing laws from colonial capitals (or later Washington, D.C.) was both necessary and often almost impossible. The most difficult problem in America became regulating land expansion as settlers, expressing their own version of "settler sovereignty," came to view their access to land as an entitlement. The Congress of the United States responded by adopting ever more liberal land laws encouraging squatting, at first called Preemption Acts (starting in 1813), and then passed the Homestead Act (1862). All of this made it more difficult to implement a policy that respected Indian sovereignty over lands even when they farmed them.

Chief Justice John Marshall of the United States Supreme Court faced the issue of whether Indians or the national government, through right of "discovery," had sovereignty over the West. In 1810 and again in 1823 his majority opinions created a legal fiction, granting that Indians were "the rightful occupants to the soil" they lived on but contending that the government was sovereign over Indian land. While in some regards this seemed a blow to any notion of Indian sovereignty—and it was—it might also be seen as a moral restraint that required the government to purchase that soil.[57] Eventually this would lead sympathetic legislators to pass the Intercourse Act of 1834, which for the first time in history granted Indians what amounted to a "title" to lands west of the Mississippi River. It created "Indian Country."[58]

The Intercourse Act of 1834 was really only meant to calm the righteous indignation of opponents of Indian Removal, a program that resulted in the forced deportation of nearly 100,000 Indians from lands east of the Mississippi River to places west of it. Many followers of President Thomas Jefferson, while avid expansionists, realized that Indian Removal might be wrong but realistically hoped that it would "save the Indian," giving time to adjust and accept a "civilized" life. This policy has often been called "assimilation."[59] Many Americans saw it as the ultimate moral restraint, implemented at a time when Americans believed that the Indian was "vanishing" as a result of continued contact with Anglos. When ethnic cleansing occurs in the world, it is always the case that moral restraints exist that to some degree prevent genocide, this being one of the best examples of the policy adhered to in the evolving young American republic.

The history of the European conquest of the New World would be filled with contending views as Europeans struggled to interpret the lessons learned from the Renaissance and the Enlightenment, as standards of private property rights slowly matured, as individual settlers argued that they had an "entitlement" to land, and as Native Americans defended their sovereignty over hunting and horticultural lands that supported their unique lifestyle. American authority, both local and national, would bend in the heavy breeze of expansion. The process of what Americans eventually called Manifest Destiny was fraught with contradictions, laws that on occasion became impossible to enforce, and a lust for land that challenged all sense of order, creating what became an agonizingly long process that led to the disenfranchisement of Native peoples. While Indians lost the lands that they had possessed so clearly in 1500, the ending would not result in the utter destruction of the Indians. They lived on, often facing removal and privation but also at times prospering.

The Indians' survival had much to do with the implementation of this dominating policy of ethnic cleansing. It was not a sudden process but one that ebbed and flowed throughout the four-hundred-year period of contact. The times of "interregnum," of static growth, allowed Indians to regroup to reform communities shattered by removal. Attempting to ascertain the political and economic views of so many different Native societies further complicates the story. American Indians fought among themselves, or alongside European nations, almost as frequently as they resisted the American policy of ethnic cleansing. Some Native groups had sophisticated social and political institutions that seemingly offered both peaceful and militant resistance, sometimes at the same time. Others had little central political power, making it difficult for Americans to negotiate with them. While it is much easier to gather facts about the motivations of colonial regimes or even the policies of the later United States, it is often impossible to replicate such conclusions when it comes to Native Americans.

To warrant any sort of just conclusions, at least some moral standard must be applied to both Indians and invading non-Natives. American Indians murdered and even raped—but on very few occasions—and attacked unsuspecting Anglo frontier communities, making them dangerous places to live. Anglos did the same to a much greater degree. Like Europeans and later Americans, however, most tribes had moral restraints when it came to killing women and children, even though they had never read the philosophers of Europe. Indeed, on occasions, such as after the destruction of the Pequot village in 1637, Native allies of the English looked on in horror as Pequot women and children burned to death in houses set on fire by Europeans. They were disturbed by the English brand of war.[60] Historians must apply the moral standard equally. Where the moral standard is known and practiced, both Indians and Europeans who abandon it should be castigated and condemned for their lack of humanity.

This study explores the process of dispossession and the conflict that it occasionally engendered. The beginning chapters focus on the rights of discovery and conquest, which entailed European use of "deeds" and treaties to acquire Indian land.[61] The growing acceptance of enlightened thought led to a more cautious approach to Indian affairs by the early eighteenth century: the ebbing of the policy tied to questions of land ownership and the development of Indian and land policies within the various colonial assemblies. The middle chapters consider how the process of treaty-making by the United States accepted the notion of Indian occupancy of land but not ownership and finally resulted in the abrogation of any legal prescripts as Manifest Destiny overwhelmed the nation. By the 1850s, 1860s, and 1870s the rejection of fair treatment of Indians led to what is probably the most brutal ethnic conflict in America, in Minnesota, Texas, and California; on the northern Great Plains; and in the deserts of the Southwest—distant lands in which people frequently defied the moral restraints that their government sought to impose upon them.

Today, nearly a century after the general acceptance of the ludicrous justifications that supported such wars and policies, we must attempt to identify those actions for what they were. Doing so requires clarity of definitions as well as the will to find a balanced history. They were cynical yet frequently peaceful manipulations that sometimes led to conflict but in sum constituted an ethnic cleansing that Americans at the time considered just and righteous. How we should judge this history now is a story worth telling.

1

THE NATIVE NEW WORLD

While en route to Asia in June 1497, the Genoese-born sea captain John Cabot—whose real name was Zuan Caboto—finally sighted land. He commanded the good ship *Matthew,* owned by merchants from Bristol, England, who, with the king's good wishes, intended to exploit the Asian spice market. In a word, Cabot epitomized a global businessman, well connected in the courts and best families of Europe and bent on obtaining wealth. Ships from England had been coasting along lands known today as North America for several decades, preceding even the voyage of the "Admiral of the Ocean Sea," Christopher Columbus, who had bumped into the Bahamas and Haiti some five years before. Indeed Cabot knew Columbus, who was himself trying to exploit his great "discovery."[1]

While Cabot never reached the Far East, he had convinced the English king Henry VII that he could do so by sailing north of the Caribbean Islands, where Columbus had landed. His exact route and the lands he visited are mostly a mystery. Cabot probably followed the course pioneered by early Vikings and cod fishers, north to Iceland and thence south along the Newfoundland coast. Possibly he put ashore near Cape Breton and planted the flag of England, claiming those lands. Cabot's claims—inexact at best—mirrored those of many more explorers over the next several centuries. European monarchies took title to the Americas according to the utterly preposterous notion that they were theirs by "right of discovery."[2]

"Discovery," and thus a string of claims, hardly ended with Cabot. The French, Spanish, Portuguese, Dutch, and even the Swedes all sent ships into the North Atlantic world in the years to follow. All these nations made claims in the name of their monarchs in one fashion or another.[3] The name "America" derived unintentionally from the pilfered and doctored letters of an Italian sea captain, Amerigo Vespucci, who sailed for the kings of both Spain and Portugal. While Italian publishers mostly forged Vespucci's letters, they did describe his four voyages to the mainland between 1497 and 1504. Vespucci, a modest man and close friend of Columbus, realized that Columbus had sensed that South America was a "continent" and not an island; Vespucci surmised the same about North America. But he likely would have been aghast to learn that the letters attributed to him were used to construct maps of the New World in Italy— with his name on them.[4]

French merchants joined the fray for New World lands in 1524 when they sent Giovanni Verrazzano in the ship *Dauphine* to search for a western route to Asia. Such a route, being heavily involved in the silk and spice trade, which connected the commercial families of Florence, Lyon, and Paris, would lead to immense profits, or so Verazzano's supporters hoped. Verrazzano landed somewhere near Cape Fear, turned north, and spent much of the spring coasting along Cape Hatteras, exploring the waters of Chesapeake Bay, the inlets around Long Island, and finally Narragansett Bay. While he returned with a wealth of information about the Native peoples and products of the land, the trip demonstrated that a route to Asia that far south did not exist. Ten years later another Frenchman, Jacques Cartier, looked even farther north, entering the St. Lawrence estuary. Here he found cod fishers from Europe who had started exchanging small items with the local inhabitants for beaver skins. Cartier returned the next year, claiming present-day Canada for the king of France.[5]

Spain remained in the best position regarding claims to the New World. Juan Ponce de León landed along the eastern coast of Florida in 1513, probably near Daytona Beach or St. Augustine (he himself, and later historians, did not really know). The Spanish king beamed with pleasure over de León's efforts and promptly gave him all the lands, including the islands of "Bimini and Florida," a gift that defied imagination: de León had no idea that Florida was a peninsula attached to the continent of North America. But dubious claims never bothered such "conquistadors." It is myth that de León sought a fountain of eternal youth; he sought gold and silver, fought with the Native owners of Florida, and abandoned his new empire when he found no wealth. Spanish missionaries and military men returned later to reclaim this enchanting land by the "right of discovery."[6]

Another Spanish conquistador, Hernán Cortés, also sought land and riches in the New World. He headed up a small force of two hundred men that landed along the Mexican coast near Vera Cruz in 1519, moved inland, and captured the magnificent Aztec capital of Mexico City. Spaniards back in Jamaica protested when Cortés defied their authority, took charge of the expedition himself, and then claimed the lands in the name of the Spanish Crown—under the obvious assumption that the Crown would reward him, which it did. Governor of Jamaica Francisco de Garay challenged Cortés. Outfitting four ships and receiving a grant from the Spanish Crown for lands discovered, Garay placed navigator Antonio de Alaminos in command of a 1519 expedition that first landed in Florida then proceeded west along the Gulf Coast the next year, landing occasionally to take notice of rivers (one being the mighty Mississippi), resources, and Native peoples who lived in large numbers along the coast. Garay's expedition completed the Spanish claim to the Gulf Coast of North America.[7]

In a few short years European monarchs and their surrogate explorers had theoretically completed the greatest real estate swindle in history. The region that they claimed title to, stretching from Mexico to the Arctic Islands, constituted nearly 10,000,000 square miles of land, while the homelands of these new rulers (the British Isles, France, and Spain) combined totaled a mere 500,000 square miles. The kings and queens of Europe would recognize the claims of other monarchs to lands in the New World mostly in order to legitimize their own, ignoring any claim voiced by the Native inhabitants.

Nevertheless, those same monarchs would occasionally fight over their claims, thus embracing a second right, often attached to a paper treaty: the "right of conquest." The justification of the right itself came from theological discussions in Europe, especially in the Roman and later Spanish realms. The flag of conquest soon rested on the crests of aristocrats, whose values played a crucial role in the development of European empires and later those in America.[8] Only after the early settlement of some coastal American lands did the issue of Indian rights surface. And even then Native claims always remained subject to Crown acquiescence.

Those European explorers who first coasted along North American shores concluded that the Native inhabitants of this new land were "uncivilized." They lacked legal order, substantial housing, proper language and religion, and even sensible dress and eating habitats. An early observer,

Martin Frobisher, reported that the Indians "live in Caves" and hunt for their dinner, occasionally reverting to the consumption of "such grasses as the countrey yeeldeth," and that they had no tables, stools, or knives and forks to eat with. The Indian, as historian Roy Harvey Pearce has so succinctly noted, became a symbol of everything that the Europeans must never be.[9] Under such circumstances, what rights could the Native peoples have to the land that they occupied?

Just what Native Americans thought of those Europeans and the vessels they arrived in is more difficult to determine. Some Indians certainly viewed early Europeans as supernatural beings, gods who rose out of ships with billowing white sails that resembled clouds. When Europeans discharged guns, Indians related the noise to the thunder and lightning, sources of immense physical power. Explorers Jacques Cartier and Hernando de Soto described occasions when Indians brought their sick and laid them at the feet of the Europeans, hoping for a cure. And Cortés, after entering the heart of the Aztec empire, took great advantage of the Aztec leaders' fear that he was the long expected god who had come to rule the earth.[10] Yet these early impressions soon gave way to a more realistic assessment of the European presence: Indians came to understand that these pseudo-gods really wanted gold and, later, land.

Europeans also occasionally turned to religion in attempting to understand the people of the New World. A few early seventeenth century European commentators ultimately put forward the logical suggestion that the Indian derived from nature, created by the Christian God. Even though the Indians did not work much of their land in the fashion that God intended, the Laws of Nature gave them protection against immediate expulsion from their lands. In addition, the kings and queens of Europe all accepted the religious responsibility of converting all subjects to Christianity, initially proposed by the pope in Rome and later accepted by Protestant offshoots. All across the newly discovered lands of North America moral restrictions anchored by religion, the Laws of Nature, and civil law prevented the mass killing of Native Americans. A few less cultured people might cross the line, but those in authority promoted these moral restraints most of the time.[11]

In addition, Indian lands seemed endless, with plenty for everyone. Europeans initially needed Indians to survive; most early colonists exchanged goods with them for food. The new invaders from Europe slowly accepted that Indians did have some rights to use the land, to live, and to have the opportunity to embrace the Christian religion and European culture. Needless to say, such concessions came only with the ultimate acceptance of Crown sovereignty over all North American land.

Yet another practical reason for not slaughtering Indians was that they did have order—legal, political, social, and otherwise. Indians had developed economies that did not overtax the land, as European measures often did, and sustained life to the extent that populations grew, especially in the period after A.D. 1000. Most historians today agree that the Native population north of the Rio Grande ranged in the millions by the time of the European voyages of invasion. Anthropologist Henry Dobyns estimated it as high as 18 million. Shepard Krech III offered a more subdued assessment of somewhere between 4 and 7 million. Whatever the real Native population size—and it will never be ascertained with certainty—Indian villages were found almost everywhere in early North America.[12] The densest populations in North America were along the California coast, along the Northwest coast, in the upper Rio Grande valley, and especially in the Southeast and Florida. Indeed a belt of settled villages existed along nearly every river that flowed into the Gulf from modern Florida to the Red River of modern Texas.

New England alone, where Frobisher landed, had a population of at least 90,000, but that number would fall precipitously in the years after European contact. Native peoples in the Americas had no immunities to European diseases such as smallpox. Some tribal groups along the coast suffered a 90 percent decline in population just as a result of contact with pathogens introduced from Europe in the sixteenth century, well before settlers arrived.[13] When Europeans came in numbers to New England, mainly after 1630, they quickly surmised that the largest tribes included the Narragansetts of western Rhode Island and the Pequot-Mohegans of the Connecticut River Valley, at 20,000 and 15,000, respectively. These were followed by the Massachusetts and Pawtuckets, tribal groups living south and north of Boston, each with a population of 12,000 people. Other smaller groups like the Wampanoags, who early on allied themselves with the Pilgrims at Plymouth Colony, had smaller villages and fewer warriors to defend themselves. The lands between these communities were well known to these Native groups, as trails and pathways stretched across most of the land, connecting towns. While many early English settlers believed that parts of New England were *vacuum domicilium* (virgin land) free for the taking, this was mostly a myth.[14]

Most Native communities in New England resembled classic riverine or coastal towns, built where water could facilitate travel by canoe. Yet villages could be found inland: the Nipmunk towns in central and western Massachusetts offer a good example. There is considerable debate today regarding the political and social organization of these people. Some scholars suggest that the southernmost bands had the most organization, with various bands working together to promote a "tribal" agenda.[15] But political fluidity existed even among these southern people. The best example comes from the off-again, on-again activities of Uncas (the Mohegan "sachem" or leader), a Pequot tribal headman. He often gave lip service to Pequot leaders and at times conspired with the English to preserve his own small band of people.[16]

The degree to which these small tribes or bands understood the boundaries of their various domains is also debated. Certainly their views conflicted to some degree with the European notion that land came with distinct boundaries, often defined by rock piles or rivers. The Native peoples of New England—and indeed Indians of most of North America—viewed land differently, seeing their domain as one defined by economic process.[17] Many small clusters of round, thatched huts called wigwams held people who spent the summer along the coast, collecting food and tending crops of corn, beans, and squash. They created horticultural plots (often only an acre or two) in areas best suited to production. The sandy-loam soil of the river valleys was ideal, because planting sticks could quickly open a deep hole for seeds. Fall and spring found the Indians in a different locale, hunting and fishing, often in the interior. This second vocation provided considerable protein to their diet. The third phase of the economic process involved the collecting of nuts, berries, and edible roots. Such an economy depended upon the availability of wild plants and animals within the prescribed territory of the various bands, which had little to do with a fixed boundary.[18]

Sachems (town leaders) often sparred with the representatives of other communities over land-use policies. If a particular river valley held considerable game or berries, agreement came easily: joint use by two or three different villages occurred. Such an agreement often evolved from kinship ties, with intermarriage bringing alliances. In this sense property rights, as Native peoples saw them, entailed an ecological value, often anchored by a social network that was shared or even transferable from year to year. Nonetheless, if two bands disputed over a given region, especially during difficult economic times, the best hunting lands could become a conflict zone, where few hunters dared to go and animals accordingly flourished. The Narragansetts and the Wampanaoags, for example, often had differences, usually associated with resource disputes. Abundance and sharing seemed to be more common, however, especially during the spawning season, when fish flourished in the rivers. Members of several villages could then share the wealth. Such times led to celebration and courting.[19] Most evidence suggests that New England Indians were seldom impoverished, at least before the white settlers came.

Those periods of celebration helped mold a sociopolitical order. Each village selected its sachem based upon lineage and experience, the position often being handed down within an elite family. The ability to speak or negotiate—a skill passed down by elders—often worked hand and hand with political success: the sachems represented their people rather than lording over them. Diplomacy became even more important in the region because the Indians of New England—and many tribes farther south— spoke variations of the same Algonquian language.

While a few villages, likely in the North, may have been patrilineal, the best evidence suggests a matrilineal society for the larger bands, where the line of descent passed from mothers to both sons and daughters. The success of women in producing food from their fields as well as by gathering gave them status. Even so, some polygyny existed. Elite sachems took multiple wives, which in turn may have promoted political alliances that reinforced relationships with the bands of their wives. Strict social taboos preventing incest certainly existed, as is the case with nearly all human societies.[20]

Indians living south of New England in what is today New Jersey and Pennsylvania had similar economies and political structures. The Florentine explorer Verazzano likely first encountered the Lenape or Delaware Indians when he landed at Delaware Bay. Consisting of three tribal groups, the southernmost Unami Lenapes inhabited the Atlantic coastal regions as well as both banks of the lower Delaware River. To the north and east in what is today New Jersey, Europeans found the Unalachtigo Lenapes. Scattered small villages of Munsee Lenapes were located even farther north, extending into northern Pennsylvania and southern New York, including Manhattan and Long Island. Europeans eventually made contact with more inland Shawnee Indians just beyond the Delaware River, extending into central Pennsylvania. Their favorite haunt was the

Susquehanna River: using canoes, they ranged along this river south into what is today Virginia.[21]

The Delaware and Shawnee people practiced limited horticulture, storing small amounts of corn for later use. Hunting and gathering likely provided more sustenance, and fishing along the tributaries of the Delaware and Susquehanna Rivers offered year-round food. Small kin groups at times joined together to create bands, which laid claim to specific hunting regions and gathering territories. But as in New England to the north, no boundaries existed. Land use rather than land title, or even occupation, defined right of possession—not unlike the rights held by European peasants. When a kin group stopped using the resources on particular lands, they could be acquired by others. While such kin groups cooperated with neighboring peoples, early European observers concluded that they lacked a centralized authority. Sachems spoke for the various matrilineally organized kin groups. They acquired this authority by their common sense and by reinforced connections with younger members of the band, through gift-giving.[22]

Just how many Delaware Lenapes and Shawnees inhabited these lands is open to conjecture. The sailors with Verazzano and those who landed with the Dutch navigator Henry Hudson along the Hudson River in 1609, and indeed many others who traveled along the Atlantic coast in the intervening years, probably carried diseases for which these Indians had no immunities. Lenape populations conservatively reached 10,000 to 15,000 people by 1607, when the first Europeans settled in Virginia; Shawnee villages may have contained more. Several thousand Munsee Lenapes died in a vicious conflict with the early Dutch that broke out in 1640. Populations of both the Delawares and Shawnees would decline to a few thousand by the late seventeenth century, perhaps as much as a 90 percent drop.[23]

The rich bottomlands of the James and Potomac Rivers of the Chesapeake Bay region offered ideal locations for Native settlements. More permanent sedentary towns existed there, unlike the more mobile Native communities farther north. Yet the coastal regions of the bay, a section of country called the "pine barren," seldom held sedentary towns, given the poor quality of the soil. Some thirty Native villages existed in what is today the "tidewater" of Virginia and Maryland, most being part of the Powhatan Confederacy, a political organization centered on the James River near present-day Richmond. Chief Powhatan of Powhatan's town, a powerful leader, ruled most of these other towns, which paid him tribute in 1600.[24] Powhatan offered both priestly and secular rulings to his people, but this also involved working closely with *werowances* (subchiefs), who ruled individual villages.[25]

The Powhatan Confederacy constituted a chieftainship: Powhatan recruited loyal *werowances* to control outlying villages. The core towns were located between the James and York Rivers. Powhatan's influence dwindled farther north and south in Maryland and modern North Carolina. The centers of power within the society were the mortuary temples, which were guarded by carved images of sacred beings. The temples remained the province of the *werowances*. These religio-political leaders collected tribute, some of which financed festivals and feasts—favorites with village people. Other goods went on to the main Powhatan village. In return villagers received protection and assistance from Powhatan. Virginians today know the locations of many of these subordinate towns by their names, which have been attached to rivers, such as the Appomattox of the Appomattox River, the Pamunkeys of the Pamunkey River, and the Piankatanks of the Piankatank River.[26]

The Powhatan Confederacy produced an abundance of food. The early English who landed near the mouth of James River in 1607 unquestionably would have starved without the Indians. At first the exchanges of a few iron goods and blankets for venison and corn seemed fair, even natural, but soon the food demands took the form of "tribute." Pocahontas, the celebrated daughter of chief Powhatan, was even kidnapped in 1613 in an attempt to extort more food from the Indians. She was placed in the house of one Reverend Alexander Whitaker, who prided himself on the draconian laws he had written on "moral and martial" duties. Under what amounted to a boot-camp regimen, Pocahontas learned the Apostles' Creed, the Lord's Prayer, and the Ten Commandants. Then she met and married settler John Rolfe and returned with him to England, where she ultimately died of smallpox.[27] While the life of Pocahontas—and its varied fictional derivatives—has been used to suggest a period of peaceful early contact between Europeans and Indians in Virginia, the reality was far different.

To the south of Virginia, in the Carolinas and Georgia, Native populations spoke a Siouan language dialect, which suggests a relationship with groups of western New York such as the Iroquois. It is possible that many migrated into the area from the north. By 1700 Tuscaroras and Yamasees inhabited the coastal plain of the Carolinas, while villages existed along the various river valleys farther inland, in the Piedmont, Westos, Catawbas, and Monacans. To their west, Muskogean-speaking groups, such as the Creeks and Choctaws, dominated lands in what would become Georgia, Alabama, and Mississippi.[28] The famous explorer Hernando de Soto and his army invaded these lands in 1539–41, disrupting villages and confiscating food, which may explain why Native populations plummeted. It is certain that Europeans introduced smallpox in the decades that followed.[29]

Just what the North American South looked like before Europeans arrived is difficult to determine. Native populations likely ranged into the millions. Large communities in Florida, Georgia, Tennessee, and Alabama had names like Apalachee, Cofitachequi, Colosa, Toa, and Tascaloosa. These towns all had massive mound structures in their center, where religious leaders held sway. The larger villages, often called "super chieftainships," controlled dozens of others in the outlying regions. One such chieftainship in north Florida dominated some ninety other communities; it could literally raise thousands of warriors. Tragically, these civilized centers were all either gone or terribly reduced by 1650.[30]

The Spanish opened dozens of missions in north Florida and eastern Georgia in the late sixteenth century, so much is known about Indians such as the Timucuas and Apalaches of this region. Their town centers included a round administrative building where councils convened. A heavily stratified political leadership existed in each chieftainship: it included the headman (called the *mico*) and a variety of other leaders, often identified by the Spanish as *caciques* or *principales*. These officials collected and stored vast amounts of food; at times they lavished this bounty on Spanish visitors, who marveled at the tables of corn, beans, squash, fish, oysters, and acorns. The Timucuas likely had the most sophisticated chieftainships, even though their individual communities were never very large. Even so, Timucua populations probably exceeded 500,000 at contact.[31]

As Spanish explorers traveled along the western Gulf Coast, they found Native communities wherever they landed. Governor Garay of Jamaica sent at least five expeditions into the Río de las Palmas (undoubtedly the Rio Grande) just between 1519 and 1523. One noted some forty Native villages within a few miles of the mouth of the river. These Indian hunters and gatherers traveled by canoe and at one point had sufficient forces to drive off a large Spanish marauding party that was searching for food. Within a few years the villages and the people disappeared, undoubtedly victims of epidemics.[32] Nevertheless, Spaniards who followed Garay's sea captains make it clear that even as late as 1750 the lower Rio Grande Valley had a population of at least 15,000 Indians (half living north of the Rio Grande and half south of it) and another 15,000 Coahuiltecan Indians (who lived in the Nueces and Colorado River valleys of present-day Texas).[33]

A better sense of the Indians of the Southwest and their cultures resulted from the violent entrada of Francisco Vázquez de Coronado, who reached the upper Rio Grande in 1540. While he searched for cities of gold, Coronado found multistoried adobe towns of the Pueblo Indians, with populations of one thousand to three thousand in a town, who tended crops of corn, beans, and squash and pulled up their ladders to their enclosed communities whenever danger appeared on the horizon. The people of the individual Pueblo communities looked inward, each town being independent of others. The inhabitants had created a strong matrilineal order, with women who possessed considerable status and a priesthood that determined times for planting and harvesting.

The Pueblo Indians had lived along the upper Rio Grande for several centuries.[34] They had domesticated dogs and turkeys and made exquisite pottery, jewelry, and cotton blankets. They even hosted "trade fairs" with mobile bands of Apaches from the plains and other Jumano Pueblos from the lower Rio Grande, who brought them dried buffalo and hides (mostly buffalo ribs, which could be strapped to dog caravans).[35] These symbiotic relationships with more mobile people to the east brought many other exotic commodities into Pueblo towns: seashells from the coast, flint arrow and spear points from quarries on the plains, and skin bags of salt.

Pueblo towns stretched from the easternmost Pecos community in eastern New Mexico to the Hopi towns of Arizona and from Taos in the north to El Paso in the south and thence eastward to the junction of the Conchos and Rio Grande (a Pueblo community called La Junta by the Spanish). While Pueblo communities may have harbored populations of several hundred thousand people in A.D. 1250, some communities had been abandoned by the time the Spanish arrived. About one hundred towns along the upper Rio Grande then housed 80,000 people, still a population that was very secure in its inward-leaning, fortified adobe hamlets. The town of La Junta alone had a population of 10,000 in 1580.[36]

The Pueblo communities suffered terribly at the hands of the first Spanish invaders. Within a year Coronado's army lacked food and clothing and began requisitioning it from the Indians, who at times resisted. Some Spaniards raped Native women, leading to insults and growing hostility. Ultimately Coronado's men stormed several of the walled communities, breaking the outside walls and setting fire to the large structures. As the Indians came out, soldiers slaughtered them with broadswords. Several hundred captured men faced death by being tied to stakes and burned— the Laws of Burgos did little to protect these Indians in far-off New Mexico. In all Coronado's troops alone reduced thirteen Pueblo communities to ashes, killing hundreds of Indians.[37]

When Coronado returned to Mexico City he faced charges for his actions. He had in fact committed some of the first war crimes in American history. The royal *fiscal* (prosecuting attorney of the Viceroyalty) listed five acts that violated the laws: hanging Indians, selecting commanding officers who mistreated Indians, waging war (obviously what Grotius would later term "unjust" war), setting dogs on Indians, execution of the Indian guide Turk, and failure to colonize Quivira (the term used for the land that Coronado invaded and then abandoned). The case went to the Royal Audiencia, where the viceroy, Antonio de Mendoza, presided. These judges absolved Coronado of blame: the first war crimes tribunal in North America ended in injustice. Yet the occurrence of such a trial in itself set the Spanish to thinking; many recognized that they could face consequences for killing Indians.[38]

Some Pueblo Indians who escaped the wrath of Coronado fled to the mountains in the middle of winter, without clothing or food. Some joined the more mobile Apaches, starting a trend that continued after the Spanish conquistador Juan de Oñate brought permanent settlers into New Mexico in 1598. Apache populations would rise while Pueblo towns suffered throughout the seventeenth century from epidemics and mistreatment. The process of ethnogenesis—of Pueblos becoming Apaches—continued into the mid-nineteenth century, when Pueblo towns had been reduced to a mere dozen or so.

The early story of Native encounters with Europeans in the Southwest had little to do with struggles over land. Most conquistadors sought gold not soil, even though they dutifully claimed North American lands for their kings and queens. Likewise English sea captains paid little attention to the quality of the soil in Virginia or Massachusetts, looking instead for waterways and commercial profit. Land seemed even less a factor in the early settlement of Quebec in Canada, as the earliest settlers, led by Samuel de Champlain, disembarked 150 miles upriver along the St. Lawrence seaway on abandoned Indian lands. Epidemics apparently had carried off the Hochelagans and Stadaconans (who had been visited by the earlier explorer Cartier years before) as a result of their constant contact with European traders.[39]

While many explorers commented on the lands that they stumbled upon, rating their productivity or even their sterileness, these issues were generally secondary during the age of exploration. For many, North America simply stood in the way of Asia, their ultimate goal because of its exotic products that would sell in Europe. Accordingly, most European explorers moved on. Even Cortés in the Southwest went back to Mexico when he found no gold. But a new age of settlement was just beyond the horizon. It would impact Indians to a much greater extent than did Vespucci, who gave the New World a name.

2

EUROPEAN PENETRATION
OF THE NEW WORLD

Europe faced a daunting new landscape as it emerged from the Middle Ages. Populations devastated by plagues in years past were once again growing after 1500. Markets coveted sugar, bananas, spices, and other exotic products. Kingdoms metamorphosed into states with established laws. All this rustling about brought a transition; Europeans turned quickly from the exploration of the New World to its settlement. Ironically, most Europeans crossed the Atlantic Ocean with little intention of settlement—they sought wealth instead. Gold, silver, furs, and products of any sort that might be marketed in Europe were at first prized. But when Europeans found little to exploit, they grudgingly turned to the land. This transition took a little over a hundred years.

The process of settlement accelerated after 1600. It started in far-off New Mexico with Oñate's invasion of Pueblo lands, and then Powhatan's people arose from their beds one morning in 1607 to learn of a European settlement taking shape at the mouth of what the English called the James River in Virginia. To the north, Pilgrims landed at Plymouth Rock along the south Massachusetts coast in 1619; Puritans followed them in 1630, founding Boston. Meanwhile the Dutch had landed at New York, claiming Long Island and lands in the Jersey countryside. North American Native peoples must have noticed the change; indeed some may have welcomed it. Others no doubt took a dim view of their new neighbors, who seemed to have an insatiable desire for exploiting the land, whether through planting much larger fields or by taking ever growing numbers of animals for their flesh and fur.

Settlers from the south of Europe differed somewhat in their view of settlement from those in the north. Settlers from Spain harbored views derived from the Middle Ages. Oñate's contract, for example, was similar to those originating during the reconquest of Spain from the Muslims, when the Crown licensed *adelantados* (captains) to conquer towns and their surrounding lands, granting them titles, governmental authority, and land when they were successful.[1] Indeed the 130 soldiers who joined Oñate's party expected to become *hidalgos,* which meant literally the "sons of someone"—in essence landowners. While grants from the king in both New Mexico and Florida were forthcoming, most of the land held limited resources and offered little if any income from mining. Yet another institution made such grants worthwhile, however, as the grantees often acquired an *encomienda* grant—while not land, it provided Indian "tribute" or "labor" from Indian towns to develop either mines or estates.[2]

Spanish missionaries—and the utter lack of gold—limited the activities of *adelantados* during the early settlement of Florida. But New Mexico, and later Texas and California, possessed lands similar to those reconquered in Spain. Historians occasionally have viewed the two institutions that the Spanish used to conquer the Southwest—the landed estates (haciendas) and the *encomiendas*—as one and the same. But *encomiendas* simply granted Indian tribute or labor to an *encomendero*. The *encomienda* first appeared north of the Rio Grande in New Mexico in the form of "tribute." The *encomendero* collected blankets and corn, which on occasion were replaced by labor when the Indians were unable to pay.[3]

While the viceroy in Mexico City limited *encomienda* grants in New Mexico to thirty-five, many Native Americans struggled to sustain tribute payments or provide the men necessary for labor. After receiving an *encomienda, encomenderos* subsequently received a land grant to the region surrounding the Indian town—or the Indian pueblo in the case of New Mexico—from which they received tribute. Initially Oñate handed out *encomiendas* and land grants to his most trusted soldiers. Francisco Gómez Robledo received grants for two of the most productive pueblos, Pecos and Esuque. As the grants became burdensome, some Indians abandoned their towns and moved onto ranches nearby, becoming landless vaqueros or joining Apache bands.[4] This promoted missions to some degree: the Franciscans who also received land grants in New Mexico tried to protect their charges from such abuse. But throughout much of the early seventeenth century Pueblo Indians could only watch as Spanish pressure on their land and society mounted—and many of their leaders plotted rebellion.

Native family units and Pueblo religion likely suffered the most. Indian men were unable to protect their women from sexual abuse, which only increased after Indians were forced to work on Spanish ranches or moved to them.[5] Worse, Indian captives, taken in raids by both Indians and Spaniards, often found themselves in the slave market of Santa Fe, being auctioned off to the highest bidders. The market encompassed adults and children taken in an area from the Grand Canyon in the far West nearly to the Mississippi River in the east and from Sonora in Mexico into central Kansas. Young, nubile females brought the highest prices, because they were free of sexually transmitted diseases.[6] An entirely new ethnic group identified as mestizo/mestiza resulted, part Spanish, part Indian. They had little status in either Pueblo or Spanish society. Given their low status, the mestizos remained mostly landless.

For the Spanish conquerors, the decline in the Native population soon became a pragmatic factor restricting the killing of Indians. But it had little impact on the institution of slavery, which also had a negative impact on Native social structures, limiting births and creating population instability. Put simply, Indians were needed for their labor. This did not prevent at least one orgy of destruction. In 1601 Oñate's soldiers, seeking retribution for the murder of several of their own, overran the western Pueblo of Acoma. The conquerors slaughtered hundreds of Indians and sentenced those men who surrendered to have one foot chopped off (to what extent the sentences were carried out is debated).[7] The massacre, decidedly opposed by authorities in Spain, was perhaps the second great war crime committed by Europeans against Native Americans.

The Spanish demands for food, unusually dry weather, and disease did more to reduce Pueblo Indian populations than did Spanish soldiers or the institution of slavery. By 1640 the number of occupied Pueblos along the Rio Grande fell to forty, with a population roughly half of what it had been just forty years before. Twenty years later more Pueblos disappeared, especially in the so-called Salinas district (the salt region of southeastern New Mexico). Declining Native populations slowed Spanish growth in the region. Ranches became untenable without Indian labor, and some ranchers gave up even though the Indian land that they claimed title to was granted gratis by the Crown.[8] Such massive population declines and shifts in the Spanish Southwest were a consequence of invasion, perhaps even a crime against humanity, given that the *encomienda* system certainly bordered on slavery.

The first English colonists who permanently settled in Virginia in 1607 had a somewhat different view of land. Those who belonged to the gentry expected to own lands in fee simple, much like the emerging gentry of England. Yet the English Crown actually gave clear title to the "Virginia Company," a corporation owned fundamentally by just four men, all members of the gentry.[9] While the question of sovereignty seemed settled—England had a viable claim against Spain, or any other foreign usurper—questions regarding property ownership arose. Colony leaders supposedly settled the issue by exchange; Powhatan's people agreed to accept goods and the English settled on lands (the titles remained in England with the company).[10]

This arrangement lasted only a few years. A guerrilla war broke out after a large number of new colonists arrived and moved fifty miles inland to build a fort at Henrico in 1611 along the James River. Soldiers from the fort invaded lands in the heart of Powhatan's confederacy. Cut off from supplies from Powhatan's people, Captain Samuel Argall opened trade relations with the Patawomekes, a strong, independent band of over a thousand people who lived in ten villages along the upper Potomac River. After making allies of the Patawomekes, Argall then forced Powhatan to sign a peace treaty in 1614, recognizing the English presence. During the fighting Argall's men burned some forty Indian houses just above Henrico and even convinced the Patawomekes to assist in the kidnapping of young Pocahontas. The marriage of Pocahontas to John Rolfe brought a temporary peace. Rolfe's access to Indian villages led to his discovery of Native tobacco plants. This produced the first commercial profit for Virginia and, unfortunately for the Indians, created a land rush.[11]

Lands inland grew tobacco much better than the barren coastal plain, so the English push into the interior increased rapidly after 1618. The Virginia Company aided the expansion by a change in land policy; stockholders who moved to the New World received land through stock purchases, paying a small, one-time quitrent.[12] But initially the Virginia Company continued to reject attempts, even by the gentry, to purchase land directly from the Indians. It finally relented about 1620 when one large purchase was secured from Opechancanough, the Pamunkey *werowance* who gradually assumed power from an aging Powhatan.[13]

The purchase of Indian lands seemingly prevented conflict, at least for a time. But as the English learned to play one group of Native villages off against another—as Argall had demonstrated—they used similar advantages in purchasing lands. The debate over whether the English had the right simply to seize lands as a result of the "right of discovery" or whether they needed to respect Indian ownership swung more and more to the former position.[14] As the English became stronger and developed more Indian allies in Virginia and an insatiable demand for land emerged, the moral restraints that moderated ethnic cleansing (of the sort that came with purchase and perhaps bribery) rapidly diminished.

Pressure on land brought on a much more destructive Anglo war with Powhatan's people in 1622, likely as the result of a misunderstanding over the sale supposedly agreed to by Opechancanough. This chief led the attack that completely surprised the English. In one day his men killed over 300 colonists. But the English regrouped and pushed the Indians farther into the interior over the next decade, taking more and more land by right of conquest. Peace finally came in 1632, but Opechancanough, old and brought into battle on a litter, tried one last time to regain the lost empire of the Powhatans, attacking the English twelve years later. Again he faced defeat: he was captured, displayed in a cage, and ultimately shot in the back by his English captors.

The Virginia governor Francis Wyatt summed up the general belief of most English in Virginia: "Our first work is expulsion of the savages." Indeed, he went on, "it is definitely better to have no heathen among us, who at best were but as thorns in our sides, than to be at peace and league with them."[15] It is difficult to determine how European philosophers such as Grotius (who was writing his famous book *The Rights of War and Peace* at the time) would assess such a conflict and such a conclusion. Powhatan's people were defending their lands: they instigated a war that some would argue was "just" and then lost the conflict and their lands. Through their newly selected sovereign, Governor Wyatt, the British had instituted a stated policy of ethnic cleansing, but one that clearly avoided the word "extermination."

The Anglo-Powhatan wars of 1622–32 and 1644–46 put a terrible strain on the Virginia Colony. Large numbers of men and women perished in the combat and other tobacco plantation workers faced ambushes while in the fields. Although minor skirmishes did occur just prior to the wars, the Virginia Colony did not purposefully adopt a policy of conflict that might lead to war. Even so, Powhatan's people realized that the continued loss of land jeopardized their entire economy, which depended upon hunting and gathering over rather vast expanses as well as farming in the fertile riverbottoms coveted by the English for growing tobacco.

War offered the English the opportunity to force Powhatan's people entirely out of the James and York River watersheds and take these valuable lands. The destruction of Indian towns and the forced relinquishment of large amounts of land only made it easier for colonial administrators to advance the stated policy of ethnic cleansing (or expulsion) by the 1640s. Within several decades of the implementation of this policy, the Anglo Chesapeake Bay region population grew from a few thousand to seventy thousand people. The hopes of slow, nonviolent assimilation symbolized by Pocahontas, as historian Daniel Richter has noted, crumbled as her fellow tribesman Opechancanough launched a futile effort to expel the invading English.[16]

The conflict of 1622 had attracted the attention of British authorities. Virginia Company proprietors, now anxious to invest elsewhere, turned the colony over to the Crown in 1624. The king thereafter selected a royal governor who had much to say about land grants and Indian policy. He first acquired the right to charge a nominal fee for signing off on the grants that the Crown sanctioned; more fees emerged later to cover the cost of surveying lands. Yet the House of Burgesses, which at times quarreled with the governor, acquired some authority over the distribution of land simply by agreeing to or resisting the institutionalization of such fees or quitrents, as they were often called.[17]

A similar pattern emerged farther north in New York and New England. The Plymouth Colony remained small. It had no charter from the king, so it quickly made peace with the nearby Wampanoag Indians, signing a treaty in 1621. The Wampanoags benefited by the treaty, because they feared the more powerful Narragansett bands to the west and the Pequots who lived beyond the Narragansetts.[18] The real story of the struggle for New England came when the Puritans settled at Boston. They selected John Winthrop as governor of the colony even before departing England and carried their charter with them, which allowed them to grant vast lands—with some question of legality—especially after England submerged itself in civil war. While the English built communities in New England, they also became expert at manipulating the various small Native bands and tribes who had never developed anything approaching a unified political system.

After arriving in 1630, the colonists who sailed with Winthrop—some of whom were of the gentry class—soon laid out towns in the vicinity of Boston harbor. The Court of Assistants, which supposedly ruled the colony, promoted these communities as some 30,000 Puritans poured into the region in the first decade of development. Common folk, anxious for lands themselves, soon found an avenue by joining church congregations and claiming that such bodies had authority to distribute lands. Within a few years land selection and titles quickly fell under the authority of town governments or church bodies, which spread rapidly into the countryside. If the Congregational or Presbyterian church accepted newcomers, their families received land.[19]

Winthrop considered the issue of land acquisition and distribution even before leaving England in 1629. He concluded that most lands in America fell under the category of *vacuum domicilium* (uninhabited land). This might have been true for lands directly in and around Plymouth, because a small-pox epidemic had carried off many of the Wampanoags, but the argument failed the farther the English went into the interior. Given the doctrine of Laws of Nature, which most English believed in, Winthrop soon conceded that Indians did have title to cultivated or highly developed lands but contended that hunting lands became incidental and rightfully might be opened to settlement and emerging town populations.[20] The council passed a law in 1634 expanding on Winthrop's views. Citing Genesis 1:28 and Psalm 115:16, the council determined that Indians could seek redress in the court for loss of farmlands or fishing stations but that all other lands could be purchased from them with a license from the court.[21] Winthrop's son soon tested the new legislation.

John Winthrop, Jr., landed at Boston in 1635, determined to seize and open new lands. Young Winthrop quickly took advantage of a treaty then being negotiated between the Pequot chief Sassacus and Massachusetts Bay officials. The Pequots agreed to sell land in the Connecticut Valley, opening the region to two English settlements. The negotiation had evolved around an attempt to settle several murders of Dutch and English traders that resulted from competition over the beaver-skin trade. The new English settlements only widened the emerging guerrilla conflict, however, and in 1636 the English militia attacked two different Pequot villages. The Pequots understandably retaliated, killing English settlers.[22]

Despite having been in existence for only one year, the Connecticut General Court ordered that a militia be formed to punish the Pequots by attacking their towns. John Mason formed up ninety settlers, most of whom had little experience in warfare, and then sought allies. He convinced the Mohegan sachem Uncas to join the expedition with his seventy warriors. Other Narragansetts joined as well; several served as guides. With the assistance of a Native force equal in size to his own, in 1637 Mason surrounded and destroyed (mainly by burning) the main Pequot village at Mystic Lake on the central Connecticut River, killing an estimated 400 to 700 Indians. Most of the dead were women and children—often historically the victims of ethnic cleansing—burned to death in their wigwams as the English slaughtered those who ran.[23]

Forced treaties and purchases allowed Puritans to claim most of central Connecticut in the aftermath of the struggle. Pressure for more land only mounted as many English fled the homeland as a result of England's Civil War. In the 1640s leaders of the Connecticut colony opened talks with the Narragansetts, who were forced to cede more land in eastern Connecticut. By this time some deeds were obtained even without presents. A "bottle of rum" often served the purpose, a circumstance that some Massachusetts Bay religious leaders and politicians decried but seemed incapable of stopping.[24]

After taking much of central Connecticut, Puritan settlers then turned on the small and demographically declining Wampanoags, who by the 1660s were led by the increasingly contrite Metacom or King Philip, as the English called him. After repeated threats and even an attempted assassination by leaders of the Plymouth Colony, King Philip agreed to another land grab in the 1660s and in the bargain was forced to pledge obedience to English authorities.[25] The Indians owned small herds of livestock, mostly pigs, and further conflict emerged over use of lands necessary for grazing. As the Wampanoags lost their best lands in southern Massachusetts, Philip plotted to stop the injustice, gathering arms for his warriors. He was dragged in front of Plymouth Plantation authorities on several occasions in the 1670s and pledged to remain at peace, but in reality he prepared for war.[26]

Philip recognized that the Wampanoags faced complete submission—the loss of a homeland, which in reality meant joining one of the Indian praying towns under the direction of English missionaries, where farming would be possible. But submission meant abandoning the Wampanoag way of life, its economy, its social structure, and its religion. In 1675 King Philip elected to fight, attacking the most exposed English towns. His coalition included elements of almost all the remaining Algonquians in southeastern New England. By fall, when it seemed as though the powerful Narragansett tribe of western Rhode Island would also join the coalition, a large English army marching in dreaded cold overran the Narragansett fort in what was called the "Great Swamp fight." Probably a thousand Indians—again mostly women and children—were killed or died of starvation thereafter.[27]

The English suffered as well. Native war parties attacked some fifty English towns and overran twelve of them. By spring 1676 the Wampanoags and Narragansetts and their allies all had been defeated, hiding in swamps and starving to death or fleeing across the Hudson River into New York. Some, like Philip, were caught and shot down. As triumphant English troops proclaimed, the dead leader of the rebellion ended up face-down, covered with mud, and looked like "a doleful, great, naked, dirty beast."[28] For good measure, his body was drawn and quartered and his head carried back to Plymouth as a trophy. That spring the colonies placed rewards on the heads of Indians living outside the praying towns. As Douglas Leach, historian of King Philip's War, has noted, "Hunting redskins became for a time a popular sport in New England." The war, begun by the Indians, erupted over land (especially grazing rights), pure and simple.[29]

A less violent fate befell the Delawares of New York and New Jersey. After suffering a terrible defeat in the 1640s, they faced the continued expansion of both the Dutch and the English into the Hudson River valley and eastward onto Long Island. Original settlers purchased much of their land in New York in small parcels, fifty acres or thereabouts. The purchaser did have to acquire permission to negotiate from colony officials. This policy continued after the English took over New Netherlands in 1664. By this time, however, a few powerful families had also bought Delaware land, creating huge estates for the Van Cortlandts, the Livingstons, and the Roosevelts. Much larger land transactions occurred in New Jersey and Pennsylvania, where proprietors literally owned the colony and purchased lands that settlers then bought. By the time the proprietor William Penn founded Philadelphia in 1680, much of the original Delaware homeland was in English hands—and Penn's colonists would slowly demand the rest.[30]

Well to the north of these Delawares and Shawnees, yet another conflict seemed in the offing, especially after the French built Quebec in 1608 and moved into the interior. By 1615 they reached the well-developed lands of Huronia, just north of Lake Erie, where a large exchange economy soon took shape. From these lands came corn, tobacco, and other foods, but the main export was beaver skins. The Huron Indians constituted the largest Native group west of the emerging French colony, some 40,000 to 50,000 Indians. Huron towns, built on hills, were heavily defended with twenty-foot bastions where bowmen could protect the permanent long houses. Most towns held several thousand people. While the French also sent Jesuit missionaries into these lands, they experienced little success or even protection from the growing numbers of Frenchmen who went native, taking Huron Indian women as wives and producing a restless new ethnic group, the *coureurs de bois* (Great Lakes Indian traders). New France proved an exception. The French were not there for land; they came to trade.[31]

As the French trade grew, it soon attracted the attention of Iroquois Indians south of Lake Erie. Their villages, nestled in the Finger Lakes area of western New York, were well protected and ideally located to send parties into the West. Obtaining arms from the Dutch, who opened a new outpost at Albany in the late 1620s, they soon competed with the Hurons for control of the Western Great Lakes fur trade. The fighting became intense in the 1640s and was soon accompanied by outbreaks of smallpox. By 1649, despite their heavy fortifications, the Huron towns faced utter destruction. Only a handful of Indians fled west beyond Lake Superior. These "beaver wars" kept New France from growing appreciably for the next fifty years. They ended to some degree only in 1700, when the Iroquois, exhausted and seeing the benefits of neutrality, agreed to peace at Quebec.[32]

A fate similar to that of the Hurons awaited those Indians who had made peace and tried to live quietly in Virginia. The Pamunkey, Appomattox, and Chickahominy Indians had settled in small communities on lands offered to them by the Crown. The governor of the colony at the time, William Berkeley, a good man who had been in Virginia off and on since 1641, pledged to protect them and maintain peace. Unfortunately, perhaps as a result of the conflict in New England, English planters on the frontier became convinced in 1675 that Delaware and Susquehannoch Indians living in Maryland had been responsible for small raids on their farms in which a handful of livestock had disappeared. Following a wealthy planter, Thomas Mathew, colonists crossed the Potomac and attacked some Delaware Indians, killing ten of them. Berkeley ordered Colonel John Washington (the ancestor of the future president) to investigate. Along with Major Thomas Truman of the Maryland militia (the ancestor of another future president), the forces surrounded a Susquehannoch town and demanded that its leaders surrender.[33]

The Susquehannochs, who had moved to Maryland to avoid conflict with the Iroquois, denied all the charges. They even sent out five unarmed sachems to negotiate. The men carried a silver metal plate inscribed with a pledge that the colonial government of Maryland would protect them. Washington and Truman captured the five men and promptly executed them. As nearly a thousand Virginia and Maryland militia then laid siege to the fort, the one hundred Susquehannoch men inside stood their ground. Seeing little hope of relief, however, the Susquehannochs quietly evacuated in the wee hours of the morning, killing ten sleeping English sentries on the way out.[34]

Conditions only worsened when a newly arrived member of the gentry from England, Nathaniel Bacon, punished several friendly Appomattox Indians whom he suspected of stealing corn. In the fall some small Indian raids, mostly inconsequential, occurred, probably revenge assaults by small numbers of Susquehannnochs. Governor Berkeley responded by ordering settlers to build stockades. He then tried to negotiate an end to the conflict. Many in the colony, however, only became convinced that Governor Berkeley himself had profited by the fur trade—a false accusation—and overtly seemed more interested in saving Indians than colonists. Bacon led the critics, organizing a rump militia and starting what is known to history as Bacon's Rebellion. His paramilitary force, like so many in history, sought land and booty.

Within a few months Bacon's men, as Wilcomb E. Washburn, the historian of the rebellion, has noted, "contented themselves with frightening away, killing, or enslaving most of the friendly neighboring Indians, and taking their beaver and land as spoils." More significant assaults occurred against Indians who were farther away, including the friendly Occaneechees. As one chronicler who witnessed the carnage reported, Bacon's force fell upon "men woemen [sic] and children . . . [and] disarmed and destroid them." In summer 1676 he turned on the Pamunkeys, seeking out their small encampments hidden in the swamps along the James River. Once Bacon's men found them, they murdered and plundered even these friendly communities.[35]

Bacon's ultimate goal included forcing Governor Berkeley from power. Bacon's movement gained momentum through the summer, as many Virginians joined him; but by fall his followers suffered from want of provisions and arms as the British Navy arrived in the bay. Just as Bacon's paramilitary force sought final victory by capturing Berkeley, Bacon died of the "bloody flux" (dysentery) on the eve of the battle. When a thousand British troops disembarked, Bacon's force fled, most disavowing the treason that had obviously occurred.[36]

A few early historians of the event saw Bacon's cause as symbolic of the growing restlessness of American settlers who wanted "liberty." Some viewed the effort as simple opposition to Governor Berkeley's supposed oppression. But Bacon seemed more intent on using turmoil as a means to plunder Indian towns and even some English towns than in fomenting a "liberal" revolution, as his men sacked Jamestown at one point. While Bacon's "army" did devastate Indian communities, driving the few Indians left in Virginia into the forests, it should be remembered that Governor Berkeley declared Bacon a "rebel" and the English government disavowed his actions. Had he been captured before his death, he would have been treated as a common criminal and executed. Nathaniel Bacon and his followers were murderers or perhaps war criminals, depending upon the degree to which his forces might be granted some military status. And these events clearly demonstrate that the British government decried the policy of extermination that Bacon attempted to institute.

Just as it took New England many years to recover from King Philip's War, Bacon's Rebellion had a lasting effect on Virginia. Lessons regarding conflict with Indians became clearer and clearer to many English as the century wore on. Plantations and farms were burned and people living farthest from the centers of English colonial government often had to flee eastward, leaving behind everything. The abject lust for land and booty caused this conflagration, moral violations that the home government in England and its governors in the New World came to recognize.

Far to the south and west, in the Spanish provinces of Florida and New Mexico, the handful of increasingly isolated Spanish settlers and missionaries learned the same lesson. The Pueblo Indians had lost more and more land to Spanish intruders, as had the Apalachees and Timucuas in Florida. Franciscan missionaries increasingly took the best farmlands and built churches with bells that daily called the Indians to the fields and to church. Ranchers in New Mexico coveted the mission lands and charged the missionaries with abusing the Indians. These accusations had some legitimacy. The missionaries used *mayordomos* (labor bosses) to whip Indians who rebelled and to chase down those who fled the missions. Charges and countercharges filled letters sent back to Havana and Mexico City: governors of the province outlined the atrocities committed by missionaries, while missionaries used the Inquisition to excommunicate governors. In Florida missionaries probably tried to prevent information about the growing conflict with their so-called neophytes in 1565, 1647, and again in 1675 from getting out.[37]

The administrative confusion seems not to have been wasted on the Pueblo Indians, who sought to remove the Spanish yoke in one swift blow in 1680. Growing religious conflict was at the center of the rebellion. Missionaries continually invaded kivas (underground religious centers) and destroyed sacred objects. The Pueblo Indians had relied upon these objects for protection during times of drought and war. And some of the worst droughts in history descended upon New Mexico in the 1660s and 1670s. When the Catholic religion offered no release, Pueblo religious leaders slowly united a number of towns, convincing their leaders to rise against the Spanish.[38]

Popé, a devout Pueblo religious leader who had been ceremoniously whipped just five years before in the square at Santa Fe for sorcery, emerged as the charismatic leader. Using knotted ropes to time the rebellion, about a dozen Pueblo townsmen fell on their missionaries on August 10, 1680, killing priests and burning churches. They soon turned to the countryside, where isolated Spanish ranches were vulnerable. In all they killed over 400 of the hated Spaniards, sending the survivors fleeing to Santa Fe. The governor, Antonio de Otermín, barricaded the town and prepared to defend it as best he could. He had only a hundred capable men and some 2,000 civilians, who soon faced perhaps 2,000 armed and angry Pueblo and Apache Indians.[39]

The siege of Santa Fe became a momentous struggle. The Pueblos took most of the town and pushed the surviving Spaniards—who had been joined by a small number of loyal Indians—into a few strong buildings. After seeing many of his men either fall or be wounded, Governor Otermín decided to flee south late in the evening of September 21. He left behind a colony in ruin. It seems inconceivable that this withdrawal of 2,000 people 300 miles to the small outpost of El Paso could have been accomplished without the Indians knowing it. Most likely some leaders within the ranks of the Pueblo rebels did not want to kill the Spanish. Getting rid of the hated Franciscans and burning the Spanish towns had been enough. Otermín's departure with his surviving people had been the goal of the rebellion.[40]

In 1680 a new era dawned in North America. The English colonies on the Atlantic Coast had seen their populations severely reduced through Indian war. The Indians who survived those times had mostly fled into the interior, where they joined other Native towns and rebuilt their shattered lives. Ethnogenesis occurred in the East much as in the Southwest, in that surviving bands of Indians joined others, molding their social and religious customs to fit the emerging majority. Evidence suggests that such restructuring occurred quickly, often within a generation or two. This melding of different groups created stronger Native societies that also knew much about the land-hungry Europeans who had produced such upheaval.

Calm settled in, resulting as much from events in Europe as in America. The English Civil War had ended by 1660; it too had devastated the land and slowed the development of the motherland. The migration of settlers from England to America slowed appreciably. Perhaps the starkest example of the changing times was the decline in religious zeal. The Puritan movement began to sputter; the generally despised Anglican Church opened its doors in Boston in 1690. To the south, in Florida and New Mexico, the rebellions had led to much less interest on the part of the Crown and the religious orders in rebuilding churches that had been destroyed or replacing martyred missionaries. The Spanish would slowly return to central New Mexico, but with a different view of colonial development. And English governors in the eastern colonies of North America were instructed on the cost of war—when ships and men had to be sent to the New World, it taxed the treasury of the king. Such occurrences were to be avoided. The colonial push into the American continent that had seen so much activity between 1600 and 1680 slowed due to exhaustion, and negotiated settlements of disputes with Indians became the norm for some time thereafter.

Yet what can be said of the destruction of the Pequots, Wampanoags, Hurons, Powhatans, and other Indians who were forced into the interior of American, abandoning their homelands? We know for sure what did not happen. There was never a concerted policy (discussed and implemented through the various colonial assemblies in North America or their colonial governors) with the goal of killing all Native men, women, and children because of their ethnicity. The nearest indictment possible under the circumstances might be applied to the Connecticut General Court, which did sanction the attack on the Pequot towns, perhaps a war crime. But this came after a guerrilla war had broken out, in which men and women on both sides were killed.

The destruction of Native peoples and the forced withdrawal of many others were the direct result of British, French, and Spanish imperial designs. These constitutional claims functioned to establish Crown authority in core areas, such as Boston, Jamestown, Santa Fe, and even Quebec. As historian Lisa Ford has argued, however, they did not "extend meaningful jurisdiction" over frontier elements such as the groups who joined John Mason or Nathaniel Bacon or even the Iroquois Indians who destroyed the Hurons.[41] Indeed, for all practical purposes, Bacon was one of the first colonists to assert a right of "settler sovereignty," defying the very Crown authority that had given him access to lands in the New World.

The generally peaceful designs of empire builders, most of whom sat in the colonial capitals of the New World, offered little consolation to Indians who had lost their lands and homes in the orgies that had constituted the first eighty years of colonial development. Those Indians had been victims of a crime against humanity, stemming from the adoption of a policy of ethnic cleansing that empire builders had sanctioned. Indians had to be removed from lands so that Europeans could expand onto them or in the Southwest moved to ranchos, where they would become vaqueros. The justification for such removal mirrored what is commonly considered the main cause for massive crimes against humanity today: Indian culture differed from European culture. Native peoples spoke a different language, prayed to a different god or gods, and had a different economy. They even built houses differently. Europeans questioned their use of the land and the degree of their civilization.

But leaders in positions of legitimate power generally did not question the right of the American Indians to live. When Indians protested or rebelled, wars erupted that both the English and Spaniards would call "just," such as the declared war agreed to by the Connecticut General Court. At times this led to abuses or war crimes, perpetrated mostly by militia units. The same colonial authorities who sanctioned expansion then often lacked the policing resources to restrain frontier elements. They frequently lost control over events, as did the parent governments in Europe, who often knew little about what was occurring in their colonies.

The Indians of Florida and New Mexico suffered a somewhat different fate, but it too often reached the level of a crime against humanity rather than genocide. Those Indians were forced to work in the fields and tend stock, bordering on a violation of section c of the Rome Statutes, which outlaws "enslavement." The Franciscans, who used force to keep Indians in missions, then sold the excess produce of the Indian laborers to purchase silver chalices and ornate figurines to adorn the recesses of these churches. When Pueblo Indians rebelled individually, they were whipped; when entire towns rebelled, they were reduced to rubble. But Spaniards needed Indian labor more than dead Indians.

Only the French resisted the inclination to conquer Native peoples, at least initially, especially after the Huron and Ottawa Indians became important intermediaries in the fur trade. Even so, French reticence had little to do with respect for Native Americans. The lands along the banks of the St. Lawrence simply were not attractive when it came to intensive cultivation, and the colony suffered accordingly, often facing starvation. The rules regarding the relationship of cultivation to possession established by Grotius, Locke, and Vattel just did not apply. Moreover, the French who came to the New World were mostly adventurers who saw the fur trade as a chance to gain wealth, much as the Spanish viewed their gold and silver mines of Mexico.

The first penetration of America brought Indian dispossession and considerable conflict and only occasionally peaceful but tension-filled negotiation. These themes seldom reach American history textbooks, which often revel in the establishment of towns and assemblies such as the House of Burgesses or the conversion of Pocahontas and the first Thanksgiving at Plymouth Rock.

3

INTERREGNUM

Natives and a Reformed Colonial Land Policy

Bacon's Rebellion and King Philip's War had exhausted European colonists along the Atlantic seaboard. Europeans had won the first contests for control of the coastal regions of America, sometimes by perpetrating "unjust" wars, but it had cost them dearly. It seemed a good time to consolidate what had been gained and avoid conflict. As the early decades of settlement led invariably to the adoption of a policy of ethnic cleansing, especially in New England and Virginia, by 1680 that policy fell into question. A period of interregnum pervaded the English settlements: government authorities gained the upper hand against such outlaws as Nathaniel Bacon, and policy fell under the control of colonial assemblies. A greater respect for Native titles to lands seemed in the offing. Half a continent away a similar reexamination was taking place. In the Southwest Spanish imperial designs and the land grab that went with them had suffered as well. The Pueblo Popé had sacked and burned missions in northern New Mexico, leading to a reexamination of Indian policy in Mexico City.

While it too would enter a period of relative peace after 1715, the southeastern portions of North America remained in turmoil throughout the period of imperial struggle known as Queen Anne's War (1702–13). The trouble erupted first in Florida, where in the late seventeenth century the seemingly mission-tamed Timucuas and Apalachees faced growing assaults from more northern tribes, such as the Yamasees and the Muskogees or Creeks. The imperial war then followed, pitting coastal and inland Indians against mission Indians, whose populations declined from more than 30,000 to less than one-third of that number before peace finally came to the region in 1715.[1] With the exception of the South, where the interregnum period came much later, American Indians in most regions of the continent, who had come to see Europeans as land-hungry aggressors, held their ground from 1675 into the middle of the next century and in some cases even retook some of it.

More significantly, the mother countries of Europe began to question the need for expansion onto Indian lands in the New World. They wished to exploit the region commercially, not to provide agricultural homes for the peasantry of their respective countries. Most of the early land policies that they had adopted were feudal in nature. European land policies appeased the gentry. When they produced wars, which cost blood and treasure, home governments often tried to rein in their colonists, including the gentry. Much new land had been abandoned by retreating Indians in Virginia, New Jersey, Massachusetts, Florida, and even New Mexico, offering sufficient ground for several decades of slow settlement. For a brief moment conflict over the continent's land subsided; pragmatic restrictions by colonists and Crown administrators led to the abandonment of a policy of ethnic cleansing in most parts of the New World.

This is not to say that Europeans (especially those of a commercial bent) entirely abandoned the imperial urge that had pushed them onto Native lands. The French sent explorer René-Robert Sieur de La Salle into the area of the western Great Lakes. Building trading posts across the west, La Salle reached the Mississippi River and canoed down it nearly to the Gulf of Mexico in 1682. Soon French traders had penetrated the Native villages of the Ohio Valley and even built posts in the far-off lands of what would become Minnesota.[2] In a rush to dominate the fur trade of the southern Indians, English traders (coming mostly from Barbados) landed on the Charles River in South Carolina in 1670 and built a small trading post. They too reached the Mississippi River in 1700 (or maybe a year or two before), meeting up with French traders who had established a base the year before at Biloxi, on the Gulf of Mexico.[3] Along with the Spanish, the English and French soon competed in the South for the two main sources of income: deerskin and slaves. Indeed the slave trade in Indians, not Africans, financed much of the early development of the Carolinas and even Virginia. It was clearly responsible for the turmoil that characterized the region until 1715.[4]

Southern colonial designs initially had little to do with land. In that sense settlements in the Carolinas or even in Alabama were not unlike the one organized by William Penn, the friendly aristocrat who had converted to Quakerism and convinced the king of England to grant a colony for a handful of Quakers in the New World. Penn founded Philadelphia in 1681 as a commercial town. Hardly any different than Charlestown, or Biloxi for that matter, Philadelphia emerged along the Delaware River, where it had access to the sea. It sent ships around the world and initially looked outward to the ocean rather than inward into the deep woods of Pennsylvania.

As further evidence of the quieting times, England and the Netherlands signed the Treaty of Westminster in 1674, ending yet another continental war. Little changed, other than the regranting of a royal charter for the colony of New York to the Duke of York, thus recognizing England's conquest of the colony from some years before. The duke, in turn, wishing to smooth the transition from Dutch control, selected a trusted advisor and military officer named Edmund Andros to serve New York as its new governor. Andros arrived just in time to help convince the Mohawk Indians, who had villages just west of Albany, to assist in putting down the Narragansetts during King Philip's War. Indian alliances with Europeans had unfortunately become a common story. While Andros might initially assist the land-hungry New Englanders in their aggression, above all he was a loyal and courageous supporter of the monarchy and his benefactor, the duke. He wanted to establish the Crown's rule in America and bring order and peace. That translated into an Indian policy that at least had little intent forcefully to push Indians west.[5]

Governor Andros had much more trouble with unruly colonists than with Indians. At times he jailed colonists who refused his orders, including a few Quakers who had settled in New Jersey and resisted the governor's new policies. He challenged faulty land grants and refused to recognize individual land titles purchased from Indians. This created quite a stir in New England, where the title to lands had been sanctioned by a Puritan Council. Andros found the Puritans to be particularly difficult; he generally believed that they were responsible for King Philip's War, which had produced "very greate" and unnecessary destruction. Worse, the war eventually involved the Abenaki Indians of Maine. The new governor thought that they should be courted as allies and their titles to land should be recognized. Andros negotiated with them in 1677 but could only watch as the Puritans in southern New Hampshire continued to raid Indian towns. Ultimately, after a Puritan militia unit suffered a disastrous defeat the next year, Massachusetts finally signed the peace accord.[6]

With conflict in the Northeast settled to some degree (more troubles over land would arise decades later) Andros sought to end the still festering conflict between the Susquehannock Indians and the colony of Maryland. This involved negotiating with the Iroquois, who had extensive trade relations with the Dutch at Albany. Dutch traders had purchased land from the Mohawks—who supposedly had conquered it from the Mahicans—and formed the community of Schenectady, some forty miles west of Albany, in 1661. This purchase marked the first Iroquois land cession and signaled the beginning of a slow European movement west into New York. Settlers pushed up the Mohawk River, opening farms some fifty miles beyond Schenectady, thanks to yet another land purchase in 1701. Individual land speculators concluded these sales with Iroquois village elders who may or may not have understood what the agreements meant. To some degree they could hardly refuse; Schenectady warehouses kept the goods that the Mohawk and other Iroquois Indians had become dependent upon.[7]

Meanwhile Andros attempted to calm another imperial expansionist: the proprietor, Cecilius Calvert (Lord Baltimore), whose Maryland colony straddled the upper Chesapeake Bay. He seemed far less willing to listen to Andros than the Indians were. Baltimore blamed the conflict with the Susquehannocks on the Indians rather than on Washington and Truman. Andros countered with the assertion that the Maryland militia had fallen on the Susquehannocks and "so near destroyed them." The governor called for a series of meetings, taking place at Albany between 1677 and 1679, in which he attempted to negotiate a general peace.[8]

The five Iroquois tribes became key players in the negotiation: the Mohawks, with villages just west of Schenectady, Onondagas, Oneidas, and Cayugas, whose villages extended into the Finger Lakes of western New York, and the far western Senecas, who had towns some forty miles east of Niagara Falls. These communities formed a political "confederacy," but one in which each individual tribe remained autonomous, unlike the Powhatan Confederacy. All five tribes often debated major decisions at a central council, where every tribal leader had a say. Andros recognized that the Iroquois held sway over much of the land west of the New York and Pennsylvania settlements. When a Mohawk leader was questioned regarding land ownership in the Susquehanna Valley, he simply replied that he was sure his people owned the land because so many of his warriors died defending it and were buried there. Consequently the Iroquois spoke for other "tributary" tribes who had been forced into the northern

Susquehanna Valley, forming what historian Francis Jennings has described as a "multiparty confederation" with the Iroquois.[9]

In council Iroquois Indians emphasized the need to proceed at a slow pace, taking days or even months to arrive at a conclusion. Indeed after two years of summer talks a Mohawk speaker summed up the growing alliance that Andros finally had concluded, which the Iroquois had pioneered among themselves some decades before. This agreement with Europeans, called the Great Covenant Chain, lasted for many decades thereafter. "The Governor Genll [General] and we are one," the Iroquois speaker began, "one heart and one head, for the Covenant that is betwixt [us]." The agreement was so strong that "the very thunder" should not "break it asunder."[10] It only remained for the English to reaffirm this alliance each summer, making Albany literally the most important diplomatic post in the northern English colonies.

Andros's role in creating this lasting agreement was based upon his realization that in Native/European politics the offering of presents—or the stuff of trade—made lasting friends. Presents became symbolic of kin adoption, literally the willingness of a "father" to bestow benefits upon his "children," leading to a growing metaphor in which the father (the Crown) developed ties with his children (American Indians). While it would seem that this made the Indians dependent upon Europeans, it actually led to obligations on both sides. The relationship helped mold alliances, which affected war, peace, and commercialism.[11] The chain also involved the exchange of many belts of wampum or "sacred" gifts that had meaning well beyond their practical use. These belts consisted of channeled whelk shell (which was difficult to collect) and the hard-shelled clam shells that Native women painstakingly strung together. The presentation of the belts indicated that the European officers as well as Native speakers were not just talking for themselves but represented the "truthful" views of the governments involved.[12] Thousands of belts of this sort would be produced by Indians over the next century, being used to signify friendship and alliance as well as to create peace where it had broken down.

Most significantly, at the conference the powerful and astute Iroquois leaders eventually convinced Andros to honor Iroquois rule over much of the lands of what would become Pennsylvania, New York, Kentucky, and even Ohio. The Susquehannocks, who had been forced to flee northward, had little choice but to accept this tributary status. The Mahicans of the upper Hudson River had little to say about it either, given their diminished indeed almost insignificant military capabilities. Other Indians in the region, including the Delawares, Shawnees, and Mingos (villages of refugee Indians, some of whom were likely part Susquehannocks and Iroquois), also seemingly accepted the rule of the powerful Iroquois towns. This determination would have lasting and far-reaching implications, as new Delaware and Shawnee leaders would reject this tributary status in a generation or two.[13] But in the late seventeenth century the conferences at Albany seemingly settled the question.

Yet another attempt to consolidate Crown authority over land came when King James II ascended to the thrown in 1685 and placed New England, New Jersey, and New York under one central "Dominion," as it was called. Andros, as the new governor-general, caused a near-riot in Boston when he announced that only authentic titles to lands coming from the Crown would be recognized.[14] Andros, like many other British officials, recognized that the slow process of removing Indians from their lands undertaken by individual colonists or speculators led only to conflict and destruction. Unfortunately for Native Americans, the Glorious Revolution broke out in England in 1688, sweeping King James from power. The Dominion collapsed in America. New royal charters followed in the 1690s for Massachusetts and other colonies. The land question, seemingly fraught with overlapping claims and lawsuits, remained relatively unchanged. The Dominion's demise had little impact on the land policies in either New York or Pennsylvania, where commerce and the sea still prevailed in legitimate enterprises, but the lessons of King Philip's War and Bacon's Rebellion lingered in the councils of European and colonial capitals.

While Andros adopted an enlightened Indian policy based upon pragmatic and legal restrictions that generally prevented ethnic cleansing, similar patterns of administrative pragmatism emerged in the Southwest. In far-off New Mexico as well as in Florida mission Indians had frequently rebelled. The rebellions spread into northern Mexico, where Sumas, Conchos, Tobosos, Julimes, and Pimas all sacked missions and then ran to the hills, often joining Apaches.[15] Spain turned the New Mexico debacle over to a new governor, Diego de Vargas, in 1691. He had few illusions about the difficulty of retaking the upper valley of the Rio Grande when he set off with a small army and a large contingent of Pueblo auxiliaries the next year. Eventually Vargas retook Santa Fe, but New Mexico would never be the same after the 1680 revolt. Vargas and those who followed him recognized that the Native populations had to be treated with more fairness and allowed some semblance of independence. A few missionaries returned to labor in the Pueblo towns that remained; unlike their predecessors, most of them allowed some measure of Native religious and economic freedom, if for no other reason than that the alternative might easily be rebellion and martyrdom.[16]

Vargas also implemented more enlightened land policies. The large estates (*estancias*) that had appeared after 1600 had been abandoned during the rebellion. Vargas and other governors who followed reverted to granting much smaller amounts of land and even assuring Pueblo towns of titles to lands that they irrigated. These smaller grants came in two varieties; one was a simple grant of land to the head of a family, usually lands designated for agricultural use. This led to the creation of *ranchos*. The title to the land was granted by the governor with the assistance of the local town council, which issued a *testimonio,* a document that gave a general description of the land and its boundaries.[17] While the few Pueblo towns that remained generally received town grants, these were also given to mixed Spanish/Indian towns that emerged after 1700.

The town grants came in several varieties. The most difficult to maintain went to *genízaro* towns (collections of ethnically mixed people, many of whom were the progenies of Indians taken during slave raids). Most of these *genízaro*s were assimilated Spaniards. As new generations of *genízaros* emerged, they agreed to form towns on the periphery of Spanish society, often entering lands that were not securely under Spanish control. Occasionally Spanish ranchers and their families settled nearby. When communities such as the *genízaro* towns or Spanish ranchers remained on their lands for four years, they received a title in fee simple.[18]

Genízaro communities remained buffers on the edge of Spanish settlement and faced constant pressure from Plains Indians and mountain people, especially Apaches and Navajos and (after 1700) Comanches. Some survived in this rather hostile atmosphere while others abandoned their land grants. Thus a give and take of land in New Mexico was the result. The colony made few inroads on Native control of the mountainous and near desert regions that bordered the upper Rio Grande valley. While Spanish officials could grant these lands for sheep herding or cattle raising, it often remained a question as to whether Spanish-bred communities could hold lands in the face of mounting Native opposition. In reality New Mexico stagnated in the eighteenth century, never attaining the level of development that had characterized the colony fifty years before.

Yet another change in New Mexico came in regard to its labor institutions. The *encomienda,* which had dominated labor relations during most of the seventeenth century, nearly disappeared, because Indian labor was no longer sufficient to sustain it.[19] In fact many Pueblo Indians had become Navajos, Apaches, or Hopis, groups independent of the Spanish. Yet a far more repressive institution replaced the *encomienda*: slavery expanded on a large scale, much as it did during the same period in the American South. Towns like Pecos, Taos, and even Santa Fe itself increasingly developed slave markets where Indians taken from the plains or the mountains, or even the distant Great Basin, were auctioned off.[20] Many were sent south to work in the mines of north-central Mexico; others toiled on small ranchos, while Franciscans purchased some for their missions. Slaves likely produced more revenue for Spanish governors than any other commodity.[21]

In many ways New Mexico became a sleepy outpost along the northern fringes of the Spanish empire after 1700. Yet Spain had not entirely given up on the region, especially after French explorers appeared along the lower Mississippi River in the 1680s and ultimately ventured into east Texas. A small group of Frenchmen even stumbled into a Spanish mission on the lower Rio Grande in 1714. The Spanish responded by founding missions in east Texas among the Caddo Indians, but they failed miserably, as both drought and smallpox forced a Spanish retreat. Nevertheless, even though smallpox continued to batter the Texas bands (Coahuiltecans, Tonkawas, and Karankawas as well as Caddos), the Crown sent Franciscans into south Texas in 1717, where they built yet another complex of five missions and a presidio or fort at San Antonio de Béxar along the San Antonio River. San Antonio eventually boasted a population of 3,000 people, the largest community in the Spanish borderlands.[22]

San Antonio, like New Mexico, suffered from the attempts of Native Americans to assert their control over the land. Apaches consistently remained outside the mission systems in both New Mexico and Texas and raided mission herds, killing cattle and taking horses. Even so, Franciscans slowly forced Coahuiltecans into the missions at San Antonio. The Crown granted lands to missions and ranchers, mostly for cattle raising. Grantees only had to demonstrate an ability to utilize the land for the good of the colony. Crown officials never considered any compensation to the Indians of south Texas, viewing them as "men without reason." This was primarily because they were hunters and gatherers, who, as Grotius, Locke, and

Vattel had argued, supposedly had no right to vast expanses of land. Spanish land grants increased in south Texas as the century wore on, mostly in the region bordered by San Antonio, the Gulf Coast in the east, and the Rio Grande in the south.[23]

While ranching provided the colony with protein, San Antonio governors found much greater profit in sending slaves to the south. This practice seemed to be on the increase across much of the Spanish borderlands and soon attracted groups of men in the emerging English colony at Charleston.

Rather than sending slaves into the mines of northern Mexico, the best market for the Carolinian traders was in the Caribbean, where sugar plantations demanded more and more labor. By 1700 some three hundred Charlestown traders worked in the interior, collecting slaves and hides. In doing so they made alliances with the Muskogeans (later called Creeks by the English) from the interior of what would become Georgia and Alabama as well as with smaller tribes, such as the Westos and Yamasees, who lived even closer to the emerging colony.

In the early seventeenth century the Westos from the Piedmont region of North Carolina had mounted raids on Spanish missions for slaves, which they sold to Virginia planters even before the founding of Charleston. The Yamasees consisted of people from various Native American groups, some of whom had fled Spanish missions in Florida and eastern Georgia and others of whom found it impossible to survive in the no-man's land that soon existed between the Spanish missions and South Carolina. Such groups were ideally situated to work for the Carolina traders, who armed them and sent them south and west to obtain deer skins and slaves. Unfortunately neither the Indians nor the English seemed to sense the problems that this would create. English rum soon inundated the Native communities south and west of Charleston, and English traders debauched Indian women when their husbands were in the interior. Even worse, the slave trade readily facilitated the spread of many different viruses that decimated Indians all across the Southeast.[24]

Perhaps even more devastating for southeastern Indians was the war that came to Europe in 1702 and lasted until 1713, called Queen Anne's War. Much of the conflict in the New World occurred in the South—Albany merchants mostly avoided the fighting. Carolina traders amassed some 500 whites and 370 Indian allies to assault the Spanish mission frontier in August 1702. While the force did not take the Spanish fort at St. Augustine, it did devastate the nearby missions, killing and pillaging and carrying into captivity scores of Timucua Indians. This victory only emboldened the English: over the next two years they destroyed the western Spanish missions among the Apalachee Indians. Some thousand Muskogeans joined them in the effort, capturing hundreds of slaves for the Caribbean markets. The Apalachee Indians, a once powerful force in western Florida, abandoned their remaining towns; some fled west to join Indians near the Mississippi delta, while others begged to be allowed into Muskogean towns. Ethnogenesis was occurring all across the South.[25]

Queen Anne's War, which continued for nine more long years, left virtually all of Spanish Florida in ruins and the lands of the Indians nearly vacated. Yet South Carolina could do little to take advantage of this situation, for it had a population of only a few thousand people. It did realize how important Indian allies had become during the war and attempted to pass laws preventing the crime of enslavement, at least of nearby Indian allies. The colony passed an Act for Regulating Trade in 1707, which required traders to apply for licenses and abstain from exchanging liquor with Indians. Perhaps more importantly, the same legislation set aside a "reservation" of land inland near Port Royal, for the exclusive use of the Yamasees, who had been so valuable during the early stages of Queen Anne's War.[26]

South Carolina's attempts to regulate contact with Indians seemed all the more important when the Tuscaroras rebelled in 1711. The causes echoed circumstances a century before in Virginia. Besides exploitation by Carolina traders, the Tuscaroras had been squeezed by the Cherokees in the West, thus finding hunting grounds increasingly difficult to protect. North and South Carolina squatters were poaching on those same lands from the east, despite laws designed to present such abuse. The Tuscaroras suddenly struck out at both the English and the Cherokees. The conflict continued into the next year, when the Tuscarora villages were overrun, with hundreds of Indians being killed. The South Carolinians and their Yamasee allies fought over the booty—some 700 Tuscarora slaves. They sold for 18 to 20 pounds apiece in Barbados, a small fortune for any frontiersman.[27]

Two years later a similar fate awaited the "trusted" Yamasees, allies of the English, who saw their reservation overrun by land speculators. While traders and settlers corrupted Yamasee men with rum and took advantage of their women, they also constructed a road through the heart of the

reservation, from Charleston to Port Royal. Protesting to Charleston officials that "white men were [illegally] settling among them," the Yamasees
tried to negotiate the expulsion of the new settlers. Becoming increasingly
exasperated at their failure to do so, the Indians struck at the heart of Carolina in 1715, killing an estimated 100 Indian traders in a few days. Only
after Virginia came to the aid of Charleston, mostly by providing arms
and munition to the Cherokees, who moved against the Yamasees, was
Charleston saved.[28] While historians have debated whether this conflict
originated from trader abuses or encroachment on lands, surely the end
result was ethnic cleansing, a product of the "right of conquest" formula
that existed after an Indian attack. The victims of the conflict were again
Native Americans, many of whom were women and children.

A minor land boom hit South Carolina by the 1720s, as the colony
slowly expanded up the Savannah River, building forts for protection.
South Carolinian forts and "rangers" took the place of the Yamasees, who
had at one time been the protective buffer defending the colony. Savannah
Town, a fort located two hundred miles up the river, became just such
a bastion. Other block houses existed farther east along the river.[29] The
rangers who occupied these outposts quickly doubled as land agents; they
knew the best lands, exploring the last crannies of what had been Indian
Country just a dozen years before.

As these new lands became available, the South Carolinian proprietors
granted much of the land as "headrights," based upon the immigrants'
ability to use it. Newly arriving immigrants paid a yearly quitrent of half
a penny an acre for the land, receiving more land if they brought along
servants to work it. Land policies across the Carolinas as well in Virginia
thus were feudal in nature. South Carolina became a royal colony in 1729,
much like Virginia and North Carolina. Thereafter the Crown allowed
the legislatures in all three of these colonies considerable leeway regarding land policies. This only increased land speculation in the West. One
Thomas Bailey in South Carolina, for example, sold nearly 12,000 acres of
land in a few years during the 1730s.[30] The consequences of the Yamasee
War had implications all across the South, even north of South Carolina.

Virginia pushed for the most liberal land policies after the Crown allowed the House of Burgesses to determine the fees that the governor
might charge for issuing land titles. In a dispute with lieutenant governor Robert Dinwiddie in the 1750s, the House asserted its authority: the
fee that Dinwiddie charged for affixing the royal signature to a title, the

House argued, was "an infringement on the Rights of the people, and a Discouragement from taking up land."[31] North and South Carolina followed suit, increasingly asserting power over land distribution. Most of this land fell under control of either the gentry or land speculators—indeed the gentry were often land speculators.

While the debates with Crown governors regarding land often erupted in all three of these colonies, they virtually never involved a discussion of Indian titles, for most of the coastal tribes that had lived in the region had long disappeared or reinvented themselves in villages in the western hills and mountains. From 1715 to 1750 the southern colonies experienced a slow growth of population inland, where the only remnants of Indian life were a few small isolated villages, disconnected and a threat to no one.[32] While conflict and ethnic cleansing had occurred prior to 1715, a period of interregnum followed, much as in the North, where Indians and whites on the frontier either ignored each other or got along.

The only conflict that surfaced during this period was in the distant West, in lands along the Mississippi River, where French colonists pushed up the river and eventually built a fort and several plantations adjacent to the Natchez Indians, a small tribe who inhabited several closely connected towns along the river. Conflict came in 1729 when the Natchez people tried to regain their lands, taking the French fort and capturing many of its inhabitants. The French then moved a small army up the river the next year, supported by Choctaw auxiliaries, and reduced the Natchez forts, making slaves of over four hundred of their people. They were sent mostly to Caribbean islands. Some Natchez Indians fled to the Chickasaws and reinvented themselves; but they no longer acted as an independent nation.[33]

At virtually the same time yet another conflict loomed in the Wisconsin country, where the Fox Indians had been increasingly alienated from French rule. Mostly they fought with Algonquian Indians to the north, who were French allies; as the Fox were pushed south, they cut off and killed several French traders and blocked French avenues into present-day Illinois. Ultimately a combined force of some twelve hundred Potawatomis, Kickapoos, Illinois, and French soldiers cornered the Fox on a prairie in northern Illinois and killed some five hundred, the majority of them women and children.[34]

The attempted annihilation of the Fox Indians was as much the product of intertribal war as it was the result of French policy. Indeed Huron and

Seneca Indians (avid enemies a century before), encouraged and armed by the French, attacked yet another Fox village and destroyed it, killing two hundred Indians and carrying others into slavery the next year.[35] Other attempts to destroy the Fox followed, but with less success. The Fox joined their allies the Sac people and continued to hold their villages near Rock River and along the lower Des Moines River into the 1750s, when their populations rebounded. While historian R. David Edmunds and French scholar Joseph L. Peyser have suggested that the Fox Wars might have constituted an attempt at "genocide," they also admit that the French effort "had failed."[36] Even so, there can be little doubt that given Fox intransigence the "intent" of French policy was completely to destroy the Fox Indians.

The conflict in Illinois and Wisconsin was spawned by intertribal fighting and the need of the French to protect their commercial monopoly. The French used Indian allies, both against the Fox and against the Natchez people. They also employed the rhetoric of "extermination" when it came to organizing expeditions against both groups. Several hundred Fox and Natchez Indians were deported to Caribbean Islands, much like the victims of English raids in the Southeast. Nevertheless, these actions occurred after a protracted period of conflict, which was vicious but hardly reached a level of genocide. In both cases a crime against humanity occurred: a clear violation of the law prohibiting "enslavement." It is also a war crime to attack villages with noncombatants in them. But a number of Indians from both tribes survived, some of whom were incorporated into other tribes.

The disruption of peace in the far West contrasted markedly with the tranquillity that existed in the East. While this peace was partly the legacy of the Andros administration, William Penn also contributed to what one historian has called the creation of a "Peaceable Kingdom" in America.[37] From the outset of his appearance in 1681 at Philadelphia, the capital of his new colony, Penn set out to make peace with the nearby Delaware Indians. He offered goods (much as Andros had at Albany), which ultimately brought purchases of land some twenty to thirty miles north and west of Philadelphia. But even the kindly Penn had difficulties convincing Indians that by signing a treaty they had relinquished the land. The famous—or perhaps infamous—Delaware chief Tammany constantly troubled Penn for goods, arguing that Penn owed him a yearly allowance for the "use" of the land. Tammany's argument was perfectly compatible with the idea that land can not be alienated but the right of use can be granted.

Penn did his best to placate Indians such as Tammany and did pay for his land. Unfortunately one questionable agreement would later do much to smudge his reputation. According to legend Penn convinced Delaware leaders to make a "walk" with him along the upper Delaware River, which in turn would mark the northernmost boundary of his colony. The group apparently walked for a day and a half rather than the three days that later negotiators would claim was entailed in the original agreement. In any case this purchase in 1686 supposedly helped establish Buck and Chester Counties, lands north of the original purchases. This early "walking purchase," if indeed it ever actually occurred, was followed by others, negotiated mostly by James Logan, who took over the administration of the colony in 1718 at Penn's death.[38] While Penn had honestly hoped to create a "Holy Experiment," even a "Peaceable Kingdom," in the New World, those who followed in his footsteps—including his sons, his grandsons, and Logan—had profit from land speculation in mind: the famous "walk" would aid them in their endeavors.

Penn left his colony to his eldest sons, John and Thomas. Unfortunately John fled England in 1734 with debtors literally chasing him to the boat. He soon saw his father's colony as the only possible solution to his troubles; bringing James Logan into the fold, he set out to end the Indian claims to land and sell Pennsylvania land for profit. First Logan acquired the assistance of Conrad Weiser, a German who had moved with his family to the upper Hudson River in 1711. There he learned the Iroquois language by living with the Mohawks. Weiser later moved to the Delaware River of eastern Pennsylvania and became a key Penn advisor. In 1736 Penn enlisted him to convince the Mohawks that they should sell claims to the upper Delaware River, land for which they had virtually no claim and said so. Nevertheless, some fifteen Iroquois chiefs signed the deed.[39]

Knowing that the Delawares feared disappointing their Iroquois benefactors, Logan invited the leading Delaware chiefs to his estate north of Philadelphia, where he harangued them the next fall. Arguing that William Penn, Sr., had actually purchased the upper Delaware River in 1686 but had only taken part of the sale that had been designated by a "walk" (in other words Penn walked only for a day and a half), Logan pressured the Indians into completing the walk. When Logan produced a faulty map indicating that such a walk would not encompass Delaware lands north of the Lehigh River valley, the browbeaten Indians agreed. John Penn then hired fit runners—in substantially better shape than his father had been some years before—and charged them to race west from the Delaware, covering some fifty miles in a day and a half: all the land between the Lehigh and Delaware Rivers in northeast Pennsylvania. The Delawares protested what was clearly a corrupt negotiation but to no avail. Penn opened the land to settlement—a region of 710,000 acres, roughly equivalent to the state of Rhode Island.[40] Much like the Tuscaroras in the south, the Delawares and their Shawnee friends to the west suddenly discovered that the period of interregnum ushered in by Governor Andros and later supported by some colonial legislation seemed on the verge of ending.

More pressure on Pennsylvania land emerged when settlers arrived from northern Ireland. They are known to history as the infamous "Paxton Boys," some being the grandsons and granddaughters of those hardcore Presbyterians who had shown a proclivity for the ethnic cleansing of the Irish in Ulster. Lutherans arriving from Germany held similar views regarding their entitlement to land. Penniless and mostly nameless to history, the Paxtons went directly to the frontier: the transition zone where remnants of Indian bands, fur traders, and settlers formed tense and ethnically disjoined communities. Mostly this region consisted of lands west and north of Lancaster County, in the Susquehanna River valley and beyond it. By the 1720s the numbers of these squatters grew; they congregated on both banks of the river around the frontier town of Paxton, some eighty miles directly west of Philadelphia. While the size of their population remains a guess, the numbers of these back-country Scots-Irish and German intruders likely reached 100,000 by 1750.[41]

The colonial government of Pennsylvania tried on numerous occasions to remove the settlers, fearing conflict. The issue became even more serious after a delegation of 300 Iroquois came to Philadelphia to complain about the Paxtons. The Iroquois renewed the Great Chain with their Pennsylvania allies. This had become commonplace by 1750. The Indians then demanded that the authorities remove these hardcore Presbyterians and Lutherans from lands that the Iroquois felt duty-bound to protect. Meanwhile the Paxtons, who often survived as much on wild game as on their farm patches, decimated deer populations in central and western Pennsylvania. Lieutenant governor James Hamilton did order a police force into the region in the late fall. The authorities expelled a few settlers and burned their cabins, but the effort proved futile. The Paxtons were embedded in the countryside; Hamilton's police could do nothing to dislodge them.[42]

The Delawares and Shawnees, after being uprooted from eastern Pennsylvania as more and more Scots-Irish settlers invaded the region, could either fight for the land or leave it. But fight against whom? Striking squatters such as the Paxtons would ultimately bring Pennsylvania and maybe even New York into the skirmish. Most Native leaders wished to avoid conflict. Accordingly, some villagers moved into the upper Susquehanna River valley, joining a settlement near the forks called Shamokin, while others moved farther west beyond the Allegheny Mountains, where another settlement, called Logstown, appeared not far from what would become Pittsburgh. Indians in these communities included Conestogas, Susquehannocks, Mingos, Delawares, Shawnees, and even some Iroquois. All of them lived by farming, gathering, and hunting.[43]

These people, now residents of upper western Pennsylvania, respected the promises inherent in the Great Chain Covenant. Unfortunately, Indian traders and groups of Paxton hunters often plied them with rum and encroached on hunting grounds, which in turn led to discussions relative to the negative impact of the European invasion. By the late 1740s some bands talked of making a stand against the Paxton Boys and even spoke disparagingly of their old friend Penn's progeny.[44] While their leaders tried to maintain peace with Pennsylvania and New York government officials and often attended negotiations at Albany and Philadelphia, many no longer trusted the New York Iroquois who had spoken for them, particularly the Mohawks, and most recognized that soon the Europeans would want more land.

Little did these Indians of Pennsylvania know, as they sat at night and smoked by their fires, that for them the period of interregnum was fast coming to an end, much as it had for the southern Indians after Queen Anne's War. The land hunger and the ethnic cleansing that had pushed the Susquehannochs out of Maryland; the Delawares and Shawnees out of Delaware, New Jersey, and eastern Pennsylvania; and even the Mohawks out of eastern New York had briefly stalled after 1680. But by 1740 the entitlement attitude that had driven Nathaniel Bacon—the general belief in "settler sovereignty"—was clearly on the rise, as evidenced by the emergence of the Paxton Boys in Pennsylvania and various "ranger" groups in the Carolinas. Even worse, the crime of "enslavement" had become standard practice among Europeans in the far West and the South. Indeed it often constituted a significant part of the European economy.

Native Americans did their best to resist the widening trends of violence committed against their people in locales closest to European settlement. And much of what historian Richard White has called the middle ground still existed in Cherokee, Creek, and Choctaw communities across the South, in the Ohio River valley, and even in Algonquin towns along the western Great Lakes. Negotiation and the exchange of wampum continued in these regions well after Governor Andros departed for Europe. When disagreement surfaced, as White has noted, Europeans and Indians often simply agreed to disagree, without fomenting violence.[45]

Nevertheless, a certain reality also seemed clear to many Indian leaders, particularly those close to European settlement. While they still could not read the treaties or deeds that were often thrust in front of them, many, indeed most, fully understood that "paper" meant land sale—Chief Tammany never got his land back from William Penn. These Indian leaders preferred to honor, touch, and share the belts of wampum that symbolized truth. Europeans, wherever they trod in North America, ultimately turned to paper. Those papers, with their legal endorsements and stamps of approval, soon became the tools of renewed ethnic cleansing.

4

A NEW KIND OF ETHNIC CLEANSING

The Frontier "Rangers" and the Assault on Native America

The period of peaceful coexistence that settled across most of North America after 1680 ended in the 1750s. Colonial populations slowly increased, especially in Pennsylvania and New York, and the surge of people to the frontiers of the continent added to tensions over land. While conflict in the past had often pitted colonial governments against Indians, the ethnic composition of frontier communities broadened significantly starting in the 1720s. The Irish, Scots, and Germans, often men and women who possessed little loyalty to the British or French Crown, became the intermediate populations, between British authorities and Native nations. They were committed to a doctrine of "settler sovereignty," a belief that they were no longer "migrants" in a new land. They saw themselves as people who had rights of possession: rights to establish their own political order in a new land that they were "entitled" to own.[1]

With such a new and diverse population, it became less likely that British, French, and Spanish authorities or those of the emerging government of the United States after 1775 could maintain the pragmatic and moral restrictions that had stalled and at times even prevented ethnic cleansing in the past. Wars accelerated this breakdown, as groups of so-called rangers emerged to fight in the West, sometimes organized by the British but just as likely coming together on their own, out of a perceived need to defend settlements. Rangers occasionally received a salary from the colonies that they defended, but they often fought for plunder. They became adept at finding Indian villages and destroying them, putting fear into the hearts of Native peoples so that they would abandon their lands. Rangers also were often land-hungry immigrants who scouted new valleys and future prospects for settlement. This new era of conflict and increased ethnic cleansing began as relations between Britain and France broke down in 1754.

By then, increasing tensions were evident across the Pennsylvania frontier. The French feared losing their empire in America, which was buttressed by the fur trade, involving kinship obligations that stressed French coffers but were absolutely necessary to maintain Indian alliances. For the Indians maintaining a balance of power between the French and the English offered the best option: both would have to maintain gift-giving or support what historian Richard White has termed "the middle ground."[2] By the early 1750s British traders hawking cheaper goods had entered the Ohio River towns of the Miami Indians as well as Indians living farther west in what is today Illinois and Wisconsin. Among these "English traders" were legitimate merchants who dealt honorably with Indians and some who were products of the frontier. But the end result was more rum entering the new towns of Shamokin and Logstown as well as other Indian communities that surrounded them. The French were losing control of the region.

Land speculators used such traders to search out good property. A number were connected to a new enterprise called the Ohio Land Company, formed in Virginia in 1747. A prime stockholder was the colonial governor, Robert Dinwiddie, and the company hoped to extend the claims of the colony's royal charter beyond the Appalachian Mountains. The governor eventually convinced the Privy Council in England (the body that set policy) that the French intended to occupy the Ohio region. The English increasingly rejected this. Concerned with possible English aggression, French officials decided to shut down the entryway—they moved a military force into the headwaters of the Ohio in the early spring of 1754 and built Fort Duquesne. The move presaged what many in Europe already suspected: England and France would soon be at war.[3]

While not officially at war, the government of Virginia sent a twenty-two-year-old aristocrat, Major (later Lieutenant Colonel) George Washington, to dislodge the French in May. The land speculators connected to the House of Burgesses in Virginia simply could not have opened the Ohio region with a French fortress blocking the way. Hearing of the impending conflict, settlers in western Pennsylvania (some living in the vicinity of Paxton) sent petitions demanding military assistance and calling for support of the Virginia forces to the mostly Quaker Pennsylvania Assembly.

That august body refused to provide funds for protecting the frontier, given Quaker pacifism. The Quakers simply waited out events.

Washington's small force of just forty men and his contingent of Indian allies faced an uphill battle. While trying to take the French fort, the major at first experienced some early success, surprising a small French patrol, killing several of its men (including its commanding officer), and taking others captive. But Washington could not control his Indians, who murdered wounded soldiers. Washington hurriedly built Fort Necessity in the woods south of Fort Duquesne, just in time to face a much larger French army and many of its Indian allies. Washington's small fort was poorly located: the French fired down on it with considerable accuracy. Rather than fight, Washington quickly surrendered and was given his parole. Ohio belonged to the French and their Indians by the summer of 1754.[4]

Washington, despite the reputation built for him by later hagiographers, offered up a bald-faced lie in the process. He had tried to recruit Delaware and Shawnee auxiliaries; about forty had joined him before the attack on the small French force and had made his initial success possible. But when a Mingo in the group boldly asked Washington what his purpose was, the colonel replied that the "only motive for our conduct . . . [was] to put you again in possession of your lands . . . to dispossess the French."[5] While Washington was too young to be a party to the original crowd of eleven Virginia aristocrats who organized the Ohio Land Company and ultimately received a land grant of 200,000 acres, he certainly knew by 1754 that the grant itself required the Virginians to found a town of 100 English families in the Ohio Valley and support them with the construction of a fort.[6]

Washington's failure and the expanding conflict over land in New York and Pennsylvania prompted British colonial officials to call a conference at Albany, New York, in fall 1754. The "congress" at Albany attracted a whole host of interesting colonial and Native American leaders, including William Johnson, a well-connected aristocrat placed at the head of Indian affairs by New York governor George Clinton. Johnson kept several Mohawk mistresses at his estate just west of Albany, reinforcing those kinship ties by giving his Mohawk relatives countless presents. Lieutenant Governor Hamilton and John Penn, William Penn's grandnephew, spoke for Pennsylvania; but the delegation had two other luminaries, Benjamin Franklin and the Indian emissary Conrad Weiser. Teedyuscung, who at one time had flirted with Christianity, represented the eastern Delawares of the Wyoming Valley, while Theyanoguin or Hendrick, as he was often called, spoke for the Iroquois. The western Iroquois, especially the Senecas and their Susquehannock allies, as well as the Delawares and Shawnees of the upper Ohio either failed to come or were not invited. They had become increasingly upset with both the French and the English, who had determined to claim all of the upper Ohio Valley.[7]

The Albany Congress is best known to American history as the place where Ben Franklin first introduced a plan of union for the colonies, which a very few historians argue influenced the writing of the American Constitution. But the meeting also witnessed one of the greatest land swindles in history. Even so, the first order of business involved the alliance. Some Iroquois had suggested that the English had broken the "Great Chain" of friendship due to prior land swindles. Johnson and the other English representatives struggled to convince the Indians otherwise, but without representation from the western tribes they only won a partial victory. Hendrick agreed to honor the chain once again; in case of war, the Mohawks, bound closely to Johnson through kinship ties, would remain in the British camp or at least would listen to Johnson.[8]

In the process of pressing the Iroquois for a return to the chain, Johnson and the other English representatives had to listen to Iroquois complaints. They all involved land. Hendrick had broached the issue of fraudulent land sales the year before with Governor George Clinton. The Iroquois had spoken to the governor in order to "relate our Grievances about our Lands." The Albany merchants, Hendrick noted, were "Devils" who could not be trusted. Because of them "the Covenant Chain is broken between you and us." The Privy Council had instructed colonial politicians to come together at Albany partly due to Hendrick's eloquent concerns. Now, in 1754, the Mohawk chieftain made it clear that no less than eight land purchases that the Indians considered fraudulent had occurred in the Mohawk River valley. Often German and Irish settlers had convinced Indians to sell lands that they did not legitimately own. Many of the sales occurred after long nights of drinking and celebrating, so the Indians likely had little idea of what they had signed.[9]

Other Mohawks complained of a massive land grant of some 800,000 acres north of the Mohawk River in lands that had been important hunting ground. The majority of the Mohawks had no intention of selling this region. Just the same, some Iroquois also complained bitterly of the French encroachment in the Ohio Valley. The French seemingly were no better than the English. "The Govr. Of Virginia, and the Govr. of Canada," as Hendrick saw it, were "both quarrelling about lands which belong to us." The grievances mounted so rapidly that William Johnson had a difficult time returning the discussion to the Great Chain. The fact that he did had much to do with the Privy Council's decision to take diplomatic affairs out of the hands of colonial governors and give them to a Crown official such as Johnson.[10]

While the Iroquois complained of land sales they also recognized their increasing dependency on English goods. They needed English presents, such as kettles, firearms, and munitions, and even money that came from land sales. Tragic as it seems, as they complained as a group, some few chiefs among them found themselves being persuaded to sell more land. The Pennsylvanians, Governor Hamilton and John Penn, approached a few Iroquois representatives and asked to purchase all Indian lands in Pennsylvania, including some west of the Allegheny Mountains. This included both branches of the upper Susquehanna River, the region known as the Wyoming Valley. Quietly, behind closed doors, yet another meeting occurred between John Henry Lydius, who represented the so-called Susquehannah Company (land speculators from Connecticut), and a handful of Iroquois chiefs. They signed the Lydius Deed, as it was called, which included roughly the same lands in the Wyoming Valley that Hamilton and Penn had supposedly sought. Ultimately, probably after bribes, five Mohawk chiefs also agreed in open council to sell the land to Hamilton and Penn. Other signatories included five Tuscaroras, whose people had no right to Pennsylvania land at all, and one Onondaga.[11]

To what degree Teedyuscung of the Delawares knew of these land sales is impossible to determine. Apparently both Hamilton and Penn and Lydius avoided discussing the issue with him or with any other Delaware or Shawnee in attendance. Only the Mohawk Hendrick complained openly of the deal, noting at one point that he would never sell "the land at Shamokin and Wyomink" because the bones of many Mohawk warriors were scattered there, testimony to their conquest of the land. Yet when Penn's compatriots read the final list of names attached to the sale, Hendrick's was there as well. Whether or not he actually signed the deed is not known.[12]

Given the serious nature of the weakened chain alliance, the officials at the Board of Trade, or its Privy Council, ordered an investigation.

As this unfolded, Pennsylvania officials protested the Lydius Deed, even convening a council at Philadelphia, where the Quaker Assembly took up the issue. Penn quickly reassured the Delawares living in the valley that they would be allowed to stay, receiving small reservations under conditions similar to those being offered to Christian Indians—a farmstead on which the new land owners would construct a small log house for each of their families. Regardless of what the grandnephew of William Penn did, Pennsylvania and Connecticut soon feuded over the Wyoming Valley, just as war broke out all across North America. The investigation ended with the outbreak of war, as did Indian sovereignty over most of northern and western Pennsylvania.[13] The issue of who owned the Wyoming Valley would only come up in colonial circles thereafter, as Indian complaints regarding the land fraud at Albany in 1754 were simply ignored by the English and French.

The war clouds that settled over Europe helped bring on the French and Indian War in America. The struggle over the Ohio River valley constituted the flashpoint. American Indians, however, saw the conflict differently; the French invasion of the valley marked a change in strategy that many western Indians did not appreciate. Neither did most Indians of the region appreciate the position of the English, who openly coveted Indian land. And a British force was ready to press the issue.[14] Led by a Scotsman, General Edward Braddock, some 1,400 British regulars and over 1,000 colonial militia led by George Washington rendezvoused at Alexandria, Virginia, in 1755. William Johnson, elevated to first "superintendent" of Indian affairs, received orders to hold the Iroquois to the British cause. Only Quaker Pennsylvania refused to participate in the war plans—it sent no soldiers and no money.[15] Braddock marched west in May 1755, often opening a road for his supply trains along the way. He hoped to take Fort Duquesne by summer, march east up the lakes toward Niagara, and end the war by fall.

Few commanders in early America could have been more ill suited for frontier combat. William Johnson had planted a rumor through Indian trader George Croghan—though it was completely untruthful—that Braddock's army was invading Ohio to "recover" Delaware and Shawnee lands for these two tribes. The claim only extended Washington's lie of the year before. Croghan convinced some Delaware and Shawnee leaders to visit with Braddock in western Pennsylvania, however, and perhaps join the British cause. When they arrived, according to one oral account of the interview, Braddock caustically stated that the British "should inhabit and inherit the land," not the Indians. Braddock knew little about fighting Indians and even less about Indian diplomacy.[16]

Braddock assumed that his regulars could easily take Fort Duquesne, which had roughly two hundred French troops. The French remained less confident; they appealed far and wide for assistance, bringing in several hundred Ottawas, Potawatomis, and Chippewas from the lakes region, who joined many of the discontented Delawares and Shawnees. Further weakening his force, Braddock left many of his more experienced colonials behind, the exception being a few hundred New York militia. A French force of some 600 Indians and a mere 200 French regulars awaited him. The Indians climbed trees and lay behind small hillocks as Braddock's red-coated regulars marched into the ambush with flags flying. In the two-hour fight, in which Braddock himself forced his men to stand in file like honorable soldiers rather than hide behind trees, nearly 1,000 British troops were soon dead or dying in a lane just eight miles from Fort Duquesne; Braddock himself lay mortally wounded.[17]

The war went no better for the British for the next two years, as confusion over command and strategy confounded war plans. The smallpox virus soon afflicted colonials and Indians alike. Ben Franklin, finding the news of Braddock's defeat extremely disheartening, could only bemoan it: the whole incident "gives us Americans the first Suspicion that our exalted Ideas of the Prowess of British Regulars had not been well founded."[18] Worse, Braddock's disastrous defeat only encouraged the Shawnees and Delawares who attacked the Pennsylvania and Virginia frontier that fall. They killed a dozen or so settlers at the Ulster settlements near Shamokin; more assaults occurred along both banks of the Susquehanna River over the next two years. Small raids became the norm and "murder" became the modus operandi, with the intent of forcefully removing settlements— ethnic cleansing in reverse. Even the peaceful Teedyuscung joined the Indian raids, hoping to regain his homeland along the Susquehanna. Within a year roughly 700 settlers had been killed, many of them squatters living in advanced western settlements, and others were abandoning their homes.[19]

During the first three years of the war the frontier people of Pennsylvania feuded as much with colonial officials in Philadelphia as with Indians. The Paxtons united under the command of various Presbyterian ministers. They saw their voluntary military service as something of a religious crusade and called their units rangers. These volunteers patrolled the river well beyond Shamokin, northward into the Wyoming Valley, generally on horseback rather than on foot. Most dressed like Indians with deerskin leggings, moccasins, and coats made from blankets. Their leaders preached the obvious: the French "Popists" were bent on destroying the Paxtons as well as their religion, Presbyterianism. The supposed atrocities that the Indians committed, in the view of the Paxtons, made them both "savages" and "Popists."[20]

Fighting such Popery had become a strong British tradition by the time of the French and Indian War, with views regarding the Catholic faith carried across the Atlantic from Europe. As Indian attacks mounted along the Pennsylvania frontier, local Paxton Rangers set out to take revenge. One such group organized by John Armstrong, an Ulster settler, was particularly active in searching out Indians and attacking them in their homes. His force even crossed over the Allegheny Mountains, where his 360 men, most coming from west of the Susquehanna River, burned the Delaware village of Kittanning to the ground in 1756. The number of women and children killed by the Pennsylvanians was never reported.[21] While western Indian raiders likely got the better of the contest with the Paxton Rangers, English settlers accomplished much of what they wanted through these revenge raids—pushing Indians farther west.

Farther north in New York, Robert Rogers, who had organized "Rogers' Rangers," marched on the Jesuit community of St. Francis on the St. Lawrence River, thought to be a headquarters for Indian raiders. Rogers tore it apart, claiming to have killed 200 Indians himself. The Jesuit priest, who resided in the village but was not there at the time, reported 22 women and children killed along with 10 men, numbers considerably smaller than Rogers's claim.[22] Rogers had embraced a common ranger practice: they often exaggerated the numbers of Indians killed when reporting results to their frontier friends. While Indian raiders had likely used the village as a place of refuge and had attacked settlements, inflicting considerable damage along the New York frontier, they still tended to take women and children captive, rather than kill them.

The rangers had implemented a unique warring strategy, similar to yet different from that of Native raiders. The men in these forces were comfortable on the frontier, acquainted with its landscape, and often held extremely prejudicial views of Indians. They could find Indian villages and destroy them, generally killing everyone in them. And they came from settlements where populations were much larger than among the Indian towns to the north. The rangers fulfilled a major role in the process of ethnic cleansing. They terrorized Indian women and children—some at St. Francis were burned to death in their houses—to such an extent that Indians removed their villages from the scene of battle. Indeed ranger actions of this sort targeted women and children, who have historically been the victims of ethnic cleansing in the modern world.

As the war dragged on, Pennsylvania authorities tried to negotiate a settlement with those Indians who would listen. Teedyuscung agreed to visit Philadelphia to talk over the issue in 1756 and returned for another conference two years later held at Easton, in the heart of the Upper Delaware River area. He explained that the problem was the Walking Purchase of 1737 and the Penn purchase of the Wyoming Valley in 1754. By this time, members of the Pennsylvania Legislature, not happy with the Penns, who had abandoned their Quaker faith, considered ways to annul the giant land purchases. William Johnson, who also came to Easton, pressured the Penns as well, ultimately convincing them at least to abandon claims to the Ohio region.[23] In essence this created the first natural boundary regarding Pennsylvania lands, agreed upon by colonial officials at least, separating Indian and colonial lands west of the Allegheny Mountains from those owned by the Penns east of the mountains. Unfortunately, Johnson's agreement with the Penns had nothing to do with slowing down Virginia speculators.

While the Easton Agreement failed to turn the tide of war, a few months later the English took Fort Duquesne. The next year British armies also captured Quebec, Niagara, and finally, in 1760, Montreal. French Canada had fallen to the British. This gave the western tribes very little bargaining power thereafter, making it impossible to play the British off against the French.[24] Once the British had won the war, they did not need to accommodate themselves to Indian whims. While the Ohio Indians argued that the British should not settle at the old French fort on the Ohio because that the land was theirs, the British promptly refused to leave the area. They built Fort Pitt on the foundation of Fort Duquesne and occupied Detroit and even far off Michilimackinac at the north end of Lake Michigan.

But William Johnson recognized a need to placate the various tribes to prevent Indian war. This became increasingly difficult when several hundred settlers from Connecticut moved into the Wyoming Valley in 1762, burning out the handful of Delawares who had remained behind. Many of these Indians had moved onto the farms promised to them and surveyed for them by the Penns. Teedyuscung, who may have been inebriated at the time, failed to escape his burning cabin and died along with his wife. Worse, Lord Jeffery Amherst, commanding all British troops in America, ordered Johnson to stop giving Indians gifts, especially alcohol. Amherst saw the dividend of British victory as a major reduction in colonial administrative costs; in his view, presents to Indians, the life-blood of the Great Chain and peace, were no longer necessary.[25]

Without powder and lead to hunt, many Indians were starving in the West by spring 1763. Most joined the charismatic Pontiac, an Ottawa warrior and mystic of sorts, who launched a rebellion against British rule that summer that nearly reversed British gains during the war. Pontiac may have heard stories of British encroachment on Indian land, but his rebellion had little to do with troubles in Pennsylvania. He disliked haughty British officers and wanted them to leave his land. The lack of supplies and a raging smallpox epidemic that had been going on for several years, however, ultimately ended hostilities. The British forts at Detroit and Pitt both survived Indian sieges. Pontiac fled west in the aftermath, only to be killed by a disgruntled Indian. Pontiac's Rebellion demonstrated that ignoring the western Indians, as Amherst had done, might prove deleterious to Crown interests. This in turn made Johnson's position more important than ever.[26]

At the height of the conflict, the British commander at Fort Pitt (formerly Fort Duquesne) exchanged letters with Lord Amherst, who encouraged his subordinate to distribute blankets laden with the smallpox virus to Indians. A few blankets had been distributed well before Amherst's letter arrived, suggesting that the notion of germ warfare was somewhat commonplace. Indeed smallpox had been raging in the colonies for some years, more frightful at some times than at others, and had attacked both Indians and Europeans. More importantly, both Indians and Europeans seemed well aware of the dangers of infection and avoided locales with the disease. Given such historic confusion, it is quite impossible to conclude that Amherst's actions constituted germ-laden genocide. No evidence has surfaced suggesting that the blankets handed out ever did any damage to the Indians surrounding Fort Pitt.[27]

During the height of Pontiac's Rebellion, however, frontiersmen in and around Paxton, usually identified as the "Paxtang Rangers," took up arms once again. Although they had been raised and equipped as militia soldiers during the war, these "troops" remained rebellious, especially when it came to the authorities in Philadelphia. They believed that Philadelphia officials, for the most part representatives of "colonial sovereignty," had failed to assist them against the Indians during the war. They also suspected that the peaceful Moravian Indians, who had been living in missionary communities, had supported the Delawares and Shawnees of the Ohio country. The Paxtang Rangers had already hacked to death six peaceful Conestoga Indians. Fearful that the peaceful Indians might fall victim to their rage, the local sheriff at Lancaster put fourteen of the Indians into the workhouse for safekeeping. On December 27, 1763, the Paxtang Rangers rode into Lancaster at night, broke down the door of the workhouse, and slaughtered the Indians—three couples and their eight small children.[28]

This failed to satisfy the Paxtang Rangers, who declared their intention to kill all the Moravian Indians, some two hundred of whom had fled to Philadelphia. John Penn and the Quaker Council argued over what must be done. The thought of Quakers taking up arms to defend the town for the sake of Indians seemed implausible. Yet the rumors increased dramatically in January 1764, suggesting that the Paxtang Rangers might start killing Quakers as well. When rumors circulated that a thousand Paxtang Rangers had organized themselves to take the city, panic broke out. Penn asked the British government for regulars. Preparing a defense as strong as possible—including a number of Quakers who did finally take up weapons—the Paxtang Rangers ultimately dispersed. In an ironic twist, the last contest of the French and Indian War in the north came when Presbyterian ruffians from the interior nearly ran the Quakers out of Pennsylvania.[29]

The British victories at Quebec and Montreal distracted most English in America from events farther south. The threat of conflict in the Carolinas had diminished considerably after the conclusion of the Yamasee War in 1715, but rapid changes had become evident forty years later, especially in western Carolina. One benefit for the Carolinians had been occasional conflicts between the Cherokees and their southern neighbors, the Creeks. Perhaps because of this, the Indians could do little to resist the establishment of the new colony of Georgia in the 1730s and the slow but steady stream of westward settlement. Even so, Cherokee leaders maintained good relations with both the Carolinians and the Virginians and the few Catawbas who remained in western Carolina, who were a threat to no one. Indeed these Indians allowed the English into their towns in the 1740s and 1750s, where these traders built fortified posts.[30]

Following the Yamasee War, some Cherokee towns had abandoned the eastern slopes of the Appalachian Mountains. They established communities in the upper Holston River of eastern Tennessee, where they could maintain contact with traders from Virginia. Yet another transition community that marked the intersection of Indian and Anglo interests was Saluda, in far western South Carolina, where contact with Carolina traders often occurred. The western ridges of the Appalachians protected the largest Cherokee communities along the headwaters of the Tennessee and Cumberland Rivers, the so-called Lower Towns and the Overhill Towns north and west of them.[31]

These communities (probably fifty or so in 1750) had a common culture and language, yet each town acted on its own through a town council. Every Cherokee had a right to speak at such a meeting, and this type of government worked well in dealing with surrounding Indian groups such as the Creeks to the south. Unfortunately, it produced too many voices when Europeans arrived. The British had difficulty understanding just where the Cherokees stood on issues of war, peace, and trade. While the Cherokees were seemingly secure beyond the mountains, the increased contact with Europeans had produced some ill effects. Smallpox invaded the communities in 1739, killing many. Cherokee populations may have dipped as low as 12,000 by this time, before experiencing a slow recovery over the next century.[32]

Cherokee-English relations remained friendly until 1751, when a series of small incidents brought growing tension.[33] Small conflicts often arose as a result of the failure of the increasing English back-country population (many of whom were of Scots-Irish origin) to reinforce relationships with Cherokee men and women with gifts; at other times the use of rum in the trade created problems.[34] Open competition—and thus the use of spirits—also occurred between Virginia and Carolina traders, sometimes spurred on by government officials, who wished to maintain alliances with this powerful tribe.[35] To keep the peace, Virginia and South Carolina built two forts among the Cherokees: Fort Prince George among the Lower Towns and Fort Loudoun near the Overhill people. But the British could not maintain an active trade—the war depressed the value of deerskin, and the cost of goods skyrocketed.

After a series of incidents in 1759, Carolina officials feared that the French had somehow attracted the Cherokees into their camp. Convinced of duplicity, South Carolina governor William Henry Lyttelton embargoed trade and concluded that the Cherokees needed to be punished. The Cherokees promptly laid siege to the British forts but did not attack them, and a full-scale war seemed in the offing. Lyttelton launched an invasion of Cherokee lands that fall with over a thousand men, but his forces soon fell victim to the smallpox and ultimately retreated after making a hasty peace.[36]

Once Canada had been secured, the Crown dispatched British regulars to South Carolina to punish the Cherokees, who had mostly wished to maintain the British alliance. Three expeditions into Cherokee lands followed; at one point a British force of 1,200 regulars, with a considerable contingent of Carolina "rangers," burned five Indian towns, killed sixty to eighty Indians, and destroyed crops, mostly at will. Another army returned in 1761 and invaded deeper into Cherokee lands, burning fifteen towns along branches of the Hiwassee and Tennessee Rivers and destroying hundreds of acres of crops. The majority of Cherokee inhabitants fled before the army, moving their communities to safer and more defensible lands.[37]

The conflict in the South had been Lyttelton's affair, plain and simple. His wish for glory and victory had ignited a conflict that would smolder for the next twenty years. Ironically, the war demonstrated to many British officials—especially those in the army—that the back-country folk of the Carolinas were just as rebellious and difficult to deal with as the Paxton Boys had been in Pennsylvania. And they had plenty of access to rum, which often was at the root of ethnic conflict in the transitional zones between Indians and settlers. While the Appalachian Mountains had held the back-country folk back to some degree, the expeditions of 1759–61 made it clear that good land existed in the West, even though it might still be Indian land.[38]

The conflict fomented further hatred between the Cherokees and the back-country folk who were their neighbors. "Ranger units" joined the British, burning and pillaging Indian towns with considerable glee. Cherokees, in turn, set ambushes for the Carolina rangers and the British regulars who seemed determined to destroy the Indians. When the Indians were successful, the Charleston newspapers reported that the Anglo dead had been "most inhumanely butchered." The newspapers also occasionally reported ranger failures; a ranger unit under command of a "Captain" Morrison was attacked on one occasion by Indians, and most of the men ran. Morrison was killed and "his body cut in two and shockingly mangled."[39]

The French and Indian War had come to mean just one thing to American Indians: both the Paxtang and Carolina Rangers fought to expand the American frontier onto Indian lands. William Johnson concluded in November 1763 that there was only one way to satisfy the western tribes. "They have repeatedly said," he noted to the Board of Trade, "that they were amused by both parties [English and French] with stories of their upright intentions, and that they made War for the protection of the Indians' rights." Indian leaders found this to be untrue, for "they plainly found, it [war] was carried on, to see who would become masters of what was the property of neither the one nor the other."[40] And the tactics of the militias, rangers, and the regulars who supported them involved attacks intentionally directed at Indian villages, a clear violation of Article 8 and thus a war crime.

The problem over land only would get worse. Migration to the English colonies skyrocketed in the postwar years. While over a hundred thousand came from England itself in the decade after the war, even more came from Germany, Ireland and Ulster, and Scotland. Perhaps forty thousand new immigrants came from Germany alone. Ben Franklin feared that Pennsylvania would become a purely "German" colony, undermining the English language. Growing land pressure occurred in New England as well, where colonists in Vermont and New Hampshire put more pressure on the very Indians attacked by Rogers and his rangers. With so many new people seeking land, it came as no surprise that the Ohio Land Company of Virginia, the Susquehanna Land Company of Connecticut, and a new group called the Mississippi Land Company renewed efforts to open up new lands. The "middle ground" had vanished by 1770.[41]

Nevertheless, the British Board of Trade recognized the problem. As speculators geared up to expand into the West, it came as sobering news when the British government issued a proclamation in October 1763. It established the Appalachian Mountains as the western boundary line of all the English colonies and supposedly gave Indians lands lying beyond that boundary. This came at an inopportune time, when immigration to America was expanding and land was one of the few commodities of value. Some in America questioned the ambiguous right of the board and its so-called Privy Council to issue such a decree.[42]

The plan apparently was the work of Henry Ellis, who argued that the Privy Council could best serve British interests by keeping settlement close to the coast, to benefit British trade. But the law went even further—it took Indian trade in the West out of the hands of royal governors and gave it to Crown administrators such as Johnson, who became Indian superintendent for the northern half of the colonies, and John Stuart, who eventually would act in that capacity in the South. No English person could purchase Indian lands or even trespass upon them. British soldiers who wished to claim bounty land for service were encouraged to migrate to Canada or Florida, where land was available.[43]

British officials certainly never meant to cede any degree of sovereignty to American Indians as a result of the proclamation. But they did follow through with a serious attempt at implementing the edict. Johnson met some two thousand Indians at Niagara in the summer of 1764 and explained the proclamation. This was one of the first times Indians had not been asked to cede land—they exchanged belts of wampum, received presents, and pledged eternal peace. While nothing akin to a "fee simple" title was discussed, the agreement suggested that Indians held rights to unceded lands. Johnson also affirmed that the same boundary had been extended into modern Canada. Indeed the First Nations of Canada today regard the agreement as reaffirming their rights to exist as self-governments.[44]

American land speculators challenged the proclamation almost from the beginning, sending a lobbyist to London. They noted that little could be done to prevent the frontier elements—such as the "rangers"—from heading west to squat on lands. Some squatters had already discovered the Cumberland Gap in far southeastern Virginia, which led into Tennessee; others moved into the upper Ohio country. "Squatter sovereignty" was in full bloom. Hoping to prevent conflict, Johnson met over three thousand Indians at the newly built Fort Stanwix, in western New York, to discuss the situation. He proposed another "permanent" boundary but attached to the agreement a demand for more land. George Croghan, one of Johnson's agents and at one time a lobbyist for the land speculators in London, pushed the issue. Using bribes and rum, Johnson convinced the Iroquois to give up claims to all lands east of the Ohio River, including much land just beyond the Appalachian Mountains and a considerable amount of land in eastern Kentucky. They did so only after Johnson agreed to leave intact most Iroquois lands in New York. The loss of the upper Ohio Valley caused an almost immediate backlash among the so-called tributary tribes, who claimed that land as hunting ground.[45]

British officials at the Board of Trade pondered the sale with considerable suspicion. "Now that the Six Nations have sold the land as lords of the soil," wrote Major General Thomas Gage to the Earl of Hillsborough, and "the white people are expected . . . to settle on their hunting grounds, these dependent Indians are exasperated."[46] Agent Croghan soon discovered that Shawnees, Delawares, and Mingos had joined Hurons, Ojibwas, Ottawas, Pottawatomis, and even some Senecas in councils near Detroit, where they talked of forming a confederacy to resist English aggression.

Croghan hired spies who attended more and more councils regarding the land sale in fall 1770 and spring 1771. He soon discovered that the so-called dependent northern tribes were sending emissaries south to meet with the Cherokees and Creeks, hoping to bring them into the fray. When approached by Croghan, these Indians complained bitterly regarding English encroachment. "Unless you can fall upon some method of governing your people [squatters] who live between the mountains and the Ohio River," they warned, "it will be out of the Indians' power to govern their young men, for we assure you, the black clouds began to gather."[47]

Just as Johnson faced pressure from squatters and speculators in the North, similar lobbying for more land came from Virginians and Carolinians who had entered Tennessee, staking out farms on Cherokee lands, or had moved up the Savannah River, grazing cattle and hunting on Creek lands. To prevent conflict, Superintendent Stuart opened negotiations with these Indians in 1765 and continued negotiations for the next five years. A boundary for the Creeks was established first; after considerable debate, on October 20, 1770, Cherokee leaders signed a treaty creating a boundary that extended up to the Holston River. The chiefs who signed the agreement realized that it set a line much farther west than they liked, but the southern Indians could do little. The British had taken both Mobile and Pensacola at the close of the war, creating a British trade monopoly that allowed their agents to decide when and if the Indians received gunpowder and lead, essential for hunting.[48]

The boundaries settled very little. Great Warrior, who spoke for the Cherokees, noted that all the chiefs of the "valley, middle, and lower" towns had agreed to give up some land in order to get a permanent boundary but that the young men of the various towns opposed any such agreement. "They seemed surprised that I would agree to give away so much of their land," Great Warrior told a visiting Virginian. Worse, "they never would take hold of the beads [wampum] which were presented to me," signifying acceptance. Some of these young men talked of joining the northern tribes and driving the settlers out. Constant turmoil existed in the few years after the boundary agreements: squatters disrespected the lines nearly as soon as they were drawn.[49]

Native Americans sensed almost before the French and Indian War ended that they might become losers from the outcome—certainly the brief discussions with General Braddock had foreordained such a conclusion. It had become unmistakably true by the early 1770s that even such powerful tribes as the Iroquois and Cherokees would have to negotiate from an impotent position. The British had replaced the French on the upper Ohio, at Detroit, and in Florida and Alabama and showed signs of being stingy with presents and goods. British officials often had good intentions when it came to Indians but—recognizing that imperial policy and the need to keep down the cost of war were best served by concentrating settlement along the coast—clearly saw the forces of "settler sovereignty" at work in the back country.

Settlers and squatters from New York to Georgia rejected the views of the English Board of Trade. So did some speculators who had influence in the various colonial legislatures. And ranger militias were ever ready to drive Indians out, regardless of what British officials tried to accomplish. These groups had become spearheads of ethnic cleansing, during a period when the British government tried to bring peace to America. While both the Fort Stanwix Treaty of 1768 and the Cherokee cession of 1770 involved lands that had been set aside for Indians by the Proclamation Line of just five years before, British officials hoped—and even asserted to Indian leaders—that these cessions would be the last.

For groups who identified themselves as "rangers," the proclamation soon represented British oppression. Yet such groups remained so diverse and so different from colony to colony that it is difficult to determine their true motivations. They certainly felt that organizing as rangers gave them a degree of independent power necessary to take land or defend themselves against perceived Indian threats—even, as some historians have asserted, the power to create their own laws and order.[50] Nevertheless, British officials had tried to use them in a strategic sense by striking out at far-off Indian groups who were French allies. Rangers were never burdened by supply trains that prodded along slowly through the forest, such as the one attached to Braddock's army. They carried their food on their backs or in knapsacks on their horses, which gave them considerable mobility.

Ranger groups, particularly in the Carolinas, also recruited other Indians to serve as guides and scouts. In the North Robert Rogers used such allies as well, suggesting that his goal was punishing French-allied Indians, not simply killing all Indians. The colonies and the British government had no "intent" to use rangers in an anticipated policy of genocide during the war. Rangers may have committed war crimes, but their intended goals were more frequently revenge and plunder in typical preemptive strikes that preceded ethnic cleansing.

It must have seemed a final irony to men like Johnson, Stuart, and even to some degree Amherst that Native Americans were easier to deal with than ranger groups or squatters. The Iroquois had negotiated the best deal possible for them at the Fort Stanwix treaty in 1768 and hoped that they could convince the Shawnees and Delawares to the west to abide by it. Cherokee leaders likewise embraced negotiation after the crushing blows inflicted on their villages in 1759–61. But British attempts at pragmatic Indian diplomacy, based upon guaranteed boundaries, only went so far. And the same British officers who had implemented the policy would soon be forced to defend it against a new force: the rebelling colonists whom their policies had been designed to contain.

5

THE AMERICAN INVASION

While the years following the French and Indian War witnessed the opening of the trans-Appalachian West to colonists, the American Revolution only expanded that nightmare for Indian peoples. Anglo patriots joined Washington's army to fight in the East for freedom and representative government—those intangible concepts that Jefferson had so ably defined in the Declaration of Independence as "inalienable rights"—while Indians faced hordes of frontier settlers whose goal often consisted of suppressing their rights to land. Along the frontier, from New Hampshire in the north to Georgia in the south, groups of Americans banded together to push into new lands, building small stockades to protect their vulnerable stock and families. Frequently they had no title to this land or any reasonable belief that the true owners, the Indians, would allow them to stay without expectation of conflict. When violence broke out, they pleaded for colonial assistance, which land speculators in the various colonial legislatures were quite willing to provide.[1]

The Revolution became general in 1775 and went on for eight long years. The peace of 1783, however, failed to bring the fighting in the West to a close. For Indians, the American Revolutionary War lasted twenty years, from 1775 to 1795. Indians fought to defend their villages and hunting grounds, often attacking advanced Anglo settlements to drive them from their lands. While Great Britain promised them assistance, it came only in the form of some guns, ammunition, and a few presents, distributed to them at Detroit or in Canada. American paramilitary groups overwhelmed Cherokee towns in western Carolina and eastern Tennessee. Shawnees and Delawares gave up ground in eastern Kentucky and

Ohio. Worse, the ink had hardly dried on the last signature on the treaty in 1783 when American land speculators huddled over their maps of the West. They wanted more land. The British Crown had ceded to the young United States a vast empire, starting at the Appalachian Mountains and extending to the Mississippi River. This meant profit for the likes of many Founding Fathers, including Washington, Jefferson, Franklin, Hamilton, and Henry. The "Deed game" of earlier colonial times reemerged in the West after American independence; the only obstacle to wealth was the American Indian.

American frontier settlers naturally opposed the Proclamation of 1763 and its ban on western migration. But they also quickly took note of Britain's announcement the next year that new lands were available in east Florida and Canada. These lands came into the realm as a result of conquest during the French and Indian War. Western Carolinian Daniel Boone was a typical responder. He and several friends traveled south into Florida in 1765, looking the region over. They found the lands inferior to what they had and returned home. Boone and his friends then turned west, settling with their families in the mountains along the Yadkin River. Moving into Tennessee, they soon built communities in eastern Kentucky. By 1775 Boone and other Carolinians had small settlements, buttressed by blockhouses, from the Holston River in east Tennessee literally to the Ohio Valley.[2]

This invasion occurred in regions (later part of West Virginia and Kentucky) that were well beyond the lands ceded in 1768—even though nothing resembling a boundary had been run for that cession. The Shawnees, Delawares, Mingos, and Cherokees all claimed this land as hunting ground. They consistently resisted the incursions of Boone and his friends. Indeed they captured Boone and many other Carolinians on several occasions and pillaged goods and furs; failing to stem the tide, some warriors captured and killed a number of Anglo invaders, including Boone's son. Governor John Dunmore in Virginia asked the House of Burgesses to declare a state of war in 1774. He set about to raise militias that would assist in bringing the western mountain regions under his control.[3]

The war in the West that escalated by 1775 was much about land and little about liberty. Kentucky, or Boone's settlements there, could raise a mere hundred men for its ranger unit in 1775—handing over command to "Captain" Daniel Boone. But as the war progressed, more settlers came, some likely avoiding fighting in the East. By 1783 Boone had over a

THE AMERICAN INVASION   89

thousand men under arms. These fell under the leadership of charismatic men such as Boone as well as the famous "ranger" George Rogers Clark. Almost every man who followed them into battle had some interest in land speculation. Clark became a deputy surveyor in Kentucky as early as 1775. The Clark family (including the youngest son, William, of Lewis and Clark fame), which had been a relatively modest Virginia clan in terms of land ownership, came to own thousands of acres of land taken from Indians in Kentucky by 1800.[4]

Many Indian leaders by this time fully understood the implications of the rising American populations in Kentucky. The growing Anglo population affected a variety of tribes in the North, some well organized and others still trying to regroup after the disastrous attempts to defend hunting grounds in Kentucky in the 1750s. While the six Iroquois tribes claimed this land, other tribes had much better claims, including the Mingos (who had many western or Ohio Senecas in their ranks), Shawnees, Wyandots (also called Hurons), Miamis (a group generally identified as the Three Fires Confederacy), Potowatomis, Ottawas, and especially Delawares, whose homeland had been Pennsylvania.[5] The Iroquois claim went back to Governor Andros's willingness to accept it, hardly a title of legal standing. While most of these groups had given up the notion of ever regaining their lands in eastern Pennsylvania, they defiantly asserted their claims to the trans-Appalachian region.

Cherokee, Creek, and Choctaw towns in the South still occupied the various river valleys that led to the Gulf of Mexico or the Little Tennessee and Hiwassee Rivers in eastern Tennessee, which drained into the Mississippi River. Their claims to land may have been challenged by Spain, France, and Britain in the map rooms of Europe but never in a military sense. This remained relatively true even after American colonists like Boone invaded eastern Kentucky. Just as war clouds appeared, Boone took advantage of the growing British distraction to work a deal with Richard Henderson, a land speculator, who represented ten of the wealthiest families in Virginia.

Offering huge numbers of presents, Boone helped bring several thousand Cherokees together in 1775, who supposedly sold Henderson (under title of the Transylvania Company) some 27,000 square miles of land between the Cumberland and Kentucky Rivers, nearly all of eastern Kentucky. While no journal of the sale has survived, many younger Cherokee hunters opposed it, as they had spoken out against any sale as early as 1770.

Henderson did deliver £10,000 worth of goods to a number of Cherokee chiefs who accepted the presents, suggesting agreement. The lands south of the Kentucky River had never been part of the Iroquois sale at Fort Stanwix, and the sale was certainly illegal under the terms of the increasingly defunct proclamation.[6]

As hundreds of Anglos moved into the Cumberland River Valley or traveled north to join Boone at his new settlement, called Boonesborough, on the northern edge of the purchase, they slaughtered deer and buffalo herds (often just for the skin or choice morsels) and opened farms. Cherokee young men retaliated. The Indians struck during the summer of 1776, burning out a few cabins and killing a few dozen frontiersmen who fought them. While these attacks conceivably started a war, offering Anglos the opportunity to retaliate, "just war" historically hinged upon the right of a people to defend their property from invasion. In this case the Cherokees and their northern allies were clearly in the right.

Whatever the justification, it certainly did not include the right to murder civilians, which occurred. The attacks gave Americans the excuse to retaliate that fall. A frontier paramilitary and militia army of 6,500 heavily armed men from Virginia, Kentucky, and the Carolinas invaded Cherokee lands from three different directions, burned dozens of villages along the Little Tennessee and Hiwassee Rivers, and slaughtered hundreds of Indian men, women, and children. They even cut down orchards in their wanton orgy of plunder. The Cherokees could do little to stop the rampaging Virginians and their allies.[7]

The lands in northern and eastern Tennessee had been disputed ground. Shawnees and Delawares had claimed it along with the Iroquois, but the Cherokees had as good a claim as the others and lived in the closest proximity.[8] Some young Cherokee warriors stood and fought the American invaders, including Dragging Canoe, Glass, Bloody Fellow, Fool Charles, and Badger. Many Cherokees perished during the onslaught, and the survivors evacuated their families to the lower Tennessee River in what is today northern Alabama. Thereafter called the Chickamauga Cherokees, they continued the fighting from more secure settlements, striking Anglo settlements in northeastern Tennessee and southern Kentucky and even the westernmost counties of the Carolinas. In the West the American Revolution would become a conflict fought over Indian lands.

After the disaster that befell those Cherokees on the Hiwassee River, some asked for peace. But their proximity to the Americans—dozens of towns still remained in southeastern Tennessee—made that almost impossible. Carolina paramilitary raiders even assaulted some of the far-off Chickamauga settlements, defended only by women at the time, as their men were on a visit to the British at Pensacola. The last raids were ordered by Governor Patrick Henry of Virginia in 1779 and by his successor, Thomas Jefferson. Many Cherokees were forced south, out of northern Tennessee; some settled in northern Georgia around what would become a Cherokee political center at New Echota. During the conflict some Cherokees signed treaties exchanging land for peace. But after 1780 Governor Jefferson of Virginia concluded that the new federal government organized at Philadelphia should head such negotiations. The active participation of eastern state officials in what were clearly ethnic cleansing campaigns in Tennessee came to an end.[9]

Also expelled from their lands by American revolutionaries, many British loyalists joined the Chickamauga settlements and fought alongside them. Young men with family names such as Ross, Rogers, Walker, McLemore, Fields, Chisholm, McIntosh, Adair, and Gunter in effect became Cherokees. They took Cherokee wives, had children, and adapted to the guerrilla war tactics of the Chickamaugas.[10] The revolution in this back-country region had become an ethnic as well as a political struggle, not unlike the struggle in Ireland two centuries before. Indians fled eastern Tennessee, abandoning towns along the Tennessee and Hiwassee Rivers and moving south and west. By almost any definition, much as in Ireland, this was "forced" ethnic cleansing.[11]

Despite the alliance with Great Britain, the southern Indians received little help. English promises of arms and munitions during the early years of the Revolution failed to materialize; meanwhile the Americans only got stronger after France joined their cause. The British superintendent of Indian affairs, Robert Stuart, who had fled to Pensacola, did try to provide supplies to both the Cherokees and their western neighbors, the Creeks, and worked closely with the Creek leader Alexander McGillivray, who convinced a small contingent of Creeks to join the British cause. But the Cherokee disaster in eastern Tennessee in 1776 made the jobs of both men almost impossible. In a famous speech given by the Cherokee chief Raven in 1781, he said simply that he sent an emissary to Virginia "to make the rebels [Americans] believe we want peace, but it was only to save our corn." On several occasions Stuart could not convince the Indians to join the British and advised them to remain neutral.[12]

The Cherokees had often quarreled with the Creeks in the past, but Creek leader McGillivray recognized that Americans were a much greater threat: they were moving inland from the Savannah River, settling lands that Creeks had claimed in Georgia. As Indian lands became threatened, the Creeks put aside some differences with both the Choctaws to the west and the Cherokees to the north and joined the British, who finally landed an army at Charleston in December 1778. McGillivray provided some 300 Creek warriors for the British cause. But the Cherokees still remained suspicious of forming any alliances. They often told British lieutenant Thomas Brown, assigned to recruit their services, that they "had not taken an active part in favor of the [British] government" because of their exposed positions. While the British capture of Charleston and their ability to supply Indians from Pensacola helped their situation, British diplomats utterly failed in their strategy of uniting the Cherokees, Creeks, Choctaws, and Chickasaws against the Americans.[13]

Any hope of obtaining massive Indian assistance took a serious blow in early fall 1780, when thousands of pounds worth of trade goods stored at Augusta, Georgia, were taken by American forces. The supplies, necessary for Indian diplomacy, were all lost to the British; thereafter even the mostly loyal Creeks seemed reticent to leave their lands to defend British ambitions.[14] Worse, the British under General Charles Cornwallis then moved northward and the Americans recovered, leaving the Creeks to face an angry retribution. As the war came to a close, the Creeks knew that an American invasion was immanent and gave up eight hundred square miles of land in a treaty in order to obtain peace.[15]

The struggle over land produced still more conflict in the North, much of it a continuation of the fighting that had erupted in the early 1770s. A lot of the fighting centered on the Ohio River and its two tributaries, the Monongahela, which headed into West Virginia and then snaked north to join the Ohio, and the Allegheny, which had its source waters in southern New York, meandering south to connect with the Ohio in western Pennsylvania. The Monongahela and the Allegheny formed a natural boundary across western Pennsylvania and western Virginia. Unfortunately, the joining of the rivers also created a natural location for a fort, still called Fort Pitt (modern Pittsburgh), occupied by Americans. And the fort and the good river bottomland nearby attracted settlers.[16]

The Iroquois of New York remained one of the most powerful Indian confederacies in America, despite suffering losses during the French and

Indian War. Their Six Nations included several thousand warriors. They claimed and patrolled land from the American-occupied Fort Stanwix in far western New York well down into the upper Ohio watershed. The remaining Shawnees and Delawares who had fled into Ohio after Lord Dunmore's War still claimed the lands in the same Ohio watershed between the Allegheny Mountains and the Ohio River. The Iroquois and the Ohio Indians increasingly argued over these lands; some Iroquois leaders agreed to the sale of the lands in the Fort Stanwix Treaty of 1768. The divisiveness aided the Americans, who coveted the Ohio Valley. Many American settlers saw the revolution as offering an opportunity to occupy the area, by force if necessary.

Even so, the hopes of some Ohio Indian leaders to retain their lands rose when rumors circulated that the British and the Long Knives (Americans) were at war. Even though British Indian superintendent Johnson had died the year before the war broke out, British officials were quick to exploit the land issue. They had exhibited a willingness to protect Indian claims—or so they said—by issuing the proclamation. Mohawks under Joseph Brant quickly joined the British cause, setting up a base used for raiding Pennsylvania at Fort Niagara, a strong British outpost. Other Iroquois, however, including most of the Onondaga, Oneida, and Cayuga tribes, opted for neutrality. This was also true of the Senecas, whose main chiefs, Red Jacket and Cornplanter, did not want war.[17]

American representatives of the Continental Congress, which met initially in 1774 and took over the prosecution of the war the next year, hoped that they might keep the Indians neutral in the West. But the American squatters who invaded Kentucky and moved up to the left bank of the Ohio made that practically impossible. Continental Congress officials tried vainly to rectify the situation by calling the Delawares and Shawnees, as well as the Iroquois, to a council at Fort Pitt in summer 1775. During the various speeches Chief White Eyes of the Delawares adamantly spoke out against the Fort Stanwix Treaty. "You say you have conquered me," he said defiantly to the American negotiators, but "I am a man!" Referring to the Monongahela-Allegheny divide, he concluded: "All the country on the other side of that river [the Monongahela-Allegheny] is *mine.*"[18]

But two other Shawnees at the convention, Blue Jacket and Cornstalk, took the presents offered by the Americans and listened to the arguments for neutrality. The Americans promised trade (the life-blood of the Indian economy), which the British could not supply given the brief American invasion of Canada that summer.[19] American success seemed even more apparent when Cornplanter and Red Jacket arrived. They spoke for the Senecas and indicated that the main council of the Iroquois Confederacy would soon debate the issues of war and peace. They said nothing about the growing efforts of the Mohawk Joseph Brant to recruit Indians for the British (Brant had already led a force against the Americans who were invading Canada).

Brant found recruitment difficult. He even turned to recruiting British loyalists; in order to disguise their intentions, the loyalists dressed as Indians when raiding along the frontier. Brant had a purely nationalistic goal—greater Indian autonomy. Ironically, however, he promoted this by using raiders acting as rangers, who took their salaries from plundering colonial communities. Despite Brant's effort, Red Jacket told the Americans that he had "clean ears" and would listen to their speeches. The Americans hoped that the Senecas could prevent their western Mingo relatives, as well as the Delawares and Shawnees, from raiding the settlers who were pouring into Kentucky.[20]

While the Continental Congress felt authorized to control the Indian trade in the West, it refused to intervene when it came to land; this was still a colonial or increasingly a state priority in 1775. And just before the council at Fort Pitt convened, surveyors from Virginia started staking out the lands immediately south of the fort in the upper Monongahela Valley. The next year the Virginia militia garrisoned Fort Henry (named for the governor), located at Wheeling, well within the Shawnee-Delaware claim. The troops constructed Fort Randolph farther south along the Ohio at the mouth of the Kanawha River, well downstream from Fort Pitt. Both forts were appropriately named for Virginia land speculator–politicians.

Despite his neutrality, Cornstalk, the one Shawnee leader who remained friendly toward the Americans, spoke passionately about the claim of his people to Kentucky and the lands north of it along both banks of the Ohio. The American invasion "sits heavily on our hearts," he told the Americans. He knew that some Shawnees and Delawares had moved their towns farther west to the Little and Great Miami Rivers, in central Ohio, preparing for war. Making one last effort to stop the fighting, Cornstalk approached Fort Randolph a few weeks later with a white flag, asking to parley. The American commander, Captain Matthew Arbuckle, promptly arrested Cornstalk, his son, and several others, holding them as hostages to ensure the good conduct of the Shawnees. Shortly thereafter a crowd of American ruffians stormed the rooms where the men were held. As Cornstalk's son trembled at the thought of his impending death, Cornstalk urged him not to be afraid, "for the Great Spirit had sent him there to be killed." The Americans then opened fire and slaughtered the defenseless prisoners.[21]

The murder of innocent and peaceful Shawnees in the custody of American militia at Fort Randoph only confirmed what the Mingos already knew—that the Americans were devils. Mingos started raiding Kentucky late in the fall 1776, concentrating on the settlements on the Licking and Kentucky Rivers, near Boonesborough. Bands of Shawnees and Delawares joined them in spring 1777. This coincided with the landing of a large British force in Canada under General John Burgoyne, who soon moved south, implementing General William Howe's plan to invade the Hudson River Valley and cut off New England. The British official James Hamilton at Detroit recruited all the Ohio tribes to the cause, delivering goods and arms that had finally reached the West. Americans increasingly portrayed Hamilton as a "scalp buyer," despite his generally successful efforts—and orders from England—to convince the Indians to take captives. Americans would constantly play on the "savage" nature of Indian warfare, despite their own tendency to slaughter Indians indiscriminately, even those held as captives.[22]

As conditions deteriorated, American settlers continued to invade the lands between the Ohio and the Monongahela and to move north from Fort Pitt, up the Allegheny. Many had land warrants from the new states of Pennsylvania and Virginia and took up what were known as "tomahawk claims," a term reflective of the difficulty in holding them against Indians. The new American Indian agent George Morgan, hired by the Continental Congress in January 1777, increasingly relayed the complaints of various Indian leaders "relative to our settling on their lands." But the states were the culprits, not the federal government, and the Continental Congress was mostly interested in fighting the British in the East.[23]

When Morgan tried to hold yet another council at Fort Pitt in July, even the once friendly Senecas under Cornplanter and Red Jacket complained of American invaders on their lands north of the fort. "I believe it is more necessary to restrain our own people," Morgan reported to Congress, "than to think of awing the different nations by expeditions." Morgan's hopes were quickly dashed after American settlers murdered many Senecas under a white flag in Pittsburgh. A Moravian missionary who witnessed the carnage could only lament: "By this step . . . the savages were again enraged at the white people, considered them altogether as traitors, and vowed revenge."[24]

Shawnees, Delawares, and Mingos took the offensive again in February 1778, assaulting the settlements in Kentucky with over eight hundred warriors. They surrounded Fort Randolph, killing all the cattle and horses that grazed outside the walls. While the fort held, the Indians turned eastward to the settlements in the Lick and Kentucky River valleys. While these campaigns resulted in the overrunning of several blockhouses and the herding of dozens of women and children prisoners back to Detroit, where they were well treated by Hamilton, the Indians failed to break the American settlement of Kentucky. The tide also slowly turned when General Burgoyne surrendered at Saratoga, New York, in late fall 1777. Yet Burgoyne's fate did not preclude a desperate struggle in western New York, which the majority of the Iroquois Indians joined the following summer.

It began with a massive attack on Fort Stanwix, the American garrison located east of the Mohawk towns. The majority of the Iroquois had finally decided to join a smaller force of New York Loyalists and regulars, led by the British commander Colonel Barry Saint Leger. While the British lacked the cannon necessary to take the fort, they soon clashed in a desperate struggle with eight hundred American reinforcements under General Nicholas Herkimer at Oriskany. Ambushed by Mohawks, the rear of Herkimer's militia broke and fled, while the center, assaulted mostly by the Senecas, stood its ground. Oriskany was a bloody carnage, often fought hand-to-hand, in which two hundred to three hundred Americans and perhaps a hundred or more Indians died.[25]

Given the inability to take Fort Stanwix, the British force of Indians and regulars turned south the next summer, invading the Wyoming Valley. Vengeance soon dominated the fighting: a group of British Tories recruited Indians to assist them in pummeling American "patriots," who had driven them from their lands.[26] Some American forces broke and ran, and Indians then came upon many others whom they had outflanked. While the Battle of Wyoming Valley was viewed as a dreaded "massacre" by many Americans thereafter, that is not the case: noncombatants, especially women and children, never faced the tomahawk. Indeed probably a thousand or such civilians were held by the British at war's end, testimony to the success of their officers in convincing Indians to take captives rather than kill them.[27] Nevertheless, the campaign became a *cause célèbre:* artists and poets depicted the supposed atrocities of the Indians, including the alleged tomahawking of women and children.[28]

While other attacks on American settlements continued into 1779, with more American communities being devastated, that spring General George Washington organized a retaliatory expedition against the Iroquois of New York. General John Sullivan took charge of nearly three thousand continental soldiers who marched into northern Pennsylvania, headed for the Iroquois towns. The British commander at Niagara, Major John Butler, had only two hundred men and his Indian allies to oppose this force. Sullivan and his men soon routed these defenders, burned some forty Indian towns, mostly Iroquois, and destroyed all the crops in the field. They slaughtered thousands of hogs, cattle, horses, and even poultry and cut down hundreds of apple trees. Sullivan's campaign increasingly became a looting expedition, in which the troops took furniture, blankets, and almost anything that could be sold. Troops from Fort Stanwix joined the carnage, invading the peaceful Onondaga communities that had remained neutral. They burned houses and raped a number of captured Indian women. The war had finally come to the Iroquois, with all the characteristics of ethnic cleansing—rape, the burning of towns, and plunder to reward troops for service.[29]

The American success in New York led to a reassessment of their alliance with the British by the Ohio tribes. The Delaware leader White Eyes promised to remain at peace in exchange for neutrality. He even signed a treaty with the American general Lachlan McIntosh, who added an article in fine print that allowed American forts to be built west of the Ohio River. Governor Henry of Virginia ordered McIntosh to build the forts, which he promptly did. When White Eyes came to McIntosh to protest the incursion into the country of the Delawares, Shawnees, and Mingos, McIntosh's militia murdered him and secretly disposed of his body.[30] Hoping to secure McIntosh's southwestern front, George Rogers Clark and 200 Kentucky "rangers" captured the British post at Vincennes. Clark's rangers operated in the Ohio country through 1780, but he failed to capture Detroit, a second objective. Clark also had supply problems, as the mostly French traders of the region ultimately rejected his continental paper dollars.[31]

The fortunes of war drifted back and forth in the West over the next two years. Outraged Indians, especially those who suffered from Sullivan's campaign, struck the Pennsylvania frontier as well as small communities in Kentucky. New York's settlements suffered the most; at one point Governor George Clinton concluded that the frontier had rolled back nearly to Schenectady.[32] Clark's ranger force on the lower Ohio also faced near annihilation at one point by Joseph Brant's Mohawks; desertions mounted among the ranger units. They were often paid by plunder; when Indian towns could no longer be found with anything to plunder, some departed for home.[33]

Worse, military order broke down in the West after the Continental Congress no longer feared losing it to the British and removed regular troops. Paramilitary ranger units, which lacked discipline, were all that remained. In April 1781 a force of less than two hundred Americans attacked unprotected Delaware towns near Fort McIntosh that had remained neutral or even pro-American. The troops took several hundred captives and, unlike the Indians, put fifteen to death in an outward display of butchery. Their commanding officer, General Daniel Brodhead, convinced many of the rangers to join the expedition by promising plunder. The pelts and livestock that they brought back sold for 8,000 British pounds in Wheeling.[34] A worse display came from Washington County, Pennsylvania, militia, who slaughtered ninety peaceful Christian Indians from the Moravian mission towns in March 1782. The Delawares, rightly outraged, soon retaliated after yet another American plundering expedition was defeated. As its troops fled, the Delawares captured several dozen, including the commander, Colonel William Crawford, and burned him at the stake.[35]

Back in London, British officials fretted over what to do regarding the brutal ethnic war that seemed impossible to end in the West. Governor Frederick Haldimand reported that rangers, when storming a Shawnee town in 1783, "indiscriminately massacred its inhabitants of all ages and sexes." Iroquois leaders at Niagara began calling British conduct "treacherous and cruel," because the British did little to stop the carnage. The Indians expressed greater exasperation when news of the peace indicated that Britain had ceded the Ohio country to the United States. "They told me," Brigadier General Allan Maclean reported, "they never could believe that our King could pretend to cede to America what is not his own to give." Joseph Brant, the intrepid Mohawk leader, raced to Quebec in May to determine the extent of the capitulation. He soon discovered that no mention had even been made of the plight of the Indians in the peace treaty. General Maclean cautioned Haldimand to keep Brant in Quebec for as long as possible, for fear that he would cause trouble in the West.[36]

News of the end of the war brought considerable relief to some set-tlers and some Indians, but it only heightened outrage among the more militant Ohio and southern Indians. In a massive Indian council at San-dusky, New York, in September 1783 British agent John Johnson told the assembled warriors and chiefs that they no longer wanted the Indians to attack American settlements but that they had the right to defend their own lands, a territory that bordered on the Ohio River. Such an explana-tion became even more unpalatable when American negotiators later told the same Indians that Great Britain had ceded all lands south of the Great Lakes, all the way to the Mississippi River, to the United States.[37]

The confusion only grew after the new federal government, under the Articles of Confederation, passed a land ordinance in October 1783 de-claring federal ownership of all lands west of the Ohio to the Great Miami and Maumee Rivers in central Ohio.[38] At the same time, New York state officials called for a council to convene at Fort Stanwix; they planned to force the Iroquois, supposedly conquered by the Americans, to cede all their lands and leave for the West. While New York eventually agreed to allow the Iroquois to stay, it did join federal negotiators as well as Penn-sylvania officials who contrived to carry out the terms of the new ordi-nance. In 1784 a small handful of Iroquois chiefs, including Cornplanter, sat stunned as they listened to the terms of peace. Commissioners Richard Butler and Arthur Lee told them: "The King of Great Britain ceded to the United States *the whole,* by the right of conquest they [the Americans] might *claim the whole.*"[39] This even included Iroquois lands

While the final treaty that the Americans demanded at Fort Stanwix allowed the Iroquois to keep reservations in New York, it forced the In-dians to relinquish all of the upper Susquehannah and Allegheny River valleys. Cornplanter and other Iroquois leaders grudgingly signed the agreement.[40] The Americans did not stop there. They convinced a few leaders of the Wyandots, Delawares (some of whom were Christians), Ot-tawas, and Ojibwas to meet them near Fort Harmar, near present Marietta, Ohio. These Indians heard the same story: the United States had taken the Ohio country "by conquest." The Ojibwas and Ottawas—Michigan tribes—had never claimed this land, and the few Wyandots and Delawares were hardly representative of those Shawnees, Delawares, and Miamis who had the best claim to it. The Indian leaders present signed the treaty, once again made with Indians who had a questionable claim to the lands involved. This started a new war in the Ohio country over land.[41]

The Americans then forced yet another treaty upon a few Shawnee chiefs at the newly built Fort Finney, constructed at the mouth of the Great Miami in January 1786. The fort itself represented a further penetration of the Ohio country. This time, the fighting nearly started during the negotiation after the commissioners noted that all of Ohio to the Great Miami belonged to the Americans. The Shawnee chief Kekewopellethy then threw a "Black Wampum" belt at the feet of the commissioners, a sign for war. George Rogers Clark angrily stomped it into the ground. Nevertheless, several Shawnees, including Molunthy, came forward a few days later and signed the so-called Peace Treaty, mostly in order to get the presents of food that the Americans distributed.[42]

While some of the Ohio Indians wanted peace, Clark recognized that many Delawares, Shawnees, and Miamis would not accept American settlement beyond the Ohio River. These Indians soon formed a confederacy to resist American invasion.[43] Clark continued to keep his rangers in action. Two bodies of rangers moved northward in the fall 1786. One, under Clark and now "Colonel" Daniel Boone, consisted of 790 men. Rather than take on the militant Shawnees or Miamis, they ultimately attacked the friendly town of Shawnee chief Molunthy, who had signed the 1786 peace treaty just months before. While at Fort Finney, Molunthy had received an American flag, which floated over his town when the rangers went in. The rangers cried out: "Spare white blood only," meaning captive Americans. Clark's rangers tore the place apart, killing indiscriminately and capturing Molunthy. While he was kneeling, a ranger split his skull open with a hatchet. Eight towns were burned in all, many of them friendly, and hundreds of Indians killed. The rangers burned several captives at the stake.[44]

To be sure, the American Revolution witnessed many noble displays of gallantry—Washington's leadership in crossing the Delaware River and his courageous stand at Valley Forge being examples. But the conflict in the West attracted American men of a different character, who joined ranger units not to defend their liberties but to drive Indians from their lands. Above all, they were devout believers in "settler sovereignty." By the summer of 1786 these ruffians had succeeded in taking the disputed regions of western Virginia, eastern Kentucky, and northeastern Tennessee and had often crossed into what is today Ohio. The American title to these regions, while fought over by various states, was based solely upon the "right of conquest" but hardly came with the sanction of the Indian occupants or by any meaningful understanding of "just war."

While this scenario played out in the North, similar land grabs occurred in the South. After the federal government under the Articles finally asserted control over western lands, it demanded that Cherokee representatives meet the leaders of the new government in council at Hopewell, Kentucky, in 1785. In those first negotiations between these two nations, the Cherokees surrendered claims to Kentucky as well as lands extending down into central Tennessee near what would soon be Nashville. In exchange the Cherokees convinced the United States to recognize their lands in far southeastern Tennessee, with the hope that the government would prevent more squatters from invading them.[45]

The federal government did try to establish boundaries separating whites and Indians, much as Great Britain had tried to do with its proclamation. The selection of Henry Knox as the secretary of war in 1788 helped; Knox and other revolutionary leaders believed that Indian war would simply bankrupt the country. He freely admitted that the breakaway state of Franklin in Tennessee, which had formed out of the Henderson Purchase, violated the Hopewell Treaty. Those frontiersmen who formed this government—which eventually was negated—had no intention of recognizing any Indian title to land. Knox asserted federal control and ordered the removal of any trespassers.[46]

In his first report to the nation as the secretary of war under President Washington, Knox went further, noting that Native peoples, "being the prior occupants, possess the right of the soil." And their lands, he declared, "cannot be taken from them unless by their free consent" or in the case of conflict only under conditions of "Just War." Knox had obviously read Grotius.[47] As the war came to an end, the American federal government began to reassert its control over the West, much as Great Britain had attempted to do after the French and Indian War.

The weak financial condition of the new republic proved a more pressing concern—indeed the British in Canada somewhat expected the new country to collapse. The Articles had left all taxing power to the states. Accordingly, the government set about to convince the various states to give up claims to lands west of the Appalachian Mountains so that this land might be sold in order to support the federal treasury. Northern states finally agreed after the government proposed passage of the land ordinances of 1785 and 1787, allowing for the surveying and sale of public lands as well as the creation of territorial governments. This created the ultimate conundrum for the federal government: Knox and others wished to prevent costly Indian wars and even protect Indian boundary claims, a commendable goal, but at the same time the government had to sell western lands in order to remain solvent.

In the South the government under the Articles found the states less cooperative in relinquishing their supposed ownership to western land. Both the Carolinas and Georgia initially refused, accepting relinquishment after several years of negotiation. Georgia became the last state to surrender claims to what would become Alabama and Mississippi in 1802. Unfortunately, in the agreement—which Native Americans never had a say in—the United States promised eventually to remove all Indians from the new state's borders. Indian Removal thus became an increasingly accepted future federal government policy or at least one that southern states would demand. But it could be argued that northern states were no better, because they agreed to "give up" lands in the West only after highly questionable treaties had supposedly opened them to speculators and settlement.

While the government under the Articles had created a fledgling land policy, it accomplished little else, leading to a political *coup d'état*—the writing of the Constitution and the adoption of a new, more powerful federal government. George Washington, who was elected the first president in 1789, sent a message to the new Congress late that year. The Constitution required that any treaties with European nations be ratified by the Senate, so "I am inclined to think," he wrote, "it would be advisable to observe it [the same procedure] in the conduct of our treaties with the Indians."[48] Nevertheless, at the same time, Washington introduced a letter from Governor Arthur St. Clair of the Western Territory, who noted the growing hostility of the Indians associated with the Ohio Confederacy. Washington recommended that Congress organize a federal army, because, as St. Clair noted, the "handful of troops" from the state militias of Virginia and Pennsylvania did not seem up to the task.[49]

Knox remained in the new government as secretary of war. He hoped to implement a new policy of negotiation, ordering yet another treaty council with the Ohio tribes, in which the United States would make the land purchases west of the Ohio River legal, rather than based on a fictitious claim of conquest. Some opposed the plan, supposedly including Governor St. Clair. But the government under the Articles had appropriated money for negotiation in 1788, and Knox ordered the talks to begin.[50] When St. Clair met with Indians near Fort Harmar in January of the next year, he rewarded those who came with lavish gifts and plenty of liquor.

The most notable leader was Cornplanter, who along with lesser chiefs signed yet another treaty giving up the same land that supposedly had been taken from the Indians in 1784 and 1785.[51]

Nearly at the same time, many leading chiefs of the Shawnee, Delaware, Miami, Mingo, Ojibwa, Ottawa and Potawatomi tribes were meeting with British officials at Detroit. Mostly members of the new confederacy, they bitterly complained of the failure of Americans to meet any of the treaty terms that had been agreed to. Indeed some almost immediately thereafter formed war parties and struck the Kentucky frontier. Governor St. Clair quickly convinced Secretary Knox of the need for a military force to punish the villagers who had settled along the headwaters of the Great Miami and Maumee Rivers. The British seemed to promote hostilities; they had built Fort Miami on the upper Maumee River supposedly to protect the Indians.

St. Clair's army fell under the command of General Josiah Harmar, a veteran of the revolution. He quickly voiced concern. Some 320 regular soldiers were joined by 1,133 militia of the worst sort: they were undisciplined and untested, and most of their arms were out of order. Even so, Harmar marched into northern Ohio, finding village after village along the Maumee abandoned and burned. Nevertheless, his troops started looting. With disorder at its height, the Shawnees Blue Jacket and Little Turtle ambushed the ragged American column not once but twice. Harmar's losses mounted, reaching 75 regulars and 108 militia killed. The expedition destroyed many Native towns, but its retreat had also bolstered the Indians, who realized that they could fight American troops even without British regulars alongside.[52]

Harmar's expedition had accomplished little, prompting Governor St. Clair to lead the army himself into northern Ohio. Knox tried to assist the general by ordering American negotiators to occupy the Iroquois by negotiating with them.[53] By October 1791 Harmar's force of over 2,000 men had built Fort Jefferson, a third of the way to the Maumee. Moving slowly northward, the command bedded down on the banks of the Wabash River. As the 200 women camp followers prepared breakfast the next morning, November 4, parting mist on the river revealed hundreds of Indians bearing down on the camp. The Indians attacked, often tomahawking the aroused troops as they left their tents. The fighting became hand-to-hand, with the women carrying on the struggle the best they could alongside the men. The chain of command immediately evaporated:

many American troops ran for their lives, some breaking out on foot, others on horse. After Governor St. Clair, who survived, made it to safety to Fort Jefferson, he noted that 623 soldiers were missing, along with nearly all the women (only 3 survived); he also counted some 258 severely wounded. St. Clair's defeat still remains the worst ever suffered by an American army in North America. To celebrate their victory, the Indians stuffed the mouths of the dead soldiers with soil, to decry the Americans' lust for land.[54]

Knox and President Washington agonized over St. Clair's debacle. Yet both men had other concerns; they anticipated that the Northwest Territory, which stretched to the Mississippi River, would one day be settled by Americans, foreordained by the debates of the 1780s and the passage of the two land ordinances. The two men hoped, however, that the lands might be taken through purchase rather than through war, because wars were so expensive. Both moral and pragmatic restraints existed: it was not right to kill Indians to take their land; nor would it be wise to risk yet another war with Great Britain in doing so.[55] When word arrived in late summer that the Ohio Indians wished to negotiate, Knox was quick to accept the offer. But the question remained: peace at what cost?

Washington decided to ask his cabinet for advice; should the United States back off on the treaties of the 1780s and give up much of Ohio to the Indians? Secretary of the treasury Alexander Hamilton, who had to finance a war, thought that was a good idea. Hamilton (despite having relatives who were heavily involved in Ohio land speculation) despised the uncouth, back-country ruffians like George Rogers Clark who started Indian wars over land. But Thomas Jefferson, who had become secretary of state, disagreed. The one man who would later be seen as the friend of the Indians refused to give an inch in Ohio. Despite a divided cabinet, Knox organized the peace commission that met the leaders of the Indian confederacy near Sandusky over the summer. The Indians continued to demand a border at the Ohio River, and the negotiations broke off by fall. By then Knox and Washington had ordered General Anthony Wayne to the Ohio frontier with a strict charge: to build a federal army that was disciplined, well armed, and capable of defeating the confederacy that the British had so deftly helped organize.

Wayne came to command naturally. He harbored none of Harmar's faults—alcohol, for example—or St. Clair's basic incompetence. Landing at Fort Pitt in summer 1792, he quickly recruited men and officers. But

Knox continually offered cautious advice to him, fearing a clash with Great Britain. Wayne, however, feared that caution might "sacrifice National Character & Justice" in order to "patch up a temporary peace."[56] Wayne recruited Cornplanter as a spy and soon found the Indian Confederacy deeply committed to preserving its land claim to Ohio. Increasingly the cautious Knox concluded that a peace that "sacrifices" the national character might not be acceptable to the nation.[57]

When Cornplanter finally returned after speaking with the confederacy leaders in March 1793, all hope of peace vanished. "My mind and heart is upon that river [the Ohio]," Cornplanter told Wayne. "May that water ever continue to run & remain *the boundary of a lasting peace* between the Americans & the Indians."[58] Such a peace—a boundary at the Ohio—had become the sacrifice that Secretary Knox had dreaded and ultimately refused to make. General Wayne prepared his army for combat. Plain and simple, the young United States was going to war to "cleanse" Ohio of its Indians.

Wayne marched north from the Ohio River in July 1794 with 3,500 men, mostly federal troops, who obeyed their officers. Wayne finally met Blue Jacket's and Little Turtle's bands and their various allies at a place along the Maumee River where a cyclone had blown down all the trees. The Battle of Fallen Timbers, fought on August 20, 1794, proved anticlimactic. The Indians, who had fasted for three days waiting for the engagement, soon broke and ran; many of them fled to the British fort some miles up the river, south of modern-day Toledo. As they reached it, the British soldiers closed the gate and warned them away. Wayne then descended upon Fort Miami, demanding that the British withdraw from American soil; but he did not provoke a fight, heeding Knox's caution. The British troops could only watch from their ramparts as Wayne's soldiers burned Indian village after village, along with food and crops that might sustain the Indians over the winter.[59]

General Wayne then waited patiently as the Indian leaders of the confederacy visited him, asking his intentions. He treated them kindly and explained that they would have to sign yet another treaty, giving up lands in Ohio forever. The Wyandots from Sandusky quickly agreed, as did many others. Finally Wayne met Blue Jacket, the noted Shawnee chief, who likewise accepted the terms. Wayne called for a massive council to be held at his new Fort Greenville, where over a thousand Indians gathered in June 1795.

As the talks began, many Indians showed signs of suffering from lack of food. Wayne fed them for several months. During the talks both Little Turtle and Blue Jacket argued vehemently that they had never surrendered their land at Fort Stanwix: "My Fathers told me not to sell our land, and we have never sold it." But this time these Indian leaders knew that the British would offer no assistance in sustaining their claims to Ohio lands. On August 3 the chiefs signed the Treaty of Greenville, giving up Ohio for an annual annuity of $9,500 and some $20,000 worth of presents.[60] Late that summer the American land rush into Ohio began in earnest. Town after town sprang up, protected by the guns of the American forts at Greenville, and later at the headwaters of the Maumee River, a blockhouse appropriately called Fort Wayne.

Fortunately for the American president, George Washington, negotiations with the southern Indians proved less taxing than the Ohio war, which consumed the four years of his first administration. After the war Spain continued to provide McGillivray and his Creeks, as well as some Cherokees, with munitions. But it seemed unlikely that Spain would join the Creeks should a general conflict erupt, much like the British in the North. And Washington's government as well as the Indian nations wanted to avoid conflict. Helping matters along, Washington did receive a concession from North Carolina in 1789 when it finally relinquished all claims to land beyond its western border. This made it much easier to negotiate with the Creeks and Cherokees and settle the boundary between them and the Carolinas and Georgia.

A solution seemed all the more possible when Alexander McGillivray agreed to visit New York and treat with Washington personally. The Creeks wanted a recognized boundary, and Georgia wanted land. When Washington agreed to guarantee Creek land claims if the Indians conceded lands to the Oconee River, in central Georgia, the treaty of New York was signed in August 1790. While the Creek lower towns remained angry over the cession—it had been their land that McGillivray had given away—they could do little to reclaim it: Americans soon swarmed over it.[61]

The struggles with the evolving United States had demonstrated to southern Indians that they would have to develop more centralized governments in order to deal with the land-hungry Americans. McGillivray had attempted to do this through organizing a national council in which every Creek town had representation. He was not quite been able to accomplish this before he died at a young age in 1793. But his successor,

Benjamin Hawkins, pushed the nation to even higher levels of organization—Hawkins created legislative districts with systematically appointed delegates and a National Council that soon provided a police force (called a "light horse") that offered some vestiges of law and order.[62]

Cherokees and Choctaws were slower to form such governments, primarily because the Choctaws had yet to be pressured for land and the Cherokees were so thoroughly disrupted in 1776 by the American invasion. The Washington government used the same tactics with the Cherokees regarding land cessions as it did with the Creeks. Officials opened negotiations with the Cherokees in 1790 that continued into the next year. The Indians ultimately agreed to give up much of the land in eastern Tennessee that Americans had already invaded and settled. A smaller cession occurred in 1798, which added to this land base.[63]

The treaties made with the Creeks, the Cherokees, and the Ohio tribes all established permanent boundaries separating Indians and whites. The Washington administration had also created an Indian service under the new Intercourse Act of 1790, orchestrated by Knox, which included selecting Indian agents to reside among the various tribes. Their mission was to prevent further conflict. While the language of each treaty seemed to make it clear that Indians had sovereign rights to use their lands, other sections of nearly every treaty foreordained more negotiations to come. Both Secretary Knox and his predecessor, Timothy Pickering, consistently stressed to negotiators the need to inform the Indians that if they ever desired to sell lands in the future they must sell them directly to the United States. Individuals like Henderson could no longer purchase Indian lands.

Washington's successor, John Adams, likewise saw the need to negotiate with Indians as reflective of Washington's general policy of remaining neutral in foreign wars—such as the one that broke out between England and France in 1793—and to reinforce that neutrality in the West with honest agreements that preserved Indian claims to land. If nothing else, these treaties reaffirmed the Indians' "right of occupancy," the phrase that occasionally crept into discussions. By the mid-1790s vast regions of land in eastern Ohio, Kentucky, and Tennessee had been made available to settlers, which further reinforced Washington's policy of negotiation. Nevertheless, Washington's "federalism" was falling out of fashion in America, considered by many to be elitist or even aristocratic. Worse, the ruffians who had illegally seized much of the frontier from Indians soon became voters and encouraged a form of "settler sovereignty" that increasingly led to local government and law. Both Kentucky and Tennessee joined the union in the 1790s as states. Such new regions supported expansion.

Federalists openly condemned these ruffians, who at the drop of a hat formed ranger units and rode west to start Indian wars. Knox, in particular, remained critical of the frontier elements. "The desire of too many frontier white people, to seize by force or fraud upon the neighboring Indian lands," he wrote in late 1794, "still continues to be, an unceasing cause of jealousy and hatred on the part of the Indians." Until the Indians could be assured that their titles to land were permanent, there would be nothing but conflict. "This," Knox believed, "appears to be a principal cause of Indian wars."[64]

What can be said about this period of raid and counterraid and destruction of frontier Anglo hamlets and Indian villages? Is it only part of the "fog of war," inevitable given the larger conflict between England and the United States? An answer may be found in assessing the locales of the conflict. Indian attacks never occurred in settled regions—Anglo communities of long standing. Indians had given up those lands. They occurred instead in the back-country lands thinly, and illegally, settled by Anglo squatters that had little to do with the Revolution itself. George Washington certainly recognized that omission—that legitimate treaties relinquishing the land being fought over did not exist.

Furthermore, in truth, Indians usually conducted a "just war" designed to protect their legal right to their lands. Their abuse of captives or cruelty was often nothing more than revolutionary propaganda. Indians took women and children as captives, many of whom wrote dozens of "captivity narratives" after their release.[65] American ranger groups, in contrast, seldom observed these rules, killing indiscriminately—on many occasions even killing men who had surrendered. And they killed to make a statement—to convince Indians to remove themselves for lands farther west. Their visions of settler sovereignty did not include Indians as part of an evolving frontier political process, even if Indians agreed to settle into farming communities, as many in Ohio did. Those Native communities were often viewed as easy targets for plundering rangers.

Thomas Jefferson mostly disagreed with the passive, appeasing policies of George Washington. He broke with Washington over neutrality in 1793, declaring his support for France in the struggle then erupting in Europe. Jefferson also had different views regarding western lands; in particular, he did not see the new union of states confining itself to the eastern seaboard and had less concern for preserving the Indians' right to land. Jefferson formed his own political faction the next year, called initially the Anti-Federalists and later the National Republicans. Jefferson, the author of the Declaration of Independence, had spoken eloquently about the "rights of man" and wrote that "all men were created equal." Yet equality to Jefferson included the Indians only if they metamorphosed into white people.

In an ironic twist, the very liberals, like Jefferson, who had formulated the intellectual arguments regarding freedom and equality for America soon embraced a policy calling for the removal of all Indians to the western bank of the Mississippi River. Once there, they would have time to change, to adopt the elements of American civilization that would be necessary for citizenship. The argument for removal matured almost immediately after Jefferson assumed the presidency in 1801. With a smugness that almost defies belief, the Jeffersonians soon promoted ethnic cleansing as a general policy that would benefit American Indians.

But as American settlers en masse pushed beyond the Appalachian Mountains, it must be said that the evolving policy of assimilating Indians to an American lifestyle by driving them farther west prevented an even worse alternative—genocide. Indeed liberals increasingly championed removal as a "moral restraint" that was best for all. Removal gave Indians time to reach the same level of "civilization," through education and religion, that existed in the rest of the United States.

6

THE JEFFERSONIANS AND
THE REMOVAL GAME

Thomas Jefferson's National Republicans won a sweeping victory in 1800, primarily because many Americans perceived them to be the emerging party of the people. From this party came a host of young, idealistic politicians, often called the Jeffersonians. They included the likes of James Madison, who would succeed Jefferson as president; James Monroe, who would succeed Madison; and even John Quincy Adams, the nation's sixth president and the son of the last Federalist president. Adams assumed the presidency in 1825 as a Jeffersonian. Four years later the party split, evolving into the Democrat Party and Whig Party. The Democrats, who would call themselves "Jeffersonians," then elected the first westerner to become president, Andrew Jackson. These men all had in common a limited belief in egalitarianism, the view that all white American men had a right to property, religious freedom, and what Ben Franklin so aptly added to the Declaration of Independence: "the pursuit of happiness." But men of color had few rights, if any, even when it came to ownership of property.

Above all, Jeffersonian politicians gloried in the accomplishments of the individual American farmer. North America had few cities, which Jeffersonians saw as a decided advantage over Europe, because urban communities often bred disorder and poverty. A farm provided sustenance for the family and allowed the yeoman owner to work the land, which Jeffersonians often saw as a spiritual pursuit. Ironically, this belief that the individual yeoman farmer constituted the future of America continued to dominate Jeffersonian ideology at the same time that much of the South was being consumed by larger agriculturalists, called "planters," who used slaves to work their fields.[1] The planter class that emerged from this agricultural revolution soon overwhelmed the influence of small farmers who lacked the capital to acquire slaves.

Jeffersonians also claimed a paternal relationship with Indians. But the Indian lifestyle, despite its naturalness and simplicity, seemed peculiar to Americans in general and even to Jeffersonians. The Indian would simply have to change, in dress, in politics, in economic pursuits, and, finally, in religious mores. Jeffersonians felt it their moral duty to help foster this change, or so the synthetic argument of the age began. This could be done through urging the development of agriculture, through discouraging communal living and encouraging democratic rather than tribal politics, and even through a conversion to Christianity.[2] All in all, by reading the rhetoric of both Jefferson and his followers, the Indians might expect fair and moral treatment from the newly elected president, even considerable assistance in adopting "white" civilization. But in reality little assistance was forthcoming, and at least some Jeffersonians abandoned the pursuit of fairness in regard to American Indians and worked instead to take much of their land.

Even so, a general hiatus on the transfer of Indian lands to the United States had occurred under both presidents George Washington and John Adams—a lull in the process of ethnic cleansing that had become so common just before and during the American Revolution. Jeffersonians to some degree continued that policy, at least before the War of 1812, convinced that Native farming communities needed to be protected but that Indians had no right to expect to retain massive tracts of hunting lands. Many Jeffersonians had read Grotius, Locke, and Vattel and accepted their basic argument that nations with expanding populations could acquire the lands of "wandering" people, but only under the general belief that they must be left a portion of land to cultivate. This became the early moral restraint on the land policies of Thomas Jefferson—to purchase lands that the Indians supposedly had no use for: hunting lands that were mostly devoid of game.

In most cases the Indians who treated with Jefferson's government received promises that a cession would guarantee continued ownership of the lands that they still held. And the government would pay for the lands with funds that could be used to purchase agricultural implements, thus furthering the stated policy that later Americans would call assimilation. Unfortunately, the men who made such promises were often replaced by others even more aggressive and committed to taking more land from Indians. And as more and more pioneers flooded into the lands beyond the Appalachian Mountains, they often squatted on Indian lands, producing yet another justification for taking these lands—the squatters were American citizens who voted and who deserved to have land.

The recognition of "squatter's rights" or "settler sovereignty" became a problem in itself. Ultimately, Jeffersonians adopted a narrow view of egalitarianism that recognized the rights of white squatters. Congress debated and finally passed the first "preemption act" recognizing squatter rights in 1813. The Supreme Court seemed to sanction such rights when it had ruled three years earlier in *Fletcher v. Peck* that a state contract to sell a vast amount of land in Mississippi, known as the Yazoo strip, could not be voided even though bribes had been used to acquire the land. The case tangentially put Indian title to any land in the West in jeopardy, and other decisions coming later would only add to this conclusion.[3] A fair Indian policy that promoted Indian rights to land and assimilation became almost impossible to enact even when federal officials, at least rhetorically, indicated a desire to do what was right.

In truth, President Jefferson inherited a messy land problem across much of this trans-Appalachian region in 1801. In the North both the British and French governments had issued land grants prior to the Revolutionary War that supposedly had to be honored—or turned their backs as individuals purchased land. Congress had passed a reasonably effective land law for the rest of the region in 1800, which opened up much of Ohio to settlement. It created four land offices at Steubenville, Marietta, Chillicothe, and Cincinnati, where once a month officials took bids on tracts of land opened by the government. The standard price reached two dollars an acre. But the successful bidder could purchase 320 acres or more, putting down one-quarter of the cost; the federal government financed the rest for a period of years.[4] With such a liberal policy in place, Ohio rapidly filled with Americans.

Jefferson's secretary of state James Madison investigated the claims of mostly the French and Spaniards in the South in 1802 and issued a report to Congress. He concluded that 52,000,000 acres of land existed between the 31st and 35th parallels: between the northern border of Spanish Florida and the southernmost border of the new state of Tennessee, a region where much of the land was still owned by Indians. Madison created a rigorous plan to recognize the legitimate land claims of only those who had settled on their lands, including the French, Spanish, and English. He suspected that this would include roughly 350,000 acres, a very small amount—the actual figure turned out to be 450,000 acres. With the exception of small tracts in eastern Georgia and western and southern Mississippi, all the remaining lands within those quadrants theoretically belonged to American Indians.[5]

Jefferson recognized that settlers were penetrating deep into Tennessee, eastern Georgia, and southern Mississippi. Unfortunately for the Indian owners, these lands were capable of cotton production, an industry that expanded dramatically after the invention of the cotton gin in the 1790s. Indian claims to this land would soon prove a problem for Jefferson's administration. Georgia's demand that all Indians be removed from the state as a condition for relinquishing claims to land farther west had been agreed to by the Jefferson administration in 1802. Thereafter, Georgia congressmen became downright belligerent about removing Indians from their state, who at the time claimed 80 percent of Georgia.[6]

Jefferson felt the pressure. In a "confidential" message to Congress in 1803, the president noted that the Indian tribes in the West were "growing more and more uneasy at the constant diminution of the territory they occupy . . . and the policy has long been gaining strength with them of refusing absolutely all further sale, on any condition." The situation remained tense, Jefferson thought: it "excited dangerous jealousies and perturbations in their minds to make any overture for the purchase of the smallest portions of their land."[7] This did not dissuade the president from trying to purchase land, however; indeed he offered two possible avenues that, if pursued, would lead to the purchase of mostly Indian "hunting lands," or so he presumed.

Jefferson suggested that Congress could help immeasurably by providing funds to expand the "factory system" of government trade houses. These trade houses had been authorized by the Intercourse Act of 1795.[8] They offered goods at cost to Indians with the intention of keeping them loyal to the United States. While these houses competed against small independent traders—who complained about the "government" competition—the president argued that those same American fur traders should move to the upper Missouri River and drive out British merchants who dominated that commerce. Jefferson then noted the advantage of having government trading houses. They would put Indian nations in debt to the United States and tribes would have to pay off their debts by selling land.

The president felt that the government's interests—indeed its great need to purchase land—superseded free enterprise.

A second solution involved encouraging Indians to give up the hunt and turn to raising stock and farming. Embracing the views of Grotius, Locke, and Vattel, Jefferson believed that this would benefit them and lead to a situation in which "less land and labor will maintain them."[9] The president did emphasize the need to convince Indians to enter "civilization" programs, but above all he urged officials who worked for him to use every means to convince the Indians to sell land. He wrote to the rising Tennessee politician Andrew Jackson in 1803 that the interests of the United States came first in this endeavor. An agent—he used the example of Benjamin Hawkins, who worked among the Creeks—must be removed immediately if "he obstructs cessions of land" from the Indians in any way.[10]

Jefferson attached a second note to his "confidential message," which included a report from the new secretary of war, Henry Dearborn. He described Dearborn's report as a statement detailing the "setting and marking of boundaries" across the West, which the Washington administration had started. It also gave an audit of the lands recently purchased from Indians, "and the prospect of further progress in marking boundaries, and in new extinguishments [sic] of title in the year to come." Jefferson quickly came to realize that Indian lands could be bought for a trifle and then sold, thereby financing the federal system. In a long letter to Governor William Henry Harrison, a close Jeffersonian ally, Jefferson even gloated to some degree over the 63 million acres of land purchased in 1801–1802 alone, for an astonishing price. "It will be found," the president reported, "that the average price we have paid and engaged to pay for Indian cessions does not amount to quite one quarter of a cent per acre."[11] The same land then went on the market at several dollars an acre.

Finally, in his "confidential" recommendations, Jefferson also included a request for $2,500 to pay the costs for exploring the lands west of the Mississippi River to the Pacific Ocean. This "voyage of discovery" by Captains Meriwether Lewis and William Clark, as Jefferson called it, had begun that spring. It had little to do with the president's evolving Indian policy east of the Mississippi River, at least in 1803, when it got under way, but it surely demonstrated a holistic approach to the development of the West. This led to the obvious conclusion that the lands beyond the Mississippi River might one day act as a safety valve for American Indians.

Rumors of such a prospect, discussed by Jeffersonians, were soon exposed in congressional debates that very year.

The news arrived of the purchase of Louisiana from France as Lewis and Clark organized their expedition in St. Louis. The French had taken back the region called Louisiana—or the lands between the Mississippi River and the Rocky Mountains—from Spain in a treaty initially kept secret three years before then sold it to the United States for a mere 15 million dollars. While the Senate promptly ratified the treaty, controversy soon erupted in Congress on how to come up with the money necessary to finance the deal. The debates, which ultimately centered on the value of the purchase and its future use, occupied Congress throughout October and November 1803.[12]

Opposition in the Senate came from the delegations from Delaware, Connecticut, and Massachusetts, the New England states where the Federalist Party still had considerable support. Senator Samuel White of Delaware saw Louisiana as an "immense, unbounded world" that probably could never be incorporated into the United States. The Constitution failed to allow such a purchase, White concluded. Even if that occurred, it would be a "curse," productive of many "evils." White especially objected to the notion, then circulating among Jeffersonians, that called for the "removing of the Creeks and other nations of Indians from the eastern to the western banks of the Mississippi." The Creeks obviously were singled out because of the Georgia compact, regarding the removal of all Indians from the state. Beyond this, the senators from New England especially feared that Louisiana would attract large numbers of people from the East. While they never admitted it, such an event would lessen the political power of their region. They also believed that it would perhaps lead to rebellion, destroying the union.[13]

This notion that Louisiana might become an Indian refuge had been discussed somewhat before the debates.[14] Senator White noted that the administration apparently backed the idea. Despite the dubious nature of the morality of Indian removal, many more senators supported the purchase and agreed to fund the treaty. They came from Virginia, Pennsylvania, New York, and especially the new states in the West, regions that generally supported National Republicans or Jeffersonians. In the House John Randolph attacked the notion that a rush to Louisiana would somehow destroy the union. The purchase, he concluded, "will tend to destroy the cause of Indian wars, whilst it may constitute the asylum of that brave and injured race of men."[15] Thus Indian Removal could both be moral and have beneficial consequences for Indians. In the end both the Senate and the House passed the appropriation bill overwhelmingly.

Overjoyed with the success of the treaty, Jefferson offered a report to Congress on the new lands just acquired in November. While Lewis and Clark were still well over two years away from returning, the president used the most recent information that he could gather. He offered a long description of the various Indian tribes, which included some interesting and likely inaccurate conclusions. Discussing the Choctaw Indians, he noted that some five hundred families had already left the South, migrating into Louisiana to hunt. The whole nation "would have migrated across the Mississippi, had it not been for the opposition of the Spaniards and the Indians on that side [west of the Mississippi River]." Furthermore, large numbers of Chickasaws apparently frequented the "neighborhood of Arkansas" and "seemed inclined to make a permanent settlement" there.[16] Jefferson seemed determined to convince himself that Indians would be better off west of the Mississippi River.

Although most eastern Indians wanted nothing to do with removal, Congress helped create the bureaucracy necessary to implement such a policy. One aspect included the creation of superintendents of Indian affairs in the West as well as agents who worked for these superintendents and served individual tribes. Jefferson determined that they should come from the locales that they administered. He selected C. C. Claiborne, William Henry Harrison, and Arthur St. Clair to act as superintendents. All three men were heavily involved in western politics, serving as governors of the Mississippi (parts of which soon became Orleans Territory), Indiana, and the Northwest Territories, respectively.[17] As such, they had much to gain from opening Indian lands and creating states: the voters would then likely reward them with political office.

With a bureaucracy slowly coming into place and pressure from more and more western pioneers to remove Indians, it is hardly surprising that the vast majority of the correspondence of Jefferson's secretary of war, Henry Dearborn, should concentrate on Indian affairs. During his first year in office Dearborn sent instructions to many different agents regarding negotiations. In particular he charged Benjamin Hawkins and James Wilkinson to approach the Cherokees, Chickasaws, Choctaws, and Creeks and negotiate for land. Dearborn left the agents considerable discretion in these talks, suggesting that the government wished to purchase as much land as possible but that at the very least the Cherokees and Chickasaws should surrender lands in south-central Tennessee, a booming region.[18]

The invasion of Indian lands by whites made such negotiations difficult. Settler intrusions on Indian lands occurred all across the trans-Appalachian region. The situation became so tense that the Cherokees sent a delegation to Washington, D.C., to see if the government intended to honor the treaties made by Federalist presidents to control squatters. Cherokee spokesman Glass noted that he had told federal officials some years before that "we had no desire to part with any more land." In an obvious attempt to placate Dearborn, Glass then noted: "We think that the United States do not want our lands, but we know well who do want them—the frontier people want them."[19] Glass understood the pressures of "settler sovereignty" better than federal officials in Washington did.

Dearborn did not disagree with Glass. He insisted, however, that the chief "must be sensible, that the white people are very numerous." The Cherokees had large amounts of land. "We [the government] never wish to buy, except when you are perfectly willing to sell." And the government had marked a boundary line that separated Indians and whites. "All beyond that line," Dearborn insisted, "we consider as absolutely belonging to our Red Brethren."[20] Dearborn hoped that the Creeks, who owed some $10,000 to the American factory, would be more pliable. He instructed James Wilkinson, Benjamin Hawkins, and Andrew Perkins to use the debt to force the Creeks to give up central Georgia. Dearborn had a clear idea of the tract that the government wanted, as he outlined in his instructions to his agents. It included all the land from the junction of the Oconee and Ocmulgee Rivers south to the Spanish border.[21]

Leaders of the Creek Nation greeted the debt argument with stiff resistance. They had already sold half of the land between the Oconee and Ocmulgee Rivers in 1802. When agent Hawkins approached them again the next year asking for more land, Creek leaders complained bitterly that the earlier cession had simply resulted in a large number of cattle owned by settlers constantly invading their lands and fields. When Hawkins forwarded this message to Dearborn, he received a stern rebuke. The secretary told Hawkins that the Creeks were at fault because they had not wanted a "strong natural boundary" to separate them from white Georgians. Dearborn wanted the land all the way to the Ocmulgee River (supposedly a natural boundary) or central Georgia and told Hawkins that it was "absolutely necessary that every means in our power should be used" to acquire that land. "They [the Indians] ought to show a friendly disposition towards us when we ask them to sell a small piece of land," the secretary fumed.[22]

As the Creeks continued to resist the government's efforts, Dearborn applied pressure. In spring 1804 he ordered General David Meriwether and United States troops to join the discussions, "for the purpose of affording Colonel Hawkins every aid in his power."[23] But the presence of a military force did little to dissuade Creek leaders, who noted that their populations were increasing like the U.S. population and that they needed all their lands for their young people. In their final answer they suggested that Jefferson send his young children to Louisiana, where the president owned plenty of land:

> We have therefore well considered the request of our father . . . we have viewed around the extent of our Country and find it not in our power to sell any part of it. We have sold lands to our White brothers so often for no more than one thousand [dollars], part of its value, and what land we now have, we have no desire to sell. If our white brothers want land send them over the Mississippi which our father has purchased from the French, indeed when the purchase was made we thought our father would not ask us for any more land.[24]

Dearborn became even more enraged by this affront. In the fall the secretary ordered that any Creek men trying to hunt temporarily west of the Mississippi River were to be turned back, "as a check on any improper or unfriendly views they have towards our government." Dearborn knew that hunting remained a significant part of the Creek economy.[25] Some Creek chiefs, in turn, feared that open conflict with the United States would result in their losing the land anyway.[26] Hawkins had formed especially close ties with younger Creek leaders from the lower towns, mixed-bloods like William McIntosh, who would one day sell more Creek land. But as the Creeks surrendered land in Georgia, the sale left them increasingly angry and divided. Factionalism increased at a time when national unity was absolutely necessary.[27]

Turning to the Choctaws, Dearborn found even more reticence to sell land. Choctaw leaders had agreed to let the government build a road through their lands in 1801, but they complained bitterly about the boundary line that the agreement helped establish.[28] Nevertheless, the British trade house at Pensacola had offered these Indians extensive credit and the Choctaws felt obligated to take care of their debts, a concern well understood by American officials. President Jefferson even became personally involved in the negotiations, explaining to Choctaw leaders in the usual flowery fashion that while the government would "take from no nation what belongs to it, our growing numbers make us always willing to buy lands from our red brethren when they are willing to sell."[29]

Secretary Dearborn then proceeded to undermine all of Jefferson's promised rhetoric, probably with the full knowledge of the president. Dearborn gave two of the treaty commissioners, James Robertson and Silas Dinsmoor, clear advice on how much should be paid for Choctaw lands, as if the debate over whether they would sell or not had ended. The secretary argued that the fur pelts taken from the southern portion of the Choctaw domain were worth about $3,000 a year. The fur trade was rapidly diminishing, so the price for the land should not be much more than that figure. Dearborn also argued that the deal benefited the Indians because the government would allow them to hunt on the lands for a few more years after it was sold.

Put simply, Dearborn believed that the Choctaws had an obligation to give up lands much like all other Indian tribes. This "hunting ground" that the government wished to purchase possessed little value to Indians — American settlers, however, would use it for agriculture. Dearborn believed that the Indians needed to surrender it, under threat if necessary and at the government's price. "The average price paid for Indians' lands, within the last four years," he concluded, "does not amount to one cent per acre." He would pay more for Choctaw lands, given their locale, but at the very most the commissioners should never pay more than two cents per acre.[30] These figures of from one to two cents per acre remained standard for land that the Jefferson administration bullied Indians into selling.

Jefferson's agents, including General Wilkinson, applied the pressure, literally flaunting bills presented by Indian traders Panton and Leslie in the face of Choctaw leaders. By this time factionalism within the tribe had become a major ally of the Americans, because some Choctaws were adjusting to the new market forces then increasingly invading their lands and others were not.[31] Choctaw leaders ultimately surrendered over 800,000 acres of land, receiving in exchange "fifteen pieces of strouds [coarse woolen cloth], three rifles, one hundred and fifty blankets, two hundred and fifty pounds of powder, two hundred and fifty pounds of lead, one bridle, one man's saddle, and one black silk handkerchief."[32] It is easy to imagine the anger of Choctaw leaders when agents Robertson and Dinsmoor approached them in 1805 and asked for yet more land. Panton and Leslie levied new charges: the Choctaws owed another $46,000![33]

Choctaw chiefs at first refused even to speak with the American commissioners, who warned the Indians that they would receive no more credit unless they paid off the debt. In late November the chiefs relented and signed the treaty. This third treaty, negotiated over three years, resulted in the surrender of 4 million more acres of land for roughly $50,000 in cash (which went to pay debts) and a $3,000 annual annuity, the sum that Secretary Dearborn originally had recommended.[34]

The story seemed little different for the Chickasaws and Cherokees, who tried to fight off treaty commissioners in 1804–1805. Dearborn informed both tribes that the government wanted all lands south and west of Nashville. The Cherokee claim rested on the Treaty of Hopewell, concluded in 1785. The Chickasaws asserted that they held title to the same land. Commissioner Robertson noted the conflict and the advantage that it gave the government: "The title[s] of these two nations to the lands in question," he wrote, "are questionable & they are both conscious of it, each is afraid that the other will sell. The Cherokees request that they may first be consulted."[35] The negotiators, aware of the conflict, did exactly the opposite—they turned to the inexperienced Chickasaws.

Nevertheless, a relatively educated Chickasaw mixed-blood named Page Colbert, who had fought with George Washington during the revolution, took over negotiations for the Indians. In head to head meetings with Secretary Dearborn, Colbert soon learned that the War Department would stop Chickasaw hunters from crossing the Mississippi River to hunt in Arkansas—a major asset—unless they agreed to a land cession. Dearborn also brought up the debt owed by tribal members to the house of Panton and Leslie. Colbert relented, especially after Dearborn agreed to pay him for his service during the Revolution, an obvious bribe. The tribe sold all lands east of the Tennessee River and north of the point where the Duck River entered the Tennessee: in essence all land within a hundred-mile radius southwest of Nashville.[36]

After convincing the Chickasaws to sell, the government turned to the Cherokees. The inducements offered to many Cherokee leaders, however, had a new ring. Commissioner Return Jonathan Meigs argued that the land cession could include many different "reservations" or farms given to

Cherokee leaders in "fee simple." They could settle on the land, become citizens of Tennessee, or sell it at a profit to whites. Other agreements were made with groups of hunters. They were offered assistance in migrating west to better hunting grounds. With all sorts of secret agreements, two treaties were signed: one at Tellico, Tennessee, in 1805 and one in Washington, D.C., the next year, in which the Cherokees gave up title to over 7 million acres of land. The tracts included the "upper" hunting grounds in central Tennessee and the "lower" hunting ground along the Duck and Tennessee Rivers in western Tennessee.[37] These final treaties opened most of Tennessee to white settlement.

This final treaty with the Cherokees in 1806 brought to an end what had become the first round of major land cessions in the South. Indians generally had resisted these sales, often telling federal authorities that they did not want to sell any more land. But federal agents had persuasive strategies, using debts or dividing Indians into factions or bribing leaders, especially mixed-bloods. Indians still held most of what would become the states of Alabama and Mississippi and roughly half of Georgia. But as roads penetrated these regions—the 1806 Cherokee Treaty granted one between Tellico, Tennessee, and the lower Mississippi Territory—and Americans traveled them, the value of these lands made protecting the Indian claim difficult because the cotton industry was then in full swing.

Dearborn had not in any way ignored the Indians north of the Ohio River as he worked to solidify the government's increased ownership of southern lands. He could see how rapidly Ohio was filling up with people. But he also knew well the struggles of the 1790s and met several times with the chiefs of the Miamis, Shawnees, Delawares, Pottawattomis, and Weas in 1802 to assure them of the government's commitment to peace.[38] In particular Dearborn ordered the boundary line of the Treaty of Greenville run—it had been ignored for many years. Nevertheless, negotiating with the Indians of Indiana and Illinois would be difficult; there were many refugee communities, including Indians who had fled from General Wayne, and mixed groups of villagers, some of whom were forming new political entities and economies. The lands west of Ohio had many discontented elements.[39]

Some of the Northwest Indians had come to understand the significance of land titles and took Jefferson's statements regarding farming to heart. The Seneca leader Handsome Lake showed up at Washington in 1802, requesting that Dearborn provide "a writing on paper . . . so that

we can hold it [the title] fast." Handsome Lake had begun a revitalization movement among the Senecas, which included embracing farming
and abstinence. Liquor had become a major debilitating influence on his
people, so those who followed Handsome Lake gave it up. Dearborn plotted the forty-two square miles of land that the Senecas claimed, putting
down the boundaries of their land and recognizing their claim, giving
them in essence a "reservation."[40] Handsome Lake's Senecas wanted to stay
in New York, a decision that divided the Senecas increasingly into eastern
and western factions.[41]

A new tactic of the federal government that came into more common
use toward the end of the Jefferson administration was the granting of
reservations to heads of families or chiefs. Obviously this promoted private
ownership and broke up tribal holdings, but it also often led the Indians
to sell their lands to whites when the government issued the titles in fee
simple. Increasingly the landscape along the south shores of Lakes Erie
and Ontario included small parcels or reservations that Indians owned
for a time and then lost. Sometimes huge land cessions would include
specific references to small tracts a mile or two square where headmen
lived with their extended families. When General William Hull purchased roughly one-quarter of the Michigan peninsula (18,000,000 acres)
for about $12,000 a year in annuities in 1807, the treaty included at least a
dozen separate parcels for the Indian leaders who signed the agreement.[42]

Yet Dearborn quickly learned that less pressure existed for acquiring
lands along Lake Erie or even in western New York. The American settlers wanted cessions to the lands around Vincennes in central Indiana and
to the south, or all the lands between the Ohio and Mississippi Rivers,
in what would become Indiana and Illinois. Some of these regions had
been granted by the French to a few settlers. Complicating matters, some
Piankashaw and Kickapoo Indians had apparently reaffirmed the French
claim by signing a contract for the sale of southern Illinois to the Wabash
and Illinois Land Company in 1795. Dearborn saw the early claims as an
opening for the United States. "It would be very desirable that the United
States should acquire the exclusive right to this tract," he wrote Governor
William Henry Harrison, "and it is the wish of the President [Jefferson]
that you learn the opinion of the Indians on this subject."[43]

Harrison needed no prodding. He first pressured the Indians of Ohio
to accept a much more liberal definition of the 1795 Greenville boundary than they had ever anticipated. His tactics garnered complaints from

Indians that Dearborn could hardly ignore, especially given their proximity to the British in Canada. In what might be viewed a reprimand, Dearborn ordered Harrison to devote more of his time to "the principle of strict integrity" that he believed had become a hallmark of the administration in dealing with Indians. Such a reprimand must have seemed comical to Harrison, although he certainly understood the geopolitical issues at stake; Dearborn had been ruthless at times in forcing Indians to sign treaties, particularly in Georgia and Mississippi.[44]

In the very next paragraph after the homily, Dearborn virtually ordered Harrison to buy as much of southern Illinois and Indiana as possible, but apparently without making any Indians angry. The land wanted now by the federal government included a triangle extending up the Mississippi River in the West and the Ohio in the East, including lands on the Wabash River and west of it.[45] It took Harrison only a few months to convince a group of Piankashaws—who complained bitterly that they were the original owners of the land—and Delaware chiefs—who had migrated west into the region—to sign a treaty giving up southern Illinois.[46] Others claimed the same land, however, including both the Miamis and Potawatomis and several other refugee villagers. The Potawatomis seemed pliable, but not the Miamis.[47]

Chief Little Turtle of the Miamis, who had been a principal leader in the Ohio Indian Confederacy in the early 1790s, expressed outrage and began spreading rumors of possible war with the United States.[48] Dearborn, despite his earlier reticence, now sided completely with Harrison. The secretary had no intention of allowing such a display, even though the very Delaware chiefs who had signed the treaty also complained bitterly of Harrison's high-handed efforts during the negotiation. "Such of the Delaware chiefs as were present at the treaty," Dearborn wrote to Harrison, "have made false or improper representations of your conduct . . . and ought to be severely reprimanded." As for the Miamis and Potawatomis, Dearborn suggested giving them some presents worth two or three hundred dollars in the hopes of quieting them. Apparently Harrison laid lavish presents at Little Turtle's feet.[49]

The sale of the lands along the Wabash and south of Vincennes led to constant complaints by 1807. The Kickapoos soon joined in threatening war, and the Sacs and Fox, in western Illinois, seemed anxious to join them. Harrison had apparently convinced the Sac and Fox Indians to surrender all their lands east of the Mississippi River, all the way to what would become the Wisconsin boundary line, and part of their lands in southeast Missouri.[50] This gigantic slice of territory even included the main Sac village at Rock Island. The cession was so vast, and the land owned by so many other Indians, that another treaty would be needed in 1815 when the claims of other tribes to the region were relinquished.[51] These negotiations and treaties clearly went beyond the supposed principle that only hunting lands should be bought and that lands should be left for the Indians to farm on—the purchases included dozens of Indian villages where farming was the predominant economic pursuit.

Harrison's lack of regard for Indian ownership of land and even village rights became increasingly obvious. He simply found a few pliable chiefs—realizing that some of them had no claim to the lands they were selling—and had them sign a document. Given the rampant fraud of such agreements, a new Native leader soon emerged who intended to stop the Indiana governor. The Shawnee Prophet had started a cultural regeneration movement in northern Indiana, trying to unify the various Indians around the leadership of his brother, Tecumseh. The Prophet preached abstinence from alcohol and emphasized the need to return to the old ways. His movement remained peaceful in 1807, but the evolving currents of conflict in the Old Northwest foreordained trouble.[52]

President Jefferson tried to smooth over the various infuriated groups. He wrote an open letter to them all, suggesting that the problem came from overlapping tribal land claims, not American aggression. Jefferson believed that all the Indians of the Northwest—Wyandots, Delawares, Shawnees, Ottawas, Chippewas, Potawatomis, Miamis, Weas, Kickapoos, and Piankashaws—needed to come together and "settle amongst themselves" their boundaries. Such advice seemed relevant to Washington officials, but it proved problematic given the mixed villages and refugee groups who lived there. Jefferson believed that the Shawnee Prophet might stand in the way of future land sales. In a lapse not usual for the president, he suggested that Governor Harrison might "gain over the prophet, who no doubt is a scoundrel, and only needs his price." If Little Turtle could be bought, the president seemed to suggest, so could the Shawnee Prophet.[53]

As Jefferson contemplated leaving office, he believed that the country was still poorly prepared to fight another conflict in the West. Accordingly, the president continued to soothe the Northwestern Indians with letters and declarations proclaiming American friendship throughout much of 1808 or offering to mediate. Part of his efforts stemmed from the growing conflict with England that had led him to enact a trade embargo, closing American ports. Such actions might lead to war. Jefferson admitted to the Indians in letters, read by agents, that relations with England were strained, but he strongly urged the northwestern tribes to stay out of any future conflict. On at least one occasion Jefferson also sent out "papers" that attested to the Indians' absolute ownership of land.[54] It only remained to be seen whether the new president, James Madison, who took over the office in March 1809, would continue this sudden change in Indian policy.

Thomas Jefferson left an interesting legacy. He had turned the country's head to the West with his purchase of Louisiana, and the country responded. The purchase by itself seemed to promise cheap land for every American. But Americans did not want to settle in far-off Louisiana; they wanted Georgia, Alabama, Mississippi, Indiana, and Illinois, lands mostly owned by Indians. Jefferson responded by introducing an Indian policy that utilized bribery, debt leveraging, and the fostering of tribal divisiveness in order to buy lands from Indians—hardly the fair and honest dealings of a philanthropist.

Perhaps even more revealing is Jefferson's willingness to employ people in the West who used unscrupulous tactics. Men like Harrison cared little about promoting Indian agricultural villages or the Christian religion and manipulated tribal political groups rather than encouraging elements of representative government. They also sensed the utter helplessness of many Indian leaders. The leaders realized that other chiefs would step forward to sign the treaties if they failed to do so and would gain the presents that such chiefs redistributed in their villages to gain status. North of the Ohio River there were simply too many villages, too many chiefs, and no Native unity, at least in the middle of the decade.[55] Harrison and others, however, sensed that this might change if the Prophet and his brother gained ascendancy.

President Jefferson never started a war over land with these sovereign nations. Hardly an Indian warrior fell protecting his lands. Yet Jefferson created a bureaucracy that acquired millions of acres of Indian land—the final tally was close to 200,000 square miles of land, more than the federal government needed to placate its rising population.[56] Jefferson sanctioned what amounted to threats, intimidation, and bribes to acquire this land. Such "benevolent" treatment of Indians hardly fit the tone of the president's often philanthropic speeches, which emphasized the need to educate the Indians and teach them farming.

Even so, Jefferson's policies mostly fit the patterns well accepted in America: purchasing lands from Indians that had been used for hunting. In a few cases Indians surrendered hunting lands that were mostly devoid of game so that Indian hunters could continue to invade lands west of the Mississippi River in pursuit of game animals. Of course, it must be noted that the government threatened to deny such hunters access to these regions if the tribes refused to sell other lands east of the river.

While such circumstances suggest that the Jefferson administration offered mostly a continuation of Washington's policies or that his years in office were characterized by an "ebb" period in the implementation of a policy of ethnic cleansing, such an argument would likely be contested by the many Creek, Cherokee, and Choctaw leaders who were browbeaten into signing treaties. Furthermore, it is difficult to see the actions of William Henry Harrison as anything less than ethnic cleansing in the North, because he made no effort to preserve Native villages, agricultural or otherwise. The Sac and Fox Indians, who supposedly surrendered lands surrounding their village at Rock Island (they later denied selling them), had been living in a farming community there for well over a century.[57]

Other evidence demonstrates that the small tributaries that ran south into the Ohio River had Indian villages on them. The mapping of the region for 1810 shows some eight villages along the upper Great Miami and nearly two dozen just north of Vincennes, along the Wabash River.[58] These were farming towns, where Indians grew corn, beans, and squash. Harrison never attempted to exempt such communities from land cessions—the issue never came up. And the time was fast approaching when the federal government would make little distinction: Indians would not be allowed to remain east of the Mississippi River, even in villages that depended mostly on farming.

At best, Jefferson's policy constituted an uneven ethnic cleansing, more pronounced in the North, where Indians were forced to give up village grounds and lands, than in the South, where they ceded mostly hunting lands. The pressure on Indian land along the fertile Ohio River delta was most obvious. At times it seemed as if Jeffersonians such as Harrison had abandoned even the fundamental principle that Indians had sovereign rights to their land in the rush to steal America from its rightful owners. Sovereign rights for Indians—those same rights that many of the ancestors of European settlers had fought to secure decades before in Europe— became increasingly marginal.

But it must be said that such a view was at least an improvement over the antics of earlier ranger groups, squatters who recognized no Native rights at all. In the decades after Jefferson left office Supreme Court opinions vacillated regarding the "right of conquest" that had been so preeminent in Wayne's taking of Ohio or even to some degree in Harrison's thinking regarding Indiana and Illinois. Justice Henry Baldwin concluded in 1835 that "holding treaties" with Indians was the only acceptable way of acquiring Native lands.[59]

But Baldwin's assessment remained in the future. It came well after the consequences of a new war that the United States entered in 1812, which—much like the American Revolution—spelled disaster for American Indians. War offered American politicians an accelerated opportunity to harness the nationalism that often led to the destruction of Indians and their loss of land as well as to the conquest of Indian lands and a violent ethnic cleansing that even defenders of agricultural expansion such as Vattell would have thought unjust.

7

THE GREAT LAND GRAB

Jefferson's retirement brought to power a new regime in Washington, D.C. The new president, James Madison, had a brilliant mind. He had authored several of the key letters, known today as the Federalist Papers, that had led to the adoption of the Constitution. He and his protégé James Monroe, who would follow him into the White House, had views similar to Jefferson's, though Madison did believe in a more expanded role for the federal government, while Jefferson thought that sovereign power should be vested mostly in the states. Friends and allies, these two men did not differ much regarding Indian affairs, at least early on. They projected themselves as "humanitarians" in regard to the Indians, as men who would do right by their Native charges. Nevertheless, both certainly agreed that the future of America lay in the West, where land could support American settlers who held democratic views regarding government. Indians would have to give up land in order for that to happen.

Madison's first inaugural address, short by almost any standard, never even mentioned American Indians. It did present a rather gloomy picture, suggesting that world troubles—war between France and England—weighed heavily on the president's mind. Like his predecessors, Madison placed much of the responsibility for conducting Indian affairs in the hands of the secretary of war, and the position became one that warranted constant correspondence with officials in the West. As the country headed into conflict with Great Britain in 1812, the secretary of war became in a very meaningful way the second most powerful man in the United States.

Madison picked for his secretary of war William Eustis from Massachusetts. Eustis was an early convert to Jefferson's party, having been elected to Congress from his home state in 1801, when Jefferson entered the White House. Eustis supported expansion to an even greater degree than Jefferson's secretary, Dearborn. But given the troubles with England in 1807, Jefferson had toned down his efforts to acquire lands in the West. Part of the reason was the emergence of Tecumseh and the Shawnee Prophet and their growing collusion with the British in Canada.[1] But just after removing the embargo on trade that Jefferson had begun in December 1807 President Madison's diplomats in London reached an accord with the British, known as the Erskine agreement. Congress considered it over the summer of 1809. The agreement supposedly rescinded the British Orders in Council that had authorized the capture at sea of American ships. While the accord would ultimately collapse, for nearly a year it offered Eustis, who assumed that the winds of war with England had quieted, the opportunity to push hard for more land cessions.[2]

Within weeks of hearing of the accord, President Madison authorized Eustis to order yet another land purchase in the Northwest. The secretary wrote Governor Harrison in July 1809: "The President authorizes and instructs you to take advantage of the most favorable moment for extinguishing the Indian title to the lands lying to the west of the Wabash River."[3] Harrison needed little prodding, calling together whatever chiefs would meet with him—and of course the most respected ones refused. Indeed, the Shawnee Prophet had urged his followers to return to the food, clothing, and implements used by their ancestors and have nothing to do with anything "American."[4] Many tribes in the region had some claim to this land—as Jefferson had clearly stated in a letter to them some two years before—and most did not want to sell it.

The Shawnees had recruited many other smaller Indian bands to their cause and the Prophet's brother Tecumseh slowly turned the group into a more aggressive political confederation, which pledged never to sell any more land to the Americans.[5] This threat seemed to make Harrison more determined. He called for chiefs of the Delawares, Potawatomis, and Miamis to meet him at Fort Wayne in September 1809 and demanded that they sell much of western Indiana, including lands well north of Vincennes. Harrison had become accustomed to browbeating Indians into submission, and these rather pliable leaders surrendered 5,000,000 acres for a mere $5,200 in goods, delivered during the negotiation, and a $1,500 a year annuity.[6] If the price is figured over the course of thirty years (a generation), the government paid one cent an acre. The Senate ratified the treaty in May 1810.

Secretary of War Eustis recognized the provocative nature of this act, but it fit President Madison's increasingly belligerent policy toward Indians. Madison had asked for and received permission from Congress to raise a militia of 100,000 men, to be ready by January 1810—quite a sizable army in that day and age.[7] Some were on active duty, so Eustis ordered Harrison to move a large force onto the newly purchased ground, occupying the strategic town of Vincennes, even though the troops had to live in lean-tos. Eustis intended to build a line of forts across the Northwest from Sandusky to Vincennes and on to the Mississippi River.[8]

Further evidence of Madison's shift away from Jefferson's late-term caution came when a mob of Americans launched a filibuster movement in west Florida. England reminded the Americans of its alliance with Spain, through a diplomatic note dropped off at the White House by the British ambassador. Madison, however, stood his ground, arguing that the region south of Mississippi Territory and including land on the left bank of the Mississippi River from Baton Rouge to the mouth of the river actually had been part of the Louisiana Purchase. "I, James Madison, President of the United States," he wrote in a proclamation, "have deemed it right and requisite that possession should be taken of the said territory in the name and behalf of the United States."[9] This new rift with Great Britain very likely was all that prevented the president from ordering Harrison to force the Indians to sell all of Indiana.

Madison's aggressive tone may in part have resulted from the growing talk of war in Congress, where a group of young newly elected lawmakers called the "War Hawks" were determined to bring on conflict with England. Mostly from the South (John C. Calhoun and William Lowndes from South Carolina) or the West (Kentuckians Henry Clay and Richard M. Johnson), they talked of taking Canada from Great Britain and encouraged Madison to legitimize the seizure of west Florida.[10] Mimicking the War Hawks, Eustis wrote Governor Harrison that the military occupation of Indiana was the "only efficient language" that Tecumseh and the Prophet would listen to. "It has indeed occurred to me," he mused to Harrison, "that the surest means of securing good behavior from this conspicuous personage and his brother [Tecumseh] would be to make them prisoners."[11]

Some Jeffersonians like Eustis had lost all thoughts of the liberal rhetoric and humanitarian tone that had once permeated the propaganda of the Revolution—such as the natural rights to life and property. Talk of attacking Indian towns and taking their leaders hostage in order to secure their land was the language of conquest and ethnic cleansing, especially when coming from the secretary of war with the blessings of the president of the United States.

Eustis continued his saber rattling into spring 1811 and pushed for a new Indian policy that had as its goal complete removal of all tribes west of the Mississippi River. He instructed agent Silas Dinsmoor in the South to prepare the Choctaws and Cherokees for "removal" to the "western side of the Mississippi." Such a solution had been seriously "contemplated by Mr. Jefferson," the secretary argued, and President Madison strongly favored implementing it. Indian agents received instructions "to consult" with the Cherokees, Creeks, and Choctaws relative to such removal. While Eustis intimated that war might delay the effort and that "a gradual migration" that did little to disrupt the peace that still existed in the South would be preferred, all the agents working for the government should prepare their charges for such a move.[12]

Removal would have to wait, however, as conditions deteriorated in Indiana. Small bands of Indians entered the supposedly ceded lands that Americans had squatted on and attacked a few wayward frontiersmen, causing havoc and prompting flight.[13] When Harrison met with Tecumseh in August 1810 to discuss these events, it became clear that the Shawnee leader, as Harrison rather amazingly admitted, "had organized a combination of all the Indian tribes . . . to put a stop to the encroachments of the white people."[14] These Indians had not signed Harrison's corrupt treaties. Over the next few months Governor Harrison continued to report attacks to the War Department. An irate Eustis called for five hundred militia troops to be sent from Pittsburgh to reinforce Harrison. The secretary then instructed Harrison: "in case circumstances shall occur which may render it necessary," Harrison was to "attack the prophet and his followers" on Tippecanoe Creek or a town known generally known as Prophet's Town, in northwest Indiana. This was the most significant Native community in the region, with some two hundred lodges and a thousand people.[15]

Harrison began planning the campaign almost immediately. He moved forces northward from Vincennes, building Fort Harrison about sixty-five miles north of the old French community, well within Indian lands. By November 7, 1811, his army had reached Prophet's Town. A hard-fought battle ensued. The Indians and the Americans both fought bravely, but in the end Harrison's troops prevailed. They then marched into the town and burned it to the ground. Ironically, the Shawnee military leader Tecumseh was absent, negotiating with the Creeks in the South, hoping to convince them to join his confederacy.[16]

Both President Madison and Secretary Eustis expressed delight over these results. In December the president conveyed his thanks for the "gallantry and good conduct of the troops" and for Harrison's zeal and bravery, though Harrison had attacked a town of Indians whose only sin was the belief that they had rights to the surrounding lands. Wars of conquest of this sort were certainly contrary to the Intercourse Acts, which in fact guaranteed at the very least the right of occupancy of those lands. But the secretary of war had authorized it. Making war on Indian communities, where Indian men had to defend their women and children, was part and parcel of a policy of ethnic cleansing. It struck terror in the minds of these women and children and many other villages that were in that vicinity and prompted them to move farther west. Prophet's Town, located in a lovely spot on Tippecanoe Creek, was abandoned thereafter.[17]

The next month Eustis considered just how the burning of Prophet's Town at Tippecanoe Creek might be used by the government to take advantage of the Indians in their defeat—to hasten their removal beyond the Mississippi River. Eustis ordered Harrison to make contact with the defeated Indians and invite their leaders to Washington, including Tecumseh and the Prophet. He intimated to Harrison that the governor should warn the Indians that President Madison had it within his power "to raise a large force in the Spring of the year, to drive beyond the great water [Mississippi] all those who have been or shall be found in arms."[18] Eustis's goal seemed perfectly clear—the objective of Harrison's attack was forcing these Indians west in order to take their land. The proposed meeting might facilitate removal without using force, the government's ultimate goal. The meeting never occurred, however, as President Madison asked Congress for a declaration of war against England in March 1812 and Congress overwhelmingly agreed.

The problems leading to the War of 1812 had been festering for years. The issue of impressment lay at the core. American sailors—some of whom had recently been in the service of the British Navy—were being taken by force from American commercial ships at sea even though they had attained American citizenship. In its struggle with France's new emperor, Napoleon, Great Britain had also used the conflict as an excuse to take ships and sell them as prizes. While the main problems leading to war were mostly commercial, conflict over Indian land in the West became a secondary issue, especially after Congress ratified Harrison's treaties.[19] Certainly, westerners—and many easterners as well—believed that Indians were conspiring with Great Britain.

Harrison's treaties had outraged Tecumseh and other leaders of the Indian confederacy. Even so, the Prophet's movement initially had been peaceful, aimed at regenerating the Native culture of the Shawnees, Delawares, and others who followed his religion. The movement did radicalize, transforming Native political culture after 1808, when some five thousand American Indians, including in particular various Shawnee, Miami, Potawatomi, Chippewa, and Delaware leaders, visited the British at Amherstburg and discussed the growing possibility of war between Great Britain and the United States. Canadian officials had concluded that Americans wished to conquer Canada (a sentiment openly expressed by many in the American Congress) and that Americans intended to take more Indian land and drive the tribes west of the Mississippi River. It can hardly be argued that this constituted saber rattling: it had become the planned and stated policy of the United States to remove Indians from lands in Indiana. To the Native tribes of the Old Northwest, the War of 1812 became a last, desperate attempt to hold these lands.[20]

Initially the war went well for the various tribes that joined Tecumseh's confederacy. They supported British colonel Isaac Brock, who convinced frightened American general William Hull to surrender Detroit in 1812. The word of the defeat spread terror through many of the upper Ohio settlements, most of these communities being on lands that had yet to be surveyed.[21] Tecumseh, who had returned from the South, stayed by the side of his British allies, fighting mostly a defensive war, and American settlers retired to a line of protection formed naturally by the Maumee and Wabash Rivers. Indians never threatened these communities thereafter. In addition, General Harrison launched a campaign in spring 1813 that resulted in the relief of Fort Meigs, at the mouth of the Maumee River, and eventually forced the British out of Detroit. In the final battle near the fort Tecumseh fell to an American sword, supposedly swung by the Kentucky War Hawk and former congressman Richard Johnson.[22]

Congress exacerbated the problem in the Northwest with its aggressive land policies. As early as 1811 it authorized the president to set aside 6 million acres as military bounty lands, to be used to help defray the cost of increasing the size of the army and navy. Tracts of 2 million acres each were set aside in Illinois, Louisiana, and Michigan, where boundaries had not been identified. Some settlers moved onto these lands early, mimicking the so-called tomahawk claims of previous decades. General William Hull at Detroit warned government officials as early as April 1811 that the policies had led to an invasion by squatters, which had infuriated the Indians living around his fort. Other congressional legislation, which authorized preemption claims in Illinois, brought an even greater land rush in summer 1813. After news of Harrison's victory and Tecumseh's death reached the Ohio settlements, the floodgates opened as thousands of settlers pushed north into Indiana and west into Illinois.[23]

Tecumseh's death spelled the end of most resistance to American expansion in the Northwest, although many of his followers migrated to Canada and hoped to continue the war. His influence in the South lingered on even after his death. Tecumseh's mother—supposedly a Creek Indian—and some Shawnee Indians lived with the upper Creeks in northern Alabama. In an attempt to create unified pan-Indian resistance to American expansion, Tecumseh had traveled south to the Upper Creek towns in fall 1811. While the speeches he gave at various councils were not recorded, he apparently convinced the Upper Creeks that the British would come to the aid of all Indians in any future war with the United States.[24]

Many Upper Creeks took Tecumseh's message to heart. A number of religious leaders emerged who adopted some of the militant songs and dances that Tecumseh had given them, precipitating a revival of traditional Creek culture among followers of the five or more new Creek "prophets." They ranted against the American government and its constant pressure on land as well as against many of the chiefs of the Lower Creek towns, who seemed to be increasingly influenced by McIntosh and his friend agent Hawkins, pliable men who had agreed to land sales. More importantly, Creek men of property—especially cattle and cotton—had helped create a National Council that at times oppressed the poorer and less literate Upper Creeks. Hawkins had been able to manipulate those men of property, resulting in the treaty of 1805. The Creek prophets increasingly seized control of the political agenda in the North and tried to force compliance among the southern Creek towns as well. They and their followers soon acquired the name "Red Sticks," for the canes they carried.[25]

Tecumseh's appearance came at a point when agent Hawkins had solidified considerable control over the Lower Creek towns. The most important chiefs among them, Bird Tail King, Little Prince, and William McIntosh, accepted Hawkins's guidance. The Lower Creek towns had been far more aggressive in adapting agriculture and seemed on the road to becoming active participants in the cotton market then exploding across the South—cotton that fed expanding British factories. As the war with Britain broke out, however, civil war erupted among the Creeks; many younger warriors of the Upper Towns seemed ready to join the British, despite the obvious logistical problems of getting support to them from Canada. The only means for supplying the Creeks was through Pensacola, far south of the Red Stick towns, along a road that led through the Lower Towns.

While the British had little if any chance of getting assistance from the Creeks, the rising nativistic movement did lead to several small attacks on Lower Creek towns, plantations, and settlements that remained loyal to the United States. The followers of the prophets especially despised the older southern chiefs who were members of the National Council. In summer 1813 the Red Sticks completely destroyed a settlement called Fort Mims, along the lower Alabama River, which was occupied mostly by Creek mixed-bloods. Along the way they burned Creek plantations and killed hundreds of cattle, the symbols of wealth that they had grown to despise. In all, some 250 people died at their hands in a violent outburst against the southern towns. Few whites, however, suffered from the onslaught.[26]

Despite the "Native" conflict, Governor David Holmes of Mississippi Territory sent several alarming reports regarding the possibility of a Creek assault on the American settlements along the lower Tombigbee River. Holmes dismissed any fear of the Creeks joining the British, but he did believe that the Red Sticks might instigate a slave insurrection.[27] In hindsight it is difficult to see how this theater of war could ever have been important: British influence in the region was at best commercial, with no perceivable military forces nearby. Nevertheless, the United States government entrusted General Andrew Jackson, a rising politician from Nashville, to assume command of the army of the South, in order to check the Creeks.[28]

Jackson's lineage was back-country, hewed from the Scots-Irish frontier element that placed a strong emphasis on protecting one's family and honor. On occasion this resulted in saloon brawling and dueling, both of which Jackson relished. He undoubtedly saw this chance at military honor as an opportunity. Jackson organized militia units from Tennessee,

Mississippi, and Georgia and invaded Creek lands. In October 1813 many Red Sticks were routed, suffering large losses—186 were slaughtered at the battle of Tallushatchee and another 300 died outside Talladega Town, a loyal Lower Creek community. The militia troops and their Indian allies—both Lower Creeks and Cherokees—were killing men, women, and children. The slaughter went far beyond what was necessary. Jackson's success was explainable: in January 1814 he reported that the Red Sticks were out of ammunition.[29]

Despite the severe punishment and the Red Sticks' lack of supply, Jackson overemphasized the Red Stick threat in letters to the War Department. A growing clique of southerners who surrounded the general saw the war as an opportunity to take Creek lands. One was William Blount, then governor of Tennessee. Jackson wrote him complaining that the war policies of the Madison administration were "insane": after mostly crushing the Creeks, the government had ordered Jackson to muster out some 2,000 men whose brief enlistments were up. The administration seemed convinced that the so-called war in the South was over. Jackson hotly disagreed: "Is it good policy to turn loose upon our defenseless frontier 4,000 exasperated savages to reek their hands once more in the blood of our fellow citizens[?]"[30] The raving and the political pressure finally brought Jackson reinforcements. In March 1814 the general ordered the destruction of the sole remaining Red Stick stronghold, even though the Indians could hardly defend themselves.

Most of the Red Sticks had selected a horseshoe bend on the Tallapoosa River as a last bastion of defense, building breastworks across the land portion. Jackson sent Cherokee, Chickasaw, Choctaw, and Creek allies around the bend to cut off escape to the north. He wisely calculated that the Red Sticks had "penned themselves up for slaughter," an observation that proved true. Jackson turned his cannon loose on the breastworks. The carnage was terrific. Jackson's infantry then went over the breastworks and took the town. Some 557 Indians—men, women, and children—lay dead, with probably 300 more dead in the river and beyond. Jackson ordered the nose cut off of each victim so that an accurate count could be made. "Having destroyed at To'hope'ka [the Creek town] three of their principal prophets leaving but two in their nation—having tread their holy ground as they termed it," the general reported to his wife, "it is probable they may now sue for peace."[31]

Andrew Jackson showed even less compassion in inflicting peace on the Creeks. He promptly declared that all lands in south Georgia (about

20 percent of the state) as well as a major portion of Alabama would have to be ceded. The Lower Creek towns—firm allies of the United States—suffered more from this loss of land than the few remaining Red Sticks. The Lower Creeks lost their homeland, which would become a prime cotton production region in the South. Jackson's actions were purely motivated by the land issue—he adopted a policy of ethnic cleansing against both the loyal Indians who had fought beside him and the Red Sticks.

Jackson gave a frivolous justification for this decision—southern Georgia was somehow important for the nation's defense:

> The hostile Creeks have forfeited all right to the territory *we have conquered* and while justice to the friendly part of the nation requires that they should be left in the peaceable enjoyment of their towns . . . humanity dictates that the conquered part of the nation should be allotted sufficient space for agricultural purposes. Still the grand policy of the government ought to be, to connect the settlements of Georgia with that of the territory and Tennessee, which at once forms a bulwark against foreign invasion.[32]

The justification was absolute gibberish for anyone who could read a map. Georgia had been connected to both Tennessee and South Carolina by lands that had been ceded in 1790 and thereafter. And Spain could not even defend west Florida, which had been overrun by Americans to the Perdido River. England, a supposed ally of Spain, had done nothing to stop the filibusters. Finally, despite Jackson's claim that "humanity dictates" that the Indians be allowed to keep their towns, the treaty he forced upon the Creeks resulted in the cession of many of the Lower Creek communities. The forced treaty violated every premise of what Jeffersonians claimed as reasonable accommodation—that Indians would have to surrender hunting lands but not their towns and fields.

While Jackson's hyperbole made little sense, his destruction of the Creeks along with Harrison's dramatic defeat of the Northwest Indian confederacy at Detroit had a chilling impact on all Indians east of the Mississippi River. Indian agent Josiah Meig's report of conditions in Illinois in January 1815 made this clear. "In a very short time the savages [Indians] will lower their tone along the whole frontier," he boldly proclaimed to his top surveyor. Surveying companies were posed to crisscross Illinois, and some had moved even farther west into Missouri. At the close of the War of 1812 the American people were poised to conduct another strong surge of settlement west of the Appalachian Mountains, similar to the gains between 1801 and 1807, and the federal government had adopted an Indian policy to make that possible.[33]

President Madison hoped to accomplish this expansion through the use of peace treaties in the Northwest as well as in London. Put simply, treaties that offered massive land cessions could not be negotiated with Indians who were at war. Moreover, the British had burned Washington, D.C., in 1814. If General Jackson had not defeated a large British force below New Orleans a few months later—the battle actually occurred after a peace had been signed—the armistice might have seemed hollow. Accordingly, Madison ordered General Harrison to negotiate a peace treaty in the Northwest, which he accomplished at Chillicothe in August 1815. The Shawnee Prophet, who had survived the war, sent word that he intended to remain with the British. He apparently got little satisfaction at Amherstburg, however, and finally showed up to listen to Harrison. The Prophet soon departed, apparently angry at Harrison's belligerent tone. While the Shawnee Prophet remained unrepentant, other Indians signed the treaty, including the Wyandots, Ottawas, Chippewas, and Potawatomis.[34]

As the British in Canada slowly admitted to their Indian friends that they would have to live under the American flag, a new secretary of war, John C. Calhoun, under newly elected president James Monroe announced that the administration would continue with an aggressive Indian policy of land purchase. Calhoun had been a staunch War Hawk and had allies in others of a similar mind. He found an extremely capable ally in this effort in General Andrew Jackson, whom he called on to negotiate a number of treaties in the South. For the northern territories Calhoun turned increasingly to rising politician Lewis Cass. Both Cass and Jackson began to move the government away from a policy in which Indian nations were recognized as sovereign to one in which treaties were simply a mechanism for obtaining land, rather than guaranteeing Indians any rights. Through this policy, which they hoped would soon be adopted, Congress simply inflicted on Indians whatever measures it deemed appropriate.[35]

Some of the first successful treaties came in the Northwest, as former soldiers flocked into the region to take up land. Indiana became a state in December 1816, and Congress created the new territory of Michigan shortly thereafter. Cass, a former colonel in Harrison's army, became Michigan's territorial governor. According to one of his early biographers, Cass would force Indians to give up more land over the next thirty years than anyone else, including Jackson.[36] Indeed, Cass became in the North the equivalent of Jackson in the South—a man who believed that expediency was always the best policy. Cass's success in taking Indian land later led Jackson to pick him as his secretary of war. Lewis Cass organized, and justified through several published writings, the forced Indian Removal policy of the Jackson administration after 1830.

Cass's first orders included trying to purchase the last remaining Indian-owned parcel of land in northwest Ohio. Most of this land, on the east bank of the Maumee River, already had been invaded by white squatters. For roughly $12,000 a year in annuities, paid over ten years, he secured nearly 2,000,000 acres of land. Even so, Cass had to make bargains. Many separate tracts were set aside as "reservations" for Native families, in fee simple, and each family was listed individually. One included 30,000 acres of land, to be divided among over a hundred Seneca Indians.[37] While Cass never invented the idea, this began the process known as "allotment": the distribution of smaller plots of ground, some rather large but others only a few hundred acres, to individual Indian families. These promises of "reservations" built into treaties made it easier for Cass to get Indian leaders to agree to the deal.

Cass reported his success to Secretary Calhoun with considerable modesty—he knew that Hull had bought nine times more land for about the same price and had not provided reservations. Cass assured the secretary that the task would get easier. "As our settlements gradually surround them [the Indians who took reservations], their minds will be better prepared," Cass thought, to sell the lands and eventually move west.[38] "Small Reservations" were simple expediencies. Whether Calhoun was impressed with Cass's patience in organizing such an effort or just pleased finally to acquire all of Ohio, he wrote Cass that his effort "far exceeds my most sanguine expectations." The treaty, Calhoun said, was "the most important of any that we have hitherto made"—at least that summer.[39] It did have some military implications, in that a stronger American presence around Detroit and a solid connection between northern Ohio and Michigan would cut off the Indians from their British allies at Amherstburg, Canada.

Calhoun liked Cass and recognized his ability to handle Indians. The secretary of war soon set Cass to work every summer thereafter, buying up land and pushing farther north and west, into central Michigan and even Wisconsin. After concluding a massive land purchase in 1819—virtually all of Lower Michigan—Cass condescendingly wrote of the Chippewas who signed the treaty: "they were anxious to receive what they could speedily dissipate in childish and useless purchases, at the expense of stipulations which would be permanently useful."[40] It is difficult to see in this rhetoric the language of a humane removal policy designed to aid the Indians' conversion to American social and political mores.

While Cass made no effort to convince the Indians to ask for plows or schools, later evidence (which surfaced when Cass negotiated with the Winnebagos in Wisconsin ten years later) suggests that the prime ingredient of the "dissipation" that he mentioned in 1819 was alcohol. One of the Winnebago leaders admonished Cass by saying: "Father, you have a kind of milk we like very much, when you hold a treaty again hold it where there will be none of this milk. Some of our young men, I am afraid, do not see the sunrise."[41] Secretary Calhoun certainly never questioned Cass's strong-arm tactics in buying land. "It is the wish of the President," Calhoun wrote the budding politician, "that the whole of the Indian titles within the peninsula of Michigan [Lower Michigan] should be extinguished."[42]

Calhoun placed even more importance on obtaining land in the South. Commissioners John Coffee, John Rhea, and John McKee wined and dined the Choctaw leaders over the summer and fall of 1815, stressing that because Creeks lands had been "conquered" in western Alabama the Choctaws should also give up their overlapping claim. The Choctaws eventually complied, ceding all their claim to lands on the left bank of the Tombigbee River.[43] This cession still left lands in southern Tennessee and northern Georgia in the hands of the Cherokees, who several times had refused to sell since their last cession in 1806. While negotiations occurred with the Choctaws, a similar discussion opened with the Cherokees. The pressure exerted by government officials on tribal leaders, however, led to a growing consolidation of political power in the hands of the Cherokee National Council, which adopted a new constitution the next year. It was signed by fifty-four Cherokee towns, virtually the entire nation. Much as in the case of their Creek neighbors to the South, the purpose of the council was to prevent the further loss of land.[44]

The Monroe administration and Secretary Calhoun were determined to force the Cherokees to give up all their lands in the East and migrate west of the Mississippi River. The Cherokees had been allies of the United States in the War of 1812, however, and no possible military justification existed for removing them. Yet Calhoun believed that if the Cherokees could be convinced to move, all the other tribes east of the Mississippi River would follow suit. Then Calhoun discovered one important document that aided him in this quest; back in January 1809 President Jefferson had outlined in a letter a proposal to the Cherokees in which they would supposedly remove to the West. No council had ever formally ratified the agreement, but now Calhoun argued that the Indians must move, because they had apparently accepted Jefferson's offer and had expressed a willingness to "exchange" eastern lands for equal ground in the West.[45]

The commission selected to convince the Cherokees to accept Jefferson's agreement included Andrew Jackson, Joseph McMin, and David Meriwether. Jackson's views on Indians were well known by this time— he believed that all of them should be sent west, forcibly if necessary. McMin, the governor of Tennessee, seemed even less sympathetic to Native concerns, given his need to open more Tennessee land. And Meriwether, a former congressman from Georgia, was determined to push all Indians west of the Mississippi River, the sooner the better. The only concession that the secretary of war suggested that these men might consider included a treaty whereby some Cherokees could remain "on reservations"—adopting Cass's strategy—if they agreed to accept the jurisdictional rule of either the state of Georgia or the state of Tennessee.[46]

Ordering General Jackson to open the negotiations is indicative of the importance that the Monroe administration put on them. But, fortunately for the Indians, Jackson became distracted in late 1817 by the growing conflict between American settlers and a few Red Stick Creeks who had joined Seminoles in Spanish east Florida.[47] Jackson invaded the region and captured Pensacola in May 1818, marched on and destroyed several Creek and Seminole communities, and later executed two British traders in the process, an act that enraged England. Positively for Monroe, however, the action quickly convinced Spain to relinquish all of Florida in a treaty with the United States the next year. As Jackson chased Indians in Florida and harassed the Spanish, he returned only occasionally to pressure the Cherokees to leave. He did formally read Jefferson's letter to members of the Cherokee council, but they responded by arguing that the letter was not a treaty and that the council had actually met in 1810 and rejected the idea.[48] In addition, by this time the 1,500 to 2,000 Cherokees who had migrated to Arkansas—some had left in 1805 and a few more joined them in 1814—sent back discouraging information about the region. Other

Indians occupied these lands, including the Osage, Quapaw, and Caddo tribes. Intertribal war had broken out.[49]

The Cherokee National Council used the conflict in the West to counter the American commissioners. It responded in writing, admitting that many Cherokees were not yet "capable" of American civilization but stating that they did not want to go west into "the same savage state of life that we were in before." They then pointed to some progress—they now had schools, mills, and missionaries who preached Christianity. Jackson and McMin scoffed at the answer, threatening the Indians. They openly told members of the National Council that if they did not agree to move, the government would cut off their annuities coming from earlier treaties (there had been drought and some famine in Cherokee lands that summer). Worse, Jackson said that the government would not protect the Indians against American intruders, which in fact remained a real and growing threat.[50]

Jackson's harsh language finally showed some signs of producing success. Some forty Cherokee representatives, many of them leading chiefs, signed the treaty of 1817. Key leaders refused, however, including Major Ridge and John Ross. The treaty surrendered two tracts of land, roughly half a million acres in south-central Tennessee and north Georgia. But the rest of the terms were masked in what appeared to be deliberately confusing language. Most Cherokees believed that they had three choices: sign a "census" that the government would take in 1818 that committed them to remove west, take up a reservation in which they would come under the control of the states, or remain in the "Nation," suffering no consequences. Jackson and McMin apparently deleted the third option when the agreement was signed.[51] Understandably, most Cherokees supported the third option. They did not wish to leave.

The treaty brought instant jubilation in Washington, D.C. Upon receiving the news, Calhoun wrote Cass in Michigan, suggesting that the agreement had ramifications for all Indians living east of the Mississippi River. After meeting with a Cherokee delegation a few months later, Calhoun confessed to Governor McMin that "its probable effects will lead ultimately to the removal of the Creeks, Chickasaws, and Choctaws."[52] The celebration soon subsided, however, after Calhoun saw the actual document. He fretted that northeastern senators were increasingly opposing removal and that the Senate might not ratify the agreement. He also questioned the tactics used by the commission. Many prominent chiefs had not signed the agreement. Calhoun even questioned the "transactions that took place in 1809," especially the emphasis that the commissioners had placed on Jefferson's letter.[53] The secretary's concerns about northeastern senators at least proved premature; the Senate quickly ratified the Cherokee treaty in 1818.

The sobering realization that the only two remaining options were removal or acceptance of a reservation evoked outrage in the Cherokee Nation. While professing to prepare for removal, Ross and Ridge quietly convinced many Cherokees that the whole governmental scheme would collapse if they refused to sign the census or take a reservation. They then convinced the National Council to issue an edict that any Cherokee who did sign would be "disenfranchised." Fortunately for them, Jackson once again was drawn away to Florida at this crucial time.

Governor McMin continued to push the Cherokees to sign the census document and move, to no avail. He even discovered that the Cherokees remained unwilling to reveal much about the numbers of people living in their towns. At one point he suggested that nearly half had either agreed to move or were already in Arkansas. He gave the number as 718 families; this seems to have been a total fabrication. When the census takers failed to get names, McMin cut off annuities for food that had become important in the Cherokee economy. This strategy also failed. He then warned tribal leaders that "they had forfeited their right to protection from the United States."[54] This too the Cherokees ignored.

The tug of war with Cherokee leaders continued into 1819. Calhoun seemed reasonably sure of solving the problem when a delegation of Cherokee leaders visited him in Washington. But the hyperbole of the event must have surprised even the secretary. The Cherokees said that they were "propelled by the dictates of reason, restrained by prudence, education & science" and were completely ready to "participate with our White Brothers in the enjoyment and advantages of the best of all earthly government." In other words, they seemed fully ready to cooperate—but in reality, once back in the nation, they refused to do so. While a few Cherokees did emigrate to Arkansas, the vast majority (well over 12,000) stayed in their towns and on their lands.[55]

While Monroe seemed intent on adopting the strategy of using debts, bribery, and (at least in the Northwest) liquor to acquire Indian land, others in government found the entire process tedious and unnecessary. Andrew Jackson stated this case clearly in 1817, in an astonishingly bold letter that he hoped President Monroe would sign off on after his inauguration. Jackson argued that the government had to negotiate with Indians when it was weak. That had changed, Jackson argued: "the arm of the government is sufficiently strong to carry into execution" a new policy—forcing Indians to give up their lands. He went on: "I have long viewed treaties with the Indians as an absurdity not to be reconciled to the principles of our Government . . . I have always thought, that Congress had as much right to regulate by acts of Legislation all Indian concerns as they had of territories." Indeed, Jackson concluded, white settlers in territories were "citizens" and Indians were "subjects." As such, Indians had "no right" to the soil but merely a "possessory right, yielded by the liberality of the United States through humanity." Jackson had studied for the law and knew that "possessory rights" were nothing more than the right to occupy land, commonly granted to peasants in Europe.[56] Jackson's letter set off a round of debates in Washington.

Jackson continued to lobby for his new views into 1819, submitting a long letter to Calhoun, in which he again expressed a belief that Indians were nothing more than *"Subjects."* "The strength of our Nation is now sufficient to effect any object which its wisdome [*sic*], humanity and justice may please to adopt with regard to those unfortunate people." Worse, Jackson believed that negotiation led to the "corruption" of the nation, because nothing could be accomplished without bribing the chiefs. Such policy went against the "principles of our Government."[57] Jackson had come to believe that forced removal was absolutely necessary, that it was humane, moral, and even righteous, and that it would save the government from the pitiful examples of corrupt negotiations that had occurred in the past.[58]

As Calhoun's frustrations built in trying to implement the Cherokee treaty, he began selecting negotiators who held views similar to Jackson's, although the secretary was not going to abandon using treaties to acquire land. Treaties were the only recognized mechanism available to him that contained elements of moral restraint. This led to a rash of land cessions between 1818 and 1825, when Calhoun finally left office. Beaten and increasingly ruled by mixed-bloods like William McIntosh, the Creeks signed another treaty ceding several hundred thousand acres in central Alabama in 1818. Calhoun went out of his way to note McIntosh's flexibility regarding such measures, an indication that the man could be bought.[59]

Calhoun ordered more negotiations with the now defeated northwest tribes. He wanted that last remaining Indian lands in Indiana and

Illinois, which were of incredible agricultural value.[60] Considerable questions existed as to who owned these lands. The meeting that Jefferson had proposed many years before, in which these tribes would determine boundaries, had never occurred. Calhoun simply attached a message to his orders to the commissioners, indicating that it would be best if these Indians just agreed to move west into Arkansas or Missouri, where lands had recently been purchased from the Quapaw Indians.[61] The Kickapoos accordingly relinquished all their claims in Illinois, some 7,000,000 acres for $3,000 in presents and $2,000 in yearly annuities. The treaty never indicated just where the Kickapoos were to move to. It seems hard to imagine that Indians would give up their homelands for lands that they had never seen or could not even find on a map.[62]

Meanwhile settlers clamored for more land in Mississippi. In May 1820 Calhoun turned to the one man who had become indispensable in forcing Indians to give up their lands: Andrew Jackson. Secretary Calhoun made it clear that even President Monroe supported his appointment—what that said about Jackson's letter is unclear. Obviously two views were emerging on Indian negotiation, one offering hyperbolic principles that included honesty and fairness mouthed by the presidents of the United States and another, crude and dishonest, in which threats, intimidation, and outright force were employed with an utter disregard for Native sovereignty. Jackson heartily agreed to go, opening up discussions with Choctaw leaders at Doaks Stand on August 20, 1820.[63]

The negotiations got off to a bad start. A missionary with the American Board of Commissioners for Foreign Missions, Cyrus Kingsbury, had apparently advised the Choctaws not to deal. Jackson furiously ordered Kingsbury to come forward. When he did, the two men finally reached an accommodation. Jackson suddenly supported the construction of mission schools—with Indian money, of course—in the new lands west of the Mississippi that the Choctaws would occupy.[64] The talks went on, with Kingsbury's approbation. But Choctaw leaders, led by Pushmataha (who had come to Jackson's assistance militarily on several occasions), seemed suspicious. For three weeks in October Jackson gave his standard speech. He assured the Indians that they would receive 13,000,000 acres of land in the West—once again without identifying it—in exchange for just 5,000,000 acres that the government wanted in Mississippi.

Finally losing his patience, Jackson berated Choctaw leaders. "If you reject this friendly proposal," he began, the president will be compelled to "treat with those [Choctaws] beyond the Mississippi." They too held title to land in Mississippi, he argued, and could easily sell it. Or worse, stamping his own views on Indian policy, Jackson said that "Congress at their next session will take the business into their own hands." By the Treaty of Hopewell (1785), Jackson claimed, "they have the right to manage the affairs of this nation, and they will do so." At this several chiefs abruptly left the council. Getting even angrier, Jackson proclaimed that their actions were "insulting" and that he would no longer treat with them. Clearly fearing that Jackson would negotiate next with the several hundred Choctaws who had migrated west of the Mississippi, or simply convince Congress to take Choctaw lands, more moderate Choctaw chiefs, including Pushmataha, agreed to sign the document.[65] The Choctaws ceded 5 million acres of prime cotton land in southern Mississippi for land in the West but still maintained ownership of 10 million acres in the northern part of the state.

Calhoun rejoiced at the completion of the Choctaw treaty. It was the first clear success in forcing Indians to exchange land in the East for land in the West. Unfortunately, total confusion existed over the exact location of those western lands—they had never been surveyed. Calhoun believed that such minor details could be worked out later. The Senate ratified the Treaty of Doaks Stand without much debate.[66] The "negotiation" was accomplished after Jackson had threatened Indians with the new policy— that Congress had the right to dictate to tribes and take their lands.

Much the same would occur in other negotiations that followed. Perhaps the most spectacular land purchase of the 1820s occurred when James Gadsden (who would later be known to history as the negotiator of the Gadsden Purchase from Mexico) bought much of Florida from Indians. Only a small remnant of those Florida Indians—some of whom were Seminoles—actually attended the negotiation at St. Augustine, many being afraid that Jackson and his army would show up. Gadsden reminded the Seminoles of what had happened when General Jackson had been forced to come in and punish them: "His [the president's] whites are strong and might exterminate his Reds."[67] Threats used to accomplish a treaty had degenerated into the use of genocidal rhetoric.

The Indians in attendance hardly represented what supposedly had become the "Seminoles." This term, adopted from a corruption of the Spanish "Cimarrones," which meant simply "wild ones," had very little real meaning. Many Indians had fled to Florida, including some Creeks, Red Sticks, and Yamasees, all of whom intermeshed with small bands of

Alachuas, Mikasukis, Tallahassees, Apalachicolas, and perhaps a thousand African American escaped slaves.[68] In all about 5,000 Indians and former slaves may have lived in the region. Commissioner Gadsden took a hard line from the start; he flatly told the assembled few that the others would be "forced to comply with its [the treaty's] provisions." While no response to this threat was ever recorded by Gadsden (he left no journal), some leaders, including Jumper, signed the treaty. Clearly also fearful of Jackson's possible return, the leaders in attendance surrendered 28,253,820 acres of land for roughly three-quarters of a cent an acre. They kept a 9,000,000-acre reserve in the middle of the state.[69]

Calhoun had one last treaty to effect before leaving office. He wanted to obtain the last tribal holdings of the Creeks in far western Georgia, most of the cession being west of the Flint River. The talks opened at McIntosh's tavern at Indian Springs in February 1825. By this time the new governor of Georgia, George M. Troup, also participated along with seasoned commissioners Duncan Campbell and James Meriwether. Rather than even calling the chiefs of the Upper Towns, McIntosh argued that the Creeks were divided, much as they were during the War of 1812. A treaty was quickly drafted, and McIntosh and a handful of his adherents signed it. Article 5 allowed for a cash payment of $200,000 to the McIntosh clique, disguised as money necessary for transportation costs. The Senate quickly ratified the agreement that fall.[70]

Outraged and stunned by the swiftness of the capitulation, the Creek National Council condemned the actions and promptly ordered the execution of William McIntosh. Creek warriors gunned him down outside his plantation a few weeks later. The new administration that came into office that March, headed by John Quincy Adams, had a somewhat different view of Indian policy. Adams had fought a long, hard battle with Jackson over the presidency, a rift that led to the creation of two new political parties: the Democrats, with Jackson at their head, and the Whigs, who slowly emerged as a political group that mostly represented northeastern commerce and industry. Being from Massachusetts, a commercial state, Adams took the minority view that the United States had enough land for itself and that the Indians' rights should be protected. Adams was appalled at the Treaty of Indian Springs. Yet he knew that Georgians quickly overran the land purchased within weeks of the signing date—settler sovereignty remained a powerful force on the frontier. In what constituted some justice to the Indians, Adams encouraged Creek leaders to come to Washington, where they signed a new treaty, abrogating the old one, in 1826. It could not restore the lost land, but at least it offered a fairer compensation.[71]

The actions of the Jeffersonians who controlled government can only be seen as appalling when it comes to the policies applied to American Indians. After Jefferson came into office in 1801, those policies were designed and implemented with one goal in mind—to acquire as much land from Indians as possible and at as cheap a price as possible, averaging perhaps one cent an acre. It has been argued that Jefferson, Madison, and Monroe all paid considerable attention to providing Indians with the means for agricultural development. Yet Jefferson himself had helped create the atmosphere in political circles, where many politicians believed that Indians would soon be moved west of the Mississippi River.

Certainly the War of 1812 had an impact on the evolving policy of ethnic cleansing that had been accepted by most politicians. It mattered little that many of the Indians affected had been allies of the United States during the war. Many American politicians viewed the acquisition of Indian lands after the war as "spoils" or additions made from "legitimate conquest." Jackson's view of removal policy seemed to be more accepted in Washington political circles after 1817, although President Monroe never publicly sanctioned the notion that the eastern Indians held only a "possessory" right to land. Certainly Jackson and many other politicians came to see Indians as "Subjects"—unfortunate "savages," as he called them. They might, out of necessity, be treated as sovereign nations when the United States was weak, but certainly should not be treated as such now that the country was strong. Indians, Jackson felt, should be subject to the laws of Congress, whatever they might be. Secretary Calhoun adopted just such a view in his last years in office, as evidenced by the negotiations with the Choctaws, Seminoles, and Creeks.

Despite the changing conceptualization of Indian Removal that was under way, presidents continued to boast in their annual addresses to Congress of their benevolent Indian "civilization" policy. The outgoing President Monroe was no different. He announced with considerable pride in December 1824 that the government—using annuity money obtained from the sale of Indian land—had built some thirty-two schools in Indian country, which had "916 scholars."[72] While such "success" hardly seems worth mentioning, given a total Indian population east of the Mississippi River of nearly 100,000 people and 200,000 more west of the river, Monroe's next admission seems even more ludicrous:

Experience has shown that unless the tribes be civilized they can never be incorporated into our system in any form whatever. It has likewise shown that in the regular augmentation of our population with the extension of our settlements their situation will become deplorable, if their extinction is not menaced. Some well-digested plan which will rescue them from such calamities is due to their rights, to the rights of humanity and to the honor of the nation.[73]

Twenty years before, Jefferson had talked of a similar plan and the need to implement it.

While John Quincy Adams had quelled the thirst for Indian lands when he took the presidency in March 1825, part of the reason for the brief hiatus was the vast quantities of land that had been forced from Indian hands under the auspices of the Jefferson, Madison, and Monroe administrations. So much land had been acquired that government surveyors could not keep up with the work required to measure it. The acquisition of both Floridas—some 34,000,000 acres in all—added significantly to the 52,000,000 acres that Madison had estimated in 1802 constituted the lands between the 31st and 35th parallels, between the Tennessee and Florida borders. Of this total domain—some 86,000,000 acres by 1826—Indians, who just two decades before had claimed virtually all of it, held roughly 25,000,000 acres, including swampland in Florida. This loss of roughly 70 percent of the land, or 85 percent of the arable land in the South, occurred under governmental regimes that claimed to be benevolent and humane in dealing with Indians.

Federal officials had taken a somewhat smaller percentage of the land north of the Ohio River, but many of the lands in Michigan and Wisconsin were heavily forested and not suited to intensive agriculture at that time. Pressures would mount in the years to come when their timber was needed in the rapidly expanding industrial towns of Pittsburgh, Cleveland, Toledo, Detroit, and Chicago.

Perhaps worse, Andrew Jackson had become a hero in the West after his destruction of the Red Sticks and the British at New Orleans. And Americans hailed his invasion of Spanish Florida, which he at the time believed would force Spain to cede the land to the United States. Jackson's mistreatment of Indians did little to quell the zeal of his supporters; indeed it only added to his political strength. And he intended to run for the presidency in 1828. For American Indians, the election of such a man could mean nothing but disaster.

Jackson's core constituency consisted of rabidly aggressive frontier settlers, expanding cotton farmers in the South, and people in general who believed in expansion in the West. In many ways the presidential choice in November 1828 between the more educated Adams and the reactionary and caustic Jackson could hardly be clearer. Jackson's victory that fall signaled the descent of what had been a corrupt, immoral Indian policy to a new level, in which Indian nations were no longer viewed as sovereign entities and treaties became mere formalities. The disguised agenda of Jeffersonian philanthropy, which had consisted of a more minimalist adherence to ethnic cleansing, no longer existed. Andrew Jackson had little patience for philanthropic rhetoric and harbored a deep-seated conviction that the lands of the nation belonged to white people, not to American Indians.

8

UNSCABBARDING THE BAYONET

Andrew Jackson and the Policy of Forced Ethnic Cleansing

The vast majority of Americans believed that voluntary removal, or even the diminishment of Indian reservations in the East, constituted fair and moral Indian policy in 1829. Most Americans also believed that Indians were human beings who might be converted to the mainstream republican beliefs of the new rising American nation at some future time. Thus Native peoples had a nominal right to the lands that they owned, which would help them to sustain themselves, given their conversion to some form of agriculture, if they made them productive.[1] These political precepts faced a serious challenge, however, with the election of Andrew Jackson, a man who fundamentally rejected any notion that Native American sovereignty existed.

Jackson's views regarding American Indians are the subject of considerable debate. After examining his rhetoric—certainly his words before the Battle of Horseshoe Bend are a good example—it becomes difficult to suggest that he held serious sympathy for the plight of Indians. Jackson even dispossessed large numbers of Lower Creeks who had fought beside him in battle.[2] Jackson's frontier views on politics seem even more problematic. He took a hardened Jeffersonian stand, putting the argument in words in his first inaugural address on March 4, 1829: "In regard to the rights of the separate states I hope to be animated by a proper respect for those sovereign members of our Union, taking care not to confound the powers they have reserved to themselves with those they have granted to the Confederacy."[3] In reality, Jackson came to believe in states' rights to the extent that states held sovereignty over Indian lands within their borders, a new and radical view in 1829 that clearly conflicted with the constitutional authority of the federal government over those lands.

Many different groups of American Indians came into the gun sights of this new policy. They included the so-called Five Civilized Tribes in the South, including Cherokees, Choctaws, Chickasaws, Creeks, and Seminoles. Numerous northern groups also were affected, including the Sac and Fox Indians, who remained on lands in river valleys just east of the Mississippi River in western Illinois and southern Wisconsin, as well as Ottawas, Potawatomis, Weas, Chippewas, and even some New York tribes that had drifted west. But statehood had come to Mississippi, Alabama, Georgia, Tennessee, Illinois, Indiana, and other regions, and Michigan, Wisconsin, and Florida would soon enter the Union. When it came to Indians, Jackson quickly demonstrated a clear unwillingness to assert federal rights to administer Indian affairs when states challenged that authority.

The federal government's recognition of some Native sovereignty began with the passage of the Trade and Intercourse Acts in 1790 and their subsequent additions.[4] They declared it illegal for any citizen to purchase lands from Indians—only the federal government had authority to buy their lands through treaties—and further regulated trade and commerce among the tribes. Most lawyers in the country accepted this constitutional authority, including the future president John Quincy Adams, who in an 1802 speech honoring the Pilgrims questioned the absolute right of Indians to hold massive hunting territories but clearly affirmed their right to their agricultural lands: "Their cultivated fields, their constructed habitats, a space of ample sufficiency for their sustenance, and whatever they have annexed by personal labor, was undoubtedly by the laws of nature theirs."[5] This mimicked the arguments of Grotius, Locke, and Vattel.

Such renditions of the "Laws of Nature" lacked legal standing, however, as the United States Supreme Court implied in the majority opinion in *Fletcher v. Peck* in 1810. The case involved a fraudulent land purchase in western Mississippi, called the Yazoo district, from the Georgia state legislature. The 1795 purchase came before Georgia had relinquished title to the United States, and the completed sale occurred after members of the Georgia assembly had been bribed by the purchasers. Chief Justice Marshall wrote the majority opinion in *Fletcher*, in which he affirmed the original contract despite its fraudulent nature but then also addressed the nature of Indian title to these lands. In conclusion, he determined that

Georgia had a "fee simple" title, by right of its colonial grant, while the Indians had only the "right of occupancy" or in his words "an Indian title."[6]

Exactly what Marshall meant by the phrase "Indian title" remained unclear in 1810. But he clarified the issue when he again wrote the majority opinion in the case *Johnson v. M'Intosh* in 1823. The issue once again involved land, this time in Illinois, purchased by speculators well before the formation of the United States. Marshall argued that the Indians maintained an "Indian title of occupancy," which meant that they could do as they wanted with the land—that is, sell it to speculators. But then he argued that this created a two-tier title. Those same speculators, he noted, would have to return to the "Indian court" under which they had purchased the land in order to obtain any compensation. The Chief Justice concluded that the United States had legally received the same land after defeating the British during the Revolution—"right of conquest." Thus, with the stroke of a pen, Justice Marshall had created the fiction of a non-existent Indian legal system that lay outside the course of American law. It remained to be seen what rights Indians might have under their so-called right of occupancy.[7]

Marshall's opinion, while on the surface seemingly contradictory and at the same time conciliatory to the evolving sense of limited Indian rights that many Jeffersonians held, had yet another caveat. In further statements, he noted that European powers obtained title in fee simple by "right of discovery"—thus negating the sale to speculators in Illinois, who would have to go to the "Indian court" for justice. Yet American Indians were still the "rightful occupants" of their land, which could only be expropriated by the federal government in one of two ways. First, it could be taken in conquest in a "just war," which Marshall defined as one started by Indians. Second, the land could be purchased legally, within the American system, which meant through a treaty. This then was the law of the land in 1823. It specifically implied, though it did not clearly state, that the government could not take the lands of Indians who remained peaceful and refused to sell them.

Jackson had distinctly different views of Indian rights, which had been evolving since his 1817 letter to newly elected President Monroe. But he needed a better legal justification for his central argument that Congress could simply legislate regarding Indian land ownership. It seemed almost silly—and morally corrupt—to suggest that the country had to negotiate treaties with Indians when it was young but did not have to do so after it had gained ascendency over those tribes. Jackson brought into his inner circle various cabinet officials who contributed to the debate, such as the secretary of war, William Eaton, his close friend from Tennessee, and especially Lewis Cass, the now middle-aged protégé from Michigan, who had a brilliant mind (Cass would later take over the War Department and implement Indian Removal in its early stages).

What all these men brought to the argument emerged in Jackson's first message to Congress on December 8, 1829. Jackson argued that the Indians within states faced constant debilitation and decline and that a similar fate awaited the "Choctaw, the Cherokee and the Creek" in the South. A better fate was complete removal to the west. "Humanity and national honor demand that every effort should be made to avert so great a calamity." Jackson asserted that the founding fathers had made a major mistake by including Indians within the boundaries of states and that several tribes had recently illegally formed constitutional governments within these sovereign states. Jackson rhetorically asked whether the federal government "had the right to sustain those people [Indians] in their pretensions." He thought not, as even the Constitution stated that "no new state shall be formed or erected within the jurisdiction of any other state." The solution seemed simple to the president—remove the Indians to lands outside the various established states, to lands "without the limits of any state or Territory now formed" that would never become part of a state.[8]

Jackson's address presaged a well-orchestrated propaganda effort to convince the nation to adopt these views. Cass led the way. A talented author who had written many articles about the West and Indians, Cass threw himself into the debate, publishing a 59-page article in the *North American Review,* parroting the virtues of Indian Removal. He argued that Indians were "diminishing" at an alarming rate, from millions of people to a few hundred thousand; those living east of the Mississippi River totaled a mere 105,060. The only means of preserving the Indians, Cass concluded, "is to remove them" from the "sphere of influence" causing their debilitation, which he identified partially as use of "ardent spirits," a problem that Cass was well acquainted with.[9]

Over the weeks that followed others joined the president and his supporters, including Thomas L. McKenney, who would become the first regular commissioner of Indian affairs. McKenney, who had been in the Indian office for several years before Jackson's election, had generally supported the implementation of the Intercourse Acts, ordering the removal of any white intruders from Indian lands. It must have been somewhat astonishing to him when his new boss, Secretary Eaton, in July 1829 ordered him to inform Indians that the federal government would no longer police such intruders in states with Indian lands, turning the duty over to local officials.[10]

Southern states greeted Jackson's address and his new Indian policies with joy. As early as 1829 Alabama passed legislation extending its rule of law over Creek lands. Mississippi soon joined in, adopting similar legislation for Choctaw lands. Jackson said nothing regarding these blatant violations of federal Indian law. But these state law makers were slow to implement the laws, fearing open conflict. The laws were undoubtedly unconstitutional; the Alabama legislation even prohibited "all laws, usages, and customs" of Indians within the state. This included calling a general council or a religious gathering.[11]

Georgia had passed a similar law extending its sovereignty over Cherokee lands in 1828—which it also had trouble enforcing—but it soon followed the lead of Mississippi and Alabama. In 1830 it added a separate measure that prohibited all whites from entering Cherokee Country, a clear challenge to the federal Intercourse Acts, which the Jackson government once again failed to enforce. Worse, the Georgia "guard" or militia soon thereafter invaded Cherokee country and arrested and removed several whites, including missionaries Samuel A. Worcester and Elizur Butler.[12] This invited a clash with federal officials and also made removal seem ever more certain, even to some Indian leaders, as southern states increased pressures on Indian lands.

Jacksonians in Congress brought out a bill calling for the removal of Indians from state lands in February 1830. Those politicians and reformers who opposed the law were slow to respond, yet various missionary groups spoke out against the measure, promoting the success of their "civilization programs." Jeremiah Evarts of the American Board of Commissioners for Foreign Missions (ABCFM) led the way. Removal, he argued, simply violated treaty obligations, some of which financially supported the various missions that the ABCFM had created.[13] ABCFM missionaries pointed with tremendous pride to the advancements made in education and agriculture among the Choctaws and other southern Indians.[14]

Senators from northeastern states especially rallied against the legislation. Theodore Frelinghuysen from New Jersey called for the "highest execution of Justice" in dealing with the southern Indians, and Daniel Webster from Massachusetts claimed that Indians held valid titles to lands that the federal government must protect. Even so, the final votes approving the bill were cast in May 1830, mostly along the new party lines that had emerged during the 1828 election. Supporters of Jackson, including Democrats from northern states such as New Hampshire, New York, and Pennsylvania, voted overwhelmingly for the measure. Opponents tended to come from New England; a major exception was Henry Clay, who would soon oppose Jackson for the presidency. The House of Representatives proved a different story, the vote tally being 102 to 97. Many northern Democrats broke with the president over the legislation.[15]

Jackson signed the measure on June 30, 1830, and promptly sent out commissioners to meet with the various tribes.[16] The legislation authorized the president to exchange unorganized land in the West for Indian lands in the East, in reality a seemingly redundant power. Presidents and the Senate already possessed the rights to do just that through the treaty process. But the legislation put both the Indians and the nation on notice that the federal government would now force the issue. Perhaps even more importantly, the legislation provided funding for the effort, something that had not existed in the past.[17]

Given the growing pressure in Mississippi, the Choctaws seemed like the perfect target for implementing the scheme. They still owned land that constituted nearly one-half of the state. Missionaries and even some local politicians defended the Choctaw land rights, noting the racist nature of the state's new law—it supposedly extended Mississippi's authority over the Indians but did not grant them suffrage. Missionary Cyrus Kingsbury was outraged, calling the new policy a "wholly and most unjust & wicked proceeding." The Choctaws had made considerable progress toward developing a "regular government"; ironically, the changes that reformers were encouraging constituted exactly the violation that Jackson used to justify removal.[18]

Nevertheless, many mixed-blood Choctaws saw the writing on the wall. This became obvious when they convinced council leaders to give absolute authority to Greenwood La Flore. Wrangling followed, when commissioners William Eaton and John Coffee opened discussions with the Indians in September 1830. They were fully aware that if they could remove the nearly 20,000 Choctaws the other southern Indians would leave as well.[19] Coffee and Eaton knew that open conflict was brewing between the mixed-bloods, led by La Flore, and the full-bloods and nurtured this by openly offering bribes of four sections of land (2,560 acres) to any leader who would sign the removal pact. Even so, the Indians rejected the offer. Coffee and Eaton announced that they were about to leave, stating categorically that the Choctaws would soon be placed under the legal authority of the state of Mississippi. If the Indians violently resisted, the federal army would be sent in.[20]

The threats worked, as Choctaw leaders asked once again to reconsider the treaty. After getting assurances that Choctaw lands in the West would be theirs forever and after carefully outlining the new boundaries of those lands—designated principally by Fort Smith in the east and the source of the Canadian River in the west—Choctaw leaders signed the treaty of Dancing Rabbit Creek in late September. The payment included a cash annuity of $20,000 for twenty years, various gifts of blankets and axes, and other items, and funds to finance migration. Those Choctaws who wished to stay on allotments in Mississippi were assured of receiving a section of land each. This "allotted" land and the Indians would thereafter fall under state authority.[21]

General confusion reigned thereafter in the Choctaw Nation, yet most leaders believed that it was the best deal that could be made. Jackson had an investment in the Choctaw removal; if it went badly, other treaties would be difficult to get. The president and Eaton, his former secretary of war (Cass had already replaced him), quickly acted to assign commissary agents and forwarded thousands of dollars to promote a smooth removal. Unfortunately, quarrels broke out among the agents, and Cass placed the army in command. Lacking sufficient steamboats, army officers proceeded to cram as many Indians onto existing boats as possible. Disease followed, and perhaps as many as 2,500 Indians died. At final count, over 12,000 Choctaws actually reached Oklahoma. Perhaps a thousand forsook the United States and crossed the Red River into Texas, where they hoped for better treatment from Mexico. A Choctaw chief who witnessed the despair dubbed the migration "the Trail of Tears."[22]

Jackson and Cass came to see Choctaw Removal as a complete success: Congress even published all the documents relative to the food and supplies purchased for the Indians to demonstrate government largesse. Life in Oklahoma offered only one benefit for the Choctaws—they were out of the grip of land-hungry southerners and could reinstitute their tribal government in a land separated from any American state.[23] But the manner in which the federal government had forced the Choctaws to leave Mississippi constituted ethnic cleansing under almost any definition.

The pressures that had forced the Choctaws out of Mississippi also mounted in Alabama. There the Creeks had resisted removal despite several articles in treaties that encouraged it. A few hundred followers of William McIntosh, who had been assassinated for signing the treaty of 1825, did agree to leave in the winter of 1827–28, but most of the 20,000 Creeks who remained stood steadfastly against being forced from their lands. Jackson wrote Creek leaders a letter in 1829, noting that Alabama "had extended their law over your country" and that he intended to do nothing to prevent this. Much of this so-called law was inflicted upon the Indians by Alabama ruffians, who answered to no one. Fearing expulsion, the Creeks signed a treaty of removal in March 1832.[24]

While Article 5 of the Creek treaty of 1832 guaranteed that the federal government would protect the Indians who decided to stay and take land allotments in Mississippi, the promise went unfulfilled. Whites invaded Creek lands, sometimes simply expelling the Indians from their houses, seizing their fields, their wagons, and especially their slaves. Local courts would not convict Alabama ruffians, and the carnage continued into 1833 and 1834. Small groups of Creeks fled into the surrounding rugged hills, where they generally starved. The evidence suggests that Secretary Cass considered the allotment article nothing more than a bribe to get the Indians to leave, a process that he had invented and used earlier in northern Ohio.[25]

As other southern tribes watched the rush to push the Choctaws and Creeks into the trans-Mississippi West, the Chickasaws and the Cherokees huddled to consider their options. Chickasaw leaders, most of whom were mixed-bloods, opted to negotiate immediately, meeting with Coffee and Eaton. They successfully negotiated an agreement in which their lands—roughly 6,400,000 acres—would be allotted: 320-acre farms were given to each Chickasaw family who wished to stay in the East. Then they signed a formal treaty in 1832, in which most of them agreed to remove as soon as suitable lands could be found in the West. This took time: by 1837 all the Chickasaws had been moved to lands west of the Choctaws in Oklahoma. The Chickasaws, though suffering their own ethnic cleansing, at least had the opportunity to sell their allotted farms in northern Mississippi before making the final migration west. A few arrived in Oklahoma with extensive amounts of cash, the only tribe to accomplish such a feat.[26]

Unlike the Chickasaws, the Cherokees took a diametrically opposite view. They hired one of the best lawyers in the country, William Wirt, to contest removal in court. Senators Webster and Frelinghuysen, both lawyers, assisted. The first problem that they faced was simply getting the case into federal court.[27] Wirt filed suit on behalf of the Cherokee Nation in 1831, arguing that it was a "foreign power" and asking the court to stop Georgia's intrusions into its lands. The case had merit, because a foreign power had the right to sue in American federal courts under Article III of the Constitution. The resulting opinion, again prepared by Marshall, dashed all hopes. In *Cherokee Nation v. Georgia* Marshall ruled that the Cherokees were in fact not a foreign nation but a "domestic dependent nation" and as such could not bring a suit. The tenacious Wirt refused to give up. He found yet another case that the Supreme Court could not refuse. The next year Wirt filed *Worcester v. Georgia*.

Marshall, who had become somewhat inflamed by the way the attorneys for Georgia had used material from his earlier opinion in *Johnson v. M'Intosh,* wrote the majority opinion. Belittling the argument of those attorneys, Marshall challenged how the minuscule settlements on the coast of Virginia, established in 1607, could constitute a legal right for the English to occupy much of a continent—of course he had written as much in *M'Intosh.* He then even rewrote much of *Johnson v. M'Intosh,* contending that "discovery" failed to result in actual ownership of Indian lands in the discovering state. Then he returned to segments of the earlier case that guaranteed some Indians title. The Cherokee Nation was a "distinct community" that had a right of occupancy, so the lands could only be taken over in a just war or by purchase.[28]

Yet Marshall did not demand, as some historians have incorrectly asserted, that Jackson defend the Cherokees' rights to their lands—although a few of the judges on the court did. The Chief Justice only struck down the Georgia law that resulted in the arrest of Worcester, ordering his release, which Georgia finally complied with. And Jackson likely never made the famous statement attributed to him: "Marshall has made his decision now let him enforce it." The federal government was not a party to the litigation, and federal courts by themselves could not direct the executive branch of government to act. But Jackson should have concluded that his office had a moral duty to defend the Cherokees in their lands because of treaty rights. *Worcester v. Georgia* changed nothing, despite Wirt's seemingly brilliant victory.[29]

Jackson and Cass stayed the course, ever pressuring Cherokee leaders to join the Choctaws, Chickasaws, and Creeks in the West. Cherokees, however, continued to stay on their farms and protect their property as best they could.[30] But when it became clear that Marshall's decision would not sway federal authorities from removing the Indians in spring 1833, even the ABCFM concluded that removal to the West was best for the Indians. This produced an openly divisive split within the Cherokee leadership; while this alone may not have doomed them to removal, it certainly did not help provide a united front in opposition to it.

The divide soon produced what became known as the pro-removal and anti-removal parties. Both groups had able men at their head; Ross became the leader of the anti-removal faction. Most full-bloods sided with Ross and utterly refused to move. The pro-removal faction, who accepted what appeared to be the inevitable, included men such as Major Ridge, Elias Boudinot, John Ridge, David Vann, and Stand Watie, many of whom could trace their ancestry back to the time when British royalists fled west to live with the Cherokees after the American Revolution. Both sides were patriotic. Boudinot was the editor of the famous *Cherokee Phoenix* newspaper printed both in English and in the Cherokee Syllabary.[31]

Once it became obvious that President Jackson would not intervene, the State of Georgia made a provocative move. It sent five hundred surveyors into Cherokee land and began dividing it up into 160-acre plots. The pro-treaty party, more than the conservative full-bloods, knew the result; Georgians would soon run the Indians off their land by force. The federal government would not prevent it—forced ethnic cleansing would be accomplished with violence. After months of wrangling and numerous attempts to compromise with Secretary Cass—all of which both the president and the secretary rejected—the pro-treaty party decided to sign a treaty in December 1835, getting the best terms possible.[32]

What would become the Treaty of Echota provided a sum of $4,500,000 as compensation for eastern Cherokee lands. In exchange the tribe received 13 million acres of new lands in Oklahoma. Ridge inserted an article that made it necessary for the Cherokee National Council to agree to the terms; Commissioner John F. Schermerhorn was just the person to apply the pressure necessary to make that happen. Even so, John Ross mustered all his friends to oppose Cherokee ratification, producing an ugly factional feud that escalated into violence.

Despite the growing infighting—which even included assassinations—Commissioner Schermerhorn convinced a number of Cherokee men from the council to sign the treaty at Elias Boudinot's house on December 29. A "committee" that supposedly represented the National Council signed off soon thereafter. While some senators suspected that the agreement did not represent the Cherokees overall, the Senate ratified the treaty, which became law. Cherokee families would received compensation for their houses and fields and transportation to the West and would have until May 1838 to complete the move. Those who refused to go would then be forced west by the army.[33]

While the Cherokees remained peaceful but defiant, Indians farther north angrily resisted forced removal. American settlement in the Northwest had been hindered by the War of 1812 and then the Panic of 1819, but by the 1820s settlers poured into Illinois, taking up land between the Illinois and Mississippi Rivers that had belonged to many different tribes, including the Sac and Fox Indians. William Henry Harrison supposedly had negotiated a treaty with this nation in 1804, purchasing the lands extending northward from St. Louis between the rivers to southern Wisconsin. In the years that followed the Sac and Fox Indians lived on their lands and when queried consistently indicated that they had no idea that the lands had been purchased, especially a group called the "British Band" led by Black Hawk, who had openly sided with the British during the War of 1812.[34]

Black Hawk's anger seemed justified when he returned from his winter hunt along the Des Moines River in 1829 to discover that his main village at Saukenuk, at the mouth of the Rock River, well north of St. Louis, had been occupied by American settlers. Whites had even taken over his house. Black Hawk protested to local Indian agent Thomas Forsyth, who only reminded him of the 1804 treaty—an agreement that Black Hawk had never signed, knew little about, and totally rejected. Tensions built over the next two years.[35] As a clash between whites and Indians seemed in the offing, Illinois governor John Reynolds ordered "Mounted Rangers" to the area in 1831; some 1,400 answered the call. Indian superintendent William Clark, fearing a war, convinced General Edmund P. Gaines, who commanded regular troops at St. Louis, to remove the Indians quickly, before the rangers arrived.[36]

Gaines reached the Rock River region in May, but Black Hawk and his 1,600 followers seemed unintimidated. Black Hawk remained in contact with the Winnebago "Prophet," who assured him that regular army infantry troops would not attack. But Black Hawk readily understood that state-raised mounted rangers often acted without orders. He told a friend that he "was afraid of the multitude of *pale faces,* who were on horseback, as they were under no restraint of their chiefs." Gaines, frustrated and searching for resolution, finally called on the Illinois Rangers to join him. Black Hawk and his people, fearing the worst, quietly crossed the Mississippi River into Iowa at night on June 25, 1831.[37]

Just when it looked as if removal had been successful, Black Hawk returned, swayed by the Winnebago Prophet. He settled some forty miles up the Rock River with his band on lands that were not part of the original cession. By spring 1832 a new commander at St. Louis, General Henry Atkinson, seemed unsure of how to proceed. Governor Reynolds, though, had no doubts; he immediately raised 3,250 volunteers, many of them mounted rangers. Reynolds reinforced greatly exaggerated stories of settlements being burned in what he concluded was an "Indian War." The governor then ordered his rangers to advance on Black Hawk's camp.[38]

These Illinois rangers, spoiling for a fight, came upon a small party of Black Hawk's men who had been sent to negotiate peace with them on the upper Rock River. Killing two warriors, rangers then thought that they could easily rout the Indians and mounted a cavalry charge headlong into an ambush set by Black Hawk. Several dozen Indian riflemen dropped a dozen troopers, and the rest fled in utter terror. Some forty troopers deserted, telling stories of the "thousands" of Indians who had attacked them. The "battle" at Stillman's Creek emboldened the Indians and greatly embarrassed the Jackson administration back in Washington. While some small raids ensued thereafter, as a few Potawatomis and Winnebagos joined Black Hawk, secretary Lewis Cass demanded that the army make an example of Black Hawk. Other Indians might resist removal if Black Hawk succeeded in staying east of the Mississippi River.[39]

General Atkinson and Governor Reynolds organized a new volunteer force in July 1832, consisting of 3,196 volunteers and 629 regulars. Major Henry Dodge commanded one of the most reliable volunteer forces; competent Colonel Zachary Taylor handled the regulars. During the summer skirmishes occurred over and over again. Black Hawk handled his small force of 300 warriors with considerable skill. But desertions and casualties occurred as well, and Black Hawk's main camp had dwindled to 600 by late July and 500 by August, when he realized that the Americans would not accept peace. His only option was to flee back across the Mississippi River.

With Taylor's and Dodge's troops at his heels, outnumbered literally fifteen to one, Black Hawk reached a point where the Bad Axe River joined the Mississippi and tried to make rafts for his people, most of whom were women and children by this time. The American gunboat *Warrior,* with cannon on board, raked the Indian positions, indiscriminately killing dozens. The militia showed even less compassion, attacking the collections of women and children who desperately sought refuge across the river. Women and babies were slaughtered. Some of the Native women were later found without a stitch of clothing. At the height of the carnage one of the volunteers screamed: "kill the nits and you will have no lice." Bad Axe was not a battle but a massacre: 300 of the final 500 Sac and Fox Indians under Black Hawk perished. In a second misfortune the 200 or so who made it across the river fell into a Dakota Sioux ambush; roughly 100 of the survivors fell victim to intertribal war.

President Jackson and Lewis Cass certainly had their example after news of the slaughter at Bad Axe River reached Washington. The event also had a profound impact on those Indians who remained along the Mississippi River and in northern Illinois and southern Wisconsin. The Sac and Fox Indians quickly ceded their eastern lands in Iowa a few weeks after the massacre. Winnebago lands in southern Wisconsin were then ceded, as these Indians had aided Black Hawk.[40] The Jackson government sent William Ewing to treat with the Chippewas, Ottawas, and Pottawatomis at Chicago in September 1833. After being told that President Jackson was the "greatest war chief amongst all, [and] the red men cannot count so great a number of scalps as your Great Father can," the clearly intimidated chiefs handed over more land, agreeing to migrate west of the Mississippi River. The rhetoric used to frighten these Indians harkened to a medieval age, when trophies of hair symbolized the strength of armies.[41]

A virtual land rush followed. The New York Indians who had been coaxed to move to Wisconsin on firm guarantees that they would receive land were approached in 1836 and virtually ordered to give up all their claims. The Stockbridge, Munsee, Brothertown, and Oneida Indians who attended were amazed at the audacity of the federal authorities. An Oneida spokesman responded:

> We have hardly laid down our packs or cleared land enough to live on, when word comes for us to go on . . . we expected to have a chance to remain where we are . . . wherever we go whites can go also, and to get away from them is impossible. . . . We wish the President to look at his wealth. . . . He possess all the lands of the Indians except a few spots and we hope he will let us rest.[42]

Such pleas changed nothing, and the New York people signed yet another treaty.

The next year the Chippewas of central Wisconsin were the targets of ethnic cleansing. No doubt aware of what had happened to the Sac and Fox Indians, they agreed to sell 10,000,000 acres of land for virtually nothing. After telling the Indians that the "land was not valuable for you," commissioner Henry Dodge then bragged to the commissioner of Indian affairs, Carey Harris, that the land "abounded in pine timber." Dodge's only concession was his solemn agreement that "you [the Chippewas] shall have the free use of the rivers and the privilege of hunting upon the lands you are to sell." This too would ultimately be challenged over a century later.[43]

The purchase of northern Illinois and much of Wisconsin evoked only feeble complaints from the Indians. But the vast majority of Cherokees still refused to recognize the mostly illegal treaty of 1835. Only a few members of the treaty party, among them the Ridge family, departed for the West during the summer of 1836. Animosity between the two factions had been growing.

That summer the army selected General John Wool to take command of what would become an increasing American military presence in Cherokee country. Wool, a veteran of the War of 1812 and an extremely efficient administrator, had a difficult task ahead and knew it. He was ordered to prepare the Cherokees for removal, by force if necessary.[44] In order to encourage emigration, Wool handed out extensive provisions to emigrating parties as they left. Some key members also received cash for their improvements, but the money soon ran out; those who left later generally received nothing.[45]

General Wool had been informed that the Georgia Guard had forcefully disarmed many Cherokees in northern Georgia, and other whites in Alabama were doing the same. They justified such actions—which also included theft of property—by suggesting that the Indians contemplated armed resistance. Once Wool arrived on the scene and saw the often pathetic condition of the Cherokees, he quickly reported to Washington that the Indians were no threat to anyone; most were families with large numbers of women and children, incapable of resistance. Wool mustered in only one regiment of volunteers, sending others, who had been sent by the War Department, home. He divided up the men, deploying several companies to Rossville, near Ross's Landing, to Valley River in the mountains of North Carolina, and to New Echota in north Georgia. Small detachments patrolled into northern Alabama, where fewer than two thousand Cherokees lived.[46]

Wool arrived at yet another conclusion when he reached New Echota. He quickly recognized that his troops needed to prevent the growing assaults on Indians by lawless elements from Georgia and Alabama. Wool forwarded a letter from Major Ridge addressed to President Jackson, which described the suffering in north Georgia and Alabama in summer 1836. The general agreed with Ridge's overall description of the situation:

> Even the Georgia laws, which deny us our oaths [rights], are thrown aside, & notwithstanding the cries of our people and protestations of innocence & peace, the lowest classes of the white population are flogging the Cherokees with cowhides, hickories & clubs. We are not safe in our house—our people are assailed by day & night by the rabble. . . . This barbarous treatment is not confined to the men, but our women are stripped also and whipped without law or *mercy*.[47]

Some of the worst state militias dispossessed Cherokees of their property, their food supplies, their fields, and even the ferryboats that they had built to carry people over rivers.[48]

Despite federal troops, north Alabama and Georgia were descending into anarchy. Wool's troops faced dozens of complaints. Cherokee women had been thrown out of their houses. Cherokees who were preparing to move routinely had their stock stolen. In one case a white man dispossessed a Cherokee man of his house then shot and wounded the work oxen so that soldiers could not restore the animals.[49] Nathaniel Smith, who was supposedly in charge of emigration, estimated that some "4 or 500 families, of the Cherokees, in Tennessee, Georgia, and Alabama, but chiefly in Georgia, have been turned out of their houses and farms by whites and who are now living in camps in the woods."[50]

Colonel Edward Buffington, on Wool's orders, established a court where Indians could ask for redress. In one day he ordered property returned to seven Cherokees, evicting whites from their property by force. Obviously such efforts only marginally addressed the problem. The confiscation of property became so general and so common that one man even agreed to pay for his thievery. Even worse, nearly a thousand Creeks had fled into Cherokee lands in 1835, refusing to remove. Some violently resisted and a so-called Creek War—certainly a misnomer—erupted, causing more difficulty for General Wool.[51]

While the Cherokees faced dispossession, various militia units were hunting Creeks and in the process abused all Indians. Colonel William N. Bishop, who commanded the Georgia Guard, had captured several dozen Creeks. Brigadier General R. G. Dunlap, Wool's second in command, came upon Bishop as he was marching the Indians off. Dunlap tried to convince the Georgia militia officer to give up the Indians, but Bishop refused. In disgust Dunlap wrote the colonel: "You must take their chains off, and treat them as friendly Indians. Your own sense of propriety and humanity would no doubt induce you to this course." The Georgia and Alabama militias were not listening: they took Creeks and sometimes Cherokee women who had Creek men as husbands, placing them both in chains and shipping them west. The roundup continued into the fall and winter of 1836–37. Twelve Indians were brought in from Hanging Dog Creek; fifty from Brass Town; thirty-eight from Frog Mountain; and several dozen from North Carolina. Lieutenant Edward Deas, who had control of the deportations, counted a total of 500 Creeks by spring 1837, all housed in a carefully guarded "containment" near Calhoun, Tennessee. The Creek ordeal—capture, confinement, and deportation—was a prelude to Cherokee forced removal.[52]

General Wool remained adamantly supportive of Jackson's removal policy even though he detested the work assigned to him. Wool did his best to alleviate the suffering of the Indians, despite the growing problems that the army faced in providing such aid. His aggressive efforts in defending Cherokee property, however, soon brought protests, especially from the governor of Alabama and its congressional delegation in Washington. Accordingly, the War Department removed Wool in summer 1837—unbelievably, on suspicion that he was harassing Alabama citizens. As he left, the general summed up the situation succinctly: "The Indians are anxious to retain and live and die on the lands of their forefathers. The white inhabitants are equally anxious to dispossess them. . . . It is truly a hard case."[53] It only got worse in spring 1838.

While the Ridge party and several others had migrated to Oklahoma by March 1838, many thousand remained behind—but how many? Wool's officers had set about carefully collecting census data relative to the size of various Cherokee communities as early as 1837, usually attaching a number (which included men, women, and children) along the course of a particular creek. Accordingly, the army concluded that exactly 11,953 Cherokees had to be deported.[54] Most in this final group were full-bloods, convinced that John Ross would save them and their lands. Ross had encouraged such a belief during open councils, which General Wool knew about. President Jackson, on hearing of Wool's failure to stop the discussions, openly berated the general. Soon thereafter Wool issued General Order 74, which forbade such councils. He even detained Ross at one point, forcing him to stop preaching against removal.[55]

After Wool's departure, Ross realized that he could no longer foment opposition to removal—he also recognized the hardening attitudes of the military. Most of the leaders of the treaty party had reached Oklahoma. Ross discovered that no one would see him anymore in Washington—the friends of the Cherokees had given up the issue. So it was that on May 23, 1838, the army began sending troops into Cherokee lands, capturing Indians, and moving them to deportation camps. General Winfield Scott took personal command, organizing an army of 4,000 men.[56] The general then divided Cherokee country into three districts: "eastern" (North Carolina, extending down into eastern Georgia); "western" (Alabama); and "middle," with the major concentration of Indians, around New Echota in north-central Georgia and in southern Tennessee.[57]

The military tried to prepare the Indians for removal with proclamations and speeches. In early March 1838 Captain Thomas J. Caldwell in North Carolina made it known that the military would no longer protect the Indians from whites unless they quickly came into the camps being set up for them; if they did not, "their property then might be seized with impunity and no relief would be afforded them."[58] General Scott did the same, issuing a proclamation in May stating that "the emigration must be commenced in haste." None could stay behind.[59] Such proclamations did no good; the Indians refused to leave.

Scott ordered Lieutenant Colonel William Lindsay to begin the roundup on the morning of May 23, 1838. Lindsay concentrated troops in the "middle" district, in southern Gilmer, Union, and Murray Counties, Georgia, and began to "drive" the Indians north, as he put it, toward the Tennessee River. Lindsay concluded that the largest concentration of "ignorant and untractable [sic] Indians" was there. Most had said that they "would rather die, than go, & so far from preparing to remove by selling their property, they are clearing, building, & getting ready for another crop . . . they intend to make it manifest that they are forcibly expelled from their country!" The troops had been ordered not to shoot unless fired upon; the "bayonet" became the weapon of forced ethnic cleansing.[60]

Few if any Cherokees resisted the roundup. Troopers invaded their homes, dragged them from their tables or beds, and forced them onto a nearby road. Most were not even allowed to take any clothing or food with them. At least one officer, Major B. M. Venables, complained to Scott that the removal created hardships: "The Indian prisoners . . . were collected with such rapidity as to preclude the possibility of bringing in any of their movables . . . I am reluctant to send them off [to Oklahoma] in their present condition."[61] In just two short weeks the army collected nearly 11,000 Cherokees in this fashion and forced them toward the transportation camps.[62]

Once the Indians were in the camps, just feeding the many mouths proved challenging; the government had never undertaken such an effort before. Some Indians, sleeping on the ground without blankets or cover, tested the troopers who guarded them. "I have as many as I can handle," one officer complained. "[T]hey run in every instance where they have the opportunity."[63] Most escapees headed for the mountains to the east, in North Carolina, where the army had little knowledge of the terrain. But young men often had to leave their families and the old behind, and many stayed behind to protect their dependents. By June the situation had worsened: the army had not provided sufficient transportation to move the mass of Indians then in the camps, and food supplies became increasingly scarce.

By this time three expeditions had been sent west under the command of the head of emigration, Nathaniel Smith. Over two thousand Indians made up these groups, their travel time being about three weeks. Then the Tennessee River ceased to be navigable as a drought set in. Worse, disease broke out in a large camp near Chattanooga that held 900 Indians. The army and the Indians both tried to construct huts to get the sick out of the weather. Wagons could not be found to move them, and one of the two flatboats brought in to be used in floating the Indians west promptly sank in the Tennessee River.[64]

A second problem surfaced when officers in the West informed General Scott that moving the Indians during the summer might submit them to epidemics, especially during the malaria season. One of the parties that departed in June suffered massive deaths from the disease.[65] Also, teamsters who owned wagons and teams wanted nothing to do with government lease offers to move Indians west. Secretary of War Poinsett ordered a delay, first until September 1 then extended until October 1.[66] Meanwhile, as the Cherokees waited in their camps through July and August, they died literally by the hundreds. The food proved a major liability; on one occasion when the army ran out of supplies, it gave the Indians heavily salted bacon that the troops at Fort Delancy in North Carolina had thrown into the fire rather than eat. The bacon was several years old, partly rancid, heavily salted, and caused massive dehydration and dysentery.[67]

The situation became so severe that the army sent doctors into the four main camps as well as the one that remained in North Carolina.[68] What they found was appalling. Nearly 600 Indians were suffering from dysentery alone, and hundreds of others had other diseases. Children especially were coming down with measles. Worse, cholera had broken out in several camps. In one camp 462 cases of "vacunea" existed, which one doctor correctly spelled "vacinia," another word for "cowpox" or smallpox. Just how many Indians had died by the end of July was impossible to determine, because many Indian women hid the illnesses of their children out of fear of the doctors' medicines. The attending physicians counted 144 dead during one two-week survey. Doctor Jonathan L. Hooker later stated that even this survey was "much understated."[69]

By fall the government had found sufficient wagons to move the final groups out of the camps and onto the trail. John Ross, who was put in charge of the final movement by General Scott, worked tirelessly to save the remainder of his people from destruction. On October 1, the deadline set by Secretary Poinsett, the various caravans associated with the Ross removal left Tennessee. They had 645 wagons, 5,000 horses, and a large number of oxen. As they departed, the army set the huts and bark-covered shelters of the camps afire. One of the conductors, William S. Coodey, described the scene as the wagons were ordered to move: "In all the bustle of preparation there was a silence and stillness of the voice that betrayed the sadness of the heart."[70]

The regular army did its best to prevent death and hardship in the ethnic cleansing of Cherokees from their eastern homes. Many Cherokees died of disease even before the removal began, however, and others were sick when the final caravans departed. Sick or elderly Cherokees received no reprieve. The administration made it clear that all Cherokees must move. Those with the worst illnesses were generally moved by water, down the Tennessee River into northern Kentucky and thence down the

Mississippi River to the Arkansas, where riverboats carried them to Fort Smith. Many died along the way and were buried in unmarked graves. The remainder of the strongest marched across Tennessee, Kentucky, and Arkansas to the new lands in the West. Much like the Choctaws before them, Cherokees soon called this forced migration the "Trail of Tears," as so many died en route. The numbers of deaths are only estimates. A good guess is that 1,000 Indians died in the camps before leaving and another 2,000 fell ill, perished along the trail, or died almost immediately after reaching Oklahoma.

While Andrew Jackson, the tormentor of Indians, left office in March 1837, his successor Martin Van Buren continued his policies. Far to the Southeast the various groups called Seminoles remained just as stubborn in their resistance to removal. In 1817 then General Jackson had pushed eastward into Pensacola and beyond, destroying some Native towns. But the Seminoles and their African American allies had regrouped in central Florida. These groups, numbering some five thousand people, had no central political organization and remained ethnically and linguistically diverse. Escaped African American slaves lived among them, which made the federal government even more determined to force them west: the African Americans challenged the existence of the expanding labor system in the South and offered refuge to other escaped slaves.

Jackson's young protégé James Gadsden had forced a final treaty on the Seminoles. At Payne's Landing, thirty miles southeast of St. Augustine, Gadsden gathered a few Seminole leaders about the same time that Black Hawk was being subdued, in 1832. Several of the so-called chiefs were leaders of the Alachua and Mikasuki bands. They supposedly signed Gadsden's removal treaty, even though two years later most of these leaders denied having ever signed the document. It mattered little: the Seminoles and others allied with them were given three years to pack up and leave and ordered to join the Creeks west of the Mississippi River.[71]

Most Seminoles had no intention of leaving. A war broke out in 1835 when the three-year period expired. Led by chiefs such as Osceola and Wild Cat, the Seminoles turned to hit and run tactics. Some 15 percent of their fighters were African Americans, fully aware that defeat likely meant a return to slavery. While Secretary Cass ordered 1,500 militia to fight the Seminoles—about half of what he agreed to for Black Hawk's War—this quickly proved insufficient. Disease soon killed more American soldiers than the Indians did.[72] The Seminoles, who knew the terrain, proved a more than worthy opponent, ambushing American troops at will.

The conflict in Florida seesawed back and forth from 1836 well into the 1840s. Some Seminoles surrendered, given the growing shortage of food. Others, after being assured of joining peace talks, often faced capture and deportation in chains when American officers violated flags of truce, which happened on several occasions. President Jackson, nearly a year after leaving office, became exasperated at the war and wrote a long letter to Secretary Poinsett, giving his views: "find where their women are . . . and capture them—this done, they will at once surrender." Ethnic cleansing in Florida, much as in Illinois, had reverted to a war against women and children. In the end the war became costly for the United States in terms of treasure—literally hundreds of thousands of dollars were expended—and lives—some 1,500 American soldiers died, more than in any other Indian war. But 3,000 Seminoles were eventually forcibly removed to the West.[73] A few hundred hid out in the Everglades—lands that Americans did not want—and were allowed to stay.

Indian Removal had begun as a voluntary policy, supposedly aimed at offering American Indians a second chance to acculturate to American values while living in the West. But in the last years of its implementation, 1830–42, it became a policy of forced deportation. This was a clear violation of Article 7 of the Rome Statutes and perhaps the most vivid example of ethnic cleansing in American history. The leading officers of the young American army faced their first combat, subduing the Native groups who resisted. Winfield Scott, Edmund Gaines, Thomas Jesup, Zachary Taylor, Henry Dodge, Henry Atkinson, Lewis Armistead, and even later protagonists Abraham Lincoln and Jefferson Davis, all served at one time or another in units that cleansed regions of Indians. Later in life Lincoln minimized his role in the slaughter of the Sac and Fox Indians, claiming that he saw little combat and spent most of his time swatting mosquitoes. But, truth be told, Illinois volunteers in general eagerly joined units, seeking glory in Indian war.

Jackson obviously got his way. By 1842 the only Indians left in the eastern states were several thousand in northern Michigan and Wisconsin; a few thousand more hiding out in Florida swamps, the North Carolina mountains, and the more rugged country of northern Mississippi; and the mostly acculturated New York tribes, which quietly farmed on small reservations. Of the roughly 100,000 Indians Cass identified in 1830, over 80,000 had been forcefully removed. The land taken from these Indians was worth billions of dollars, and its sale financed the federal government for years to come.

The stated policy that led to this conclusion was literally written into American law and took a dozen years to implement. While this was a violation of the Rome Statutes, it needs to be noted that no government official ever called for the extermination of all the Indians in the East—officials wanted them removed, peaceably if possible. Indians did at times defend their lands against crooked treaties and invading rangers, but such acts, as in Florida, only made war "just" in the eyes of most Americans. Nevertheless, the Illinois Rangers, who had been ordered not to kill women and children, did so anyway. Georgia and Alabama militiamen indiscriminately stole land, animals, and personal property from the Cherokees and Creeks and on occasion raped their women. And American officers who offered flags of truce in Florida frequently violated them. War crimes, unsanctioned by the federal government, did occur despite efforts to prevent them—such as those attempted by General Wool. They were frequently committed by rangers and government regulars alike.

At the end of the Seminole War in 1842 most government officials assumed that the so-called Indian Problem had been solved. During the height of the implementation of the policy Congress had even passed the Intercourse Act of 1834, a thirty-section bill that clearly outlined "Indian Country" as being west of the Mississippi River.[74] It seemingly existed on lands that were not part of any state or territory. Yet within seven short years restless Americans, some floundering after the Panic of 1837, organized at St. Joseph, Missouri, in 1841. Several wagon trains moved onto the Oregon Trail that spring, headed for new lands in the West. Other Americans had moved into Mexican-owned Texas, driving Indians before them. The policy of ethnic cleansing would soon take on a new meaning in the West, while adapting many of the same justifications that had proved so successful in implementing it in the early colonies and in eastern states.

9

THE WESTERN DOMAIN

Indian Country

Anglo-Americans nurtured a fundamental belief in their own "exceptionalism"—a view reinforced by the continuous progress of the nation across the continent. Most Americans also embraced a simple truth: all people had "natural rights," especially to life and property. A bare majority of American politicians and voters approved of Indian Removal; but the vast majority believed that the process included the moral obligation to give land in the West to the Indians who were removed. There they could begin a new life, perhaps even what most Americans perceived as an "industrious" one, modeled on a Christian-capitalistic ethic. But those "removed" Indians soon found that others inhabited their new homes— the Plains Indians of the horse culture and the buffalo hunt.[1]

Soon after the arrival of the removed tribes, a trickle of white settlement appeared west of the Mississippi River. The invasion of western Indian land by Americans began as early as the 1820s and skyrocketed in the 1840s. The first settlement came along the lower Missouri River. American fur traders then moved into the Rocky Mountains about the same time that land-hungry pioneers were entering Mexican Texas. Fur traders, the army, and pioneers had marked the Oregon Trail by 1841, fought a war with Mexico from 1846 to 1848, and seized a vast empire in the Southwest, including several future states—New Mexico, Arizona, California, Nevada, Colorado, and Utah. The gold rush the following year cemented the American hold on the Pacific Slope.

Well before the rush of '49, Congress considered the ownership of the Great Plains. In a solemn pledge it gave virtually all lands between the Mississippi River and the Rocky Mountains to American Indians.

Theoretically this ended debate in the East regarding the viability of the Indians' title. The pledge came in legislation known as the Intercourse Act of 1834. Section 1 of the act, which was written in part to satisfy opponents of removal, defined all lands west of the Mississippi River—with the exceptions of Missouri, Arkansas, and part of Louisiana—as "Indian Country."[2]

Despite Congress's good intentions—the Intercourse Act was a product of legislators mostly opposed to removal—Americans soon challenged the concept that Indian Country was only for Indians. Pressures mounted to open at least some lands on the west bank of the Mississippi River in what would become Iowa and Minnesota, followed some years later by settlement along both banks of the Missouri River in what would become Kansas and Nebraska. This region, close to St. Louis where the Western Superintendency of Indian Affairs was headquartered, could be monitored.[3] But settlers from the American South moved into Texas in 1821, even though it belonged to Mexico at the time.

Texas remained outside American jurisdiction until 1845, when it became a state. Even then Texans thought that the federal government had no right to establish Indian Country within its boundaries. Texans believed strongly in the "right of conquest" and the "settler sovereignty" that it seemingly guaranteed, which gave them all of Texas—even the part generally identified as eastern New Mexico, which still belonged to Mexico at least until 1846. The notion of Anglo "entitlement" to land became deeply ingrained in the Texas psyche, even at times superseding efforts by the government of the Republic of Texas and later the United States to control expansion into the West. For the Native population of the southwestern Plains, some forty thousand people, and even many of the Tejano communities that had been in the land for nearly a century, this led to a violent policy of ethnic cleansing.[4]

The American Indians who inhabited the lands between the Rocky Mountains and the Mississippi River differed markedly from the Cherokees who suffered through removal. On the northern prairies and plains, Dakotas, Nakotas, Lakotas, Crows, Mandans, Pawnees, and Cheyennes often contested with each other for control of the massive buffalo herds that sustained them. Their combined populations likely surpassed 60,000 people in 1840. Farther south Comanches, Kiowas, Southern Cheyennes, and remnants of smaller tribes had similar populations in 1780, but disease reduced them by nearly half at mid-century.[5] Nevertheless, the Southern

Plains people tenaciously held onto lands in west Texas, what would become Oklahoma, and even Nebraska and Kansas.

All of these Plains bands and tribes had claims to land based more on their mobile resources—mainly buffalo—than on their agricultural value, making them excellent examples of the land doctrines espoused by Grotius, Locke, and Vattel. Exceptions did exist, such as the Mandans, who grew corn and beans along the upper Missouri River. Other semisedentary village Indians included the Pawnees, Poncas, Omahas, Kansas, and Osages, all of whom had similar riverine economies, but their populations remained small. The areas of the upper Brazos, Arkansas, and Red Rivers also held some village Indians, including Wichitas, Caddos, and Quapaws and some transplanted eastern Indians.

The first Indians to face forced expulsion from their lands west of the Mississippi River were in Texas. "Gone to Texas" became a refrain often repeated in the American states after Stephen F. Austin received a massive land grant from the Mexican government in 1823. He distributed these lands to pioneer settlers. His colony, along the lower Brazos and Colorado River waterways, grew to thousands of people.[6] When Mexico, fearful of an Anglo insurrection, tried to halt migration in 1830, radical Texas political leaders fanned the conflict into open rebellion. With the defeat of the Mexican dictator General Antonio López de Santa Anna at San Jacinto (near Houston) in April 1836, the Republic of Texas came into being.[7] Texas, which originally contained fewer than 25,000 people, ballooned to 140,000 people within a decade, and voters in the republic agreed to enter the American union in 1845. This brought on the Mexican War a year later, when Americans, consumed by an orgy of what became known as "Manifest Destiny," conquered Mexico and took the Southwest and California.

Those pioneers who went to Texas constituted a hearty breed. Many were of Scots-Irish background and fiercely defended kinfolk and hearth and home. Fighting with Indians seemed natural—indeed many came from the very southern states that expedited the expulsion of Indians in the 1830s. Several small volunteer parties, called rangers, cleared the lower Brazos and Colorado River valleys of Indians in the 1820s and 1830s. Along the way, they massacred a hundred or so Karankawa and Tonkawa Indians and forced the survivors to flee into Mexico.[8]

After independence, Sam Houston, the first president of the Republic of Texas, tried desperately to make peace with the remaining tribes in the area. The republic had little money and few arms and many of the remaining Indians, especially those in the West, were warrior societies with far more military prowess than the coastal Karankawas.[9] Houston even signed a treaty in 1836 with the so-called immigrant tribes—Cherokees, Creeks, Shawnees, Delawares, Kickapoos, and their neighbors, all refugees from ethnic cleansing in the East—guaranteeing their right to land in northeast Texas. Unfortunately Houston's plans collapsed after he left office. Mirabeau B. Lamar, openly racist and an advocate of Indian "extinction," became president of Texas in 1838. The Texas constitution prevented Houston from running for a second term.[10]

Lamar turned immediately to the expulsion of Indians. Even though many Native immigrant people had established farms, Lamar rejected Houston's pledges. Parroting the American removal act of 1830, President Lamar gave these Indians an ultimatum: leave Texas or face forced expulsion. He made no pretense of adopting Jackson's argument that Indians had written constitutions and formed governments, which could not exist within the Republic of Texas. Lamar ordered General Thomas Rusk and an army of a thousand men to attack, as the president said, beginning "an exterminating war upon their warriors, which will admit of no compromise." Rusk expelled the Kickapoos in 1838 and the Texas Cherokees and their allies the next year, often in bitter fighting. Rusk's threats were enough to convince the passive Caddos and Wichitas to leave. Several hundred Indians died during the conflict and flight that followed.[11]

Claiming that Texas owned all of the lands between the Rio Grande and Red River—which included eastern New Mexico—Lamar then turned on the Plains tribes, mostly Comanches, Kiowas, and (in south Texas) Apaches. Captain John Moore's renegade ranger force proved the most successful: his mounted rangers hit Indian camps in the dead of winter in 1839 and again in 1840. They marched without orders from any government and killed hundreds of Indians. They also burned Indian camps, forcing their occupants, if they survived, into a brutal plains winter without food, clothing, or even tents. Women and children suffered the most, the usual victims of ethnic cleansing.[12]

The so-called Texas Rangers of this age, so often glorified in the hagiography that is often part of early Texas history, rode not so much to remove western Indians from their homes—the goal of Lamar and Rusk—but for the booty that came with capturing Indian camps. The rangers took horses, mules, buffalo hides, and the like. Although they are heroes in

Texas, they acted mostly like renegades, like the rangers of the Carolinas, Virginia, and Kentucky. Henderson Yoakum, an early Texas writer who rode with Moore and used the ranger's words to describe the carnage of one attack, concluded: "As this was a war of extermination, the bodies of [Comanche] men, women and children were seen on every hand, dead, wounded, and dying."[13] Indeed the Texas Rangers would have killed more Indians had they not been sidetracked to collect animals and goods that were later sold for profit. Moore's men brought back some five hundred horses from one raid, easily worth $15,000 in cash-strapped Texas.[14]

While Rusk did not exterminate the Indians of east Texas and Moore did not kill all Comanches, they did force these Indians to evacuate their homelands. These actions clearly resembled ethnic cleansing; some acts were more forceful than others, but all led to the removal of villagers. Often these Indians had signed a solemn treaty with Houston guaranteeing their lands, and many Texans wanted to adopt Houston's more lenient Indian policy. Indeed some of the eastern tribes who had settled in east Texas contributed to the local economy.

Lamar's role in the policy of forced deportation is more difficult to pin down. He did order Rusk into east Texas and is just as guilty of forcibly removing Indians as the general was. Lamar added another dimension by using this language of "extermination." Whether rogue Texas Ranger units heard these pronouncements and later acted upon them is impossible to determine; some groups struck Indian camps, killing women and children. Lamar was likely guilty of the same offenses for which men in Rwanda received lengthy prison terms, being convicted of crimes against humanity for "inciting" others to commit genocide, which is today an international crime.[15]

Sam Houston, reelected president of the republic late in 1841, tried one last time to make peace with the now understandably distrustful Plains Comanches. He set up a trade house along the upper Brazos River and stocked it with food and goods, coaxing Indian leaders to visit. Meanwhile Houston attacked Lamar for his attempted policy of "extermination," noting its failure and its extreme cost. Ultimately Houston convinced the Indians to accept a boundary line separating Indian lands from those belonging to Texans. It ran north and south, roughly on the west edge of the Cross Timbers. While United States officials tried with some success to reinforce this boundary in 1846, Texans violated the line. Although fighting in Texas had subsided, the line had virtually disappeared by the

1850s as cattle ranchers moved onto what had been Comanche, Kiowa, and Apache land.[16]

While Texans took land by conquest, the federal government still preferred to purchase it. One of the earliest land cessions in Iowa came in the aftermath of the Black Hawk War, when the Sac and Fox Indians ceded all their lands along a fifty-mile strip on the west side of the Mississippi River. The government "negotiation," if it can be called such, was meant to pay for the Indian war, which, as the treaty indicated, had been perpetuated by "the hostile band who have been so conquered and subdued." Further Sac and Fox cessions, along with lands ceded by the Missouri and Iowa bands, opened much of Iowa to settlement. Congress made Iowa a state in 1846 and three years later created Minnesota Territory.[17] The valley lands of the Des Moines, Rock, and Minnesota Rivers, rich almost beyond imagination in terms of their agricultural value, soon became coveted by land-hungry settlers.

The federal government had few places to put these newly removed Indians. Most preferred to maintain a mixed economy with hunting, gathering, and some modest horticulture. One solution involved moving them to the prairies of Kansas and Nebraska. Some of this land had been ceded to the United States by the Kansas Indians as early as 1825. But other tribes already lived there, in particular the Osages and Pawnees, who had villages on the periphery of the plains and hunted buffalo along the upper Solomon, Republican, and Smoky Hill Rivers. But they too were suffering: the Lakotas had mostly expelled the Pawnees from the Platte River valley and later from the Republican and Solomon Valleys.[18]

Securing a boundary line in Texas, settling the so-called border tribes, and even making the newly created Oregon Trail safe for wagon trains were looming problems for concerned officials in the Indian Office in Washington. One remedy adopted in 1849 was transferring the agency from the War Department, which had done a miserable job with removal, to the Department of the Interior. Commissioner of Indian affairs William Medill had offered other solutions in 1848. He believed that if the border tribes could be congregated on small reservations, with specific boundaries, the government could protect them from both more western Indians and Anglo intruders. The plan, often called "colonization," contemplated purchasing and breaking Indian Country up into smaller, manageable reserves.[19]

The new policy gained considerable support the next year from Medill's Whig successor, Orlando Brown, who stressed the need to create "boundaries" and to move the border tribes—Iowas, Omahas, Otos, Missouris, Poncas, Osages, and Pawnees—to reservations. This would create a central corridor for American travel and settlement, especially securing the Santa Fe and Oregon Trails. That same year the Upper Platte Indian agent, Thomas Fitzpatrick, cautioned that the government also had to contend with the more western Plains tribes, who were complaining about the "numerous travelers passing on the different thoroughfares of their country." The Cheyennes, Arapahos, Sioux, Kiowas, and Comanches all complained about the "destruction and dispersion of game, the cutting down and destroying of wood, and other minor cases."[20]

Although it would take a number of years for the Medill-Brown plan to materialize in full, with the creation of Minnesota Territory in 1849, the Whig territorial governor and Indian superintendent Alexander Ramsey proposed implementing it in part. The Dakota or Sioux Indians closest to St. Paul (Mdewakantons and Wahpekutes) had signed a treaty in 1837, ceding lands in Wisconsin; the agreement gave the Eastern Sioux annuities in the form of food and agricultural equipment. They came to depend upon the food but preferred to hunt rather than plow land. The food annuities created considerable jealousy among their western relatives, the Sisseton and Wahpeton Dakotas, who hunted the western prairies of what would become Minnesota all the way to the Missouri River. At times they faced starvation.[21]

Ramsey recognized that his future as a Minnesota politician rested upon opening the lands of Minnesota to anxious American settlers. Henry Sibley, who controlled many commercial interests in the territory, convinced the governor to approach the westernmost Dakotas, the Sisseton and Wahpeton tribes, in late July 1851 and offer annuities for their land. Less savvy than their eastern relatives, they quickly agreed and surrendered all their lands in western Minnesota and northwest Iowa. Their leaders were heavily influenced to sign by their mixed-blood relatives and their traders, who were promised compensation by Sibley.[22] Now faced with federal lands on either side of them, Mdewakanton and Wahpekute leaders—who were often threatened by their young men not to sell anymore land—reluctantly sold the regions between Traverse de Sioux and the Mississippi River in exchange for a reservation and food annuities. Little Crow, the dynamic chief whose village lay on the western banks of the Mississippi River, was the first to sign.[23]

The federal government purchased the southern half of Minnesota for roughly six cents an acre. These 25,000,000 acres represented some of the most valuable agricultural lands on the continent. In a shocking move, the U.S. Senate took out the clause giving the Dakotas a reservation in the western portion of the territory, theoretically pushing them out onto the plains. In a compromise that the Indians surely did not understand—a negotiation sometimes even more deceitful and corrupt than the original treaty signing—the president allowed the Dakotas to occupy the designated reservation land for five years. Not unlike the Cherokees some twenty-five years earlier, the Dakota Sioux slowly gave up their villages along the Mississippi and lower Minnesota Rivers and moved west, often followed or even overtaken by white pioneers who rushed on to claim town-plots and farms. These Indians could only hope that the government would eventually establish a permanent reservation for them.

The greed that Minnesota politicians exhibited in taking land from Indians had yet to subside. Chippewas still held the northern half of the territory. In 1854 and 1855 they succumbed to treaty negotiations at La Pointe, Wisconsin, granting to the United States lands nearly equal in size to the lands that the Dakotas had relinquished in southern Minnesota. This time lumber interests rather than farmers lobbied for the cessions. The Chippewa lands held virgin pine in large quantities, and mills for processing it already existed in the territory.[24]

It may seem peculiar that Native peoples would give up most of what would become an entire state in a few short years. Government negotiators often used veiled threats with both the Dakota and Chippewa people. Perhaps 10 percent of both tribes by this time were also of mixed blood, functioning in both the Indian and capitalist worlds, and saw payoffs coming in the form of direct payments built into the treaties. Also, many of these Indians nearly starved to death during the winter and needed food annuities to survive. Some Native leaders, depending upon such goods from earlier treaties, were told that annuities would be cut off if they refused to sign. Although this treachery might be viewed as something other than ethnic cleansing, the negotiations certainly resulted in the removal of Indians.

While Dakota Indians struggled to maintain a small reservation in the West, surprisingly, some progress toward establishing a working reservation system finally appeared in Texas. Texas editors, congressmen, and even governors frequently charged that Plains Indian raiders murdered and raped citizens. Senator Edward Burleson was most vocal: Texans had been "butchered before their wives and children, and they inhumanely violated [raped]." But the United States built a chain of forts across Texas in 1849, extending from the Red River to the Rio Grande, and General George M. Brooke, sent to command the department, soon challenged Texan assertions regarding such raids. Brooke deemed the charges nothing more than propaganda; they "proceed from very interested motives, such as that additional troops may be called out, bringing money into the country."[25]

Other generals who followed Brooke continued to modify defensive strategy in Texas. When General Persiphor Smith took command in Texas in October 1851, he realized that the threat of large Indian attacks had long since vanished all along the Texas frontier. Small bands of about half a dozen Indians occasionally tried to enter the frontier communities on foot, steal a few horses, and ride west to safety. Smith's solution was novel: send the mounted troops a hundred miles to the rear and use infantry in the most advanced locations to control and lay ambushes at the few waterholes that existed across the high plains. With this new strategy Smith had brought minor Indian raiding—and ranger attacks on Indians—to an end by summer 1853.[26]

The federal government had committed over three thousand troops to Texas from a national army of just eleven thousand, which in turn provided the means for General Smith to carry out his strategy. It also benefited the Indian Office of the Interior Department, which could thereafter make a simple argument: peace in Texas would only be lasting when Indians were granted their own lands in the West as reservations. With a new Democratic administration in Washington, D.C., in 1853, yet another opportunity appeared. The new secretary of war, Jefferson Davis, was a southern Democrat, well aware of the trouble in Texas. Davis penned a long letter to Texas governor Hansborough P. Bell in September 1853, noting that "while the Indians have no territory of their own, they have virtually the right to roam where they will." They needed to be confined to a reservation where the army could watch them.[27] Davis's argument expanded upon the earlier views of Medill and Brown, who saw small reservations as a way to compensate Indians for lands increasingly taken for white settlement. The secretary believed that reservations could also be places of confinement where Indians could be watched by the army.

With raiding virtually contained, Governor Bell conceded the argument. He convinced the legislature to provided twelve leagues of land for two Indian reservations to be located on the upper Brazos River. Congress then appointed a new federal Indian superintendent for Texas, the likeable and energetic Robert S. Neighbors, who laid out the reserves, which consisted of a total of 17,000 acres each, that summer. Wacos, Wichitas, Delawares, Shawnees, and a few Tonkawas quickly moved onto the first reservation, located just west of Fort Belknap. Neighbors then hired John R. Baylor to bring in the southern Comanches (who had been mauled by Moore), who would occupy the second reservation, which had been staked-out farther up the Brazos River. Congress appropriated money for a large "civilization" program for each reserve.[28]

While these actions seemed humane on the surface, they led to an obvious conclusion that Southern Plains Indians hardly understood. The creation of the two Texas Indian reservations led to acceptance of the Texas argument—almost by default, the state thereafter argued that it owned the high plains, lands that had never been surveyed or conquered by Mexico, and lands that rightfully belonged to the nonreservation Comanches, Apaches, and Kiowas who still lived on them. No one asked the Indians for their approval.

With reservations being established along a line from Texas in the south, north into Indian Territory, and in Minnesota—where at least the promise of reserves existed—former commissioner Medill's policy seemed to be taking shape nicely. Yet many Southern Plains Indians had not acquiesced to the notion that they had to settle on a reserve, especially the Comanches and Kiowas and even some of their southern relatives, who refused to stay on the Brazos River Reserve. Other Indians, who had been forced to move on numerous occasions, found the new reservation policy not only confusing but immoral. The Winnebagos had agreed to move west of the Mississippi River and found themselves stuck in central Minnesota, between the Dakotas to the south and the Chippewas to the north, who were traditional enemies. The Winnebagos faced removal several more times in the future.[29]

Despite complaints, policy-makers pushed ahead, intent on confining Indians to what they perceived as permanent reservations. If the Indians ceded valuable lands during the process, so much the better. The treaty negotiators always seemed to have the same justification: Indians owned too much land, mostly hunting lands, more than they could use for agriculture. By 1850 the Indian Country created by Congress in 1834 was being threatened as some Americans cast their eyes on the valuable lands in the West. But the tribes held an advantage—at least politicians were not parroting the words of Andrew Jackson, who proclaimed that Indians had only a "possessory right" to their lands. Legally they owned Indian Country, and most would defend their title.

As to lands north of Texas, Washington officials hoped to create some sense of tribal boundaries in order to validate future treaty agreements. Superintendent David D. Mitchell received the task of doing this. He convinced Lakota Sioux, Northern Cheyennes, Arapahos, Crows, Mandans, Gros Ventres, Arikaras, and Assiniboins to join him at old Fort Laramie in fall 1851. Some 10,000 Indians showed up. With presents and promises of annual annuities of food, Mitchell produced a signed treaty that determined the future boundaries for these Indians. He also obtained pledges from them to allow the government to build roads and military posts within their respective territories.[30]

The boundaries created under the agreement had vague definitions, primarily because few reliable maps of the region existed. The Lakotas, being the largest group, received the largest slice of land, bordering the Missouri River in the east and north, the eastern edge of the Big Horn Mountains in the west (central Wyoming), and the Platte River in the south. Yet they frequently hunted south of the Platte River well into Kansas and into the Rocky Mountains. The Lakotas would have objected to the treaty if they had any knowledge of its boundaries. Making matters more confusing, Mitchell outlined boundaries for other nations that overlapped what he had given the Sioux. This necessitated including a clause that allowed various tribes to trespass on the lands of others. Finally, the treaty required Indians to "make restitution" for any depredations against wagon trains and their occupants even though most traffic had been undisturbed along the Oregon Trail. The superintendent even demanded that each tribe select a "Head Chief" who would be responsible for rectifying offenses.[31]

Seemingly successful at Fort Laramie, the government moved to establish the same good relations with the southern Indians in 1853. Here they picked the gruff, unsmiling mountain man Thomas Fitzpatrick to offer the Comanches, Kiowas, and Apaches a similar agreement. At old Fort Atkinson, located near present Dodge City, many Indians gathered in July to negotiate. The Indians received eighteen thousand dollars a year in annuities in exchange for allowing wagon train traffic along the Santa Fe Trail and giving the military the right to build depots and military posts along the route. Agent John Whitfield, who distributed the first food and clothing in July 1855, sensed that the newly created peace was fragile, because wagon trains used scarce firewood and scared the game. One accounting suggests that some 300,000 Americans and a staggering 1.5 million draft animals took to the Santa Fe Trail between 1841 and 1859.[32]

While immigrant parties and Indians along both the Oregon and Santa Fe Trails had generally gotten along, this suddenly changed on August 18, 1854, when a Mormon wagon train discovered that one of its oxen had been slaughtered and eaten by some hungry Brulé Sioux. When informed of this the commanding officer at Fort Laramie sent the Brulé chief Conquering Bear—supposedly the chief in charge of the camp—along with newly commissioned West Point lieutenant John Grattan to catch the culprit. Grattan's squad of twenty-nine men marched up to the camp, demanded the offending Indian, and then opened fire when Conquering Bear failed to convince him to surrender. Grattan had told bystanders that he "hoped to God they would have a fight," and he got one. The Sioux soon overwhelmed Grattan and his entire command. The "massacre," as the action was dubbed by the army, stunned the country.[33]

The army called upon Brevet Brigadier General William Harney to head up a campaign to "chastise" the offending Brulés. Harney, later nicknamed "Mad Bear" by the Sioux, was impetuous, racist, and at times brutal. After fielding a force of six hundred troops, he sought out a known peaceful Brulé camp on Blue Water Creek, a small tributary of the North Platte. Harney then pretended to parley with the leading chief, Little Thunder. But at his signal his men attacked the village on the morning of September 3, 1855, killing at least eighty-six Indians and wounding many more. Although the army praised the action, the new commissioner of Indian affairs, George Manypenny, openly declared that Harney had attacked "peaceful Indians, men, women and children," hardly the reasonable action of a humane nation.[34]

Harney continued to campaign against the Lakota Sioux, even invading the Dakotas, lands that supposedly had been given to these Indians in 1851. Back at Fort Laramie, Indian agent Thomas Twiss tried to reconstruct the peace that Grattan had so unfortunately broken and Harney had threatened to dismantle.[35] Twiss found that both the Lakota and Cheyenne-Arapaho Indians were stunned by the attack. Twiss's counseling, however, infuriated General Harney, who concluded that both commissioner Manypenny and Twiss were conspiring against him.[36]

In a fit of rage Harney ordered the post commander at Fort Laramie to arrest Twiss.[37] "I will not remove the Indian agency into the garrison,"

Twiss responded, "unless compelled to do so by the strong arm of military force."[38] The agent, dumbfounded by the order, refused to surrender. The officer in command also found the order problematic. The Twiss-Manypenny dispute with the army only widened as years passed. The Indian Office and the army had differing views of how to implement the policy of ethnic cleansing. The Indian Office wanted to create reservations slowly when the Indians were ready to settle upon them, convert them to farming, and open lands purchased from them for white settlement. The army saw the task differently, being convinced that brute force of the sort Harney had inflicted on the Brulés would bring peace and settlement to the plains more rapidly and at lower cost.

If the Blue Water Creek massacre had not been enough, the very next year similar conflict between the army and the Indian Office erupted on the southern plains. Two young Cheyennes had approached a mail coach along the Platte River road and asked for tobacco, but the driver panicked, fired a six-shooter, and raced into Fort Kearny. With tensions high, Secretary Davis ordered the elite First Cavalry under Colonel Edwin Sumner into the field to "chastise" the Cheyennes. Sumner found some of them along the Solomon River in June 1857. While the Indians sent out a chief to negotiate—who was apparently shot by the troopers—Sumner ordered a regimental charge, with sabers drawn.

The Indians' medicine men had assured the warriors that the bullets from the carbines would never pierce their shirts, but the sabers brought total confusion; the Indians fled from the field, with only a few dead. Sumner then took their camp, burning lodges and dried meat. He finally reached Bent's Fort, where the annuities for the Southern Cheyennes and Arapahos and Comanches, Kiowas, and Apaches were held. Sumner confiscated it all, distributing the food to his men and throwing much of the rest into the Arkansas River.[39] The army seemed opposed to any sort of agreement with Indians that preserved the peace and offered food for right-of-way and land.

The loss of annuities led to considerable suffering for the Indians in the winter of 1857–58. It also led to a separation of bands: those who wished peace and relied on annuities, frequently held council with agents, and even wanted a new treaty and those who remained defiant, who often harassed trail traffic. The Kiowas had even instituted a systematic program of harassment. They had established "regular stands on the road where they exact and enforce the payment of toll in the way of sugar, coffee, etc.," reported agent Whitfield. The country was "almost destitute of buffalo," and Cheyennes even invaded the Rocky Mountains and seized 2,000 head of sheep, which they promptly ate.[40]

After Colonel Sumner had departed for Utah to subdue the Mormons, who were in a state of rebellion, the army nearly abandoned the Santa Fe Trail, leaving only a few infantry at Fort Larned and Fort Wise. Indian agents once again took control of policy. One newcomer to the scene was William Bent, who knew the circumstances on the upper Arkansas better than anyone. He wrote to the superintendent of Indian affairs in 1857, using his own unique vernacular: "the Shyane [*sic*] Indians had a meeting, begging . . . to let you know as irlay [early] as possible . . . that they wish peas [peace] and a new treaty." Some Cheyennes and Arapahos especially had come to equate a "reservation" with annuities, all of which seemed to be a solution to the growing lack of game on the plains.[41] The Indian Office's implementation of the new policy, using a carrot and stick approach, seemed more than feasible.

Meanwhile Commissioner Manypenny settled various Indians who would be in the way of Anglo wagon traffic on new reservations in Kansas and Nebraska, which had recently received territorial status. Manypenny, a good man with honest intentions, recognized that the tribes of the lower Missouri Valley needed small reservations with firmly surveyed boundaries. He began with the Oto and Missouri tribes in March 1854, convincing them to accept a reservation along the Big Blue River of northern Kansas, "not less than ten miles wide by twenty five miles." Such small reservations led to confinement and, Manypenny hoped, agricultural progress, of the sort that came from raising stock and farming.[42]

Other negotiations then followed with the Omaha, Sac and Fox, Delaware, Shawnee, Kickapoo, Peoria, Wea, Iowa, Menominee, and Miami Indians, and several bands of Chippewas, all concluded by Manypenny in 1854–55. These agreements allowed for reservations ten to twenty miles in length and width. Manypenny even accommodated the increasingly resentful Winnebagos by finding land for them in southwestern Minnesota.[43]

But as Manypenny himself stated in his memoirs—with considerable pride—"all the lands of the Indians, except in the aggregate about one million three hundred thousand acres, reserved for their homes, were ceded to the government." Ethnic cleansing in the West thus differed from the implementation of the policy in the East: tribes faced massive reductions in land—or "diminishment"—while generally staying within their homelands. This, of course, was not true of those "border tribes," who had been forced into the region from places like Illinois, Wisconsin, and Michigan.

Almost all these agreements provided for the "allotment" of the reservations, often at the will of the president of the United States. Even lands mostly valuable for timber—such as the reserves given to the Menominees in Wisconsin and the Saginaw Chippewas in central Michigan—called for allotments, giving each family 160 acres of land with separate titles. While much of the land given to the Chippewa Indians in Michigan and Wisconsin was forested and not worth much agriculturally, most of these Indians had no reservations at all.[44] Manypenny gave them lands that had already been ceded to the federal government—in the case of the Saginaw Chippewas, six townships. This was one of the few occasions when a "civilization" policy superseded ethnic cleansing.

While some negotiations under the Medill-Brown plan produced positive results, this was not the case in Minnesota. Chief clerk Charles Mix, who replaced Manypenny as acting commissioner, invited Eastern Dakota tribal leaders to Washington, D.C., in 1858 for yet another council. The five-year period in which the president had allowed the Dakota Indians to remain on their reserve had expired. And settlers wanted all of the rich bottomlands of the upper Minnesota River, where the reservation was located. The commissioner told these Indians—to their utter dismay—that they owned nothing within the boundaries of Minnesota. Their shock clearly demonstrated that politicians had lied to them about the Senate changes to their 1851 treaty, which they had supposedly agreed to. Mix then offered them another treaty in which the Indians would relinquish claims to over a thousand square miles of land on the north side of the Minnesota River, leaving only a strip ten miles wide and a hundred miles long on the south side for a reservation. These lands were supposedly to house 6,000 Indians.[45]

The Dakota chiefs had no choice but to accept the reduction in land. Upon arriving home, however, they found that tensions were building on the smaller reserve as settlers invaded the lands just north of them, taking over old village sites and hunting grounds. Worse, Indian traders bribed agents in order to establish houses that gave out credit to Indians on the assumption that annuity money would be paid directly to them for debt. Indian agents also caused considerable excitement when they introduced a "civilization" program that encouraged Indians to cut their hair, don pantaloons, and become farmers. Several hundred did so and then received preferential treatment from government agents and farmers who handed out food annuities.

Missionaries added to the problem by preaching against Indian dances and trying to induce Indian children to attend church and school. Those Indians who wished to sustain their traditional ways soon discovered that the agent denied them the very annuities that they had come to depend upon in order to feed their families.[46]

Almost simultaneously trouble came to the Texas reservations, established with such fanfare in 1854. The conflict seemed increasingly confusing, as groups of mostly renegades—some Americans, some Mexicans, and some mixed bloods—turned to thievery to make a living.[47] The army's Department of Texas, falling under the command of sixty-seven-year-old General David Twiggs, became less vigorous in trying to halt the growing violence. At one point mostly white Texans killed hundreds of Mexican carters in the so-called Cart War, stealing their cargoes. Twiggs considered this growing violence to be a state problem for the police not the army; but he also increasingly lacked the troops to stop it, given the reallocation of troops to Utah.[48]

At this point Texas newspapers returned to the fray, offering reports that increasingly blamed Indians from the two Brazos Valley reservations for the loss of stock from ranches all along the western frontier.[49] Soon the growing hysteria led to the organization of volunteer Texas Ranger units, most of which were organized in the saloons of the frontier towns of northwest Texas. The leading light in this mobilization was John R. Baylor, who had been fired as Indian agent for the Comanches after cattle assigned to the reserve mysteriously ended up on his ranch. Baylor soon began planning an assault on the reservation, which had a good source of water for ranching, being located on the Brazos River. Baylor invited John Ford, the most respected ranger captain in Texas, to join his "Weatherford Rangers." Some of Baylor's men even suggested that the group might dress as "Indians" and attack a few ranches, starting a war that would drive the Indians out.[50]

Ford had been selected by Governor Harden Runnels to investigate the depredations. To Baylor's dismay, however, Ford became utterly convinced of the innocence of the reservation Indians, concluding that renegades were mostly at fault.[51] Despite the setback, Baylor continued to stir up trouble by reporting that hundreds of Texans had been killed in his new newspaper, called the *Whiteman*. One manifesto, republished in many leading Texas newspapers, proclaimed: "We regard the killing of Indians of whatever tribe to be morally right and that we will resist to the last extremity the infliction of any legal punishment on the perpetrators."[52] Over the coming winter, 1858–59, Baylor's forces grew, as he attracted many of the Kansas ruffians who had been expelled by the army from that locale some years before. Baylor's ranger force finally rode to the south edge of the Brazos River Agency and began pillaging the small Indian communities that had been built there. Just before they arrived, a handful of army troops under Captain Joseph Plummer rounded up the Indians, took them to the central agency grounds, and created a defensive position. Baylor led the final assault into the agency compound on May 23.[53]

As the ranger force of over three hundred men neared the buildings that housed the Indians and the small regular army force, it captured an Indian man and a woman, both about eighty years old. They killed the woman and then tied a rope around the man's neck and yanked him up in the air, strangling him. This infuriated about sixty Indians, who, along with a few army troopers, ferociously attacked the rangers. One of the officers was young West Point graduate Lieutenant William E. Burnet, the son of the first president of Texas, David Burnet. To Captain Plummer's astonishment, the rangers broke, many of them unnerved by the blood-curdling yells of the Indians. As Burnet later wrote to his obviously proud father: "There was never a more cowardly thing done, by any set of men."[54]

As Baylor's motley force fled, the Indian Office determined to remove the reservation Indians to Indian Territory, where land had been leased from the Choctaw and Chickasaw tribes. The exodus began in late July: nearly 1,500 Indians from both reservations packed what they could and departed for Oklahoma. The army provided an escort, but Baylor's men could be seen along the route, waiting for an opportunity to attack. Superintendent Neighbors, who had fought for the reservations, helped build them, and tried to protect the Indians, led the exodus. He wrote his wife: "if you want to hear a full description of our Exodus . . . read the Bible where the children of Israel crossed the Red Sea."[55] After Neighbors returned to Texas, a Baylor disciple shot him in the back with a shotgun.

Texans had nearly accomplished the ethnic cleansing of their state. And the government's removal of the reservations gave Texans an even stronger claim on other lands in the Panhandle. But Comanches and Kiowas still claimed this land. These Indians continued to raid into Mexico and occasionally attack Texas, assaults that would increase after the Civil War. Unfortunately for these increasingly cornered Plains Indians, a severe drought struck the Great Plains in 1858 and lasted into the Civil War. And more epidemics followed, depleting populations. While Texans continued to complain about Indian raids, most frequently the rustlers had white skin.[56]

The new reservation policy, introduced into the West with such fanfare in 1849, became more and more a system used to oppress Indians, just fifteen years after Congress had granted Indians the entire Great Plains as Indian Country. Nevertheless, both congressional and Indian Office officials never considered a policy of extermination—government policy-makers generally abhorred such language, which usually emanated from men such as Lamar and Baylor, whom many Texans deplored for their racist and inhumane views. Moreover, some Plains tribes found themselves in an increasingly difficult situation and welcomed negotiations that might lead to annuities. As agent Twiss reported, the buffalo were disappearing, being completely gone from the Upper Platte River basin and the Arkansas Valley.[57] Starvation loomed in many Plains Indian camps. The government's solution—ethnic cleansing through "diminishment"—meant pushing these people onto ever shrinking pieces of lands called reservations. While some would go willingly, others would fight to remain free on the plains.

A "West" to which Indians could be removed no longer existed, so they would have to be confined on their own lands. But other questions remained. Was it possible, for example, to avoid the rancor brought on by Jackson's removal policies? And what of the actions of Harney and Sumner, officers who despised what the Indian Office was trying to accomplish? Some officials obviously believed that it was much easier, and less expensive, to wait out the demise of the Plains Indian economy—based on the buffalo herds—rather than carry fire and sword to their villages. Fighting Indians and destroying villages where women and children lived tested the moral restraints that many American citizens still believed were necessary in dealing with Indians. Many military officers took a dim view of such restraint.

The policy of patience did have its problems, however. Allowing whites to settle next to Indian reservations in Texas, Kansas, Nebraska, and Minnesota produced tensions. Often the sense of "entitlement" of white settlers loomed so large that trouble seemed inevitable. But violence mostly had been avoided, at least before the Civil War. Indeed the army remained small, whereas the Indian Office grew in size throughout the 1850s, hiring large numbers of doctors, farmers, and blacksmiths to work on reservations, to mend tools, open lands to crops, and look after the welfare of Indians. The question apparent to many officials in the 1850s seemed to be not whether a somewhat benevolent policy of ethnic cleansing and the creation of reservations would work but whether the American people would sustain the Indian Office in implementing the policy and hold the likes of Harney, Baylor, and Sumner in check.

Along the western trails, Indian leaders debated the new policies as well and also considered the patience of their young men. While small numbers of Indian leaders talked of joining reservations, others saw their people as conquering nations, not people bound for a quiet reservation life. Entering such reserves and settling down to a life of farming seemed abominable to them. It would take considerable time, the utter depletion of the buffalo herds, and many negotiations by agents and commissioners to convince such Indians to give up the chase.

Yet another problem arose at the far ends of those trails, along the newly opened Pacific Slope. Government officials in both the army and the Indian Office soon discovered that California represented a new challenge that could lead to the "extermination" of Indians or "genocide," a repulsive conclusion that almost all civilian officials and most army officers thought immoral. The rush into California had been conducted by miners who had an ultimate sense of entitlement. Through a "settler sovereignty" mentality, they believed that they and their comrades could claim land anywhere, open mines, and kill or run off Native occupants. This new situation soon tested the very tenets of the new reservation policy, which was designed to protect Indians from whites. Miners waited for no authority to make their own courts and laws and establish their own boundaries on lands that Indians still lived on and claimed.

10

THE STEALING OF A GOLDEN LAND

Ethnic Cleansing in California

Wagon trains with American settlers reached the Willamette River of Oregon in 1841, a beautiful stream that flowed northward just east of the coastal mountains into the Columbia River.[1] Then workers discovered gold in the California mountains in 1848, producing a mad rush west. The wagon trains, and increasingly single men on horseback, thereafter mostly broke to the south after reaching Salt Lake and passed over the Sierra Nevada to reach the new "El Dorado" in California. Western Argonauts, as the miners were often called, constituted a mixed lot, but most gold seekers were men. Some 50,000 Americans mounted the trail in 1849 alone. Others from the Pacific rim, Hawaii, and Mexico, in particular Sonora, came by water and land, boosting the population to 250,000 non-Indians within two years. While the rush into the Pacific Slope may have originated as a sweeping quest for gold, it quickly led to a massive land grab of an Indian domain.

California possessed incredible resources, majestic mountains with rushing rivers, and two inland valleys between those mountains—the Sacramento and San Joaquin. The rivers dominated the interior, creating an eight-hundred-mile central valley that ran nearly from Oregon in the north to the Mexican border. While Spaniards had settled coastal bays and constructed a few inland cattle ranches, mostly north of San Diego, the regions above Sonora and most of the central valley and mountains east of it remained in Native hands even into the latter 1840s, when California became part of the United States. While resources remained scarce along the high peaks of the Sierras, the intermediate rivers, rushing westward into the central valley and fed by winter snows, had game and plenty of foods to gather, especially acorns, and the streams were often packed with salmon, seemingly making California a natural paradise.

Anthropologist Sherburne Cook estimated that California alone held 150,000 Indians in 1845—some former mission people, often working as stock herders, and the majority fishers, hunters, and gatherers. Over the next ten years Cook suspected that those numbers fell rapidly to 100,000 in 1850 and then to 50,000 in 1855. Census figures suggest only 30,000 Native survivors in all of California by 1860. If we believe Cook's numbers, 50,000 Indians perished between 1845 and 1850, another 50,000 between 1850 and 1855, and 20,000 in the five-year period after 1855. Yet Cook himself admitted that these numbers came from "personal estimates, based upon outright interpolation."[2] He obviously thought in terms of an orderly progression of population loss, roughly 10 percent a year.

Historians have not seriously questioned Cook's numbers to date. Part of the reason is that early California newspapers often suggested that Native populations ran in the hundreds of thousands. Two new Indian agents, who had been in California less than a month, sent such figures to the commissioner of Indian affairs in Washington. Another agent, who had been there longer, believed that only 80,000 (slightly less than Cook's estimate) were within the state's boundaries in 1852. The agents initially thought that the largest populations existed in the "mining district" along the tributaries of the San Joaquin River.[3] Much like Cook, they all relied heavily on exaggerated newspaper accounts rather than on actual observations.

In hindsight Cook's numbers—and even those of agents, who soon revised their figures downward—lack supportable evidence. New sources, never considered by Cook or by historians, strongly suggest that population figures for California Indians were significantly lower at the time of the inflow of the gold rush population. That evidence also demonstrates that disease took many more Indians in the late 1840s than Cook's "interpolations" suggest. Native bands had been reduced to mere remnants of their former selves, and Americans often exploited this residue for labor.[4] While conflict occurred, it never reached the point that mass murder or genocide can be used as an explanation for the large population loss in California.

Although Cook's numbers are problematic, he correctly blamed disease for Native decline, noting that venereal disease was rampant among

Indians. But this particular virus infected Indians in California well before Americans arrived, which raises the question of why it suddenly became such a killer after 1845. Cook also attributed Native population decline to "malaria," which he said "was widespread." Cholera, measles, and small-pox epidemics occurred too. The only factor that Cooke substantially discounted was murder or genocide. He estimated that between 1845 and 1860 only 4,000 Indians died from conflict, roughly 3 percent of the base population, and even this number is unsupported by reliable evidence.[5]

Cook's population estimates are crucial to recent scholarship asserting that invading Americans committed genocide against Native populations in California. One historian has argued that murder accounted for 90 percent of Yuki Indian deaths—up to 20,000 Indians just in Round Valley, an isolated region north of Sonoma.[6] Other historians have assumed much the same, based primarily upon vague reports. Some such reports unfortunately were true, but the killings—mostly committed by miners— were usually in isolated regions, where confirmation is difficult. With the exception of about a dozen incidents, the conflict seldom resulted in more than a handful of deaths. Nevertheless, over the fifteen-year period of 1845 to 1860, Native populations declined rapidly. The question becomes which of the two arguments accounts for it: genocide or disease?

To answer this complex question requires an objective assessment of Native populations in early California and, perhaps just as important, an analysis of what the federal government did to prevent the destruction of Indians and to what degree that government protected them. While Indi-ans in California today have some thirty-four federally protected reserva-tions and another twenty-six "rancherias," these are generally very small in terms of acreage. Most of the rancherias are less than a hundred acres in size. Fully 98 percent of the land in California is controlled by non-Natives today.[7] Population decline and loss of Native lands unquestionably occurred on a large scale.

The argument for malaria first broached by Cook has substantial merit. In February 1829 the brigantine *Owhyhee,* which had sailed from Chile, landed at Fort Vancouver along the Columbia River. While the ship was in the South the sailors contracted malaria, which they carried into Oregon. By late spring the disease had overwhelmed the valley. Over the following four years fully 90 percent of the 20,000 Indians in the region died. David Douglas, a botanist, witnessed the carnage, noting that Indian bodies could be seen floating along rivers, abandoned, all having perished from "fever and ague."[8] Fur traders apparently carried the "scourge" southward into California, where it struck with a vengeance in 1833, and malaria returned in the following years. Malaria was transmitted by the *Anopheles* mosquito, which existed in massive swarms both along the coast and in California's central valley. California Indians suffered terribly.[9] After the Americans arrived in numbers in 1846, reports of measles, mumps, cholera, smallpox, and likely typhoid fever, which acted much like malaria in its early stages, were common throughout California.[10] Most California Indians simply lacked immunity to any of these viruses.

American military officers witnessed the impact of the malaria as early as 1846. It attacked John C. Frémont's men, then involved in the famous "Bear Flag Revolt," near John Sutter's Fort on the American River. A party of Walla Walla Indian allies contracted both malaria and measles and carried them north, no doubt infecting other Indians along the way.[11] These volunteers, committed to driving Mexican sympathizers from the region, soon occupied San Diego, Los Angeles, Santa Barbara, and Sacramento. The "sickly season" hit in late May and lasted well into the fall. On June 14, 1847, thirty-nine soldiers at Los Angeles—virtually the entire garrison—were "fever cases." Two men had died by July, and the commanding officer thought of abandoning the post.[12] The forces at Sacramento suffered even worse, being reduced to just three standing soldiers by September 1847—they evacuated the city. Monterey fared better, being on the coast, but by August the epidemic had reduced the garrison substantially. The assistant surgeon struggled to nurse the "severe cases of low fever" that had incapacitated many troops.[13]

Serious problems with "fever and ague" continued in California for the next three years, abating only in 1852. But the question remains: to what degree did the disease affect Indian populations? If the scenario that occurred in Oregon was repeated in California, it is possible that fully 80 to 90 percent of the Native population might have perished in the four to five years after 1845, as they did in Oregon. Fortunately, combined reports of American army officers and Office of Indian Affairs officials provide a nearly complete picture of those populations.[14]

General Persiphor S. Smith joined with military governor Bennet Riley to administer the region until California became a state in 1851. After the war with Mexico ended in 1848, Smith recognized that the main concern was to control Indians. He wanted to know the strength and location of Native populations to determine where to assign his limited numbers of troops. Smith wrote to Washington requesting especially topographical engineers who could survey the entire region. Captain W. H. Warner, Lieutenant Robert Williamson, and Lieutenant George Horatio Derby, all trained at West Point, were assigned to Smith.[15] These officers joined many others, such as Captains Newton Lyon, W. W. Wessells, and E. D. Keyes, all of whom led patrols into California's interior, offering an unusually complete assessment of early Native populations and locations. They left journal accounts, often fifty to sixty pages long. These were all produced between 1848 and 1851 and offer some of the best sources available for studying Native populations.

Agents of the Office of Indian Affairs joined these patrols or asked for army escorts—both Wessells and Keyes provided protection for Indian agents as they mounted expeditions into the interior. The first federal Indian agent, Adam Johnson, reached California in 1850 and soon gathered information for reports sent east. Redick McKee, George Barbour, and O. M. Wozencraft came next, as political appointees of President Millard Fillmore. While they had never been in California before, these "commissioners" negotiated eighteen treaties with California Indians in 1851, which provided reservations. They generally conducted negotiations without competent interpreters, but a serious examination of the journals that they kept shows that the commissioners saw representatives of 80 to 90 percent of California Indians and counted them.[16]

The journals and reports of these military and civil officers overwhelmingly demonstrate that malaria, in combination with dehydration, proved fatal and caused a massive collapse of Native populations, much as it had in Oregon. By June 1849—literally a few months before the massive gold rush that fall—Derby found malaria so prevalent along the San Joaquin River and its tributaries that even the handful of white settlers were heavily infected, and some were dying from it. The mosquito swarms were "so excessively thick and vicious," Derby wrote, that no one could sleep at night. "The whole region of this country upon these rivers," the lieutenant reported in late summer, "is now becoming unhealthy, fever and ague being the prevalent disease, from which many die."[17] In summer 1849 those "many" were clearly Indians, because the large influx of miners came that fall.

The situation farther north seemed hardly any different. At Sutter's Hock Farm and along the Feather and Yuba Rivers malaria flourished even in the late fall—as had been the case since 1846, when it even incapacitated Sutter himself. In the small Indian villages that Derby visited in October and November the Indians "howled" all night for their dead: "they were suffering much with the prevalent fever," he wrote, as were the American occupants of Sutter's farmhouse.[18] In 1850 agent Adam Johnston reported that of the "numerous tribes" once within two hundred miles of San Francisco "scarcely an individual is left." After reaching the upper Yuba and Feather Rivers, where Derby had been the year before, he reported that the "red man [is] fast fading away . . . many have died of disease." In an interview with an "Old Indian" survivor, the man lamented that his people "have all passed away. They have died like the grass . . . [and] I am all that is left of my people."[19]

While some Indians had fled to the mountains, the exodus did not protect them from malaria. Major Wessells found it raging in epidemic proportion in northwestern California in 1851. Hordes of mosquitoes greeted his survey party as it came down the Eel River, reaching Humboldt Bay. The Indians nearby were "loathsome from disease."[20] Commissioner Redick McKee, whom Wessells was protecting, found the twelve bands of Indians both above and below the junction of the Klamath and Trinity Rivers—rugged mountainous country—all suffering in early October 1851. "Owing to the prevalence of sickness among many of the bands," he had to go to them. They were so weak that leaders could not travel "from the sickness."[21]

Once army troops entered the mountains, building posts and patrolling, they suffered while in the high ranges of both the coastal mountains and the Sierra Nevada. Lieutenant George Stoneman's patrol of two dozen men all collapsed from fever just west of Lake Tahoe in 1851. Lieutenant Henry Judah's command suffered from "fevers" while at Fort Jones on the Scott River. Indians ambushed and killed Captain Warner in the mountains east of Goose Lake—wild and mountainous country—because most of Warner's escort was left back in a mountain camp, down with fever. When reporting on the health of the troops in California in 1850, Surgeon R. O. P. Murray noted: "I do not recollect a single instance of a person visiting this region during the sickly season who did not have an attack of fever." He wrote the note from army headquarters at Benicia then added that "fevers are as common high up the Sacramento as they are here."[22] While troops got medical attention—citrus fluids and quinine—Indians did not, at least before 1851.

Native populations north of Los Angeles suffered catastrophic collapse between 1845 and 1851, which only differs from Cook's "interpolations" in that the collapse did not follow a simple 10 to 12 percent loss each year but came earlier than he suspected.[23] If the circumstances in California in any way mimicked those of Oregon twenty years before, it seems plausible that the influx of people (starting in 1846 with the outbreak of the Mexican War and reaching fifty thousand to a hundred thousand by 1849–50) brought in the malaria virus with nearly every boat that landed in California. Most ships had stops in Mexican and Central American ports, which commonly suffered from malaria and cholera.[24]

Military officers were far more inclined to report the sickness of their troops than that of Indians and also noted the surgeons' efforts to treat their men with quinine, but agent McKee understood that the disease debilitated Indians to the point where they could not exert the energy necessary to survive. While in the Eel River valley in September 1851, he noted that the Yuki Indians were in a "destitute condition," facing starvation, and literally unable to come down to his camp to negotiate a treaty. Very little food was available in the mountains, even though they had fewer mosquitoes. McKee sent runners to inform the Yukis that he was leaving a supply of hard bread and beef for them, to help stave off hunger.[25]

A few Indians obviously fled to the mountains, hoping to avoid being victims of disease, but the Native economy of California was tied to the lower river valleys and their salmon runs. The Indians had to take salmon or starve. While other gathered foods were also important, many of the mountainous areas were "acornless," lacking the oak trees that provided the most important gathered protein for the Native diet.[26] Moreover, emigrants who came through those upper mountain passes, via the Truckee Route or Lassen's Route to the north of it, nearly starved to death while in the Sierra Nevada. Few if any game animals were available there. Even their cattle died for lack of forage. The army organized several major rescue parties to save emigrant lives in 1849, 1850, and again in 1851, commandeering hundreds of wagons and mules to meet trains in the mountain passes with food.[27] Indians simply could not survive for long in the higher mountain ranges.

The malarial outbursts subsided about 1851 but reappeared in later years. Yet the disease thereafter never reached the magnitude of the infections that existed between 1845 and 1851. Settlers and Indians alike developed some immunities, but medicine also became available to fight the scourge. By the early 1850s the army surgeon at San Francisco normally ordered massive amounts of "Sulph Quinin" (quinine sulfate). He estimated that each post in California needed 88 grams of quinine per year. It was mixed with iron and wine and then given in three doses a day to cure soldiers.[28] The drugs helped reduce the impact of fevers and fought dehydration caused by dysentery, another common ailment associated with fevers. While hundreds of soldiers were incapacitated by malaria in 1847–51, and many died, by summer 1852 the report of the chief surgeon in California cited just four cases of malaria, eight cases of dysentery, and five cases of consumption throughout the entire command.[29]

By 1852, the army had thirteen doctors on staff in California prescribing quinine, and the Office of Indian Affairs also hired doctors to treat Indians. Agent Johnston traveled over 1,500 miles in 1851, beginning a vaccination program among Indians to prevent smallpox. Malaria remained a nagging problem, but it had subsided considerably in comparison to what Derby had observed just two years before. Indeed Johnston believed that smallpox was at that time the "most dangerous" disease infecting the various Native bands that he visited.[30] Seeking assistance, Johnston hired a local physician from Stockton, Dr. W. M. Ryer, to cover the region south of San Francisco east into the mountains, vaccinating Indians wherever he found them. In a year Ryer administered serum to over seven thousand Indians, living from the Stanislaus River south to the Mexican border. He claimed to have missed only a "a few stragglers."[31]

Documenting the existence of diseases, and even noting Derby's, McKee's, and Johnston's descriptions of their impact in specific villages, says little about the demographic impact of epidemics: the numbers who died and who survived. California nearly equals Texas in size. Fortunately for historians, both military officers and Indian agents alike were forced to deal with many specific trouble spots that offer an even better sense of the Native demographic collapse.

The upheaval following secularization of the missions in 1834 set many Indians adrift. Some of them went into the interior, where they communed with bands who raided ranches for stock, which they ate. During February and March 1847 dozens of Native attacks on towns and ranches were reported in and around Santa Clara, Los Angeles, San Juan Bautista, Sacramento, San Jose, and Sonoma.[32] American officials tried to negotiate with various tribes, selecting John Sutter and Mariano Guadalupe Vallejo as temporary Indian subagents. Sutter worked with some success to pacify the tribes in what would become the northern mining district, east of the San Joaquin River, while Vallejo tried to ameliorate conditions north of Sonora, a second trouble spot.[33] Remarkably, the raids declined appreciably four months later. Military officers attributed the change to the impending "sickly season." The commanding officer at Los Angeles, Colonel J. D. Stevenson, confidently concluded that Native perpetrators of future thefts could easily be tried by "military commissions," then in use in Mexico to try civilians. He believed that Indians from the Tulare Lakes region (the southern portion of the central valley) lacked the means with which to mount the raids.[34]

One significant trouble spot remained: the region north of Sonoma. These lands extended into the Clear Lake region and beyond into Round Valley. Major James Hardie negotiated a treaty with the bands north of Sonoma in 1848. Some early residents of Sonoma suggested that Native populations reached 10,000 north of them. These were gross exaggerations, as later evidence demonstrates, but such figures often found their way into newspaper reports. Once on the ground near Clear Lake Hardie found just twelve bands of Pomo Indians remaining, with whom he parleyed. Two had an average population of only fifty people, which seemed to be the norm for the others as well. Hardie also reported the existence of "scourges" that had obviously reduced their numbers. The major thought that the villages north of Sonoma—which included parts of the upper Russian River and the headwaters of the Eel River valley—contained just 2,000 Indians, literally one-fifth the number that observers in Sonoma had estimated.[35]

Hardie's treaty lasted roughly two years, and then more trouble broke out. Some warriors from the Clear Lake and Russian River tribes had attacked wagon trains coming south from Oregon and had killed two Americans named Stone and Kelsey. Kelsey's ranch was just west of Clear Lake. General Persiphor Smith ordered Captain Lyon into the field to "chastise" these people. Lyon sent his dragoons northward around the west side of the lake, while he marched infantry overland on the eastern shore. He surrounded the Clear Lake Indians, but they escaped to an island stronghold on the north end of the lake. Here Lyon assaulted the village by boat, killing many warriors. The captain jubilantly reported that they numbered "not less than sixty." Even so, in his journal of the assault, Lyon noted that just fifty Indians attacked his men with bows and arrows, hardly a significant force. Thereafter Lyon moved over the mountains to the Russian River, to attack the "Yohaiyah" (a Yokaia Pomo village), "their position being entirely surrounded." The assault led to "a perfect slaughter pen," with nearly a hundred Indians being killed.[36]

Only a few Pomo Indians managed to escape into the mountains. Lyon supposedly killed over 150 to 200 Indians, probably including many women and children. It was the worst slaughter of Indians in a single campaign ever recorded in California, supposedly justified by the attacks on two ranchers by these Indians. Yet the expedition demonstrates the obvious: very few Indians were left in the Clear Lake and Upper Russian River valley—a handful of villages with perhaps a thousand to fifteen hundred people. The small bands that Major Hardie had observed just two years before had likely joined together, given their diminishment from disease. They could not easily survive as a gathering band unit with so few people. But even then they could not defend their town against seventy-five American troops.

After subduing the Pomo people, the Indian commissioner Redick McKee moved north from Sonoma to negotiate treaties. Major Wessells joined him with a command of troops. They spent much of the summer and fall in the region, examining the Russian, Eel, Trinity, Klamath, Salmon, and Scott River valleys, intent on getting an accurate picture of the region. Wessells found just "700 souls" around Clear Lake, Pomo Indians who had survived Lyon's assault. The official journal of the military expedition also noted that "they have been generally represented by the whites as exceeding 1,500 and even 2,000" or even 10,000 some three years earlier. In the valley of the Russian River the captain reported just 200 Indians, also Pomos.[37]

The Wessells-McKee party then proceeded into the Eel River or Round Valley, a rugged mountainous region that extended from Clear Lake in the south to Humboldt Bay, roughly one hundred and fifty miles. Here they first met with the Yuki Indians. After spending five days surveying the upper river and the mountains surrounding it, Wessells reported just "5 tribes," with a mere "400 souls." Moving over to the South fork of the Eel River, he found another "500 people," probably Pomos. Yuki populations in 1851 might have been larger than 400, as at least one historian claims. But when the government established Nome Cult farm for them in the center of Round Valley in 1855, the numbers of Yukis attached to it ranged between 200 and 300. Including the much larger numbers of Pomo Indians, who also inhabited parts of the valley, populations reached several thousand. When Indian superintendent Thomas Henley visited the region in 1857, he estimated that 2,000 Indians lived in the valley. His count included the lands from just north of Clear Lake to Humboldt Bay.[38]

The Wessells-McKee party moved northward, giving little attention to the regions surrounding Mendocino Bay. Later efforts by the Indian Office to organize these Pomo coastal Indians on the Mendocino Indian Reservation in 1855 revealed much larger populations than in the valley, some 3,000. The coast held a bounty of food resources, especially shellfish. Indian Office inspector J. Ross Browne, who visited the area in 1857, hardly mentioned the Yukis at Nome Cult farm in Round Valley—he gave their numbers as "several hundred Indians"—but he did marvel at the success on the Mendocino Reservation on the coast, where wheat farms and houses for Indian occupants were being constructed.[39]

Most of the lands north of Round Valley were rugged, so Native habitation in the 1850s was grounded in the river valleys, which had a bounty of salmon. Actual census data reported by a longtime trader in 1851 reveal sixteen small Yurok towns with 1,062 people along the Trinity River. McKee, who reported 1,400, believed that they consisted of twelve bands, half above the junction with the Trinity River and half below. They were all deathly sick.[40] Even so, Wessells was impressed with their engineering, especially those living at "the bottom of an immense chasm" formed by the junction of the Klamath and Trinity Rivers. These Yurok people built substantial plank houses and log dams used to trap salmon. Wessells offered a demographic figure more in line with the estimate of the trader: these Yuroks numbered "only a thousand souls."[41]

As Wessells and McKee moved even farther north along the Trinity and Klamath Rivers and into the mountains near the Oregon border, they found more Indians. Some villages existed on the upper Klamath, with small populations. McKee treated with four bands along the Salmon River, numbering just 250 people in all. Miners had moved into the lower Scott's River area, forcing many of the Indians farther up the river. The miners reported to Wessells that a few Indians stayed "in the mountains" and remained "hostile." After spending several weeks in the Salmon, Scott, and Klamath valleys—virtually the entire region from the coast to the Sacramento Valley—McKee concluded that the occupants of these lands, mostly Shasta Indians, numbered 4,000 in all. In an 1856 survey completed for Superintendent Henley, the entire Native population between the Humboldt coast and the Sierras, north of Round Valley, reached just 5,000 Indians.[42]

The small number of people in these towns was ominous, typical of communities that had suffered from what Hardie called "the scourge."

And the mountains north of Sonora were more isolated than the mining district, which John C. Frémont believed to have the largest Native populations.[43] Here Derby found just one Native "rancheria" with a mere "forty or fifty" people on the entire upper Mokulumne River in 1849. Derby also found that some towns had been abandoned, including one "built of boughs of trees, long since withered." While many more Indians lived to the south, in the lower San Joaquin River watershed, even these were small populations. The several villages on the east side of Taché and Ton Taché Lakes (both since drained) totaled just 800 people. Derby found what was likely the largest rancheria in the region, well back in the mountains. It housed just seventy Yokuts or Yosemite warriors. In all Lieutenant Derby reasoned in 1849 that the entire eastern watershed of the Sierra Nevada from Sutter's Fort south to the Kern River contained just "4,000 Indians."[44]

Such a figure seems astonishingly low, given the numbers reported by both Wozencraft and Johnston two years later. But the evidence demonstrates that Derby was right, and the Indian agents, who had not visited the region when they gave their estimates, were terribly wrong, as they soon discovered. Captain E. D. Keyes, who provided an escort for Barbour and Wozencraft, found 200 Miwok Indians on the upper Tuolumne River in 1851 as well as 600 more on King's River, most being pushed south by miners. A few had "mild cases of fever and ague," but most were healthy. Some 170 Indians, likely Miwoks, came in to treat with Keyes's party on the Fresno River. In May a major treaty was signed with some eight tribes, consisting of 1,240 Indians, according to Keyes. The largest group encountered by Keyes was on the Tule River—where Derby had reported a number of villages—some 1,660 Indians in what Keyes thought were four "tribes," consisting of many bands. Finally, Keyes counted 597 Indians in twelve bands along the Kern River, totaling just over 4,000 people in all.[45]

Even agents Barbour and Wozencraft came to recognize the folly of their earlier estimates. When they spent the summer of 1851 negotiating with all the Indians from the mining district—between the American and Kern Rivers—they counted exactly 4,120 Indians, broken down into twelve tribes, almost identical to the numbers reported by Derby and Keyes. Barbour then turned south into the Tejon Pass region just northeast of Los Angeles. Here he found and signed treaties with 1,200 to 1,500 more Indians, some from the vicinity of Los Angeles. His explanation to Washington for the small numbers strongly reinforced what earlier observers had noted. "The ravages of disease, intentionally spread among them by the Spaniards . . . have in some instances . . . almost annihilated [them]." He too met an old Indian man who was "the last of his tribe."[46]

Derby's initial trip into the mining district was followed by yet another expedition in late fall 1849 into the regions north of the American River—the Feather, Bear, and Yubo Rivers as well as lower Butte Creek, in the "Butte" country of northeastern California. His observations often reflected the bias of most Americans. He found "100 wretched Indians, playfully termed Christian" on the lower Feather River. Above them on John Sutter's Hock Farm were 300 more, similarly described. Two rancherias on Butte Creek had perhaps 300 Indians. To the east of them, in "Lawson's Route" (a misspelling of "Lassen"), he found another three rancherias with perhaps 500 Indians. All of these, he contended, numbered "under one thousand Indians." Derby learned of just "two or three thousand" in the mountains to the east, making a total for the eastern upper Sacramento watershed of fewer than 4,000 Indians.[47]

Over the following years, much as in the southern mining district, Indian agents followed Derby's tracks. Agent Johnston counted just seven tribes, or roughly a thousand Indians, on the Bear River and north of it in 1850. The next year Wozencraft spent over a month concluding treaties with those Indians as well as with various tribes on the Yuba, Feather, Butte, and Sacramento Rivers. He estimated their population at just 3,900 in all. Finally, in 1852 McKee did a survey of Indian populations in Sierra, Placer, and Nevada Counties—virtually the entire region—and found just 3,220. Disease in the region, in particular smallpox, likely accounts for the decline—Dr. Ryer had not penetrated that area.[48]

This left only the lands north of Sacramento relatively unknown to either the Indian Office or the War Department. General Smith assigned Captain Lyon the job of surveying this region in 1850, after he returned from his slaughter of the Pomo Indians near Clear Lake. Lyon hoped to inflict a similar "chastisement" upon the Indians who had killed Lieutenant Warner. Lyon's "Pitt River Expedition" moved up the Sacramento River in June 1850, found only a few isolated Indians, and then scoured the lands about Goose Lake and Clear Lake (both nearly on the Oregon border). His report indicates that he found no Indian villages between Redding and Goose Lake—as he put it, "*no signs* of probable Indian presence within a long time, & apparently in the last five years, could be discovered."

Lieutenant Williamson, collecting evidence from both Warner's notes and Lyon's expedition, concluded the next year that the only Indians in the region were Modocs, found well north of Goose Lake in Oregon.[49] Wozencraft did negotiate a treaty with a handful of Indians from the west side of the Sacramento River at Redding, but he found their numbers to be so small that he never even reported them.[50]

From the work of the army and Indian Office surveys it is possible to calculate an accurate assessment of Native populations in California by summer 1851, a year and a half after the gold rush. Some 4,000 Indians survived along and south of the San Joaquin River and its tributaries, while 1,200–1,500 Indians occupied the southern lakes and Tejon Pass. Another 4,000 lived north of the American River, in the Feather and Yuba Valleys. The Pitt, Salmon, Scott, Trinity, and Klamath Rivers had villages that protected another 5,000 people. Another thousand or so lived in the foothills west of the upper Sacramento. When Round Valley, Clear Lake, and the coastal regions of today's Mendocino County are added—another 5,000 people—the total Native population then living outside the ranching community in California north of Los Angeles was at most 19,500.

This number seems confusing given that the 1860 census revealed roughly 30,000 Indians in California. But it makes sense when it is realized that the census included Indians south of Los Angeles—likely another 7,000—as well as large numbers of Indians who were working and living on ranches and those that the army was not concerned with. When these are added to the mix, the total number of Indians in California in 1851 probably was somewhere near 35,000, declining by a factor of 10 percent over the course of the decade.[51]

If these numbers are accurate, then Sherburne Cook's estimates that 100,000 Indians lived in California in 1850 and 50,000 in 1855 are simply incorrect. Cook knew of the impact of early diseases, but he lacked the evidence to analyze the significance of these epidemics. Furthermore, if Cook's foundation figure of 150,000 Indians for 1845 (which may also be inflated) is accepted, then 75 to 80 percent of Native peoples had died from disease by 1851. Such numbers fundamentally discount the argument that thousands of Indians in California were killed in fits of mass murder by miners after 1849. Another way to approach the problem is to ask what evidence for genocide exists. What policies did the federal government adopt to prevent such killings, to halt the massive decline that seemed to lead to extinction for California Indians?

The federal government formulated two policy changes after 1851. First, with Mexican aggression no longer a threat, the new problem became separating Indians and miners. Moreover, because Native bands no longer threatened settlers, the army devoted more energy to protecting Indians rather than fighting them—indeed the Lyon escapade was the last of its kind conducted by the regular army in California. Second, as Indian Affairs officials moved into California they adopted policies similar to those in the East. They turned to the Medill-Brown plan for "colonizing" Indians on small reservations—in essence, ethnic cleansing. Such a solution seemed even more appealing in California because federal officials were convinced that the California bands lacked "tribal" political organizations and thus had no tribal homelands. They could be legitimately removed to almost anywhere, even out of the state, by force if necessary.

General Smith, who seemed to sense the massive collapse of Native populations, saw the need to protect the survivors. He issued a "circular" in 1849 decreeing that all "adventurers" who trespassed on government lands would be arrested. The army in particular wished to bring order to the mining districts, especially the valleys of the Mokelumne, Calaveras, Stanislaus, and Tuolumne Rivers.[52] Politically, however, Smith's powers were weakened after Congress granted California statehood in 1850. While Congress appropriated money for the creation of an Indian Superintendency, it agreed only to apply the Intercourse Acts of 1834 to Oregon and Washington, making Smith's decree unenforceable.[53] Federal jurisdiction—applied through the Intercourse Acts, which defined Indian Country—would have provided the legal foundation for his decree. Another problem emerged out of the Treaty of Guadalupe Hidalgo with Mexico in 1848. The treaty sustained the large, and often vague, Mexican land grants. What exactly constituted the "public domain" was often fought over in court.[54]

Newly arrived miners generally ignored decrees and issues of jurisdiction anyway. They set up their own "miner law," which led to the creation of "mining districts." Each district kept track of mining claims and established rules relative to the number of days that miners had to work their claims in order to hold them. Believing that no law existed, miners became the ultimate examples of those who felt "entitled" to the land and its resources. Some even argued that the gold-producing riverbeds belonged only to Americans and proceeded to run off foreigners, including many Sonorans, who were forced south. Others claimed emphatically that

Indian Country, or lands generally off limits to whites, did not exist in California.[55] California had no "frontier," no definable line where Indian and miner interests collided along demarcated boundaries.[56]

Enforcing a federal Indian policy that maintained peace between miners and Indians became extremely difficult under such circumstances. Given the information from the surveys, General Smith quickly set out to rectify this problem by establishing military posts at San Diego, San Francisco, and Benicia (on the estuary of the lower Sacramento River), on Bear Creek (in the Northern Mining District), and, finally, on the Fresno River (in the Southern Mining District). At first there seemed to be no reason to occupy northern California. Wessells had been quite surprised to see miners operating in the Scott River valley in late fall 1851, but they had just arrived.

The peaceful relations that existed between Indians and whites in summer 1849 slowly deteriorated, but they never reached the point where mass murders occurred to any great degree. General Riley held negotiations with large numbers of tribal leaders on the Stanislaus River in late September 1849 and soon realized that many of the bands were being "forced to the south," as Derby confirmed that fall. He concluded that "troops in this position to meet Indian difficulties will probably not exist much longer."[57] Indeed, Captain Henry Day, commanding Cantonment Far West along Bear Creek in the Northern Mining District, confirmed that small Indian raids had occurred there, mostly to steal stock, and that miners had retaliated during the summer of 1850. California volunteers had been called in, but fewer than a dozen people were killed on both sides in three different clashes. As Agent Wozencraft reported on the conflict, the war was "declared happily ended," as the volunteers failed to dislodge the Indians. The Miwok Indians involved in the skirmishes agreed to a treaty of peace, and some went to work in the mines.[58]

The situation in the Southern Mining District proved more difficult. Miwok, Yokut, and Yosemite bands became enraged over the invasion of miners along the Merced, Mariposa, and Fresno Rivers. The so-called Mariposa Indian War broke out in January 1851 and continued into the next year. As some of these Indians acquired firearms, attacks on mining camps escalated, with dozens of miners being killed. Indian trader James Savage, who had married into three different Native bands, raised volunteers and Indian auxiliaries to beat back the assaults. His men were mostly ineffective, however, as was a state volunteer force. Governor

John McDougal called for restraint in his instructions to its commander, J. Neely Johnson, noting that "an Indian war is at all times to be deprecated." The appearance of an Indian Commission that summer of 1851 led to negotiated settlements, including the establishment of reservation lands along the Fresno River. To support the effort, General Smith established Fort Miller on the San Joaquin River just north of the reserve, to some degree straddling lands between the miners and the Indians.[59]

Meanwhile, as minor clashes broke out, Governor Riley reported them to Washington, pleading with authorities that they should "immediately recognize" Indian land titles and "remove them [Indians] from the immediate vicinity of the white settlements."[60] But even Riley realized that solutions became more difficult after he turned over authority in California to the newly elected state governor, Peter H. Burnet, in September 1850. California officials seemed intent on enacting their own Indian policy and immediately lobbied Washington for funds to form militias. Officers such as General Smith, and even the secretary of war, opposed these efforts. When it came to paying troops that the governor had authorized for expeditions into the Bear River area in the north and along the lower San Joaquin in the south, state officials were aghast to discover that the bill came to $100,000, which the federal government initially refused to pay and which the state did not have.[61]

Newly elected state politicians then turned to other options. The California legislature passed "An Act Relative to the Protection, Punishment, and Government of the Indians" in 1851. Dividing the state into ten districts, the law allowed local justices of the peace to grant Indian labor contracts, much like the "indentures" of past centuries. While employers supposedly had to pay the Indians for labor, the law led to abuses, particularly abuses of Indian women by miners.[62] Those "contracted," or more correctly kidnapped, often served as prostitutes.[63] Even worse, gangs emerged in 1852. Rather than pan for gold, a tedious and difficult process, they turned to kidnapping Indian children and selling them as servants.

A variety of groups—including unsuccessful miners—worked this form of virtual slavery. But some of the most successful were identified as Sonorans. They dominated the slave trade between 1852 and 1854 north of Clear Lake, even striking fear into the hearts of Indians living east of the coastal range in the Central Valley. One group of Sonorans worked out of the Berryessa Valley near Napa. District attorney R. W. Wood, who had indicted the men, pleaded for assistance in arresting them. Both the sheriff and the army refused to help.[64] One report in 1854 put the number of Indian children seized at 150.[65] American miners and Mexicans became involved in human trafficking as a direct result of a law supposedly designed to provide agricultural labor for California farms and ranches. Unfortunately, the practice had existed in the Spanish borderlands for centuries and was sometimes used even by missionaries to train surrogates. How many Indians were victimized is impossible to determine.[66]

The kidnapping seemed to be more pronounced in some regions than in others. Indian superintendent Henley noted on a few occasions the Indians' wish to move to safe havens to protect their women and children, particularly those living north of Sonoma. Some white farmers and ranchers did try to protect and pay their Native laborers.[67] Superintendent Thomas Henley investigated a number of cases, looking for abuse. He visited a farm owned by one Brown Smith near Clear Lake where several hundred Indians were working in the fields, seemingly all content. Several hundred other Indians in the Yuba River valley as well as some near Nevada City, west of Lake Tahoe, also maintained themselves through work. W. P. Crenshaw from Nevada City, an Indian subagent, gave a long, detailed account of how Miwok Indians near Nevada City made a living. They maintained their tribal identity while at the same time working for ranchers haying in the spring and summer, digging potatoes in the fall, and making deals with miners who had claims much of the rest of the year, which allowed Indian women to pan for gold (Native men refused to do so). The dust was then used to purchase flour and meat. Crenshaw was convinced that no one in the region around Nevada City wanted the Indians to leave. A very similar situation existed on the Yuba River, where Indians, who still retained a communal identity, often worked for wages.[68]

The Indian Office hired more and more agents to investigate and prevent labor abuses when possible. Those Indians who were sold—the numbers may have stretched into the low thousands—could bring as much as $100 each. This was slavery—a clear crime against humanity. The state law was finally rescinded when it became obvious that it conflicted with the 14th Amendment of the United States Constitution, adopted just after the Civil War.[69]

California Indian policy entered a new phase when Congress authorized Barbour, McKee, and Wozencraft to make treaties with Indians to establish reservations in 1851. The commissioners negotiated eighteen agreements, providing detailed descriptions of Indian lands that would supposedly become Indian Country. Wessells, who observed the process in the North, thought the negotiations almost laughable; very few of the Indians could understand the treaty rhetoric. But Keyes and other Indian Officials had a very different experience in southern California, where many Indians spoke Spanish. Miwoks and Yokuts were well aware of the land that had been set aside for them on the Merced River and defended it. Despite the effort, the Senate failed to ratify the very treaties it had authorized. Governor John Bigler and virtually the entire California delegation lobbied against ratification.[70]

Barbour and Wozencraft both exceeded their authority when they offered contracts for the delivery of beef to various Indian groups who signed treaties in spring 1851, well before they had been sent east for ratification. The contracts were mostly with John C. Frémont, who seemingly had political clout in Washington and could convince Congress to pay for the beef. The contracts offered a massive opportunity for corruption and explain to some degree the two agents' attempts to report large Indian populations, at least early on. Each treaty included annuity clauses: the more Indians, the more beef needed to be purchased. Probably because of their corruption, the Indian Office replaced both men with Edward F. Beale, who became superintendent of Indian affairs in California in 1852.[71]

Beale offered a unique solution, which he presented to General Ethan Allen Hitchcock, the new commanding officer of the division. Beale proposed putting Indians under the charge of the military on what came to be known as "military reservations." While the army seldom cooperated with the Indian Office in later years, Hitchcock enthusiastically embraced the plan.[72] By 1853 military reserves were being staked out, 5,000-acre sanctuaries that would allow the Indian Office to concentrate Indians in specific areas. While the Native peoples would not be removed from the state—deportation was rejected—they would be urged and even at times forced to move to the new reservations. The plan continued into the early 1860s, when Congress established permanent reservations and placed Indians under the complete authority of the Indian Office.[73]

While Superintendent Beale had suggested the solution, the new Democratic administration of Franklin Pierce replaced him in 1853 with Thomas Henley. Over the next six years Henley worked tirelessly to establish both Indian military reservations and farmlands, which were removed from the public domain for "military" purposes. Congress also appropriated hundreds of thousands of dollars—Beale's first appropriation in 1852 had been $350,000—to help create the reserves. This led to the employment of hundreds of mostly white men—farmers, carpenters, millwrights, and doctors.[74] These men opened fields and built housing for Indians. Agents then purchased large cattle herds, most Indians being capable herders.

The two earliest reservations took shape in 1854 at Nome Lackee southwest of Redding and near Tejon Pass, on a reservation called Sebastian.[75] Hired farmers broke more than 2,000 acres of land at both reserves. A year later agents opened large farms on the Fresno and Kern Rivers; the first wheat crop at Fresno came in at 16,200 pounds.[76] Indian Office inspector J. Ross Browne visited the reserves in 1854 and was pleased with progress. Similar success came at Nome Cult Farm in 1856 on the Eel River in Round Valley and at the Mendocino Reservation, located on the coast. Agent McKee had set out a final reservation along the lower Klamath River that was occupied in the late 1850s. Most Indians who came onto these reserves expressed appreciation for the food that they provided as well as the protection. Populations fluctuated widely, as Indians came and went, but most reserves and farms had at least a thousand Indians. The Mendocino Reservation counted 3,000 in 1856.[77]

Collecting the Indians at these reserves did prove problematic. Some Americans did not want to see them leave areas where ranches and farms were being built. They represented cheap labor in a state where labor was generally very expensive. Henley worked with such prominent local citizens as John Sutter to negotiate removal. Sutter, a decent man, originally concluded that it was best for all those Indians on Yuba River and at his Hock Farm to be removed to Nome Lackee, where they would be well cared for. But then he changed his mind. The debate reached the newspapers in 1856, and Henley held meetings with local groups to discuss alternatives. Ultimately he convinced Sutter to allow the removal of the Indians on the Yuba River, who were often taking their pay in whiskey, and allowed Sutter to keep his Indian workers at Hock Farm, where he agreed to take care of them. Bargains of this sort had to be made, for General John Wool, who took command of California troops in 1853, refused to use the bayonet to force any Native peoples to move.[78]

Given Henley's success, it seemed likely that the reservations would solve California's "Indian problem." But criticism of Henley's reservation solution mounted in the late 1850s. While Henley's agents generally received praise for their treatment of Indians, some California newspaper editors criticized the efforts mercilessly, claiming that Henley allowed corruption in beef and flour contracts and even permitted some whites to run cattle on reservation lands. Title to the lands where farms and reserves were laid out often proved problematic, leading to white invasion. Other critics claimed that Henley had failed to give much attention to Indians south of Los Angeles, near San Diego.

Inspector Browne, who remained above the criticism, stood by Henley at first, lauding him for his "great energy" in an 1857 report to the commissioner of Indian affairs. Visiting all the reserves and farms, Browne noted that he "had never seen Indians of California better fed or better satisfied" and that reservation doctors had put a clear "check on disease." Indeed doctors reported no diseases at Nome Lackee and Sebastian, not even social ones.[79] Browne mostly saw Indians on the reservations, who numbered perhaps seven to ten thousand out of the nearly twenty thousand who remained north of Los Angeles in 1857.

Given the military presence, Indians who remained off the reservations also received better treatment from white ranchers, who likewise did not want conflict. The 4,000 or so Tulare and Yokut Indians frequently worked on ranches by the mid-1850s, but many remained in the mountains. Somewhat less than half of them often showed up at the Tejon reserve or the Fresno and Kern River farms to help at harvest, collecting grains that would get them through the winter. This remained the case farther north as well, as agent Crenshaw reported from Nevada City. A native cycle of subsistence had emerged that integrated farm work, gathering, fishing, and food from reservation lands.[80]

Historians over the years often have been critical of the California reservation system. Sherburne Cook began the attack in 1976, claiming the reservations "were nothing more than concentration camps into which as many Indians were herded as could be caught and transported."[81] While Cook relied mostly on newspaper accounts, often the source of negative information, Indian Office reports and army documents paint a different picture. Indeed the army had much to do with running the reservations in the 1850s, and most officers were sympathetic with the Indians' plight. Officers like Lieutenant Henry Judah spent time on several reserves. Judah often lamented his inability to keep the Indians on the reserves, where they were safe from child poachers and violent miners. He realized that the Indians often preferred a more mobile life, moving about the countryside. Judah also understood that one reason for the abrupt departure of

Indians from reservations was that they were forced to work in the fields, to plough, plant, and harvest. For Indians in northern California, it was labor that they were not accustomed to doing.[82]

As California's white population matured and turned to ranching and farming, some reservation lands became more valuable, which explains some of the criticism of the reservation system.[83] Put simply, a minority of Californians wanted Indians removed so that farmland or pristine streams that might hold gold would be returned to the public domain. In January 1855, for example, miners interested in working around the junction of the Klamath and Trinity Rivers invaded a series of Native towns there that had impressed Major Wessells and burned several of them. While Lieutenant Judah, who investigated the atrocity, gave no account of murder at the towns, the occupants had fled to the hills. In like fashion the farms on Fresno and Kern Rivers to the south soon became particularly attractive regions. The so-called Woodville and Visalia Rangers briefly tried to drive the Indians off the lands in 1856, but the rangers were soundly defeated and promptly departed the field, because the reserve Indians had obtained firearms.[84]

Despite such reports, historians who have cited examples of Indian murders—and tried to make an argument for genocide—have generally failed to note the many different attempts to prevent killings made by California settlers, particularly ranchers and farmers, the army, and the Indian Office. A petition signed by five settlers who lived near "the mouth of the Trinity" demanded that the military punish the miners who had burned out the Indians nearby. The miners had acted "without any general consultation." The citizens "of the upper River," they wrote to General Wool, "altho' in favor of disarming the tribes, were most earnestly and bitterly opposed to firing [Indian] ranches or destroying property." Judah found a large number of settlers, who feared Indian reprisals, quite willing to prevent the "murderous schemes" of a few miners.[85] One of the leading citizens of Humboldt Bay, Walter Van Dyke, had stated the case of many settlers along the Klamath River some years before. He wrote to Governor John Bigler: "Our Citizens from experience are fully aware of the evil consequences of an Indian war and its destructive effects on every branch of business."[86]

Lieutenant Judah coaxed a hundred of so Klamath River Indians who had fled to return with him to Fort Jones. Most were women and children. One report suggested that some of their men had been killed in the fighting, defending their burning towns. Judah fed them throughout the summer, because most of their food stores had been lost. The reservation along the Klamath was staked out that fall and became the place of refuge for these people and others from Scott River.[87] Miners, mostly condemned by more upright local citizens, killed a number of Indians along the Klamath and Trinity Rivers during summer 1855, but the army had the situation under control by August.

One mostly isolated trouble spot still remained, however. Colonel George Wright at Fort Reading had sent patrols into Round Valley on numerous occasions. Lieutenant L. Q. Hunt, who entered the valley in early 1854, found very few Indians, much like Wessells a few years before. He did uncover evidence that some Yuki or Pomo Indians had been crossing over the coastal mountains and stealing horses and mules from wagon trains. Lieutenant Judah patrolled the region in late fall 1854, again finding little evidence of Indian occupation. He did rescue four Indian men, literally held in chains by kidnappers from Napa Valley. Judah demanded and got the Indians' release.[88] On receiving Judah's report, General Wool lamented that "there is not so much as a justice of the peace in that section." The white community consisted of only a few ranchers.[89]

Settlers moved into Round Valley in more considerable numbers after 1855. It soon became the scene of what would become a brutal ethnic conflict.[90] As deer herds declined from both Indian and white hunting and the acorn harvest became increasingly unreliable, Pomos invaded the gardens of settlers in Mendocino County and slaughtered livestock in 1857.[91] Settlers then made a "foray" against the Indians, killing "a number" of Pomo people. More such incidents occurred in the months that followed, although casualty figures are difficult to assess.[92]

The final phase of the struggle erupted when a prime stallion belonging to a wealthy rancher named Serranus Hastings was killed and eaten by Yuki Indians. A small number of Yukis refused to remain on the government farm, where two hundred or three hundred Yukis lived. Other ranchers, who had also lost stock, apparently corroborated Hastings's claim. They lobbied Governor John B. Weller to organize a state ranger company to roam the Eel Valley, ostensibly to stop thievery. Although Weller had strong reservations—to some degree because respectable men seemed to spurn the need for troops—he finally agreed, giving the job to the only man who would lead the force, a ruffian named Walter S. Jarboe. A known confidence man of sorts, Jarboe soon styled himself "captain" of the "Eel River Rangers." While he could recruit only about two dozen men, his force went into the field that fall and supposedly began killing Indians indiscriminately, remaining out until December.[93]

Governor Weller had suspicions about Jarboe's willingness to shoot Indians first rather than find the few Indians who might be pilfering livestock. In his instructions—clear indications of what the state government hoped to accomplish—Weller cautioned Jarboe that "human lives must not be taken when it can possibly be avoided." Weller was certain that "an indiscriminate warfare against the Ukah [Yuki] tribe could not be justified by the facts now in my possession." The governor knew that the depredations had been minimal. Jarboe, however, with the braggadocio that commonly came with being a ranger captain, soon claimed to have killed nearly 300 Indians, very likely an exaggeration. No one ever witnessed the killings, and no evidence at that point even suggested that that number lived in the hills. The army ordered troops from Fort Vancouver south to the Eel Valley and notified Governor Weller that his rangers were a pack of murderers. The governor withdrew the men in January 1860.[94] While some ranchers and settlers in the region lauded the murders committed by "Ranger" Jarboe, many Californians did not. And the governor made it clear that he did not support a campaign of "extermination," despite the tendency of some historians to call the event genocide.[95]

While small numbers of Yukis remained in the hills and might have suffered during fall 1859, the "intent" of the policy of the United States government as well as the state government was to stop the killing of livestock when it occurred, separate Indians and whites, and put Indians on reservations—in essence ethnic cleansing. Nome Cult remained a viable alternative for the Yukis just as the Mendocino Reservation provided a refuge for the Pomo Indians. Small numbers of Indians preferred to remain in the mountains rather than move to a reservation or a farm where the agent made them participate in plowing. They did not wish to become farmers.[96]

Some conflict continued into the period of the Civil War. While searching for Indians, one out-of-control group of volunteers killed thirty Indians outright and knifed the wounded to death. In a horrible massacre another group supposedly killed eighty Wiyot women and children on an island off Humboldt Bay. And after three white children were killed by a war party from the Pitt River Yahi band, their small village was discovered and destroyed. One survivor of the Yahi band, an Indian named Ishi, remained outside the reservation for decades thereafter, later telling his story to anthropologist Theodora Kroeber in an award-winning book. But even some Californians in this region so remote that news of the attacks hardly reached San Francisco protested against such violence—killing Indians was simply inhumane. One was the poet and writer Bret Harte, who was a journalist at the time.[97]

While occasional killings occurred in the regions east of Humboldt Bay after 1857, most Indians throughout the rest of California transformed themselves into farm laborers or dependents who lived on reservations. Federal officials continued to consolidate them, abandoning some reservations and farms as more and more Indians became laborers. By the early 1860s those Indians at Nome Lackee and Mendocino were moved into Round Valley, where Native peoples from the Sacramento Valley were brought to join them. The Indians who came and went from the Sebastian Reservation and the farms on Fresno and Kern Rivers found themselves removed to a remote valley to the south, on Tule River. Farther north the Klamath River Reservation provided a refuge for the Indians from that area as well as for those from the region of the Scott and Salmon Rivers. Native peoples metamorphosed, many becoming more like Californios than Indians. This process in California had variants not found in other regions of the United States, where a similar Hispanic population did not exist and ethnic differences remained more obvious.

While reservations offered refuge for Native peoples, attacks on Indian camps and towns by so-called rangers, miners, and volunteers did occur. But they never reached a point that even approached extermination. In a pattern often repeated on other frontiers around the world, the men who committed these assaults frequently exaggerated the numbers of Indians killed. Killing became a badge of honor among such men, an expression of their sense of entitlement. Gangs of the sort that committed such acts are often found on all frontiers (even those pioneered by people who proclaim a penchant for democracy): such groups are disconnected from community life, consume large amounts of alcohol, and are prone to braggadocio.[98]

Many such unattached miners left for Oregon—soon to become another troubled spot—in the mid-1850s and went to Montana and Colorado a few years later. With the possible exception of the far Northwest, California's Anglo population also changed very quickly from transient miners to a more business- and agriculture-oriented community. Given these rapid changes, it is ironic that the most appalling attempts to exterminate

California Indians came in 1859 in Round Valley, well after the boom era had passed, and in the far Northwest during the Civil War. Neither attempt succeeded: the descendants of those bands live on today on reservations near their homelands.

Evidence suggests that approximately two thousand Indians were murdered in California during and after the gold rush. The numbers are indisputably disturbing, but it is highly questionable that they were the product of a policy of genocide. As abhorrent as such numbers are, they hardly equal the numbers of those killed under other regimes across the globe in either the nineteenth or twentieth centuries. In these cases government policies, often debated and even put in writing, were implemented for the purpose of exterminating all or most of a particular racial, ethnic, or religious group.[99] Furthermore, statistics show that Native California populations were much smaller than previously thought: bands and tribes were remnants of their former selves as early as 1851. Based on the demographic evidence available, it is not convincing to argue that tens of thousands of California Indians disappeared after the gold rush began and less convincing still to assume that genocide explains their disappearance.[100]

The failure of state and local government to control the actions of militia groups contributed to the scale of the human carnage. Nonetheless, the governmental policies that promoted the removal of thousands of Indians to confined reservations certainly fall within the modern definition of ethnic cleansing. The acts of state-sponsored militia groups should be condemned as war crimes, however, and those miners and militias who acted on their own volition, without state sanction, quite simply committed murder. There is no evidence that any state or federal governmental entity ever supported the militias or miners in their murderous endeavors or "intended" to implement a policy of extermination in California. A series of inhuman acts—murder, war crimes, and certainly ethnic cleansing—occurred, extending over a dozen years, but collectively they do not amount to state-sanctioned genocide.

The Indian policy adopted by the federal government reflected what the majority of citizens in the region wanted. White Californians wanted Indians to be removed from valuable lands and at the same time wanted docile Indian laborers; given their need for labor and moral prohibitions against killing people, the majority of settlers sought to prevent extermination.[101] At most it might be argued that federal reservations, feeding programs, and medical care came far too late for many California Indians.

However humane its intent, such policy should be condemned for failings, not crimes, even though those failures might be responsible for the deaths of hundreds of innocent Indians from disease and even starvation.

The harsh realities of ethnic cleansing in California might have been mitigated had the government simply implemented the reservation system attempted in 1851. It failed to do so. This failure, which led to massive dislocation and resettlement, was horrendous in itself. In addition, the "Eel River Rangers" and others of a similar sort should have been indicted for murder—they were not. Perhaps Governor Weller should have known what the rangers intended to do in Round Valley in 1859; if so, he might be charged with collusion. But his instructions advocated restraint and police action, not murder, and the same was true in the early 1860s.[102]

In addition, given the efforts of men like Beale, Henley, McKee, Judah, Wright, and Wool, thousands of California Indians found sanctuary on the reservations created for them, which were in turn protected by the army. According to the army's surveys, Native populations leveled off fairly early in the 1850s and declined only slightly thereafter. In reality federal officials treated California Indians no differently than they did Indians elsewhere. They moved them at will and forced farming upon them, even apparently using the whip at times to drive them into the fields. While this process was well under way in California by 1853, it took a bit longer to implement farther north in Oregon and Washington. And it would be attended by similar levels of violence, some of which was prompted by the same old groups—rangers and volunteers.

11

THE "DIMINISHMENT" OF
THE NATIVE DOMAIN

Oregon and Washington

"Gone to Oregon" appeared frequently in every newspaper in America by the early 1840s. The press portrayed the region as an enchanting land, with lush river valleys full of salmon, and a mild climate that contrasted markedly with the variations that existed just west of the Mississippi River, on the treeless prairies and plains. Financial depression had helped spur the move to Oregon, as a near-collapse of banking and land development had hit the nation in 1837 and lingered on into the early 1840s. To the north another region took shape, named Washington in honor of the first president. Coastal shipping had entered Puget Sound many years before, and the term "Boston" came into common usage among Indians to identify the non-Natives, mostly Americans, whose ships set down anchor. The political future of these two new regions was settled when Oregon gained territorial status in 1849, and statehood nine years later, and Washington became an organized territory.

European epidemics of smallpox, malaria, and measles were reported in Oregon during the 1770s, 1820s, and late 1830s, continuing well into the 1850s. They had redefined the region demographically, causing a massive decline in Native populations that continued even after 1850. While the tribes west of the Sierra Nevada fared quite well, actual census data suggest that fully one-half of the Indians in southwestern Oregon in 1853—those in the Rogue River watershed—had disappeared by 1858.[1] Such a decline, differing from the decline in California that occurred in the years prior to 1853, brings forward once again the issue of genocide versus disease. Certainly smallpox played a major role in the loss of life, as did other diseases. But in Oregon disruption by war became a real problem. The surviving tribes in the southwestern part of the territory lost habitat rapidly after 1853, as miners destroyed the salmon runs. This led to malnutrition and starvation.

The Willamette River valley had become mostly void of Native communities by the 1840s. Tribal or band organization had disappeared, allowing white settlers to occupy the region without conflict.[2] The largest surviving Native groups existed in southwestern Oregon, living in the small tributaries of the Rogue and Umpqua Rivers that penetrated the coastal range of mountains. They were identified by their linguistic affiliation—Coos, Coquilles, Tututnis, Umpquas, Nahankuotanas, and Shastas. Indian Office officials estimated the total population of those living on both the eastern and western slopes of the Cascades at roughly 3,500 people in 1853. Another 700 to 800 Shastas lived on the Oregon-California border but claimed lands extending into the upper Rogue River valley. When the 3,000 or so Umatilla, Wasco, Wishram, Warm Springs, and Cayuse Indians of eastern Oregon are added, the total Native population of the new territory perhaps reached 7,000 people.[3]

Native populations had also suffered to the north in Washington. The coastal Salish and Chinook people had experienced degradation from epidemics as well as an influx of alcohol brought in by the "Bostons" over the years after 1800. But their villages still contained nearly 5,000 people, who existed primarily by fishing and hunting. Farther inland were more Salish people, such as the Coeur d'Alene and Spokane tribes, as well as some villagers who straddled the Columbia River and especially the plateau to the west of the river's upper waters. The most prominent groups on the inland plateau were the Klikitat, Cayuse, Walla Walla, and Yakama (sometimes spelled Yakima) people. While they suffered from epidemics, their populations had stabilized to some degree, numbering perhaps 10,000 or more by the early 1850s. Moreover, the plateau people were horsemen and warriors, a force to be reckoned with when the American military occupied the region in 1849 and established Fort Vancouver in the south and Fort Steilacoom on Puget Sound.[4]

While peaceful relations generally existed between whites and Indians in Oregon, trouble started after the region became a territory. The new territorial governor, Joseph Lane, a Democrat, did little to placate Indians. After arriving in March 1849, Lane found considerable concern among the settlers in the region: elements of the Cayuse tribe had massacred the missionaries at the Whitman Mission in the upper Columbia basin a year and a half earlier. The Indians blamed the Whitmans for introducing smallpox. Lane did coax five Cayuse men to surrender in 1850 and take responsibility for the act. Under questionable authority, he promptly tried them for murder at Oregon City. While the Indians were given counsel—a lawyer who later objected to their convictions—the jury convicted them and the governor hanged them.[5]

Tensions then mounted in the Rogue River valley, especially with the Shasta Indians, who were harassing travelers along the increasingly important route from central Oregon into California. An army patrol that reached the region some two years before had suggested the need for a military garrison. After the gold rush began, such a garrison became even more important. Considerable migration occurred southward, out of the Willamette Valley. Wagon trains were attacked, especially in order to steal their stock.[6] Major Philip Kearny and his dragoon force briefly answered the call and attempted to assault a fixed position of Indians who had defied them, along the Rogue River in June 1851. He lost several men, including Captain James Stuart, who had led the charge.[7]

Governor Lane arrived with volunteers a few days later, bent on punishing the Rogue River bands. But the Indians were once again ready, and neither side gained much advantage in several brief skirmishes. After a standoff of sorts Kearny finally withdrew and Lane went on into California to try his hand at mining. The new territorial governor, John Gaines, and the new superintendent of Indian affairs, Anson Dart, negotiated a treaty in September that ended this first round of conflict. Gaines reported to the president of the United States that the Rogue River Indians seemed to have divided into two groups, one that remained mostly north of the river and had peaceful relations with whites and one south of it, who, he feared, had formed a "combination." The willingness of this second group to stand and fight demonstrated that many of the Rogue River people would not easily give up their land to invading whites.[8]

Prospectors had moved into the upper Klamath and Scott Rivers by spring 1851—Major Wessells reported them as being at Scott's Bar—and gradually invaded the Illinois and Rogue Rivers areas as well as the Oregon coast. These miners and their Indian neighbors had competing economic strategies: the Indians were trying to preserve the watersheds and the salmon in the rivers, while the miners were destroying the spawning beds in their search for gold. Federal government officials had reached the upper Klamath River in 1851 and negotiated treaties that created a

reservation in northwestern California, but the treaties had not been ratified by the Senate. The only federal official who remained behind after the
negotiations was Indian agent Redick McKee, who had been one of the
original commissioners in 1851. McKee, a good man doing a difficult job,
blamed the miners for the troubles and called upon Governor John Bigler
of California to restrain them. But given the failure of Congress to ratify
the 1851 treaties, McKee could do little else, especially in Oregon, where
an entirely different territorial government was taking shape.[9]

McKee did note that many of the miners moving into southern Oregon
were coming through Humboldt Bay or Port Orford, up the Oregon
coast. He condemned most of them as "[b]rave warriors," who indiscriminately killed Indians. He had learned of one attack where some twenty
Indians had been slaughtered.[10] After McKee traveled far up the Klamath
River, where many of the miners had located themselves, he called once
again on the government to send in troops. While Humboldt Bay already
had a small garrison, the army soon occupied Port Orford on the Oregon
coast and established Fort Jones, along the Scott River, west of Yreka,
California.[11] With the military bringing some stability, it became possible
for agents such as McKee to work toward establishing a reservation system.
He quickly found an ally in this endeavor when Joel Palmer was selected as
Indian superintendent for Oregon in 1853. Palmer agreed that the Medill-
Brown plan of "colonization" would soon be needed in southern Oregon.

McKee and Palmer both could see that three fundamentally different
groups had emerged in northern California and southern Oregon. Some
generally wanted peace in order to protect their farms and ranches and
supported a reservation policy; others cared little about the Indians but
perhaps exaggerated or even instigated Indian troubles, hoping to benefit
from the markets that new military garrisons offered; members of the
third group exaggerated and often bragged of their success in seeking revenge by killing Indians, partly to impress fellow miners. Unfortunately,
less need for Indian labor existed in the northernmost reaches of California
and in southern Oregon, and miners were entering regions that were almost impossible to police, given the ruggedness of the mountains and the
deep canyons where they sought gold.[12]

After federal troops arrived at Fort Jones, Lieutenant W. H. Stanton
launched a patrol into the Rogue River valley in late summer 1852. It was
exceedingly difficult just to travel in the region. Stanton did discover that
conflict between Indians and miners had frequently occurred. Yet just

to the east of the coastal mountain range, near the major ferry over the upper Rogue River along the Oregon-California trail, a white settlement of twenty families at a place later called Jacksonville had maintained good relations with the Indians. It was the generally violent nature of the miners and their tendency to kidnap Indian women that created problems.[13]

A so-called captain of paramilitary volunteers, Ben Wright, was one of the most infamous provocateurs. Wright, a troublemaker with a small group of followers, believed that Modocs from Klamath Lake in southern Oregon regularly raided the California-Oregon road—there were reports that nine whites had been killed by a Modoc war party. Wright organized a volunteer force of thirty-two men and eight Shasta Indian allies and met a large party of Modocs along the trail near the border. The Indians "paraded in sight sixty-five strong, twelve on horse back and the others on foot." They fought in an open field, then the Indians fell back to Goose Lake, where Wright claimed to have killed ten or twelve. He set out to parley with the leaders of the war party, coaxing roughly thirty-five to assemble and receive goods. Wright's men then pulled revolvers and killed virtually all of them.[14] Wright's treachery, and similar incidents, brought on the first phases of the Rogue River War, which lasted throughout the summer of 1853.[15]

Territorial officials acted quickly to raise volunteer forces but had little success, even after Joseph Lane returned to stir up resentment and encourage attacks on Indian villages. The Rogue River Indians at times raised several hundred men, some of whom were armed with muskets. They easily fended off miners sent to punish them and often inflicted considerable losses on the miners, seven of whom were killed near Jacksonville in one ambush. When troops from Fort Jones arrived to assist the miners, some negotiations occurred. At one point several Rogue River Indians, likely belonging to bands that promoted peace, were captured; four were executed. Superintendent Palmer dutifully reported the deaths of the miners and the Indians, losses that hardly merited the description "Indian War." These events did convince the superintendent to accelerate his anticipated policy of reservation confinement.[16]

After receiving permission from the commissioner of Indian affairs to expand the number of agents in Oregon, Palmer began assigning men to various locales. He sent Samuel A. Culver to the Rogue River, which was likely the most problematic trouble-spot. Palmer gave Culver strict instructions to make sure that any Indians arrested received a "fair trial"—which apparently had not been the case with the four who were executed—in order to "convince the Indians that their reliance on you for protection and redress is well placed." Palmer believed that negotiation would solve the problem, but he was also convinced that it would be necessary to persuade many of these bands to surrender their lands before removal to reservations could begin.[17]

The military impasse in the south allowed Superintendent Palmer to bring most of the bands along the Oregon rivers to a peace council in September and October, where they signed the first of seven treaties relinquishing much of southeastern Oregon to the federal government. Once Congress acted on these agreements, the land sales would finance the development of reservations. Acting mostly on good faith—in the past Congress had rejected such agreements—Palmer then established the first reservation at Table Rock, two buttelike plateaus located just north of the Rogue valley along Evans Creek. A second reserve was set aside for the Umpquas farther north, not far from the newly created town of Roseburg.[18] Just who signed these treaties is difficult to determine. Several small bands cooperated, peaceful Indians for the most part, who were willing to be consolidated on either of the two reserves. But those Indians south of the Rogue River were not yet ready for peace, and many likely avoided the negotiations.

The terms of the agreements suggest that the Indians knew little about what they signed. Most of southern Oregon was purchased for roughly two cents an acre, although gold in recoverable quantities existed on the lands and much of this region had valuable timber. But Palmer also noted that many of these bands were "wretched, sickly, and almost starving." A massive smallpox epidemic had raged throughout the summer, making "fearful ravages among the Indians south of the Clapsop Plains [the wetlands and sand dunes of northwest Oregon]." While Palmer convinced the Indian Office to hire doctors, they could do little to stem the death toll. When the physician failed to save the wife and children of an Umpqua chief, he threatened to kill the doctor. Near-starvation added to health problems, resulting from the loss of habitat. Promises of food and assistance on a supposedly safe reservation likely seemed an alternative to starvation for some of the Rogue River people.[19]

The federal army had strengthened its forces in northern California, Oregon, and Washington to nearly a thousand men by 1854, with the intention of aiding the Indian Office in its evolving reservation policy.

General John Wool commanded all forces within the Division of the Pacific. Wool had been in charge of Cherokee Indian Removal and had
demonstrated considerable sympathy for American Indians. When the
general arrived, he found conditions in central and southern California to
be mostly peaceful, allowing him to shift more troops to the north. Colonel George Wright (no relation to Ben, the volunteer), who commanded at
Fort Reading along the upper Sacramento River, informed Wool that he
thought the Pitt, Scott, and Rogue River Indians wanted peace.[20] Not all
raiding had ceased: small groups did at times steal stock, mostly for food,
and miners retaliated. But Colonel Wright believed that peace could be
maintained if Palmer's reservation plans were implemented and if renegade
white miners would simply leave the Indians alone.[21]

Wright's views did little to placate General Wool, who received increasingly critical inquiries from superiors in the East. While problems
in California had mostly been solved, Oregonians were clamoring for
more troops. Miners made the situation even worse: in early spring 1854
they attacked a peaceful Indian town located just south of Port Orford,
apparently to plunder it. After surrounding the town, they opened fired
as the men came out, killing fifteen. After agent F. M. Smith and a small
army force from the fort arrived on the scene, peace was restored. Smith
believed that "well disposed" whites were anxious to stop such outrages
but that they were afraid of the miners. The agent condemned the miners
as "murderers," which in fact they were. Palmer agreed, identifying them
as "miscreants" who "slaughter these poor, weak, and defenseless Indians"
with impunity.[22] Nothing was done to arrest the miners, who numbered
in the hundreds and were well armed.

Reports of such atrocities, along with constant newspaper stories that
blamed the Indians and the army's inability to punish either the Indians
or the miners, even convinced secretary of war Jefferson Davis to question
Wool's leadership.[23] Davis demanded that the general stop such outrages
against peaceful Indians, rein in the hostile tribes, and control the miners.
The Oregon issue had become an embarrassment to the army. Wool defended the actions of the military in several letters in January 1855, noting
that his men had saved hundred of peaceful Indians and prosecuted hostile
ones.[24] Worse, the violence in Oregon, Wool argued, was perpetrated by
bands of renegade miners, considered repulsive even by the local citizenry.
Some were carrying on the California practice of kidnapping, especially
taking Indian women.

In one long letter General Wool outlined just how depraved the miners of the region had become. In their circles they readily embraced the name "Squaw Hunters," because they kidnapped Indian women for sexual services.[25] In one incident that Wool related to the secretary of war "Squaw Hunters" tried for several days to dislodge seven Indian women from a cave where their men were protecting them. When a nearby army commander, who had been convinced to join the miners, negotiated with the Indians, he discovered the true nature of the struggle. The women had been kidnapped and forced to serve the miners but ultimately made their escape. The army officer in command disarmed the miners, sent them away, and left the Indians in peace.[26]

Wool's defense of his troops came as yet another problem emerged. Lane, as the Democratic territorial delegate for Oregon, had convinced Congress to pay roughly $200,000 in salary to the volunteers who were raised in 1853. The arrival of the money in spring 1855 evoked a frenzy of activity in which the leaders of various frontier groups lobbied to organize more volunteers—volunteer work paid better than mining. With miners expecting remuneration, various groups emerged in both northern California and Oregon that began stalking Indians. Killing started on both sides in early October: some small parties of Indians were waylaid and massacred while off the reservation gathering food. Finally, a force of forty miners bent on murder entered the Table Rock Reservation, where several bands of peaceful Rogue River Indians had been disarmed and were living peacefully. They had mostly broken from those Indians who remained outside the reservation. The miners committed an "indiscriminate slaughter" of the peaceful Indians, as one observer described, killing 106 men, women, and children.[27] It was the worst massacre of the conflict.

The new territorial governor, George Curry, learned of the fighting a few days later—but not the extent of the massacre—and called for the organization of a volunteer battalion of several hundred troops. They were ordered to cooperate with a few dozen army regulars who were in the region. Curry, however, was aghast to learn of the killing of peaceful Indians on the reservation. He issued a proclamation on October 20, noting that "armed parties have taken the field in southern Oregon with the avowed purpose of waging a war of extermination again the Indians." Curry condemned the action taken against a "friendly band" and pledged that "no countenance or support from the executive" was to be expected. Yet a war was now under way with Rogue River Indians who had not joined those friendly groups on the reservation. Curry ordered his troops south to end it.[28]

Some two hundred relatively well armed Indians awaited the volunteers and regulars, picking the ground for battle: a bluff covered with downed trees and shrubs. The volunteers decided to charge the position, being aware that they would soon run out of supplies. In a pitched battle at "Hungry Hill" (a name suggesting that the men had already run out of food) just south of Roseburg the Indians got a modicum of revenge. Various reports put volunteer losses at anywhere from twenty to fifty men, with an equal number wounded.[29] The Rogue River Indians had won the day, but they had lost the issue. Within weeks, as snow fell and food became impossible to find, more and more of them turned to Superintendent Palmer and his agents in a starving condition. Removal got under way by January 1856, although many Rogue River and Umpqua Indians lacked the clothing and even shoes necessary to migrate. Nevertheless, they were congregated at the Table Rock and Umpqua reservations and prepared for removal out of the Rogue River valley.[30]

Curry's proclamation and the reports regarding the murder of women and children became widely circulated, and many people in Oregon turned on the volunteers. When the men returning from the Battle of Hungry Hill passed through the thriving new town of Roseburg, the citizens shunned them, refusing them food and even prohibiting them from sleeping in their barns. Meanwhile General Wool ordered more soldiers to the region to do whatever they could to protect the Indians. Lieutenant Judah, ever an active officer, forced several small volunteer groups still in the field to disarm. After President Pierce approved the location of the new Klamath Indian reservation in northern California in December, Judah helped move Indians to it.[31]

After Wool's exchange with Secretary Davis, the War Department sent some two hundred more troops. Wool dispatched them to Crescent City, in far northwest California, and to Fort Orford. The troops moved inland under the command of Lieutenant Colonel Robert Buchanan, who sent Captain Edward Ord out on a number of patrols to both subdue miners and pacify and collect the scattered Rogue River bands. These Indians were removed to the new Grande Round Reservation, which Superintendent Palmer opened that fall. It included a vast domain, extending along the northwest coast of Oregon from Florence in the south to Point Lookout, some fifty miles north. The Rogue River Wars, if they should even be called that, were slowly grinding to a halt. Some three hundred Indians were killed, maybe more, along with well over a hundred volunteers and miners. It had been a destructive conflict for both sides.[32]

While ethnic cleansing served as a solution to the problems in Oregon, similar to the situation in California, many Rogue River Indians did not want to leave their homelands. Some protested, declaring a desire to remain near the bones of their ancestors. But soldiers such as Colonel Wright at Fort Reading and Captain Ord served as positive forces initiating removal to the new reservations on either Klamath River or at Grand Ronde. Wright's so-called horseback diplomacy started with the distribution of clothes and food to Indians in isolated areas, which led to discussions and ultimately to surrender.[33] But these actions generally went unnoticed back east as a fight loomed for the appropriation of more money to pay the volunteers.

At the height of the trouble General Wool both vocally and in published reports condemned the miners and volunteers and their chief spokesman, delegate Lane. The general said nothing of Governor Curry, who had sworn not to reward the men who had slaughtered innocent Indians at Table Rock and elsewhere. The infighting reached the halls of Congress, where Lane argued for another $300,000 to pay for the volunteers. Wool's assessment included the open charge that the miners were the cause of the trouble, not the Indians. To Wool's delight, one of the first "civil rights" reformers in American history came to his defense. John Beeson had been in Oregon in 1855 and had seen the carnage. In published newspaper accounts and a later book he gave detailed descriptions of the so-called Squaw Hunters or "Bostons," as they were also called, who terrorized peaceful Indians and at times even decent white citizens. On one occasion at Jacksonville, Beeson wrote, Squaw Hunters invaded the town, pillaged it, and burned much of it down. Beeson noted that the good citizens of the town totally disavowed what the "Boston" thugs were up to. Beeson thought these men "on a low plane of development, with all the selfish or animal passions."[34]

In a strong defense of his forces and an indictment of the local Squaw Hunters, Wool offered the secretary of war a dramatic and truthful conclusion that ended any thoughts of criticism from Secretary Davis, even though he privately sided with Lane, a staunch defender of southern Democratic policies and slavery.[35] "In a thousand instances, the Indians were not to blame," Wool reported. "The contest is between a party of whites [renegades], few in number, who would wantonly 'exterminate' after dis-arming them [Indians], and the more right-minded [citizens] who would protect them [Indians] more out of humanity and to avoid the disastrous consequences of retaliation."[36]

As the conflict ended, Superintendent Palmer negotiated several more treaties with Oregon Indians throughout 1855 and 1856, designed to cre-ate reservations. He convinced most of the Indians of southern Oregon to move north to the coastal reserves near Grand Ronde, where there had been little white settlement. While the Indians "urged serious objections against leaving their accustomed haunts," as Palmer noted, fear of miner attacks, loss of fishing and hunting habitat as miners disrupted river flows and salmon migration, and starvation prompted the migration. Within a year Palmer had removed almost all of the southern bands. In order to set-tle the "Indian question" in Oregon permanently, Palmer also convinced the handful of so-called Confederated bands, or remnants of such, to sell all of central Oregon on much the same terms as the Rogue River tribes received.[37]

Unfortunately, the death rate from disease and malnutrition at the new reserves remained high. Unlike the situation on the reserves in California, agents had initially done little to plant grain at either Table Rock or the Umpqua reserves. This changed when the Indians reached Grand Ronde, where large wheat fields were quickly put in. Even so, many Indians were "sick" and many were dying when they arrived at Grand Ronde in 1856. Initially the agents relied on schooners from Portland to bring in flour and beef. But such a diet, without the Indians' common fare of roots and salmon, often produced "a bloody flux and an intermittent fever." Those Indians arriving at Grand Ronde were routinely reported as being "sick" for a solid two years after the reserve was established. In late 1857 chief To-qua-he-ar could only lament: "My People are all dying."[38] Office of Indian Affairs inspector Browne, who visited Grande Ronde in 1858, counted 1,925 Indians (roughly half those in eastern Oregon a decade before), but he too noted that "much sickness has prevailed among them, venereal and consumption." Some 800 were sick at the time of his visit, most likely from flu or malaria.[39] Disease had become the ally of ethnic cleansing, weakening Indians to the point where they had few choices but to move.

With conflict in Oregon subsiding, more and more attention shifted to Washington Territory, where General Wool increasingly spent his time, organizing the new forts: Vancouver, Steilacoom, on a bay east of Tacoma, and the Dalles, well upriver from Vancouver.[40] When Washington territorial governor Isaac I. Stevens arrived in 1853, he set out to negotiate treaties that relinquished land with all the tribes in the territory. He held his first council with Indians in the vicinity of Olympia and thereafter negotiated nine other major treaties, ending in January 1856.[41]

Stevens's negotiation with Chief Seattle provides a good example of how the governor worked. Stevens opened the discussions on January 22, 1855, after he and his assistants had already written up the treaty terms. "We want to give you houses, and having homes you will have the means . . . to cultivate the soil," he began. "The Great Father wishes you to send him back a paper showing your desires and wishes." Stevens apparently never mentioned land cessions, assuring the Indians that they could continue fishing for salmon, hunting, and gathering nuts and berries.[42]

How much of this rhetoric Seattle understood is difficult to determine. A trader translated Stevens's words into a Chinook trade jargon, and a mixed-blood Indian then related it to Seattle. Seattle supposedly responded: "I look upon you as a father . . . All of the Indians have the same good feeling towards you and will send it on paper to the Great Father. All of them, old men, women & children rejoice that he has sent you to take care of them." Seattle very likely failed to understand that "the paper" that he signed gave up his homeland—some 5 million acres—for three cents an acre. In return Stevens organized three small reservations and promised yearly annuities.[43]

By spring 1855 Superintendent Palmer from Oregon joined Stevens near Walla Walla, on the upper Columbia River, and opened a rather stormy week-long discussion with the powerful Columbia River Indians, including the Klikitat, Yakama, Cayuse, Walla Walla, Nez Perce, and Pelouse tribes, numbering well into the thousands.[44] The two men made the same promises—presents, annuities, and small reservations. But these Indians were not poor or subdued by liquor and other debilitating influences, like some of the Puget Sound bands; they had large cattle and horse herds and a vast country. And they seemed to understand the rhetoric of the governor to a much greater degree. Thus Stevens initially faced a stone wall: the chiefs all refused to take presents or even tobacco, a clear "no" in Indian terms.[45]

But Stevens hammered away, often speaking for several hours a day. The chiefs patiently listened—headmen of Native tribes became headmen primarily because of their ability to listen and put off making a decision. Finally, after many days, Chief Peopeomoxmox of the Walla Walla challenged Stevens's rhetoric. Peopeomoxmox, joined by Kamahkan of the Yakamas, openly charged Stevens with trying to distribute presents in an effort to take Indian land. "Goods and the earth are not equal," Peopeomoxmox angrily retorted. The earth was their mother–how does one sell one's mother?[46]

At that point a large contingent of Nez Perce Indians arrived from Idaho. They claimed hunting land in eastern Washington and Oregon and rode into the council on beautiful horses, "gaily dressed and painted and all mounted. . . . They approached in columns, two abreast." They also carried an American flag, as some Nez Perces had joined Americans in the earlier struggle to subdue the Cayuses who had killed the Whitmans. The entire mood of the council changed. On June 7 a Nez Perce chief, Lawyer, announced that he would sign a treaty. A further breakthrough occurred when Superintendent Palmer assured the Cayuses, Umatillas, and Walla Wallas that they would have their own reservations in eastern Oregon.[47] On June 9 the Walla Walla chief Kamahkan finally signed along with other leaders. Stevens had purchased most of Washington, over 30,000 square miles, and parts of eastern Oregon for several hundred thousand dollars.[48]

Tensions along the Columbia River as well as in the Puget Sound region increased dramatically by fall. Whites moved immediately onto Indian lands, taking over fisheries and prospecting for gold. Local newspapers in Oregon incorrectly reported that the treaties allowed miners immediate access, even before the Senate ratified the agreements. As miners invaded Indian lands, expressing their right of "entitlement" in the usual manner, clashes occurred, resulting in the Yakama Indian War.[49]

Governor Stevens quickly wrote the president for help, noting that the white population had fled to blockhouses.[50] The Nisquallys provided the bulk of the fighters, joining the Klikitats and Yakamas. They even laid siege to the infant town of Seattle, where settlers barely held on. Indians burned houses and fired on ships in the harbor. Wool quickly ordered Colonel Silas Casey and 400 troops to sail for Fort Steilacoom and save the white communities on Puget Sound. When Casey arrived, he defeated the Indians in a brief skirmish but seemed unsure of the future and concluded: "The Whole country between the Green and White Rivers and the Payallup south to within five miles of Ft. Steilacoom was captured and occupied by the Indians."[51]

The war also attracted attention in Oregon, where settlers had little reason to be concerned with these Indians. Seemingly intent on coming to the aid of the white people of Washington, territorial governor Curry ordered out the Oregon Mounted Rangers to reinforce Fort Dalles. Yet a combined force of rangers and regulars was unable to overawe the plateau Indians. In a curious move Governor Curry then ordered the Rangers against the Walla Walla, who were far to the west and only lightly implicated in the fighting.[52] General Wool, however, opposed putting volunteers or rangers into the field. After learning of the violent activities of the volunteers in the Rogue River War, Wool remained convinced that they would only widen the conflict in Washington. In a private letter to his wife he concluded: "[U]nless extermination is abandoned, private war prevented and the volunteers withdrawn from the field, the war may be continued indefinitely."[53] In a wise move Wool ordered Colonel Wright, the "horseback diplomat," from Fort Reading, to take command at Fort Dalles.[54]

Wright moved his now nearly 600 troops cautiously to a region just east of the main Yakama villages, along the Naches River in central Washington. "My presence here disturbs these Indians very much," he wrote to Wool in May 1856. "If hostilities are to continue, they cannot fish in safety on any of these rivers. This river, the Naches, is famous for fish, the bank for miles is lined with their old lodges." Wright did not intend to attack the Indians—although he did skirmish with them—instead he denied them access to their fisheries.[55] His tactics worked. Kamahkan sued for peace in July, and Wright acceded. The colonel then marched east to the Walla Walla country, where he reached a similar agreement.[56] The war had supposedly ended.

While negotiating peace Colonel Wright soon ran afoul of the Oregon and Washington Volunteers. The Washington militia under Lieutenant Colonel Ben Shaw—whom Wright had forced from the field while dealing with the Yakamas—assumed that the less protected Cayuse and Walla Walla bands of eastern Oregon might be easy pickings. He heard of a small village of mostly Cayuse Indians situated in the Grande Ronde River valley (not to be confused with the Grand Ronde of northwest Oregon). Shaw surprised the Indians in their camp on July 17, 1856, shot down forty, mostly old men, women, and children, and then plundered the camp of food, ammunition, tools, and livestock. Upon hearing of the attack, Wool ordered Wright to "disarm the volunteers and drive them out." He intended to stop their "plundering."[57]

While Wool feared retribution for disarming volunteers, he detested the war crimes that they often inflicted on Indians. To this end he sent several letters back east to friends that were published in the *New York Herald* as well as the *New York Tribune*. The editors of the papers noted the massive cost of the conflict—some 4 million dollars—and that whites had "shamelessly butchered" Indians. With strong support in both military and journalistic circles, pressure finally convinced Stevens to step down and return to Washington, ostensibly to defend his treaties, which had yet to be ratified. As the fighting came to a conclusion, the army eventually granted General Wool's request to be relieved of command. Congress awarded the general a sword for his service, to some degree a vindication of his efforts to protect the Indians of the Pacific Northwest.[58]

This still left the War Department in a quandary as to how it should proceed in the future. Colonel Townsend, who had been Wool's adjutant, brought the question to the secretary of war, who agreed that the army's role did not include forcing Indians onto reservations—in essence ethnic cleansing—although continuously pushed to do so by territorial officials. Rather the army should only deal with "hostile" Indians.[59] Nevertheless, the army exacerbated the situation further when a decision was made to connect troops then located on the upper Columbia River with those in Montana by building a road between the two commands. The road soon took shape, meandering east through the mountains over Lookout Pass into the Bitterroot Valley, near Missoula, Montana. Miners soon followed. Yet another Indian war broke out in 1858, this time with the Spokane Indians.

The Spokane and Coeur d'Alene Indians had killed several miners. Hurried messages reached Colonel Edward Steptoe at Fort Walla Walla on the upper Columbia, who marched against the Indians. Steptoe underestimated the Indians' strength and soon found himself surrounded and forced to retreat. The disgrace seemed all the more apparent when it was learned that Steptoe had abandoned cannon during his retreat. Colonel Wright received orders to avenge Steptoe's misstep, much in the fashion of what Harney accomplished at Blue Water Creek. Wright lit into the Spokanes and Coeur d'Alenes, defeating them in two engagements. These Indians had been in contact with missionaries for many years and had planted crops for their subsistence. Wright laid waste to their country. "Many barns filled with wheat, or oats, also several fields of grain with numerous caches of vegetables, dried berries and Kamas, all destroyed or used by my troops."[60] The devastation brought the Indians' immediate surrender.

Far from authority, Wright assumed that he had the right to convene a count-martial, which theoretically could only be used in trying soldiers. His officers found eleven Indians guilty, and Wright promptly hanged them all.[61] While on shaky legal ground, Wright seemed totally unaware of the availability of using a "military commission" to try Indians, which had been done in California for several years. General Winfield Scott had written the procedures for using such commissions for trying civilians in Mexico in 1847. But Washington officials, consumed by the problems in Kansas and the Mormon revolt in Utah in 1857–58, gave the issue little attention. In any case Wright's actions quickly ended the conflict, and the eastern Spokanes and Coeur d'Alenes never went to war again.[62]

The struggles over land in the Northwest slowed by the time the Civil War broke out. Most Indians had been placed on reservations or at least assigned to various reserves. Pressure from miners subsided appreciably as well, as new strikes in Colorado in 1859 and Montana a year later siphoned off troublemakers who had helped start the wars of 1855 and 1858. The only conflict of note came when miners invaded Nez Perce lands, in far eastern Oregon and north-central Idaho. Oregon senator James W. Nesmith—who had commanded one of the Oregon Volunteer regiments during the 1855 war—called for a new treaty negotiation in 1862 to reduce the size of the original Nez Perce reservation. Commissioners arrived the next year to purchase lands, ignoring the more western Nez Perce groups called the Lower Bands whose lands were sought and negotiating instead with those Indians who generally followed Chief Lawyer, a Christian. In a stunning display of obvious deceit the federal negotiators convinced Lawyer's followers to give up 90 percent of the original reserve, some 7 million acres of land. The Senate quickly ratified the agreement, although the signatories represented less than one-third of the Nez Perce Nation.[63]

The Nez Perce treaty of 1863 in some ways represented what had happened to many Indians along the Pacific Slope following the gold rush, but in other ways it was an exception. The Nez Perces, Umatillas, Walla Wallas, and other tribes in Washington faced the diminishment of their homelands but at least were allowed to maintain some of those lands. The general belief among American negotiators was that Indians had no right to own vast expanses. This was not the case with the huge numbers of Indians in western Oregon or California, where reservations were ultimately created in regions that were isolated from white settlers, such as the Tule and Klamath River valleys or even Round Valley. Most of the survivors on these reserves had been forcefully removed without much consideration by government officials as to the willingness of these people to give up their ancestral lands. Indeed most officials considered the ethnic cleansing of these people to be a humane resolution of a perplexing problem.

Very few officials—either in the army or in the Indian Office—seemed to sense the moral implications of such actions. Most officers saw the actions as being progressive solutions. The main objective was to provide land sufficient for Indians to become farmers, so that they might support themselves much like the "civilized" settlers who drove the Indians from their homelands. Even so, most officials along the Pacific Slope, even many state and territorial officers, did decry the random killing of Indians, which was more a problem in southwestern Oregon and northern California than elsewhere. Men like General Wool wrote angry letters back to Washington demanding action, disarmed rangers, and ordered his troops to prevent violence. It cannot be denied that Wool and other representatives of the Indian Office, such as Superintendent Palmer, tried to uphold a federal policy that had elements of humanity while it deported people to new lands. Some tried to a greater degree than others, perhaps reflecting their own sense of what was right and what was wrong or perhaps reflecting the degree of individual influence that they had in Washington. These men certainly felt that they had taken a morally correct stand against genocide, and they did.

Once again, much as in California, most state and territorial officials in the Northwest never offered up written policy statements that promoted genocide. Indeed Governor Curry openly opposed such a policy in published proclamations. While delegate Lane in Oregon and Governor Stevens in Washington certainly embraced language that promoted the "extermination" of Indians, neither had the opportunity to create such a policy or put it into effect. The plateau Indians of eastern Oregon and Washington mostly were powerful enough to resist the state-led troops and at times defeated them, and Lane was never an executive in charge of territorial affairs after 1851. Wool viewed both men as what they were— troublemakers who incited rangers and volunteers to acts that constituted war crimes. In today's world they probably would face prosecution for such collusion.

Surely Indian leaders all along the Pacific Slope who had resisted federal policies of deportation, diminishment, and reservation confinement felt much the same as military officers, who mostly had tried to protect their people. They had done what they could to preserve their people and their rights to land and resources during a most trying decade. Despite their raids on wagon trains and their waylaying of isolated miners, we can hardly blame Indians for defending what was rightfully theirs—the land and its resources. Indeed it hardly seems fathomable to sit back today and try to comprehend what it must have been like for Indians to see river streams that had once provided vast stores of dried salmon muddied, destroyed, and altered even in their courses by miners. The patient reserve of Native peoples in the Pacific Northwest during an incredibly difficult period is a marvel to behold.

12

THE GREAT PLAINS

War Crimes, Reservations, Peace Commissions, and Reformers

The Yakama War cost 4 million dollars, just as Wool had predicted. Worse, the government soon faced a crisis of much greater magnitude—the American Civil War. When war clouds appeared in the East, Indian Office officials assumed that many problems in the West had been settled, particularly in Texas, in Minnesota, and on the Pacific Slope. But conflict had been festering; serious trouble soon broke out all across the plains and even in Minnesota. By 1865 an exhausted America faced turmoil in the West, in particular on the Great Plains, where war loomed.[1] While treaties in 1867 in the South and in 1868 in the North brought some reprieve, allowing reformers at least to offer peaceful solutions, the 1860s brought to the fore a newly accepted policy—"diminishment" of Indian Country, even though lands on the Great Plains had been solemnly promised to their Indian occupants in 1834.

The chaos of the war often superseded any effort to create an effective Indian policy, even one that promoted ethnic cleansing. Both the Union and the Confederate states maintained Indian offices and hired agents, but military officers often took charge of agencies or regions. President Abraham Lincoln and later President Andrew Johnson both were distracted from Indian policy issues during the war and the Reconstruction period that followed. The executive branch, which had often served as a mediator between the Indian Office of the Interior Department and the Department of War, simply had more pressing issues—winning the war, Reconstruction, and impeachment.

Just before the firestorm of war, rumors of gold along the eastern watershed of the Rocky Mountains surfaced in 1858 in what would become eastern Colorado. A rush into the region reached its height the following summer, as 100,000 miners scoured the mountains just west of the new town of Denver. Hopes of administering the Intercourse Laws on mostly Cheyenne and Ute Indian land faded.[2] Indian agent William Bent at Fort Wise, in southeastern Colorado, reported increasing miners' invasions of the eastern watershed of the Rockies in December, "making large and extensive settlements and laying off and building towns all over the best part of their [the Indians'] country." Even more galling, the Indians did not understand the invasion, as "they have never been treated with for it [the land]."[3] Indians near Fort Laramie had similar concerns. Here agent Twiss noted that these tribes had "extreme suspicion in all matters relating to the preservation of game, their only means of subsistence." They even had a "suspicious belief that the buffalo will not return to the same place again where he may have scented the white man."[4]

As miners overran eastern Colorado, Twiss concluded that a treaty negotiation might prevent war. The outgoing Buchanan administration did send commissioners who reached an agreement with the Cheyennes and Arapahos in February 1861. Rather than attempt to define Indian Country, the treaty simply stipulated that the Indians ceded "all the lands owned, possessed, or claimed by them." They, in turn, received a reservation along the upper Arkansas River of some 1,500 square miles, a major "diminishment" of their homeland.[5] The signers included Black Kettle for the Cheyennes and Little Raven for the Arapahos, but the Cheyenne Dog Soldiers mostly stayed away. It is likely that none of these Indians realized that the agreement ceded west-central Kansas, a major hunting ground.[6]

Captain John Hayden, commanding Fort Larned, soon spoke with these Indians. He believed the Arapahos and Cheyennes led by Little Raven, Wolf, and Big Mouth to be "friendly" and sympathized with their plight: "These Indians have been much annoyed by the intrusions of organized parties of New Mexicans, who pursue the buffalo as a matter of business."[7] But Hayden could do little to prevent conflict; he had few troops, mostly infantry. Other commanders in the West at the outbreak of the Civil War were in a like circumstance. As fighting erupted in the East, Forts Cobb, Arbuckle, and Gibson in Indian Territory were all abandoned by the Union for lack of supplies and troops to protect them.

Confederate officials soon filled the gap left by the Union, commissioning Albert Pike from Arkansas to negotiate new treaties with the Indians in Indian Territory. Pike found the Cherokees divided when he reached

Tahlequah, their capital. Head Chief John Ross opted for neutrality. Ross received strong encouragement from the secret society of mostly full-bloods called the Keetoowahs. They met quietly at night to discuss the evolving events, attaching the insignia of a cross pin to their shirts and thus being referred to as the "pins."[8] Ross hoped to convince Union authorities to reinforce Fort Gibson, but it never happened.[9]

The old Treaty Party of 1835 still remained strong. Elias Boudinot and his brother, Stand Watie, formed the "Southern Rights Party" in 1861. Watie quickly took a colonel's commission in the Confederate Army. He organized an "Indian Home Guard" armed by the Confederacy. Pressure then mounted on Ross to join the Confederacy.[10] Unlike the Cherokees, who remained divided, the Chickasaws, Choctaws, and Seminoles readily signed treaties with Pike under the promise that they would retain their lands. Pike even convinced some Comanches and Kiowas to sign a treaty attaching them to the Confederacy in 1861, although some of these Indians apparently thought that they were negotiating with the United States. Nevertheless, Confederates had mostly taken over Indian Territory by Christmas; Indians, like Ross, who wanted neutrality had been defeated by Confederate troops and sent fleeing into Kansas.[11]

With few options, Ross finally agreed to call a Cherokee National Convention on August 21. With Stand Watie and some of his well-armed regiment in the audience, the National Council signed a treaty with the Confederacy.[12] The Union forces that Ross had hoped for finally arrived in March 1862, when General Samuel Curtis and some 12,000 men soundly defeated a larger Confederate force under General Earl Van Dorn at the Battle of Pea Ridge. This offered Ross an opportunity to visit Washington and confer with Abraham Lincoln, arguing to the president that the Cherokee Nation had been "forced for the preservation of their Country and their existence to negotiate a Treaty" with the Confederacy.[13] Ross hoped that Lincoln would understand and that he would guarantee Cherokee rights to their Oklahoma homeland, which the Confederate treaty had certainly put in jeopardy.

Sensing the continuing need to convince Washington naysayers of their loyalty, Ross helped muster in several brigades of Cherokee and Creek Indians as soldiers in the Union Army and formed a new National Council in 1863. It met at Ke-too-wha, the stomp grounds of the society that had resisted Confederate conscription. Reconstituting themselves as a nation, they then sent several petitions to the federal government asserting their loyalty to the Union and begging for protection. "Our people have rallied to the standard of the Union," one read. "Fifteen hundred loyal Cherokee men are now in the service of the United States, . . . and thousands more are ready to enlist." Finally, the new council abolished slavery in the Cherokee Nation.[14]

Confederate setbacks in eastern Indian Territory did not deter their efforts to invade the far West. President Jefferson Davis sent regiments under General Henry Hopkins Sibley and the notorious Colonel John R. Baylor into El Paso and thence north up the Rio Grande into Colorado. While Union troops sent Sibley reeling at Glorieta Pass and retook New Mexico, the Confederates in the meantime had started a war with the Apaches.[15] Some of these Indians—in particular the Navajos in the north—had horticultural plots, herded sheep, and even nurtured fruit trees. Chiricahua Apaches lived in small bands that roamed the mountains and valleys, gathering food and raiding Spanish settlements for horses.[16] By 1862 the Chiricahuas Cochise, Victorio, Mangas Coloradas, and Geronimo all led bands, attacking supply trains and cutting off settlements in southern Arizona (such as Tucson) from New Mexico.[17]

A California column arrived at Tucson with 2,300 troops late in 1862, too late to fight Confederates. Its red-headed and ruthless commander, General James Carleton, issued orders: "hunt [Apaches] and destroy all but the women and children." One of his troops surprised an entire Arivaipa Apache town, killing fifty Indians. Carleton's men killed another two dozen Chiricahuas in eastern Arizona. Nevertheless, as Cochise's biographer Edwin Sweeney has noted, "we must not overlook the fact that Cochise and Mangas [Coloradas] practiced the same policy." A vicious guerrilla war had erupted, with evidence of the war crime of killing civilians on both sides. The conflict would not end for another twenty years. Meanwhile Carleton's men soon faced an even greater challenge from the Navajos.[18]

General Carleton ordered mountain man Christopher "Kit" Carson and 4,000 New Mexican volunteers to invade the Navajo heartland at the Canyon de Chelly in far northeastern Arizona. They slaughtered hundreds of sheep and destroyed crops. From the newly established Fort Wingate, in northwestern New Mexico, Carson convinced the Indians to surrender. He then herded 11,612 Navajos onto what history has recorded as the "Long Walk," an exodus from northwestern New Mexico to the desolate Bosque Redondo in the southeast. The deportation eventually caused the lives of 3,000 Indians, who perished from the heat and poor food.[19]

No one in Washington questioned these policies, which were certainly crimes against humanity or ethnic cleansing. The mass deportation of people is today an international crime. But even with the loss of life, the policy was designed to confine Indians, not exterminate them. Despite attempts by some historians to argue for genocide, the majority of the Navajos survived. Indeed General Carleton had boasted of his ability to use the nonfertile lands of Bosque Redondo to make the Navajos into farmers. And Carleton had mostly followed the stated policy of Colonel E. R. S. Canby, who earlier had concluded: "There is now no choice between [the Navajos'] absolute extermination or their removal and colonization at points so remote . . . as to isolate them entirely from the inhabitants of the territory."[20] The Navajos survived primarily because the officers who led these campaigns considered genocide to be an unacceptable alternative.

The violence that characterized the Southwest seemed a continent away in peaceful Minnesota, where roughly 6,000 Dakota Sioux tried to adapt to their newly "diminished" reservation. A new aggressive Indian agent, Joseph R. Brown, organized an active "civilization" program in 1858, mostly forced upon the Mdewakanton people under Chief Little Crow, known by his Dakota name Taoyateduta. Some of these Indians joined the "farmer" band, cutting their hair, putting on pants, and moving into new clapboard houses. Brown poured annuity resources into the farmer band, which constituted a small minority on the reservation, ignoring other Indians.[21] Soldiers from nearby Fort Ridgely had to be called in to quell disturbances, especially when annuity distributions for the other Indians were too late and too little.[22]

Many Mdewakantons opposed the new policies by 1862, especially those from two traditional villages under Red Middle Voice and Little Six, who formed an akicita (soldiers' lodge). This group of warriors contemplated breaking up the farmer band and removing the thousands of settlers who had taken up land on both sides of the ten-mile-wide reservation. When four young members of the lodge arrived late in the evening of August 17, explaining that they had killed four whites after being refused liquor, the soldiers' lodge decided for war and pressured Taoyateduta to join them. He did so reluctantly. "You will die like rabbits when the hungry wolves hunt them in the Hard Moon [January]," he proclaimed. "Taoyateduta is not a coward: he will die with you."[23]

A hundred warriors marched into the Lower Agency compound at 8:00 A.M. on August 18, 1862, and started killing the traders and government workers. They then turned on the settlers. By nightfall some four hundred pioneer families had been murdered, many with knives and hatchets.[24] Pitched battles followed at Fort Ridgely and the mostly German town of New Ulm, but they both held out. Nevertheless, panic struck Minnesota, which faced the most brutal ethnic war in American history.[25]

State authorities organized a relief column commanded by Henry Sibley, the man who nearly dictated the removal treaties of 1851. As Sibley's army of 1,600 men moved west, he encouraged Indians who had not killed civilians to surrender, sending emissaries with the message into Taoyateduta's camp.[26] After Sibley's army defeated those who wished to fight at Wood Lake on September 23, some two thousand Dakota Indians surrendered, mostly innocent people. With state newspapers calling for "extermination," Sibley broke his promise and created a military commission. It tried 392 Dakota men in just thirty-five days, condemning 303 to death. Sibley fully expected to execute them as soon as the President Abraham Lincoln authorized it.[27]

A military court-martial could only be used to try military personnel, so Sibley organized a "commission" consisting of five officers. Such commissions had been sanctioned during the Mexican War. General Winfield Scott's General Orders Number 20 outlined the way in which the courts should proceed. All defendants were to have legal council, including assistance from the judge advocate of the court. Cross-examination was allowed, and hearsay evidence not admitted. All questions from the military officers of the court had to be put in writing several days before the commission met. Scott believed that a Military Commission needed procedures similar to those found in civil courts in the United States, complete with "discovery" before the trial proceeded. And as the Civil War broke out, judge advocate general John F. Lee reissued General Order Number 20 in April 1861, sending copies of it to all commands.[28]

Colonel Sibley violated every procedural rule of General Order Number 20. Hearsay evidence, taken in the Dakota language and translated in court by mixed-bloods, was commonly accepted. Indians incriminated themselves at every turn; well over a hundred admitted to carrying a gun and firing at Fort Ridgely and received death sentences. They had never been advised that they did not have to testify against themselves. No Indian had a lawyer or was offered one. Even worse, some forty trials had been conducted in a single day. When President Lincoln saw the trial records, he was aghast. The trial records of such commissions supposedly had to be reviewed by the Judge Advocate General's Office, which had the authority to demand new trials. In the end Lincoln made a political decision, agreeing to execute thirty-eight Dakota men mostly deemed guilty by association with others who might have killed civilians. A crowd of three thousand Minnesotans gathered at Mankato, as the floor of the square-shaped gallows dropped from beneath the feet of the condemned men on December 26, 1862, the largest mass execution in American history.[29]

Besides the prisoners, who were moved in wagons to Mankato, some 1,658 Dakota women, children, and old men were sent east to Fort Snelling.[30] A few commentators have suggested that the long walk to Fort Snelling replicated the Cherokee "Trail of Tears" or even the Navajos' "Long Walk." In reality, thousands died in these other two events, compared with just one Dakota child and one Dakota man during the Dakotas' deportation.[31] In spring roughly 1,300 mostly Dakota women and children climbed aboard riverboats bound for Crow Creek, Dakota Territory; several hundred died from disease and starvation during the process of deportation and resettlement in the West. Large numbers of women survived only by prostituting themselves to nearby army personnel. The remaining 260 mostly male prisoners at Mankato served mostly three-year sentences in a Union camp at Davenport, Iowa, where about half of them died, again of disease.[32]

Minnesota politicians convinced Congress to confiscate the Dakota reservation as well as that of the Winnebagos. They then turned on the Chippewas. Commissioner of Indian affairs William P. Dole asked them to cede their remaining lands. Chief Shaw-bus-cum gave an angry reply while in council at Fort Ripley: "How can it be possible to abandon our reservations. . . . We demand that we should be allowed to live on our reserves."[33] Although Dole relented, Governor Alexander Ramsey traveled north in late summer 1863 and demanded that the Chippewas sign two more treaties. "They have lands here which many of them never see," Ramsey began. He then argued that since a handful of Chippewas had assaulted a steamboat along the Red River, the "Great Father" demanded restitution. Fearing expulsion, as had happened to the Dakotas to the south, band leaders of the Red Lake and Pembina Chippewas finally ceded more land, receiving a number of small reservations in the northernmost portion of the state.[34]

The Minnesota-Dakota War had been a tragedy for all concerned. The root cause of the conflict was the Medill-Brown reservation scheme, which in this case provided too small a reservation, and encouraged white settlements to form quickly around it. The policy of ethnic cleansing led to confusion, outrage, and violence. Nevertheless, the actions of the roughly one hundred Dakota men who killed civilians must be condemned as homicide. Taoyateduta had counseled against murdering civilians, but he had failed to prevent it. Even so, General Sibley's failure to follow legal procedure, as prescribed by General Order Number 20, also made a mockery of American justice.

While Minnesota's frontier recovered slowly, miner "entitlement" soon caused trouble in southern Idaho.[35] By early winter 1862 Colonel P. E. Connor and his California Column reached Salt Lake, where the chief justice of the Territorial Supreme Court issued an order for the arrest of three Shoshone chiefs, Bear Hunter, Sampitch, and Sagwitch, who were implicated in several murders along the northward trail to the Montana mines.[36] Territorial marshal Isaac L. Gibbs set about to arrest the men, asking for assistance from Colonel Connor, who brushed Gibbs aside and noted his intention to march against the Indians. He openly proclaimed that he would solve the problem and "take no prisoners." Meanwhile the oracle of the Mormon Church, the *Desert News,* publicly announced that it would be best if the Indians were "wiped out." Even more ominously, Porter Rockwell, one of Brigham Young's military officers, agreed to assist Connor in finding the Indians' camp. Since the *News* never published anything that the Mormon Church did not sign off on, its sanction seemed clear.[37]

Descending upon the Shoshones at Bear River in January 1863, Connor's California militia tore the camp apart, killing men, women, and children, often at close range. An orgy of rape followed, as the soldiers forced Indian women to the ground and shot them if they resisted. Connor reported that 235 Shoshones lay dead in the cold snow, 90 of them women and children, but the count likely reached over 300. Federal officials never ordered the attack and indeed wanted to use civil law to prosecute the perpetrators of the murders. But the Bear River Massacre goes down in history as the worst war crime ever committed by American soldiers against Indians.[38] Whether the Mormon Church played a role in the slaughter is impossible to determine.

Unfortunately, news of Connor's massacre—deemed a great victory in the West—soon reached Denver; conflict in western Kansas and eastern Colorado had subsided after the Fort Wise Treaty of 1861. The new governor of Colorado Territory, John Evans, met several times with the main leaders of the Dog Soldiers in 1863 and 1864. Tall Bull, Big Wolf, and Two Crows refused to sign anything. The tone of Governor Evans's letters suddenly changed: he now feared Indian war.[39] Evans noted that cattle and horses had been run off from ranches near Denver, a firefight had occurred with some 400 Cheyennes near Fort Larned, and a rancher named Hungate and his wife and two daughters had been brutally murdered. Even though the evidence for a "war" was certainly slight, Evans received federal permission to muster in the Third Colorado volunteers, placed under command of Colonel John Chivington.[40]

While Governor Evans headed east for meetings, the "bloodless Third," the whimsical moniker that Denverites gave to Chivington's troops, sat out the fall in saloons. General Conner arrived from Utah, flush from "Indian" victory. While Conner had come to consult regarding protection of the overland mail, his braggadocio riled Chivington. With criticism over inactivity growing, Chivington marched 700 troops out of town on November 14, 1864. Rather than chase the troublesome Dog Soldiers, Chivington headed south to Fort Lyon, finding Black Kettle's peaceful band camped along Sand Creek. His force hit the large scattered camp at dawn on November 29. The slaughter never reached the level of the massacre at Bear River—Chivington never did outdo Connor, and one captain even refused to allow his men to commit mass murder. But many of the "bloodless Third" killed and mutilated Indians, particularly women, who were raped and even had their private parts carved out for trophies.[41] Chivington murdered some 150 Indians in the snow that day.

Indian policy had reached its lowest level in the West by 1864, seemingly falling into the hands of a few murdering militia colonels determined to commit war crimes. Fortunately, new attention came to the region at war's end, as reformers gained ascendancy. Senators such as James Doolittle and John Henderson joined army officers, including Generals Henry Sibley, John B. Sanborn, and William Harney, and supported the Indian Office's effort to expand the reservation system.[42] A hopeful sign came when a new agent, Colonel Jesse Henry Leavenworth, convinced the Southern Plains Indians to negotiate, bringing them together with a peace commission, headed by Sanborn and Harney, in fall 1865. The commission signed a treaty with Cheyennes and Arapahos at the mouth of the Little Arkansas River in October 1865. Black Kettle (who had survived Sand Creek), Little Raven, and several of the more compliant leaders made the necessary marks.[43]

In an unusual turn the treaty actually offered an expanded Indian reservation, giving the Indians lands lying between the Arkansas and Cimarron Rivers, which included roughly one-tenth of the state of Kansas as well as lands lying south of the Arkansas River.[44] A few days later the commission met Comanche and Kiowa leaders and concluded a similar agreement. In what the commission must have seen as a serious reproach to Texas, the reservation set aside for these Indians included most of the Texas Panhandle eastward to the 98th degree of west longitude.[45] These agreements seemed designed to protect Indian hunting grounds, a new twist in United States Indian policy that temporarily rejected "diminishment."

With momentum for peace building everywhere, the government turned to the mess in Indian Territory. Although Union Cherokee troops had recaptured much ground from the Confederacy, federal officials demanded that the Cherokees cede lands, including their western "Outlet." The Choctaws, Creeks, Chickasaws, and Seminoles also gave up land in order to regain some semblance of sovereignty.[46] The commissioners then included clauses that sanctioned railroads in Indian Territory. The West was quickly being transformed from Indian Country to a region where white settlement would soon challenge Native territorial rights. A second result of the war was criticism of the army, which was increasingly blamed for the violence that occurred there. By the late 1860s some easterners saw the Indians as the somewhat noble defenders of their lands.

The selection of General John Pope to head up the new Military Department of Missouri in 1865—which included most of the Great Plains north of Texas at the time—signaled that the War Department seemed less convinced than those who wanted peace with the Indians. Pope had suffered an inglorious defeat at the hands of Confederates at the second Battle of Bull Run in 1862—and then blamed subordinates for his failures. He had been banished to Minnesota thereafter to organize the Department of the Northwest after the Minnesota-Dakota War broke out.[47] Early on, he ordered a subordinate to enlist Canadian "half-breeds . . . in exterminating the Sioux."[48]

Once at his new command at Omaha, General Pope learned that Indians had been raiding almost at will along the Oregon and Smokey Hills Trails. News of the Sand Creek Massacre had arrived at every camp on the plains, and Lakotas and Cheyennes in particular were out to avenge the killings. Complicating matters, both the Union and Kansas Pacific Railroads were headed west along the trails, eventually reaching Indian hunting grounds. Also, after gold had been discovered near Virginia City, Montana, freighter John Bozeman determined to find a route into the goldfields. He started running wagons north from Fort Laramie, hugging the eastern hills of the Big Horn Mountains, into the Yellowstone Valley and thence western Montana.[49] His route, which also invaded Indian hunting grounds, soon became known as the Bozeman Trail.

General Pope believed that protection of the trail warranted punishing the Indians who had been assaulting Bozeman's wagons. But with troops being mustered out of the military, his only hope included using General Connor's California column, which he ordered to punish a large collection of tribes, including Red Cloud's Oglalas, Sitting Bull's Hunkpapas, and the Cheyenne Dog Soldiers.[50] Sending one force of some 1,400 splendidly dressed cavalry under Colonel Nelson Cole east of the Black Hills and thence into the upper Powder River, Connor then advanced north from Fort Laramie and constructed Fort Reno on the headwaters of the Powder. But he lost all contact with Cole, whose troops soon faced several thousand angry Indians. As the battle unfolded, Cole's men broke and ran.[51] By fall both columns had lost their horses and faced starvation.[52] Connor was sent back to Utah and his force disbanded.

Plains Indians had mastered horse combat, using decoys and even at times massing into cavalry charges. They had the added advantage of having little formal contact with whites, helping to sustain their strong traditional moral and religious conviction. While the Dakotas of Minnesota (who mostly surrendered in October 1862) and even the Indians of California and Washington had years of contact with missionaries and traders, the High Plains peoples had a different history. The Dog Soldiers allowed only one or two white men among them, and no missionaries had reached them or Sitting Bull's Lakotas or Buffalo Hump's Comanches. The one exception came with Father De Smet, whom Sitting Bull welcomed into his camp on an occasion or two.[53]

After Connor's retreat, Senator Doolittle worked to bring together a Peace Commission in the North, much like the one that had apparently worked so well under Leavenworth's direction in the South. The American delegation included Indian superintendent Edward B. Taylor, Thomas Wistar (a Quaker philanthropist), and several army officers. To everyone's surprise, in early March 1866, well before the delegation had arrived, Colonel Henry Maynadier at Fort Laramie awoke to see Red Cloud, Spotted Tail (whose Brulé Lakotas increasingly promoted peace), Brave Bear,

Standing Elk, and several hundred mounted Lakota warriors at the river below the fort. They wanted to negotiate.

Maynadier opened the gates and watched as the Indians formed "like a regiment in a line of battle."[54] While the military officers wanted to host the assemblage inside the quarters of the commanding officer, Red Cloud noted that he had never been in a "white man's" house before. Once he reluctantly agreed, Spotted Tail opened discussions by voicing grave concern that the whites must stop driving off the buffalo. After Superintendent Taylor and the commission arrived on May 30, they too met Red Cloud (a shirt wearer at that time, which signified important political and military leadership), Spotted Tail, and Man Afraid Of His Horses, who was the most influential civil chief among the Oglalas. The Indian leaders loudly complained of growing traffic near Fort Laramie and along the Bozeman Trail.[55]

Unfortunately, both Maynadier and Taylor knew that the several companies of infantry under Colonel Henry B. Carrington that had escorted the superintendent west were intended to occupy the very road that Red Cloud and the others opposed—Indian Country at the time.[56] By mid-June Red Cloud learned Carrington's purpose and exploded. Taylor tried to calm him, sending messages explaining that the Great Father was not asking that you "give up the country, or sell it." The treaty that Taylor wished the Indians to sign only offered "Peace." Both Red Cloud and Man Afraid Of His Horses bolted the council. Several days later Spotted Tail and other Brulé leaders, who had no claim on the Powder River country, readily signed the 1866 "Peace Treaty" in exchange for more food annuities.[57]

Just as Red Cloud feared, Colonel Carrington quickly moved north to the headwaters of the Powder River. Some sixty miles north of Fort Reno, he constructed Fort Phil Kearny. The site had the advantage of wood and water and lay at the foot of the Big Horn Mountains, which rose majestically to the west. They were mostly impassable, but rugged hills to the east could hide a thousand warriors, as Carrington soon discovered. For good measure Carrington dispatched even more troops, moving farther north into southern Montana to build Fort C. F. Smith, a stone's throw from the soon-to-be famous Little Big Horn River. All three forts fell under siege by July 1866, as bands of a hundred to three hundred Indians assaulted teamsters and especially the more exposed firewood details.[58] The move into northern Wyoming, legal or not, had started a war along the Bozeman Trail.

While Carrington struggled to get supplies for the winter, the War Department ordered Brevet Brigadier General William B. Hazen to investigate the situation. He found that the treaty of 1866 had accomplished little, concluding that "Indian policy" was "unsettled." He argued for a "vigorous final campaign against these fellows [the northern Indians] as soon as it can be organized—say about November."[59] Such talk invigorated the officers at Fort Laramie. Major James Van Voast recruited Indian spies to go into the camps to determine their exact locations and warrior strength.[60] A full-blood brother-in-law of the Indian trader James Bordeaux provided important information. The informant soon reappeared with interesting news. The now middle-aged war leader (*blotaunka*) Red Cloud and Man Afraid Of His Horses, a major civil chief (*itancan*), had lost influence to the "soldiers' lodge" (*akicita*). The soldiers, commanded by Bad Horse (likely Bad Heart Bull of other accounts), High Backbone, and young Crazy Horse, controlled the largest Lakota camps, even regulating who could come and go.[61]

Surprisingly, Bordeaux's brother-in-law then reported that both Red Cloud and Man Afraid Of His Horses wanted peace.[62] As they told Van Voast's informant: "Big men and old men want peace." Then Red Cloud offered a startling assessment, which the informant repeated: "See all those men [the *akicita*], I have preached to them ever since I went in to make peace and since I took the hand of the White man in peace [a reference to the negotiations in 1866], which I intend to follow, but it's of no use, they have committed depredations all summer. I expect to suffer with them but won't help them. I have talked to them many times, but it's of no use I cannot do anything with them."[63]

Van Voast, who forwarded the report to Colonel Carrington, failed to send it to headquarters back east. The colonel probably discounted it, as he obviously wanted more troops from the War Department—indeed he begged for them on many occasions—which made it unwise to suggest that a peaceful alternative might exist.

Seemingly helping his case, the shrill report of "Indians" came from the ramparts of Fort Phil Kearny on December 6, 1866. A war party had assaulted the wood detail some miles away. Carrington ordered Captain William J. Fetterman and thirty cavalrymen to rush to its rescue. After relieving the train, the young Fetterman, fresh from West Point, followed them, suddenly facing an onslaught of a hundred yelling Indians, who had used decoys to spring a trap. What followed next was unforgivable to a cavalry officer: in Fetterman's own words, "in the most unaccountable manner the cavalry turned and commenced a retreat." While Carrington arrived with reinforcements, Fetterman lamented the actions of his men and sought to restore honor to himself and the troop.[64]

High Backbone, Bad Horse, Crazy Horse, and others probably noted Fetterman's rashness. They decided to draw the cavalry north, if possible, beyond Lodge Tail Ridge, a high butte that ran for five miles to the northeast of the post. Mustering perhaps 900 men, they descended upon Fort Phil Kearny on the morning of December 21, concealing their men in deep crevices northeast of the ridge. Crazy Horse had been picked to lead the ten decoys. The now expected attack on the wood train commenced about 11:00 A.M. Carrington had sent ninety men with the detail—more than usual—so he showed little apprehension. Nevertheless, he eventually ordered Fetterman to relieve the woodcutters, ordering him not to pass over Lodge Tail Ridge. Once out of the fort, Fetterman at the head of eighty-one men chased the decoys over the ridge, where hundreds of Indians surrounded them. On the eastern slope, a spot now known as "massacre hill," Fetterman and his entire command were destroyed.[65]

Army officers bristled at any thoughts of negotiation thereafter and wanted retribution.[66] General Sherman wrote his commander of the newly created Department of the Platte, General C. C. Augur, that he "may construe all the Sioux near the Powder and Yellowstone as hostile, and may punish them to the extent of utter extermination if possible."[67] Yet Sherman had on hand only 2,000 infantry in the whole department, and they also had a responsibility to protect the construction of the two railroads heading west. What cavalry Sherman could deploy went to General Winfield Scott Hancock, of Gettysburg fame, then commanding troops in the Department of Missouri. Sherman hoped that Hancock, who was a long way from the Bozeman Trail, might offer some vindication, writing: "Our troops must get amongst them, and must kill enough of them to inspire fear, and then must conduct the remainder to places where Indian Agents can and will reside amongst them, and be held responsible for their conduct."[68]

To Sherman's chagrin, Congress passed legislation on July 20, 1867, funding another peace commission. The commissioners included Commissioner Taylor, Senator John Henderson from Missouri, reformer Samuel Tappan, and Generals Sherman, Harney, Augur, and Alfred H. Terry. Sherman expected the peace commission to fail, but he soon had to assume the defensive.[69] While at Fort Larned Hancock had learned of a Cheyenne and Lakota village on the Pawnee River. Eager to show off the new troops, Hancock confronted the village leaders and burned their village and food stores when they disappeared at night—the women and children feared another Sand Creek. Hancock's excuse was "their treachery."[70] The incident started an Indian war in Kansas that went on into 1869. Reformer Samuel Tappan thought the actions smacked of Chivington's massacre. Sherman soon replaced Hancock with General Philip Sheridan.

Phil Sheridan, as he was often called, soon gained ascendancy over military affairs. He was shrewd, political when necessary, and determined. General Sherman soon clashed with the Grant administration (he despised the secretary of war), so Sheridan, as general of the Division of the Missouri (literally the entire West), assumed an inordinate degree of influence. Yet he ruled an army officer corps that remained divided over strategy and tactics, much as it had been in the 1850s. Many of his generals had friends in Washington, D.C., much like General Wool nearly two decades before. Sheridan came to distrust many of his department commanders and maintained a small inner circle of officers who remained totally loyal to him. While Sheridan and Sherman remained on the same page—both generally hated Indians—some officers put the Natives' concerns ahead of those of invading settlers. As a result extended arguments often erupted over policy within the army command structure. The army was far from a monolithic organization despite its "chain of command."

The peace commission, which contained both reformers and army officers, met Spotted Tail and other Lakota chiefs at the North Platte Hotel in September 1867. General Sherman surprisingly admitted that some Sioux had not agreed to the Montana road and that some peaceful tribes deserved fair treatment. Then he offered an ominous solution to Spotted Tail: "We therefore propose to let the whole Sioux Nation, you included, select a country on the Missouri River, embracing the White Earth and Cheyenne Rivers." Spotted Tail said nothing in return, but the suggestion implied that lands including the Black Hills and most clearly the Republican and Platte River hunting grounds would not be part of such a new Lakota homeland.[71]

Feeling somewhat relieved at this modest success, the commission moved south into Southern Cheyenne, Arapaho, Kiowa, and Comanche country. In October at Medicine Lodge Creek, in southern Kansas, Senator Henderson opened yet another council, announcing the intent of the government to create a new reservation with houses and fields. He wanted to hear from the Native delegations before, as he put it, "we tell you the road to follow." The Kiowa chief Satanta spoke first. "All the land south of the Arkansas belongs to the Kiowas and Comanches, and I don't want to give away any of it." As to the offer of houses and fields, Satanta said: "I don't want any of these Medicine homes built in the country. I want the papooses brought up just exactly as I am."[72]

Many other chiefs spoke as freely. Ten Bears, a mostly compliant Yamparica Comanche chief, noted that the Great Father had assured him that "all the Comanche land was ours . . . so why do you ask us to leave the river, the sun, and the wind, and live in houses?" Housing and farming became synonymous with the abandonment of the Native way of life to Indian leaders. A day or so later Satanta offered a final comment: "If you build us houses, the land will be smaller. Why do you insist on this?"[73] These Indian chiefs sensed a change in government policy, driven by the coming of the railroads and the need to convince the Indians to settle on diminished reservations.

But the Indian delegations, despite the rhetoric of a few chiefs, also possessed older, pliable men, who had become used to food annuities after the 1865 treaty.[74] Among them were Toshewa (Silver Brooch), Horseback, and Iron Mountain of the Comanches and Kicking Bird, Stumbling Bear, and even Satank of the Kiowas. The more militant—and younger— Comanches, such as Homeah, Cheevers, Mowway, and Paracoon, all failed to attend the discussions. The drought and diseases of the early 1860s and the awful death rates that they created had left leadership voids—historians have even had difficulty determining the realignment of bands that survived into the period after the Civil War.[75] More militant leaders of both tribes certainly did not attend the council with the commissioners.

In the end the peace commission easily convinced the chiefs in attendance to sign the Treaty of Medicine Lodge Creek on October 21, 1867. Article 1 pledged peace—an element that the commission often stressed— but Article 2 established the Comanche-Kiowa Reservation lying between the Washita and Red Rivers from north and south and between the 98th and 100th meridians from east to west—about 12,000 square miles (Congress would later move it south and west from the original location). This agreement took from these Indians land granted to them in Texas under the 1865 treaty—roughly 45,000 square miles. In exchange for the land the government offered more annuities. The Indians could hunt on the lands ceded until the buffalo disappeared, no doubt a clause (if it was correctly understood) that convinced many Indians that little had changed.

Before leaving, the commissioners then obtained signatures on a treaty with Cheyenne and Arapaho chiefs. While Black Kettle remained a principal chief, a number of Dog Soldiers increasingly poked fun at his passivity, especially men like Tall Bull, Roman Nose, and Bull Bear. The final treaty resulted in the creation of a reservation lying just north of the Comanche-Kiowa reserve, lands that constituted roughly half of what the 1865 agreement had guaranteed.[76] The Cheyennes and Arapahos received the right to hunt northward to the Arkansas River or on lands that had been their former reservation.[77] Obviously the Dog Soldiers never agreed to this. Indeed west-central Kansas contained some of their best hunting grounds. During the discussions the Dog Soldier Tall Bull made clear his "shame" and "disgust" at letting Hancock burn his village a few months before. His hatred for the army loomed above any rational discussion relative to which lands were allowed for hunting.[78]

The Medicine Lodge Creek treaties created reservations much smaller than the Indians' claim to land—the agreements were good examples of the new policy of diminishment. Commissioners made vague promises regarding hunting, but most Indians never understood them. The commissioners believed that the Indians would need annuities far more than hunting ranges in the future, obvious indications of their belief that they, rather than the Indians themselves, knew what was best for these government "wards." The commissioners departed, headed north to deal with the Lakotas once again at Fort Laramie.

Reaching the fort on November 12, 1867, Commissioner Taylor could see that the government had an uphill battle. Even the friendly Crows seemed upset, as their chief Bear's Tooth, who spent considerable time near Fort C. F. Smith, noted: "Look at me right. . . . Your young men scare away the game and I have none left. . . . I want you . . . to call back your young men from the country of the Big Horn. Your young men have destroyed the young grass and have set the country on fire. They kill the game not because they want it. They leave it to rot on the roadside. Suppose I went into your country and destroyed your cattle?"[79]

Similar remarks came from the Crow Black Foot, who rejected reservation life: "You speak of putting us on a reservation and teaching us to farm. We were not brought up for that and are not able to do it. That talk does not please us. We want horses to run after the game, and guns and ammunition to kill it. I would like to live just as I have been raised. . . . I am talking with a good, honest heart now."[80]

Sensing resistance and seeing few Lakotas, the commission headed back east, stopping briefly to speak with Spotted Tail. He too remained friendly but resisted a reservation life. "We want to live as our fathers have lived," he concluded, "on the buffalo and the deer that we now find on our hunting grounds."[81] Spotted Tail's Brulés hunted south of the Platte River, which was now part of Kansas, rapidly invaded by homesteaders.

Regrouping in Washington, the commissioners convinced Congress that the Plains Indians needed "two Grand Reservations," the one that the southern Indians had supposedly already agreed to and one that the northern Indians must accept. Returning west, the commission then laid the proposal for a "Grand Reservation" in front of a small gathering of northern Lakotas at Fort Laramie on April 13, 1868. Almost immediately the issue became the Bozeman Trail. The Brulé Iron Shell spoke first: "We want you to take away the forts from the country." Ironically, this concern had actually been addressed in Washington. The Union Pacific Railroad had reached Salt Lake, which made the Bozeman Trail obsolete and costly. Even General Sherman agreed, ordering General Augur to abandon the trail forts in March 1868. He wanted the posts broken up "with the utmost deliberation"; Sherman feared that Indians "may attribute the withdrawal to the wrong motives!"[82]

Senator John Sanborn broke the news to the Indian delegation. On April 29 virtually every Indian representative in attendance, White Bull, American Horse, and even the leader of the Loafers, Big Mouth, agreed that they would sign if the forts were removed. As he stepped forward, the Oglala chief American Horse warned the commissioners: "You know very well that if the treaty is signed by only a portion of our people, it is not likely to stand." He made it clear that Red Cloud and Man Afraid Of His Horses, the two most honored Oglala leaders, who remained in the North, would also have to sign. This seemed unlikely.[83]

Flushed with limited success, some members of the commission headed west to negotiate with the Shoshones in Utah, who were still reeling after the Connor massacre, and settle them on a reservation. Others left for New Mexico, where they resolved issues with the Navajos. The Navajo Treaty of 1868 allowed the remaining Indians to return to northwest New Mexico; the agony of the Long Walk had finally ended. By fall, even after all the forts except Reno had been abandoned, Red Cloud had not come in. The treaty document had been left with the new commanding officer at Fort Laramie, Colonel William Dye. He, like his predecessor, had been trying to coax Red Cloud in by sending him messages of friendship and peace, assuring him that the treaty did not relinquish land.[84]

Only muddled and sometimes contradictory reports can help reconstruct what might have occurred in the camps along the Powder River, but apparently most of the members of the Lakota *akicita* had no intention of making peace, refusing to allow men to leave the camps (which partially explains Red Cloud's failure to appear at Fort Laramie). Indeed, when Red Cloud and Man Afraid Of His Horses spoke of such a possibility the young soldiers supposedly became more suspicious of them. When the *akicita* selected new shirt wearers, they ignored Red Cloud and selected Crazy Horse, "young" Man Afraid Of His Horses, "young" American Horse, and Sword Owner, all men still committed to pressing for war.[85]

Perhaps bitter, Red Cloud and the elder Man Afraid Of His Horses led their bands into winter quarters on the northern edge of the Black Hills. The *akicita* could do little to prevent this, as the Lakotas broke into smaller units during the winter months. Red Cloud learned that some Lakota leaders had signed the treaty at Fort Rice, on the Missouri River, and returned to their villages with large numbers of presents. Concerned about the need to acquire ammunition to fight the Crows and to hunt, and favoring peace, Red Cloud appeared at Fort Laramie on November 4, 1868, with seven lesser chiefs. Major Dye, who met the delegation, indicated that "Red Cloud affected a great deal of Dignity and disinterestedness, while the other chiefs arose, advanced and shook hands." Red Cloud refused a formal handshake: he "remained seated and sulkily gave the ends of his fingers to the officers who advanced."[86]

As Major Dye proceeded to explain the articles of the treaty, he was cut off by Red Cloud. "In answer to whether he wished to hear all the points in regard to the reservation and farming," Dye reported, "he stated that he had learned from others all he cared to know." Dye's Indian messengers had outlined the terms, stressing that the paper was simply a "peace treaty." Those same messengers expected to be rewarded for convincing Red Cloud to come in and likely had never seen the treaty terms themselves. They obviously convinced Red Cloud that he was only agreeing to peace. Nevertheless, the established procedures of the Department of Interior dictated that treaties normally had to be read to the signers in their language, which Dye tried to do but quickly abandoned (Dye, as a military officer, likely knew little about the regulation). When Dye met the delegation on the second and third day, he apparently stressed the "benefits" of the treaty rather than attempting a careful reiteration of its terms. The Indians and military officers argued over the "desires" of the Indians to obtain powder for their guns.

A careful perusal of the Dye report reveals other interesting aspects of Red Cloud's concerns. He notes that he had come in peace in 1866 to treat with the Americans at Fort Laramie and found instead that they were sending in troops to build forts. The forts and the Bozeman Trail that they protected had been the cause of war. All Red Cloud wanted from the negotiations with Dye was "peace" and presents in the form of ammunition to fight the Crows—he dismissed virtually every attempt to discuss the development of a "reservation," the "benefit" that Dye stressed. Indeed Red Cloud noted that Crows had recently killed "five and fifteen" of his warriors and that above all he wanted the wherewithal to get revenge. Dye struggled to explain that only General Harney could authorize the distribution of ammunition, certainly a disappointment for the Oglala chief.

Perhaps the most interesting aspect of Dye's report involved his failure to explain the boundary lines established by the new reservation for the Indians and Red Cloud's belief that he would be able to return to the Powder River country and live thereafter. Apparently Red Cloud heard nothing regarding the article defining the so-called Great Sioux Reservation, which placed the Bozeman Trail outside the reserve. In parting Red Cloud said that he expected to go back to the Powder River country and continue to live by the hunt over the new year.

Red Cloud noted that "they [his people] did not wish to leave their present home, abounding in game, to go to a new country . . . and that he [Red Cloud] thought it wrong to try to induce them to abandon the chase and go to farming . . . that his name to the paper would mean peace and therefore he did not wish to make any promises to the Government which in justice to the Red Man he could not execute."[87]

Without question Red Cloud failed to understand that Article 2 of the agreement placed the westernmost border of the reservation on the western edge of the Black Hills—well east of the Bozeman Trail—and that the northern boundary cut the Indians off from the Yellowstone River Valley and one of its main arteries, the Powder. Article 4 stated that the Lakotas would have to move to that reservation, which Red Cloud completely rejected. Article 11 indicated that the very lands that Red Cloud wished to go back to—the Powder, Big Horn, Tongue, and Rosebud River valleys—could not be "occupied" by the Lakota people. Article 16 identified these lands as "unceded Indian Territory." The Indians might hunt these lands only while buffalo existed. Finally, the Indians reserved the "right to hunt on any lands north of North Platte, and on the Republican Fork of the Smoky Hill," a clause that certainly seemed to contradict other articles.[88] Analyzing Articles 2, 4, 11, and 16 in terms of what they said about land and hunting would keep a good legal team busy for months. Moreover, quite a few Lakotas felt betrayed by the chiefs who signed the agreements. Colonel Jonathan E. Smith, who commanded Fort Laramie in 1871, concluded that "all the Indians unite in saying that nothing was said to them of the limits defined as their reservation by the Treaty of 1868."[89]

While the Civil War had brought nothing but conflict to the plains, the peace commissions had at least temporarily ended the fighting. The commissioners had also witnessed the departures from the field of men like Chivington, Connor, and even Carleton. The treaties also included a rhetoric that preached peace and the eventual settlement of Indians on large reservations in their own homelands. Nevertheless, the treaties brought the diminishment of those homelands—hunting lands could be used but Indians no longer owned them. As such the treaties constituted a new form of ethnic cleansing, even though it lacked the aspects of deportation that eastern Indians or even those in California had suffered through. Worse, most tribal members had little idea that these lands in Kansas and west and north of the Black Hills had been ceded, even as they continued to hunt on them.

More ominously, Congress had authorized more troops for the West not fewer. Western citizens squarely supported the army, unlike the "softhearted" reformers. Sherman's old friend Ulysses S. Grant was a frontrunner for the presidency in fall 1868. Despite their tempered views on tactics, then, army generals would look for ways to regain ascendancy in the West and overcome what many saw as the temporary expediency of peace commissions and treaties. Trouble lay ahead for all concerned.

13

THE "PEACE POLICY"

Benevolent Ethnic Cleansing

Most Americans celebrated the signing of the peace treaties in 1867 and 1868. The Union Pacific and Central Pacific Railroads had nearly joined in Utah, and the treaties, along with the railroads' success, suggested the beginning of a new era. The peace soothed the concerns of intellectuals and reformers who believed that Indian war led to a moral decline and the abandonment of the principles of natural rights. The triumph seemed even more secure when Americans elevated General Grant to the presidency. He had seen enough of war and courted the very reformers despised by Sherman. Henry Ward Beecher triumphantly stated that Grant would go down in history more for the wisdom of his "civil administration" than for his victories in war. William Lloyd Garrison, the great abolitionist, endorsed Grant wholeheartedly. Samuel Tappan, Hancock's critic, seemed ecstatic. Tappan knew that Grant had condemned the massacre at Sand Creek as "murder." To cap it off, Grant's campaign promise included the statement "All Indians disposed to peace will find the new policy a peace-policy."[1]

And so it was that the United States embarked on a Peace Policy—not war or extermination—for the eight long years of the Grant Administration. A few caveats did exist. The treaties of 1867 and 1868 granted railroad rights-of-way through the various reservations and so-called unceded Indian lands. While this did not initially pose problems with the Lakotas or the southern tribes, it was an issue with the Sisseton and Wahpeton Indians of eastern Dakota, who finally agreed to a Northern Pacific right-of-way in 1871.[2] Nevertheless, even as this agreement was being reached, road engineers remained relentless. Within a year they had moved their wagons and instruments west into the Dakotas and southwestern Kansas where Indians expected to be left in peace to hunt.

On the central plains the railroads initially seemed less a threat than American settlement. The Cheyenne Dog Soldiers, increasingly identified as "nontreaty" Indians—because they openly disavowed the 1867 treaty—believed that white settlement foreordained the destruction of the buffalo. Spotted Wolf, Dull Knife, Cut Nose, Roman Nose, and even Tall Bull led small raids into exposed Kansas settlements such as Plum Creek, Big Springs, and Downer's Station in 1867.[3] The army responded by constructing Fort Wallace astride the Kansas-Colorado border, along the Smoky Hill Trail in the very heart of Cheyenne hunting lands. That summer, troops from the 7th Cavalry reached the post in time to engage the Cheyennes.

At dawn on June 26 Cheyennes struck at the stage station near the fort. The fifty cavalrymen sent out soon faced three hundred Cheyennes. Forming like "platoons" on the plains, the Indians charged headlong into the troopers. The fight was hand-to-hand, sabers versus lances; at one point a cavalryman literally put his carbine against the chest of an Indian warrior and blow him off his horse.[4] The firefight presaged conflict. Colonel George Armstrong Custer, sent to the central plains to protect the towns and railroads, spent much of that summer hunting for Native villages. In mid-August he received word of an overdue patrol of just eleven men. When Custer reached Beaver Creek, "a most horrible stench was observable, at the same time numerous vultures or buzzards were to be seen flying in the air." Custer found the men: "They had been stripped of all their clothing . . . ten had been scalped and their skulls broken in the most horrible manner." The scene horrified Custer's men and reflected the growing hostility that Hancock's war had wrought.[5]

Unfortunately, the killing had just begun. Joining with others, a mixed party of Dog Soldiers and renegades swept down onto the newly built cabins along the Saline River in August 1868, killing fifteen men over several days and raping four or five women.[6] While most historians have concluded that the perpetrators of what became a historically important crime were perhaps fifty Dog Soldiers, that seems unlikely. General Alfred Sully made a complete investigation at the scene and reported that a considerable number of the attackers were Anglo renegades. A number, "speaking in English," as Sully put it, vowed to "clear out all the settlers on the Saline." And a memoir taken from a boy who survived the killings indicated that one of the raiders passed around the boy, who was feigning death, remarking: "Now the d[amned] little b[astard] is dead."[7]

What Sully learned at the cabin of one Simeon Shaw confirmed that the perpetrators were renegades. The raiders raped Shaw's wife and his sister-in-law, while Shaw stood in the corner watching—suspicious behavior for Indians. As they raped the women, as Sully reported, they had a conversation with Shaw: "At Mr. Shaw's, white men overhauled his trunks, read his letters, and papers, took what they thought valuable—amongst his papers was his marriage certificate. This they handed him back, telling him in a joking way, that they 'guessed they would have no use for that.' I do not think this attack was made by any organized band of Indians, but was only a raiding party consisting of the rascals of different bands & outlawed white men."[8]

Groups of renegades pervaded the plains by this time, disguised or acting as buffalo hunters and "bushwhackers," as they were often called, remnants of Civil War paramilitary units who operated in Missouri and Kansas. They had invaded Indian Territory and at one point threatened to burn the town of Baxter Springs. Thousands of such men had overrun the Osage and Cherokee Reservations along the south Kansas border, and many got involved in rustling. Indeed, both cattle and horse rustling would be a terrible problem in Indian Territory for the next thirty years.[9]

Whatever the makeup of the group, it struck terror into the Kansas settlements. The army never released Sully's report to settlers or newspaper reporters. Sully likely learned that his report failed to mesh with General Sheridan's plans.[10] Not surprisingly, Generals Sheridan and Sherman blamed the entire Cheyenne and Arapaho Nations and planned to punish them. As these generals sat down with the Peace Commission in Chicago in October 1868, even Tappan shuddered at the reports of rape. A terribly subdued Tappan and the other commissioners accepted the need to strike the Indians, even agreeing to rescind the 11th article of the 1867 treaty, which allowed the southern Indians to hunt on ceded lands.[11]

The treaty 1867 never clearly determined who had authority to end the hunting privileges of these Indians, but the commission, acting for Congress, obviously assumed that it did. Certainly no one questioned the decision, which further diminished the treaty rights of the Cheyennes and Arapahos. Signaling the importance of the meeting, presidential candidate Grant showed up and became just as upset as Tappan over the reports of rape. He warned that the railroads and immigrants had to be protected, "even if the extermination of every Indian tribe was necessary." This hardly seemed the rhetoric of "peace," and it surely indicated that the August raids had swung the control of Indian policy away from the peace advocates, at least temporarily.[12]

As the commissioners departed, General Sheridan issued his final orders to General Sully: to "clean out the Indians—families and lodges—in the Big Bend of the Arkansas" and to push south into Indian Territory, to the Canadian River. While the orders might have been warranted for the upper Arkansas or even western Kansas—indeed later evidence suggests that this is where Tappan and others expected the army to campaign— they were a direct violation of the 1867 treaties, the reservations at least being under the charge of the Indian Office of the Interior Department. A delay set in when Sully, who commanded the District of the Upper Arkansas, clashed with Custer, who commanded the 7th Cavalry, which had discovered the massacred patrol the year before. Sheridan no longer trusted Sully: he would never be a member of the inner circle, especially after his report on the Kansas massacres. He sent Sully packing, back to Fort Harker, which gave Custer a free hand.[13]

Custer ordered "Boots and Saddles" on the morning of November 23, 1868. A Norther had descended onto the plains, leaving a foot of blowing snow and freezing temperatures. As the troops headed south, a determined Custer ordered his band to play "The Girl I Left Behind Me." Custer's scouts soon found a trail that led to the Washita River, deep inside the Cheyenne Indian Reservation.[14] Black Kettle and some 250 followers were in the village, about seventy miles south of the Kansas line. At intervals of five and ten miles both north and south of them were other camps, some holding warriors who had fought in Kansas. After finding the camp, Custer ordered an attack at dawn on November 27. Custer's force outnumbered the Indians some four or five to one. As Captain Edward Myers later exclaimed, his men were "killing them [Indian men, women, and even children] without mercy."[15]

While the numbers will never be known exactly, about one hundred Cheyennes lost their lives at the Washita (other estimates are both higher and lower), including the peaceful Black Kettle and his wife. Some fifty Native women and children were marched off as captives.[16]

Sheridan, who remained back in Kansas, was jubilant at the success, reviewing the troops as they marched into Camp Supply. But controversy erupted almost immediately. Commissioner of Indian affairs Nathaniel G. Taylor quickly announced to the press his belief that Black Kettle's village had been friendly and that Custer's attack constituted yet another Sand Creek. Reformers such as Tappan agreed; they had sanctioned campaigns against the Indians who had raided Kansas, not against those on the reservation.

In another example of repulsive behavior, as troopers herded the Indian captives back to Camp Supply, army officers took the younger females into their tents at night for comfort. Custer took young Monahseetah, about seventeen years of age, and kept her in his tent until his wife arrived in the spring.[17] While this dalliance seemed inoffensive to Sheridan—indeed Custer's officers took part in the ravishment with the same pleasure as their colonel did—the slaughter of innocents prompted General Sheridan to move Custer to another command. Custer's attack, though authorized by military authorities, was roundly condemned by government representatives, in particular the Peace Commission. When Custer allowed his men to rape scared and defenseless girls and women, this, like his attack, constituted a war crime. While the colonel's actions bordered on genocide, much like those of Connor and Chivington, it is doubtful that the soldiers or those who ordered them into the field could ever be charged with a crime of that level even given Sheridan's order to "clean out the Indians."

Sheridan continued to defend Custer's actions as a "victory" over hostile Indians and ordered Colonel Benjamin Grierson, the new commander of the District of Indian Territory, who was scouting to the south, to find a suitable place for a military post. Within a month of the Washita conflict Grierson began construction of Fort Sill, just south of the Wichita Mountains, literally on the Comanche Indian Reservation.[18] Camp Supply in the north became a second depot for counseling with and feeding Indians, and agencies were soon established for the Comanches and Kiowas and Cheyennes and Arapahos. Some bands of Kiowas and many Kwahadi and Kotchateka Comanches continued to roam the plains west of Fort Sill and refused to settle on the reservation. They soon communed with refugee Dog Soldiers, after they suffered a major defeat in central Kansas in July 1869 at the hands of Colonel Eugene Carr.[19] These "nontreaty" Indians numbered perhaps three thousand, with many visiting the reservation at various times of the year. General Sherman's stated policy of "killing a few Indians" to force them away from the railroads apparently had led to the successful ethnic cleansing of Kansas.

After the defeat of the Cheyenne Dog Soldiers in Kansas, the war entered a period of great flux. The newly elected president, Ulysses S. Grant, was under extreme pressure to implement the Peace Policy that he had promised during his campaign. Sherman, who was placed in charge of the War Department by Grant, found himself succumbing to the new policy. He even issued orders in May 1869 that prevented army assaults on Indian villages, a direct result of the criticism of Custer's attack. The new rules of engagement made a clear statement: no Indian was to be attacked "unless he manifests a hostile intent."[20] Grant obviously hoped to implement the moral restraints found in what civilized nations had often called the "Rules of War," which prevented the punishment of civilians during war.

Even more ominously for the Sherman and Sheridan faction, Congress appropriated money for establishing yet another commission to study the situation in the West after President Grant called for a "civilization" policy in his inaugural address. The group, organized in May 1869, became known as the Board of Indian Commissioners and included many leading clerics and reformers. It generally set in motion the new Peace Policy. Grant took advice from commissioner Nathaniel G. Taylor—whom Sherman and Sheridan despised—and his former aide-de-camp during the war, Ely S. Parker, a Seneca Indian who became commissioner of Indian affairs. The policy became a check against men like Sherman and Sheridan, a moral restraint on the future actions of the army. More importantly, many of Parker's selections as superintendents and agents were Quakers or Protestant clerics, such as Enoch Hoag, who took over the Central Superintendency.[21] Such men supposedly would build western Indian agencies into agents of assimilation, distributing food, organizing farm programs, and building schools and housing.

The Quaker Peace Policy, as it is often called, had many different twists and turns. Clerics, intellectuals, newspaper editors, and even former abolitionists joined the crusade to end the violence. Ironically, their goals seemed very similar to that of Generals Sheridan and Sherman—to convince Indians to give up their occupations as hunters, to settle on reservations, and to take up farming and tend livestock. Yet unlike a number of army officers—certainly those loyal to Sheridan—the Peace Policy advocates adhered to a strategy of patience. They still endorsed the need to confine the Plains Indians on reservations—diminishment, in effect—but thought that this process might take years. Even reformers thought that

Indians could hardly claim the vast Great Plains as a hunting preserve forever.

Nevertheless, these reformers had little understanding of the commitment of several thousand Plains Indians to maintain their lifestyle—even though such views had been stated time and again in treaty negotiations. More revealing, those Indians who had signed treaties, such as the Lakotas Red Cloud and Spotted Tail and the Comanche Silver Brooch, had mostly given up following the buffalo.[22] Indian men who had decided to stay on reservations had no right to cede eastern Wyoming (which Lakota and Cheyenne soldier societies had successfully defended), the Yellowstone Valley, western Kansas, the Platte River valley and its tributaries, the Texas Panhandle, or the lands lying between the Arkansas River and the new reservation for the Cheyennes and Arapahos.

The winter of 1869–70 offered new hope of a peaceful resolution. Even General Sherman seemed to moderate, suggesting the need to arrest individual Indians rather than punish entire villages or tribes for the actions of a few—police actions, rather than war. Reformers applauded this transformation, agreeing that an Indian who committed a crime needed to stand trial. Sheridan remained unrepentant, however, even defending the actions of Colonel Eugene Baker, whose command had attacked and massacred 170 Piegan Blackfeet Indians in far-off Montana in fall 1870. Baker led the assault while intoxicated.[23] Troubled by this slaughter, Congress passed a law forbidding army officers from serving on any reservation, leaving the reserves solely in the hands of the Indian Office. This was a strong indication of the influence of reformers in Washington and a decided change from a year before, when Sheridan seemingly had been given carte-blanche authority in Indian Territory.[24]

Even before this policy went into effect, a Quaker agent appeared at Fort Sill to take charge of the Comanche-Kiowa Reservation. Laurie Tatum had been a farmer in Iowa and knew little about Indian affairs, but he arrived eager to learn more. Colonel Grierson had made progress on the construction of Fort Sill; while some Indians saw it as a thorn in their side, others saw it as a place to obtain rations. Grierson had also effected an understanding with Indian Office officials. While Indians on the reservations fell under the authority of the agents, "the Indians still out" or off the reservation, he argued, "are to be entirely under the control of the military." Grierson knew that Comanches and Kiowas had been raiding in Texas. He would use food as bait to bring them in and turn them over to Tatum. Tatum agreed to these terms, and the two men got on quite well.[25]

Grierson's patrols that summer made contact with the more militant Comanches and Kiowas, then still on the Staked Plains. Accordingly, some 309 lodges of Quahadas came into Fort Sill in late August. Destitute, they readily accepted beef, sugar, and coffee. Grierson then sent messages to others left behind: "The country they occupied was no longer theirs, and if they persisted in remaining there, it would not be well for them." Grierson's authority was never questioned, although it was debatable whether the Peace Commission had only suspended the right of Cheyennes and Arapahos as well as Kiowas and Comanches to hunt on ceded land. By November estimates suggested that some 6,000 Indians had settled either on or very near the two major reservations in Indian Territory, leaving perhaps 2,000 still out on the plains. The numbers caused an immediate crisis for the Indian Office, which was not prepared to feed that many Indians. Rations soon became scarce at both agencies.[26] Nevertheless, Texas raiding diminished at least for the time being.[27]

The situations at both the Comanche and Kiowa Reservation and the new Cheyenne and Arapaho Reservation remained somewhat in flux. The new Quaker agent to the Cheyennes and Arapahos, Brinton Darlington, often quarreled with the commanding officer at Fort Supply, Colonel A. D. Nelson. Even so, both men agreed that the captive Cheyenne Indians taken by Carr and Custer and held at Fort Hayes should be returned. Their release set off a brief celebration at the agency.[28] Nelson saw the goodwill that this engendered and sought to placate Indian leaders, even allowing them to distribute food, which sustained their tribal positions. Quite intrigued by the process, the colonel gave a wonderful description of how tribal social and political etiquette meshed with the Peace Policy:

> The various parts of the rations were placed in separate piles and the distribution made by the young chiefs—The women and children were seated in a huge circle, the rations being about the center. The warriors were seated within smaller circles—I remained several hours on the ground watching the proceeding with much interest and was satisfied that the distribution was equitably made. It was done by the young chiefs with their own hands, the whole tribe looking on.[29]

But the goodwill of the summer and fall 1869 soon faded. The first herds of Texas cattle showed up in western Indian territory in January 1870; many others followed along the so-called Chisholm Trail. It headed into the railhead in Abilene, Kansas, at times entering the eastern boundaries of the reservations. The thousands of cattle devastated valuable grass. Satanta's Kiowa men rode into a herd in January and killed and ran off some 270 head; along with some Comanches, they struck several other herds in June and July. Kicking Bird, a more amenable Kiowa chief, arrived and prevented the murder of sixteen Texas herders. Nelson, who mostly lorded over the Cheyennes and Arapahos, quickly condemned the entire Kiowa tribe—he even jailed Kicking Bird at one point. Grierson at Fort Sill seemed far more understanding. He sent out a military patrol that forced the Kiowas away from the herds.[30]

Angry Comanches, Kiowas, and Cheyennes held a council at their Medicine Dance in spring 1870. Some war parties formed and attacked the Utes, while others went south into Texas. A third force made a foray against Camp Supply, where Nelson drove them off, killing six warriors. Tatum, who had spies at the dance, reported that the Cheyenne Whirlwind called upon all the Comanches and Kiowas to join together so that they "once more [might] have an open country."[31] Similar talk came in councils at Fort Sill, where the Kiowa Black Eagle told Tatum that they must have an end to "the boundary lines of all reservations [the surveys] . . . so that the Indians can have the country in common." The Kiowa Lone Wolf offered even stronger talk, as Tatum reported: "The Qua-ha-da claimed that the Texans had stolen their country, & they would get some of it back!"[32] The Americans could have peace, Black Eagle noted in closing, when they gave back the country, at which point he "swept the road between here and there, of all traces of the blood stains" so that we could "forget and forgive the past."[33]

Obviously many Kiowas, Comanches, and Cheyennes had finally come to understand the meaning of the treaties of 1867 and roundly rejected them. By spring 1871 Tatum's "civilization" policy increasingly became one in which Indians who remained on the reservations received annuities, but those who left it were refused. Many Indians, Tatum reported, went away "much displeased." A party of these men, under the mostly friendly Kiowa chiefs Satanta, Satank, and Big Tree retaliated in mid-May by waylaying a wagon train of supplies in north Texas. They killed seven teamsters, burning one tied to a wagon wheel; but five wagoners escaped to tell their story at Fort Richardson, Texas. Coincidentally, General Sherman had arrived there hours before on an inspection tour. While the war party let him pass unmolested, they waylaid the supply train, obviously in search of food that had been denied them at the agency.[34]

Sherman moved on to Fort Sill, where he quickly learned that Satanta had swaggered into the fort and boasted of leading the attack. The teamsters had killed several of his men, and he considered the fight a draw. Once informed of this, Sherman had the three Kiowa chiefs arrested. One was shot dead as he bolted. Satanta and Big Tree were sent back to Texas for trial, in which a biased Texas jury sentenced them to death. Yet the Interior Department convinced Texas governor E. J. Davis that the chiefs would do more good as hostages held for the good behavior of their people. Davis incarcerated both men in the Huntsville state prison for the time being.[35] These events helped convince agent Tatum that he could no longer control his Indians, and he anxiously waited to turn over the agency to yet another Quaker, James Haworth.

When it became clear that Grierson's threats would not bring in the Plains bands, Colonel Ranald Mackenzie led a large force out of Texas into the Panhandle and surprised a large Quahada Comanche village in October 1872. While his troops killed only two dozen Indians, they took captive 124 Indian women and children, who became hostages along with Satanta and Big Tree, held in Texas to ensure the good behavior of their people.[36] Although this was a clear violation of the rules of war, Mackenzie became a hero in Texas; the attack did lead to some suppression of Indian raids. While Grierson did not openly criticize Mackenzie's success, he did continue to council with Indians and tell their side of the story. They "continually brood over the diminution of their territory by the whites," he reported. Lone Wolf even went so far as to say: "The Government must remove Fort Sill and all the troops out of the Indian Country. The Reservation must be extended to the Rio Grande on the South and the Missouri . . . on the north."[37] While these were seemingly impossible demands, Grierson realized that the Indians wanted the old Comanche domain back and that their views had to be at least considered for the Peace Policy to work.

Such a noncompromising position by Indians led to growing attacks on the Peace Policy by the officers in the army who originally had opposed it. Sent to survey the situation, inspector general James Hardie, who some years before had negotiated with Indians near Clear Lake, California, thought that the Kiowas were nothing more than a "thieving and plundering" people, incapable of advancement toward "civilization." General Augur recommended that "the whole Kiowa tribe be taken possession of and disarmed and taken entirely out of the Indian Country."[38] To such officers, allies of General Sheridan to be sure, the capture and internment of women and children as hostages even became acceptable policy. It was certainly true that Southern Plains Indians had been taking captives and selling them. But the Indian Peace Commission still controlled the politics of Washington. The secretary of the interior convinced the War Department to return all captives held by Mackenzie in Texas by spring 1873. And Governor Davis agreed to release Satanta and Big Tree on parole.[39]

The promised release of the captives led to some peacefulness, and events elsewhere distracted Sherman. The outburst occurred in far-away northern California. At the close of the Civil War the government negotiated a treaty with the Klamath, Shasta, and Modoc Indians, moving the Modocs from their homelands around Tule Lake to a new Klamath reservation in southern Oregon.[40] The Modocs found the confinement intolerable—in particular they feuded with the more numerous Klamaths—and ultimately fled back to the Lava Beds near Tule Lake. In fall 1872 and into 1873 a war broke out, as the Modocs led by Captain Jack tried to sustain their control of lands contested by settlers. Ridiculed by other would-be leaders, Jack ultimately agreed to kill a negotiating team led by General Edward R. S. Canby, the commanding officer of the Department of the Pacific.[41] Perhaps Jack had a long memory, recalling the day in 1853 when Wright and his men had coaxed several dozen Modocs into a negotiation only to slaughter them. Canby and two others died during the peace council, as Modoc men, including Jack, drew concealed weapons and fired.

Army troops finally forced some 150 Modocs to surrender. General Sherman immediately sought permission to hang all Modoc men with Captain Jack, while their women and children were to be dispersed onto other reservations so that the Modoc tribe "would no longer exist." This inflamed reformers, including civil rights activist John Beeson, who lobbied President Grant for leniency. The judge advocate general ultimately concluded that only the men who had killed Canby could be tried by a military commission, because they had allegedly committed murder. Four men, including Captain Jack, were convicted and executed in early October 1873. Yet Sherman retained control of the remaining Modocs. He put most of them on a train and deported them to the Quapaw Indian Reservation in northeastern Indian Territory.[42] This drastic solution had little precedent in that day and age. It surely violated Article 7 of the Rome Statutes, which today make "deportation" a crime against humanity.

Meanwhile reservation "agencies" took shape for the Lakota Sioux in the early years of the 1870s. The southern Lakota bands (Red Cloud's Oglalas and Spotted Tail's Brulés) refused to settle along the upper Missouri, as the army desired, and instead convinced the Indian Office to open agencies south of the Great Sioux Reservation, along the White River.[43] General Sheridan lobbied strongly for a location closer to the Missouri, making it easier to dispatch troops to the region and to provide annuities. But the Indians, being protective of their right to hunt in the Republican River valley, even refused to allow the agents to get an accurate assessment of their populations. It is likely that some 8,000 Indians lived at these two agencies, most coming and going.[44]

All the army could do was expand the number of forts in the region. Along with Forts Rice and Sully, built on the central Missouri River during the Civil War, the army advanced up the Missouri in the late 1860s, constructing Forts Buford and Stevenson and occupying the old trade post called Berthold, in what is today eastern North Dakota. General Sherman finally relented and ordered the construction of Fort Robinson to protect Red Cloud's and Spotted Tail's Agencies in north-central Nebraska. Along with smaller, often temporary garrisons at various agencies along the Missouri River, the forts became symbols of invasion for the Lakotas; the northern, nontreaty Indians increasingly demanded that the forts and the steamboats that serviced them be removed, much as Indians had protested the Bozeman Trail forts and similar in many ways to the demands being made by the southern Indians.[45]

Efforts to force the Lakotas to settle on their reservation proved difficult. Spotted Tail claimed a right under the treaty of 1868 to hunt during the summer in the Republican River valley. To General Sherman's chagrin, the Indian Office agreed, counseling patience and remaining hopeful that Spotted Tail might preach peace among the other off-reservation Indians. But when settlers complained that horses and cattle disappeared from nearby ranches, the Indian Office tried to end Lakota hunting south of the Platte River, only to reverse itself when it was reported that Spotted Tail's people were starving and needed to hunt.[46] In other words, even when the Indian Office was able to bring Indians onto reservations in the South and again in the North, it was often unable to bring in sufficient supplies to feed them. Sheridan's concerns shifted momentarily to the more northern Lakota bands, who demonstrated increasing unhappiness with the army's presence. Most, according to one report, "refuse positively to locate on reservations."[47] Sitting Bull's Hunkpapas even planned to force the abandonment of Fort Rice and to destroy the new Northern Pacific Railroad then under construction from Fargo.[48]

Colonel David Stanley, who commanded the District of the Upper Missouri from Fort Sully, took such information very seriously. He repeatedly warned that besides the Hunkpapas, who had determined to force the army from the upper Missouri, even "the Ogallallas [Oglalas], a part of the Brulés who are with the Ogallallas, and about half the Minneconjous are decidedly hostile."[49] Violence erupted farther west as well, near and north of Fort Laramie. Some four hundred miners from eastern Wyoming proclaimed their right to prospect in the Big Horn Mountains and east of them—a classic example of "settler sovereignty," as the region was still part of ceded Indian lands. The army seemed perplexed by the demand. General Augur noted that "the country they propose to visit" was in Wyoming and not "as I understand it" on an Indian reservation. Yet under the treaty of 1868 Americans had no right to enter unceded Indian lands. The miners soon clashed with Lakotas, Cheyennes, and even some Arapahos. Greybull Creek and the various tributaries of the Wind River had become a dangerous place to live.[50]

While commissioner of Indian affairs Francis Walker asked for patience—the standard refrain of the advocates of the Peace Policy—farther east serious trouble erupted over the growing invasion of the West by railroad surveyors. The officers of the Northern Pacific Railroad had asked the army for protection for its surveying teams. They had reached the Red River, were rapidly laying track west of it, and wanted to begin surveying a line through the Yellowstone River valley. While some of this land had been purchased by treaty from the Crow Indians, it ran across hunting grounds claimed by northern, nontreaty Lakotas, who had never seen the treaty of 1868 and had no understanding of its boundaries. Colonel David Stanley at Fort Sully received orders to take all measures to protect the surveyors during the summer of 1871.[51]

Staying closer to the Missouri River than to the Yellowstone, the surveyors encountered little trouble, at least during summer 1871. But the next year General Sheridan sent more infantry troops up the Missouri River to occupy the mouth of the Yellowstone River, challenging the northern tribes. Major Eugene Baker advanced east from Fort Ellis with one survey team and four hundred soldiers. Just as he passed Rosebud Creek, sentinels gave the alarm in the early hours of August 14. A fierce firefight with Lakota warriors broke out and lasted into the next day. The soldiers dug rifle pits in the riverbank to save themselves. It was here that Sitting Bull, arriving at daybreak, made his famous walk down the other side of the riverbank, sat down in leisurely fashion, and took out his pipe and lit it while army bullets rained down on him. Just two days later the Hunkpapa *akacita* war leader Gall struck Stanley's camp. The advance into Montana had started another Indian war over land.[52]

The surveyors attached to both Baker's and Stanley's commands were unnerved by the massive numbers of Indians involved. Chief surveyor John Hayden ordered a swift withdrawal to Fort Ellis. Stanley moved forward for a few more days but also withdrew. Telegrams from Stanley notified General Hancock of the need for more troops to complete the task.[53] Stanley had talked on and off with several representatives of the nontreaty Indians, who spoke for Sitting Bull and Gall. Spotted Eagle had pointedly warned the colonel that the Northern Pacific surveyors would not be allowed into the Yellowstone Valley; the Lakotas would fight for the land.[54]

So it was that by late fall 1872 eastern reformers seemed convinced that the Peace Policy was working at the same time that the army called for more troops, in particular to support the surveyors working in the Yellowstone River valley. The situation on the southern plains looked more stable, yet the Quaker agents in charge had practically no control over the buffalo hunting bands in the West, who continued to raid in Texas. And when small raiding parties did appear, the army at times was pressured to treat such groups as felons, trying to capture their leaders for trial in civil courts. General Sherman had tried to convince the judge advocate general's office that a military commission—used only in the case of war— might apply to the Modocs, but the lawyers in Washington had generally refused to allow such trials for incidents like the Kiowa raid led by Satanta, Satank, and Big Tree, which were now viewed as felonies or murder.

In reality the only issue bound to promote major conflict was use of hunting grounds, which the nontreaty Indians refused to surrender, and the failure of the government to recognize the Indians' right to that land. It might be argued that war would settle the issue, but even the founding fathers of the nation had argued that such conflict had to be "just war." The attacks in western Wyoming and even the defense of hunting grounds along the Yellowstone River hardly constituted war, and an American invasion of these lands could not be seen as just. Furthermore, the Lakotas had a right to be on ceded hunting lands in the Yellowstone River valley under the treaty. While the treaty also gave the railroad a right-of-way through those very ceded lands, the Lakota people who occupied them never signed the agreement. When such circumstances had arisen in the past, the government had treated for the land.

Given the terms of both the treaties of 1867 and 1868 and the views of the northern and southern tribes, as well as those of at least some army officers and railroad officials, the treaties passed with such promise became virtually untenable. The rush to build railroads across the West attracted cattle onto Indian lands in the southern area and surveyors onto lands in the Yellowstone Valley; the reservations "diminished" to the point where major buffalo hunting grounds were cut off from the various tribes. This situation made it impossible for the Peace Policy to succeed. But many army officers—particularly those within Sheridan's inner circle—and the railroad builders who worked with them lacked the patience necessary to make a slowly evolving reservation system work. To them, the Peace Policy was simply a failure from the start—it did not "civilize" Indians and failed to allow for progress.

As the Peace Policy became more untenable, the conflict that it engendered led to war crimes and crimes against humanity. This conflict even hatched conspiracies on the part of some army officers to keep information from the public that might change the way it viewed Indian policy. Army attacks on peaceful villages, such as Black Kettle's village or the Piegan camp, had somewhat negated the influence of the generals, but the perpetrators of such crimes were never punished and the reformers of the day lacked the influence to obtain indictments. Worse, General Sheridan sanctioned Custer's attack and a year later defended Baker's murder of Piegan Indians. These were war crimes, sanctioned by the commanding officer of the western armies. And holding hostages in return for the surrender of their relatives and using the deportation of people to foreign lands in order to control them violated Article 7 of the Rome Statutes. While civilian authorities of the central government ultimately restored some hostages—but not others—the government's failure to remove the perpetrators of such crimes, or even recognize them as crimes, made it an accessory.

It is true that some Cheyennes likely had joined renegades in attacking settler houses in Kansas, Satanta and his fellow Kiowas had committed heinous crimes, and some Comanches had attacked helpless settlers in west Texas. Unfortunately, the perpetrators of these were just as difficult to punish as were those officers who sanctioned and participated in attacks on Indian villages. General Sherman did sanction the use of civil law as a means of punishing some of these individuals but did so reluctantly, only because of the moral restraint placed upon him by civilian authorities. And when individuals responsible for crimes could not be captured, expediency rather than any observance of the rules of war became policy: Sheridan and Sherman blamed entire tribes for what they fully knew were the acts of a few Indians, occasionally in concert with renegades.

Finally, it must be said that all of this confusion—whether the Indians were at war, as Sheridan and Sherman tried to argue, or were committing simple crimes—existed because of the new Peace Policy adopted by President Grant and the type of treaties that its commissioners negotiated. The agreements allowed for the recognition of Indian rights to hunt on lands that the government claimed the Indians had ceded, even though the majority of tribal members had no idea that the agreements had clauses that ceded these lands. And to the government negotiators, the lands in question had become crucial for the advancement of the railroads, lines of communication that would benefit the army in its contest with both northern and southern Indians, and also roads and land that would open the West to settlement.

But reformers pleaded for time and patience: in the view of the secretary of the interior it would take three years for the extinguishment of buffalo herds and the capitulation of Indian hunters. Reformers thought that this would occur slowly, leading to the settlement of Indians on reservations. The reformers thus championed a benevolent ethnic cleansing that would end conflict in the West. Given the men in command of army troops and the divided nature of government authority, they got war instead.

14

THE RED RIVER "WARS"

The Collapse of the Peace Policy

The Southern Plains Indians signed the treaties of 1867 for two obvious reasons. First, the Indians who understood at least part of the rhetoric during the negotiations assumed that the agreements preserved the status quo, meaning that they could live and hunt on the plains as they had in the past. Second, the treaties offered annuities, which the Plains Indians increasingly needed.

During the fall of 1872 and into the spring of the next year the awful truth became more evident: while nontreaty Comanches and Kiowas had little idea of the terms of the treaty, others who had been at the negotiations saw surveyors establish boundaries. Indians theoretically no longer owned land in west Texas, a reduction that left them with one-sixth of what had been guaranteed under the Little Arkansas Treaty of 1865. Cheyennes and Arapahos also increasingly learned that their lands constituted less than half of what the treaty had allotted them two years before. The goals of the Peace Policy, even if administered with "patience," ran directly counter to what most southern Indians expected. They would not accept a form of ethnic cleansing that offered houses, farms, and food in place of hunting land and created drastically diminished reservations that forced a dramatic change in lifestyle.

The Indian Office and its increasing number of Quaker agents, who had been recruited because war was anathema to them, had no intention of abandoning the government policy of eventually forcing the Indians onto the new reservations. They did hope to do it peacefully by convincing the nontreaty Indians that they could no longer sustain themselves on the plains west of the reserves as hunters. This seemed possible in spring 1873. Schoolteacher Thomas Battey, a Quaker who was writing a book on the Southern Plains Indians, spent considerable time feasting with Indians and observing their various dances. As was customary, Comanche men entertained Battey. The women passed the food through a slit in the lodge, not being allowed in. "The bill of fare consisted of wild plums stewed, boiled corn and pumpkins, bread and coffee."[1] Battey reported to his friend James Haworth, the new Quaker agent, that he thought that the Indians would in the end accept the Peace Policy.

The only rumors that suggested upcoming problems appeared in late July 1873 when it became obvious that Governor Davis had second thoughts regarding the release of Satanta and Big Tree. While Colonel Mackenzie had complied with orders to relocate the Comanche prisoners whom he had taken and held in Texas to their Oklahoma reservation, Davis's upcoming "pardon" suddenly had serious political repercussions in Texas. Davis, a Republican kept in power mostly by a Reconstruction regime, was trying to be reelected. When the governor finally—and reluctantly—arrived at Fort Sill in early October, with the two Kiowa chiefs in tow, Davis made excessive demands. He wanted all reservation Indians dismounted, including even Cheyennes and Arapahos, and their weapons taken from them. More importantly, Davis demanded that five Comanche Indians supposedly involved in raids (he had no indication of who they really were) be arrested and put in prison to replace the two Kiowa leaders he proposed to pardon.

Commissioner of Indian affairs Edward Smith, who came west to orchestrate the release, reluctantly accepted Davis's demands. He then asked that an army patrol find the raiders and have them arrested. Sheridan recognized the folly of such a venture—the army had no idea who had committed recent raids and did not even know particulars of those raids. When the patrol returned empty-handed, Smith again agonized over the situation. Finally he ordered that Haworth stop issuing annuities to any Indians who seemed hostile and called upon the army to force the surrender of all Plains Indians. While Mackenzie had violated the hunting clause of the 1867 treaty by attacking a Comanche plains camp, Smith created new policy guidelines that seemingly allowed military intervention in the lands "ceded" but still legally claimed and used by the Indians as hunting grounds. No one in Washington, D.C., challenged the order or even attempted to argue that the buffalo no longer existed on those lands.[2]

A new military commander, Lieutenant Colonel J. W. Davidson, replaced Grierson that fall at Fort Sill. Davidson, a hothead, quickly argued with agent Haworth. As Cyrus Beede, another Quaker who acted as a "special" agent for Superintendent Hoag, noted: "Col. Davidson manifests his open hostility to the President's Indian policy by recommending that . . . these Indians . . . receive at the hands of the military a 'good threshing.'"[3] Given the demeanor of Davidson, who completely lacked Grierson's patience, and Smith's growing impatience, the Peace Policy (for which Indian Office officials had such hopes in spring 1873) seemed to be unraveling, mostly as a result of the changing personalities involved in administering the reservations.

Fortunately for the Indians, winter descended early upon the plains that fall. The army could accomplish little until spring 1874. Colonel Davidson waited for orders, while conflict festered on several fronts, both within and off the reservation. The military openly plotted against agents: some officers even wrote critical letters to newspaper editors regarding the handling of Indian affairs. Some Indians, aware of the army–Indian Office feud, accordingly became more intractable. At times they turned to living in camps on the very western fringes of the reserve, collecting annuities but being in constant contact with nontreaty Indians west of them. It did not help when troublemakers who lounged around the agencies and fort spread the news that the army hoped to disarm any Indian who remained off the reserves. Many of these "reservation" Indians communicated with more western, nontreaty bands, bringing them the news.

An event then occurred that disrupted the reserves. A report from the south indicated that the Kiowa chief Lone Wolf's son had been killed in a raid in Mexico. When his party encountered two separate army patrols in Texas, nearly two dozen other Kiowas, mostly from Lone Wolf's camp, had been killed. The village went into mourning. Many Kiowas commiserated with Lone Wolf, who wanted to head up a party to recover his son's bones. The young man could never mount the journey to the afterlife unless he had a proper burial, attended by the food and supplies necessary for the trip.[4] Other Kiowas and Comanches wanted to avenge the loss: some came into the reservation, armed and angry, to confront Agent Haworth, especially after he refused to give them annuities.

At this crucial moment some of the more conciliatory Kiowas approached Haworth, nearly begging for permission to retrieve the bodies, to soothe Lone Wolf's grief. Big Bow, Satanta, Kicking Bird, and Big Tree were among them. Recognizing how important this was to the Kiowas, Beede telegraphed Commissioner Smith asking for permission to send a delegation south. But Smith—who had already turned to the army for help, believing that the Plains bands needed punishment—ignored the situation. Lone Wolf departed with a war party in May 1874. Big Bow and other Kiowas had joined him. Later reports indicated that they fought with Texans and rustled several hundred horses.[5]

As word of Lone Wolf's departure spread among the Kiowas, Comanches and Cheyennes held a joint Medicine Dance in late May 1874. The Quaker teacher Battey, ever inquisitive, attended. He noted that the Comanches had never before "made medicine as a tribe": it was generally done by small groups of men or soldier societies. It was also unusual, according to Batty, that a "young medicine man made bold pretensions" during the verbal displays that attended such dances. This man, Eschiti, claimed that he has been "raised from the dead" and that he had "raised from his stomach nearly a wagon-load of cartridges at one time." Even more boastfully, he bluffed that his medicine would prevent any Comanche from being killed by American rifle-fire, "even though he stands just before the muzzle of the white man's guns."[6] The boasts struck fear into friendly reservation Comanches. Asahabit, Quirts Quip, and Toshaway fled to Haworth and asked for protection—they had obviously been threatened as factionalism erupted among the various Plains bands.[7]

As the dancers got up their courage, a large war party of perhaps a hundred men turned on the Texas frontier. The Indians invaded the ranches northwest of Decatur, rustling hundreds of horses.[8] But a second party, including Eschiti, went after Anglo buffalo hunters, who had dramatically increased in number. Once the railroad reached Dodge City, Kansas, in September 1872, massive destruction of buffalo herds began. Groups of men (sometimes numbering thirty or forty) killed thousands of animals each month. Agent Haworth noted the "Great Complaints" made by the Indians and wondered if the government might stop the carnage, because these hunting lands were still guaranteed the Indians under the 1867 treaty.[9] One report by an army officer put the number of hides being loaded at just one Kansas depot at 500,000.[10]

Little did agent Haworth know that some in the army actually encouraged the slaughter, recognizing the economic impact that it would have on the nontreaty Indians. Confusing matters, some army officers questioned whether they had authority to remove the hunters—the land had been designated as "ceded" Indian hunting grounds, even though the region remained part of the state of Texas.[11] The grounds guaranteed by treaty had become a no-man's land, without any enforcement of the Intercourse Acts. No one in government, other than Haworth, even wanted to discuss the confusing state of affairs. Meanwhile a large contingent of hunters occupied Adobe Walls, an abandoned old trading establishment on the Canadian River. It quickly become a place where stolen stock could be redeemed and whiskey obtained in large quantities. Introducing spirits onto Indian lands violated the Intercourse Acts, had they been enforced, and so did non-Indians who slaughtered buffalo in great quantities.[12]

The Comanche medicine man Eschiti foreordained swift victory against such men, whatever guns they brought to bear. Influenced by the excitement of the Medicine Dance, with its promise of rejuvenation and regeneration—not unlike that offered by the Creek Prophets almost exactly fifty years before—a large Comanche and Cheyenne war party approached the walled trade center on the morning of June 27, 1874. Their leaders included a number of men who had professed peace at one time or another, including Mowway. Supposedly among them as well was a novice warrior named Quanah, the son of a white woman named Cynthia Ann Parker taken in a Texas raid in 1836. Quanah's time to lead, however, would come later, on the reservation. Eschiti led the attack. As the sun approached the horizon that morning, two buffalo hunters rose to prepare breakfast. They saw the Indians approach in a body and shouted out a warning. A desperate fight ensued, which lasted into the afternoon. At one point Eschiti had his horse shot out from under him and had to be rescued. Over a dozen Indians fell to the accurate rifle fire of the hunters, and many others were wounded. By afternoon the Indians withdrew. The prophet Eschiti had proved his bravery, but his medicine had failed.[13]

When the news reached the agencies, Haworth expected conflict and called upon Colonel Davidson for the protection of troops. Davidson reported the circumstances and asked for orders, telling his superiors that it might simply be a "Quaker scare."[14] The request opened an opportunity for General Sheridan even though he sensed the delicate nature of the situation. Reformers such as John Beeson, Alfred B. Meacham, and Wendell Phillips had published pieces relative to "Indian Rights," picking up considerable steam after the Modoc War and the execution of Modoc leaders. Meacham, despite being severely wounded in the affair, had decried the way in which the Modocs had lost their lands and then been deported. The reformers forced President Grant publicly to announce that he would never abandon the Peace Policy, as long as he was president.[15] Even so, Sheridan also recognized that the secretary of the interior, Columbus Delano, wanted a solution to the constant problems in Indian Territory. He also knew that the commissioner of Indian affairs, Edward P. Smith, had been accused of fraud by reformers and was virtually incapacitated.[16] This left a Sheridan ally, secretary of war William Belknap, with little opposition.

Sheridan convinced Belknap to order the army to separate "friendly" Indians from "hostile" ones.[17] Sheridan proposed "enrolling" all friendly Indians at their agencies—literally giving them papers that proved their loyalty to the United States. Belknap agreed to this and also issued Sheridan "authority" to punish the "hostiles" if they refused to enroll, even to the extent of invading reservations and western hunting lands.[18] Some debate as to the level of the response necessary ensued within military circles. Most Indian raids had been carried out by a very few warriors, although the attack in Texas had involved a larger body. The question still remained whether this constituted an act of war or whether the Indians involved should have been handled much as the army dealt with Kiowa leaders in 1871.

Of the field officers, it was surprisingly General Pope—who was not a part of Sheridan's inner circle—who seemed most committed to proceeding carefully. He blamed renegades for the fight at Adobe Walls and for some of the raids, because renegades encouraged Indians to steal livestock. The lawlessness, Pope thought, involved ruffians at a new town called Arkansas City, south of Wichita, Kansas. He ordered his troops in southwest Kansas to be "very careful, besides protecting settlers and preventing outrage, to do nothing to bring on hostilities with the Indians." Pope even lobbied Governor Thomas A. Osborn of Kansas to arrest and remove the whiskey traffickers and hunters. While there seemed to be considerable confusion over just who was responsible for policing the Texas Panhandle and southwest Kansas, Pope believed that state authorities certainly had jurisdiction within the borders of Kansas, where many of the renegades trafficked in stolen stock.[19]

Sheridan disagreed and quarreled with Pope, suggesting that he should have sent troops to support the buffalo hunters not remove them. The commanding general of the Division of Missouri clearly had no intention of enforcing the federal Intercourse Acts, which were an Indian Office responsibility. Sheridan also viewed the instability on the reservation as an opportunity to settle the "Indian problem," urging Pope to join the campaign. "We will keep at them [the Indians] so long as we have the present authority [from Belknap]," he bragged, "and will be sure to get them in the end."[20]

Brandishing his "authority," Sheridan then ordered all three agents in western Oklahoma to cooperate in enrolling the peaceful Indians, starting on August 3.[21] Captain George Sanderson reported that some 29 Comanches had enrollment certificates by mid-August—a rather pitiful showing—and 165 Kiowas. The numbers indicated the growing fear of army troops that many of the bands living on the fringe of the reservation felt.[22] The vast majority refused enrollment and moved farther away from the agencies.

While the Arapahos remained peaceful and had willingly moved to their new agency near El Reno in the early 1870s, many Cheyennes watched from villages well west of the agency as Sanderson put some recalcitrant warriors in prison and disarmed others. Some under Stone Calf and Heaps of Birds seemed willing to surrender; but others would not, especially after Sanderson "ironed" a number of Indians and put them in prison. Their new agent, John Miles, argued for patience, concluding that these Cheyennes lingering just outside the reservation "would prefer to die rather than submit to prison life." Sanderson had a very different view, declaring that any Indian who surrendered thereafter would be arrested and kept as a "prisoner of war"—as he put it, "it will not do to upset their minds with any peace promises!"[23] To army officers it seemed that Sheridan's "authority" virtually ended the Peace Policy.

Any hope of peace vanished on August 20, when forty troopers under Davidson's direct command arrested a number of Kiowas and Comanches when they showed up to get annuities at the Wichita Agency. Most of the young men seemed agreeable to surrender and willingly gave up their carbines; but when asked to surrender bows and arrows, a number simply refused—those weapons were used for hunting buffalo. As one broke and ran, the troops fired into a crowd of Indians, killing six or seven. Chaos ensued as Satanta, Big Tree, and others joined their relatives in fighting the army. Davidson fortified the agency as best he could and sent word for reinforcements. Army troops had started the melee, a firefight in which nearly all the Kiowas thereafter broke for the plains. Sheridan used the incident as an excuse to order a massive campaign onto the plains that fall, using no fewer than five separate military columns.[24]

Despite Sheridan's decision, General Pope still believed that the "difficulty" could be settled by simply removing the white renegades then on the Staked Plains. "There can be no doubt," he responded to Sheridan in September, "from the facts that have reached this headquarters from good authority, that the present difficulties with the Cheyennes were mainly caused by the unlawful intrusion and illegal and violent acts of the white hunters." Sheridan viewed this as insubordination and leaked unpopular aspects of Pope's letters to the press. Subsequently General Sherman had to step in and mediate what had become an embarrassing dogfight. At that point, the upstart General Nelson Miles openly sided with Sheridan, blaming the Red River "War" on the incompetence of the agents and their Peace Policy. Not surprisingly, Miles quickly became part of Sheridan's "inside" group. Miles rather than Pope received the assignment to go after the Indians.[25]

After the fight at the Wichita Agency, Sheridan began referring to the situation as an "outbreak," and soon the language escalated to "war."[26] This allowed for a large-scale response. General Mackenzie went into the field that fall with a column from Texas. Lieutenant Colonel George Buell advanced into the lower Red River with units of the so-called Buffalo Soldiers (African American cavalry). Colonel Davidson pushed west from Fort Sill, Major William R. Price scouted east from Fort Union in New Mexico (with many Navajo scouts), and General Miles, with the largest force of eight companies of cavalry, launched a campaign from Fort Supply into the upper Canadian and Red Rivers. In a classic pincher movement, military forces descended upon the Indians from all directions. Sheridan even ordered his officers to refuse the surrender of Native women and children, which would force their men to defend them. Such rhetoric against civilians was and is typical of campaigns that constitute ethnic cleansing.[27]

Miles's force quickly routed a combined village of perhaps a thousand Comanches and Cheyennes on August 30. He then followed the fleeing men and their families, burning lodges and buffalo meat at will. "From Sweetwater to the head of south Fork of Red River, a distance of 110 miles, the trail is strewn with their property, abandoned and destroyed," he boasted.[28] Indians fled for their lives, trying to return to the safest haunts or breaking for the three agencies in the hopes of being saved. Miles remained dogged in pursuit: "Now that the policy of protecting them at their agencies has been abandoned," he wrote to Sheridan, "if we deprive the Indians of the territory which they have used as retreat for their families and herds, . . . there can be no resource left them except extermination or submission."[29] Of course, this supposed "territory" still remained protected "hunting grounds," a circumstance that all concerned seem to have completely ignored.

Supposedly one of the safest haunts was Palo Duro Canyon, a mysterious deep, rough depression lying south of present-day Amarillo, Texas. In late September Mackenzie found the refugees, mostly Comanches, there. While he never closed with the retreating Indians, who fled by foot to the rocks, he did capture their horse herd and much of their camp.[30] He ordered fifteen hundred animals shot and all camp equipment burned. By Christmas the "Red River Wars," as they came to be known, were mostly over: destitute Indians, many on foot, straggled back to the reservations in hopes of being fed.

The weeks and months of surrender that followed revealed the beaten and desperate condition of all the southwestern Plains peoples. Some sixty families of Kiowas came in first, refugees from the firefight at the Wichita Agency. Then Satanta, Big Tree, and other Kiowa leaders gave up their arms. Colonel Thomas H. Neill noted how little threat they were to anyone: "Satanta with twenty-four lodges of Kiowas consisting of 145 men, women and children (37 warriors, 40 squaws and 66 children, and two old men) came to this camp and surrendered . . . I disarmed them of 13 rifles, 3 pistols, 18 bows and four lances." Satanta said: "I am tired of fighting and do not want to fight anymore. I came in . . . to give myself up. . . . I want to cultivate a farm at the Cheyenne Agency here."[31]

Satanta was not destined to become a farmer, however: Secretary Delano made the decision to ship him back to Texas. Sheridan seemed convinced that holding Satanta in the state prison for life was a just punishment, apparently for running from military gunfire. Four years later, while at the Huntsville prison, Satanta committed suicide by jumping out a window.[32]

Indians surrendered in small family groups thereafter. Most of the Cheyennes following Stone Calf and Heaps of Birds gave up in April 1875. Their leaders were incarcerated in the guard house. Mowway and Eschiti, the prophet, came in a month later.[33] A few captive Indians would attempt a breakout in April, but the army moved in a Gatling gun and raked their position, killing about a dozen Dog Solders who refused to be "ironed"—as their agent had predicted. A second group of Cheyennes, while in flight, thought themselves safe while camped at Sapa Creek. Cavalry troops soon surrounded them and massacred roughly two dozen people, mostly women and children, during the so-called battle. This was the last stand of the Cheyennes on the southern plains.[34]

As agent Haworth noted, somewhat in disgust, those who surrendered "unconditionally" were "brought to the post [Fort Sill], the young men put in the Ice House prison, the chiefs in Irons in the Guard House." The only remaining question was what the army would do with these "prisoners of war," as they called them.[35]

Early on, military officers attempted to separate out those Indians that they considered to be the worst offenders, collecting evidence that warranted prosecution for murder in either military or civilian courts. In reality only in two instances—the incident at the Wichita Agency and the attack on a family named German—could cases even be made. Texans could provide no further evidence of a credible nature that might convict individual Indians. Some evidence did exist in regard to three Kiowas who had killed civilians during the Wichita Agency affair in August—a charge of murder was drawn up for Bird Medicine, Double Vision, and Bear in the Cloud. After their repatriation the two teenaged German girls identified several Cheyenne men and one woman as those who murdered their parents and brother. But most of the Indians held as prisoners were simply considered "turbulent," an unusual category of crime.[36]

General Sheridan telegraphed President Grant in early October, suggesting that he intended to put all the incarcerated men—likely to range into the hundreds—in front of a "military commission," much like what had been done with the Dakota Sioux in 1862 as well as with the four Modocs. Sheridan brought in General Augur, an ally then in command of the Military Department of Texas, to organize the effort. The younger officers in his command wanted to start the trials almost immediately. But Augur argued that the commissions, and possible executions, would only hinder the surrender of those warriors still on the plains, so he waited. Increasing "philanthropic sentiment," as Sheridan soon put it, forced him to reconsider the issue again in December: he concluded in a letter to Secretary Delano that perhaps only "a few" of the worst offenders should face commissions and executions. "If a few of the murderers can be hanged the effect will be very salutary," the general wrote. The remainder he hoped to "select for imprisonment or surveillance at some of the forts on the sea-coast."[37] A few weeks later all Kiowa, Comanche, and

Cheyenne prisoners—supposedly the worst of the raiders and "turbulent" men alike—were moved to Fort Sill.

There General Augur had them investigated, case by case. Three categories were established for judging the Indians: (1) "those against whom there is any evidence, either by accusation of Indians, or other evidence, of having committed murders"; (2) "those who have notoriously been engaged in such crimes, but against whom no evidence can be had"; and (3) those who were simply "turbulent, insolent, and disobedient."[38] Most courts refused to allow Indians to testify under any circumstance; "hearsay" evidence from Indians had been allowed in the commission trials in Minnesota in 1862, but the Lincoln administration became fully aware of the problematic nature of those trial records. In any case all three categories raised many red flags to any legal mind with an ounce of respect for legal procedure.

Hundreds of other Indian men, supposedly not "turbulent," spent the winter in camps: disarmed, dismounted, and watched by the military. They had no opportunity to hunt, which had become an important food subsidy even for the agency Indians. The federal government had never provided sufficient food to feed all the Indians on the reservations, despite the treaty's promise to do so, primarily because so many Indians had fed themselves in the past by hunting in the West. Food ran out by February, prompting a crisis and even near-starvation. General Pope, never much in support of the war, was appalled when an order from the War Department arrived. "Your telegram is an order to me to stop the issue of food to Indian prisoners," he defiantly answered. "Of course, we cannot hold them as prisoners and starve them to death!" Colonel Neill had some five hundred prisoners at the Cheyenne Agency alone—these were not of the sort who had been sent to the Ice House at Fort Sill. The army simply had not planned for its own success.[39]

By December some decisions had been made regarding those in shackles. The War Department had assigned a judge advocate general to the case: Captain E. C. Emory was a lawyer by training. When he finally arrived in March 1875, he found the categories created by General Augur to be at least problematic. Emory did find evidence that might stand up in court regarding the killings of three civilians near Wichita Agency. And the German girls would later identify their captors. But he fumed over the possibility that he would have to rely upon the testimony of "uncivilized" persons, including "Indians" and the main witness against the three Kiowas, a "Mexican." He questioned the reliability of such men and seemed unwilling to go to court using their testimony.

Then Emory addressed a final legal hurdle: "Granting the evidence sufficient," he concluded, "it is doubtful whether a military commission can have cognizance of the offenses as it will be difficult to establish that the *state of war* necessary, in my opinion, to give vitality to a trial by military commission then existed."[40] Indeed the violence against civilians had been minimal, of the sort where civilian trials had been used in the past—without a "state of war" no trials could be conducted by a military commission. To what degree this conclusion discombobulated General Sheridan was never recorded. But even he probably declined to cross swords with lawyers in the army. This only added to the growing difficulties surrounding the prisoners.

Meanwhile both reformers and the military were discussing what to do with the prisoners. Some hoped to move them to Fort Leavenworth. The Ice House at Fort Sill held thirty-one Cheyenne men, one Cheyenne woman (charged with killing Mrs. German), thirty-one Kiowas, and five Comanches (four more Comanches would be added as they surrendered late in the spring).[41] Others had simply been disarmed and were carefully watched. As the attempt to use commissions was abandoned, a decision was made to ship those in the Ice House to Florida. The group included the Cheyenne chiefs Grey Beard and Heaps of Birds as well as the Kiowas Woman's Heart and Lone Wolf.[42]

These men were moved by wagon to Caddo, Oklahoma, where a train awaited them. What these men must have felt as the doors of the boxcars swung shut can hardly be imagined—many had never been in a house before. Most had fought to keep their hunting grounds, lands necessary to feed their families. When surrendering, most assumed, as Satanta had, that they would be disarmed and eventually allowed to join their families. Moreover, no legal grounds existed to hold them—the army had concluded that evidence did not exist to try the vast majority of them, and even the judge advocate general's office of the United States Army had concluded that a "war" never occurred. How could these Indians then be held as "prisoners of war" and deported to another land?

Hardly anyone in America had an answer for this perplexing question or noticed the illegality of these actions taken against Indians (even Confederate prisoners had been allowed to go home after the cessation of hostilities in 1865). General Sherman, as usual, seemed most determined to inflict a severe punishment. When discussing the deportations, he concluded that there should be "no end to this punishment, until death."[43] Yet the public did not forsake the southern Plains Indians completely. Indeed reformers came to their rescue.

While en route to the East reporters from various towns scrambled to get access to the prisoners, mostly just to observe them. One from the *St. Louis Republican*, however, pleaded for some leniency. The men had been chained together for days in the boxcars. Even "prisoners of war" deserved better, he wrote, yet it appeared that they were not "to receive [fair] treatment."[44] But conditions gradually improved as the Indians settled into their new life within the walls of Fort Marion, Florida. The army even allowed some of their dependents to join them—over the objections of General Sheridan, who called their requests "tweedle." A sympathetic Lieutenant Richard Henry Pratt assumed charge of the Indians in Florida and conducted personal interviews with all of them. They were allowed to request that spouses and children be sent to the fort. One enterprising Kiowa young man simply said: "Tell Woman's Heart to bring him a wife." Another told Pratt that, of his two wives, he should "bring the one that wants to come the most." Some forty-six women and forty-six children ultimately made the same trip to Caddo and then rode the train to Florida to join their relatives.[45]

Young Lieutenant Pratt became an ideal choice for directing the Indians' imprisonment and their educational advancement. He soon set up schools at Fort Marion: the men and their dependents learned to read and write. Many took up ledger art, filling books with pictures of their experiences, which Pratt later sold for them. Pratt soon concluded that some men might be repatriated to Oklahoma, and nearly half of them returned in 1878. Others would be sent to Pratt's new Indian school, then being established in Pennsylvania.[46]

If judged by today's standards, the American government violated numerous international laws in punishing Comanches, Kiowas, and Cheyennes. By acquiescing to the army's solution, civil authorities in the Interior Department committed a crime against humanity by agreeing to the deportation or forcible transfer of a significant portion of captured Indians.[47] General Sheridan also concocted a plan that clearly deprived "a prisoner of war or other protected person of the rights of fair and regular trial," as the Rome Statutes so clearly state today, which in effect constituted a war crime.[48] And an officer from the judge advocate general's corps concluded that martial law had not been established and a "war" had not occurred, leaving little defense for Sheridan's conclusion that the Indians were "prisoners of war." Indeed calling the struggle the "Red River Wars" is a misnomer.

The end result was the taking of Native peoples' lands, which they rightfully had possession of: ethnic cleansing. While they retained reservation lands in western Indian Territory, they lost hunting grounds in the Texas Panhandle and even in western Kansas. Article 11 of the 1867 Medicine Lodge Treaty gave the Indians the right "to hunt on any lands south of the Arkansas River so long as the Buffalo may range thereon." It also expressly excluded "white settlement" in this region. All of these promises were abandoned by the government in pursuing its policy of ethnic cleansing, facilitated to a large degree when civilian authorities, represented by the secretary of the interior and the commissioner of Indian affairs, turned the so-called Indian problem over to the army.[49]

Sheridan's manipulation of government policy and his determination to start a "war" could have been avoided. General Pope offered an alternative. By removing the white buffalo hunters, two evils would have been mostly averted. Markets for stolen livestock, which only encouraged Indian raiding in the South, would have declined appreciably and buffalo herds would have been gradually reduced rather than annihilated in a few years. Most of the Indians roaming in the Panhandle would eventually have moved to the reservation, as many had done. The army also had the troops by 1873 to build a barrier across the southern plains and prevent raiding parties from going south—it was very close to achieving such a solution when Sheridan launched his invasion of Indian hunting lands. The policy of patience would have given Indians a choice. Forcing them from the land and then deporting them to Florida were crimes that cannot be defended, even given Native intransigence.

It is ironic, given Pratt's supposed success, that the violation of Indians' rights by use of deportation became yet another strategy that would be employed many times in the future when recalcitrant Indians refused to give up their lands. Even some reformers viewed it as a moral restraint because it blunted the bluster of army officers who demanded much greater retribution, such as starvation or trials that led to executions. Deportation even worked much better than military commissions, which offered far too much transparency and had questionable legality. And at least some reformers likely viewed Sheridan's solution as being necessary: how could

Indians justifiably be allowed to hold vast acreage in the Texas Panhandle as hunting ground? It violated the agrarian principle that remained so much a part of Indian-white relations in America, going back hundreds of years.

President Grant and Generals Sherman and Sheridan all supported the decision to confine the Indians in the East. In substance they became hostages that guaranteed the behavior of their kin in the West. This decision would force all the nontreaty Indians onto the reservations assigned to them—and it worked. Indeed Sheridan's "authority," as he called it, soon became the model for dealing with the northern nontreaty Indians, who were next on his list. The only likelihood of difficulty came in numbers. Forty thousand Lakota Sioux and Cheyennes hunted on lands that they too had been guaranteed through treaty. To remove them from those hunting lands would be more difficult. Nevertheless, General Sheridan seemed confident as early as 1874 that he had found the strategy: he only needed the "authority" to force these Indians onto their reservations and then control those agencies where they were fed, deporting many or even withholding food to keep them in line.

As the nation headed into the centennial of 1876, after one hundred years of national development, the army still saw the need to flex its muscles on the northern reaches of the Great Plains. The Peace Policy was in full retreat, and the winds of war were blowing stronger than ever. Success in the South foreordained a similar policy for the northern plains.

15

GENERAL SHERIDAN AND THE ETHNIC CLEANSING OF THE NORTHERN LAKOTA SIOUX

Colonel David Stanley was a learned man who graduated toward the top of his class at West Point. He traveled to the academy with fellow Ohioan Philip Sheridan.[1] Stanley, who had assumed command of the new District of the Upper Missouri, dutifully reported to his superiors, including Sheridan, the news regarding the threat to the American presence posed by Lakota Indians. Many Indians vehemently opposed American travel on the upper portions of the Missouri and especially the work of surveyors in the Yellowstone River valley, which began in 1871 and continued for the next two years. The Northern Pacific was now poised to move west beyond the Missouri River, so General Hancock, commanding the Department of the Northwest in St. Paul, pressed Stanley for more information regarding the attitude of the various Native bands. Stanley's reports became more pessimistic, predicting major conflict. The colonel's information, gleaned from Indian confidants, led to a provocative solution to the "problem" that the military faced, as he saw it.

Stanley, who certainly trusted Sheridan and remained somewhat within his circle, seemed uncertain of General Hancock's views, at first testing him. In November 1872 he wrote: "Since the Department Commander has had the manners to ask my views . . . [the] two great mistakes" regarding Indian policy involved "breaking up the posts along the Bozeman Trail in 1868" and "allowing traders to go amongst the northern non-treaty Indians" and provide them with arms and munitions.[2] This criticism might easily have been deemed insubordinate, because General Sherman had agreed to abandon the Bozeman Trail forts. But Stanley likely knew that Hancock and Sheridan (who would also have access to his reports) agreed with him. Receiving only encouragement, Stanley then launched into a much more detailed assessment of the situation in his district two months later in a long letter sent directly to Hancock, dated January 4, 1873.[3]

In a twelve-page assessment Stanley carefully spelled out the policy that the army should pursue. Despite the various attempts to feed the Indians at reservations, he began, "the spirit of lawlessness" among them "has increased." Stanley contended that ambushes of soldiers at the Upper Missouri River agencies and forts had grown in number. He listed thirteen individual assaults, without the arrest of any Indian. Stanley was obviously suggesting that treating these assaults as individual actions or felonies was foolish—he believed that they were acts of war. Stanley's second point reflected directly upon the land. "The great difficulty is the immensity of the Sioux Country," he argued. While the treaty limited the reservation to a manageable 200 miles east to west and 300 miles north to south, a clause "prohibits [white] settlements north of the Platte, and as far west as the summit of Big Horn Mountain," making the "Great Sioux Reservation" immense.[4]

Stanley then noted that the attack on Baker's command the previous summer was undertaken by "northern Cheyennes and warriors from every band of Sioux I could name!" Trying to subdue individual bands or warriors, even by recruiting a massive force of Indian auxiliaries, would be impossible "and probably meet so much opposition from the class of womenlie [sic] philanthropists . . . that the plan would fail." Unlike the Indians of the South, who raided in small groups, the nonreservation Lakotas and Cheyennes were a formidable force. And the recently published argument of commissioner of Indian affairs Francis Walker that "three years will see the end of Indian hostilities" seemed ludicrous to Stanley. Unless the Indian landholdings were reduced, "Not three nor thirty years" would bring the end of fighting.[5]

This brought Stanley to his "third and last consideration . . . the remedy." Stanley proposed opening the entire "mountain section" to settlement from the head of the Cheyenne River to the Yellowstone: fundamentally the Black Hills, Powder River country, and the old Bozeman Trail north to the Yellowstone. He continued:

> Always do the thing your enemy dreads most, and the settlement of the
> place of refuge from justice by the whites, is above all what these murdering

Sioux most dread. The immediate incentive for explorers would of course be gold. I have sifted the reports of gold in the Black Hills pretty carefully, and have no white man's evidence that any gold has been found there or in the Powder River Mountains. . . . The Indians state that they have found gold on the north fork of the Cheyenne, and an Indian (White Bear) now at Cheyenne Agency gives a very intelligent account of finding gold dust on the same stream. . . . But whether gold be found or not, the grazing facilities, the fine timber, and the healthful climate . . . would soon attract settlers.[6]

Settlement, Stanley assumed, will come someday: "Why postpone it longer to favor a people who are practically and professedly assassins?" He urged army officials quietly to encourage the gold stories, which obviously would create a rush into the Black Hills that would force the army to defend the citizens and eventually diminish the size of the "Great Sioux Reservation."[7]

Sheridan shared Stanley's views, but he shrewdly realized that his scheme could seriously damage the army. It would cause outrage among those "womenlie [sic] philanthropists." Sheridan looked for ways to accomplish Stanley's goal of "diminishment" in other ways. Obviously the Northern Pacific's demands for military protection for the summer's survey work in the Yellowstone Valley created opportunities, and even reformers supported the railroad's advance. Perhaps a gold rush would be unnecessary, especially if the expedition found gold along the Yellowstone or the surveyors themselves provoked an Indian war that the army had to fight.[8]

Reinforced with troops who were being removed from the South, Sheridan ordered Colonel Custer (who had been detached to duty in Memphis) to move his cavalry to the upper Missouri to support the surveyors. In spring 1873 Custer joined Stanley's support troops to defend the surveyors who were headed into the Yellowstone Valley. They got on poorly at first, squabbling over the use of the cavalry, but Stanley soon recognized Custer's daring and his ability to handle troopers. While sources do not reveal just when Custer and Stanley discussed the final solution to the "Indian problem," as Stanley saw it, there can be little doubt that they did—probably even before they left Fort Rice in late May 1873. Custer, Sheridan's favorite cavalry officer, was certainly part of the general's inner circle of officers that he trusted with sensitive information.[9]

The acting secretary of war wrote Stanley a personal letter directing him to take along geologists and scientists, "sound, active, and intelligent officers" who would survey the natural resources of the region explored. The group included Harvard mineralogist Joel Allen and geologist Lionel Nettre. While they found no gold or minerals of value, the expedition's newspaper reporters did much to promote the need of the railroad to proceed on to the Pacific. A host of others tagged along, including Indian scouts such as Bloody Knife, recruited by Indian agent John Tappan at Fort Buford. Bloody Knife soon became Custer's favorite scout.[10]

Stanley's force consisted of 1,300 men, including 275 six-mule wagons. By early August they had crossed the Yellowstone River, moving along its northern bank. There Custer's lead element fell under attack, ultimately being surrounded and cut off. Bloody Knife proved his value by urging Custer into a defensive position. As Stanley came to their relief, the Indians broke off. But Stanley ordered Custer to pursue them, hardly the actions of a commander bent on protecting surveyors.[11] With "hostile" Indians in his front, Custer, leading several companies of men, reveled in the opportunity. They sacked several abandoned villages and drove Indians under Gall and Crazy Horse from the field. Sitting Bull and others, who watched from afar, knew the accuracy of Stanley's artillery. The Indians dispersed, crossing over the Yellowstone to safety.[12] The Indians avoided the "war" that Stanley tried so hard to produce.

While the surveyors mapped their final route to the mountains, startling news ran back and forth along the telegraph wires from New York to Philadelphia to Washington, D.C. The financial empire of Jay Cooke—over a dozen banks, several railroad companies, and of course Cooke's "gem," the Northern Pacific Railroad—all collapsed into bankruptcy on September 18, 1873.[13] The controversial way in which Cooke had financed the road through stock foreordained his downfall. As the indomitable financier and railroader Cornelius Vanderbilt reportedly said: "Building railroads from nowhere to nowhere at public expense is not a legitimate undertaking!"[14] Legitimate or not, the collapse forced the army to turn its attentions elsewhere. Campaigning in the Yellowstone Valley thereafter—Indian hunting lands guaranteed by treaty—would only seem to be a provocation that reformers were sure to denounce.

The retreat of the Lakota Indians in front of Custer hardly signaled defeat. Agent A. J. Simmons noted that some seven hundred Métis Canadians had crossed the line to trade for buffalo hides, offering in exchange exactly what the Indians wanted—ammmunition and guns. Sitting Bull, according to Simmons, "declares his purpose of fighting to the last, opposing the

NPRR [Northern Pacific Railroad] and the settlement of that country. He forms the nucleus around which the disaffected and renegades from all the other bands of Sioux gather."[15] Yet another area of contention, which likely brought reinforcements to Sitting Bull, emerged late in the summer 1873. Smith sent a commission to convince Red Cloud and others to surrender their hunting rights outside of the Great Sioux Reservation. The commissioners came away shocked, reporting that the Indians "will not relinquish their right to hunt or cede the territory outside of their Reservation" and that the government should prepare for a "serious struggle."[16]

Aware of the rebuff, Sheridan planned a new approach. He tried to convince Congress to provide funds to build military forts on lands considered vital by the army, especially in the Yellowstone River valley and the Black Hills. Such garrisons would be necessary to protect the railroad when it reemerged from bankruptcy, just as the army had done for the Union and Kansas Pacific. Sheridan felt that garrisons along the Yellowstone and in the Black Hills were essential and expected to get authority for the forts sometime in the future. Meanwhile he quietly assigned his trusted aide Major James Forsyth—another member of the inner circle—the job of selecting locations. Forsyth spent much of 1873 to 1875 reconnoitering the Yellowstone River. He found locations for garrisons, all on land well within the guaranteed hunting grounds of the Lakota Sioux.[17]

Realizing that only Congress could authorize the forts, Sheridan set out to develop a plan that might bring about such a result. Major "scientific" surveys of the West by the likes of John Wesley Powell, Clarence King, George M. Wheeler, and Ferdinand Hayden had been undertaken, were under way, or were being organized in the late 1860s and 1870s. Americans clamored to read the published reports of these men and to view the photographs of the Grand Canyon and the geysers of Yellowstone. Sheridan had legitimately promoted science, even courting the friendship of famous geologists and botanists who collected specimens for various museums. He had convinced the secretary of war to provide $7,350 in funding for scientists who had accompanied Colonel Stanley into the Yellowstone valley in 1873.[18] Two of Sheridan's new recruits included Newton H. Winchell, the state geologist of Minnesota, who later wrote one of the first full histories of his state, and the famous writer George Bird Grinnell, at the time a young Yale paleontologist.[19]

Using scientific enquiry as a guise, Sheridan requested permission for an exploration party to enter the Black Hills, considered a mysterious land by some. In discussions with President Grant, he presented the army's case: most observers expected war with the nontreaty Lakotas, which would require a military presence in the hills. President Grant finally relented after Sheridan assured cabinet officers, including the secretary of the interior, that rumors of gold in the hills were unconfirmed.[20] Given authority, Sheridan picked Colonel Custer to lead the expedition. Custer organized a massive column of men, some ten companies of the Seventh Cavalry, two infantry companies, three Gatling guns, and a three-inch Rodman cannon. Over much of July and August 1874 the expedition explored the various valleys and peaks of the hills but found little gold. Indeed, the date of the only find—a handful of specks that had to be viewed with a magnifying glass—was never recorded.[21]

Yet if doubt ever existed relative to the purpose of Custer's mission, it soon faded when he sent runners into Fort Laramie who announced a massive gold strike. Once the colonel reached Fort Abraham Lincoln in August, he reported to the *Bismarck Tribune* that the strikes matched "the richest regions in Colorado."[22] Custer's messages and comments were absolute falsehoods, as the expedition's chief geologist, Professor Winchell, declared openly in the press a month later. Winchell had seen no gold at all and doubted that it existed in the hills in any quantity.[23] The reports proved so disturbing to reformers in the East who feared a gold rush that Sheridan was forced to publish a notice in newspapers indicating that the hills were on an Indian reservation and therefore off-limits to miners.[24]

What Custer and his superiors hoped to accomplish has often been the stuff of historical speculation. The Stanley letter of January 1873, however, reveals that several senior army officers all along had discussed using the discovery of gold in the Black Hills as a means to start a rush and an Indian war that would settle the "Indian problem."[25] Indeed it can hardly be imagined that Custer spend most of the summer of 1873 with Stanley and never discussed Stanley's plan to promote just such a gold rush into the hills. The very fact that Sheridan's choice of Custer to lead the expedition rather than General Crook is suspicious: Fort Abraham Lincoln and Custer's command were nearly 200 miles from the Black Hills, while Fort Laramie and General Crook were a mere 60 miles away. Sheridan did write Sherman a rather elusive and apologetic letter in September, noting that he had contemplated using Laramie as the point of embarkation but concluded that the "condition and temper" of the Indians would not allow this. Custer's massive force would not disturb the Indians, he suggested, even though it penetrated the very hunting lands that they vowed to protect. Even Sherman must have smiled at Sheridan's fib.[26]

It took little time for miners and adventurers to press for admission to the Black Hills. News of Forsyth's job of finding fort locations leaked to officials in Montana, prompting the first invasions, led by Montana hunters and miners who moved down the Yellowstone from Fort Ellis (present-day Bozeman) and constructed Fort Pease during the early summer 1875, nearly at the mouth of the Big Horn River. The occupants of Fort Pease included a host of men who had exhibited a strong sense of entitlement. Some were so-called wolfers, former mountain men who hunted for a living. They used strychnine-baited carcasses to kill wolf packs, just to acquire their pelts. A number of the wolfers also panned for gold on the side but soon found that the Lakota Sioux were determined to force them to leave. Most miners defied authority of any kind, in particular that of the American military, even though the army at Fort Ellis came to their rescue at a crucial moment. They exhibited the same attitude of "settler sovereignty" that had traditionally existed along the American frontier—they believed that they had a right to take game and search for gold wherever their rambling took them.[27]

Custer's so-called discoveries and contemplated miner invasions of the Black Hills prompted some military officers to weigh in on the issue. Unlike General Sheridan and the members of his circle, at least a few army officers believed that troops should protect the Black Hills from miner invasion, much as General Sully had recommended in the case of the buffalo hunters in the South. General Alfred Terry, a trained lawyer who commanded the Department of Dakota, openly disagreed with many of Sheridan's schemes. He signaled his views in a long letter, arguing that "it is of the greatest importance that any attempt to defy the law and to trample on the rights secured by the Sioux . . . should be met with the most vigorous manner *at the very outset*." Terry believed that the Black Hills should be "absolutely closed to intruders."[28] Sheridan surely knew at the time that General Crook, a fellow Ohioan who had just taken command of the Department of the Platte, agreed with Terry, leaving two important commanders in the field who could not be ignored.

After Custer's return, Crook also acted decisively. He ordered his troops to inspect the Black Hills early in spring 1875. Captain John Mix found twenty-eight people at French Creek—dubbed the Gordon Party—and escorted them out in April, the first evictions to take place.[29] The invasions, which evoked severe criticism from reformers, had also embarrassed President Grant, who had issued a personal order the month before explaining that the hills were on Indian lands and all miners were to be expelled. Even so, he discussed the issue with his cabinet, agreeing that a more thorough exploration was necessary—it seemed strange to the administration that the lead geologist would contradict Colonel Custer. This time, however, General Crook was asked to organize the expedition, given the Custer-Winchell feud then taking place in the newspapers. Crook picked Colonel Richard Irving Dodge to conduct the survey. Dodge brought along young Professor Walter Jenny from the Columbia School of Mines.[30] Jenny (Dodge later concluded that he was a bit "crazy") had a host of other scientists along with a military contingent of 452 men. The party spent the summer panning in nearly every small stream that came out of the hills.

Americans followed the progress of Dodge and Jenny in national newspapers and reports in June and July 1875. And Jenny's dispatches enthralled the nation: "Gold Reported to Have Been Found in Large Quantities—One Hundred Miners at Work."[31] Young Lieutenant John G. Bourke, a personal friend of Sheridan who accompanied Dodge, sent a quick note to the general, which in itself is telling: "The main purpose of the expedition, as I understand it, has been accomplished, in the discovery of gold." This seemed to be a vindication of Custer. Bourke even included some "color" (gold dust) for Sheridan's amusement and concluded: "all the cavalry in the department, all the mounted force of the army, will be unable to retard their [the miners'] ingress much less drive them out." The letter obviously pleased Sheridan, who expected that the discovery would eventually lead to the settlement of the hills and to the "diminishment" of Indian lands.[32]

Jenny continued to survey the hills, and many miners joined him. A report printed in the newspapers on July 28 suggested that even more were welcome. Jenny noted: "About 200 miners have deserted French Creek and followed me here. They are pouring into the hills from all directions." More reports, often several weeks old, appeared in newspapers in late July, August, and even on November 12, when Jenny's final report was printed on the front page of the *New York Times*, emphasizing the "paying quantities" of precious metal in the hills.[33] While Jenny's assessment that there was gold in the Black Hills would eventually prove correct, he never really found quantities; his reports were mostly gross exaggerations.

While miners and the government sparred, Congress appointed William Allison to chair a commission sent west to extinguish Lakota title to the Black Hills. The group met Red Cloud and Spotted Tail, who quickly rejected the government's offer. The nontreaty Indians to the north, including Sitting Bull and Crazy Horse, had sent word to the commission even before it arrived, through the scout Frank Grouard. According to Grouard, Sitting Bull replied in a message aimed at Allison: "Are you the great God who made me; or was it the great God who made me who sent you? If he [God] asks me to come to see him, I will go; but the big chief of the white men must come see me. I will not go to the reservation. I have no land to sell. There is plenty of game for us. We have enough ammunition. We don't want any white man here."[34]

Sitting Bull's stubborn refusal to sell anything likely influenced Red Cloud and Spotted Tail, who had become reservation Indians. Nevertheless, they too had visited the Black Hills in August, spending time with Crook and Dodge, and had become aware of the great value that Americans put on the region. That observation in itself made them less likely to agree to a sale.[35]

Back east, some newspaper editors fumed over Lakota obstinateness, suggesting that a gold rush might alleviate economic wows. The *National Republican,* the arm of the administration in Washington, concluded that the "stubbornness" of the Indians left the government little choice but to "develop the resources of the Black Hills." And it would be impossible to keep the miners out: "the Black Hills will continue to be a source of perplexing trouble" until they were opened to miners. The *New York Times* agreed and added a simple justification: "the government need not concern itself too strictly to keep the White man out of the Black Hills," as the Indians remained "hostile" to any negotiation.[36]

Given the miners' invasion, it seems logical that they could not possibly be kept out of the region. Most historians have taken this view. One of the earliest, Watson Parker, concluded that the few troops in the hills "could accomplish little more than their own survival," as miners snuck by them at will.[37] Nearly all later historians have cited Parker, including Robert Utley, who concluded that the army made "only a token effort to keep them [the miners] out." Jeffrey Ostler's award-winning book had little new to suggest. "Although the army officially discouraged miners from trespassing on the Great Sioux Reservation," Ostler wrote, "its pursuit of violators was halfhearted." If this were true, it left the president of the

United States with little choice other than to authorize military action. But this history is terribly flawed.[38]

Many army officers did not hold views similar to those of Custer, Stanley, or Sheridan. Both Generals Crook and Terry, who controlled the troops who were assigned to protecting Indian rights in the hills, sought to carry out the president's order. Young army officers such as Captain Fergus Walker, obeyed orders from Crook, forcing several large parties back to the Missouri River in April and May 1875. Lieutenant Colonel L. D. Bradley arrested the members of the so-called Gordon Party a second time, placing Gordon in a guard house at Spotted Tail's Agency. Throughout the summer the army evicted hundreds of miners, despite newspaper reports to the contrary.[39] General Crook arrived in late July and convinced several hundred miners to leave of their own volition (which, incidentally, pleased Red Cloud and Spotted Tail). When Colonel Dodge departed for Fort Laramie, he turned over several cavalry units to Captain Edwin Pollock, whose job it was to scout the hills in the fall and remove the few miners who remained.[40]

Pollock's large cavalry force explored nearly every creek and crevasse in the hills over the fall. After removing a number of parties, he focused on groups of two or three men, who hid in the hills. "I have endeavored to gather all the information possible concerning any miner that may be known or supposed to be yet in the hills," he reported, "the result being that all agree with Colonel Dodge that but few remain."[41] By late September Pollock had determined that Rapid Creek and Castle Creek were "entirely clear" of miners. Four men were arrested and tied up at one point; and a lone straggler ("an elected delegate of the Dakota legislature") surrendered. While Pollock was virtually certain that no miners remained in the hills by late September, his final report of November 27, 1875, concluded definitively that all intruders had been removed.[42]

This turn of events, totally unknown to newspaper editors, did not dissuade General Sheridan. He informed General Terry that a "meeting" with the president would occur after the Allison Commission had returned to Washington. "If congress does not open the country," the general concluded, "then a post will have to be established." Such a conclusion seemed unwarranted given the diligence of the troops. Nevertheless, the meeting with President Grant occurred on November 3 and included the new secretary of the interior, Zachariah Chandler (a former senator from Michigan who was deeply implicated in swindling Chippewa Indians out of timber); Secretary of War Belknap; and Sheridan (Sherman, feuding with both Grant and Belknap, apparently refused to attend). No known notes of the meeting have survived.[43]

The Black Hills were crucial to the discussion. The press continued to offer a general picture that the hills had been overrun by miners. Sheridan, of course, knew better, being privy to all the reports coming in from junior officers. For his part, Grant had serious political consequences to think of—the presidential election, which was proving to be a difficult one for the Republicans, given the economy, was exactly a year away. Reformers continued to hound the president regarding the need to preserve Indian lands guaranteed by the Sioux Treaty of 1868. Given Grant's support of reformers, and even his continued rhetorical support for the Peace Policy, a legitimate question exists as to what General Sheridan actually told the president. Did Sheridan admit that Generals Terry and Crook could easily keep the Black Hills free of miners or did he simply report that the newspapers had offered an accurate assessment of the situation? In other words, what did Grant know when considering options regarding the hills?[44]

Unfortunately, the sources end at the question. But some hints do surface. Grant wanted the army to keep the March 1875 order prohibiting access to the hills in place—a political necessity—but allowed Sheridan to stop enforcing it. This strongly suggests that Sheridan argued that he could not prevent the invasion, which would have been a fabrication. As Sheridan's biographer Paul Hutton succinctly stated: "The meeting gave Sheridan all he had hoped for."[45] Indeed it gave Sheridan presidential "authority" to begin preparing for military operations against the nontreaty Lakota and Cheyenne Indians, the only option that the president apparently believed was on the table. But the president knew that the decision would not be well received in reform circles in the East.

Sheridan's lobbying also included winning over Secretary Chandler, which probably took little effort: Chandler had worked hand in hand with the timber interests in Michigan who were pillaging the Isabella Indian Reservation.[46] Legally the secretary had to create a crisis in order to turn the Indians over to the army. He did this by issuing another order, requiring all nontreaty Indians in the Yellowstone River valley and its tributaries immediately to move onto the reservations by January 31, 1876. All who refused would be declared hostile. The order went out by telegram to the various agencies on December 3, during the dead of winter in the

Dakotas. Indian agent John Burke complained vociferously about the tim-
ing—it was impossible to get the information to the Indians and convince
them to move in such a short period.[47] Agent James Hastings at Red Cloud
Agency actually received a response, sending the news east on January 28.
Oglala leaders Crazy Horse and Black Twin had agreed to come in, but
the snow was so deep that reaching Indian camps was nearly impossible.[48]

Sheridan hardly waited for the response, pressing Chandler for "authority" to start military action. He wanted to get his troops into the field by
March. Chandler theoretically had to wait until February 1 to issue the
order, but when he did so he ignored the news from Red Cloud's Agency
and noted simply that Sitting Bull had refused the original order. Two
days later, on February 3, the secretary of war ordered the army to "take
immediate measures to compel these Indians [Lakotas and Cheyennes] to
return to their reservations." Both Sheridan and Stanley admitted in letters
that buffalo still existed in the valleys northwest of the Black Hills, making
it perfectly legal for the Indians to be there. In essence the government
was breaking the treaty of 1868 and had declared an "unjust" war on the
Lakota Sioux and Cheyenne Indians over land, in the dead of winter.[49]

The war went badly from the start. General Crook ordered Colonel
J. J. Reynolds with six companies of cavalry into the field ahead of him.
With the temperature plummeting to 26 below zero, Reynolds stumbled
onto roughly a hundred lodges of Cheyennes on March 17, nestled into
the banks of the Powder River. Reynolds charged, ran the Indians off,
and took the camp. Then most troopers attempted "to go to the rear with
plunder," as Captain Anson Mills later reported. When the Cheyennes
saw the confusion, they counterattacked and drove the army out, even
regaining most of their horses. Crook and Sheridan were both apoplectic.
Reynolds faced a court-martial and left the army in disgrace.[50]

Sheridan expected better results after the weather moderated. By mid-
May General Terry and General John Gibbon moved nearly a thousand
infantry to the north bank of the Yellowstone River. Crook's force of
roughly 1,500 men moved north, up the Powder River and into the Rosebud Valley. Custer and 700 troopers of the 7th cavalry searched the tributaries of the Yellowstone, looking for villages. Sheridan expected these
three armies to drive the Indians out of the Yellowstone River valley,
toward the agencies. As in the South, the families of the hostile Indians
would be prevented from coming in, as Sheridan put it, unless by "unconditional surrender"—in other words, only when men, women, and

children all surrendered together. The general added that "the ringleaders [were] to be punished as were the southern Indians."[51] It all seemed so simple, so precise. Sheridan likely already knew where Sioux leaders such as Sitting Bull would be deported to in the East.

Sheridan's simple plan suddenly seemed in jeopardy, however, when news arrived that General Crook had left the field. On the morning of June 17, while Crook's forces were camped along the Rosebud River, some eight hundred mounted Lakota and Cheyenne warriors hit the camp. The only thing that prevented panic and disaster was that many of the cavalry troops had unsaddled their horses and could not run. Captain Anson Mills, who had been with Reynolds just weeks before, wrote that "we were lucky not to have been vanquished." With dozens of wounded and dead on both sides, the Indians withdrew in the afternoon. Crook announced the battle a victory and then ordered "retreat."[52]

Worse, while Terry's and Gibbon's forces hoped to join up with Custer's, the rendezvous never occurred.[53] Custer acted rashly much as he had at Gettysburg and on the Washita, using maneuvers that had succeeded in those engagements. Custer found the main Lakota and Cheyenne camp along the Little Big Horn River on June 25 and then divided his command into thirds. Captain Frederick Benteen, who had chased miners in the hills the year before, was ordered south with most of the ammunition. Custer then sent Major Marcus Reno, with just three companies, to attack the village on its south end. Custer, with five more companies, moved north around a large hill with bluffs extending to the north. The bluffs disguised the presence of 10,000 Indians in the camp.[54]

As Reno's troops got on line several hundred yards to the south, pandemonium broke out in the huge Sioux village. Children ran looking for their mothers. Women, prepared for such an occurrence, turned to tearing down their lodges, getting ready to leave as quickly as possible. But the Lakota soldier societies and the Cheyenne Dog Soldiers had trained all of their lives for such an event. Indian warriors quickly routed Reno, sending him reeling to the rear with fifty dead and many wounded. The well-armed warriors, many with new Winchester rifles, then turned on Custer and drove him northward. By five P.M. the fate of Custer's entire command of 204 had been decided. Indians killed every soldier. Later that evening Lakota women came onto the battlefield, joining in the general mutilation of the corpses and taking pants and shirts and whatever else of value the dead American soldiers possessed.[55]

Custer's forces attacked a village of roughly 10,000 people, most of whom were women and children. Their scouts had reported the existence of soldiers hours before Reno's assault. Even though some of these Indians had skirmished with Crook's army just days before, they seemed confident of their own safety and perhaps even assumed that the officers of the army coming from the East would negotiate.[56] The Indians were camped on a hunting preserve that the treaty of 1868 guaranteed to them. Custer's attack itself was a clear violation of the rules of war as they were known at the time and constituted a war crime by today's standards. Had Custer been successful, the same criticisms of his actions would undoubtedly have emerged as those that came after his "victory" on the Washita River.

After the Custer debacle a number of narratives surfaced that offer glimpses into how the Lakota people felt about their land and their defense of it. A number have been published, while others remain mostly unused by historians.[57] Most show that the Lakota people camped on the Little Big Horn remained divided; many hoped to maintain peace, even though several hundred had attacked General Crook a week earlier. Many young men and women who joined the camp from the agencies came to hunt and trade rather than to fight American soldiers. One such visitor was Kills Eagle, a Hunkpapa chief who reached the camp in April with two dozen lodges of his people. He went to trade for buffalo hides and moccasins, which he obtained by bringing ammunition into the camp.[58]

While other Hunkpapas originally offered Kills Eagle a feast after his arrival, Sitting Bull believed that he was a friend of the white people. In the center of the three-mile-long assemblage of lodges was a main "soldiers' lodge." It contained literally hundreds of followers who policed the camp and held a council every night. Soldiers came and told Kills Eagle that he could not return to the agency any time soon. Many other Indians were in a similar circumstance, confined by the soldiers' lodge. One, Medicine Lodge, sent with a message to Sitting Bull from the agent at Fort Peck, even had a guard posted over him. When Kills Eagle attempted to leave, he reported that Sioux soldiers "took some of my horses, killed 8 of them. . . . They abused and whipped my men." During the battle with Custer Kills Eagle and his men stayed in camp, as did others. Sitting Bull and other Lakota leaders were well aware that some of their people were sympathetic to reservation life.[59]

In the weeks after the battle, however, the leaders of the nontreaty Indians wanted to make peace. They needed time to hunt and feared more attacks. Accordingly, the soldiers' lodge released a goodly number of reservation Indians, giving them messages to bring to the Americans. As these Indians returned to the agencies, they often related verbatim the words of war leaders like Crazy Horse and Sitting Bull. One of the most forthright messages was carried back by Man That Smells His Hand, who reached Standing Rock Agency in early September with a message from Sitting Bull. It said simply:

> This land belongs to us. It is a gift to us from the Great Spirit. The Great Spirit gave us the game in this country. . . . The White man came here to take the country from us by force. He has brought misery and wretchedness into our country. We were here killing game and eating, and all of a sudden we were attacked by white men!
>
> Sitting Bull says he was out there because there was game, but he did not want to fight. He had to fight because he was attacked. Perhaps the Whites think they can exterminate us, but God, the Great Spirit, will not permit it.[60]

Although the Lakotas had prevailed in this one encounter, they too had suffered. Custer's men had inflicted considerable casualties: fourteen Lakotas died outright in the skirmish with Reno, and thirty-nine others were killed overcoming Custer. Many wounded died in camp in the days that followed.[61]

Kills Eagle estimated that as many as six hundred Indians had been wounded—perhaps an exaggeration. Kills Eagle gave descriptions of the chaos in the main Indian camp that supported the claim that Custer's men had inflicted considerable damage. "They kept coming in continuously with wounded Indians, thrown over their horses, with their heads hanging down and the blood running out." Kills Eagle noted that when they moved the wounded on the day after the Custer fight, "there were twenty-seven on travois and thirty eight on horseback" just among the Oglalas, Crazy Horse's lodge group. While the other seven lodge groups may not have suffered as severely—no reports exist on their numbers—overcoming Custer had obviously taken a severe toll on the Indians.[62]

The interviews with Kills Eagle suggest considerable factionalism within the Lakota community, some Indians being for war and others preferring to remain mostly peaceful. But the vast majority of Indians wished to protect their access to the hunting grounds in the West. As the army reinforced troops on the reservations by summer, many tribal spokesmen came forward to challenge the army's occupation of both the reserves and the hunting grounds. At Cheyenne River, a rather peaceful reservation, White Swan told army officers: "We want to know if the Great Father ordered his troops to make trouble." Push the Clouds was more emphatic: "We have been driven by the Whites to where we are now, we ran away from them and they took all we had, our land, and our game. . . . We were told that this was to be our land, that we could live here in peace, that we could hunt and not be molested. Why don't you keep your promise?"[63]

As military troops attempted to arrest certain leaders, even peaceful young men and their chiefs encouraged resistance. Chief Grass responded to Captain R. E. Johnson at Standing Rock that "his men would not come in and be arrested by the military, that they would not be slaves." Grass and fellow chief Running Antelope were both then arrested.[64]

All the evidence suggests that the large number of Lakota and Cheyenne Indians who stayed at home on the reservations during the spring campaigns also demonstrated a willingness to defend their lands and rights, often being closely related to those on the Little Big Horn River. Many had adopted a mobile economy, remaining on the reservations during the winters and turning to their western hunting grounds come spring, to hunt and trade with the nonreservation Indians. This lifestyle was being threatened by both the armies in the field and those on the reservations. By fall General Sheridan concluded that the "settlement of the Sioux troubles" was simple: "*running them down*" and then inflicting "stern punishment" on those who resisted his troops, even on reservations, which supposedly belonged to the Indians.[65]

Beyond doubt, the destruction of Custer and his five companies did much to crush any sympathies that might have existed regarding Lakota claims to land, even those of leaders who had not participated in the battle. Custer's demise came at an awful time. Philadelphia had officially opened the Centennial International Exposition or world's fair. It celebrated American progress and ingenuity. American politicians demanded explanations regarding the Custer debacle. The job of explaining fell to Commissioner Smith, who labored over a letter that eventually offered many mischaracterizations.

Smith contended that the "non-treaty Sioux" consisted at most of a mere 3,000 Indians, describing them as exceedingly different in their views from the reservation people. They had made "disastrous raids" on friendly tribes such as the Crows and had "engaged in a long series of depredations upon white settlers." Even worse, "the hostiles are not a distinct band of Indians, but a *set of desparados* [*sic*] consisting of the disaffected and outlaws from all the different bands . . . held together by a common love of plunder." The Indian Office had no choice, he argued; it felt obligated to turn the Indians over to the army, as it did on February 1, 1876.[66]

Smith's explanation, with all its falsehoods, hardly touched on the real issues surrounding Plains Indian policy. Westerners and army officers for years had been arguing that the agencies should be administered by the Department of War, not by the Department of the Interior. Congress had nearly made the change in 1875; Grant, however, seemingly remained steadfast—at least in public—in his support for the Peace Policy. By summer of the year after the Custer disaster even some reformers had doubts. The reform-minded E. L. Godkin of the *Nation* could only lament: "Our philanthropy and our hostility tend to about the same end, and this is the destruction of the Indian race."[67]

Yet not all the reformers flip-flopped on their long-held views. While they withheld their criticism of the president—who was supposedly one of them—they attacked the army viciously in the summer and fall of 1876. Wendell Phillips in a letter to the *Boston Evening Transcript* reprimanded newspapers for using the term "Custer Massacre": "What kind of war is it, where if we kill the enemy it is death; if he kills us, it is a massacre?" Then he turned to the newly forming international laws being published and debated in Europe, governing the actions of army troops and established army policy. "We have violated every rule of civilized war, massacring women and children with worse than savage brutality."[68] General Sherman tried to respond; but both he and Sheridan had been guilty of using terms like "extermination" many times in the past, and they both knew it. While President Grant finally dismissed Commissioner Smith, who increasingly took the brunt of criticism from reformers, he also gave General Sheridan authority to lock down all Indian reservations on the northern plains in order to bring the war to an end.[69]

The army quickly moved to consolidate its control over the northern plains reservations. Sheridan ordered all officers to arrest, dismount, and disarm any warriors coming in for annuities.[70] As Sheridan put it: "the subjugation of the hostile Indians is an absolute necessity."[71] To facilitate this, army officers took command at all agencies. When a disgruntled agent, John Burke, posed a question as to exactly who would try these Indians and what would be their "final disposition" if found guilty of something, he was jailed and eventually ordered to leave.[72] Sheridan believed that the "worst offenders" should be deported to Fort Snelling in Minnesota but soon abandoned this idea. As Indian parties came in that fall, hungry and in need of annuities, the army often held three or four as "hostages" under guard, guaranteeing the good behavior of their relatives.[73]

Late in the fall Colonel Nelson Miles, with fresh troops in Montana, caught up with Sitting Bull and the main nontreaty camp. At one point Sitting Bull left a note along the road. In an almost childlike manner, he said: "I want to know what you are doing traveling on this road." Miles was scaring the buffalo. Some days later the two men met briefly near the confluence of the Missouri and Yellowstone Rivers. Miles accused the chief of being "strongly against the White people." Sitting Bull retorted that whenever the army came into his country "they came to fight."[74] Miles unleashed his troops and forced some four hundred Indians to surrender in several days of running fights. In the usual fashion four chiefs were taken as hostages to ensure the proper behavior of the others.[75] In December Colonel Mackenzie, with troops fresh from the south, surprised the Cheyenne camp of nearly two hundred lodges on the Tongue River. Much as with the Comanches, he only killed two dozen Indians, but he burned the entire village, destroying all of its winter food supply.

What remained of the camp that Sitting Bull and the other chiefs had so effectively put together in June broke up completely in February 1877, when fifty-two lodges of Sans Arcs and Minneconjous surrendered. The Lakota soldiers' lodge, still numbering hundreds, drove the Minneconjous and Sans Arcs back into camp, but they regrouped and demanded to be allowed to leave. After the shooting of some horses failed to prevent the exodus, the main camp broke up entirely.[76] By spring only a few holdouts remained. Crazy Horse was one, but even he surrendered in May 1877. After being arrested some months later he tussled with soldiers and was bayoneted in the back.[77] Over the next few months Sitting Bull and his followers fled into Canada, refugees from their homeland. Most would eventually surrender. Sitting Bull was the last to give up in 1881. As he did so, he placed his rifle into his son's hands and turned to the attending officer, saying: "I wish it to be remembered that I was the last man of my tribe to surrender his rifle."[78] With this gesture the plains wars seemingly came to an end, a conflict almost entirely over land.

Meanwhile yet another Indian commission set out to divide up the very land that so many Lakota leaders had vowed to preserve. Congress passed legislation in August 1876, stating that it would refuse to fund the treaty of 1868—and its annuities—should Lakota leaders fail to surrender all lands south of the reservation border (the South Dakota line) and west of 103 degrees longitude, including the Black Hills and the Yellowstone Valley and its tributaries. The commission of seven men, headed by the former commissioner and so-called reformer George Manypenny, reached Red Cloud Agency in early September.[79]

At the council, commissioner and Episcopalian bishop Henry B. Whipple—a staunch supporter of the Peace Policy—opened the proceedings by asserting that the Great Father did not wish to "throw a blanket over your eyes." Whipple suggested that the president believed that the Lakotas had started the war and that he wanted all Lakota Indians to move south to Indian Territory. Finally, a number of Lakota speakers—who were not always identified—rose to challenge the commissioners. "If the white men had a country," one retorted, "and men of another race came to take it away by force . . . would you fight?" Another, with a obvious gift for humor, responded: "Since the Great Father promised that we should never be moved we have been moved five times. I think you had better put the Indians on wheels and you can run them about wherever you wish."[80]

While a small Lakota delegation in charge of commissioner Jared Daniels did visit Indian Territory, they returned in a sullen mood. After a number of the young Lakota soldiers who had just arrived heard the news, the situation became tense. The young Oglala *blotaunka* Sitting Bull (not to be confused with the Sitting Bull who headed to Canada) raced into the meetings, armed to the teeth, and denounced the suggestion. By mid-September it had become obvious that a deal could be struck for the Black Hills if the commissioners were to allow the Lakotas to live on reservations close to the Missouri River. The failure of the Indian Office and the army to hand out food also had a decided effect on the discussions. Hungry Indian chiefs finally stepped forward and signed the new agreement, diminishing the Great Sioux Reservation. But protests abounded. Fire Thunder, mocking Bishop Whipple, covered his eyes with a blanket and then touched the pen.[81]

The commission's work grew easier thereafter, as many Lakota leaders at Cheyenne River and Standing Rock had been imprisoned. In addition, Indian inspector William Vandever noted the heavy military presence and its impact: "The Indians are evidently somewhat alarmed at the large military force assembled . . . but there is no alternative left them." General

Sheridan in a private letter called the process "an ultimatum."[82] Many Indian leaders recognized their lack of choices: "The country upon which I am standing is the country upon which I was born," Little Wound from Standing Rock responded. To sell it would mean that "I should be a man without a country." And Wolf Necklace said: "I never want to leave this country; all my relatives are lying here in the ground, and when I fall to pieces, I am going to fall to pieces here."[83]

Some commissioners found their task distasteful. In their final report they lambasted the federal government and its policies. They started by listing the historical events that led to the war, criticizing especially the decision to send Custer into the hills in 1874. If the goal was to further American civilization, the plan brought about that end "by falsehoods and violence." The decision to offer a deadline of January 31, 1876, for the return of the Indians to their reservations was ludicrous, the commissioners felt. "It does not appear that anyone of the messengers sent out by the agents was able to return to his agency by the time which had been fixed." Finally, they addressed the sentiment of some Americans, perhaps even a few in Congress, who called for the "extermination" of the Indian. "We would remind such persons that there is only *One* [God Almighty] who can exterminate . . . the Indian is a savage, but he is also a man."[84]

Interestingly, these critics never sensed that Sheridan, Stanley, and Custer concocted a conspiracy to bring about the war over the Black Hills. Perhaps Custer's martyrdom influenced their critiques. President Grant certainly had political reasons for avoiding an Indian war. It seems clear that Sheridan's counsel—which very likely failed to give an honest assessment of conditions in the hills—led Grant to sanction such a conflict. Sheridan had promoted military action on the plains at every turn. It will never be known what credence Sheridan placed in the Stanley letter, although he certainly looked for excuses to create the scenario that Stanley envisioned. Sheridan—unlike Stanley—was simply too shrewd to leave heavy tracks.

The Peace Policy had failed miserably by 1876, both in the North and in the South. But even if it had succeeded, it also promoted ethnic cleansing. The policy clearly involved using inordinate amounts of pressure to force Native peoples to move to smaller confined reservations on lands that at times would not even support them, to change their ways, to abandon their cultural mores, and even to abandon their religion. Reformers watched and wrung their hands over the actions of the army, but most continued to accept the agrarian principle that permeated all policy toward Indians: Indians had no rights to hunting lands and must give them up and become farmers. The army's acceleration of these events hardly mattered in the long run: both the reformers and the army reverted to policies that were violations of international law and the rules of war as they were being defined in the nineteenth century when the conflict loomed. Wars of aggression to seize land were no longer condoned by the international community, a group of nations that the United States joined when it signed the first Geneva Convention of 1864.

Worse, in order to implement the more aggressive military policies that ultimately won out, the army reverted to illegally imprisoning leaders of the Lakota people without trial or benefit of habeas corpus. Some in government, including special agent Vandever, complained openly of the way Indian prisoners were treated. "Considering the fact which is undoubtedly true, that the war was forced on the Indians," he concluded in a special report to the commissioner of Indian affairs in fall 1876, "they should not be required to do more than lay down their arms." In an interesting comparison Vandever wrote: "Sitting Bull is entitled to as liberal treatment as we gave Jeff Davis [president of the Confederacy]. He is a better man than Davis and he had real grievances to complain of at the hands of government."[85] Vandever, a government functionary, saw the actions of the army as inflicting "unjust war" upon the Lakota people: attacking their villages, harming noncombatants, and imprisoning their young men and leaders. These were all violations of the statutes defined today as crimes against humanity and war crimes.

After Sitting Bull's surrender, he too was incarcerated—albeit loosely guarded—for four years. As more events unfolded, the policy of ethnic cleansing was being implemented not on the Great Plains but in the mountains to the west and in the southwestern desserts where Indians still roamed at will. They too would soon face the ever-invading white people and face their military prowess. The tug-of-war continued between reformers who preached patience and justice for the Indians (along with a few military officers who increasingly sympathized with them) and a few army officers who sided with Sheridan and Sherman and their younger protégés, who considered such policy "womenlie [sic]."

16

THE INDIANS' "LAST STAND" AGAINST ETHNIC CLEANSING

The miners' invasion of the West that began in 1849 led to the exploration of every mountain stream and valley. Miners looked for gold and found silver in quantity as well. Congress responded with a new mining act of 1872 allowing miners to take up land claims. Politicians then debated the degree to which silver should be minted into coins. While the rush into the Black Hills in the mid-1870s produced many headlines, other prospectors entered the mountains in Colorado, Idaho, and eastern Oregon, as well as the deserts and mountain country of Arizona and New Mexico. These were mostly Indian lands, some belonging to tribes that had recognized claims, and others to groups, such as the Chiricahua Apaches in the Southwest, that had never agreed to the Spanish grants that supposedly gave away many of their lands.

The mountain regions held smaller Native populations in comparison to the Great Plains, perhaps fewer than 25,000 people in all, inhabiting a vast region from Canada to Mexico. A few thousand Nez Perce Indians dominated west-central Idaho and the rugged mountain regions extending into eastern Oregon, bordered on the north by Spokane, Coeur d'Alene, and Flathead Indians, who had sparred with the army in 1857–58. The Nez Perces had received a huge reservation in 1855 under the Stevens treaty and stayed largely out of the fray when the Plateau Indians went to war. But miners and the government had forced a new agreement upon them just eight years later: the reserve was reduced by fully 80 percent, to just under 100,000 acres. Many Nez Perce people lived in more isolated regions, off the reservation, including those who would later be connected to their eloquent leader Chief Joseph. The government called them the "nontreaty" Indians, because they had not signed the 1863 treaty and continued to hunt, gather foods, and fish, as in the past.[1]

South of the Nez Perces in Colorado, the Utes held nearly 20 million acres of land under their 1868 treaty—an immense reserve that covered most of western Colorado but not the eastern watershed lands that other Plains tribes had supposedly ceded. Other Utes and Paiutes, to the north and west, had settled on much smaller reservations. But miners and ranchers, ever convinced of their entitlement to lands, were encroaching, forcing the Utes into the Brunot Agreement of 1873, in which they lost nearly a third of their homeland. Miners had made discoveries in the San Juan Mountains of southern Colorado, which the government convinced the Utes to give up.[2] In reality the agreements of 1868 and 1873 left the Utes with four reservations, but they were separated. The two largest held the followers of Chief Ouray in the upper Gunnison River valley, and other close relatives were confined to North Park in northern Colorado and eastern Utah, isolated locations.

The transition to smaller, more confined reservations seemed relatively easy for the Utes, who occupied a diverse environment conducive to herding, hunting, and gathering.[3] Even so, nearly a dozen of their bands still clung to the ceded regions. And as usual the federal government allowed the Indians to hunt on off-reservation lands and made little effort to survey and establish boundaries. Squatters, though small in number, became a common problem within both the Nez Perce and Ute Reservations, as prospectors and ranchers claimed mining rights and brought in herds. A few entrepreneurs also introduced liquor by the wagonload; Indian Office employees made little effort to enforce the Intercourse Acts, which forbade it.

Trouble with intruders also existed in the far South as they prospected and settled in Arizona and New Mexico establishing claims. After the Civil War Tucson became a center of activity. The rest of the non-Indian population of southern Arizona and New Mexico consisted of a few ranchers and sheepherders. In early 1871 General Pope was asked to assess the situation in these lands. "The depredations of the Apaches," he wrote, "have been continuous for twenty-five years past, but they are insignificant in extent and generally confined to plunder of a few sheep and mules and the occasional murder of a lonely sheep herder." The herders, Pope thought, had no sense, being "sent with their herds many miles into the Indian Country, wholly unprotected." The only reason more were not killed was "the fact that the Apaches are a squalid race, with little courage."[4] Pope opposed military action to protect herders and seemed convinced that most of the region was Indian Country, even though the government had not sanctioned such a claim.

While a few tribes in northern New Mexico and Arizona, such as the Jicarillas, Hopis, and Navajos, made peace with Americans and accepted reservations just after the Civil War, the southern groups congregated in small bands. They remained restless and committed to raiding, which defined their livelihood. To the east in New Mexico were Mimbres, Gila, and Warm Springs Chiricahua Apaches; west of them—mostly in southern Arizona and northern Mexico—were central and southern Chiricahua bands, which frequently migrated into Mexico.

Many Western Apaches coalesced around their most famous leader, Cochise, although splinter groups continued to come and go. Those within Cochise's rather extended kin group included the bands of Mangas Coloradas (his father-in-law), Loco, Nana, Victorio, and Geronimo, who was little known at the time. These people created a dual but chaotic existence, developing symbiotic relationships with some Pueblo and Mexican communities while raiding others for horses, sheep, and mules.[5] Whenever Apaches entered a Pueblo or Mexican village, the exchanges of goods occurred under tense circumstances—so many double crosses had occurred by 1860 that neither side trusted the other. While Apaches perhaps disliked Mexicans more than Americans, they also often raided Anglo ranches; such attacks could and did lead to the ransacking of houses or even murder and kidnapping.

Despite General Pope's seemingly cavalier attitude, two serious threats to Chiricahua Apache dominance emerged in the late 1860s. First, Sonoran officials sent troops into the field (the Mexican intervention of Maximilian I had finally ended), forcing Cochise and his followers to spend more time raiding in southern Arizona. Second, in late fall 1869 Captain Reuben Bernard received orders to subdue the Chiricahuas. After several engagements Bernard challenged Pope's desk-bound view of the Apaches, concluding that Cochise was "one of the most intelligent hostile Indians on this continent." Nevertheless, Bernard adopted a new strategy that generally worked; he recruited Apache scouts from unrelated western bands and surprised several camps, killing dozens of Cochise's allies.[6] Cochise soon recognized that no place was safe anymore for his southern people, at least while they remained in southern Arizona.

A major concession occurred in fall 1870 when Loco sued for peace and was granted a reservation in the Tularosa Valley of New Mexico for his people. But the momentum this brought to the region quickly changed when a Tucson mob unleashed a vicious attack, murdering 150 peaceful western Apaches near Camp Grant a year later.[7] The attack stunned Washington officials, many of whom were still committed to the Peace Policy, prompting President Grant to create by decree (Congress had stopped using the term "treaty" with Indians that very year) a massive Indian reservation in central Arizona and ordering a "peace commission" to depart for Arizona and move the Indians onto it.[8]

General Oliver Otis Howard ultimately took over negotiations. Howard struck a noble pose, having lost an arm during the Civil War and often carrying a Bible under the stump. The general sought out Cochise, finally making the rendezvous after eliciting the help of frontier scout Thomas Jeffords. Howard convinced the aging chief to select a reserve—the boundaries of which Howard drew on a map. The Howard agreement set aside land from Fort Apache just east of Tucson south to the border with Mexico, a vast domain some fifty miles square that Cochise agreed to police. He kept his word, preventing raiding and keeping the Tucson road into New Mexico open, working in close cooperation with his friend Jeffords.[9]

Just as the Apache troubles in the Southwest seemed manageable Cochise died, supposedly of stomach cancer. Lesser leaders soon made his Chiricahua reserve a base for raiding northward into Arizona and New Mexico.[10] To make matters worse, army officers such as Crook and Pope castigated the Howard agreement, displaying yet another example of the divergent views of senior officers. The criticism drew considerable support from citizens and led to the removal of agent Jeffords. Crook argued that all Apaches should be moved to the San Carlos Reservation or the southern portion of Grant's reservation in central Arizona. A new agent, John P. Clum, began the removal in 1877.[11]

Clum initially marched troops to the reservation in New Mexico, where they surprised Loco, Victorio, Nana, and other chiefs, including Geronimo, and forced them to remove to San Carlos in Arizona. Geronimo and sixteen others were chained to wagons for fear that they might protest. While Clum made advancements in agriculture at San Carlos, the earlier mistreatment of Victorio and Geronimo led to many late-night discussions. The two Apache leaders ultimately fled back to the mountains, taking along many of their relatives. They refused to give up the

Apaches' age-old claim to much of the American Southwest or their raiding lifestyle.[12]

As trouble simmered in the Southwest, violence erupted farther north. Christian missionaries had made a number of converts along the Snake River on the Nez Perce Reservation. Nevertheless, they found stiff resistance from Native prophets, who increasingly combined older traditional belief in visions and other practices with Christian rituals such as baptism and the sacraments. Some prophets insisted that their followers wear their hair long, as a symbol of a commitment to the old way of life. Other Nez Perce men turned to raising cattle and flirting with Christianity when it suited them. The cultural turmoil took yet another turn when a growing debate erupted over the rights of the nontreaty Nez Perces to stay off the reservation on lands mainly in Oregon that they had always claimed as a homeland.[13]

The reservation Indians under Chief Lawyer had relinquished the lands west of the reservation in the Wallowa River valley in the 1863 treaty, but they had little right to do so. Many Nez Perce bands remained in eastern Oregon when President Grant arbitrarily opened the land to settlement in 1876. General Howard, who had been reassigned to the region, recognized the potential for conflict as he traveled west to Fort Walla Walla in April to meet Ollicut, the brother of Chief Joseph. Howard explained that the army had clear orders: the Indians would have to move to the reservation. Howard even arrested Dreamer Leader, a traditional prophet who had openly defied him in council.

Howard knew much about the nontreaty Indians, consisting of Joseph's band, White Bird's band, and the Hush-hush-cute band. Most of these people saw Looking Glass as their natural leader, Joseph being less dynamic.[14] Howard seemed confident that he could persuade them all to settle on the reservation when he arrived at Fort Lapwai on the Nez Perce reservation in May, for what he hoped would be the final negotiations. Recognizing that White Bird's band had yet to arrive, Howard humored Joseph by explaining that his early arrival would allow him to pick out the best land available. But Ollicut, Joseph's brother, preferred instead to discuss grievances: "We have respect for the whites but they treat me as a dog . . . there should be one law for all." Howard rebuked him, saying that there was but one law of the Great Father in Washington. At that point the general got impatient, literally threatening Ollicut "with as much severity of manner as I could command."[15]

The next day the sparring got worse. Two older men, described as "Medicine Men," disputed the notion that the nontreaty Indians had surrendered any land. Another "dreamer," as Howard identified him, Too-schul-hul-sote, said much the same: "You white people get together and measure the earth and then divide it. . . . Part of the Indians gave up their land; I did not." Howard turned to both Looking Glass and White Bird in desperation, hoping that they would shut the old man up. Instead they agreed with him, encouraging Too-schul-hul-sote, who responded: "I never gave the Indians authority to give away my lands. . . . I am *not* going to the Reservation." Howard promptly had Too-schul-hul-sote arrested.[16]

While band leaders such as Joseph mulled over Howard's demands to remove to the reservation, trouble erupted in early June. When miner Larry Ott killed an Indian, the government did nothing to punish the crime. Other whites had beaten Indians and even set their dogs on them. As tension mounted over removal on June 14–16 a few young Nez Perce men went into the settlements and started killing their oppressors—eighteen in all. Panic struck the white settlements, as many fled. One drew an ominous conclusion: "We are in the midst of an Indian war."[17] As historian Elliott West has noted: "To whatever extent it was justified, the violence was a release of generations of building tensions, intense and ugly, and poisonous, less an outbreak than a lanced boil."[18] But the lanced boil soon brought in the army.

General Howard sent two companies of cavalry under Captain David Perry to restore order. Indian leaders seemed confused and disorganized; indeed the Nez Perce young men had obtained a considerable quantity of liquor and became terribly drunk. White Bird and Looking Glass struggled to maintain order and avoid conflict. Nevertheless, the foolish Captain Perry, much in the tradition of Fetterman, lit into the Indians. The encounter quickly turned to disaster, as the Nez Perces routed the captain's force, killing thirty-four and wounding many.[19] Several veterans of such skirmishes called it the "worst managed affair" ever.[20] The event greatly embarrassed Howard, who tried desperately to reorganize his troops and start after the Indians, who were retreating eastward toward Montana.

After the firefight several groups who had remained on the reservation joined Joseph and the others. Looking Glass even reentered the reservation, seeking recruits, but the reservation Nez Perces, many of whom were Christians, would have nothing to do with the war that was unfolding.[21] Nevertheless, a formidable force of Indians came together under White

Bird and Looking Glass and engaged Howard in "battle" over two days, July 11–12. During a lull Chief Joseph sent out a white flag, whereupon Howard called for "unconditional surrender," noting that Indians who committed murders would be "tried and punished." At this point eighteen Indians deserted, returning to the reservation only to face arrest. Howard promptly ordered a "military commission" to try them, but the judge advocate general, W. M. Duran, refused to sanction the court. Instead they were shipped to Fort Vancouver, held in chains, and later released.[22]

While Howard dallied, Colonel John Gibbon received orders to collect troops from Forts Shaw and Benton in Montana, as well as volunteers, and proceed west to Missoula, where the Indians had appeared in force by July 23.[23] They traded peacefully with Montanans, who had often dealt with these Indians in the past. This exchange left the Nez Perces with a false sense of security as they traveled south, up the Bitterroot Valley. But Gibbon, ordering grueling marches, caught up with the Indians on August 8 near Big Hole, Montana, a shallow depression with a small creek covered mostly on both sides with brush and willows. The troops cautiously approached the quiet camp in early morning. Gibbon ordered a full-fledged charge at dawn, catching the Indians in their tepees.[24]

The Battle of Big Hole came on suddenly and was fought at close quarter. Gibbon noted in his initial report that "the surprise was complete & many were killed in the tepees or running out." Troopers did little to differentiate women and children from adult men. As Gibbon's men fought their way into the camp, however, the Nez Perces rallied, taking up positions above the camp in brush. They poured deadly fire down upon the troops, wounding Gibbon and forcing what amounted to a disordered retreat. Gibbon later claimed that eighty-nine Indians were dead; while he failed to differentiate between men and noncombatants, one account suggests that nearly two-thirds were women and children. It had been a slaughter.[25] Despite the hurried exit, Gibbon had severely damaged the Nez Perces—and created serious questions regarding the leadership of White Bird and Looking Glass, who now sought ways to avoid combat at any cost. Worse, they were on the run with dozens of wounded, many of them women and children.

Back east, criticism built over Howard's inept handling of the crisis. General Sheridan responded by mobilizing more troops. Infantry regiments from as far away as New York and Alaska were ordered to stand ready, and General Sherman sought more money for what had now become a very brutal and costly war. The frustration led to yet another Sherman outburst. He demanded in a letter to General Sheridan that the Indians be captured "without terms . . . their leaders executed preferably by sentence of a civil court."[26] Sherman at least had given up on the use of "military" justice.

In the weeks that followed the remaining four hundred Nez Perces disappeared into Yellowstone National Park and then skirted east of the Absaroka Mountains, completely avoiding yet another army sent to capture them, under Colonel Samuel Sturgis. Reaching the high plains of the Judith Basin, they then traveled north into the Bear's Paw Mountains, just fifty miles from their final destination—Sitting Bull's camp in Canada. It had been a masterful retreat, avoiding large contingents of military troops and their Indian scouts.[27] But once they reached the Bear's Paw Mountains, with many wounded as well as exhausted horses and mules, Nez Perce leaders finally allowed a rest—this was a second fatal mistake.

To the east General Nelson Miles, who had chased Sitting Bull into Canada, mounted his own campaign to capture the Indians. Miles, who had over five hundred men, mountain howitzers, and fresh horses, surprised the resting Indians on September 30, running off some seven hundred horses. Looking Glass had picked an excellent campsite to rest his people before the final push into Canada, in a deep ravine. But after Miles opened up with artillery and sent in his infantry, both Looking Glass and Too-shul-hul-sote were killed in the fight that followed, along with fifteen others.[28] Miles, who lost twenty-two men dead to the stubborn Nez Perces, soon saw the futility of frontal attack and decided upon negotiations.

While speaking with Joseph under a flag of truce, Miles first violated the flag by seizing the chief and then turned him loose when it became obvious that the Indians held one of his officers as a hostage. On October 5, after several days of talks, Joseph came out and laid down his arms. The war was over. As he spoke with Lieutenant Charles Wood, Howard's aide-de-camp and an interpreter, it became obvious that he had wanted to avoid conflict almost from the start. Joseph said simply, "I am tired of fighting," and then he went on to make a famous speech.[29]

Historian Elliott West has argued that Joseph's address compares well with other orations of the age, including President Abraham Lincoln's Gettysburg Address. But West strongly suggests that Lieutenant Wood played a part in writing it, putting words into Joseph's mouth. Wood later claimed that his notes regarding the speech had gone missing, leaving only a somewhat literary version in the *Bismarck Tri-Weekly Tribune,* published on October 26, 1877. West's suspicions multiplied after realizing that Wood went on to have a literary career, writing novels and poetry, which made him far more suited for the brilliant oratory than an Indian leader. Even more telling, according to West, Joseph never spoke English; the speech was translated by two Nez Perce men who knew him well and gave the rendition of it to Lieutenant Wood.[30]

General Howard's final report in the army records of the National Archives, however, gives a far different rendition. Howard reported that Lieutenant Wood took the statement down "verbatim" from Joseph; given that Howard was there, his statement merits serious consideration. Howard also notes that he recorded the speech in his report from Wood's "Jottings" or notes.[31] When Howard's version is compared to the version published in the Bismarck newspaper, the differences not in words but in punctuation are striking, leading to the obvious conclusion that Howard did take the version from Wood's notes rather than from the newspaper's account (it may have been the newspaper editors who made changes). In addition, most sentences are only five to seven words: short, choppy, language that reflected the efforts of the interpreters—so different from the literary version found in the newspaper. The vast majority of the speech is classic Indian oratory. To some degree the tendency of historians like West to question the speech's validity comes from the very last sentence, which is admittedly poetic. Howard's version, or the original version found in his *Supplementary Report,* is worth repeating:

> Tell General Howard I know his heart. What he told me before, I have it in my heart. I am tired of fighting. Our chiefs are killed. Looking Glass is dead. Too-schul-hul-sote is dead. The old men are all dead. It is the young men who say yes or no. He who led on the young men is dead. It is cold and we have no blankets. The little children are freezing to death. My people—some of them—have run away to the hills and have no blankets; no food. No one knows where they are—perhaps freezing to death. I want to have time to look for my children and see how many of them I can find. May be I shall find them among the dead. Hear me, my chiefs, I am tired. My heart is sick and sad. From where the sun now stands I will fight no more forever.[32]

General Howard had assured Joseph that he and his people would be allowed to return to Idaho after they surrendered. Negotiations had gone on for several days: the chief and his followers refused to lay down their arms until Howard made that exact assurance. Howard even issued an order that Miles treat the Indians as "prisoners of War" and then move them west in the spring. He concluded that all the "bad" Indians, who had killed civilians in Idaho, had themselves been killed during the fighting, thus making trials unnecessary. Those who remained camped in the ravine were not the instigators of the war.[33]

Howard's belief that he possessed such authority likely came from the military's acceptance—at least initially—of his agreement with Cochise. Generals Sheridan and Sherman quickly reminded Howard, however, that they commanded the army and would make final decisions regarding the prisoners of war. Sheridan noted that it would be impossible to march them back through the mountain passes in winter. Sherman, with the acquiesce of the commissioner of Indian affairs, ordered the captives—some 87 men, 184 women, and 147 children—first to Fort Lincoln then to Fort Leavenworth, where they spent the winter in a camp similar to the camp of the Dakota Sioux in 1862–63 at Fort Snelling. Even General Pope, who had control over the Sioux at Fort Snelling fourteen years before, believed Leavenworth to be a horrible place for a prison camp, infested with mosquitos. Much worse, Nez Perce women faced repeated sexual assaults from soldiers. The abuse became so blatant that a report regarding the crimes was even presented to Congress.[34]

Congress finally deported the Nez Perce captives to the Quapaw Reservation in northeast Oklahoma, a land that had become a dumping ground for Indians. Many Modocs still remained there, and some Poncas were on the way, being removed from Nebraska. The Nez Perces would endure eight long years in what would later become the largest mining wasteland in America, the so-called Tar Creek Superfund Site. Poor rations, contaminated water from lead and zinc outcroppings, and even the heat contributed to a growing death rate.[35] Of those Indians who made the trip south, 153 had died by 1880; deaths totaled 282 three years later. While roughly 200 defeated and mostly wounded Indians avoided the fate of Joseph, reaching Sitting Bull's camp, they too suffered from near-starvation while in Canada. Joseph and the captives were finally repatriated to eastern Washington in 1885, where the chief died of old age, never again living in his homeland that the federal government had taken from him.[36]

Even though the army suffered substantial embarrassment in its failure to capture the Nez Perces, Generals Sherman and Sheridan had made considerable strides in wresting control of Indian affairs from the Interior Department. It became commonplace by the mid- to late 1870s for the commissioner of Indian affairs to abdicate authority. Whenever violence erupted on or near a reservation, the commissioner handed over responsibility to the army. Part of the reason for the change involved the army's new policy of simply confining Indian "troublemakers" to military prisons either at Fort Leavenworth or in Florida, something that the Indian Office did not oppose and often supported. And even Sherman, who blustered at times, gave up advocating immediate execution of Indian leaders, a solution that was repugnant to Indian reformers. Imprisonment and deportation met the criteria for moral restraint, and this form of ethnic cleansing became acceptable Indian policy.

That policy would next be employed with the Utes in Colorado, who had been quite peaceful until the Brunot Agreement allowed miners into the San Juan Mountains in 1873. Chief Ouray of Los Pinos (the Uncompahgre Valley Agency) had initially refused to consider another land sale but acquiesced after the government bumped the price up to half a million dollars.[37] This only led to more miners and more trouble, especially in North Park or at the White River Agency, some one hundred miles north of Ouray's Agency. Here the Utes under their leader Johnson spent considerable time off the reservation, sometimes simply visiting with relatives who lived on the Uintah Reservation in Utah. They mostly rejected Ouray's progressivism, especially his embracing of cattle herding and farming. Ouray had moved into a house and seemed ready to accept much that American civilization had to offer.[38]

Ouray's people remained calm even after news of trouble at the northern agency on White River arrived. Sixty-five-year-old Nathan Meeker became the agent in 1878. A religious zealot and unbending man, Meeker had trained at the church-affiliated Oberlin College. He began using annuities—much as agent Brown had done in Minnesota—to induce the northern Utes to farm. Unfortunately, most of the land around the agency had been set aside for grazing, especially for Ute horses used in gambling competitions that attracted Indians from the other reservations.[39]

Other problems complicated Meeker's efforts. By early summer 1879 drought devastated much of Colorado, with forest fires destroying grassland and timber stands and even burning out some settlers. Coloradans blamed the Utes for the fires, which seemed to foreordain trouble. This prompted agent Meeker to send alarming letters east, some addressed to

Major Thomas L. Thornburgh at Fort Fred Steele, situated just north of the Colorado border in Wyoming, and others to the new commissioner of Indian affairs, E. A. Hayt. The agent claimed that the Utes associated with "ruffians, renegades, and cattle thieves" and that they had to be prevented from leaving the reservation. On September 13 Meeker reported that Johnson had physically attacked him. "Life of self, family and employees, not safe," Meeker pleaded in a hurried report. Major Thornburgh mostly discounted the reports, having met Meeker in the past and judged him to be a man who was prone to exaggeration. Evidence later surfaced that the agent had ordered his farmers to break land in the very pasture where Johnson grazed his racehorses, certainly a provocative measure.[40]

As the Ute problem gained the attention of the army, General Pope, who then headed the Department of New Mexico, noted that it might be good policy to move all the Utes in Colorado into either New Mexico or Utah. Mining, logging, and ranching had attracted settlers in numbers, and Colorado was also on the verge of a lead and copper boom. Sheridan, who had sparred with Pope in the past, quickly sided with him. As had been happening frequently, Sheridan asked for and received permission from the commissioner of Indian affairs to send troops to assist Meeker. Major Thornburgh received the order to enter the agency, departing Fort Fred Steele with four companies of troops, almost 200 men, on September 21.[41]

Thornburgh likely had little idea of the firestorm that lay ahead. Johnson had married the sister of Ouray and possessed a reasonably good understanding of American ways. Other Ute leaders such as Douglas, Colorow, and Chief Jack were nearly as savvy. These men, often dressed in white man's clothes, spent time in Denver, where they collected the latest news. There they learned of the circumstances surrounding the deportation of the Nez Perces, as well as the army's handling of Kiowas and Comanches. Oral history accounts some years later suggest that White River Ute leaders concluded that Thornburgh's mission included removing the Utes to Utah. Not surprisingly, Ute leaders quickly confronted agent Meeker, telling him that trouble would result if a large military force showed up at the agency.[42]

Meeker quickly dispatched a messenger to Thornburgh on September 25, recommending that he keep his troops in camp well away from the agency and come with a small detail of four or five men. Thornburgh either misunderstood the message or, more likely, had little faith in

Meeker's advice, because he had pleaded for help on so many occasions. Thornburgh countered with a letter of his own, sent to Meeker on September 28. "Under my orders," the major concluded, it is required that "I march this command to the Agency. I am not at liberty to leave it at a point where it would not be available in case of trouble." It was a fateful decision, given the Utes' state of mind. Meeker barricaded himself and family in his house and waited for Thornburgh's cavalry to arrive.[43]

Several hundred mounted Utes attacked Thornburgh's troops at Mill Creek well before they reached the agency. The major, a cool West Point–trained officer, ordered an immediate retreat to a wagon train, some two miles back. Just as his men reached it, Thornburgh fell dead from a bullet. Nearly a dozen other cavalrymen had been killed. Once at the train the men quickly turned over wagons and shot wounded horses to use as breastworks. For three days they withstood a determined Ute assault, taking nearly sixty casualties from the Indians' accurate rifle fire. Finally, on October 5, Colonel Wesley Merritt fought his way into the wagon enclosure. Yet even when Merritt met Ute leaders under a flag of truce, they declared a willingness to "fight to the death" to stop him from taking the agency.[44]

Just as Merritt spoke with several Ute leaders, a curious letter arrived from the southern Ute agencies. Ouray and other chiefs demanded that the White River Utes retreat and kill no more whites. And the Utes did so. They quickly moved south into the Gunnison River valley and awaited events. Meanwhile Merritt moved his command into the agency, where an awful scene awaited him: Meeker and six other male employees all had been killed, some burned to death in buildings.[45] General Sheridan reacted to the events predictably, writing Sherman that "no stone" should be left unturned in the "punishment" of these brutal Indians.[46] Sherman soon began amassing troops, several thousand in all.

Events then took another curious turn. Rather than sanction the anticipated war on the Utes—inflicting army "punishment" as Sheridan called it—the new secretary of the interior, Carl Schurz, ordered Sherman to hold Merritt's force at White River Agency. Schurz, reasserting the Interior Department's authority, issued similar directives to Colonels Edward Hatch and Ranald Mackenzie, who had large armies along the New Mexican border (2,500 soldiers in all, when Merritt's command is included). Schurz, unlike Zachariah Chandler, whom he replaced, sought to reform Indian affairs, not turn them over to the army. He also heeded the advice of agent W. M. Stanley, who remained at Los Pinos Agency. Stanley had called for the establishment of a commission; unlike the situation in previous conflicts, President Rutherford B. Hayes sided with Schurz.[47]

For the commission Schurz selected former Civil War general Charles Adams to journey west and join Colonel Hatch and agent Stanley in the investigation. Adams reached Los Pinos Agency in late October and, with Ouray's assistance, convinced the leaders of the White River Utes to hand over female hostages taken at the agency.[48] But when Adams approached Ouray and asked that the men responsible for killing Meeker and his staff also be surrendered, Ouray objected and demanded a hearing in Washington in front of Secretary Schurz, whom he had met in the past and trusted. Ouray wanted to give the Ute side of the story, which he outlined in a speech to Adams: "He says no white man had been killed, nor had Indians malicious intentions, until after the approach of the military upon their country, that before the Thornburgh engagement one of his nephews and another peaceable Indian were killed by soldiers and that if the military are withdrawn, there will be no more bloodshed."[49]

In January 1880 hearings opened, initially controlled by the secretary but eventually taken over by Congress. Ouray had the opportunity to make his case, which solved little. The former female captives, when first questioned at Los Pinos Agency, stated that they had been well treated. But they completely changed their stories later, stating that they had all been raped. The allegations, whether true or not, created a firestorm in the nation when published on newspaper front pages. The news brought demands for the immediate expulsion of the Utes from Colorado, despite Ouray's strong protestations that the women were lying (there is some suggestion that editors offering book contracts for the women's stories played a role in their revised testimony).[50]

Ouray and half a dozen other Ute delegates, worn down and reeling under accusations of rape, signed an agreement in which they ceded 80 percent of their remaining reservation land in Colorado to the United States.[51] Just how Congress got the signatures on this compact was irrelevant, because three-fourths of the tribe had to ratify it in Colorado. Unfortunately, at a time when diplomacy and leadership were most needed, Ouray passed away. But just before he died he encouraged his people to sign the compact. George Manypenny was once again called upon to implement the agreement through bribery and the usual threats (commissioner Otto Mears of Colorado actually paid Indians two dollars in silver for their signatures) and ultimately obtained the necessary names.[52]

In late summer 1880 Sherman ordered Hatch to prepare to remove the Utes. The colonel first constructed a army post in the Uncompahgre Valley then determined where the Utes lived and how many of them had to be removed, much as Wool had done with the Cherokees. This took nearly a year. Sherman gave the final order to gather the Indians in late August 1881.[53] Threatening to use force if necessary, Colonel Mackenzie collected all the Utes, some fifteen hundred Uncompahgres (the vast majority of whom had never even participated in the conflict), and several hundred Indians from White River. With bayonets they forced the reluctant caravan west, crossing the Colorado and Green Rivers into Utah and reaching the Uintah Reservation on September 13.[54]

After cleansing the Utes from Colorado, the army finally turned its attention to the Southwest and the Apaches. Both Geronimo's and Victorio's bands, while small in number, had begun to raid all across the border region, dipping down into Mexico and then moving north of the boundary back into the United States. Throughout 1879 and 1880 reports of ambushes and stock thievery skyrocketed. Troops from Fort Huachuca, aided by White Mountain Apache scouts, sent out patrol after patrol, without much success. But the fortunes of raiding suddenly changed in 1880 when a strong Mexican force found Victorio's camp and killed him and most of his followers. Being left alone, Geronimo agreed to return to San Carlos, where he stayed for over a year trying to adjust to reservation life.[55]

Life on the San Carlos Reservation at first seemed acceptable to Geronimo and his close compatriot, Juh. But various plots surfaced that created suspicions. One involved General Sherman: upon receiving exaggerated reports of conflict along the border, he ordered a large army force to the reservation—these troops had the same impact on the Apaches that they had on the Utes. While Juh was told that it meant nothing, other Apaches told him that the army intended to take both him and Geronimo captive, put them in irons, and deport them. A frenzied council then occurred one night, in which the rumors seemingly were confirmed. On September 30, 1881, yet another "breakout" occurred: nearly four hundred Chiricahua Apaches fled, including Juh and Geronimo. The next year Geronimo secretly returned to the reservation and quietly convinced several hundred more Chiricahuas to flee. By 1883 most of the Chiricahua Indians were in the southern mountains of Arizona and New Mexico or in Mexico and had returned to their old livelihood of raiding. While this new "Apache war" had resulted in at least a hundred Americans being killed, the losses of Geronimo's people were nearly the same.[56]

General Sherman assigned General Crook the job of restoring peace to Arizona and New Mexico. Crook approached the job diplomatically, obtaining permission to enter Mexico to speak with the Indians. But when Crook crossed the border, invading the very sanctuary of the Chiricahua people, he ordered 143 Apache scouts, under the command of Captain Emmet Crawford and Lieutenant Charles Gatewood, to find the Apaches. They overran several camps, killed a dozen or so men, and captured several women and children.[57] This had never happened before: the attacks brought overtures of peace and the eventual return of several hundred Indians to San Carlos, including Geronimo, who surrendered again in 1884.[58]

But late-night discussions and the increasing attempts of agents and army troops to stop the "Tiswin" or mescal parties that often led to violence only brought more suspicion and talk of deportation. Ultimately Geronimo bolted again: his last breakout occurred in May 1885. By this time the army had a routine to follow. They adopted Crook's strategy by hiring large numbers of Apache scouts and sending them out under the direction of army officers, such as Lieutenant Gatewood, Captain Crawford, and a newcomer, Lieutenant Britton Davis. Over 200 Chiricahuas had stayed behind, so 57 of the 76 Chiricahua men and boys on the reservation signed up as scouts. Another 100 or so scouts came from Western Apache groups who had traditionally worked for the army. As the scouts paraded in front of General Crook at San Carlos, he assured them that they would be able to live in peace on their lands when they finally brought in Geronimo. Over the next year Gatewood tracked Geronimo and a handful of his relatives with Chiricahua and White Mountain Apache scouts.[59]

Crook may have spoken the truth, but there was more to his story. He had been fighting with General Miles over strategy. Miles had little respect for Indians, frequently abandoning the rules of war—especially flags of truce—in dealing with them. He could not understand why Crook used scouts rather than regular troops to track Apaches. Crook's peaceful attempts to subdue these Indians in 1883 and 1884 also fell under attack after Geronimo fled a year later. Given the criticism, Crook and General Sherman corresponded frequently about what to do with the Apaches.

They both agreed that a military commission would likely be rejected by the judge advocate general or the evidence would simply be too faulty to stand up in court. Civilian trials for a few of the leaders might be feasible, however. Ultimately, as General Sheridan became involved in the debate, he argued for shipping any surrendered Indians off to either Fort Leavenworth or Florida. They all agreed that President Grover Cleveland would have the final word, a curious conclusion to what should have been a legal issue.[60]

While Gatewood and the other scout leaders knew nothing of these discussions, Geronimo entered New Mexico on a raiding venture. He had very few active fighters with him: a census count revealed that only 144 Apaches had fled San Carlos, including women and children. One of those fighters, however, was Ulzana, whose men killed 38 Americans and drove off 250 head of stock in just a few months. Ulzana's raid embarrassed the army generals no end. Meanwhile Gatewood's scouts hounded Geronimo. The harassment ultimately convinced him to meet once again with General Crook. The historic meeting was held on March 26, 1886. After Crook assured the Apache leader that he would be held in the East for a mere two years or less and then allowed to return to his homeland, Geronimo, Nana, and several others formally surrendered, only to disappear that same night.[61]

An exasperated Crook asked to be relieved of command, prompting Sheridan to bring in General Miles. Meanwhile President Cleveland acquiesced to Sherman's demands to deport all Chiricahua Indians at San Carlos to Florida—many of the women and children in this group were kin of Geronimo, Nana, and Ulzana. Hearing of the order and fearful that they would not see their families again, Geronimo and two dozen others surrendered on August 18, 1886, and were disarmed and imprisoned.[62] To what degree the army used deceit to convince Geronimo to surrender is still debated. Certainly offers in the past had included a light sentence. Such a concession no longer existed after Crook's departure, and Crook, who at times displayed an unusual level of humanity toward Indians, certainly knew it. But whether Geronimo knew it is a serious question.[63]

While the Chiricahua scouts had played a major role in finally obtaining Geronimo's capture, in a surprise move the army also disarmed and incarcerated them in a horse barn. On September 8 Geronimo and a handful of followers departed Bowie Station by train, bound for Florida. Farther north, on the same day, 383 other Chiricahuas, including the loyal scouts, left Holbrook for the same destination. Most would remain in confinement, first at Fort Marion and later at Mobile, Alabama, for nearly two decades.[64]

The Apache odyssey in the American West, much like that of the Nez Perces and the Utes, was characterized by a common defense of homeland. With the exception of the Nez Perce flight into Montana, virtually all the conflict with Anglos or the American army occurred on lands that these Indians had just claims to and often legitimate titles to even according to American law. The conflict with the Utes occurred when their homeland was threatened, and much of the trouble with the Apaches came after the Chiricahuas under Victorio and Loco were removed from their lands in New Mexico.[65]

The American government committed international crimes against all the mountain people—the Nez Perces, the Utes, and the Apaches. Individual Indians did commit crimes in Idaho, Utah, and New Mexico and Arizona, and the perpetrators of those crimes should have faced trial in civil courts. But the government, fearing its inability to convict anyone, instead deported and removed thousands of Indians, many of whom were completely innocent of any crimes, including the army's Apache scouts and Ouray's band of Utes. In both the Nez Perce and Apache cases army officers either made promises that they could not keep or fabricated scenarios in order to bring about surrender.

At the hands of the army in the years following the Civil War nearly four thousand Indians were deported to lands other than their homelands, such as the Missouri River area, Indian Territory, Alabama, and Florida, or sent to prisons such as those at Davenport, Iowa, and Fort Leavenworth. Most never faced a jury or military commission. Once deported or imprisoned, many died as a result of climate change and disease—a death rate of 20 percent may be too conservative. In the case of the Apaches another violation of the surrender agreement came when the men shipped to Fort Pickens found themselves separated from their families, who were sent to Fort Marion. And how can it possibly be justifiable to force women and children to experience the same punishment as their men, putting them in a situation where many—especially the very young—would die?

Within a year of the deportation of the Apaches the Indian Rights Association investigated the living conditions of these Indians and filed a scathing assessment. Some of the Chiricahua Apaches ultimately would be allowed to return to the West in 1894, settling at Fort Sill in Oklahoma.

Others reached the Mescalero Reservation in New Mexico a few years later. Both Ulzana and Geronimo died at Fort Sill after the turn of the century, a long way from the places of their births in the Southwest.[66]

While the deportation of peoples from the plains and mountains admittedly pales in comparison to the numbers of Indians removed from the American South, it was still significant given their smaller populations. Whether discussing the removal of the Chiricahuas or the Cherokees, it must always be remembered that these acts in every way constitute crimes against humanity or ethnic cleansing. And such international violations occurred within a nation that prided itself on its "democratic" principles.

Of course we must always be aware that democracy and the oppression of ethnic groups within a democratic nation are two very different issues. Nations often launch nationalistic crusades—even democratic ones—in order to "cleanse" themselves of unwanted people—to make them seemingly more united, more secure, more ethnically pure. But within such a mentality lies a crime waiting to be implemented, in the belief that such unwanted people have no right to the homes and lands that they historically have held. This is a lesson of history that the world must come to understand, for no justification can promote forced removal—ethnic cleansing.

EPILOGUE

Allotment and the Final Ethnic Cleansing of America

At an idyllic spot in upstate New York called Lake Mohonk, reformers regrouped after the failures of the Peace Policy and the ascendancy of the army. These men set out to retake control of the Indian business. In 1883 the group formed the "Friends of the Indian," an organization that quickly attracted some of the most powerful politicians and public officials in America, including former president Rutherford B. Hayes, Senator Charles Dawes of Massachusetts, and Merrill E. Gates, president of Rutgers University. They joined a host of reformers who had further access to Congress, including Lyman Abbott, Herbert Welsh, William Strong, and the wealthy Quaker owner of the Lake Mohonk estate, Albert A. Smiley.[1] Holding annual meetings and working closely together, these men soon offered solutions to what they saw as the "Indian problem" in America.

Unlike those who had approached Indians demanding treaties that led to dispossession, these men called upon the government to provide Indians with schools, farm equipment, and the guidance necessary for American citizenship. Perhaps the most persistent, and certainly the most controversial, part of their plans involved what is generally called "detribalization." Many Indian nations, particularly those on the Pacific Slope, in the Rocky Mountains, and on the Great Plains, held their reserves "in common." This arrangement reinforced tribalism, which the reformers believed must be destroyed in order for individual citizenship to benefit Indians. The reformers proposed breaking up the common reservations into 160-acre farm plots: every Indian family would be given a farm. Once participating in the free market, they believed, Indians would then naturally be absorbed into the fabric of American democratic life. The process is called assimilation.

Allotment, or the act of dividing up reservations, had often been included in treaty negotiations in the early nineteenth century. Usually land plots were given to important Indian families or mixed-bloods, who in turn sold them for profit. The allotment process fit well into the agrarian philosophy that dominated nineteenth-century American Indian policy. But early in the century it became more a tool to acquire Indian signatures on treaties than a real policy designed to assimilate Indians. Most of the Indians who received plots "in fee simple" ended up selling them to Anglos and moving west with other tribal members. Only a few groups remained who still had their farms, most living in New York, North Carolina, Mississippi, and Wisconsin.

A major change in policy did occur for some Indians but not all in the 1850s, when the new commissioner of Indian affairs, George Manypenny, took office. In 1854 and 1855 Manypenny undertook the resettlement of roughly two dozen Native bands and tribes that had been driven into Iowa and Kansas or north into upper Michigan, Wisconsin, and Minnesota. While virtually all of these negotiations resulted in the diminishment of previously granted reservations, they offered a new, "experimental" approach to dealing with Indian assimilation. Manypenny included clauses that called for the "allotment" of reservations into 80- to 160-acre plots. The land was to be distributed to all families of the band or tribe, not just to a few leaders.[2] Excess land would then be sold to settlers, resulting in the eventual closure of the reservation. While most of these bands were small, and some even asked for allotments, Manypenny's treaties never affected the large reservations on the plains or those in the far West.

Manypenny's allotment clauses took a variety of different forms. One of the earliest, negotiated in March 1854 with the Oto and Missouri Indians, called for lands to be "surveyed off into lots, and assigned to such Indians . . . as are willing to avail the privilege" of land ownership. Still, the clause concluded that the president had authority to issue "patents" or titles, leaving the issue of whether the individual Indians could then sell the land or not up to the future state government that would write a constitution supposedly dealing with this issue. Manypenny's treaties became less flexible later that year, when his agreement with the Omahas stated that the land would be "surveyed into lots" and the president would "issue a patent," thus removing the process from state control, which might take years. The

agreement with the Kickapoo Indians of May 18, 1854, put all the authority for allotment into the hands of the executive branch of government,
and the patents in fee simple would then be issued by Congress.[3]

Most of these treaties proved a disaster for the Indians involved. When
the patents were issued in fee simple, the Indians sold the land and were
soon landless. Many then migrated to Indian Territory, where the government once again tried to help them with land. Those Indians who stayed
within the confines of their reserves fared little better. The Iowa Tribe,
after receiving nearly 12,000 acres for a reservation in Kansas, had a tribally owned domain of just 714 acres by the 1930s, with another 643 acres
still in the hands of the original allottees. A similar story held for the Sac
and Fox Tribe of Kansas, whose original reserve was 32,000 acres. Eighty
years later they owned just over 3,000 acres. The Fond du Lac Chippewas
received 100,000 acres in 1855, but non-Indians had possession of over
78,000 acres soon thereafter.[4] In general Manypenny's early allotment of
lands through fee-simple titles resulted in Anglo purchasing of anywhere
from 70 to 90 percent of the former reservation land well before 1880,
often leaving the Indians destitute or on lands considered marginal.

An 1875 investigation of the allotment process applied at the Saginaw
Chippewas' Isabella Reservation of central Michigan offers several explanations of how so much land could be lost so quickly through allotment. The tribe had signed a treaty with Manypenny at Detroit twenty
years earlier, creating a reservation of six townships. But a revision of the
original agreement, signed in 1864, allowed the Indian agent to determine
just who was considered to be a "competent" Indian and who was "not-
so-competent." So-called competent Indians received titles in fee simple,
while those not-so-competent had "restrictions" placed upon the land
title, which made it impossible to sell the land unless the secretary of the
interior's office agreed to the sale.[5]

Most allotments within the Isabella Reservation occurred between
1871 and 1875. Well over a 1,000 titles were handed out to Indians, over
90 percent of whom were declared competent by agent George Betts,
even though the vast majority could not read or write, had no idea what a
"contract" looked like, and often signed away their land on the same day
they received the title. Contracts that have survived indicate that 160–acre
plots often sold to speculators for as little as five dollars.[6] Indians often had
no idea that they had even received land. Agent Betts, who worked with
the speculators, and his interpreter both received fifteen dollars each for

every sale to speculators that they helped engineer. The "timber ring" in Mount Pleasant, Michigan, then sold the land a second time to large timber companies.[7] In this way the Saginaw Chippewas lost nearly 100,000 acres of prime timber land in just four years. Such "timber rings" became common in Wisconsin and Minnesota as well as in Michigan.

While this "legal" dispossession occurred in the 1870s, George Manypenny reassessed the state of affairs regarding Indian policy in the United States. His twenty or so treaties dealt with only a small portion of Indian lands, sometimes reservations as small as 10,000 acres. The vast majority of land held by Indians—literally hundreds of millions of acres—existed on the Great Plains, in the Rocky Mountains and Southwest, and on the Pacific Slope. Manypenny realized this and hoped to influence future Indian policy by publishing *Our Indian Wards* (1880). While this long book justified the policy of "assimilation" that resulted in the diminishment of reservations, it also pointed to the excesses of the army in subduing Indians in the West, arguing vehemently that reservations should never be turned over to military officers.

Surprisingly, Manypenny commented only marginally regarding the treaties that he negotiated—and the land loss that occurred. He did admit to one fatal flaw: they gave titles in fee simple to Indians who, because of the legal ramifications and avarice of non-Indians, were not ready for them. "The title to the land [individual allotments] should remain in the tribe," Manypenny concluded, "since the Indians are generally not prepared for fee-simple titles." Because he worked as an "Indian Commissioner" at various times in the 1870s, helping to negotiate the Lakota surrender of the Black Hills in 1876, for example, it seems likely that he had considerable knowledge of the rings that were operating in many states. Nevertheless, Manypenny stayed the course. He continued to advocate that Indian reservations should be reduced and that land be given out in allotments rather than held in common. Manypenny's book was read by many reformers who took an interest in Indian affairs.[8]

Reformers pushed for new legislation to further the Indians' evolution toward citizenship within a year or two of the publication of Manypenny's memoir. During their first Lake Mohonk meeting in 1883 the reformers roughed out basic premises: allotment would lead to self-sufficiency for Indians, individual land ownership, and citizenship. The reformers soon attracted successful authors and literary figures, including Helen Hunt Jackson, whose sentimental book *A Century of Dishonor* had been published to immediate acclaim in the same year as Manypenny's memoir. The reformers gained support from the National Indian Defense Association (created by Alfred Meacham) and from missionary societies, including former missionary Stephen Return Riggs, in whose Washington, D.C., house the men writing the legislation worked. Senator Dawes unveiled the new legislation, entitled the General Allotment Act, in 1887.[9] It quickly passed Congress that year and became law.

The law stressed that the federal government would maintain its "trust responsibility" as long as necessary for individual Indians to become citizens. Nevertheless, while the allotments would be held as "restrictive titles" for twenty-five years, the "trust responsibility" of the federal government would end when these were converted to fee-simple titles. More ominously, it was widely believed that western reservations contained more land than needed to satisfy individual Indian families, so surplus land would be sold to white settlers. Thus the large reservations of the West would eventually cease to exist. When allottees adopted "habits of civilization" and lived on their land apart from Indian communities, they would supposedly be granted citizenship.[10]

The Dawes Allotment Act did not affect every reservation in America. Some tribes, such as the Red Lake Chippewas and the Arizona Navajos, claimed successfully that their lands simply would not support 160-acre farms and were incapable of agricultural development. But most Indian groups in America found it difficult to stop the process, which was particularly successful on the Great Plains, because so much new land would be opened to ranchers and farmers. In all some sixty-seven Indian tribes had their reservations allotted. Some critics of allotment, notably minority members of the House Committee on Indian Affairs, noted that just giving Indians a farm would not make them into farmers. "The real aim of this bill," the minority report claimed, "is to get at the Indian lands and open them to settlement."[11] But hardly anyone noticed the minority report.

The pressures of "settler sovereignty" first became obvious in Indian Territory, where Indian tribes claimed thousands of acres of land that many whites coveted within the borders of defined reservations. Congress created the Cherokee or "Jerome" Commission in 1888, to begin the process of diminishment. At issue initially was the vast Cherokee Outlet, which the tribe theoretically owned but could not settle upon after the 1866 treaty. Feeling pressure from thousands of so-called "Boomers" who wanted the land, Congress finally took it from the Cherokees, paying compensation. The legislation set the tone for five years of negotiation with over two dozen tribes then in Indian Territory. In the end the tribes gave up 23,595 square miles of land in modern Oklahoma—nearly the equivalent of the size of the state of Indiana.[12] These tribes then faced allotment, their reservations being surveyed and handed out in 160-acre farms to Indian families. The process was not completed until after the turn of the century. With a new "Boomer" population, Indian Territory merged with Oklahoma Territory to become the state of Oklahoma in 1907.[13]

While the Jerome Commission worked its way across Oklahoma, other commissions went into the West to force allotment upon more than forty other Indian tribes. In Minnesota the Chippewa Commission convinced the Indians of some twelve small reserves to congregate on one large reserve, called White Earth. Allotment occurred there in the 1890s. While the titles handed out were all restricted, speculators worked to change this. They were successful in 1906, when the Clap Rider to a congressional bill determined that virtually all Indians in northern Minnesota were "Mixed Bloods" and capable of handling their own affairs, thus dismantling restrictions on titles. Land rings quickly formed in Detroit Lakes, just south of the reservations: Indians were given liquor and convinced to sell their lands. By 1920 non-Indians owned 780,000 acres out of some 836,000 acres or roughly 93 percent of the former reservation.[14]

While White Earth had valuable timber land and western portions of the reserve included excellent farmland, other reservations held less valuable land. Indians on Great Plains reservations fared much better with allotment, because most of their lands were marginally suited even for grazing. At Crow Creek and Rosebud Reservations today Indians and the federal government still jointly own 90 percent of the land. And even on Pine Ridge Reservation the Lakota people control 50 percent of the land that constituted the original reserve.[15] Allotments continued on some of these reservations well into the 1920s, as some agreements allowed Indians to retain land for future generations. But much like the Indians at White Earth, even those who received allotments were soon subject to a new law, the Burke Act, which allowed for the cancellation of the twenty-five-year restriction of land titles if Indians so requested. The law only provided more opportunity for speculators to acquire lands that Indians could be manipulated into selling.[16]

The Board of Indian Commissioners sent out investigators after 1900 to examine just how well the allotment process was working. Edward Ayer, David Smiley, Malcolm McDonald, and others made many different surveys, including investigations into land use and loss among the Pueblo Indians in New Mexico, the Blackfeet Nation in Montana, the various California bands, many of whom remained landless, and dozens of other tribes. What they found was both depressing and problematic. On the Blackfeet Reservation in northwestern Montana most of the best grazing land was controlled by mixed-bloods, who leased it illegally to white ranchers. Indians lacked the cattle, which the ranchers provided. The Pueblo Indians constantly lost legal battles over interpretations of old Spanish land grants, often as a result of surveyors being bribed. Allotment thus solved few problems and created many new ones.[17]

A recent study of two Rocky Mountain reservations, homes to the Nez Perce and Jicarilla Indians, demonstrates uniquely different results. The Nez Perces, who had excellent land, lost fully 70 percent of it through allotment, while the Jicarillas, whose reserve was isolated and less valuable, retained almost the entire reserve: some 352,000 acres were allotted, leaving no surplus.[18] In the final analysis allotment simply affected over sixty reservations west of the Mississippi River differently: some lost massive amounts of land, others retained many of the acres of the original reserves, and in other cases whites exploited the lands that still remained in Indian hands.

Despite claims that the allotment process would speed up Native American assimilation, the prediction outlined in the minority report coming out of the debate over the Dawes Act became reality. The process of Indian land alienation began with the first European settlements, at a time when Indians owned all of North America—some 3 billion acres of land. That empire had been reduced to a mere 150 million acres by 1887. When allotment finally ended in 1934, Indians in the continental United States owned a mere 48 million acres.[19] Put another way, American Indians lost 98.4 percent of their land in roughly three hundred years.

But should the loss of land that resulted from the allotment program be considered ethnic cleansing? Is it correct to imply that the Dawes legislation constituted a crime against Indians? The federal government never deported Indians as a result of the law; nor were they harmed, though a few were killed. Sitting Bull, for example, was killed not long after he physically tried to prevent the land selections at Standing Rock. Roughly

150 other Lakotas were horribly massacred at a place called Wounded Knee in South Dakota in 1890, to some degree because of their resistance to allotment, even though their dedication to the Ghost Dance and its hope of revitalization is often considered the root cause of the carnage.[20]

Resistance even broke out in Oklahoma, where full-blood Creeks under Chitto Harjo fomented the "Crazy Snake" Rebellion, which lasted from 1900, when allotment began, until 1910. Harjo, who convinced his followers to whip any Creek Indian who accepted an allotment, was finally arrested and given a two-year suspended sentence along with ninety-six of his followers.[21] When armed resistance failed, Oklahoma Indians, much like the Cherokees in Georgia in 1831, turned for relief to the courts. In 1903 Kiowa leader Lone Wolf sued the secretary of the interior, trying to block allotment by arguing that the policy violated the sacred treaty of 1867, which it did. The Supreme Court disagreed and ruled in *Lone Wolf v. Hitchcock* that Congress had plenary rights to break Indian treaties.[22]

There is no doubt that many Indians became landless within the confines of what still constituted their reservations. These Indians mostly lost sovereignty to states where the federal government concluded that no Indian lands existed anymore. Indeed after 1900 the Indian Office began defining Indian land as either "tribally owned" or "restricted" allotment lands, which mostly disappeared on many reserves. The Indian Office even discontinued its "Michigan Superintendency," believing that federal officers were no longer necessary to take care of Indian charges. Theoretically all Indians who held a title in fee simple were citizens of the United States, or so the Dawes Act decreed.[23]

In the real world it should have been clear to anyone who read George Manypenny's book that allotment would fail. The reformers and politicians who devised the process and pushed it through Congress must have known that many Indians were simply not ready for land ownership and that land rings would prey upon them. Indeed critics of the legislation made that very argument. Thus the reformers and politicians who devised the policy are guilty of forcing Indians to surrender parts of their homeland—they too contributed to the ethnic cleansing of America even though it does not appear to have been their "intent" to do so. They worked under the illusion that individual Indians would prosper once they owned their own farms—testimony to the powerful belief in the agrarian paradigm that guided early America. While the very nature of the politics and the results from the Dawes Act need more study, based upon what we know the intent of the legislation was good—its results a disaster.

All of the individuals who participated in the great land grab in the United States from 1540 to 1920 are now gone, taken by the ages. But perhaps we should take a moment to revisit what they did to American Indians. The crime that Winston Churchill attributed to Adolph Hitler, the one that he could not name, certainly was genocide. But the crime that Indians in the United States suffered never reached that level, even though some might argue that various incidents approached genocide. The crime was ethnic cleansing, at times violent. No sustained policy of genocide was ever promoted by colonial, state, or federal governments in the United States. Having said that, treatment of American Indians was and still is a crime that haunts American society. For certain, knowledge of that crime needs to be incorporated into an understanding of American history.

NOTES

AGO	Adjutant General's Office
CS	California Superintendency
DD	Department of Dakota
DM	Department of Missouri
DP	Department of the Platte
DP, PS	Division and Department of the Pacific, Pacific Slope
DRNRUT	Documents Relating to the Negotiation of Ratified and Unratified Treaties
DUA	District of the Upper Arkansas
DWWD	Department of the West and Western Department
KA	Kiowa Agency
LR	Letters Received
LS	Letters Sent
MD	Military Department
NARG	National Archives Record Group
OS	Oregon Superintendency
SW	Secretary of War
UAA	Upper Arkansas Agency
UPA	Upper Platte Agency
WDD	Western Division and Department
WS	Washington Superintendency

INTRODUCTION: DEFINITIONS OF GENOCIDE, CRIMES AGAINST
HUMANITY, ETHNIC CLEANSING, AND WAR CRIMES IN
MODERN WORLD HISTORY

1. Samantha Power, *"A Problem from Hell": America and the Age of Genocide* (New York: Basic Books, 2002), 29.

2. Lemkin created the phrase while a refugee in the United States. Yet he feared that expanding the definition to include murder for social and political reasons—such as in civil wars or even murder carried out by oppressive regimes, as in the Soviet Union—would make it difficult to gain recognition from world powers. When considered by the United Nations in 1947, Lemkin's omission remained, resulting in a watered-down definition. See the discussion in Norman M. Naimark, *Stalin's Genocide* (Princeton: Princeton University Press, 2010), 15–29.

3. See Norman M. Naimark, *Fires of Hatred: Ethnic Cleansing in Twentieth-Century Europe* (Cambridge, Mass.: Harvard University Press, 2001), 3. The United States finally ratified a severely watered-down version of the convention in 1988.

4. See James Belich, *Replenishing the Earth: The Settler Revolution and the Rise of the Angloworld, 1783–1939* (New York: Oxford University Press, 2009), 28.

5. See Robert A. Divine et al., *America, Past and Present* (New York: Longman, 2011).

6. Patrick Wolfe, "Settler Colonialism and the Elimination of the Native," *Journal of Genocide Research* 8 (December 2006): 387–409.

7. See John R. Wunder, *"Retained by the People": A History of American Indians and the Bill of Rights* (New York: Oxford University Press, 1994), 16–18; Jeffrey Ostler, *The Plains Sioux and U.S. Colonialism from Lewis and Clark to Wounded Knee* (New York: Cambridge University Press, 2004), 3.

8. "Rome Statute of the International Criminal Court" (2002), available at www.preventgenocide.org/law/icc/statute/part-a.htm. The court was originally called the International Criminal Tribunal for the Former Yugoslavia.

9. Ibid.

10. See Edith M. Lederer, "US Supports War Crimes Tribunal for First Time," *Washington Post,* March 2, 2011.

11. See Power, *"A Problem from Hell,"* 65–67.

12. Ibid., 4; "Rome Statute," Article 7.

13. See Robert M. Hayden, "Schindler's Fate: Genocide, Ethnic Cleansing, and Population Transfer," *Slavic Review* 55 (Winter 1996): 732–743; Andrew Bell-Fialkoff, "A Brief History of Ethnic Cleansing," *Foreign Affairs* 72 (Summer 1993): 110–21. Naimark suggests that Serbs used the term "cleansing" as early as 1807, when discussing the removal of Turks, Jews, and Roma (*Fires of Hatred,* 201).

14. See Naimark, *Fires of Hatred;* and A. Dirk Moses, ed., *Genocide and Settler Society: Frontier Violence and Stolen Indigenous Children in Australian History* (New York: Berghahn Books, 2004).

15. "Rome Statutes," 5–9.

16. David E. Stannard, *American Holocaust: the Conquest of the New World* (New York: Oxford University Press, 1992), 75 (suggestion that more Indians died in the Americas than in all other genocidal efforts), 255 (quotation).

17. Russell Thornton, *American Indian Holocaust and Survival: A Population History since 1492* (Norman: University of Oklahoma Press, 1987), xvi. Some scholars consider it an affront even to use the term "holocaust" (which derives from the Hebrew and Yiddish languages meaning "catastrophe" or "destruction") to describe anything other than what happened to Jews in central Europe.

18. Ward Churchill, *A Little Matter of Genocide: Holocaust and Denial in America* (San Francisco: City Lights, 1998), *Struggle for the Land: Indigenous Resistance to Genocide, Ecocide and Expropriation in Contemporary North America* (San Francisco: City Lights, 2002), and *Kill the Indian, Save the Man: The Genocidal Impact of American Indian Schools* (San Francisco: City Lights, 2004).

19. "What befell the Pequots in 1637 and afterwards," Hauptman has argued, "clearly fits the most widely accepted definition for genocide, one set by the United Nations Convention on Genocide in 1948." See Lawrence M. Hauptman, "The Pequot War and Its Legacies," in *The Pequots in Southern New England: The Fall and Rise of an American Indian Nation,* ed. Lawrence M. Hauptman and James D. Wherry (Norman: University of Oklahoma Press, 1990), 76; Robert H. Jackson and Edward Castillo, *Indians, Franciscans, and Spanish Colonization: The Impact of the Mission System on California Indians* (Albuquerque: University of New Mexico Press, 1995), 109. See also William E. Coffer, "Genocide among the California Indians," *Indian Historian* 10 (Spring 1977): 8–16; James Rawls, *Indians of California: The Changing Image* (Norman: University of Oklahoma Press, 1984), chapter entitled "Extermination."

20. Barbara Alice Mann, *George Washington's War on Native America* (Lincoln: University of Nebraska Press, 2008), 52, 152. Mann in particular notes the murder of 126 Lenape and Mahican Indians in 1782, calling it "pure genocide." Hauptman, "Pequot War and Its Legacies," in *The Pequots in Southern New England,* ed. Hauptman and Wherry, 76–77.

21. Benedict Kiernan, *Blood and Soil: A World History of Genocide and Extermination from Sparta to Darfur* (New Haven: Yale University Press, 2007), 310.

22. This field has led to the development of several journals devoted to the issue of genocide, including the *Journal of Genocide Research*, which began publication in 1999.

23. Kiernan, *Blood and Soil,* 322, 327.

24. The best discussion of the allied group of Indians and English who attacked the Pequot town is found in Michael Leroy Oberg, *Uncas: First of the Mohegans* (Ithaca: Cornell University Press, 2003), 58–69.

25. See Wolfe, "Settler Colonialism," 402.

26. Ferdinand Nahimana and Jean Bosco Barayagwiza were convicted under the Rome Statutes, Article 7, section a. The owner of a "newsletter," who also incited genocide, was also convicted under the same statute. These trials were popularly called the "media cases" and can be followed on the Internet. It could

not be proven that any of the three men "had effective control" over the forces committing genocide.

27. The studies on both events are too numerous to cite. Kiernan has offered some of the best analysis of the genocide in Cambodia in *The Pol Pot Regime: Race, Power, and Genocide under Khmer Rouge, 1975–1979* (New Haven: Yale University Press, 1996). The genocide in Europe received renewed interest after the publication of Christopher R. Browning, *Ordinary Men: Reserve Police Battalion 101 and the Final Solution in Poland* (New York: Harper, 1992). See also his main critic, Daniel J. Goldhagen, *Hitler's Willing Executioners: Ordinary Germans and the Holocaust* (New York: Knopf, 1996).

28. See, for example, John A. Berry and Carol Pott Berry, eds., *Genocide in Rwanda: A Collective Memory* (Washington, D.C.: Howard University Press, 1999).

29. Power asks this very question, noting the difficulty involved with the "numbers problem": Power, *"A Problem from Hell,"* 65.

30. See Raymond Evans, "'Plenty Shoot 'Em': The Destruction of Aboriginal Societies along the Queensland Frontier," in Moses, *Genocide and Settler Society,* 150–73; Robert Gellately and Ben Kiernan, eds., *The Specter of Genocide and Mass Murder in Historical Perspective* (New York: Cambridge University Press, 2003); and Sharon Morgan, *Land Settlement in Early Tasmania: Creating an Antipodean England* (New York: Cambridge University Press, 1991). For a controversial assessment of British imperialism worldwide and its often negative impact on Native cultures, see Richard Gott, *Britain's Empire: Resistance, Repression, and Revolt* (New York: Verso, 2011).

31. Naimark, *Fires of Hatred,* 3–4; conversation with the author and lecture entitled "Stalin's Genocide—Reconsidered" at the University of Oklahoma, November 8, 2012. Timothy Snyder provides the newest discussion of the "ethnic cleansing" of Poland, Czechoslovakia, and Hungry by the Soviet Union in 1945: *Bloodlands: Europe between Hitler and Stalin* (New York: Basic Books, 2010), chapter 10, "Ethnic Cleansing."

32. Some indication of how the discussion evolved just ten years ago and how definitions continue to evolve can be gleaned from Christoph Schiessl, "An Element of Genocide: Rape, Total War, and International Law in the Twentieth Century," *Journal of Genocide Research* 4 (2002): 199.

33. Lisa Ford, *Settler Sovereignty: Jurisdiction and Indigenous People in America and Australia, 1788–1836* (Cambridge, Mass.: Harvard University Press, 2010), 14.

34. Anthony Pagden, *Lords of All the World: Ideologies of Empire in Spain, Britain, and France, c. 1500–c. 1800* (New Haven: Yale University Press, 1995), 63. An interesting modern take on state building and peace is Charles T. Call, *Building States to Build Peace* (London: Lynne Rienner, 2008).

35. The Supreme Court of the United States concluded in 2005: "Under the 'doctrine of discovery,' fee title to the lands occupied by Indians when the colonists arrived became vested in the sovereign" and eventually the United States, as it conquered these lands from England. See *Sherrill v. Oneida Indian Nation*

(2005), 544 U.S. 197; quotation from N. Bruce Duthu, *American Indians and the Law* (New York: Viking, 2008), 73.

36. See Henry Kamen, *Empire: How Spain Became A World Power, 1492–1763* (New York: HarperCollins, 2003), 3–47. Kamen argues that the German-invented printing press not only helped create a state, as it did in northern Europe, but also tied Spain into Renaissance thought.

37. Micheline R. Ishay, *The History of Human Rights: From Ancient Times to the Globalization Era* (Berkeley: University of California Press, 2004). See also Lewis Hanke, *Aristotle and the American Indian: A Study in Race Prejudice in the Modern World* (Bloomington: Indiana University Press, 1959), 15–17, and *The Spanish Struggle for Justice in the Conquest of America* (Boston: Little, Brown, 1965), 41.

38. Pagden, *Lords of All the World,* 20–21.

39. Ibid., 24–26, 75–76.

40. Hans S. Pawlisch, *Sir John Davies and the Conquest of Ireland: A Study in Legal Imperialism* (Cambridge: Cambridge University Press, 1985), 12–59.

41. James M. Rosenheim, *The Emergence of a Ruling Order: English Landed Society 1650–1750* (London: Longman, 1998), 1–17; Richard Hoyle, "Introduction: Aspects of the Crown's Estate, c. 1558–1640," in *The Estates of the English Crown, 1558–1640,* ed. R. W. Hoyle (Cambridge: Cambridge University Press, 1992), 1–23.

42. Nicholas Canny, "The Permissive Frontier: Social Control in English Settlements in Ireland and Virginia, 1550–1650"; and Karl S. Bottigheimer, "Kingdom and Colony: Ireland in the Westward Enterprise, 1536–1660," in *The Westward Enterprise: English Activities in Ireland, the Atlantic, and America, 1480–1650,* ed. K. R. Andrews, N. P. Canny, and P. E. Hair (Detroit: Wayne State University, 1979), 21–27 and 47–58. In an age before the term "ethnic cleansing" entered the literature, Bottigheimer describes what happened in Ireland as a policy of "conquest and recolonization." Francis Jennings was one of the first American historians to compare the conquest of lands in Ireland with English policies in the New World: *The Invasion of America: Indians, Colonialism, and the Cant of Conquest* (New York: W. W. Norton, 1976), 7–9. See also Bernard Bailyn, *Atlantic History: Concept and Contours* (Cambridge, Mass.: Harvard University Press, 2005), 67.

43. Eric Gethyn-Jones, *George Thorpe and the Berkeley Company: A Gloucestershire Enterprise in Virginia* (London: Alan Sutton, 1982), 75–110; Belich, *Replenishing the Earth,* 60–61.

44. Ford, *Settler Sovereignty,* 17. See also Christopher Tomlins, *Freedom Bound: Law, Labor and Civil Identity in Colonizing English America, 1580–1865* (New York: Cambridge University Press, 2010).

45. Naimark, *Fires of Hatred,* 4–5.

46. Kiernan, *Blood and Soil,* 23–33, 377–79, 422–32, 563–67. See also Gellately and Kiernan, *Specter of Genocide,* 39–46.

47. Mark Levene, *Genocide in the Age of the Nation-State: Volume II, The Rise of the West and the Coming of Genocide* (New York: I. B. Tauris, 2005), 10–15;

Lorenzo Veracini, *Settler Colonialism: A Theoretical Overview* (New York: Palgrave Macmillan, 2010), 3–5 (quotation on 4).

48. Ford, *Settler Sovereignty,* 1–6 (quotation on 6).

49. Quotations from Belich, *Replenishing the Earth,* 146–47.

50. Hugo Grotius, *The Rights of War and Peace: Including the Law of Nature and of Nations,* trans. A. C. Campbell, with an intro. by David J. Hill (Washington, D.C.: Walter Dunne, publisher, 1901; reprint Nabu Public Domain Reprint, n.d.), 17–31, 73–85, 267–74, 290–307, 334–45, 365.

51. David J. Hill, "Introduction," in ibid., 1–16.

52. Tomlins, *Freedom Bound,* 145–47. For a general assessment, see Fred Anderson, *The Dominion of War: Empire and Liberty in North America, 1500–2000* (New York: Viking, 2005).

53. Ford, *Settler Sovereignty,* 15–16.

54. Emer de Vattel, *The Law of Nations: Or, Principles of the Law of Nature, Applied to the Conduct and Affairs of Nations, and Sovereigns, with Three Early Essays on the Origin and Nature of Natural Law and on Luxury* (1758; reprint Bèla Kapossy and Richard Whatmore, eds. [Indianapolis: Liberty Fund, 2008]).

55. Ibid., 69–129 (quotations on 75, 76, 77).

56. Ibid., 213–18.

57. David E. Wilkins and K. Tsianina Lomawaima, *Uneven Ground: American Indian Sovereignty and Federal Law* (Norman: University of Oklahoma Press, 2001), 57. See also Lindsay G. Robertson, *Conquest by Law: How the Discovery of America Dispossessed Indigenous Peoples of Their Land* (New York: Oxford University Press, 2005), 29–116; G. Edward White, *The Marshall Court and Cultural Change, 1815–1835* (New York: Oxford University Press, 1991), 674–75, 681; Blake Watson, *Buying America from the Indians: Johnson v. McIntosh and the History of Native Land Rights* (Norman: University of Oklahoma Press, 2012).

58. 4 Stat. 729.

59. See Bernard W. Sheehan, *Seeds of Extinction: Jeffersonian Philanthropy and the American Indian* (Chapel Hill: University of North Carolina Press, 1973); and Frederick E. Hoxie, *A Final Promise: The Campaign to Assimilate the Indians, 1880–1920* (Lincoln: University of Nebraska Press, 1984): see the discussion of "assimilation" on 33.

60. See Oberg, *Uncas,* 68–70.

61. Wilkins and Lomawaima, *Uneven Ground,* 19–22.

CHAPTER 1. THE NATIVE NEW WORLD

1. Peter E. Pope, *The Many Landfalls of John Cabot* (Toronto: University of Toronto Press, 1997), 13–24.

2. Ibid., 24–32. For the issue of "discovery," see Wilkins and Lomawaima, *Uneven Ground,* 19–63. See also Carl Sauer, *Sixteenth Century North America: The Land and the People as Seen by the Europeans* (Berkeley: University of California Press, 1971); and J. H. Elliott, *Empires of the Atlantic World: Britain and Spain in America, 1492–1830* (New Haven: Yale University Press, 2006), 3–28.

3. Wilkins and Lomawaima argue that "discovery" had little to do with Indians but rather worked for the benefit of European nations, who used it to sort out claims. The Supreme Court even upheld such a view in 1835: *Uneven Ground,* 56–57.

4. Felipe Fernández-Armesto, *Amerigo: The Man Who Gave His Name to America* (London: Weidenfeld and Nicolson, 2006), 183–95.

5. Sauer, *Sixteenth Century North America,* 52–61, 77–83. The evolution of the early fur trade in Canada is best followed in Bruce G. Trigger, *Children of Aataentsic: A History of the Huron People to 1660,* 2 vols. (Kingston, Canada: McGill–Queen's University Press, 1987).

6. Ibid., 1:27; see also David Weber, *The Spanish Frontier in North America* (New Haven: Yale University Press, 1992), 33.

7. Weber, *The Spanish Frontier,* 34.

8. Pagden, *Lords of All the World,* 63–69.

9. The quotation from Frobisher is from Roy Harvey Pearce, *Savagism and Civilization: A Study of the Indian and the American Mind* (Baltimore: Johns Hopkins University Press, 1953), 5.

10. Bruce G. Trigger, "Early Native North American Responses to European Contact: Romantic versus Rationalistic Interpretations," *Journal of American History* 77 (March 1991): 1200–1204.

11. Pearce, *Savagism and Civilization,* 8–12; Tamar Herzog, *Defining Nations: Immigrants and Citizens in Early Modern Spain and Spanish America* (New Haven: Yale University Press, 2003), 119–40, 164–72. Turning to the English colonies, historian Christopher Tomlins has argued that "medieval Christian natural law teaching allowed that both as men and as nations non-Christians no less than Christians enjoyed reason and hence possessed rights—to hold property, [and] to exercise governance over their own territories": Tomlins, *Freedom Bound,* 100.

12. Henry Dobyns, *Their Numbers Become Thinned: Native American Population Dynamics in Eastern North America* (Knoxville: University of Tennessee Press, 1983); Shepard Krech III, *The Ecological Indian: Myth and History* (New York: W. W. Norton, 1999), 93–94. Daniel Richter puts the population east of the Mississippi River at just 2 million, which seems very low: *Facing East from Indian Country: A Native History of Early America* (Cambridge, Mass.: Harvard University Press, 2001), 7.

13. Jennings, *Invasion of America,* 26–29. Anthropologist Kathleen J. Bragdon has carefully considered Jennings's population numbers and mostly agrees with them. The only difference is Jennings's conclusion that the Narragansett and Massachusett populations were a few thousand higher. See Bragdon, *Native People of Southern New England, 1500–1650* (Norman: University of Oklahoma Press, 1996), 24–27.

14. Jennings, *Invasion of America,* 15.

15. This argument that Native political organization passed through an evolutionary process from small kin groups to bands to tribes to chieftainships and finally to states comes from Elman Service, *Primitive Social Organization: An Evolutionary Perspective* (New York: Random House, 1962).

16. A good discussion of the various views on political organization is found in Bragdon, *Native People,* 40–41.

17. Richter, *Facing East from Indian Country,* 51–52. French anthropologists have a good sense of how this process worked, calling Native economies "modes of production," in which a social system, replete with various status levels, managed the economy. For a general discussion, see William Roseberry, *Anthropologies and Histories: Essays in Culture, History, and Political Economy* (New Brunswick: Rutgers University Press, 1991), chapter 6.

18. Bragdon, *Native People,* 16–17, 36–37; William A. Starna, "The Pequots in the Early Seventeenth Century," in *The Pequots in Southern New England,* ed. Hauptman and Wherry, 35–41.

19. William Cronon, *Changes in the Land: Indians, Colonists, and the Ecology of New England* (New York: Hill and Wang, 1983), 60–63.

20. Bragdon, *Native People,* 156–59. For a discussion of incest, see Robin Fox, *Kinship and Marriage: An Anthropological Perspective* (New York: Cambridge University Press, 1967), 54–76.

21. Steven Craig Harper, *Promised Land: Penn's Holy Experiment, the Walking Purchase, and the Dispossession of the Delawares, 1600–1763* (Bethlehem: Lehigh University Press, 2006), 17–18.

22. Robert S. Grumet, "The Selling of Lenapehoking," in *Proceedings of the 1992 People to People Conference* (Rochester, N.Y.: Research Division of the Rochester Museum, 1992), 19–20.

23. Ibid., 20–21.

24. A detailed study of the Powhatan Confederacy is Helen C. Rountree, *The Powhatan Indians of Virginia: Their Traditional Culture* (Norman: University of Oklahoma Press, 1989). See also Richter, *Facing East from Indian Country,* 70–73.

25. Steven R. Potter, "Early English Effects on Virginia Algonquian Exchange and Tribute in the Tidewater Potomac," in *Powhatan's Mantle: Indians in the Colonial Southeast,* ed. Gregory A. Waselkov, Peter H. Wood, and Tom Hatley (Lincoln: University of Nebraska Press, 1989), 216–17.

26. Ibid., 217–18.

27. Richter, *Facing East from Indian Country,* 71–73.

28. James H. Merrell, *The Indians' New World: Catawbas and Their Neighbors from European Contact through the Era of Removal* (New York: W. W. Norton, 1989), 8–48.

29. Paul Kelton, *Epidemics and Enslavement: Biological Catastrophe in the Southeast, 1492–1715* (Lincoln: University of Nebraska Press, 2007), chapter 2.

30. Jerald T. Milanich, "The European Entrada into Florida: An Overview," in *Columbian Consequences: Volume 2, Archaeological and Historical Perspectives on the Spanish Borderlands East,* ed. David Hurst Thomas (Washington, D.C.: Smithsonian Institution Press, 1990), 3–29.

31. David Hurst Thomas, "The Spanish Missions of La Florida: An Overview," in *Columbian Consequences,* 357–98. Anthropologist Henry Dobyns puts the Timucua population at nearly 800,000, a controversial figure that most scholars question. See the discussion in Thornton, *American Indian Holocaust,* 32.

32. Martín Salinas, *Indians of the Rio Grande Delta: Their Role in the History of Southern Texas and Northeastern Mexico* (Austin: University Texas Press, 1990), 22–24.

33. Ibid., 138. For the demographic debate, see Gary Clayton Anderson, *The Indian Southwest, 1580–1830: Ethnogenesis and Reinvention* (Norman: University of Oklahoma Press, 1999), 39.

34. For a newer assessment of the Spanish invasion, see Colin G. Calloway, *One Vast Winter Count: The Native American West before Lewis and Clark* (Lincoln: University of Nebraska Press, 2003), 119–63.

35. Anderson, *Indian Southwest,* 30–56.

36. Ibid., 55, 64, 95; John L. Kessell, *Pueblos, Spaniards, and the Kingdom of New Mexico* (Norman: University of Oklahoma Press, 2008), 9–13.

37. The so-called Tiguex War marked a significant event in the Native history of early New Mexico, devastating the largest Pueblos in the region. A good account is Herbert E. Bolton, *Coronado: Knight of Pueblos and Plains* (Albuquerque: University of New Mexico Press, 1949), 201–30. Bolton concluded: "The Tiguex War was a deplorable episode in Spanish empire building, but lest we make invidious comparisons we must not forget analogous chapters in the epic story of our own [American] 'Westward Movement,' which we regard as so heroic" (230). While Bolton dedicated nearly thirty pages to the conflict, revisionist historian David Weber limited his comments to one paragraph: Weber, *Spanish Frontier,* 48; Marc Simmons, *The Last Conquistador: Juan de Oñate and the Settling of the Far Southwest* (Norman: University of Oklahoma Press, 1991), 91–111.

38. Bolton, *Coronado,* 380–81.

39. W. J. Eccles, *The Canadian Frontier, 1534–1760* (New York: Holt, Rinehart and Winston, 1969), 13–14, 23–24; Trigger, *Children of Aataentsic,* vol. 1.

CHAPTER 2. EUROPEAN PENETRATION OF THE NEW WORLD

1. Weber, *Spanish Frontier,* 81–82.

2. Ibid., 87–91. Herzog emphasizes the need for any citizen who wanted land to be a citizen in good standing in a town. As the *encomienda* system became obsolete, this eventually included Indians, who did receive town grants in New Mexico: Herzog, *Defining Nations,* 43–46, 61–63.

3. Kessell, *Pueblos, Spaniards, and the Kingdom of New Mexico,* 61.

4. Ibid., 60–61, 66–67, 84–85. The differences between the hacienda and the *encomienda* are dealt with in James Lockhart, *Of Things of the Indies: Essays Old and New in Early Latin American History* (Stanford: Stanford University Press, 1999), 1–26. See also the older but still useful François Chevalier, *Land and Society in Colonial Mexico: The Great Hacienda* (Berkeley: University of California Press, 1963).

5. For Spanish frontier society in early America, see Ramón Gutiérrez, *When Jesus Came, the Corn Mothers Went Away: Marriage, Sexuality, and Power in New Mexico, 1500–1846* (Stanford: Stanford University Press, 1991), 51–66.

6. James F. Brooks argues that slavery was key to understanding the entire economy and social structure of the Southwest: Brooks, *Captives and Cousins:*

Slavery, Kinship, and Community in the Southwest Borderlands (Chapel Hill: University of North Carolina Press, 2002), 31–35. Gutiérrez notes the value of female Indian slaves for their sexual service in *When Jesus Came*, 179–87.

7. Kessell, *Pueblos, Spaniards, and the Kingdom of New Mexico*, 40–43. The Pueblo Revolt is covered in considerable detail in Calloway, *One Vast Winter Count*, 165–211.

8. While Oñate received the right to grant land, this was rescinded after he resigned as governor in 1607. The Crown took over the colony thereafter. Kessell notes that some grants were either inherited or given to single women who operated ranches: Kessell, *Pueblos, Spaniards, and the Kingdom of New Mexico*, 56–57, 84.

9. Gethyn-Jones, *George Thorpe*, 112. The four men were Sir Thomas Gates, Sir George Sumers, Richard Hakluyt, and Edward Maria Wingfield.

10. Stuart Banner, *How the Indians Lost Their Land: Law and Power on the Frontier* (Cambridge, Mass.: Harvard University Press, 2005), 14–15.

11. Richter, *Facing East from Indian Country*, 72–73; Potter, "Early English Effects," 222–23.

12. Gethyn-Jones, *George Thorpe*, 82–84.

13. Banner, *How the Indians Lost Their Land*, 16.

14. Banner, while not recognizing the differences between killing Indians to get their land and simply running them off of it, nevertheless has an excellent discussion of English views on "conquest." Both quotations are from *How the Indians Lost Their Land*, 16–17.

15. Wyatt's quotation is from Richter, *Facing East from Indian Country*, 75.

16. Ibid., 76–77. See also Tomlins, *Freedom Bound*, 24–26.

17. Jack P. Greene, *The Quest for Power: The Lower Houses of Assembly in the Southern Royal Colonies, 1689–1776* (Chapel Hill: University of North Carolina Press, 1963), 150–68. The other southern colonies followed Virginia by charging quitrents, which the colonial assemblies either agreed to or resisted.

18. Richter, *Facing East from Indian Country*, 98–99.

19. Darrett B. Rutman, *Winthrop's Boston: Portrait of a Puritan Town, 1630–1647* (New York: W. W. Norton, 1965), 46–47.

20. Jennings, *Invasion of America*, 82.

21. Banner, *How the Indians Lost Their Land*, 44. For a general study, consult John Grenier, *The First Way of War: American War Making on the Frontier, 1607–1814* (New York: Cambridge University Press, 2005).

22. The best description of the struggle in the Connecticut River valley is Oberg, *Uncas*, 47–58. See also Hauptman, "Pequot War and Its Legacies," in *The Pequots in Southern New England*, ed. Hauptman and Wherry, 71–74.

23. Oberg, *Uncas*, 58–68. Colin G. Calloway has argued that Mason learned his trade of burning houses to destroy an enemy in the feuds and conflicts in Scotland: Calloway, *White People, Indians, and Highlanders: Tribal Peoples and Colonial Encounters in Scotland and America* (New York: Oxford University Press, 2008), 35.

24. Hauptman, "Pequot War and Its Legacies," in *The Pequots in Southern New England*, ed. Hauptman and Wherry, 62–78.

25. Richter, *Facing East from Indian Country,* 99–104.

26. Douglas Edward Leach, *Flintlock and Tomahawk: New England in King Philip's War* (New York: W. W. Norton, 1958), 28–29. For an assessment that focuses on the emergence of American identity, see Jill Lepore, *King Philip's War and the Origins of American Identity* (New York: Knopf, 1998). An excellent discussion of the conflict over grazing land is found in Virginia DeJohn Anderson, "King Philip's Herds: Indians, Colonists, and the Problem of Livestock in Early New England," *William and Mary Quarterly* 51 (October 1991): 601–24.

27. Leach, *Flintlock and Tomahawk,* 112–44.

28. Ibid., 236.

29. Ibid., 237. See also Richter, *Facing East from Indian Country,* 104–105.

30. Grumet, "The Selling of Lenapehoking," 19–21.

31. Eccles, *Canadian Frontier,* 23–30.

32. For a detailed study of the Huron wars, see Trigger, *Children of Aataentsic.*

33. Wilcomb E. Washburn, *The Governor and the Rebel: A History of Bacon's Rebellion in Virginia* (New York: W. W. Norton, 1957), 20–23.

34. Ibid., 24–25.

35. Ibid., quotations on 38 and 45; see also 70–79.

36. Edmund S. Morgan, *American Slavery, American Freedom: The Ordeal of Colonial Virginia* (New York: W. W. Norton, 1975), 250–70.

37. Weber, *Spanish Frontier,* 131–33; Kessell, *Pueblos, Spaniards, and the Kingdom of New Mexico,* 53–54, 68. The view that Franciscan missionaries punished with a whip has been a contentious historical issue. See Anderson, *Indian Southwest,* 78–81.

38. A good general discussion of the period is found in Weber, *Spanish Frontier,* 134.

39. Of the many sources on the Pueblo Revolt, the best is still Charles Wilson Hacket, ed., *Revolt of the Pueblo Indians and Otermín's Attempted Reconquest, 1680–1682,* trans. Charmion Clair Shelby (Albuquerque: University of New Mexico Press, 1941).

40. Weber carefully outlines the various views of scholars on the causes of the Pueblo Revolt, the leading two factors being the *encomienda* (forced labor) and religious persecution: Weber, *Spanish Frontier,* 415–16.

41. Ford, *Settler Sovereignty,* 17.

CHAPTER 3. INTERREGNUM

1. Steven J. Oatis, *A Colonial Complex: South Carolina's Frontiers in the Era of the Yamasee War, 1680–1730* (Lincoln: University of Nebraska Press, 2004), 19.

2. Eccles, *Canadian Frontier,* 109–10.

3. Oatis, *Colonial Complex,* 11–19. The meeting between the two contesting European trading parties came at the Natchez Villages and is recorded in the unpublished journal of Pierre Charles Le Sueur, titled "Mémoires de Mr le Sueur," 1700–1702, Archives Nationales, Paris, France.

4. Kelton, *Epidemics and Enslavement.*

5. Mary Lou Lustig, *The Imperial Executive in America: Sir Edmund Andros, 1637–1714* (Madison: Fairleigh Dickinson University Press, 2002), 36–40.

6. Ibid., 81–83.

7. Thomas E. Burke, Jr., *Mohawk Frontier* (Albany: State University of New York Press, 1991), 1–32, 210–22; Banner, *How the Indians Lost Their Land,* 34–35.

8. The relationships that developed between the Dutch and the Mohawks at Schenectady did not prevent a French and Indian force from overrunning the town and killing sixty people in 1690: Burke, *Mohawk Frontier,* 92–108.

9. Francis Jennings, *The Ambiguous Iroquois Empire: The Covenant Chain of Indian Tribes within English Colonies from Its Beginnings to the Lancaster Treaty of 1744* (New York: W. W. Norton, 1984), 7–9. Alan Taylor has a good description of the Iroquois notion of land ownership in *The Divided Ground: Indians, Settlers, and the Northern Borderlands of the American Revolution* (New York: Alfred A. Knopf, 2006), 36–38.

10. Jennings, *Ambiguous Iroquois Empire,* 166. See also Taylor, *Divided Ground,* 22–28.

11. The best general description of how the relationship worked as it expanded across the Great Lakes is found in Richard White, *The Middle Ground: Indians, Empires, and Republics in the Great Lakes Region, 1650–1815* (New York: Cambridge University Press, 1991). White defines the middle ground as the creation of a "common, mutually comprehensible world" where Indians and Europeans overlapped, creating a "system of meaning and of [commercial] exchange" (52–53).

12. Jennings, *Ambiguous Iroquois Empire,* 145–71. Jennings argues that Andros's manipulation of the chain agreement made New York a dominant colony in the region and suppressed the aggressive tendencies of Lord Baltimore. But Jennings is less certain regarding the absolute rule of the "Great Chain" in that other tribes, such as the Shawnees and Delawares, did negotiate on their own. See also Richter, *Facing East from Indian Country,* 136–38.

13. Jennings, *Ambiguous Iroquois Empire,* 170–71.

14. Lustig, *Imperial Executive,* 183–207.

15. David Weber has compiled a list of the rebellions, pointing out that Spanish officials were often so embarrassed about them that some probably were not even reported: Weber, *Spanish Frontier,* 133–37.

16. Kessell, *Pueblos, Spaniards, and the Kingdom of New Mexico,* 173.

17. Malcolm Ebright, "New Mexican Land Grants: The Legal Background," in *Land, Water, and Culture: New Perspectives on Hispanic Land Grants,* ed. Charles L. Briggs and John R. Van Ness (Albuquerque: University of New Mexico Press, 1987), 21–26.

18. Ibid., 25; Roxanne Dunbar-Ortiz, *Roots of Resistance: A History of Land Tenure in New Mexico* (Norman: University of Oklahoma Press, 2007), 51–54.

19. Ebright, "New Mexican Land Grants," 21.

20. Ned Blackhawk, *Violence over the Land: Indians and Empires in the American West* (Cambridge, Mass.: Harvard University Press, 2008).

21. Ibid. See also Brooks, *Captives and Cousins.*

22. Jesús F. De La Teja, *San Antonio de Béxar: A Community on New Spain's Northern Frontier* (Albuquerque: University of New Mexico Press, 1997), 31–48.

23. De La Teja has an excellent discussion of the "Ranching Frontier" in south Texas in ibid., 97–117. The land grants of the missions are the subject of Félix D. Almaráz, Jr., *The San Antonio Missions and Their System of Land Tenure* (Austin: University of Texas Press, 1989); and Anderson, *Indian Southwest,* 211–15.

24. Alan Gallay, *The Indian Slave Trade: The Rise of the English Empire in the American South, 1670–1717* (New Haven: Yale University Press, 2002). The argument that the slave trade produced catastrophic consequences for Native peoples, due to the many infectious diseases that it spread, is found in Kelton, *Epidemics and Enslavement,* 126–59. Kelton calls the decade of the 1690s the "Great Southeastern Smallpox Epidemic" (158).

25. Oatis, *Colonial Complex,* 47–51; John H. Hann, *Apalachee: The Land between the Rivers* (Gainesville: University of Florida Press, 1988), 304–17.

26. Oatis, *Colonial Complex,* 54–56.

27. Ibid., 88–91.

28. The Carolina rangers are found in ibid., 147.

29. Ibid., 148–49.

30. Robert K. Ackerman, *South Carolina Colonial Land Policies* (Columbia: University of South Carolina Press, 1977), 5–55.

31. Quotation from Greene, *Quest for Power,* 161.

32. Greene concludes that Indian land titles never became an issue in these colonies. This argument certainly holds for land taken from Indians early on, but it does not apply to lands beyond the Appalachian Mountains, which came under dispute about the time the revolution broke out: ibid., chapter on "Fees," 148–68.

33. George Edward Milne, "Picking Up the Pieces: Natchez Coalescence in the Shatter Zone," in Robbie Ethridge and Sheri M. Shuck-Hall, eds., *Mapping the Mississippian Shatter Zone: The Colonial Indian Slave Trade and Regional Instability in the American South,* ed. Robbie Ethridge and Sheri M. Schuck-Hall (Lincoln: University of Nebraska Press, 2009), 388–417; Kathleen DuVal, *The Native Ground: Indians and Colonists in the Heart of the Continent* (Philadelphia: University of Pennsylvania Press, 2006).

34. R. David Edmunds and Joseph L. Peyser, *The Fox Wars: The Mesquakie Challenge to New France* (Norman: University of Oklahoma Press, 1993), 138–57.

35. Ibid., 167.

36. Ibid., 158–201. Edmunds and Peyser's conclusion about a "failed" genocide comes on 201.

37. Kevin Kenny, *Peaceable Kingdom Lost: The Paxton Boys and the Destruction of William Penn's Holy Experiment* (New York: Oxford University Press, 2009).

38. Harper, *Promised Land,* 13–14, 33–43.

39. Ibid., 60.

40. Ibid., 61–71. Banner gives a figure of fifty-five miles covered in the walk, noting that the Delawares expected the lands sold to be one-third of that amount: Banner, *How the Indians Lost Their Land,* 67.

41. Kenny, *Peaceable Kingdom Lost,* 3, 30. The best study of the various elements that made up these settlements is Peter Silver, *Our Savage Neighbors: How Indian War Transformed Early America* (New York: W. W. Norton, 2008). While the writings of Grotius and Vattel were often found in colonial libraries, Silver notes that these back-country settlers hardly ever questioned the notion that Indian attacks constituted the crime of "murder" or were violations of the "laws of war" (56–57).

42. Ibid., 51.

43. James H. Merrell, "Shamokin, 'the Very Seat of the Prince of Darkness': Unsettling the Early American Frontier," in *Contact Points: American Frontiers from the Mohawk Valley to the Mississippi, 1750–1830,* ed. Andrew R. L. Cayton and Fredrika J. Teute (Chapel Hill: University of North Carolina Press, 1998), 16–59.

44. Kenny, *Peaceable Kingdom Lost,* 48–53.

45. White, *Middle Ground,* 94–185.

Chapter 4. A New Kind of Ethnic Cleansing

1. Ford, *Settler Sovereignty,* 17–20. See also Veracini, *Settler Colonialism,* 3–5. Veracini offers essentially the same argument as Ford: "settler colonialism" is different from "colonialism" per se in that the so-called "migrants" evolve into the "settlers," who are "founders of political order and carry their sovereignty with them" (5).

2. White, *Middle Ground,* 223–25.

3. Fred Anderson, *Crucible of War: The Seven Years' War and the Fate of Empire in British North America, 1754–1766* (New York: Vintage Books, 2001), 33–41.

4. Ibid., 50–65; Kenny, *Peaceable Kingdom Lost,* 53–54; Francis Jennings, *Empire of Fortune: Crowns, Colonies and Tribes in the Seven Years War in America* (New York: W. W. Norton, 1988), 65–69.

5. John C. Fitzpatrick, ed., *The Diaries of George Washington, 1748–1794,* 4 vols. (Boston: Houghton Mifflin, 1925), 1:93–95.

6. Anderson, *Crucible of War,* 27–29; Jennings, *Empire of Fortune,* 10–14.

7. White, *Middle Ground,* 238–39.

8. Kenny, *Peaceable Kingdom Lost,* 57–58.

9. Timothy J. Shannon, *Indians and Colonists at the Crossroads of Empire: The Albany Congress of 1754* (Ithaca: Cornell University Press, 2000), 30–49, 163. One of Henrick's long diatribes regarding land sales in 1753 is reprinted in Jennings, *Empire of Fortune,* 81.

10. Shannon, *Indians and Colonists,* 163. William Johnson seems to be one of the few "winners" to come out of the Albany Conference, in that the British government had confidence in him to do what was good for the Crown and not necessarily for the colonies.

11. Shannon, *Indians and Colonists,* 58–59; Jennings, *Empire of Fortune,* 104–105.

12. Shannon, *Indians and Colonists,* 59–61.

13. Banner, *How the Indians Lost Their Land,* 54.

14. Kenny, *Peaceable Kingdom Lost,* 60–61.

15. Jennings, *Empire of Fortune,* 142–45.

16. Anderson, *Crucible of War,* 86–95.

17. For Braddock's defeat, I have followed Anderson, *Crucible of War,* 94–107; and Kenny, *Peaceable Kingdom Lost,* 67–69.

18. Quotation from Jennings, *Empire of Fortune,* 159.

19. Ibid., 188–97; Kenny, *Peaceable Kingdom Lost,* 72–75.

20. Kenny has an excellent description of the Paxton Rangers: Kenny, *Peaceable Kingdom Lost,* 76–77.

21. Ibid., 88–89.

22. Jennings, *Empire of Fortune,* 201; John R. Ross, *War on the Run: The Epic Story of Robert Rogers and the Conquest of America's First Frontier* (New York; Bantam Books, 2009), 250–51.

23. Kenny, *Peaceable Kingdom Lost,* 88–89, 102–109; Jennings, *Empire of Fortune,* 276–80. The minutes to the 1756 and 1758 meetings have been published, along with many other Pennsylvania documents, in Susan Kalter, ed., *Benjamin Franklin, Pennsylvania, and the First Nations* (Urbana: University of Illinois Press, 2006), 181–225, 290–333.

24. White suggests that the middle ground "died in bits and pieces," over the years following the French defeat: White, *Middle Ground,* x–xi, 516–17. But the loss of the French alliance was certainly a bitter blow, particularly to the Lakes Indians.

25. Jennings, *Empire of Fortune,* 441–47.

26. For the best study of Pontiac, see Gregory Dowd, *War under Heaven: Pontiac, the Indian Nations, and the British* (Baltimore: Johns Hopkins University Press, 2002); Kenny, *Peaceable Kingdom Lost,* 115–21.

27. The notion that the British made concerted efforts of a genocidal nature to destroy Indians by distributing smallpox-laden blankets is argued in Churchill, *Little Matter of Genocide.* The correct historical assessment is found in Elizabeth A. Fenn, "Biological Warfare in Eighteenth-Century America: Beyond Jeffrey Amherst," *Journal of American History* 86 (March 2000): 1552–80. See also her book *Pox Americana: The Great Smallpox Epidemic of 1775–1782* (New York: Hill and Wang, 2001).

28. Kenny, *Peaceable Kingdom Lost,* 130–41.

29. Ibid., 147–55; Richter, *Facing East from Indian Country,* 206.

30. Thomas M. Hatley, *The Dividing Paths: Cherokees and South Carolinians through the Era of Revolution* (New York: Oxford University Press, 1993), 42–51, 70–71.

31. John Philip Reid, *A Better Kind of Hatchet: Law, Trade, and Diplomacy in the Cherokee Nation during the Early Years of European Contact* (University Park: Pennsylvania Sate University Press, 1976), 1–3.

32. Ibid., 4–5; Hatley, *Dividing Paths,* 80–86; David H. Corkran, *The Cherokee Frontier: Conflict and Survival, 1740–1762* (Norman: University Oklahoma Press, 1962), 14.

33. Corkran, *Cherokee Frontier,* 13–24.

34. Gregory Evans Dowd, "'Insidious Friends': Gift Giving and the Cherokee-British Alliance in the Seven Years' War," in *Contact Points*, 114–50.

35. Corkran, *Cherokee Frontier*, 54–55.

36. Hatley, *Dividing Paths*, 120–25.

37. Ibid., 119–40; Corkran, *Cherokee Frontier*, 209, 253–54.

38. Hatley, *Dividing Paths*, 141–53.

39. The quotations are from extracts in Hatley, *Dividing Paths*, 121–35.

40. Quotations from Colin G. Calloway, *The Scratch of a Pen: 1763 and the Transformation of North America* (New York: Oxford University Press, 2006), 48.

41. Ibid., 56–61.

42. Ford, *Settler Sovereignty*, 20.

43. Calloway, *Scratch of a Pen*, 94.

44. Canadian Indians are able to argue different views because nothing changed regarding their relationship with the British government after the American Revolutionary War, whereas the new American government theoretically claimed sovereignty over Indians by "right of conquest" over England. See Calloway's lively discussion of the situation in ibid., 94–97.

45. Taylor, *Divided Ground*, 43–45. Taylor also notes the meddling influence of missionaries in the land deal, especially Samuel Kirkland, who also had an eye on Indian land.

46. Gage to Hillsborough, January 6, 1770, in K. G. Davis, ed., *Documents of the American Revolution, 1770–1783,* 21 vols. (Shannon, Ireland: Irish University Press, 1972–81), 2:22–25.

47. Ibid., 2:27. See also Gage to Stuart, October 16, 1770, Gage to Hillsborough, December 4, 1771, and Delaware, Munsie, and Mohican chiefs to Colonial Governors of Pennsylvania, Maryland, and Virginia, December 4, 1771, ibid., 3:203–204, 3:253–54 and 3:254–55.

48. Stuart Council notes, October 29–November 2, 1771, ibid., 3:212–15.

49. William Nelson to Hillsborough, October 18, 1770, and Alexander Cameron to Stuart, March 9, 1771, ibid., 3:205–15, 3:70–73. Great Warrior's response is found in Cameron's letter.

50. James Belich, "The Rise of the Angloworld: Settlement in North America and Australia, 1784–1918," in *Rediscovering the British World,* ed. Phillip Buckner and R. Douglas Francis (Calgary: University of Calgary Press, 2005), 39–57.

Chapter 5. The American Invasion

1. Reginald Horsman has argued that the American victory in the Revolution was "a disaster to the Indians." Native peoples in the West, in particular, were left alone to face the wrath of "land speculators and farmers": Horsman, *Expansion and American Indian Policy, 1783–1812* (Norman: University of Oklahoma Press, 1992), 3–4.

2. The story of Boone's ventures in Tennessee and Kentucky is wonderfully told by John Mack Faragher, *Daniel Boone: The Life and Legend of an American Pioneer* (New York: Henry Holt, 1992), 64–73.

3. Ibid., 99–106.

4. Frederick Palmer, *Clark of the Ohio: A Life of George Rogers Clark* (New York: Dodd and Mead, 1929), 76–80; Jay H. Buckley, *William Clark: Indian Diplomat* (Norman: University of Oklahoma Press, 2008).

5. For a discussion of these various groups that takes issue with the way previous historians have described them, see Mann, *George Washington's War,* 111–13.

6. While some Virginia politicians believed that the Henderson sale would stand in the courts, including later governor Patrick Henry, Henry worked against the sale when he was denied a partnership in the company; Virginia reasserted its claim to the region under its royal charter. The Henderson Purchase briefly became known as Transylvania, with its capital at Bonnesborough. Stephen Aron, *How the West Was Lost* (Baltimore: Johns Hopkins University Press, 1996), 59–64.

7. Archibald Henderson, *The Conquest of the Old Southwest* (New York: Century, 1920), 265–68; Thurman Wilkins, *Cherokee Tragedy: The Ridge Family and the Decimation of a People* (Norman: University of Oklahoma Press, 1970), 10–11.

8. William G. McLoughlin, *Cherokee Renascence in the New Republic* (Princeton: Princeton University Press, 1986), 19.

9. R. S. Cotterill, *The Southern Indians: The Story of the Civilized Tribes before Removal* (Norman: University of Oklahoma Press, 1954), 44–45.

10. Ibid., 20–21.

11. See Charles C. Royce, *Indian Land Cessions in the United States* (Washington, D. C.: Government Printing Office, 1900), 652; Charles L. Kappler, *Indian Affairs: Laws and Treaties.* 2 vols. (Washington, D.C.: Government Printing Office, 1903), 2:22–26.

12. A discussion of the diplomacy is found in David H. Corkran, *The Creek Frontier, 1540–1783* (Norman: University of Oklahoma Press, 1967), 288–325. See also Michael D. Green, *The Politics of Indian Removal: Creek Government and Society in Crisis* (Lincoln: University of Nebraska Press, 1981), 32–33. A rendition of the Raven's speech is in Brown to Germain, April 6, 1782, in Davis, *Documents of the American Revolution,* 19:280.

13. Brown to Germain, March 10, 1780, and Germain to Brown, July 5, 1780, in Davis, *Documents of the American Revolution,* 18:55–56 and 18:115.

14. Charles Shaw to Germain, September 18, 1780, and Governor James Wright to Germain, October 27, 1780, in ibid., 18:168–69, 18:211. In a later assessment of Creek and Cherokee assistance Alexander Cameron, one of the British agents, could only lament that "they are really an insolent, wavering set": Cameron to Germain, May 27, 1781, in ibid., 18:149–51.

15. Royce, *Indian Land Cessions,* 652; Kappler, *Indian Affairs,* 2:19–22.

16. The prerevolutionary history of the upper Ohio valley is covered in Michael N. McConnell, *A Country Between: The Upper Ohio Valley and Its Peoples, 1724–1774* (Lincoln: University of Nebraska Press, 1992).

17. Thomas S. Abler, *Cornplanter: Chief Warrior of the Allegheny Senecas* (Syracuse: Syracuse University Press, 2007), 9–10.

18. A good description of the speech is found in Randolph C. Downes, *Council Fires on the Upper Ohio: A Narrative of Indian Affairs in the Upper Ohio Valley until 1795* (Pittsburgh: University of Pittsburgh Press, 1940), 184–85 (emphasis in the original).

19. John Sugden, *Blue Jacket: Warrior of the Shawnees* (Lincoln: University of Nebraska Press, 2000), 50–51.

20. Abler, *Cornplanter,* 37; Taylor, *Divided Ground,* 90–91.

21. Downes, *Council Fires,* 207.

22. Ibid., 193–96; Silver, *Our Savage Neighbors,* 232–60.

23. Quotation from Downes, *Council Fires,* 202.

24. Ibid., 200–203.

25. Abler, *Cornplanter,* 44–45.

26. Mann, *George Washington's War,* 16–19.

27. The number is speculative but based upon the report of Governor Frederick Haldimand to Germain, October 12, 1780, in Davis, *Documents of the American Revolution,* 18:208–209. Haldimand gave a figure of four hundred captives taken in Kentucky by northern tribes; nearly as many were probably taken at Wyoming Valley.

28. Ibid., 16–17; Abler, *Cornplanter,* 46–47. See in particular the famous painting *Massacre at Wyoming Valley* by Charles Weimar (1828–98) or read Campbell's poem "Gertrude of Wyoming" in *The Poetical Works of Thomas Campbell,* ed. Rufus W. Griswold (New York: Leavitt and Allen, 1865).

29. Abler, *Cornplanter,* 49–52. Mann, *George Washington's War,* has the best descriptions of the Sullivan Campaigns, which are the main focus of her book.

30. Mann, *George Washington's War,* 214–18.

31. Ibid., 224–47.

32. Abler, *Cornplanter,* 56.

33. Downes notes the near-destruction of Clark's force in 1781: *Council Fires,* 269.

34. Louise P. Kellogg, *Frontier Retreat on the Upper Ohio, 1779–1781* (Madison: Wisconsin Historical Society, 1917), 549.

35. Downes, *Council Fires,* 273–74.

36. Haldimand to Thomas Townshend, February 14, 1783, and Maclean to Haldimand, May 18, 1783, in Davis, *Documents of the American Revolution,* 21:155–56 and 21:169–72. See the translation of the Brant speech in Haldimand to Lord North, June 2, 1783, in ibid., 19:404–405.

37. Ibid., 21:284; Abler, *Cornplanter,* 71.

38. Downes, *Council Fires,* 286–88; Horsman, *Expansion and American Indian Policy,* 16.

39. Quotation from Horsman, *Expansion and American Indian Policy,* 19 (emphasis in the original).

40. Abler, *Cornplanter,* 63–73.

41. Horsman, *Expansion and American Indian Policy,* 20.

42. R. Douglas Hurt, *The Ohio Frontier: Crucible of the Old Northwest, 1720–1830* (Bloomington: Indiana University Press, 1996), 96–97.

43. Richard White has argued that the Ohio "confederacy" perhaps began to form as early as 1783, consisting primarily of Delawares, Shawnees, and Miamis. But he suggests that each group still maintained village autonomy, taking on a common identity only when they opposed other groups such as the Americans: White, *Middle Ground*, 413–68.

44. Hurt, *Ohio Frontier*, 98–99.

45. McLoughlin, *Cherokee Renascence*, 21.

46. Horsman, *Expansion and American Indian Policy*, 32–39.

47. Report of Henry Knox on the Northwestern Indians, June 15, 1789, *American State Papers: Indian Affairs*, 2 vols. (Washington, D.C.: Gales and Seaton, 1832–34), 1:13–14.

48. Washington to the Senate, September 17, 1789, *Annals of Congress: The Debates and Proceedings of the Congress of the United States, The Senate*, Library of Congress Internet Source: http://memory.loc.gov/ammem/amlaw/lwaclink.html.

49. Washington to the House of Representatives, September 16, 1789, *Annals of Congress: The Debates and Proceedings of the Congress of the United States, The House of Representatives*.

50. See Knox's reports to Congress, May 25 and August 7, 1789, *Annals of Congress, The Senate*.

51. For biographical information on Cornplanter, see Taylor, *Divided Ground*, 246–49; Hurt, *Ohio Frontier*, 103–104.

52. There are many descriptions of Harmar's defeat. See Hurt, *Ohio Frontier*, 105–107.

53. The negotiations are covered in Taylor, *Divided Ground*, 242–66.

54. Ibid., 259.

55. Horsman has a good discussion of the concerns of both Knox and Washington: *Expansion and American Indian Policy*, 95–96.

56. Wayne to Knox, August 14, 1792, in Richard C. Knopf, ed., *Anthony Wayne, A Name in Arms: Soldier, Diplomat, Defender of Expansion Westward of a Nation* (Pittsburgh: University of Pittsburgh Press, 1960), 71–78.

57. Knox to Wayne, December 1, 1792, in ibid., 142.

58. Cornplanter in Wayne to Knox, March 22, 1793, in ibid., 206.

59. Hurt, *Ohio Frontier*, 121–42.

60. Kappler, *Indian Affairs*, 2:30–34.

61. Ibid., 2:19–22, 36.

62. Claudio Saunt, *A New Order of Things: Property, Power, and the Transformation of the Creek Indians, 1733–1816* (New York: Cambridge University Press, 1999).

63. McLoughlin, *Cherokee Renascence*, 26–31. See also Kappler, *Indian Affairs*, 2:22–26, 39–41.

64. Knox address to Congress, entitled "Preservation of Peace with the Indians," December 29, 1794, in *Annals of Congress, Appendix, Senate and House*, 3rd Congress, 1400–1403.

65. Many of the narratives are found in Wilcomb E. Washburn, ed., *The Garland Library of Narratives of North American Indian Captives*, 103 vols. (New York: Garland Publishing, 1975).

CHAPTER 6. THE JEFFERSONIANS AND THE REMOVAL GAME

1. President Washington had begun a small "civilization program" for Indians that encouraged agriculture. See Francis Paul Prucha, *American Indian Policy in the Formative Years: The Indian Trade and Intercourse Acts, 1790–1834* (Cambridge, Mass.: Harvard University Press, 1962; reprint Lincoln: University of Nebraska Press, 1970), 46–53. The dominance of the "plantation" South is the theme of Roger G. Kennedy, *Mr. Jefferson's Lost Cause: Land, Farmers, Slavery and the Louisiana Purchase* (New York: Oxford University Press, 2003).

2. The argument outlining the Jeffersonian philosophy is found in Sheehan, *Seeds of Extinction.* While Sheehan's study often has been criticized for suggesting that Jeffersonians offered the Indian a helping hand, he focuses on the philosophy of the age rather than on the policies adopted by these men, which often ran contrary to their philosophy.

3. For the preemption act of 1813, see Malcolm J. Rohrbough, *The Land Office Business: The Settlement and Administration of the American Public Lands, 1789–1837* (New York: Oxford University Press, 1968: reprint Belmont, Calif.: Wadsworth Publishing, 1990), 50; Robertson, *Conquest by Law,* 30–44.

4. Rohrbough, *Land Office Business,* 21.

5. Ibid., 33–34. For Madison's report, see "The Georgia Land Claims," February 14, 1803, in *Annals of Congress, Appendix, Senate and House,* 7th Congress, 2nd session, 1342–52.

6. Green, *Politics of Indian Removal,* 73.

7. Jefferson to Congress, January 18, 1803, in *Annals of Congress, The Senate,* 7th Congress, 2nd session, 24–25.

8. Prucha has the best discussion of the trading house or factory system: Prucha, *American Indian Policy in the Formative Years,* 46–49.

9. Jefferson's views are further discussed in the main text below based on the same source: Jefferson to Congress, January 18, 1803, *Annals of Congress, The Senate,* 7th Congress, 2nd session, 24–27. These views are expressed again with little change in a letter to Governor William Henry Harrison, dated February 27, 1803, in *Territorial Papers of the United States,* 18 vols. (Washington, D.C.: Government Printing Office, 1934–62), 7 (*Indiana*): 88–92.

10. Jefferson to Jackson, February 3, 1803, in *The Writings of Thomas Jefferson,* ed. Andrew A. Lipscomb, 20 vols. (Washington, D.C.: Thomas Jefferson Memorial Association, 1903–1904), 10:358–60. Jefferson warned Hawkins not to side with the Indians on land issues in a personal letter. For Jefferson's views, see ibid., 360–65.

11. Jefferson to Harrison, February 27, 1803, in *Territorial Papers of the United States,* 7 (*Indiana*): 88–92.

12. For a good overview of how Jefferson and his western agents tied removal to Louisiana primarily from secondary sources, see Anthony F. C. Wallace, *Jefferson and the Indians: The Tragic Fate of the First Americans* (Cambridge, Mass.: Harvard University Press, 1999), 241–75. Wallace, however, fails to note the debates in Congress regarding the issue.

13. Senate Debate of October 17, 1803, entitled "The Louisiana Treaty," *Annals of Congress, The Senate,* 8th Congress, 1st session, 29–74.

14. Merrill D. Peterson, *Thomas Jefferson and the New Nation: A Biography* (New York: Oxford University Press, 1970), 771.

15. House Debate, October 25, 1803, entitled "The Louisiana Treaty," *Annals of Congress, The House,* 8th Congress, 1st session, 432–40.

16. "An Account of Louisiana," sent to Congress on November 14, 1803, in ibid., *Appendix,* 1497–1516.

17. Dearborn to Claibourne, Harrison, and St. Clair, February 23, 1802, NARG 107, LS, SW.

18. Dearborn to Hawkins and Wilkinson, June 24, 1801, NARG 107, LS, SW.

19. Glass to Dearborn, June 1801, NARG 107, LS, SW.

20. Dearborn response, June 1801, NARG 107, LS, SW.

21. Dearborn to Claibourne, June 7, 1802, and Dearborn to Wilkinson, Hawkins, and Perkins, April 12, 1802, NARG 107, LS, SW.

22. Dearborn to Hawkins, February 19, 1803, NARG 107, LS, SW.

23. Dearborn to Governor John Milledge, April 2, 1804, NARG 107, LS, SW.

24. Creek response, Negotiations with the Creeks, NARG 75, 1804, DRNRUT.

25. Dearborn to Hawkins, November 11, 1804, NARG 107, LS, SW.

26. Kappler, *Indian Affairs,* 2:62–63.

27. Saunt, *New Order of Things.* Saunt argues that considerable differences in wealth emerged: the Lower Creeks slowly came to own slaves and plantations, in comparison to the Upper Creeks, who were more involved in hunting, which helps explain the factionalism. See also Green, *Politics of Indian Removal,* 36–41. Dearborn also argued that after the Creeks sold these lands to the United States a fort and trade factory could be established along the Ocmulgee River in the vicinity of what would become Atlanta, which naturally would attract more settlers. See Dearborn to James Wilkinson, Benjamin Hawkins, and Robert Anderson, May 5, 1803, NARG 107, LS, SW.

28. "Minutes," December 12, 1801, NARG 75, DRNRUT.

29. Jefferson to the Choctaw Nation, January 1804, NARG 107, LS, SW.

30. Dearborn to Robertson and Dinsmoor, March 20, 1805, NARG 107, LS, SW.

31. Richard White argues that this factionalism would become increasingly obvious by 1820, when mixed-bloods (who were developing herds and needed grazing land) opposed selling land and moving to Indian Territory and full-bloods (who utilized the hunt as an important part of their economy) seemed more willing to sell: White, *The Roots of Dependency: Subsistence, Environment, and Social Change among the Choctaws, Pawnees, and Navajos* (Lincoln: University of Nebraska Press, 1983), 64–147.

32. The list is written into the agreement: Kappler, *Indian Affairs,* 2:51.

33. Arthur H. DeRosier, Jr., *The Removal of the Choctaw Indians* (Knoxville: University of Tennessee Press, 1970), 31; White, *Roots of Dependency,* 95–96.

34. DeRosier, *The Removal of the Choctaw Indians,* 32.

35. Robertson, "Journal of Commissioners," 1805, NARG 75, DRNRUT.

36. Dearborn to Chief Page Colbert, February 21, 1806, and Dearborn to Robertson, Meigs, and Thomas Wright, May 27, 1806, NARG 107, LS, SW; "Journal of Commissioners," 1805, NARG 75, DRNRUT. See also Royce, *Indian Land Cessions,* 668–69.

37. McLoughlin, *Cherokee Renascence,* 97–107. See also McLoughlin's map, based upon Charles C. Royce's map, on 28. The various reserve tracts were added to the treaty of 1806, one being given to Cherokee chief spokesman John Hicks. See Kappler, *Indian Affairs,* 2:66–67.

38. Dearborn's discussions and the message of President Jefferson to these Indians, January 2 and 23, 1802, NARG 107, LS, SW.

39. Dearborn to William Henry Harrison, February 23, 1802, NARG 107, LS, SW.

40. Handsome Lake address to the President and Dearborn's reply, March 13, 1802, NARG 107, LS, SW. The story of Handsome Lake's regeneration movement is found in Anthony F. C. Wallace, *The Death and Rebirth of the Seneca* (New York: Vintage Books, 1969).

41. The sale in 1802 involved only 640 acres; the government paid $1,200, a reasonably fair price. Kappler, *Indian Affairs,* 2:46.

42. Ibid., 2:68–69.

43. Dearborn to Harrison, June 17, 1802, NARG 107, LS, SW.

44. Dearborn to Harrison, February 21, 1803, NARG 107, LS, SW.

45. Ibid.

46. Robert M. Owens, *Mr. Jefferson's Hammer: William Henry Harrison and the Origins of American Indian Policy* (Norman: University of Oklahoma Press, 2007), 84–86.

47. R. David Edmunds, *The Potawatomis: Keepers of the Fire* (Norman: University of Oklahoma Press, 1978), 166–70, argues that several Potawatomi chiefs were pro-American and willing to negotiate.

48. Dearborn to William Wells, December 24, 1804, NARG 107, LS, SW.

49. Dearborn to Harrison, May 24, 1805, NARG 107, LS, SW; Owens, *Mr. Jefferson's Hammer,* 105.

50. Kappler, *Indian Affairs,* 2:54–56.

51. Royce, *Indian Land Cessions,* 680–81.

52. R. David Edmunds, *The Shawnee Prophet* (Lincoln: University of Nebraska Press, 1983).

53. Jefferson to the Shawnees, February 19, 1807, NARG 107. LS, SW; Jefferson to Secretary of War Dearborn, August 12, 1807, in *Writings of Thomas Jefferson,* 11:324–25.

54. Jefferson's statements to Northwestern Indians, April 1 and November 23, 1808, NARG 107, LS, SW.

55. Richard White has an excellent discussion of the way chiefs were manipulated: *Middle Ground,* 494–517. See also Owens, *Mr. Jefferson's Hammer,* 128–54.

56. The figure comes from Wallace, *Jefferson and the Indians,* 239.

57. This was a major village at the time of the Fox Wars in the 1730s. See Edmunds and Peyser, *Fox Wars,* 121, 189.

58. Helen Hornbeck Tanner, *Atlas of Great Lakes Indian History* (Norman: University of Oklahoma Press, 1987), map 20 (after 97).

59. Wilkins and Lomawaima, *Uneven Ground,* 56.

CHAPTER 7. THE GREAT LAND GRAB

1. For biographies of Tecumseh and the Shawnee Prophet, see R. David Edmunds, *Tecumseh and the Quest for Indian Leadership* (Boston: Little, Brown, 1984), and *Shawnee Prophet.*

2. The British minister to the United States, David M. Erskine, negotiated the agreement without the authority to do so. See the discussion in Reginald Horsman, *The Causes of the War of 1812* (New York: A. B. Barnes, 1962).

3. Eustis to Harrison, July 15, 1809, NARG 107, LS, SW.

4. Edmunds, *Tecumseh,* 78–79.

5. Horsman, *Expansion and American Indian Policy,* 165.

6. Owens has argued that the treaties at Fort Wayne "represent the zenith of Harrison's negotiating style": Owens, *Mr. Jefferson's Hammer,* 188–210 (quotation on 204); see also Kappler, *Indian Affairs,* 2:73–74.

7. Madison's message to "The Senate and House of Representatives of the United States," January 3, 1810, in *A Compilation of the Messages and Papers of the Presidents, 1789–1902,* ed. James D. Richardson, 10 vols. (New York: Bureau of National Literature and Art, 1904), 1:463.

8. Secretary Eustis to Harrison, October 26, 1810, NARG 107, LS, SW.

9. Madison Proclamation, October 27, 1810, in *Compilation of the Messages and Papers,* 1:465–66.

10. For a discussion of the War Hawks, see Horsman, *Causes of the War of 1812.* The best new social history of the war is Alan Taylor, *The Civil War of 1812: American Citizens, British Subjects, Irish Rebels, and Indian Allies* (New York: Vintage, 2011).

11. Secretary Eustis to Harrison, October 26, 1810, NARG 207, LS, SW.

12. Secretary Eustis to Silas Dinsmoor, April 20, 1811, NARG 207, LS, SW.

13. Taylor has a long discussion of the impact of Indian raids: Taylor *Civil War of 1812,* 204–209.

14. Quoted from Edmunds, *Tecumseh,* 132.

15. Eustis to Harrison, July 11, 17, 18, and 20, 1811, NARG 107, LS, SW. A second order to attack the town was sent out by the secretary of war on September 18, 1811: ibid. For a study of the conflict, see Alvin M. Jortner, *The Gods of Prophetstown: The Battle of Tippecanoe and the Holy War for the American Frontier* (New York: Oxford University Press, 2012); Owens, *Mr. Jefferson's Hammer,* 213–14.

16. Edmunds, *Tecumseh,* 135–60.

17. Secretary Eustis to Harrison, December 25, 1811, NARG 107, LS, SW.

18. Eustis to Harrison, January 16, 1812, NARG 107, LS, SW.

19. Horsman, *Causes of the War of 1812.* Taylor focuses on biography, contending that it was a "civil" war in that Great Britain believed that "subjects" owed allegiance to the Crown for life and that those who became "citizens" of the United States were simply deserters: Taylor, *Civil War of 1812,* 4–10.

20. Horsman, *Causes of the War of 1812,* 161–67.

21. Taylor, *Civil War of 1812,* 204–10.

22. Ibid., 236–46; Rohrbough, *Land Office Business,* 47.

23. Rohrbough, *Land Office Business,* 65; Hull to Secretary of War, April 25, 1811, in *Territorial Papers of the United States,* 10 (*Michigan Territory*): 355–56.

24. Saunt, *New Order of Things,* 234–35.

25. Ibid., 149–52; Green, *Politics of Indian Removal,* 40–42.

26. Bruce G. Trigger and Wilcomb E. Washburn, eds., *The Cambridge History of the Native Peoples of the Americas,* 2 vols. (New York: Cambridge University Press, 1996), 1:497; Saunt, *New Order of Things,* 258–64.

27. Holmes to the Secretary of War, June 29, 1812, and Holmes to James Wilkinson, July 22, 1812, in *Territorial Papers of the United States,* 6 (*Mississippi*): 297, 298–300.

28. Robert V. Remini, *Andrew Jackson and His Indian Wars* (New York: Penguin Books, 2002), 38–60.

29. McLoughlin, *Cherokee Renascence,* 192–93. The military history side of the story is found in Remini, *Andrew Jackson and His Indian Wars,* 66–67; Jackson to Thomas Pinckney, January 9, 1814, in Sam B. Smith and Harriet Chappell Owsley, eds., *The Papers of Andrew Jackson,* 17 vols. (Knoxville: University of Tennessee Press, 1980), 3:12–13.

30. Jackson to Blount, January 2, 1814, in Smith and Owsley, eds., *The Papers of Andrew Jackson,* 3:5.

31. Jackson to his wife, Rachel, April 1, 1814, in ibid., 3:54–55; Remini, *Andrew Jackson,* 78–79.

32. Jackson to Colonel John Williams, in Smith and Owsley, eds., *The Papers of Andrew Jackson,* 3:73–74 (emphasis added).

33. Meigs to Edward Tiffin, January 1, 1815, in *Territorial Papers of the United States,* 8 (*Indiana*): 339–40.

34. "Journal of Proceedings of Peace Talks," August 8–September 5, 1815, NARG 75, DRNRUT. Harrison's instructions for the talks are found in Crawford to Harrison, Duncan McArthur, and John Graham, June 9, 1815, NARG 75, DRNRUT. The Shawnee Prophet returned from Canada to live in the United States and followed his people into Kansas, where he died in 1836. Owens, *Mr. Jefferson's Hammer,* 247.

35. Crawford to General Duncan AcArthur, February 16, 1816, NARG 107, LS, SW.

36. "Lewis Cass," in James Grant Wilson and John Fiske, eds., *Appleton's Cyclopaedia of American Biography,* 6 vols. (New York: D. Appleton, 1888), 1:552–53.

37. See the treaty in Kappler, *Indian Affairs,* 2:101–108.

38. Secretary of War John C. Calhoun to Cass, March 23 and July 30, 1817, NARG 107, LS, SW; Cass and Duncan McArthur to Secretary of War, September 18, 1818, NARG 75, DRNRUT; Kappler, *Indian Affairs,* 2:100–108.

39. Calhoun to Cass, October 17, 1817, NARG 107, LS, SW.

40. Cass to Calhoun, September 30, 1819, NARG 75, DRNRUT.

41. Journal of a Council with the Winnebago at Green Bay, July 18, 1828 (council date August 21), NARG 75, DRNRUT.

42. Secretary of War Calhoun to Cass, June 1, 1819, NARG 107, LS, SW.

43. Secretary of War William H. Crawford to Coffee, Rhea, and McKee, May 20, 1816, including a journal of the negotiations, NARG 75, DRNRUT; see also DeRosier, *Removal of the Choctaw Indians,* 37; Kappler, *Indian Affairs,* 2:94–95.

44. McLoughlin, *Cherokee Renascence,* 214–17.

45. Ibid., 229.

46. Secretary of War George Graham to Jackson, McMin, and Meriwether, May 16, 1817, NARG 75, DRNRUT.

47. Secretary of War to Jackson, January 13, 1817, NARG 75, DRNRUT.

48. McLoughlin, *Cherokee Renascence,* 229; John K. Mahon, *History of the Second Seminole War, 1835–1842* (Gainesville: University of Florida Press, 1967), 24–25.

49. McLoughlin has a good discussion of the Cherokees in the West: McLoughlin, *Cherokee Renascence,* 217–21.

50. Ibid., 230.

51. McLoughlin concludes that Cherokee leaders signed the treaty only under the belief that the third option was available: ibid., 231. See Kappler, *Indian Affairs,* 2:96–100.

52. Calhoun to Cass, July 30, 1817, and Calhoun to McMin, March 16, 1818, NARG 107, LS, SW. In the euphoria over the treaty Indian agent Meigs hired several men to assist in the Cherokee removal, including young Samuel Houston, who later moved to Oklahoma to live with a Cherokee band before fomenting revolution in Texas. Calhoun to Meigs, September 29, 1817, NARG 107, LS, SW.

53. Calhoun to Jackson, McMin, and Meriwether, August 1, 1817, NARG 107, LS, SW.

54. McMin to Calhoun, November 29, 1818, in Robert L. Meriwether, ed., *The Papers of John C. Calhoun,* 28 vols. (Columbia: University of South Carolina Press, 1959–91), 2:316–17.

55. McLoughlin, *Cherokee Renascence,* 232–34; Calhoun council with Cherokee leaders, February 5, 1819, in *Papers of John C. Calhoun,* 2:544–45.

56. Jackson to Monroe, March 4, 1817, in John S. Bassett, ed., *Correspondence of Andrew Jackson,* 7 vols. (Washington, D.C.: Carnegie Institute, 1926–35), 2:277–82.

57. Jackson to Calhoun, August 24, 1819, in *Papers of John C. Calhoun,* 4:271–72 (emphasis in the original).

58. Remini asserts that Jackson's views came from a pragmatic sense that removal was the only solution, since allowing the Indians to stay would lead to extinction: Remini, *Andrew Jackson,* 277–81.

59. Calhoun ordered commissioner David Mitchell to buy any land "too which they may at present be disposed to relinquish": Calhoun to Mitchell, August 4 and October 31, 1817, NARG 107, LS, SW.

60. Calhoun to William Clark and Ninian Edwards, November 1, 1817, NARG 107, LS, SW.

61. Kappler, *Indian Affairs,* 2:119–21. While the Miami Indians signed this treaty, other agreements would have to be made in the 1820s to quit the claims of other tribes.

62. Kappler, *Indian Affairs,* 2:127–29.

63. Calhoun to Jackson, May 24, 1820, and Jackson to Calhoun, June 19, 1820, in *Papers of Andrew Jackson,* 5:137–38 and 196–97.

64. DeRosier, *Removal of the Choctaw Indians,* 62–63; Kingsbury to Jackson, October 18, 1820, in *Papers of John C. Calhoun,* 5:401–402.

65. Jackson and Thomas Hind's "Treaty Journal," at Doak Stands, August 20–October 18, 1820, NARG 75, DRNRUT.

66. Kappler, *Indian Affairs,* 2:138–39.

67. "Journal of Negotiations with the Seminoles," August 30, 1823, NARG 75, DRNRUT.

68. John Missall and Mary Lou Missall, *The Seminole Wars: America's Longest Indian Conflict* (Gainesville: University Press of Florida, 2004), 7.

69. Mahon, *History of the Second Seminole War,* 46–47.

70. Green, *Politics of Indian Removal,* 82–91.

71. Kappler, *Indian Affairs,* 2:151–53, 188–91.

72. Monroe Message, December 7, 1824, *Compilation of the Messages and Papers,* 1:817–25 and 2:826–33.

73. Ibid., 2:830.

CHAPTER 8. UNSCABBARDING THE BAYONET

1. A number of states would offer citizenship and voting rights to American Indians, with certain restrictions. Admittedly, these laws came mostly after the period of removal in the 1850s. States adopting such laws included Michigan and Minnesota.

2. Some historians have argued that Jackson enjoyed the company of mixed-bloods. He and his wife did literally adopt a young Indian girl. Ronald Satz makes the argument for Jackson's compassion: Satz, *American Indian Policy in the Jacksonian Era* (Lincoln: University of Nebraska Press, 1975), 9.

3. Jackson Inaugural Address, March 4, 1829, in *Compilation of the Messages and Papers,* 2:1000.

4. The classic study of the acts is Prucha, *American Indian Policy in the Formative Years.*

5. John Quincy Adams, "Oration of the Anniversary Festival of the Pilgrims," in Royce, *Indian Land Cessions*, 2:527.

6. The quotations come from *Fletcher v. Peck*, cited in Robertson, *Conquest by Law*, 36–40; Banner, *How the Indians Lost Their Land*, 174; Ford, *Settler Sovereignty*, 135–37.

7. Eric Kades, "History and Interpretation of the Great Case of *Johnson v. M'Intosh*," *Law and History Review* 19 (March 2001): 67–116; Ford, *Settler Sovereignty*, 135–37. Legal historian N. Bruce Duthu argues that *Johnson v. M'Intosh* "created a legal framework that, at its core, assumed the racial inferiority of Indian people" and further sanctioned the so-called doctrine of discovery: Duthu, *American Indians and the Law*, 73–74. The Supreme Court in 2005 cited the case and agreed with its basic notion that "discovery" by Europeans, and later "conquest," provided legal title to Indian lands for the United States: *Sherrill, New York v. Oneida Indian Nation*. See also Watson, *Buying America from the Indians*, 290–95.

8. Jackson Address, December 8, 1829, in *Compilation of the Messages and Papers*, 2:1019–22.

9. Lewis Cass, "Removal of the Indians," *North American Review* (January 1830): 62–121. Historians have often used Cass's population numbers to represent total Native populations.

10. Satz, *American Indian Policy*, 14–15; DeRosier, *Removal of the Choctaw Indians*, 101–102; Green, *Politics of Indian Removal*, 146.

11. DeRosier, *Removal of the Choctaw Indians*, 100–104; Green, *Politics of Indian Removal*, 146–47.

12. See Ford's excellent discussion of the assumption of state authority over Indian lands in *Settler Sovereignty*, 183–96; Satz, *American Indian Policy*, 3, 18.

13. Various authors and poets also joined the debate. See Satz, *American Indian Policy*, 21–25.

14. DeRosier, *Removal of the Choctaw Indians*, 108.

15. Ibid., 25; Banner, *How the Indians Lost Their Land*, 218.

16. DeRosier, *Removal of the Choctaw Indians*, 26–31.

17. Banner has argued that the legislation was really all about financing removal, which would be costly: Banner, *How the Indians Lost Their Land*, 217.

18. Quotations from Clara Sue Kidwell, *Choctaws and Missionaries in Mississippi, 1818–1918* (Norman: University of Oklahoma Press, 1995), 133.

19. DeRosier, *Removal of the Choctaw Indians*, 116–19.

20. Ibid., 122–24; Kidwell, *Choctaws and Missionaries*, 136–41.

21. DeRosier, *Removal of the Choctaw Indians*, 124–25.

22. Ibid., 133–35, 148–58. The estimate of 2,500 deaths, and the description of its impact, comes from Sandra Faiman-Silva, *Choctaws at the Crossroads: The Political Economy of Class and Culture in the Oklahoma Timber Region* (Lincoln: University of Nebraska Press, 1997), 19.

23. Ibid., 156–67; see also *Correspondence on the Subject of the Emigration of Indians, between the 30th November, 1831, and 27th December, 1833, with Abstracts of*

Expenditures by Disbursing Agents, 5 vols., Senate Document 512 (Washington, D.C.: Dub Green, 1834).

24. Green, *Politics of Indian Removal,* 148–51, 169–73.

25. Ibid., 180–84.

26. Arrell Morgan Gibson, *The Chickasaw* (Norman: University of Oklahoma Press, 1971), 171–80.

27. Banner, *How the Indians Lost Their Land,* 218–19.

28. See the arguments in Wilkins and Lomawaima, *Uneven Ground,* 56–63.

29. Banner, *How the Indians Lost Their Land,* 220–23.

30. McLoughlin, *Cherokee Renascence,* 438.

31. Ibid., 450.

32. Wilkins, *Cherokee Tragedy,* 260–61.

33. Ibid., 268–90.

34. Patrick J. Jung, *The Black Hawk War of 1832* (Norman: University of Oklahoma Press, 2008), 17–50. See also Roger L. Nichols, *Black Hawk and the Warrior's Path* (Arlington Heights, Ill.: Harlan Davidson, 1992).

35. Jung, *Black Hawk War,* 56–59; Gary Clayton Anderson, *Kinsmen of Another Kind: Dakota-White Relations in the Upper Mississippi Valley, 1650–1862* (Lincoln: University of Nebraska Press, 1984), 134–35. Part of the reason for the unwillingness of many Sac and Fox Indians to attend the meeting was that Eastern Sioux warriors had killed ten of their delegates who were traveling to Prairie du Chien.

36. Jung, *Black Hawk War,* 59–63.

37. Quotation from ibid., 63 (emphasis in the original).

38. Ibid., 78–83.

39. Ibid., 84–86, 96–119.

40. Royce, *Indian Land Cessions,* 736.

41. William Ewing, "Journal of Proceedings, Treaty of Chicago, September 10, 1833," NARG 75, DRNRUT.

42. Oneida Spokesman, Journal of a Treaty with the New York Indians, August 31, 1836, NARG 75, DRNRUT.

43. Dodge to Harris, August 7, 1837, NARG 75, DRNRUT; Royce, *Indian Land Cessions,* 766. The challenge came in the form of a lawsuit filed by the State of Minnesota demanding that Chippewa fishing rights be abrogated. The Supreme Court ruled in favor of the Indians in 1998.

44. Wool's role in the Cherokee Removal is debated. Those who generally see Wool as a humanitarian include Grant Foreman, *Indian Removal: The Emigration of the Five Civilized Tribes of Indians,* rev. ed. (Norman: University of Oklahoma Press, 1972); Francis Paul Prucha, *The Sword of the Republic: The United States Army on the Frontier, 1783–1846* (Bloomington: Indiana University Press, 1965); and Harwood E. Hinton, "The Military Career of John Ellis Wool, 1812–1863" (Ph.D. dissertation, University of Wisconsin, 1960). A new critic of Wool, suggesting that he was "no humanitarian but a professional soldier," is Laurence M. Hauptman, "General John E. Wool in Cherokee Country, 1836–1837: A Reinterpretation," *Georgia Historical Quarterly* 85 (Spring 2001): 1–26.

45. Wool had a list of the heads of the families, which included dependents. See Ledger of Cherokees Receiving Food, 1836, Papers of John E. Wool, State Library of New York, Albany (hereinafter Wool Papers).

46. Wool to Secretary of War Lewis Cass, July 19, 1836, Wool Papers. In spring 1837 the War Department adopted a plan, recommended by Wool, for using volunteer troops from "a point distant from the scene of operations" or volunteers from states other than Georgia, Alabama, and North Carolina. Secretary Joel Poinsett to Wool, marked "private," May 18, 1837, Wool Papers.

47. John Ridge to Jackson, June 30, 1836, Wool Papers (emphasis in the original).

48. General Order No. 46, September 11, 1836, Wool Papers.

49. Reports of dispossession are too numerous to list. For a few, see Major C. H. Nelson to Wool, September 13, 1836, Catharine Vaught to Major Benjamin Currey, October 11, 1836, John Bell to Committee on Indian Affairs, November 20, 1836, Nathaniel Smith to Wool, May 4, 1837, and C. D. Terhune to Wool, May 6, 1837, Wool Papers.

50. Smith to Harris, May 10, 1837, NARG 75, Special Files No. 31; Captain Edward Buffington to Wool, April 30 and May 8, 1837, Wool Papers.

51. The proceedings of the court and its handling of Creek prisoners are found in the Wool Papers.

52. Dunlap to Bishop, July 28, 1836, Colonel John Byrd to Wool, April 17, 1837, and Lieutenant Edward Deas to Wool, April 20, 1837, NARG 75, Special Files No. 31. Colonel Bishop, a lackey of Georgia governor Wilson Lumpkin, wrote several letters describing the purported role of the Georgia Guard, which he argued was to protect Major Ridge and his party from assassination by the Ross party. These letters are in private hands but can be viewed at www.roots web.ancestry.com/~gachatto/corr/cherokee.htm.

53. Wool asked for a "Court of Inquiry" to defend himself. Embarrassed, the new secretary of war Joel Poinsett twice refused. After Wool acquired the assistance of his friend Lewis Cass, who had fought with him in the War of 1812, the court was finally convened. The governor of Alabama, content with getting Wool removed, declared that he had no evidence against the general; Wool was exonerated. Wool to Miss Warren, December 20, 1836, Adjutant General R. Jones to Wool, July 26, 1837, Poinsett to Wool, July 27 and August 11, 1837, Wool Papers. The court's decision was published as "Proceedings of Court of Inquiry," 25th Congress, House of Representatives, 2nd session, Document 82.

54. Captain John Page to Major General Winfield Scott, July 13, 1838, and Nathaniel Smith to Scott, September 21, 1838, NARG 393, LR, Department of the East (hereinafter Scott Correspondence).

55. Wilkins, *Cherokee Tragedy,* 296–97; General Order No. 74, Wool Papers.

56. Major General Alexander McComb to General Scott, April 1, 1838, NARG 393, Scott Correspondence.

57. General Scott Order No. 25, May 17, 1838, NARG 393, Scott Correspondence.

58. Captain Thomas J. Caldwell to Lieutenant Colonel Charles S. Lovell, March 12, 1838, NARG 393, Scott Correspondence.

59. Wilkins, *Cherokee Tragedy,* 317.

60. Colonel William Lindsay to Secretary of War Poinsett, March 26, 1838, NARG 393, Scott Correspondence.

61. Major B. M. Venables to Scott, May 28, 1838, NARG 393, Scott Correspondence.

62. General Abraham Eustis puts the number of Indians captured in North Carolina at just over 3,000: letter to Col. Worth, June 24, 1838, NARG 393, Scott Correspondence. Colonel Lindsay put the number of Cherokees taken from Alabama at 1,500: Lindsay to Scott, June 24, 1838, NARG 393, Scott Correspondence. There were 3,636 Cherokees at Ross's Landing on June 9, 1838, all from the "Middle District"; but two or more other camps housed Indians from that district, one housing least 900.

63. Captain A. S. Derrick to Captain W. S. Worth, May 28, 1838, NARG 393, Scott Correspondence. Some Indians fought the troops, mostly by hand because they had no guns to speak of. On one occasion a Cherokee woman attacked a trooper with a "large stick." When the trooper beat her, the news reached headquarters, where an investigation was ordered. See Derrick to Brigadier General Curtis, June 4, 1838, NARG 393, Scott Correspondence.

64. Colonel Lindsey to Colonel Worth, June 2, 1838, in ibid.; Wilkins, *Cherokee Tragedy,* 322.

65. John Drew, who was with this party that arrived in the West in August, reported that the change in environment "caused them to die in great numbers shortly after their arrival in the West." Later evidence suggests that the culprit was malaria. See Nathaniel Smith to Scott, June 18, 1838, NARG 393, Scott Correspondence.

66. Poinsett to Scott, June 27, 1838, NARG 393, Scott Correspondence.

67. For the "bacon riot" at Fort Delancy and the subsequent decision for bacon "to be issued to Indians," see Lieutenant George Montgomery to Lieutenant J. McKay, May 23, 1838, NARG 393, Scott Correspondence.

68. Wilkins lists just four camps (the number listed in a military report), but a fifth camp was kept in North Carolina: Wilkins, *Cherokee Tragedy,* 320.

69. Sick Report at Eastern Camps, July 1838, Report of Sick at Camp Ross, July 17, 1838, Report of Sick at Ridge Encampment, July 31, 1838, Monthly Report of Sick at Fort Prague, Alabama, July 31, 1838, Monthly Report of Sick at Bedwell Spring, July 1831, and Report of Jonathan L. Hooker to Major M. Wilson, August 31, 1838, NARG 393, Scott Correspondence.

70. Quotation and description of the caravan from Wilkins, *Cherokee Tragedy,* 324–25.

71. Mahon, *History of the Second Seminole War,* 76–77.

72. Missall and Missall, *Seminole Wars,* 13, 87, 105, 117. For the best biography of Wild Cat, see Susan A. Miller, *Coacoochee's Bones: A Seminole Saga* (Lawrence: University Press of Kansas, 2003).

73. Missall and Missall, *Seminole Wars,* 127–29, 135, 141, 143, 149, 205. Osceola was eventually captured in 1837 and died in prison, while Wild Cat was

first captured then made an incredibly daring escape and was tricked into captivity once more in 1841.

74. Prucha, *American Indian Policy in the Formative Years*.

CHAPTER 9. THE WESTERN DOMAIN

1. The early history of Plains Indians, the adaptation to the horse, and intertribal relations are covered in Calloway, *One Vast Winter Count*, 267–312.

2. Section 1 of the Intercourse Act of 1834 reads as follows: "All that part of the United States west of the Mississippi, and not within the states of Missouri and Louisiana, or the territory of Arkansas, and also, that part of the United States east of the Mississippi river, and not within any state to which the Indian title has not been extinguished, for the purposes of this act, be taken and deemed to be the Indian Country." All thirty sections of the law are found at *4 United States Statutes at Large*, 729. the final version is debated in *House Journal*, 23rd Congress, 1st session, 645, 833, 852, 869.

3. See Jay H. Buckley, *William Clark: Indian Diplomat* (Norman: University of Oklahoma Press, 2008).

4. Arnoldo De León and Kenneth L. Stewart, *Tejanos and the Numbers Game: A Socio-Historical Interpretation from the Federal Census, 1850–1900* (Albuquerque: University of New Mexico Press, 1989); Galen D. Greaser and Jesús de la Teja, "Quieting Title to Spanish and Mexican Land Grants in the Trans-Nueces: The Bourland and Miller Commission, 1850–1852," *Southwestern Historical Quarterly* 95 (April 1992): 445–64; Suzanne Starling, *Land Is the Cry: Warren Angus Ferris, Pioneer Texas Surveyor and Founder of Dallas County* (Austin: Texas State Historical Association, 1998).

5. Southern Plains Indian populations began to decline after 1780 when the first reliably reported smallpox epidemic occurred. Others appeared at nearly-twenty year intervals, in 1800, 1818, and again in the 1830s and 1840s. Elizabeth Fenn has argued that a vast epidemic ravaged virtually all of North America during the 1770s and early 1780s: Fenn, *Pox Americana*; Anderson, *The Indian Southwest*, 15–16, 40, 108, 180, 197, 219–20.

6. Many good biographies of Austin are available, including Gregg Cantrell, *Stephen F. Austin: Empresario of Texas* (New Haven: Yale University Press, 1999).

7. Stephen L. Hardin, *Texas Iliad: A Military History of the Texas Revolution* (Austin: University of Texas Press, 1994); Paul D. Lack, *The Texas Revolutionary Experience: A Political and Social History, 1835–1836* (College Station: Texas A&M University Press, 1992).

8. Kelley F. Himmel, *The Conquest of the Karankawas and Tonkawas, 1821–1859* (College Station: Texas A&M University Press, 1999). While some Texas historians assume that they invented the term "rangers," the word itself was long used in the East, probably first applied to the British ship HMS *Ranger,* commissioned in the 1740s.

9. James L. Haley, *Sam Houston* (Norman: University of Oklahoma Press, 2002).

10. Pekka Hämäläinen, *The Comanche Empire* (New Haven: Yale University Press, 2008), uses mostly secondary sources to describe this crucial period. He does make one major error, noting that Lamar defeated Houston for the presidency of the Republic in 1838, which produced a pivotal change in Texas Indian policy. Constitutionally, Houston was unable to run. See 214–38.

11. Gary Clayton Anderson, *The Conquest of Texas: Ethnic Cleansing in the Promised Land* (Norman: University of Oklahoma Press, 2005), 173–84.

12. Ibid.

13. Henderson Yoakum, *History of Texas from the First Settlement in 1685 to Its Annexation to the United States in 1846,* 2 vols. (New York: Redfield, 1855), 2:304–305.

14. Anderson, *Conquest of Texas,* 190–91.

15. On November 28, 2007, Ferdinand Nahimana and Jean Bosco Barayagwiza were given thirty- and thirty-two-year terms respectively for their genocidal rhetoric at Radio Télévision Libre des Mille Colline in Rwanda. They were acquitted of genocide. The court concluded that the linkage between the radio announcers and the actual men who massacred Tutsis was difficult to document, as would have been the case with President Lamar.

16. Houston's attempts to negotiate peace can be followed in Anderson, *Conquest of Texas,* 198–225.

17. Kappler, *Indian Affairs,* 2:253, 348–94.

18. Royce, *Indian Land Cessions,* 708–709, 778, 818; White, *Roots of Dependency,* 200–211. A good discussion of the various treaties is found in William E. Unrau, *The Kansas Indians: A History of the Wind People, 1673–1873* (Norman: University of Oklahoma Press, 1971).

19. Robert A. Trennert, Jr., *Alternative to Extinction: Federal Indian Policy and the Beginnings of the Reservation System, 1846–1851* (Philadelphia: Temple University Press, 1975), 30–31.

20. Fitzpatrick to D. D. Mitchell, May 22, 1849, NARG 75, LR, UPA. For an excellent account of how the Cheyennes and Arapahos viewed this invasion, and tried to protect their resources, see Elliott West, *Contested Plains: Indians, Goldseekers, and the Rush to Colorado* (Lawrence: University Press of Kansas, 1998).

21. Anderson, *Kinsmen of Another Kind,* 177–202.

22. Ibid., 184–87.

23. Historians have viewed the two 1851 treaties with the Dakota Sioux as a monstrous conspiracy. Anderson, *Kinsmen of Another Kind,* 184–99; William Watts Folwell, *A History of Minnesota,* 4 vols. (St. Paul: Minnesota Historical Society Press, 1921–30), 1:303–304.

24. Folwell, *History of Minnesota,* 1:305–309. See also Melissa L. Meyer, *The White Earth Tragedy: Ethnicity and Dispossession at a Minnesota Anishinaabe Reservation, 1889–1920* (Lincoln: University of Nebraska Press, 1994).

25. Brooke to General Winfield Scott, July 19, 1849, in NARG 393, LS, WDD, 1830, 1848–53.

26. Anderson, *Conquest of Texas,* 246–58.

27. Ibid., 256.

28. Ibid., 262–64.

29. Trennert, *Alternate to Extinction,* 155–57.

30. "Articles of a Treaty Made and Concluded at Fort Laramie," in NARG 393, LR, Fort Laramie. Lengthy discussions of the negotiation are found in Douglas C. McChristian, *Fort Laramie: Military Bastion of the High Plains* (Norman: Arthur H. Clark, 2008), 52–60; and R. Eli Paul, *Blue Water Creek and the First Sioux War, 1854–1856* (Norman: University of Oklahoma Press, 2004), 13–17.

31. "Articles of a Treaty Made and Concluded at Fort Laramie," NARG 393, LR, Fort Laramie; Michael L. Tate, *Indians and Emigrants: Encounters on the Overland Trails* (Norman: University of Oklahoma Press, 2006).

32. John Whitfield to Superintendent of Indian Affairs, July 1, 1855, NARG 75, LR, UAA; Kappler, *Indian Affairs,* 2:445–47; West, *Contested Plains,* 87–88.

33. Several firsthand accounts by Man Afraid Of His Horses, Little Thunder, Big Partisan, Paul Carrey, James Bordeaux, and Captain William Hoffman are available, as well as the "Statement of Mr. Obridge Allen," which contains Grattan's comments. NARG 393, LR, DWWD. On who fired the first shot, see Bordeaux to Whitfield, August 29, 1854, Colonel Edward Steptoe to Jefferson Davis, September 29, 1854, Second Lieutenant H. B. Fleming to Lieutenant Colonel William Hoffman, November 29, 1854, Hoffman to Major N. F. Page, November 19, 1854, and A. Cummings to Manypenny, March 8, 1855, NARG 75, LR, UPA.

34. Paul, *Blue Water Creek,* 88–110; Harney to AAG Lieutenant Colonel S. Thomas, September 26, 1855, NARG 393, LS, Sioux Expedition, DWWD. Manypenny's memoir notes that the entire command was "not without stimulant, the interpreter being in such condition that he talked to the Indians in a very indiscreet manner . . . that the soldiers had come there to 'cut the d——d hearts out of them'": George Manypenny, *Our Indian Wards* (1880; reprint, New York: Decapo, 1972), 157.

35. Council notes in Twiss to Manypenny, October 18, 1854, and Council Notes in Jefferson Davis to the President, May 10, 1856, NARG 75, LR, UPA. See also Gary Clayton Anderson, *Sitting Bull and the Paradox of Lakota Nationhood* (New York: HarperCollins, 1996; reprint, Pearson-Longman, 2007), 15.

36. Paul, *Blue Water Creek,* 61.

37. Paul notes that Harney once beat a female household slave named Hannah to death: Paul, *Blue Water Creek,* 164.

38. Twiss's responses are found in Twiss to Colonel William H. Hoffman, March 6 and September 15, 1856, NARG 393, LR, Fort Laramie.

39. The Cheyenne side of the story, including the report that a chief had been sent out to negotiate, is found in White Antelope, High Back Wolf, Tall Bear, and Starved Bear to Colonel John Haverty, October 28, 1857, NARG 75, LR, UAA. See also Whitfield to the Superintendent of Indian Affairs, August 15 and Colonel Sumner to Agent Robert C. Miller, August 19, 1857, NARG 75, LR, UAA. The best description of the campaign is William Y. Chalfant, *Cheyennes*

and Horse Soldiers: The 1857 Expedition and the Battle of Solomon's Fork (Norman: University of Oklahoma Press, 1989).

40. Whitfield to Superintendent of Indian Affairs, August 15, 1855, NARG 75, UAA.

41. Bent to John Haverty, December 11, 1857, Robert Miller to Charles Mix, April 30 and July 30, 1858, and Bent to Superintendent A. M. Robinson, August 4, 1858, NARG 75, UAA.

42. Kappler, *Indian Affairs,* 2:451. Congress appropriated $5,000 for these negotiations in 1853. Mitchell to Manypenny, April 4, 1853, NARG 75, LR, UPA.

43. Kappler, *Indian Affairs,* 2:518–20. The tract of land received by the Winnebagos was eighteen miles square. Folwell, *History of Minnesota,* 1:303.

44. The sequence of these treaties is best followed in Kappler, *Indian Affairs,* 2:451–83, 515–18, 545–52.

45. Anderson, *Kinsmen of Another Kind,* 228–31.

46. Ibid., 236–60.

47. Wood to Post Adjutant, July 27, 1857, NARG 94, LR, AGO. See also Anderson, *Conquest of Texas,* 292–95.

48. Anderson, *Conquest of Texas,* 294–95.

49. See, for example, the Austin *Southern Intelligencer,* April 14, 1858, and the *Dallas Herald,* April 1 and July 25, 1858.

50. Anderson, *Conquest of Texas,* 304.

51. The best account of the attack, a classic in Texas Ranger lore, is found in Ford to Runnels, May 22, 1858, Governor's Papers, Texas State Archives, Austin.

52. The manifesto can be found in the Austin *Southern Intelligencer,* May 25, 1859.

53. Anderson, *Conquest of Texas,* 307, 320.

54. Raymond E. Estep, ed., "Lieutenant William E. Burnet Letters: Removal of the Texas Indians and the Founding of Fort Cobb: Part II," *Chronicles of Oklahoma* 38 (1960): 371–74.

55. Neighbors to his wife, August 8, 1859, Neighbors Papers, Eugene C. Barker Library, University of Texas, Austin.

56. Anderson, *Conquest of Texas,* 310–11.

57. Twiss to A. B. Greenwood, August 16, 1859, NARG 75, LR, UPA.

CHAPTER 10. THE STEALING OF A GOLDEN LAND

1. For the trail experience, see Tate, *Indians and Emigrants.*

2. Cook's first attempt at "interpolation" came in a study entitled "The American Invasion, 1848–1879," published as vol. 23 of *Ibero-Americano* (quotation on 7). For his rather extensive use of newspapers as sources, in particular the *Sacramento Union, San Francisco Bulletin,* and *Alta California,* see the reprint, Sherburne F. Cook, *The Conflict between the California Indians and White Civilization* (Berkeley: University of California Press, 1976), 261–62 and 351–56. These population numbers are restated with minor changes in Sherburne F. Cook, *The*

Population of the California Indians, 1769–1970 (Berkeley: University of California Press, 1976), 44–45.

3. Days after reaching California, agents G. W. Barbour and O. M. Wozencraft concluded that the populations ranged in the hundreds of thousands, but they quickly rethought these numbers. After entering the region south of the American River, they settled on a figure of 50,000 for Indians south of San Francisco. The report of 80,000 was a compromise. The agent stated that he had heard several estimates, ranging from "forty thousand to two hundred thousand." He added that "these vast discrepancies show a great want of correct information." See Barbour and Wozencraft to the Commissioner of Indian Affairs (hereinafter CIA), March 5, 1851, and Adam Johnston to CIA, January 30, 1852, NARG 75, LR, California Superintendency (hereinafter CS).

4. Two historians who have looked at the subject of Indian labor agree that California Indians were generally too valuable as laborers to become the victims of mass murder. See Albert L. Hurtado, *Indian Survival on the California Frontier* (New Haven: Yale University Press, 1988); and William J. Bauer, *We Were All Like Migrant Workers Here: Work, Community, and Memory on California's Round Valley Reservation, 1850–1941* (Chapel Hill: University of North Carolina Press, 2009).

5. Cook, "The American Invasion, 1848–1879," in Cook, *Conflict between the California Indians and White Civilization*, 268–74, 352.

6. This argument is found in Benjamin Madley, "California's Yuki Indians: Defining Genocide in Native American History," *Western Historical Quarterly* 34 (Autumn 2008): 303–32.

7. For a description of each reservation and rancheria, see Confederation of American Indians, *Indian Reservations: A State and Federal Handbook* (Jefferson, N.C.: McFarland, 1986), 28–74.

8. Douglas letter, October 11,1830, Oregon Historical Quarterly 6 (March 1905): 192; Robert Boyd, *The Coming of the Spirit of Pestilence: Introduced Infectious Diseases and Population Decline among the Northwest Coast Indians, 1774–1874* (Seattle: University of Washington Press, 1999).

9. Sherburne F. Cook, "The Epidemic of 1830–1833 in California and Oregon," *University of California Publications in American Archaeology and Ethnology* 43, no. 3 (1955): 303–25.

10. Cholera was reported in November 1850 by assistant surgeon H. S. Hewitt. The disease had struck along the upper Sacramento River. Hewitt wished to "visit the upper country and observe and treat the cholera which now prevails in that part of California." Another major cholera epidemic hit the Trinity River in the early 1850s. Smallpox cases were reported virtually every year after 1849. W. P. Crenshaw noted that it had become the "greatest scourge" for Indians in the mining district. Hewitt to Lieutenant Colonel J. Hooker, November 8, 1850, George Horatio Derby Journal, October 1849, "Sacramento River," NARG 393, LR, DP, PS; Crenshaw to Thomas J. Henley, December 16, 1854, NARG 75, LR, CS; James J. Rawls, *Indians of California: The Changing Image* (Norman: University of Oklahoma Press, 1984), 175. The Department of Pacific records are

actually the "Division and Department of the Pacific" records in the National Archives.

11. Albert L. Hurtado, *John Sutter: A Life on the North American Frontier* (Norman: University of Oklahoma Press, 2006), 196–203.

12. Assistant Surgeon John G. Griffin to Colonel L. D. Stevenson, June 14, 1847, Stevenson to Colonel R. B. Mason, July 23 and 27 and September 8, 1847, NARG 393, LR, 10th MD.

13. Stevenson to Mason, July 23 and September 7, 1847, Assistant Surgeon R. O. Murray to AAG, August 5, 1847, and Major James Hardie to Lieutenant W. T. Sherman, September 7, 1847, NARG 393, LR, 10th MD.

14. The force included the 2nd Infantry and two companies of the 3rd Artillery. Colonel R. Jones to Mason, October 2, 1848, NARG 393, LR, 10th MD.

15. Derby's four journals (his last was a survey of the lower Colorado River Basin) are being published by the University of Oklahoma Press. While Derby gained fame under the pen name "John P. Squibob" for his humorous renditions of California life, his early life in California as a topographical engineer is not well known. His many columns published in the mid-1850s were brought together as *Phoenixiana; or, Sketches and Burlesques* (New York: D. Appleton, 1856) and became extremely popular reading in the day.

16. The various reports of McKee, Barbour, and Wozencraft are in NARG 75, LR, CA. For the treaties, see Thomas McCorkle, "Intergroup Conflict," in *Handbook of North American Indians,* vol. 8, *California,* ed. William Sturtevant, 694–700 (Washington, D.C.: Smithsonian Institution, 1978).

17. Derby Journal, July 1849, the Mining District, NARG 393, LR, DP, PS.

18. Derby Journal, October 1849, the Sacramento Valley, NARG 393, LR, DP, PS. Hurtado notes that Sutter employed twenty-eight people at Hock Farm besides the Indian laborers, most of whom Derby likely never saw due to their illness: Hurtado, *John Sutter,* 288.

19. Johnston to CIA, September 16, 1851, NARG 75, LR, CS.

20. Wessells report to Kearney, November 14, 1851, NARG 393, LR, DP, PS.

21. McKee to CIA, October 7, 1851, NARG 75, LR, CS.

22. Major Edward Fitzgerald to Hooker, August 27, 1851, and Murray to Captain Henry Day, April 20, 1850, NARG 75, LR, CS. Judah himself was recovering from "chills and fever": Lieutenant Colonel Robert Buchanan to Wool, August 23, 1855, Wool Papers.

23. Cook suggests that the "nadir," or the point where population loss leveled off, came in 1855, but it obviously occurred some four years earlier: Cook, *Population of the California Indians,* 44.

24. Derby mentions 2,000 Sonorans in one camp alone: Derby Journal, July 1849, the Mining District, NARG 393, LR, DP, PS.

25. McKee to E. H. Howard, Kennerly Dobbins, and N. A. Dupern, September 18, 1851, NARG 75, LR, CA.

26. Kroeber notes the "acornless" nature of the mountains: Alfred Kroeber, *Handbook of California Indians* (Washington, D.C.: Smithsonian Institution, 1925), 320–23.

27. The reports of these rescue efforts are found in NARG 393, LR, DP, PS.

28. Thomas L. Tripler to the Surgeon General, July 12, 1853; and Medical Division Letterbook, NARG 393, DP, PS.

29. Tripler to Surgeon General, September 23, 1852, NARG 393, DP, PS.

30. Medical Supply list at Sonoma, 1847, NARG 393, LR, 10th MD; Report of Adam Johnson, 1851 (misfiled 1855) and Crenshaw to Indian Superintendent Thomas J. Henley, December 16, 1854, NARG 75, LR, CS. Despite the decline in malaria after 1851, several hundred Concow Indians who fled from the Round Valley to their homeland near Chico, California, in 1862 quickly contracted the disease when passing through the Sacramento Valley. Bauer, *We Were All Like Migrant Workers Here,* 54.

31. Ryer's efforts confirm much smaller populations. Note that Wozencraft put the number for the same territory at 50,000. Ryer was so successful because, as he understood it, Spanish padres had begun vaccinating Indians well before secularization, so the Indians understood the value of taking the serum. Ryer, reports dated June 1–September 26, 1851, *Senate Executive Document* No. 61, 32nd Congress, 1st session, vol. 9, 19–26.

32. For example, M. J. Vallego to General Stephen Watts Kearny, April 18, 1847, Lieutenant A. F. Smith to Lieutenant Colonel Philip St. George Cooke, March 29, 1847, Cooke to Captain L. S. Turner, March 25, 1847, Testimony of José María Sanches, March 19, 1847, George McKinthy to Captain J. B. Hull, March 13, 1847, John H. Nash to Captain S. F. DuPont, March 1, 1847, and Petition of Citizens of San Jose, February 19, 1847, NARG 393, LR, 10th MD.

33. Hurtado, *John Sutter,* 207–14.

34. See Stevenson's many letters, but especially his reports to Mason for June 16, July 12, and August 11, 1847, NARG 393, LR, 10th MD. A peculiar case regarding the use of commissions came when a sergeant shot and killed an Indian, seemingly on purpose. See Captain Francis Lippitt to Lieutenant Sherman, December 31, 1847, NARG 393, LR, 10th MD.

35. Hardie to Sherman, May 28 and June 1, 1848, NARG 393, LR, 10th MD. For the grossly exaggerated numbers, see L. W. Boggs to Mason, May 22, 1848, NARG 393, LR, 10th MD.

36. Reports from "The Clear Lake Expedition," by Captain Lyon, May 22 and 25, 1850, NARG 393, LR, 10th MD. See also Hurtado, *Indian Survival,* 105–106.

37. Wessells to Major Kearny, November 14, 1851, NARG 393, LR, DP, PS. Indian Superintendent Henley counted 700–800 Pomo Indians about Clear Lake in 1854, working mostly on ranches by this time. See Henley to George Manypenny, October 14, 1854, NARG 75, LR, CS; Kroeber, *Handbook of California Indians,* 237.

38. Wessells to Kearny, November 14, 1851, NARG 393, LR, DP, PS; Henley to Denver, September 28, 1857, and J. Ross Browne Report, June 1857, NARG 75, LR, CS. New agent Simon P. Strong estimated that the entire valley might hold 5,000 Indians in 1856, but he had just arrived and had not traveled through it. He had 200 or 300 under his charge at Nome Cult farm. See Strong to Henley, October 27, 1856, NARG 75, LR, CS.

39. Henley to Manypenny, December 19, 1855, Strong to Henley, June 20, 1856, Report of Labor at Mendocino Reservation, 1856, and J. Ross Browne report, 1857, NARG 75, LR, CS.

40. Kroeber, *Handbook of California Indians,* 16–17. Henley put the number at nearly 1,500 in 1855: Henley to Manypenny, September 19, 1855, NARG 75, LR, CS. McKee's population figures are in McKee to CIA, October 7 and 8, 1851, NARG 75, LR, CS.

41. Williamson to Kearny, November 14, 1851, and Wessells to Hooker, October 15, 1851, NARG 393, LR, DP, PS.

42. Wessells to Hooker, October 5, 1851, NARG 393, LR, DP, PS; James P. Goodall Report, August 30, 1856, NARG 75, LR, CS.

43. Frémont's claim is in a letter to Orlando Brown, June 17, 1850, NARG 75, LR, CS.

44. Derby's Journals, July 5–August 9, 1849, and April 26–June 8, 1850, NARG 393, LR, DP, PS.

45. Keyes to AAG, March 19, April 11, and June 11, 1851, NARG 393, 10th MD. Figures collected by the Indian Office in 1854 include 400 Indians on the San Joaquin, 500 on the Fresno River, 1,000 on Kings River, 500 on Four Creek, 300 on Tule River, and 100 on Kern River. Another thousand still lived around the lakes to the south of this region, again making roughly 4,000 people. See Henley to George Manypenny, August 28, 1854, NARG 75, LR, CS.

46. Barbour to Luke Lea, May 14 and July 28, 1857, NARG 75, LR, CS.

47. Derby Journal, September 22–November 10, 1849, NARG 393, LR, DP, PS.

48. Johnston to CIA, July 6, 1850, Wozencraft to CIA, July 18, 1851, and McKee to Edward Beal, November 1852, NARG 75, LR, CS.

49. Lyon's report on the "Pitt River Expedition" is dated August 1, 1850: NARG 393, LR, DP (emphasis in the original). See Williamson report to Hooker, February 14, 1850, in *Secretary of War Report, Senate Executive Document No. 47,* 31st Congress, 1st session. The report is also found in AAG Irwin McDowell to Smith, April 26, 1850, NARG 393, LR, DP, PS.

50. Report in Wozencraft to CIA, October 14, 1851, NARG 75, LR, CS (emphasis in the original).

51. The state census for 1860 offers a figure of 31,338. See Cook, *Population of the California Indians,* 46.

52. See Smith's reports for March, n.d., and April 11 and 28, 1849, NARG 393, LS, DP, PS. While desertions generally hindered the implementation of this policy, the military had informed miners that they at least should help bring deserters into custody if they were to be left alone on government land; and a number of absent soldiers who went to the mines were turned in. See Mason Proclamation, July 25, 1848, NARG 393, LR, 10th MD.

53. Some challenges to the Intercourse Acts did occur, but they were upheld in the courts. See Stephen Dow Beckham, ed., *Oregon Indians: Voices from Two Centuries* (Corvallis: Oregon State University Press, 2006), 126–30.

54. Paul Kens, "The Frémont Case: Confirming Mexican Land Grants in California," in *Law in the Western United States,* ed. Gordon Morris Bakken (Norman: University of Oklahoma Press, 2000), 326–31. Kens describes California land law as being "in an almost hopeless state of turmoil" (331), which obviously affected any Indian claims.

55. See John Bull petition to Governor Riley, October 28, 1849, NARG 393, LR, 10th MD.

56. Andrew P. Morris, "'Miners' Law': Informal Law in Western Mining Camps," in *Law in the Western United States,* ed. Bakken, 209–11.

57. Riley to Lieutenant Colonel W. G. Freeman, September 20, 1849, NARG 393, LR, DP, PS.

58. See the many reports of Captain Day, such as Day to the AAG, May 16, May 28, July 1, and November 1, 1850, NARG 393, LR, 10th MD; Day to AAG, April 16, 1850, NARG 393, LR, DP, PS; and Wozencraft to CIA, July 12, 1851, NARG 75, LR, CS. See also George Harwood Phillips, *Indians and Indian Agents: The Origins of the Reservation System in California, 1849–1852* (Norman: University of Oklahoma Press, 1997), 37–56.

59. For a careful analysis of the "war," see Phillips, *Indians and Indian Agents,* 37–108; Smith to McDowell, June 30, 1850, and Smith to AG Jones, January 27, 1851, NARG 393, LS, DP, PS.

60. General Riley to Adjutant General Freeman, October 1, 1850, NARG 393, LR, DP, PS.

61. For the debate over volunteers, see William F. Strobridge, *Regulars in the Redwoods: The U.S. Army in Northern California, 1852–1861* (Spokane, Wash.: Arthur H. Clark, 1994), 30–31. See also Phillips, *Indians and Indian Agents,* 61–67; Hurtado, *Indian Survival,* 132–34.

62. These abuses are covered in Hurtado, *Indian Survival.*

63. Rawls, *Indians of California,* 86–94; Bauer, *We Were All Like Migrant Workers,* 51–57.

64. General John Wool responded to the request by noting that he would need "an order from the President" to act. Henley to Manypenny, April 9, 1855, NARG 75, LR, CS.

65. R. W. Wood letter in Edward F. Beale to CIA, November 22, 1852, and Henley to Manypenny, October 4, 1854, NARG 75, LR, CS. Henley spelled Berryessa Valley "Barressa."

66. Rawls mentions the "Hispanic" origin of the practice: Rawls, *Indians of California,* 84–96. I am indebted to my colleague Raphael Folsom at the University of Oklahoma, whose study of northwestern Mexico and the practice of child exchange will soon be published.

67. Ironically, Sutter found it difficult to keep his Native laborers by 1856, because they were getting paid more, in cash, to work for others. Hurtado, *John Sutter,* 308.

68. Henley to Manypenny, October 14, 1854, and Crenshaw to Henley, December 16, 1854, NARG 75, LR, CS.

69. Robert F. Heizer, ed., *The Destruction of the California Indians: A Collection of Documents from the Period 1847 to 1865 in Which Are Described Some of the Things That Happened to Some of the Indians of California* (Santa Barbara: Peregine Smith, 1972).

70. Hurtado, *Indian Survival*, 138–39. See Robert F. Heizer, *The Eighteen Unratified Treaties of 1851–1852 between the California Indians and the United States Government* (Berkeley: University of California, Department of Anthropology, 1972). All eighteen had reservations, as one agreement noted, "set apart and forever held for the sole use and occupation of the said tribe" (treaties in ibid.). See also Phillips, *Indians and Indian Agents*, 68–108; Strobridge, *Regulars in the Redwoods*, 23–25. Bigler's defense of the state's position can be found in Bigler to McKee, April 15, 1852, NARG 75, LR, CS.

71. The corruption was revealed when the man Barbour hired testified that he was ordered to "take receipts for double the number actually delivered, and to make no second delivery." John C. Frémont provided the cattle from his ranch and was likely involved in the scam. Wozencraft testified that he was unaware that many of the cows he purchased were actually resold to miners. See Frémont to Barbour, Mary 19, 1851, Wozencraft Testimony, September 14, 1852, and Statement of Joel H. Brooks, September 21, 1852, NARG 75, LR, CS.

72. Beale to Luke Lea, October 29, 1852, NARG 393, LR, DP, PS. Hitchock's willingness to cooperate with the BIA in implementing the plan, unusual at best, is found in Hitchcock to Hooker, November 29, 1852, NARG 75, LR, CS.

73. For Beale's efforts, see Gerald Thompson, *Edward F. Beale and the American West* (Albuquerque: University of New Mexico Press, 1983), 42–49; Strobridge, *Regulars in the Redwoods*, 52–54. See Confederation of American Indians, *Indian Reservations*, 28–74.

74. The debate over expenditures led to criticism of both Beale and Henley and several investigations. Ultimately it resulted in the dismissal of Henley in 1859.

75. George Harwood Phillips, *"Bring Them under Subjection": California's Tejon Reservation and Beyond, 1852–1864* (Lincoln: University of Nebraska Press, 2004).

76. Beale to Manypenny, February 4, 1854, P. Edward Connor to James Scofield, February 22, 1854, M. B. Lewis to Henley, December 15, 1855, Henley to Manypenny, December 18, 1855, and Henley to Lewis, August 7, 1856, NARG 75, LR, CS.

77. Henley to Manypenny, October 14 and 15 and December 1, 1854, and J. Ross Browne Report, 1857, NARG 75, LR, CS.

78. Henley to Manypenny, January 15, 29, April 9, December 29, 1855, John Sutter to Henley, February 9, 1856, and *Daily Herald* clipping, November 25, 1856, NARG 75, LR, CS.

79. Browne Report, 1857, NARG 75, LR, CS. Browne became a critic of the administration of the reservations two years later, which is impossible to explain. Other historians have also criticized Henley's efforts. See Richard L. Carrico, "San Diego Indians and the Federal Government: Years of Neglect, 1850–1865,"

San Diego Historical Quarterly 26 (Summer 1980): 47–62; and Michael A. Sievers, "Malfeasance or Indirection: Administration of the California Indian Superintendency's Business Affairs," *Southern California Quarterly* 53 (Fall 1974): 277–80.

80. "Report on the Condition and Management of Indians and Reservations in California" (1860), in *Senate Executive Document* 46, Serial 1033, 10. See also Bauer, *We Were All Like Migrant Workers;* and Hurtado, *Indian Survival,* 152.

81. Cook, *Population of the California Indians,* 45.

82. See Judah's many reports for 1855 and 1856, NARG 393, LR, DP, PS.

83. Superintendent Henley blamed the newspapers for what he perceived as unfair criticism. See Henley to C. E. Mix, September 19, 1855, NARG 75, LR, CS.

84. J. Ross Browne's report, 1857, NARG 75, LR, CS. Judah's report is found in General Wool to Colonel Thomas, February 26, 1855, Wool Papers.

85. Walter McDonald, Alex H. Carnelton, George A. Somes, Thomas Munroe, and John G. Suddington to General Wool, January 13, 1855, Wool Papers.

86. Van Dyke to Bigler, May 31, 1852, NARG 75, LR, CS.

87. Lieutenant Colonel Robert Buchanan to Wool, August 23, 1855, Wool Papers.

88. Judah to Buchanan, October 10, 1854, NARG 393, LR, DP, PS.

89. Wool to Lieutenant Colonel Thomas, February 26, 1855, Wool Papers.

90. Two army patrols in the Eel River valley in 1853 found little evidence of penetration by either miners or ranchers. See Lieutenant Hunt to Buchanan, June 25, 1853, and Lieutenant Edward Underwood to Buchanan, July 26, 1853, NARG 393, LR, DP, PS.

91. Petition to Robert White, May 1, 1855, NARG 75, LR, CS.

92. See Henley to J. W. Denver, September 28, October 28, and December 27, 1857, and Vincent E. Gieger to Henley, September 24, 1857, NARG 75, LR, CS. The first phase of the "war" (if it can be called that) or struggle over the winter of 1858–59 can be followed in Madley, "California's Yuki Indians," 316–18. Special agent Browne estimates the number of Indians killed at 150 (ibid., 317).

93. A blow-by-blow account of Jarboe's Ranger activity is found in Lynwood Carranco and Estle Beard, *Genocide and Vendetta: The Round Valley Wars of Northern California* (Norman: University of Oklahoma Press, 1981).

94. Ibid., 90–92; Brigadier General N. S. Clarke to Lieutenant Colonel L. Thomas, October 19, 1858, NARG 393, LR, Department of Oregon; Weller quotation from Madley, "California's Yuki Indians," 320–21.

95. The historians who call it genocide (including Carranco and Beard, Rawls, and Madley) define the act based upon the 1948 Convention. See also Clifford E. Trafzer and Joel R. Hyer, eds., *Exterminate Them!: Written Accounts of the Murder, Rape, and Enslavement of Native Americans during the California Gold Rush* (East Lansing: Michigan State University Press, 2000).

96. Strobridge, *Regulars in the Redwoods,* 139–210. See Major Edward Johnson to Captain William Mackall, August 21, September 16, and October 18, 1859, NARG 393, LR, DP, PS; and "Browne Report," 1858, NARG 75, LR, CS.

97. Theodora Kroeber, *Ishi in Two Worlds: A Biography of the Last Wild Indian in North America* (Berkeley: University of California Press, 1962). See also Gary Scharnhorst, *Bret Harte: Opening the American Literary West* (Norman: University of Oklahoma Press, 2000). This conflict in the 1860s mostly occurred in the wild regions of the Klamath and Trinity River valleys. It is best followed in Rawls, *Indians of California,* 171–81.

98. See the discussion of such groups, which are common to many frontiers, in Belich, *Replenishing the Earth,* 348–51.

99. Good comparisons for the nineteenth century might be Australia, where 80,000 Aborigines were killed in Queensland, or even Algeria, where over 500,000 Native people died as a result of French colonization. These numbers pale in comparison to twentieth-century genocides in central Europe, Cambodia, and South Africa. This was genocide. See Kiernan, *Blood and Soil,* 249–309, 364–92.

100. Madley concludes that up to 20,000 Indians might have inhabited the Round Valley of California in 1850 and only a few hundred were alive ten years later. He argues that no evidence of disease could account for their disappearance, concluding: "So, what killed them?" The argument builds from many other earlier sources, including James Rawls, who unlike Madley fails to give figures but says only that "thousands of California Indians were killed": Madley, "California's Yuki Indians," 309; Rawls, *Indians of California,* 171.

101. Rawls argues that the strongest opposition to killing Indians came in settled areas, especially bigger cities such as San Francisco and Sacramento: Rawls, *Indians of California,* 183.

102. Madley argues that Weller should have known what the rangers were intending to do; Madley, "California's Yuki Indians," 329.

Chapter 11. The "Diminishment" of the Native Domain

1. This figure is determined by analyzing the various population counts for bands found in the Oregon Superintendency records. Superintendent Joel Palmer sent subagents into the various river valleys of the coast and Cascades Mountain region, counting Indians. See his reports in NARG 75, LR, OS.

2. The lands of "Middle Oregon" were purchased from the surviving Indians of the valley in June 1855. The treaty did not stipulate tribal or band names, probably because such organizations had ceased to function. Kappler, *Indian Affairs,* 2:714.

3. E. A. Schwartz, *The Rogue River Indian War and Its Aftermath, 1850–1980* (Norman: University of Oklahoma Press, 1997), 5–12, 148–49. The best survey of populations is found in S. H. Culver to Joel Palmer, July 12, 1853, NARG 75, LR, OS.

4. Population figures for these tribes are difficult to find. One source puts the Spokane Indians at roughly a thousand people in the 1850s. See Robert H. Ruby and John A. Brown, *The Spokane Indians: Children of the Sun* (Norman: University

of Oklahoma Press, 1970), 29. See also Thornton, *American Indian Holocaust,* 104–14; Nancy Bonvillain, *Native Nations: Cultures and Histories of Native North Americans* (Upper Saddle River, NJ: Prentice-Hall, 2001), 445.

5. The lawyer, one K. Pritchell, later claimed fees of $500 for defending the men. The trial apparently lasted five days. See Charles E. Mix to R. M. McClelland, June 23, 1853, NARG 75, LR, OS.

6. George Abernathy to Lieutenant James Hardie, April 5, and Hardie to Colonel R. B. Mason, April 27, 1848, NARG 393, LR, 10th MD; and Schwartz, *Rogue River Indian War,* 25–30.

7. Kearny to Hooker, June 20, 1851, NARG 393, LR, DP, PS.

8. Dart managed to negotiate the peace only after Lane captured a few Indian women and children who were used as hostages. See Gaines to the president, June 13, 1851, and Kearny to Hooker, June 29, 1851, NARG 393, LR, DP, PS; Schwartz, *Rogue River Indian War,* 30–43.

9. Schwartz, *Rogue River Indian War,* 44–49.

10. McKee's long report is dated April 7, 1852, NARG 393, LR, DP, PS. For a journal of these events, see Robert F. Heizer, ed., *George Gibb's Journal of Redick McKee's Expedition through Northwestern California in 1851* (Berkeley: University of California Press, 1972).

11. Gibbs to Hitchcock, May 3, 1852, and McKee to John Bigler, April 5, 1852, NARG 393, LR, DP, PS.

12. McKee's report, April 7, 1852, NARG 393, LR, DP, PS.

13. Lieutenant W. H. Stanton to Captain E. D. Townsend, August 29, 1852, NARG 393, LR, DP, PS.

14. Wright to "Gentlemen," September 2, 1852, Captain Edward H. Fitzgerald to Lieutenant N. H. Davis, November 6, 1852, and Bvt. Major Robert Buchanan to AAG, April 15, 1854, NARG 393, DP, PS. There are several descriptions of Wright's treachery. See Manypenny, *Our Indian Wards,* 155; Strobridge, *Regulars in the Redwoods,* 45; Keith Murray, *The Modocs and Their War* (Norman: University of Oklahoma Press, 1959; reprint, 1984).

15. Lane to Hitchcock, September 30, 1853, NARG 393, LR, DP, PS; J. Ross Browne, "Report of the Secretary of Interior, Communicating an Answer to a Resolution of the Senate, the report of J. Ross Browne on the late Indian War in Oregon and Washington Territories" (1858), in *Senate Executive Document 40,* serial 929, 6–7; and "Report of the Secretary of Interior, including the Report of J. Ross Browne on the late Indian War in Oregon and Washington Territory" (1858), in *House Executive Document* 38, 36th Congress, 2nd session, serial 955, 7 (hereinafter "Browne Report"). For broader studies, see Stephen Dow Beckham, *Requiem for a People: The Rogue Indians and the Frontiersmen* (Norman: University of Oklahoma Press, 1971), 47–123; Schwartz, *Rogue River Indian War,* 44–112.

16. Palmer to Manypenny, July 8, 1853, NARG 75, LR, OS.

17. Palmer to Culver, August 22, 1853, NARG 75, LR, OS.

18. Treaty with the Rogue River Indians, September 8, 1853; and Palmer to Manypenny, September 10 and October 8, 1853, NARG 75, LR, OS. The

various treaties, most of which simply relinquished lands and guaranteed reservations at some site to be selected, are found in Kappler, *Indian Affairs,* 2:603–714.

19. Schwartz, *Rogue River Indian War,* 58–59; Palmer to Manypenny, May 27, 1853, and E. P. Drew to Palmer, June 1, 1855, NARG 75, LR, OS; Palmer to Manypenny, December 30, 1854, NARG 75, DRNTUT.

20. Wright to AAG Townsend, September 10, 1854, NARG 393, LR, DP, PS; Carl P. Schlicke, *General George Wright: Guardian of the Pacific Coast* (Norman: University of Oklahoma Press, 1988). The fort north of Reading was built by Lieutenant Davis in spring 1852. See Davis report, April 5, 1852, NARG 393, LR, DP, PS.

21. Wright to Townsend, September 20 and December 10, 1854, NARG 393, LR, DP, PS.

22. Smith to Palmer, February 5, 1854, and Palmer to Manypenny, March 11, 1854, NARG 75, LR, OS; Lieutenant August Kautz to Townsend, February 3, 1854, NARG 393, LR, DP, PS; Beckham, *Oregon Indians,* 131–39.

23. Davis to Wool, January 12 and 29, 1854, Wool Papers. General Wool's role in Pacific Slope military affairs was mostly castigated by local historians of the region. A major revision started with the publication of Robert M. Utley, *Frontiersmen in Blue: The United States Army and the Indian, 1848–1865* (New York: Macmillan, 1967), 186–210.

24. In one case Wool learned that Lieutenant Henry Judah had driven away miners who "insisted on retaining squaws" who had fled for protection to his reservation. Quotation from Townsend (AAG) to Wool, August 23, 1855; Wool to Davis, January 29, 1855, Wool Papers.

25. Wool to Davis, January 29, 1855, Wool Papers.

26. Ibid. The incident is reported with somewhat different details in Strobridge, *Regulars in the Redwoods,* 71–72. See also Gray H. Whaley, *Oregon and the Collapse of Illahee: U.S. Empire and the Transformation of an Indigenous World, 1792–1859* (Chapel Hill: University of North Carolina Press, 2010), 191–216.

27. Palmer to Manypenny, October 20, 1855, NARG 75, LR, OS; Schwartz, *Rogue River Indian War,* 73–117. Agent George Ambrose counted 305 Indians on the Table Rock Reservation just after the massacre and suspected that some 500 might still be outside the reserve. Ambrose to Palmer, October 20, 1855, NARG 75, LR, OS.

28. Proclamation of Governor Curry, October 20, 1855, NARG 75, LR, OS.

29. Schwartz has a good discussion of the various accounts in *Rogue River Indian War,* 91–103.

30. Palmer to Manypenny, January 9, 1856, NARG 75, LR, OS.

31. Ibid.; Wool to AAG, April 11, 1855, Henley to Manypenny, August 17, 1855, Henley to Wool, September 19, 1855, Judah to Henley, December 13, 1855, and Henley to Manypenny, December 19, 1855, NARG 75, LR, CS.

32. Schwartz, *Rogue River Indian War,* 117–29.

33. Wright did believe that the Indians of northern California were being neglected, as most government money set aside to feed Indians went to those

in the South. See Wright's many reports in NARG 393, LR, DP, PS. See also General Wool to Lieutenant Colonel A. Thomas, May 30, 1854, and Wright to Townsend, September 20, 1854, Wool Papers.

34. John Beeson, *A Plea for the Indians: With Facts and Features of the Late War in Oregon* (New York: John Beeson, 1857), 45–71.

35. In an interesting twist, Democrat John Breckinridge selected Joseph Lane as a running mate in the 1860 presidential election, with the hope that Lane would bring in the new states of Oregon and California. Abraham Lincoln won both states.

36. Wool to Adjutant General Lieutenant Colonel S. Thomas (War Department), February 26, 1855, Wool Papers.

37. Royce, *Indian Land Cessions,* 808.

38. Quotation in A. Y. Hedges to Manypenny, November 7, 1856, NARG 75, LR, OS. See also Culver to Palmer, July 20, 1854, and Palmer to Manypenny, January 9, 1856, NARG 75, LR, OS.

39. J. Ross Browne "Report," 1858, NARG 75, LR, CS.

40. Townsend to Colonel Benjamin Bonneville, September 13, 1854, Wool Papers. For a good description of the land and resources, see Bonneville to Wool, January 7, 1855, Wool Papers.

41. For all the treaties, see Royce, *Indian Land Cessions,* 798, 804, 806.

42. Journal of Negotiation with the Dwamish, Suquamish, and others, January 22, 1855, NARG 75, DRNRUT. After the signing one S'Komanish approached one of Steven's assistants, complaining of the reservation location that he was to move to. The assistant responded: "We shut them up by telling them it was too late to talk about it." George Gibbs to Stevens, January 6, 1855, NARG 75, DRNRUT.

43. Ibid. See also Alexandra Harmon, ed., *The Power of Promises: Rethinking Indian Treaties in the Pacific Northwest* (Seattle: University of Washington Press, 2008), 3–31.

44. Kent Richards, *Isaac I. Stevens: Young Man in a Hurry* (Provo, Utah: Brigham Young University Press, 1979); Jacilee Wray, ed., *Native Peoples of the Olympic Peninsula: Who We Are* (Norman: University of Oklahoma Press, 2002). "Yakama" is often spelled "Yakima," but most early documents use the older version with an "a," which is used here.

45. Journal of Negotiations with the Yakama, Walla Walla, Umatilla, Cayuse and Nez Perce, May 28, 1855, NARG 75, DRNRUT; Elliott West, *The Last Indian War: The Nez Perce Story* (New York: Oxford University Press, 2009), 62–68.

46. The name "Kamahkan," a key player in the treaty negotiation and thereafter, has various spellings, including "Kamiakin." The same is true for Peopeomoxmox.

47. Journal of Negotiation, June 9–11, 1855, NARG 75, DRNRUT.

48. Palmer and Stevens to Manypenny, June 12, 1855, NARG 75, LR, WS; Harmon, *Power of Promises,* 3–31; Kappler, *Indian Affairs,* 2:521–31. Special agent Browne later erroneously claimed that the "Treaties were not the cause" of the

war that followed, but his assignment of blame to the Klikitats and the Mormons made little sense: "Browne Report," 1858, 10–12, NARG 75, LR, CS.

49. Wool to wife Sarah, December 9, 1855 (written from Fort Vancouver), Wool Papers.

50. Stevens to Manypenny, January 29, 1856, NARG 75,LR, WS.

51. Colonel Casey to Wool, March 9, 1856, Wool Papers.

52. Captain Edward O. O. Ord later filed charges against Rains for basic incompetents in the campaign. Ord charges, April 25, 1856, NARG 393, LR, DP, PS. For an account of the Oregon rangers, see John C. Jackson, *A Little War of Destiny: The First Regiment of Oregon Mounted Volunteers and the Yakima Indian War of 1855–1856* (Fairfield, Wash.: Ye Galleon Press, 1996). The official report of their commander is James Willis Nesmith, "Report of First Regiment, Oregon Volunteers," November 19, 1855, Nesmith Papers, Oregon Historical Society.

53. Wool to his wife, Sarah, March 4, 1856, Wool Papers.

54. Schlicke, *General George Wright,* 112–37.

55. Colonel George Wright to Wool, May 18, 1856, Wool Papers.

56. Wright "Extract" of Report on War, July 16, 1856, Wool Papers.

57. Frances Fuller Victor, *The Early Indian Wars of Oregon: Compiled from the Oregon Archives and Other Original Sources* (Salem: Frank C. Baker, 1894), 479–80; Robert H. Ruby and John A. Brown, *The Cayuse Indians: Imperial Tribesmen of Old Oregon* (Norman: University of Oklahoma Press, 1972), 238–41; Wool to Sara, August 18, 1856, Wool Papers.

58. Colonel Townsend, Wool's adjutant, was in Washington at the time, surveying the political landscape. See Townsend to Wool, April 19, 1856, Wool Papers.

59. Townsend to Wool, April 19, 1856, Wool Papers.

60. Wright to Major W. W. MacKall, September 30, 1858, NARG, 393, LR, Department of Oregon.

61. S. Congiato to Colonel Steptoe, September 15, 1858, and Wright to Major W. W. Mackall, September 30, 1858, NARG 393, LR, Department of Oregon; Ruby and Brown, *Spokane Indians,* 114–40; Schlicke, *General George Wright,* 165–85.

62. The use of such commissions to try Indians is dealt with in subsequent chapters, because there is no evidence of how Wright conducted his trials.

63. A good discussion of the treaty is found in West, *Last Indian War,* 90–95.

CHAPTER 12. THE GREAT PLAINS

1. For a general survey, see Laurence M. Hauptman, *Between Two Fires: American Indians in the Civil War* (New York: Free Press, 1995).

2. West, *Contested Plains,* 13–15, 144–46.

3. Bent to A. M. Robinson, December 17, 1858, and July 23, 1859, NARG 75, LR, UAA.

4. Quoted in West, *Contested Plains,* 147.

5. Kappler, *Indian Affairs,* 2:614–17. An original copy is in A. G. Boone to A. M. Robinson, February 18, 1861, NARG 75, LR, DRNRUT.

6. Thom Hatch, *Black Kettle: The Cheyenne Chief Who Sought Peace but Found War* (New York: John Wiley, 2004).

7. See Hayden to Assistant Adjutant General, September 2, 1861, NARG 393, LR, DWWD; and Agent A. G. Boone to Dole, December 30, 1861, NARG 75, LR, UAA.

8. Ross asserted his neutrality on many occasions during the spring and summer of 1861. See Ross to William P. Ross, Thomas Pegg, John Spears, and Lewis Downing, February 12, 1861, Ross to David Hubbard, June 17, 1861, and Ross to Benjamin McCulloch, June 17, 1861, all in John Ross, *Papers of Chief John Ross,* ed. Gary E. Moulton, 2 vols. (Norman: University of Oklahoma Press, 1984), 2:462, 472–75.

9. Ross to John B. Ogden, February 28, 1861, NARG 75, LR, Cherokee Agency; Grace Steele Woodward, *The Cherokees* (Norman: University of Oklahoma Press, 1963), 253–67. The Union did appoint a new Cherokee agent, one John Crawford, in May 1861, but he could do little to change the course of events. See Crawford to Dole, May 20, 1861, NARG 75, LR, Cherokee Agency.

10. Trevor Jones, "In Defense of Sovereignty: Cherokee Soldiers, White Officers, and Discipline in the Third Home Guard," *Chronicles of Oklahoma* 82 (Winter 2004–2005): 412–27; Clarissa W. Confer, *The Cherokee Nation in the Civil War* (Norman: University of Oklahoma Press, 2007), 62–65.

11. Pike's treaty with the "Pen-e-tegh-ca Band or the Heum, Wichita, Caddo-ha-da-chos, Hue-cos, etc.," August 12, 1861, John Grimes to Charles Johnson, November 18 and 21, 1861, and General E. H. Cooper to Johnson, January 12, 1863, Edward Ayer Papers, Newberry Library, Chicago; Bent to George Hyde, April 17, 1905, Bent Papers, Denver Public Library, Denver; A. G. Boone to Dole, October 26, 1861, NARG 75, LR, UAA; Angie Debo, "The Location of the Battle of Round Mountains," *Chronicles of Oklahoma* 41 (Spring 1963): 70–104. The total number of Indian refugees fleeing into Kansas was estimated at nearly 16,000.

12. See Evan Jones to Dole, January 21, 1861, NARG 75, LR, Cherokee Agency.

13. Ross to Pike, April 10, 1862, and Ross to Lincoln, September 16, 1862, in Ross, *Papers of Chief John Ross,* 2:511, 516–17.

14. Petition signed by "Lewis Downing and Others," July 30, 1862, John Ross to Dole, April 2, 1863, and Petition of James Vann and representatives of the "Ketoo-what Cherokee Nation," October 20, 1863, NARG 75, LR, Cherokee Agency.

15. Don E. Alberts, *The Battle of Glorieta: Union Victory in the West* (College Station: Texas A&M University Press, 1998); and John Taylor, *The Battle of Glorieta Pass: A Gettysburg in the West, March 26–28, 1862* (Albuquerque: University of New Mexico Press, 1998).

16. Edwin R. Sweeney, *Cochise, Chiricahua Apache Chief* (Norman: University of Oklahoma Press, 1991); Kathleen Chamberlain, *Victorio: Apache Warrior and*

Chief (Norman: University of Oklahoma Press, 2007); Bud Shapard, *Chief Loco: Apache Peacemaker* (Norman: University of Oklahoma Press, 2010).

17. Chamberlain, *Victorio*, 92–95.

18. Quotations from Sweeney, *Cochise*, 204, 220; Robert M. Utley, *The Indian Frontier of the American West, 1846–1890* (Albuquerque: University of New Mexico Press, 1984), 83–85; Tom Dunlay, *Kit Carson and the Indians* (Lincoln: University of Nebraska Press, 2000), 240–45. See also Kit Carson, *Navajo Roundup: Selected Correspondence of Kit Carson's Expedition against the Navajo, 1863–1865,* ed. Lawrence Kelly (Boulder, Colo.: Pruett Publishing, 1970).

19. Dunlay, *Kit Carson,* 262–303; Utley, *Indian Frontier,* 83–85.

20. Dunlay, *Kit Carson,* quotation on 267; see also 304–305. For the genocide argument, see Clifford E. Trafzer, *The Kit Carson Campaign: The Last Great Navajo War* (Norman: University of Oklahoma Press, 1982).

21. Joseph R. Brown to Commissioner W. J. Cullen, February 4, August 30, 1858, and March 28 and August 2, 1859, NARG 75, LR, St. Peters Agency; Anderson, *Kinsmen of Another Kind,* 226–60. Brown has left a long description of his program in his personal papers: Joseph R. Brown Papers, Minnesota Historical Society, St. Paul.

22. Lieutenant Colonel John Abercrombie to Assistant Adjutant General, June 4, 1858, NARG 393, Fort Ridgely Letterbook.

23. While seemingly dramatic, the statement is confirmed by family members of Little Crow: Gary Clayton Anderson, *Little Crow: Spokesman for the Sioux* (St. Paul: Minnesota Historical Society Press, 1986), 132, 221 n. 34.

24. Lieutenant Timothy J. Sheehan commanded Fort Ridgely. The day of the outbreak he had been ordered to take forty soldiers to Fort Ripley in northeastern Minnesota. Sheehan received word of the war the evening of his first night out and reversed his march, reaching the beleaguered garrison of a few dozen men at dawn. See the Timothy J. Sheehan Diary, Minnesota Historical Society, St. Paul.

25. Some of the better primary accounts are "Brave Defenders from Leavenworth," *New Ulm Review,* October 12, 1912; Various Memoirs and Journals, Fort Ridgely Historical Association Papers, Minnesota Historical Society, St. Paul; Sheehan Papers, Minnesota Historical Society, St. Paul; Big Eagle's Account and Lightning Blanket's Account, in *Through Dakota Eyes: Narrative Accounts of the Minnesota Indian War of 1862,* ed. Gary Clayton Anderson and Alan R. Woolworth (St. Paul: Minnesota Historical Society Press, 1988), 147–57.

26. Sibley's move up the Minnesota River is documented in his letterbook. See entries for September 13–September 23, 1862, NARG 393, District of Iowa, 1862–65.

27. Sibley believed that the trials were fair, even though some forty men faced the commission in one day. He wrote his wife: "We are trying the prisoners as rapidly as fair play and a due regard to justice will admit": Sibley to Sarah, October 30, 1862, Henry Hastings Sibley Papers, Minnesota Historical Society, St. Paul (hereinafter Sibley Papers). Virtually every newspaper in Minnesote called for the "extermination" of the Sioux. There are too many examples to cite.

Sibley's biographer has recently argued that he hesitated in executing the entire lot of 303 men because he had recently been mustered into the federal army as a brigadier general: Rhoda Gilman, *Henry Hastings Sibley: Divided Heart* (St. Paul: Minnesota Historical Society Press, 2004), 184–85. For his letters to the Indians, see Sibley Letterbook, September 13 and 24, 1862, NARG 393, District of Iowa, 1862–65.

28. Some two thousand trials by Military Commissions of white civilians occurred during the Civil War: Erika Myers, "Conquering Peace: Military Commissions as a Lawforce Strategy in the Mexican War," *American Journal of Criminal Law* 35, no. 2 (2008): 201–40. See also Louis Fisher, *Military Tribunals and Presidential Power* (Lawrence: University Press of Kansas, 2005); Carol Chomsky, "The United States–Dakota War Trials: A Study in Military Justice," *Stanford Law Review* 43 (November 1990): 13–98.

29. Anderson, *Kinsmen of Another Kind,* 276–78.

30. Samuel J. Brown's Recollections, in *Through Dakota Eyes,* 227; Mary H. Bakeman and Alan R. Woolworth, "The Family Caravan," in *Trails of Tears: Minnesota's Dakota Indian Exile Begins,* ed. Mary H. Bakeman and Antona M. Richardson (Roseville, Minn.: Prairie Echoes, 2008), 53–78.

31. Sibley to his wife, November 12, 1862, Sibley Papers. The argument for genocide is found in Angela Wilson Waziyatawin, *In the Footsteps of Our Ancestors: The Dakota Commemorative Marches of the 21st Century* (St. Paul: Living Justice Press, 2006).

32. Corinne L. Monjeau-Marz, *The Dakota Internment at Fort Snelling, 1862–1864* (St. Paul: Prairie Smoke Press, 2005), 57; Newton Edmunds, Edward B. Taylor, S. R. Curtis, Henry H. Sibley, Henry R. Reed, and Omni Guernsey to James Harlan, October 27, 1865, NARG 75, DRNRUT; Colette A. Hyman, "Survival at Crow Creek, 1863–1866," *Minnesota History* 61 (Winter 2009): 148–61.

33. William P. Dole Discussions with the Chippewa, Fort Ripley, March 5, 1863, NARG 75, DRNRUT.

34. Ramsey, "Journal of Negotiation with Red Lake and Pembina Bands of Chippewa," September 4, 1863, NARG 75, DRNRUT.

35. Hale and Charles Hutchins Council with the Nez Perce, May 25, 1863, NARG 75, DRNRUT; Charles Mix to Edward R. Geary, July 2, 1860, and Geary to Colonel George Wright, August 25, 1860, NARG 393, LR, Department of Oregon; West, *Last Indian War,* 86–92.

36. Brigham D. Madsen, *Glory Hunter: A Biography of Patrick Edward Connor* (Salt Lake City: University of Utah Press, 1990), 78–80.

37. Ibid. Rockwell supposedly had been an assassin for Joseph Smith and was one of Brigham Young's most trusted assistants. Will Bagley, *Blood of the Prophets: Brigham Young and the Massacre at Mountain Meadows* (Norman: University of Oklahoma Press, 2002), 13, 15, 80, 243, 253.

38. Scott R. Christensen, *Sagwitch: Shoshone Chieftain, Mormon Elder, 1822–1887* (Logan: Utah State University Press, 1999), 41–52; Kass Fleisher, *The Bear*

River Massacre and the Making of History (Albany: State University of New York Press, 2004); Blackhawk, *Violence over the Land,* 266–69.

39. Leavenworth to Dole, June 27, 1863, NARG 75, LR, UAA; Evans to Major General S. R. Curtis, April 11, May 24, June 16 and 22, and August 18, 1864, and Colley to Evans, July 26, 1864, Evans Letterbook, Colorado Historical Society, Denver; West, *Contested Plains,* 290–94.

40. West, *Contested Plains,* 294–99; Stan Hoig, *The Sand Creek Massacre* (Norman: University of Oklahoma Press, 1961). See also Evans to William H. Seward, October 18, 1864, Evans Letterbook.

41. West, *Contested Plains,* 300–305. While the army wanted to prosecute Chivington, the issue was dropped when he resigned from service.

42. Robert Winston Mardock, *The Reformers and the American Indian* (Columbia: University of Missouri Press, 1971), 19–23.

43. Leavenworth to Dole, October 30, 1864, and May 6 and 10, 1865, Jesse Chisholm to Leavenworth, July 14, 1865, and Leavenworth to D. W. Cooley, November 9, 1865, NARG 75, LR, KA; Treaty with the Arapahos and Cheyennes, August 18 and 23, 1865, James Root Doolittle Papers, Colorado Historical Society, Denver.

44. Kappler, *Indian Affairs,* 2:679–82.

45. Charles Bogy and S. R. Irvin to Louis V. Bogy, December 8, 1866, NARG 75, DRNRUT; William T. Hagan, *United States–Comanche Relations: The Reservation Years* (New Haven: Yale University Press, 1976), 21–23; Anderson, *Conquest of Texas,* 343.

46. Woodward, *Cherokees,* 302–12. See also Annie Heloise Abel, *The American Indian under Reconstruction* (Cleveland: Arthur H. Clark, 1925; reprint, Lincoln: University of Nebraska Press, 1993), 301–63.

47. Richard N. Ellis, *General Pope and the U.S. Indian Policy* (Albuquerque: University of New Mexico Press, 1970); and Peter Cozzens, *General John Pope: A Life for the Nation* (Urbana: University of Illinois Press, 2000).

48. Pope to Norman Kittson, September 23, 1862, NARG 393, LS, Department of the Northwest.

49. Utley, *Indian Frontier,* 94–96.

50. McCristian, *Fort Laramie,* 238–41.

51. Reports of the cowardliness of Cole's troops failed to reach the newspapers, but they soon began to filter down through the ranks of the army. See Major James Van Voast to Brevet Major H. G. Litchfield, November 21, 1866, and Brevet Brigadier General William B. Hazen to Litchfield, August 13, 1866, NARG 393, LR, DP.

52. David E. Wagner, *Powder River Odyssey: Nelson Cole's Western Campaign of 1865: The Journals of Lyman G. Bennett and Other Eyewitness Accounts* (Norman: Arthur H. Clark, 2009).

53. Father Peter John De Smet was allowed into Sitting Bull's camp with a peace proposal in 1868: Robert Carriker, *Father Peter John De Smet: Jesuit in the West* (Norman: University of Oklahoma Press, 1998); and Report "Presented

to the Commissioners," John B. Sanborn Papers, Minnesota Historical Society, St. Paul. West notes the reticence of Dog Soldiers to allow any whites into their camps in *Contested Plains,* 198.

54. McChristian, *Fort Laramie,* 258.

55. Ibid., 258–61.

56. John D. McDermott, *Red Cloud's War: The Bozeman Trail, 1866–1868,* 2 vols. (Norman: Arthur H. Clark, 2010), 1:57–77.

57. Ibid., 1:52–59; McChristian, *Fort Laramie,* 266–70.

58. Carrington to AAAG Major H. G. Litchfield, July 30, 1866, Captain Henry Hayward to AAAG Captain F. Phisterer, July 20, 1866, Carrington to General William Tecumseh Sherman, July 30, 1866, Carrington to Littlefield, July 30, August 29, and September 25, 1866, NARG 393, LR, DP.

59. General Hazen to Litchfield, August 13, 1866, NARG 393, LR, DP.

60. Van Voast to Litchfield, November 21, 1866, NARG 393, LR, DP.

61. "Notes taken of a conversation with the Indians, one of whom was sent to the village of the hostiles, by the Indian agent—and returned—this Indian is Bordeau's Brother-in-law," enclosed with Van Voast to Carrington, September 22, 1866, NARG 393, LR, DP. For contrast, see Kingsley Bray, *Crazy Horse: A Lakota Life* (Norman: University of Oklahoma Press, 2006), 93–95.

62. Both McDermott and James C. Olson were convinced that Red Cloud remained solidly behind the war effort: McDermott, *Red Cloud's War,* 1:148–49; Olson, *Red Cloud and the Sioux Problem* (Lincoln: University of Nebraska Press, 1965), 36–47.

63. "Notes Taken . . . [from] Bordeau's Brother-in-Law," in Van Voast to Carrington, September 22, 1866, NARG 393, LR, DP.

64. Captain William J. Fetterman to Brevet Captain William H. Bisbee, December 7, 1866, and Carrington to Litchfield, December 6, 1866, NARG 393, LR, DP. For a good account of the battle, see McDermott, *Red Cloud's War,* 1:184–89.

65. Carrington Report, January 3, 1867, NARG 393, LR, DP. Carrington's report proved controversial because it implied that General Philip St. George Cooke, commanding the Department of the Platte, had not given Carrington the men that he needed. See also Shannon D. Smith, *Give Me Eighty Men: Women and the Myth of the Fetterman Fight* (Lincoln: University of Nebraska Press, 2008).

66. Utley, *Indian Frontier,* 106–107.

67. General Sherman to General Augur, February 19, 1867, NARG 393, LR, DP. See Robert G. Athearn, *William Tecumseh Sherman and the Settlement of the West* (Norman: University of Oklahoma Press, 1956), 115–211.

68. General Sherman to AAGeneral Lieutenant Colonel George W. Leet, March 13, 1867, NARG 393, LR, DP.

69. Francis Paul Prucha has called the group "a reasonable mixture of firmness and humanitarian leniency": Francis Paul Prucha, *The Great Father: The United States Government and the American Indians,* 2 vols. (Lincoln: University of Nebraska Press, 1984), 1:488–90. Two years later Cora Daniels Tappan, Samuel's

wife, would condemn the entire army as being committed to an "atrocious and infamous proposal to exterminate them [Indians]." Quoted in Mardock, *Reformers and the American Indian,* 61.

70. William Y. Chalfant, *Hancock's War: Conflict on the Southern Plains* (Norman: Arthur H. Clark, 2010), 157–236. Agent Leavenworth concluded that Hancock had started an Indian war. "He has burned nearly 300 lodges and I should think *that* was *glory enough* for him": Leavenworth to CIA, September 2, 1867, in NARG 75, LR, KA (emphasis in the original).

71. Ibid., 273–74; Vine Deloria, Jr., and Raymond DeMallie, eds., *Proceedings of the Great Peace Commission of 1867–1868* (Washington, D.C.: Institute for the Development of Indian Law, 1975), 10–31.

72. Ibid., 68–69.

73. Ibid., 68–76 (quotation on 72); Anderson, *Conquest of Texas,* 348–52.

74. Utley has asserted that "almost every chief of importance on the southern Plains" signed the Comanche-Kiowa treaty, but that statement is questionable: Utley, *Indian Frontier,* 115; Anderson, *Conquest of Texas,* 346–50; L. S. Walkley to Hazen, December 28, 1868, and Leavenworth to Taylor, May 21, 1868, NARG 75, LR, KA.

75. Anderson, *Conquest of Texas,* 351.

76. Kappler, *Indian Affairs,* 2:754–64.

77. This right quickly proved problematic and was never accepted by the army. No doubt the peace commission recognized this, because it promptly sent a letter to General Sherman informing him of the concession. See Ashton J. H. White (secretary of the commission) to Sherman, November 2, 1867, NARG 393, LR, DM.

78. Jerome A. Greene, *Washita: The U.S. Army and the Southern Cheyennes, 1867–1869* (Norman: University of Oklahoma Press, 2004), 36–37. George Bent suggests that the Dog Soldiers were represented in the treaty negotiations by Tall Bull and Bull Bear, who signed the agreement. But such "chiefs," he notes, "were selected to keep peace and be friendly to everybody," so they represented the Dog Soldiers but were not militants. Bent to George Hyde, August 9, 1904, and July 8 and September [1], 1905, Bent Papers.

79. Deloria and DeMallie, *Proceedings of the Great Peace Commission,* 82.

80. Ibid., 88.

81. Ibid., 101–102.

82. Oliver Ames to E. W. Stanton, August 7, 1867, W. Snyder to Ames, August 7, 1867, and General Sherman to General Augur, March 7 and November 19, 1868, NARG 393, LR, DP.

83. Deloria and DeMallie, *Proceedings of the Great Peace Commission,* 110.

84. McDermott, *Red Cloud's War,* 506–507.

85. Catherine Price, *The Oglala People, 1841–1879: A Political History* (Lincoln: University of Nebraska Press, 1996), 82; Bray, *Crazy Horse,* 119–25.

86. Second Lieutenant E. R. P. Shurly to Captain Thomas B. Dewees, August 22, 1868, and Major Dye to General G. D. Ruggles, November 20, 1868, NARG

393, LR, DP. While the original copy of the negotiations is in the Department of the Platte papers, a copy can be found in Deloria and DeMallie, *Proceedings of the Great Peace Commission*, 173–76.

87. Red Cloud quoted in Dye to Ruggles, November 20, 1868, NARG 393, LR, DP. A printed version of the Dye report was published in the *Proceedings*, but most historians have failed to see the significance of the document in terms of Dye's repeated failure to outline the treaty's major points regarding boundaries to Red Cloud. For Red Cloud, the agreement restored peace, ended the occupation of the Bozeman Trail, and allowed him and his people to go back to feuding with the Crows. He openly rejected the notion that he and his people should move to a "reservation," as is clear from his response. Ostler, *Plains Sioux*, 51–52; McDermott, *Red Cloud's War*, 534–35; Olson, *Red Cloud*, 80.

88. Kappler, *Indian Affairs*, 2:770–75.

89. Smith to Ruggles, July 5, 1871, and Lieutenant Colonel George A. Woodward to AAAG, May 3 and August 2, 1871, NARG 393, LR, DP.

CHAPTER 13. THE "PEACE POLICY"

1. The quotation is from Mardock, *Reformers and the Indian*, 48–50.

2. Richard White suggests that the Indian leaders initially refused to sign because their agent, former missionary Moses Adams, demanded that they end polygamy. When the government forced Adams to give in, the Indians signed: White, *Railroads: The Transcontinentals and the Making of Modern America* (New York: W. W. Norton, 2011), 61–62.

3. The reports of raids are almost too numerous to list. See Captain M. W. Keogh to AAAG, January 1, 1867, and Captain A. B. Carpenter to AAAG, June 2 and July 18, 1867, Lieutenant W. H. Hoffman to General A. L. Smith, June 12, 1867, and Captain V. K. Hart to Lieutenant Thomas B. Weir, June 17, 1867, NARG 393, LR, DUA); and Brevet Lieutenant Colonel J. K. Mizner to AAAG, January 15, 1867, NARG 393, LR, DP.

4. Captain Albert Barnitz to AAAG Lieutenant T. B. Weir, June 28, 1867, NARG 393, LR, DUA.

5. Custer to Lieutenant T. B. Weir, August 7, 1867, NARG 393, LR, DP.

6. Greene, *Washita*, 52–54.

7. Sully to Brevet Brigadier General Chauncey McKeever, August 18, 1868, NARG 393, LR, DM; E. F. Hollibaugh, *Biographical History of Cloud County, Kansas: Biographies of Representative Citizens* (N.p.: Wilson Humphrey, 1903), 44.

8. Sully to McKeever, August 19, 1868, NARG 393, LR, DM. For other observations on the possible identity of these raiders, see Captain Simon Snyder to Brevet Captain Mason Howard, August 20, 1868, NARG 393, LR, DM; and the account in Greene, *Washita*, 51–54.

9. Sherman to Pope, August 6, 1870, and John B. L. Skinner to Schofield, February 27, 1869, NARG 393, LR, DM. Descriptions of the invasions of both the Osage and Cherokee Reservations are found in W. F. Cady to J. D. Cox, July

23, 1870, and Brevet Major J. J. Upham to AAG, February 28, 1870, NARG 393, LR, DM. Estimates placed the number of whites on the Osage Reservation at 6,000, all squatters of questionable character who answered to no law enforcement.

10. Historians have overlooked the military investigations of the Kansas raids. Utley's description is typical of many: "they [Cheyennes and Lakotas] ripped through the white settlements on the Saline and Solomon rivers in Kansas. In a two-day raid, they looted and burned cabins, ran off stock, ravished five women, and killed fifteen men": Utley, *Indian Frontier*, 122. An even more distorted version is found in Jeff Broome, *Dog Soldier Justice: The Ordeal of Susanna Alderdice in the Kansas Indian War* (Lincoln: University of Nebraska Press, 2003). Broome argues that Cheyennes traditionally used ritual rape as punishment for women who committed adultery, citing E. Adamson Hoebel, *The Cheyenne Indians of the Great Plains* (New York: Holt, Rinehart and Winston, 1960), 95–96. While it may seem trivial, Colonel Eugene Carr interviewed captive Maria Weichel, who said that she was laid on the ground "and with four holding her arms and legs they all ravished her." The ritual, in contrast, took time and involved "staking" the woman out as punishment, at least according to Hoebel, a far cry from the description left by Carr. Several of the descriptions collected by Broome do not correspond with the ritual described by Hoebel. See Carr to "My Dear Cody," July 2, 1906, Carr Papers, Military History Institute, Carlisle Barracks, Pennsylvania.

11. Prucha, *Great Father*, 1:496.

12. Quotation from Athearn, *William Tecumseh Sherman*, 228. More than likely Sheridan never allowed Grant to see the Sully Report, a strategy of keeping information from the president that became more common as the Peace Policy unfolded. This animosity over the policy also drove old friends Grant and Sherman farther apart.

13. The ensuing Battle of the Washita might have been quite different history had Sully remained in command, because he did not believe that those Indians were responsible for the Kansas raids. See Paul Hutton, *Phil Sheridan and His Army* (Norman: University of Oklahoma Press, 1985), 61–62, for the dispute.

14. Greene, *Washita*, 96–105.

15. Quoted in Greene, *Washita*, 119. Many eyewitness accounts of the battle are found in Richard G. Hardorff, *Washita Memories: Eyewitness Views of Custer's Attack on Black Kettle's Village* (Norman: University of Oklahoma Press, 2006).

16. The most complete discussion of the battle is found in Greene, *Washita*, 126–38.

17. Ibid., 162–71.

18. The official order was dated February 18, 1869, the camp first being designated as "Camp Wichita." See "Inspection Report for Fort Sill," Major George Gibson, 1872, NARG 393, LR, DM.

19. See Colonel Carr's "Official Report," July 25, 1869, and "Journal of the March up the Republican River," September 15–October 28, 1869, NARG 393, LR, DP.

20. AAAG to Custer, Mary 24, 1969, NARG 393, LS, DM.

21. Prucha, *Great Father,* 1:488, 508–11.

22. Olson, *Red Cloud,* 144–70; Price, *Oglala People,* 102–20.

23. For the Baker massacre, see Hutton, *Phil Sheridan,* 188–91.

24. The law passed in July 1870, but by this time the Quaker Policy had already been put into play: many military men had been replaced by men selected by religious organizations: Prucha, *Great Father,* 1:514.

25. Grierson to Assistant Adjutant General, Department of Missouri, March 18 and April 7, 1869, and Hazen to Major General John M. Schofield, April 8, 1869, NARG 75, LR, KA. Schofield had replaced Sully that spring: NARG 393, LR, DM. For the raiding into Texas, see Report of William E. Doyle, NARG 393, LR, DM.

26. See "Receipt" for feeding Indians, February 1, 1867, in NARG 75, LR, Wichita Agency; Grierson to Assistant Adjutant General, August 4 and 25, October 25 and 31, and December 21, 1869, NARG 393, LR, DM.

27. Grierson to Assistant Adjutant General, November 23, 1869, NARG 393, LR, DM; Tatum to Eli S. Parker, July 24, 1869, NARG 75, LR, KA.

28. AAG to Nelson, June 8, 1869, NARG 393, LS, DM; Nelson to McKeever, May 28, June 2 and 22, 1869, and Grierson to the AAG, April 3 and May 25, 1869, NARG 393, LR, DM. See Robert C. Carriker, *Fort Supply, Indian Territory: Frontier Outpost on the Plains* (Norman: University of Oklahoma Press, 1970), 40–43.

29. Nelson to Brevet Brigadier General C. McKeever, May 28, 1869, NARG 393, LR, DM.

30. Grierson to Colonel W. W. Mitchell, January 28 and June 24, 1870, and Tatum to Hoag, July 1, 1870, NARG 75, LR, KA; Nelson to Assistant Adjutant General, January 15 and 16, 1870; Affidavit of Jacob Hirshfield, January 15, and Major M. H. Kidd to Post Adjutant, January 19, 1870, NARG 393, LR, DM.

31. For the quotation, see the Journal of Interpreter John Smith and Nelson to AAG, June 4 and 12, 1870. For the attack, see Captain Nicholas Nolan to the Post Adjutant, Camp Supply, June 11, 1870, and Grierson to AAG, June 24 and August 19, 1870, NARG 393, LR, DM.

32. For the Black Eagle quotation, see "Statement Relative to a Talk with Black Eagle," July 14, 1870, forwarded by Tatum, NARG 75, LR, KA. Tatum reported Lone Wolf's "talk" in Tatum to Hoag, November 15, 1870, NARG 75, LR, KA.

33. "Statement Relative to a Talk," July 14, 1870; Tatum to Hoag, November 15, 1870, and Horace Jones to Tatum, December 6, 1870, NARG 75, LR, KA.

34. Sherman to Colonel William H. Wood, May 19, 1871, NARG 393, LR, DM; Sherman to Pope, May 24, 1871, NARG 75, LR, KA. See also Athearn, *William Tecumseh Sherman,* 290–91.

35. Davis to Sheridan, April 11, 1872, NARG 48, Special Files of the Interior Department Relating to Indian Affairs. Sheridan wrote on the side of the letter: "It will always be a matter of regret to me that I did not hang Satanta when I had him a prisoner."

36. Schofield to AAG, June 19, July 6, and August 5 and 19, 1872, and Mackenzie to AAG, October 12, 1872, NARG 94, LR, AGO; Anderson, *Conquest of Texas,* 354–56.

37. Grierson to Assistant Adjutant General, September 21, 1872, NARG 393, LR, DM.

38. Hardie to Lieutenant Colonel J. B. Fry, July 3, 1872, and Augur to Sheridan, June 10, 1872, NARG 94, LR, AGO. General Sheridan wrote on the back of Augur's letter that he thought such a radical idea unwise. Obviously he would later change his mind, finding deportation perfectly acceptable.

39. Haworth to Hoag, July 21, August 18 and 21, September 8 and 9, 1873, NARG 75, LR, KA. For Governor Davis's quandary over the Kiowa captives, see Anderston, *Conquest of Texas,* 357–58; and Hagan, *United States–Comanche Relations,* 92–97. The "council" involving the handover of the captives is "Records of an Indian Council," October 6, 1873, NARG 75, LR, KA.

40. Keith A. Murray, *The Modocs and Their War* (Norman: University of Oklahoma Press, 1959; reprint, 1984), 38–40. For an interesting firsthand account, sees Jefferson C. Davis Riddle, *The Indian History of the Modoc War* (reprint, Mechanicsburg, Pa.: Stockpole Books, 2004).

41. Murray, *Modocs,* 82–200.

42. Ibid., 252–317; Utley, *Indian Frontier,* 170.

43. Olson, *Red Cloud,* 152–53. The Standing Rock, Grand River, and Cheyenne River Agencies on the upper Missouri were established in 1875. Paul L. Hedren, *After Custer: Loss and Transformation in Sioux Country* (Norman: University of Oklahoma Press, 2011), 67–68.

44. Just before the removal west of Spotted Tail's band, the commissioner of Indian affairs put the population of this group at 4,000. The Oglalas numbered about the same: Walker to Secretary of Interior, January 12, 1872, NARG 393, LR, Fort Buford; Price, *Oglala People,* 90–92.

45. For the forts, see Robert G. Athearn, *Forts of the Upper Missouri* (Englewood, Cliffs, N.J.: Prentice-Hall, 1967). See also Jerome A. Greene, *Fort Randall on the Upper Missouri, 1856–1892* (Pierre: South Dakota State Historical Society, 2005); and Thomas R. Buecker, *Fort Robinson and the American West, 1874–1899* (Norman: University of Oklahoma Press, 1999); Hedren, *After Custer,* 68–69.

46. J. W. Washburn to Augur, May 8 and September 13, 1871, Lieutenant E. M. Hayes to Lieutenant W. C. Forbush, May 27, 1871, Forbush to Captain S. C. Kellogg, July 27, 1871, Sheridan to Ord, March 21 and 27, 1872, Captain James Egan to Colonel J. J. Reynolds, March 22, 1872, Reynolds to AAG, March 24, 1872, Captain Charles Meinhold to Lieutenant J. B. Johnson, April 27, 1872, Captain Alex Moore to Post Adjutant, May 28, 1872, Francis Walker to B. R. Cowen, April 26, 1872, and Townsend to Sheridan, April 29, 1872, NARG 393, LR, DP.

47. Captain W. Clifford to Eli Parker, NARG 393, LR, Fort Hale.

48. Lieutenant Colonel S. B. Hayman to AAG, March 21, 1871, NARG 393, LR, Middle District of the Department of Dakota.

49. Quotation from Colonel Stanley to AAG O. D. Greene, February 12, 1870, NARG 393, LR, Fort Buford. See also Captain W. C. Clifford to Governor J. A. Burbank, January 11, 1870, NARG 393, LR, DM; AAG O. D. Greene to Stanley, February 7, 1870, Captain S. A. Wainwright to Greene, May 4, 1870, Hancock to Stanley, April 24, 1870, NARG 393, LR, DD; and Captain DeWitt C. Poole to Assistant Adjutant General, July 7, 1870, NARG 393, LR, DP.

50. Augur to General George L. Hartsuff, January 27, 1870, Captain D. S. Gordon to AAG, May 16, 1870, William J. Kuykendall to Lieutenant J. N. Wheelan, July 19, 1870, Colonel Jonathan E. Smith to General G. L. Ruggles, July 5, 1871, and Lieutenant George T. Woodson to AAG, August 2, 1871, NARG 393, LR, DP.

51. Greene to the Commanding Officer at Fort Stephenson, April 18, 1871, and Greene to Stanley, April 21, 1871, NARG 393, LR, DD.

52. Greene to Stanley, June 30, 1872, and Hancock to Stanley, July 3, 1872, NARG 393, LR, DD; John M. Lubetkin, *Jay Cooke's Gamble: The Northern Pacific Railroad, the Sioux, and the Panic of 1873* (Norman: University of Oklahoma Press, 2006), 118–39; Robert W. Larson, *Gall: Lakota War Chief* (Norman: University of Oklahoma Press, 2007), 82–85; Robert M. Utley, *The Lance and the Shield: The Life and Times of Sitting Bull* (New York: Henry Holt, 1993), 100–109.

53. Lubetkin, *Jay Cooke's Gamble,* 141.

54. Spotted Eagle's speech is often quoted. The original is in Stanley to Commissioner Walker, April 7, 1872, NARG 75, LR, Cheyenne Agency. See also Bray, *Crazy Horse,* 160; Utley, *Lance and the Shield,* 107; and Lubetkin, *Jay Cooke's Gamble,* 115.

CHAPTER 14. THE RED RIVER "WARS"

1. Thomas C. Battey, *The Life and Adventures of a Quaker among the Indians* (Boston: Lee, Shepard, and Dillingham, 1875), 126–27.

2. Haworth to Hoag, July 7 and December 1, 1873, Henry E. Alvord to Edward P. Smith, September 20, 1873, Smith to Governor Davis, October 7, 1873, Philip McCuster to Commissioner of Indian Affairs, October 25, 1873, Haworth to Smith, December 3, 1873, and Governor Davis to Smith, December 7, 1873, NARG 75, LR, KA; Battey, *Life and Adventures,* 196–228; Hagan, *United States–Comanche Relations,* 100–102.

3. Beede to Smith, January 1, 1874, NARG 75, LR, KA; Hagan, *United States–Comanche Relations,* 92–94. The Quakers also demanded the closing of the saloon at Fort Sill, which irritated Davidson in the extreme.

4. The raid can be pieced together from Battey, *Life and Adventures,* 245–86. McCusker to Smith, January 19, 1874, Haworth to Smith, January 28, 1874, and Haworth to Davidson, February 19, 1874, NARG 75, LR, KA.

5. Haworth to Hoag, May 9 and June 11, 1874, Beede to Smith, May 6, 1874, James E. Rhoads to Hoag, April 13, 1874, and McCuster to Lieutenant J. W. Mason, July 30, 1874, NARG 75, LR, KA; Battey, *Life and Adventures,* 289–92.

6. Battey, *Life and Adventures,* 302–305. Hagan researched Eschiti's family, thus providing the spelling used here for his name. George Bent offered another rendition as Isatac. See Hagan, *United States–Comanche Relations,* 105; Bent to George Hyde, October 24, 1913, Bent Papers, Denver Public Library; Haworth to Hoag, May 25, 1874, NARG 75, LR, KA.

7. Clerk J. Connell to Beede, July 7,1874, NARG 75, LR, Wichita Agency; Haworth to Smith, July 14, 1874, and Haworth to Hoag, July 28, 1874, NARG 75, LR, KA. Comanches generally raised war parties from among the "Residence Bands," which represented the highest level of political authority. For a discussion of the independent nature of these bands, see Morris W. Foster, *Being Comanche: A Social History of an American Indian Community* (Tucson: University of Arizona Press, 1991), 59–89, 164–70.

8. The attack was likely both the largest and the last major raid to hit northwest Texas. See Major Jonathan B. Jones to General William Steele, July 14, 1874, and G. B. Pickett to Adjutant General Steele, August 26, 1874, Adjutant General's Papers, Texas State Archives, Austin.

9. Haworth to Hoag, June 27, 1874, NARG 75, LR, KA.

10. Bison populations on the southern plains were probably only a few million to begin with: Dan Flores, "Bison Ecology and Bison Diplomacy: The Southern Plains from 1800 to 1850," *Journal of American History* 78 (September 1991): 465–85. The report of 500,000 hides being loaded is in Miles to Post Commander, Fort Supply, March 4, 1875, NARG 393, LR, DM.

11. Sheridan to Pope, August 21, 1874, Philip Sheridan Papers, Library of Congress, Washington, D.C. (hereinafter Sheridan Papers).

12. Such laws were clearly stated in the Intercourse Act of 1834: Prucha, *Great Father,* 300–302.

13. Descriptions of the battle can be found in Hagan, *United States–Comanche Relations,* 108; Anderson, *Conquest of Texas,* 358; James L. Haley, *The Buffalo War: The History of the Red River Indian Uprising of 1874* (Garden City, N.Y.: Doubleday, 1976); Davidson to Assistant Adjutant General, July 7, 1874, and McCusker to Jones, July 20, 1874, NARG 94, LR, AGO.

14. Davidson to AAG, July 6, 1874, NARG 75, LR, Wichita Agency; Hagan, *United States–Comanche Relations,* 105–12.

15. Mardock, *Reformers and the American Indian,* 134–38.

16. Ibid.; Henry Fritz, *The Movement for Indian Assimilation, 1860–1890* (Philadelphia: University of Pennsylvania Press, 1963), 154–55.

17. Acting Secretary B. R. Cowen to Belknap, July 18, 1874, NARG 393, LR, DM. See General Augur to General Sheridan, September 9, 1874, NARG 75, LR, KA.

18. Sheridan to Pope, July 24, 1874, Sheridan Papers.

19. Pope to the Commanding Officer of 6th Cavalry, Fort Hays, May 6, 1873, and Pope to Osborn, July 8, 1874, NARG 393, LS, DM. A good discussion of the liquor problem and the elements from Dodge City who were involved in it is found in Agent John Miles to Commanding Officer, Fort Supply, April 4, 1874, NARG 393, LR, DM.

20. Sheridan to Pope, July 24, 1874, NARG, LR, DM. Sheridan's views and his argument with Pope are discussed in detail in Hutton, *Phil Sheridan,* 245–49.

21. Some officers, including Colonel Thomas Neill at the Cheyenne Agency, were chided for turning over the decision to the agents. See Neill's defense in Neill to AAG, August 27, 1874, NARG 393, LR, DM.

22. Sanderson to Post Adjutant, August 1, 1874, and Haworth to Smith, August 3, 1874, NARG 75, LR, KA.

23. Quotation from Miles to Haworth, August 10, 1874. See also the long description of enrollment in Sanderson to Post Adjutant, August 8, 1874, and Davidson to AAG Jones (of Texas), August 15, 1874, NARG 75, LR, KA. The best discussion of the growing separation between so-called friendly and hostile Cheyennes is Colonel Neill to AAG, August 20, 1874, NARG 393, LR, DM. See also Donald J. Berthrong, *The Southern Cheyennes* (Norman: University of Oklahoma Press, 1963), 396–400.

24. Haworth to Smith, August 24, 1874, and Davidson to AAG, August 27, 1874, NARG 75, LR, KA; Clerk J. Connell to Richards, August 22, 1874, NARG 75, LR, Wichita Agency. There are conflicting reports as to the army's response. Davidson's official report fails to point out that his troops fired into a friendly crowd of Indians after the prisoner ran. A "Special Agent" sent to the scene reported that "the Order to fire was given [by the military] and a volley sent into the crowd composed to a large extent of friendly Indians." Casualties included several women. Davidson was outraged and filed several subsequent reports. See J. W. Smith to Smith, September 3, 1874, NARG 75, LR, KA; Davidson to Lieutenant Colonel Thomas Neill, August 25, 1874, NARG 393, LR, DM. Hagan adopts the military side of the story in *United States–Comanche Relations,* 111, but then he identified the incident as "almost" a "Wounded Knee."

25. Pope to Colonel R. C. Drum, September 7, 1874, NARG 393, LS, DM; and Miles's Final Report, March 14, 1875, NARG 393, LR, DM.

26. Sheridan to Pope, August 21, 1874, and Sheridan to AAG, October 1, 1874, NARG 393, LS, DM; Hutton, *Phil Sheridan,* 248.

27. Pope to Hoag, July 27, 1874, and Pope to Miles, July 29, 1827, NARG 393, LS, DM. When receiving the order, Colonel Neill at Cheyenne Agency apparently misunderstood Sheridan, responding: "in regard to the event of these Indians sending their women and children into the Agency, or near it, . . . I consider them as hostile and will arrest them should they come in." Sheridan's point was to force them to stay out, so that their men would have to defend them. See Neill to AAG, September 14, 1874, NARG 393, LR, DM.

28. Miles reported only seventeen dead bodies but thought that many more were killed in the various engagements. See Miles's reports, September 1, 5, and 9, 1874, NARG 94, LR, AGO. The day-by-day journal of his movements in the fall is found at "Journal," October–December 1874, NARG 393, "Special Files," Headquarters, DM.

29. Miles to AAG, September 17, 1874, NARG 94, LR, AGO.

30. Perhaps the best account of Mackenzie's attack is still Robert G. Carter, *The Old Sergeant's Story: Winning the West from the Indians and Bad Men in 1870*

to 1878 (New York: Frederick Ritchcock, 1926), 105–10; see also Sherman to General E. D. Townsend, October 14, 1874, NARG 94, LR, AGO.

31. Lieutenant Colonel Thomas H. Neill to Assistant Adjutant General, October 4, 1874, NARG 94, LR, AGO.

32. For the surrender of the other Kiowas, see Sanderson to Assistant Adjutant General, September 25, 1874, and Haworth to Smith, September 26, 1874, NARG 75, LR, KA; Sheridan to General W. W. Belknap, October 5, 1874, Belknap to Sheridan, October 5, 1874, NARG 94, LR, AGO; Sheridan to Delano, November 14, 1875, NARG 393, "Special Files," Headquarters, DM. For an excellent discussion of the "colonial" forces that came to dominate the reservation after surrender, see Jacki Thompson Rand, *Kiowa Humanity and the Invasion of the State* (Lincoln: University of Nebraska Press, 2008).

33. Neill to AAG, February 7, 12, 18, and March 7, 1875, and Jesse J. Sturm journal, 1875, NARG 393, LR, DM; Berthrong, *Southern Cheyennes,* 398–400.

34. The story of the Sand Hill fight is found in Neill to AAG, April 7 and 10, 1874, NARG 393, LR, DM. See also William Y. Chalfant, *Cheyennes at Dark Water Creek: The Last Fight of the Red River War* (Norman: University of Oklahoma Press, 1997).

35. Haworth to Smith, November 11 and 14 and December 7 and 23, 1874, and Augur to Sheridan, November 8, 1874, Smith to Secretary of Interior, November 9, Miles to General Pope, November 17, 1874, and Davidson to Augur, November 23, 1874, NARG 94, LR, AGO.

36. Charges, "in violation of the Laws of War," August 22, 1874, and Neill to AGG, October 1 and 11, 1874, NARG 393, LR, DM.

37. Sheridan to Delano, November 14, 1874, Sheridan to Augur, November 20, 1874, and Sheridan to General Pope, December 3, 1874, Sheridan Papers; Augur to Colonel R. C. Drum, December 10, 1874, NARG 393, "Special Files," Headquarters, DM.

38. Augur to Davidson, December 12, 1874, NARG 393, "Special Files," Headquarters, DM.

39. Augur to Davidson, December 12, 1874, and Pope to General E. D. Townsend, February 20, 1875, NARG 393, "Special Files," Headquarters, DM.

40. Emory to AAG, March 30, 1875, NARG 393, "Special Files," Headquarters, DM (emphasis added). The German girls had been surrendered on March 1, 1875, but Emory was unable to interview them. See Neill to AAG, June 11, 1875, NARG 393, "Special Files," Headquarters, DM.

41. Brad D. Lookingbill has an excellent description of the debate over what to do with the prisoners. He gives a figure of twenty-seven for the number of Kiowas sent east, however, when the original list filed in the Department of Missouri correspondence gives thirty-one. This suggests that four either died in prison or were left behind: Lookingbill, *War Dance at Fort Marion: Plains Indian War Prisoners* (Norman: University of Oklahoma Press, 2006), 24–40.

42. The two lists of the prisoners are dated March 12 and April 23, 1875, NARG 393, LR, DM. When it came to charges, especially for those deemed

"turbulent," the term "common report" was attached to their names, suggesting that other Indians had identified them as such.

43. Quotation from Lookingbill, *War Dance,* 26.

44. Quotation from ibid., 47.

45. Pratt to AAG, June 11, 1875, Sheridan to Belknap, June 26, 1875, and Pratt List of "Requests" for women and children, July 19, 1875, NARG 393, LR, DM.

46. Lookingbill, *War Dance,* 82–129.

47. Rome Statutes, Article 7, Section d.

48. Rome Statutes, Article 8, Sections a: vi and vii and Section B, i.

49. Kappler, *Indian Affairs,* 2:988.

CHAPTER 15. GENERAL SHERIDAN AND THE ETHNIC CLEANSING OF THE NORTHERN LAKOTA SIOUX

1. See the assessment of the Sheridan-Stanley relationship in Lubetkin, *Jay Cooke's Gamble,* 118–19.

2. Stanley to Hancock, November 7, 1872, NARG 393, Letters and Telegrams Received, DD.

3. The letter, written from "Headquarters, Fort Sully," is signed simply "DLS," suggesting that it should be considered "informal" military correspondence. It ended up in a "Letters Received" file, separate from regular correspondence. Stanley to Hancock, January 4, 1873, NARG 393, LR, "Letters and Telegrams Received," DD.

4. Ibid.

5. Ibid. Francis Walker had resigned as commissioner in November 1872.

6. Ibid.

7. Ibid. The Stanley letter helps explain the actions of Colonel Custer a year later, when his expedition claimed to have found gold in the hills when in fact they found very little.

8. Historian Paul Hutton seems to agree. Interestingly, when the secretary of war suggested to Sheridan that the Sioux leaders of the attacks on the surveying party be arrested, the general responded by saying that this would bring war. The secretary demurred: Hutton, *Phil Sheridan,* 286; John S. Gray, *Custer's Last Campaign: Mitch Boyer and the Little Bighorn Reconstructed* (Lincoln: University of Nebraska Press, 1991), 94–97.

9. Lubetkin, *Jay Cooke's Gamble,* 180–94. See Custer to the AAG, July 9 and 19, 1873, NARG 393, Letters and Telegrams Received, DD.

10. Acting Secretary George M. Roleeson to Stanley, May 6, 1873, and Major George Forsyth to Lieutenant Colonel James B. Fry, April 12, 1873, NARG 393, LR, Letters and Telegrams Received, DD; Tappan to Commanding Officer at Fort Buford, April 28 and July 2, 1873, NARG 393, LR, Fort Buford; Ben Innis, *Bloody Knife: Custer's Favorite Scout* (Bismarck, N.D.: Smokey Water Press, n.d.).

11. Lubetkin, *Jay Cooke's Gamble,* 248–51. There is some debate over whether Custer was in serious trouble and whether he realized the value of Stanley's

arrival. See Custer's report, August 15, 1873, NARG 393, Letters and Telegrams Received, DD.

12. Lubetkin, *Jay Cooke's Gamble,* 264–67. For another account, which emphasizes Crazy Horse's role, see Bray, *Crazy Horse,* 165–67.

13. Lubetkin, *Jay Cooke's Gamble,* 268–93.

14. Quotation from ibid., 287.

15. Simmons to Hazen, September 2, 1873, NARG 393, LR, Fort Buford; Colonel Jonathan Smith to AAG, May 5, 1874, NARG 393, LS, DD.

16. Olson, *Red Cloud,* 157.

17. Ibid., 166–67; Gray, *Custer's Last Campaign,* 116–17.

18. Estimate of Costs of Yellowstone Expedition, Approved Secretary of War, May 6, 1873, NARG 393, General Correspondence of Detachment of Scouts, DD.

19. Hutton, *Phil Sheridan,* 166–68.

20. Sheridan to Sherman, September 25, 1874, Sheridan Papers.

21. Watson Parker, *Gold in the Black Hills* (Norman: University of Oklahoma Press, 1966), 26.

22. Quotation from Hutton, *Phil Sheridan,* 168–69.

23. On the gold discovery, see Wayne R. Kime, *Colonel Richard Irving Dodge: The Life and Times of a Career Army Officer* (Norman: University of Oklahoma Press, 2006), 186–87.

24. See Lieutenant Colonel Pinkney Lugenbell to AAG, September 23, 1874, NARG 393, "Special Files," Headquarters, Military Division of Missouri.

25. Historians have often theorized regarding Custer's and Sheridan's motives but apparently had never seen or used the Stanley letter. Parker, in *Gold in the Black Hills* (26), suggests that the riders sent into Fort Laramie exaggerated the gold claims, somewhat exonerating Custer. Hutton, *Phil Sheridan* (291), stresses Sheridan's scientific interest in the region. Utley notes that Custer only later joined the chorus of supporters after realizing that the gold issue would ultimately lead to the occupation of the hills but may not have been aware that a conspiracy existed: Robert M. Utley, *Cavalier in Buckskin: George Armstrong Custer and the Western Military Frontier* (Norman: University of Oklahoma Press, 1988), 140–41. Ostler, who apparently searched the Department of Dakota records that housed the Stanley letter, never discovered it. Nevertheless, he is circumspect regarding Custer's motives and Sheridan's role, concluding: "It is inconceivable that a man with Sheridan's acumen for long-range strategic planning would have failed to grasp the implications of a Black Hills bonanza" (*Plains Sioux,* 60).

26. Sheridan to Sherman, September 25, 1875, Sheridan Papers. For Custer's subsequent attack on Winchell, which appeared in the *New York World,* December 13, 1874, see Kime, *Colonel Richard Irving Dodge,* 186.

27. Gray, *Custer's Last Campaign,* 117–19.

28. Terry to AAG, March 9, 1875, NARG 393, "Special Files," Headquarters, Military Division of Missouri (emphasis in the original).

29. Commissioner Smith demanded actions against miners who were "rumored" to be in the hills. See Smith to Delano, November 20, 1874, and Delano

to the Secretary of War, November 23, 1874, NARG 94, LR, AGO. Sheridan supported the decision, releasing a letter to the newspapers affirming the commitment of the army to remove miners from the reservation. *New York Times,* May 24, 1875.

30. Mix report, April 19, 1875, and William D. Whipple to AG, April 16, 1875, NARG 94, LR, AGO; General Sherman's Telegram regarding president's order, March 17, 1875, NARG 393, "Special Files," Headquarters, Military Division of Missouri; Kime, *Colonel Richard Irving Dodge,* 188–89.

31. *New York Times,* May 26, June 23, and July 3, 1875.

32. Bourke, who had won the Medal of Honor in the Civil War at the age of sixteen, was a Sheridan favorite for several reasons. Bourke to Sheridan, June 15, 1875, Sheridan Papers; Captain C. W. Foster to Major O. D. Greene, April 12, 1875, NARG 393, "Special Files," Headquarters, Military Division of Missouri.

33. *New York Times,* July 22 and 28, August 11 and 16, and November 12, 1875. Colonel Dodge, who watched the process carefully, disagreed, concluding that he saw no quantity of gold that "would pay the ordinary miner." He also concluded that Jenny was "a crazy man" in terms of his desire to find gold. Crook Proclamation, July 29, 1875, Dodge to Crook, August 7, 1875, and Dodge report, October 10, 1875, NARG 393, LR, DP.

34. Quotation from the Walter Stanley Campbell Papers, Western History Collection, University of Oklahoma (hereinafter Campbell Papers).

35. *National Republican,* August 13 and 26, September 30, and October 2, 1875; *New York Times,* October 1, 1875; Price, *Oglala People,* 149–54; Report of the Secretary of Interior, October 31, 1875, *House Executive Document* 1, part 5, 44th Congress, 1st session, 5–10.

36. *National Republican,* September 30 and October 18, 1875; *New York Times,* November 19, 1875.

37. Parker, *Gold in the Black Hills,* 70.

38. Utley, *Indian Frontier,* 175; Ostler, *Plains Sioux,* 61. An obvious misstatement of the number of miners is found in Bray, *Crazy Horse:* "The fifteen hundred prospectors in August had, before winter's end, grown to fifteen thousand" (192).

39. Captain Fergus Walker to Captain Anson Mills, May 20, 1875, Captain Mills to AAG, May 23, 1875, and Lieutenant Frederick Schwatka to Post Adjutant, July 1, 1875, NARG 393, LR, DP; Walker to Post Adjutant, April 22, 1875, Captain C. W. Foster to Greene, April 12, 1875, Lieutenant T. H. Bradley to AAG, May 27, 1875, Greene to C. O. Fort Randall, July 8, 1875, and Captain Benteen to AAG, September 16, 1875, NARG 393, "Special Files," Headquarters, Military Division of Missouri.

40. Kime, *Colonel Richard Irving Dodge,* 212–15; Dodge to Crook, August 10, 1875, NARG 393, LR, DP.

41. Pollock to Crook, August 23, 1875, NARG 393, LR, DP; Terry to Lieutenant Colonel Pinkney Lugenbeel, October 17, 1875, NARG 393, LR, Fort Hale.

42. Dodge to Pollock, August 25, 1875, Pollock to Crook, August 27 and October 5, 1875, Lieutenant W. W. Robinson to Post Adjutant, September 22, 1875, and Pollock to Crook, November 27, 1875, NARG 393, LR, DP.

43. Sheridan to Terry, August 7 and November 9, 1875, Sheridan Papers; Commissioner Smith to the Secretary of Interior, November 27, 1875, NARG 94, LR, AGO. For the best description of the meeting, see Hutton, *Phil Sheridan,* 299.

44. Other historians have seen this meeting differently. Jeffrey Ostler argues that Grant was the instigator, not Sheridan, but offers no evidence or footnote for the assertion: Ostler, *The Lakotas and the Black Hills* (New York: Viking, 2010), 94.

45. Hutton, *Phil Sheridan,* 299.

46. This issue is discussed in the epilogue.

47. John Burke to Commissioner of Indian Affairs, January 30, 1876, NARG 393, LR, DP. Chandler and others later recognized the criticism of their premature actions and tried to justify them. See Secretary of War J. D. Cameron to the President, July 8, 1876, NARG 94, LR, AGO.

48. Hastings to Smith, January 28, 1876, NARG 75, LR, Red Cloud Agency.

49. Sheridan to Sherman, December 31, 1875, and January 3, 1876, and Sheridan to Terry, February 8, 1876, Sheridan Papers; Chandler to the Secretary of War, February 1, 1876, Secretary of War Belknap to Chandler, February 3, 1876, and Sheridan to A. C. Barstow, March 11, 1876, NARG 75, LR, Dakota Superintendency. A recent study of the Lakota domain after the war in 1877–80 indicates that massive buffalo herds could still be found throughout the Yellowstone Valley and north of it. Hedren, *After Custer,* 92–110.

50. Several reports on the Reynolds engagement have survived. See Reynolds's two reports, March 28 and April 15, 1876, Captain Henry Noyes to Adjutant, Big Horn Expedition, March, n.d., 1876, Captain Anson Mills to Adjutant, Big Horn Expedition, March 27, 1876, and Captain Alex Moore to Commanding Officer, Fort Reno, March 22, 1876, NARG 393, LR, DP.

51. Sheridan to Sherman, May 27 and 29, 1876, Sheridan Papers; Terry to Sheridan, NARG 393, LR, DP.

52. Captain Mills to Adjutant, June 18, 1876, NARG 393, LR, DP; Bray, *Crazy Horse,* 205–12.

53. Major Marcus Reno, in a confidential letter, described Gibbon as "scared": Reno to Sheridan, July 4, 1876, Sheridan Papers.

54. The size of the village is still much debated. Captain D. W. Benham, who walked the ground on June 27, indicated that it was three miles long. "Besides the lodges proper, a great number of temporary brushwood shelters were found in it indicating that many men besides its proper inhabitants had gathered together there": Benham to C.O. at Fort Ellis, June 27, 1876, NARG 393, "Special Files," Headquarters, Military Division of Missouri. Just before his death Crazy Horse apparently made a very similar statement, saying to a companion that "the village consisted of eighteen hundred lodges, and at least four hundred wickiups, a lodge made of small poles and willows." Such a group could easily produce 3,000 warriors if not more. Crazy Horse statement, May 24, 1877, in Richard G. Hardorff, ed., *Indian Views of the Custer Fight: A Source Book* (Norman: University of Oklahoma Press, 2005), 35.

55. The historiography of the Custer debacle would constitute a book in itself and would include Gray, *Custer's Last Campaign,* 280–372; Utley, *Cavalier in Buckskin,* 165–93; Bray, *Crazy Horse,* 212–34; and more specifically Paul Hutton, ed., *The Custer Reader* (Lincoln: University of Nebraska Press, 1991); and Paul L. Hedren, ed., *The Great Sioux War, 1876–1877* (Helena: Montana State Historical Association, 1991). George Bent relates a possibly apocryphal incident regarding the abuse of Custer's body by Indian women, which involved urinating on him: Bent to George Bird Grinnell, March 4, 1914, Grinnell Papers, Braun Research Library, Southwest Museum, Los Angeles.

56. While the Indian Office had difficulty in getting a proper census of these Indians, Commissioner Smith uses the figure of 41,000 as the total population of all bands. Smith to Secretary of Interior, July 7, 1876, NARG 75, Report Books.

57. Many reports are found in government documents, particularly reports coming out of Fort Rice. See also Campbell Papers; Hardorff, *Indian Views of the Custer Fight;* and David Humphreys Miller, *Custer's Fall: The Native American Side of the Story* (New York: Duell and Pearce, 1957; reprint, New York: Meridian, 1992).

58. Kills Eagle's account of forty-nine pages is one of the most intriguing sources: Captain R. E. Johnson, "Statement of Kills Eagle," September 17, 1876, NARG 75, LR, Standing Rock Agency.

59. Ibid., September 26, 1876; Statement of Thomas J. Mitchell, September 5, 1876, NARG 75, LR, Dakota Superintendency. Kills Eagle had rescued a white woman some years earlier and was richly rewarded by the military, which explains Sitting Bull's animosity. See John Burke to Smith, July 29, 1876, NARG 75, LR, Standing Rock Agency.

60. Lieutenant W. P. Carlin, "Statement of Man That Smells His Hand," September 7, 1876, NARG 393, "Special Files," Headquarters, Military Division of Missouri.

61. Ibid.

62. "Statement of Kills Eagle," September 17, 1876, NARG 75, LR, Standing Rock Agency; second interview with Kills Eagle, September 21, 1876, NARG 393, "Special Files," Headquarters, Military Division of Missouri.

63. Proceedings of a Council with Two Kettles, Sans Arcs, Minneconjou, and Blackfeet Sioux at Cheyenne River Agency, July 29, 1876, NARG 393, "Special Files," Headquarters, Military Division of Missouri.

64. Johnson to Commissioner of Indian Affairs, September 7, 1876, NARG 75, LR, Standing Rock; Lieutenant Colonel W. P. Carlin to Ruggles, September 12, 1876, NARG 393, "Special Files," Headquarters, Military Division of Missouri.

65. Sheridan to Sherman, August 10, 1876, NARG 75, LR, Dakota Superintendency (emphasis in the original).

66. Smith to the Secretary of Interior, July 7, 1876, NARG 75, Report Books (emphasis in the original).

67. Quoted in Mardock, *Reformers,* 145.

68. Quoted in ibid., 147.

69. AAG Drum to Colonel Wesley Merritt, July 15, 1876, NARG 393, LR, DP; Terry telegram to all agencies, July 24, 1876, NARG 393, LR, Fort Hall.

70. Sherman to Sheridan, July 25, 1876, NARG 75, LR, Dakota Superintendency; Sheridan "Instructions," August 8, 1876, Sheridan Papers.

71. Sheridan to Crook, July 16 and August 23, 1876, NARG 393, LR, DP.

72. Sheridan to Sherman, July 28, 1876, NARG 75, LR, Dakota Superintendency; Burke to Commissioner, August 15 and 30 and September 1, 1876, NARG, LR, Standing Rock Agency. Lieutenant Colonel W. P. Carlin justified the arrest of Burke by suggesting that he had issued rations to a large party of "hostile" Indians under Kills Eagle, the same chief who had rescued a white captive female and was held hostage in Sitting Bull's camp during the spring. See Carlin to Major George Ruggles, September 2, 1876, NARG 393, "Special Files," Headquarters, Military Division of Missouri.

73. Captain R. E. Johnson to Commissioner, September 7, 1876, NARG 75, LR, Standing Rock Agency.

74. Miles report, October 25, 1876, NARG 75, LR, Dakota Superintendency; Anderson, *Sitting Bull*, 116.

75. "The Cedar Creek Councils and the Battle of Cedar Creek," October 20–21, 1876, in Jerome A. Greene, ed., *Lakota and Cheyenne: Indian Views of the Great Sioux War, 1876–1877* (Norman: University of Oklahoma Press, 1994), 97–112; Sheridan to Sherman, November 9, 1876, NARG 75, LR, Dakota Superintendency; Lieutenant Theo F. Forbes to AAG, November 17, 1876, and Colonel H. B. Hazen to Post Adjutant, June 7, 1877, NARG 393, LR, District of Yellowstone.

76. There is a long description of this struggle, given by Etehpo or Swelled Face, in Colonel W. H. Wood to AAG, February 21, 1877, NARG 393, LR, Fort Buford.

77. Anderson, *Sitting Bull*, 114–15.

78. Ibid., 117–40. For an excellent discussion of the various small bands that remained on the plains, refusing to surrender, see Hedren, *After Custer*, 133–75.

79. Daniels receipt, September 10, 1876, NARG 75, LR, Dakota Superintendency.

80. Commission Report, Senate Executive Document 9, 44th Congress, 2nd session, printed December 26, 1876, 8–12.

81. Price, *Oglala People*, 156–75; Lieutenant Horace Neide to Commissioner, December 15, 1876, NARG 75, LR, Spotted Tail Agency. Of the signing, Sheridan noted: "not a single Indian who signed the ultimatum of the commissioners [felt any different] than the Indian who covered his eyes with his blanket when he signed the paper." Sheridan to Sherman, September 30, 1876, NARG 75, LR, Dakota Superintendency.

82. Vandever to Commissioner, September 6, 1876, NARG 75, LR, Dakota Superintendency; Vandever to Commissioner, September 15, 1876, NARG 75, LR, Red Cloud Agency; Sheridan to Sherman, September 30, 1876, NARG 75, LR, Dakota Superintendency.

83. Commission Report, Senate Executive Document 9, 44th Congress, 2nd session, Filed December 26, 1876, 33–55.

84. Ibid. (emphasis in the original). These comments are at the front of the 90-page report.

85. Vandever to Commissioner, September 15, 1876, NARG 75, LR, Red Cloud Agency.

CHAPTER 16. THE INDIANS' "LAST STAND" AGAINST ETHNIC CLEANSING

1. West, *Last Indian War,* 67–95.

2. Virginia McConnell Simmons, *The Ute Indians of Utah, Colorado, and New Mexico* (Boulder: University Press of Colorado, 2000), 132–52; Blackhawk, *Violence over the Land,* 221–25.

3. Jared Farmer, *On Zion's Mount: Mormons, Indians, and the American Landscape* (Cambridge, Mass.: Harvard University Press, 2008).

4. Pope to AGG, May 22, 1871, NARG 393, LS, DM.

5. Sweeney, *Cochise,* 5–7.

6. Ibid., 272–82.

7. For the attack, see Karl Jacoby, *Shadows at Dawn: A Borderlands Massacre and the Violence of History* (New York: Penguin, 2008).

8. Dan Thrapp, *The Conquest of Apachería* (Norman: University of Oklahoma Press, 1975), 78–94. The reservation was later separated into the Fort Apache and San Carlos Reservations.

9. Shapard, *Chief Loco,* 50–63.

10. Sweeney, *Cochise,* 367–97.

11. Shapard, *Chief Loco,* 97–100.

12. Edwin R. Sweeney, *From Cochise to Geronimo: The Chiricahua Apaches, 1874–1886* (Norman: University of Oklahoma Press, 2010), 107–46.

13. For a good discussion of the turmoil, see West, *Last Indian War,* 75–97. See also the now dated standards Alvin M. Josephy, *The Nez Perce Indians and the Opening of the West* (New Haven: Yale University Press, 1965); and Merrill D. Beal, *"I Will Fight No More Forever": Chief Joseph and the Nez Perce War* (Seattle: University of Washington Press, 1963).

14. Howard's final report, written from his notes, was published privately in Portland: Howard, *Supplementary Report (Non-Treaty Nez-Perce Campaign),* dated January 26, 1878 (Portland, Ore.: Assistant Adjutant General's Office, 1878). It is sixty-eight pages long and gives detailed accounts of the various councils that Howard had before the conflict broke out. An original copy is found in NARG 94, LR, AGO, Special File 3464. See also J. Diane Pearson, *The Nez Perces in the Indian Territory* (Norman: University of Oklahoma Press, 2008), 31–32.

15. Howard, *Supplementary Report.*

16. Quotation from Howard's Council Notes, May 3–9, 1877, NARG 94, LR, AGO, Special File 3464 (emphasis in the original); West, *Last Indian War,* 115–20. Yet another rendition of these councils is found in O. O. Howard, *Nez Perce Joseph: An Account of His Ancestors, His Lands, His Confederates, His Enemies, His Murders, His War, His Pursuit and Capture* (Boston: Lee and Shepard, 1881), which West has relied upon.

17. Quotation from Howard, *Supplemental Report,* 29–31. Reports of the rape of white females captives promptly surfaced, most coming from unreliable sources. Norman B. Atkison, *Nez Perce Indian War and Original Stories* (Grangeville: Idaho County Free Press, 1966); and John D. McDermott, *Forlorn Hope: The Battle of White Bird Canyon and the Beginning of the Nez Perce War* (Boise: Idaho State Historical Society, 1978).

18. West, *Last Indian Campaign,* 130. Howard exaggerated the number of killings at thirty, as well as the number of Indians involved. Howard to AAG, June 18, 1877, NARG 94, LR, AGO, Special File 3464.

19. West, *Last Indian War,* 162.

20. West called it *The Last Indian War.* His argument is valid only if we conclude that the later Ute and Apache conflicts were something less than wars. Ibid., 123–36.

21. Watkins to CIA, July 8 and 20, 1877, NARG 94, LR, AGO, Special File 3464.

22. Watkins to CIA, July 30, 1877, Howard Report, July 14, 1877, Jonathan B. Monteith to Smith, July 31, 1877, and Judge Advocate General W. M. Duran to AAG, August 28, 1877, NARG 94, LR, AGO, Special File 3464. Information coming from the eighteen men suggested that Joseph wished to surrender. See Watkins's report of July 20 and Howard to General Irvin McDowell, July 17, 1877, NARG 94, LR, AGO, Special File 3464; Pearson, *Nez Perces,* 42.

23. Gibbon to AAG, July 22, 1877, NARG 393, LS, District of Montana.

24. See Gibbon's Report, September 2, 1877, NARG 94, LR, AGO, Special File 3464.

25. West, *Last Indian War,* 186–200; Pearson, *Nez Perces,* 35. Gibbon to Terry, August 9, 11, 1877, NARG 393, LS, District of Montana; Gibbon's Report, September 2, 1877, NARG 94, LR, AGO, Special File 3464.

26. Sherman to Sheridan, August 31, 1877, NARG 94, LR, AGO, Special File 3464.

27. Colonel Sturgis had troops in position along the Yellowstone but misjudged the ability of the Nez Perces to descend the very rugged Clark Fork. See his reports at Sturgis to AAG, August 21, 25, and 30, and Agent George Frost to General Miles, September 10, 1877, NARG 393, LR, District of Yellowstone; Sheridan to Lieutenant Colonel Robert Williams, September 25, 1877, NARG 94, LR, AGO, Special File 3464.

28. Miles Reports, October 5 and 6, 1877, NARG 94, LR, AGO, Special File 3464.

29. Howard's Report, October 17, 1877, NARG 94, LR, AGO, Special File 3464.

30. West, *Last Indian War,* 283–89.

31. The "Jottings" that Howard mentions are briefly discussed in a Howard manuscript draft, Howard Papers, Bowdoin College, Brunswick, Maine. This explains why Wood responded that he no longer had them.

32. Howard, *Supplementary Report,* 57.

33. Howard to Miles, October 7, 1877, NARG 94, LR, AGO, Special File 3464.

34. Sheridan to General E. D. Townsend, October 10 and November 14, 1877, CIA Hoyt to Secretary of Interior, November 16, 1877, General Pope to AAG, December 4, 1877, and Sherman to Secretary of War, April 4, 1877, NARG 94, LR, AGO, Special File 3464; Sheridan to Terry, October 10, 1877, NARG 393, LR, District of Yellowstone; Pearson, *Nez Perces,* 77–101.

35. Pearson, *Nez Perces,* 120–27; West, *Last Indian War,* 301–14.

36. White Bird led the exodus to Canada, fleeing at night. Some sources suggest that 230 escaped, while historian Jerome Greene puts the number at 290. But Major A. G. Irvine of the Mounted Police reported just 100 in Sitting Bull's camp in April 1878. The numbers obviously vacillated, as Indians came and went, some trying to return to the Idaho Reservation. West, *Last Indian War,* 281, 296; Anderson, *Sitting Bull,* 126–27; Jerome A. Greene, *Beyond Bear's Paw: The Nez Perce Indians in Canada* (Norman: University of Oklahoma Press, 2010), 67; Gibbon to Terry, December 23, 1877, NARG 393, District of Montana; Major Irvine message, in Colonel John Brooke to AAG, April 9, 1878, and Major H. C. Chipman to AAG, July 26, 1878, NARG 94, LR, AGO, Special File 3464.

37. Simmons, *Ute Indians,* 148–50.

38. Ibid., 139–49. See also Ned Blackhawk's discussion of Ouray's growing influence in *Violence over the Land,* 202–206.

39. For Meeker, see Marshall Sprague's classic *Massacre: The Tragedy at White River* (Boston: Little, Brown, 1957), 168–72; as well as Robert Silbernagel, *Troubled Trails: The Meeker Affair and the Expulsion of the Utes from Colorado* (Salt Lake City: University of Utah Press, 2011), 78–83.

40. Colonel Edwin Hatch to AAG, May 2, 1879, Meeker to Hayt, July 7, August 11, and September 13, 1879, and Major Thornburgh to AAG, July 27, 1879, NARG 94, LR, AGO, Special File 4278.

41. Pope to Adjutant General, September 13, 1879, and Sheridan to the Adjutant General, September 26, 1879, NARG 94, LR, AGO, Special File 4278; Mark E. Miller, *Hollow Victory: The White River Expedition of 1879 and the Battle of Milk Creek* (Boulder: University of Colorado Press, 1997), 22–25.

42. Simmons, *Ute Indians,* 186.

43. Thornburgh to Meeker, September 25 and 28, 1879, and Meeker to Thornburgh, September 27 and 29, 1879, NARG 94, LR, AGO, Special File 4278.

44. Miller, *Hollow Victory,* 84–143. The most useful immediate reports of the encounter are Captain J. Scott Payne to AAG, October 5, 1879, Captain Francis Dodge to Pope, October 8, 1879, and General Crook to AAG, October 8, 1879, NARG 94, LR, AGO, Special File 4278.

45. Agent W. M. Stanley to Henry Page, October 9 and 12, 1879, and Merritt telegram, October 13, 1879, NARG 94, LR, AGO, Special File 4278.

46. Sheridan to Sherman, October 26, 1879, NARG 94, LR, AGO.

47. Army officers in the West, in particular both Merritt and Pope, were furious with Schurz's meddling. Merritt concluded that "being equipped for a

campaign by one arm of the government and halted in its execution by another" was inexplicable. See Sheridan to Sherman, October 17 and 23, 1879, Schurz to Sherman, October 18, 1879, Merritt to Crook, October 22, 1879, and Pope to Sheridan, November 17, 1879, NARG 94, LR, AGO, Special File 4278. See also Simmons, *Ute Indians,* 188–89.

48. Adams to Schurz, October 21, 1879, Sherman to Sheridan, October 22, 1879, and Sheridan to Sherman, October 26, 1879, NARG 94, LR, AGO, Special File 4278.

49. Ouray speech in Inspector W. J. Pollock to CIA, October 24, 1879, NARG 94, LR, AGO, Special File 4278.

50. For the captives' story and the debate about the possible rape of the four women, see Silbernagel, *Troubled Trails,* 89–118.

51. Miller, *Hollow Victory,* 157–59.

52. Sherman to Schurz, April 27, 1880, Pope to Colonel W. D. Whipple, May 7, 1880, Christopher Gilson to MacKenzie, May 11 and 17, 1880, and Manypenny to MacKenzie, July 13, 1880, NARG 94, LR, AGO, Special File 4278.

53. Miller, *Hollow Victory,* 158–59; Simmons, *Ute Indians,* 192–93.

54. Pope to W. D. Whipple, February 16, 1880, NARG 94, LR, AGO, Special File 4278; Silbernagel, *Troubled Trails,* 160–70; Simmons, *Ute Indians,* 195–97.

55. Sweeney, *From Cochise to Geronimo,* 147–80. Sweeney's encyclopedic study of the period 1874–87 is essential and is used heavily here in understanding the various negotiations that went on between Geronimo and the army.

56. Ibid. 180–298.

57. Lieutenant Gatewood later wrote an interesting account of his dealings with Geronimo, including his final surrender in 1886: Gatewood, *Lieutenant Charles Gatewood and His Apache Wars,* ed. Louis Kraft (Lincoln: University of Nebraska Press, 2005).

58. Sweeney, *From Cochise to Geronimo,* 341–428.

59. Ibid., 429–54.

60. Ibid., 465–67.

61. Ibid., 510–23. Crook naturally believed that the war was over and telegraphed that to superiors. See Angie Debo, *Geronimo: The Man, His Time, His Place* (Norman: University of Oklahoma Press, 1976), 243–63.

62. Sweeney, *From Cochise to Geronimo,* 552–68. For a good description of the deportation, see Douglas C. McChristian, *Fort Bowie, Arizona: Combat Post of the Southwest, 1858–1894* (Norman: University of Oklahoma Press, 2005), 204–209.

63. Sweeney, *From Cochise to Geronimo,* 572–73.

64. Ibid., 574–75.

65. Kathleen Chamberlain makes the point that the loss of this reservation led to the massive outbreak in the early 1880s: Chamberlain, *Victorio,* 208–209.

66. Geronimo, *Geronimo, His Own Story: As Told to S. M. Barrett,* ed. Frederick Turner (New York: Duffield, 1906; reprint, New York: Meridian Books, 1996), 309.

EPILOGUE: ALLOTMENT AND THE FINAL ETHNIC CLEANSING OF AMERICA

1. Much has been written on this group. See Brian W. Dippie, *The Vanishing American: Attitudes and U.S. Indian Policy* (Lawrence: University Press of Kansas, 1982); D. S. Otis, *The Dawes Act and the Allotment of Indian Lands* (Norman: University of Oklahoma Press, 1973); Fritz, *Movement for Indian Assimilation;* Wilcomb E. Washburn, *The Assault on Indian Tribalism* (Philadelphia: Lippincott, 1975); and William T. Hagan, *Taking Indian Lands: The Cherokee (Jerome) Commission* (Norman: University of Oklahoma Press, 2003).

2. For most of these treaties, see Kappler, *Indian Affairs,* 2:606–755.

3. Ibid., 2:608–609, 611–14, 634–36.

4. Confederation of American Indians, *Indian Reservations,* 89–92, 107, 113.

5. The agent's role in selecting competent and not-so-competent Indians was written into the treaty of 1864 with the Saginaw Indians, a slight revision from the 1855 accord, which included moving several smaller bands onto the Isabella Indian Reservation. For both treaties, see Kappler, *Indian Affairs,* 2:733–35, 868–71.

6. Nearly sixty "Warranty Deeds" have survived in the papers of one of the speculators, Alexander Andre. See Andre Deeds, 1871 and 1872, Bentley Library, University of Michigan, Ann Arbor.

7. Kappler, *Indian Affairs,* 2:733–35. The official report, dated February 22, 1876, was written by Indian Office troubleshooter Edward C. Kemble: NARG 75, LR, Michigan Agency.

8. Manypenny, *Our Indian Wards,* xxvi.

9. Fritz, *Movement for Indian Assimilation,* 198–213; Prucha, *Great Father,* 224–32.

10. Forty-Ninth Congress, 2nd session, Statutes at Large, 24, 388–91.

11. Quoted in Arrell Morgan Gibson, *The American Indian: Prehistory to the Present* (Lexington, Mass.: D. C. Heath, 1980), 497.

12. Hagan, *Taking Indian Lands,* 5–17, 235–40; W. David Baird and Danney Goble, *Oklahoma: A History* (Norman: University of Oklahoma Press, 2008).

13. Kent Carter, *The Dawes Commission and the Allotment of the Five Civilized Tribes, 1893–1914* (Oren, Utah: Ancestry.com, 1999), 39–67.

14. Meyer, *White Earth Tragedy,* 53–63, 140–201; Confederation of American Indians, *Indian Reservations,* 121.

15. Confederation of American Indians, *Indian Reservations,* 252–57.

16. Hoxie, *Final Promise,* 217–21.

17. See Box E in Ayer Papers, Newberry Library, Chicago.

18. Emily Greenwald, *Reconfiguring the Reservation: The Nez Perces, Jicarilla Apaches, and the Dawes Act* (Albuquerque: University of New Mexico Press, 2002), 80–82, 114–17, 170–74.

19. Ibid.

20. A good discussion of the Wounded Knee Massacre, clearly a war crime, is found in Ostler, *Plains Sioux,* 338–60. See also Robert M. Utley, *The Last Days of the Sioux Nation* (New Haven: Yale University Press, 1963).

21. Mark K. Megehee, "Creek Nativism since 1865," *Chronicles of Oklahoma* 56 (Fall 1978): 289–90.

22. Blue Clark, *Lone Wolf v. Hitchcock: Treaty Rights and Indian Law at the End of the Nineteenth Century* (Lincoln: University of Nebraska Press, 1994).

23. Citizenship, and its benefits, fell under the province of state law, so very few Indians, even those who retained their allotments, ever were allowed to vote in most states well into the twentieth century.

BIBLIOGRAPHY

PRIMARY SOURCES: ARCHIVAL

Adjutant General's Papers, Texas. Texas State Archives, Austin.

Andre, Alexander. "Warranty Deeds." Bentley Library, University of Michigan, Ann Arbor.

Ayer, Edward. Papers. Newberry Library, Chicago.

Bent, George. Papers. Denver Public Library, Denver.

Brown, Joseph R. Papers. Minnesota Historical Society, St. Paul.

Campbell, Walter Stanley. Western History Collection. University of Oklahoma, Norman.

Carr, Eugene. Papers. Military History Institute. Carlisle Barracks, Pennsylvania.

Doolittle, James Root. Papers. Colorado Historical Society, Denver.

Evans, John. Papers and Letterbooks. Colorado Historical Society, Denver.

Fort Ridgely Historical Association Papers. Minnesota Historical Society, St. Paul.

Governor's Papers. Texas State Archives, Austin.

Grinnell, George Bird. Papers. Braun Research Library, Southwest Museum, Los Angeles, California.

Howard, O. O. Papers. Bowdoin College, Brunswick, Maine.

National Archives Record Group 48. Special Files of the Interior Department Relating to Indian Affairs. National Archives, Washington, D.C.

National Archives Record Group 75. Documents Relating to the Negotiation of Ratified and Unratified Treaties, 1801–69. National Archives, Washington, D.C.

National Archives Record Group 75. Letters Received, California Superintendency, 1849–60. National Archives, Washington, D.C.

National Archives Record Group 75. Letters Received, Cherokee Agency, 1859–64. National Archives, Washington, D.C.

National Archives Record Group 75, Letters Received, Cheyenne River Agency, 1871–80. National Archives, Washington, D.C.

National Archives Record Group 75. Letters Received, Dakota Superintendency, 1861–77. National Archives, Washington, D.C.

National Archives Record Group 75. Letters Received, Kiowa Agency, 1864–76. National Archives, Washington, D.C.

National Archives Record Group 75. Letters Received, Michigan Agency, 1828–80 (sometimes identified as Mackinac Agency). National Archives, Washington, D.C.

National Archives Record Group 75. Letters Received, Oregon Superintendency, 1853–61. National Archives, Washington, D.C.

National Archives Record Group 75. Letters Received, Red Cloud Agency, 1871–76. National Archives, Washington, D.C.

National Archives Record Group 75. Letters Received, Spotted Tail Agency, 1875–77. National Archives, Washington, D.C.

National Archives Record Group 75. Letters Received, Standing Rock Agency, 1875–77. National Archives, Washington, D.C.

National Archives Record Group 75. Letters Received, St. Peter's Agency, 1845–67. National Archives, Washington, D.C.

National Archives Record Group 75. Letters Received, Upper Arkansas Agency, 1855–74. National Archives, Washington, D.C.

National Archives Record Group 75. Letters Received, Upper Platte Agency, 1846–70. National Archives, Washington, D.C.

National Archives Record Group 75. Letters Received, Washington Superintendency, 1853–61. National Archives, Washington, D.C.

National Archives Record Group 75. Report Books of the Office of Indian Affairs. National Archives, Washington, D.C.

National Archives Record Group 94. Letters Received (Main Series), 1861–80. National Archives, Washington, D.C.

National Archives Record Group 107. Letters Received by the Secretary of War Relating to Indian Affairs. 1800–24. National Archives, Washington, D.C.

National Archives Record Group 107. Letters Sent by the Secretary of War Relating to Indian Affairs. 1800–24. National Archives, Washington, D.C.

National Archives Record Group 393. Fort Ridgely Letterbook. National Archives, Washington, D.C.

National Archives Record Group 393. Letters Received, Department of Oregon, 1858–61. National Archives, Washington, D.C.

National Archives Record Group 393. Letters Received, District of Iowa, 1862–65. National Archives, Washington, D.C.

National Archives Record Group 393. Letters Received, District of Montana, 1867–79. National Archives, Washington, D.C.

National Archives Record Group 393. Letters Received, District of the Yellowstone, 1876–81. National Archives, Washington, D.C.

National Archives Record Group 393. Letters Received, Fort Bufford. National Archives, Washington, D.C.

National Archives Record Group 393. Letters Received, Fort Hale. National Archives, Washington, D.C.

National Archives Record Group 393. Letters Received, Fort Laramie. National Archives, Washington, D.C.

National Archives Record Group 393. Letters Received, Middle District of the Department of Dakota. National Archives, Washington, D.C.

National Archives Record Group 393. Letters Received and "Special Files," Military Division of Missouri, 1871–76. National Archives, Washington, D.C.

National Archives Record Group 393. Letters Sent and Letters Received, Department of Missouri, 1861–75. National Archives, Washington, D.C.

National Archives Record Group 393. Letters Sent and Letters Received, Department of the West and Western Department, 1853–61. National Archives, Washington, D.C.

National Archives Record Group 393. Letters Sent and Letters Received, District of the Upper Arkansas, 1864–69. National Archives, Washington, D.C.

National Archives Record Group 393. Letters Sent and Letters Received, Division and Department of the Pacific, 1848–61. National Archives, Washington, D.C.

National Archives Record Group 393. Letters Sent and Letters Received, Western Division and Department 1820–54. National Archives, Washington, D.C.

National Archives Record Group 393. Letters Sent and Received, Department of Dakota. National Archives, Washington, D.C.

National Archives Record Group 393. Letters Sent and Received, Department of the Northwest, 1862–65. National Archives, Washington, D.C.

Neighbors, Robert S. Papers. Eugene C. Barker Library, University of Texas, Austin.

Nesmith, Willis. Papers. Oregon Historical Society, Portland.

Sanborn, John B. Papers. Minnesota Historical Society, St. Paul.

Sheehan, Timothy J. Diary and Papers. Minnesota Historical Society, St. Paul.

Sheridan, Philip. Papers. Library of Congress, Washington, D.C.

Sibley, Henry Hastings. Papers. Minnesota Historical Society. St. Paul.

U.S. Congress. House and Senate Documents and Reports. Serial set.

Primary Sources: Published

American State Papers: Indian Affairs. 2 vols. Washington, D.C.: Gales and Seaton, 1832–34.

Annals of Congress: The Debates and Proceedings of the Congress of the United States. The Senate and the House of Representatives. Library of Congress Internet Source. http://memory.loc.gov/ammem/amlaw/lwaclink.html.

Bassett, John S., ed. *Correspondence of Andrew Jackson.* 7 vols. Washington, D.C.: Carnegie Institute, 1926–35.

Battey, Thomas C. *The Life and Adventures of a Quaker among the Indians.* Boston: Lee, Shepard, and Dillingham, 1875.

Beeson, John. *A Plea for the Indians: With Facts and Features of the Late War in Oregon.* New York: Published by John Beeson, 1857.

Browne, J. Ross. "Report of the Secretary of Interior, Including the Report of J. Ross Browne on the Late Indian War in Oregon and Washington Territory" (1858). In *House Executive Document* 38, 35th Congress, 1st session. Serial 955.

Campbell, Thomas. *The Poetical Works of Thomas Campbell.* Ed. Rufus W. Griswold. New York: Leavitt and Allen, 1865.

Carson, Kit. *Navajo Roundup: Selected Correspondence of Kit Carson's Expedition against the Navajo, 1863–1865.* Ed. Lawrence Kelly. Boulder, Colo.: Pruett Publishing, 1970.

Carter, Robert G. *The Old Sergeant's Story: Winning the West from the Indians and Bad Men in 1870 to 1878.* New York: Frederick Ritchcock, 1926.

Cass, Lewis. "Removal of the Indians." *North American Review* (January 1830): 62–121.

A Compilation of the Messages and Papers of the Presidents, 1789–1902. 10 vols. Ed. James D. Richardson. New York: Bureau of National Literature and Art, 1904.

Correspondence of the Subject of the Emigration of Indians, between the 30th November, 1831, and 27th December, 1833, with Abstracts of Expenditures by Disbursing Agents. 5 vols. Senate Document 512. Washington, D.C.: Dub Green, 1834.

Davis, K. G., ed. *Documents of the American Revolution, 1770–1783.* 21 vols. Shannon, Ireland: Irish University Press, 1972–81.

Deloria, Vine, Jr., and Raymond DeMallie, eds. *Proceedings of the Great Peace Commission of 1867–1868.* Washington, D.C.: Institute for the Development of Indian Law, 1975.

Estep, Raymond E., ed. "Lieutenant William E. Burnet Letters: Removal of the Texas Indians and the Founding of Fort Cobb: Part II." *Chronicles of Oklahoma* 38 (1960): 369–96.

Fitzpatrick, John C., ed. *The Diaries of George Washington, 1748–1794.* 4 vols. Boston: Houghton Mifflin, 1925.

Gatewood, Lieutenant Charles. *Lieutenant Charles Gatewood and His Apache Wars.* Ed. Louis Kraft. Lincoln: University of Nebraska Press, 2005.

Geronimo. *Geronimo, His Own Story: As Told to S. M. Barrett.* Ed. Frederick Turner. New York: Duffield, 1906; reprint New York: Meridian Books, 1996.

Hollibaugh, E. F. *Biographical History of Cloud County, Kansas: Biographies of Representative Citizens.* N.p.: Wilson Humphrey, 1903.

Howard, O. O. *Nez Perce Joseph: An Account of His Ancestors, His Lands, His Confederates, His Enemies, His Murders, His War, His Pursuit and Capture.* Boston: Lee and Shepard, 1881.

Kalter, Susan, ed. *Benjamin Franklin, Pennsylvania, and the First Nations.* Urbana: University of Illinois Press, 2006.

Kappler, Charles L. *Indian Affairs: Laws and Treaties*. 2 vols. Washington, D.C.: Government Printing Office, 1903.

Knopf, Richard C, ed. *Anthony Wayne, A Name in Arms: Soldier, Diplomat, Defender of Expansion Westward of a Nation*. Pittsburgh: University of Pittsburgh Press, 1960.

Manypenny, George. *Our Indian Wards*. 1880; reprint New York: Decapo, 1972.

Meriwether, Robert L., ed. *The Papers of John C. Calhoun*. 28 vols. Columbia: University of South Carolina Press, 1959–91.

Ross, John. *Papers of Chief John Ross*. 2 vols. Ed. Gary E. Moulton. Norman: University of Oklahoma Press, 1984.

Sherrill v. Oneida Indian Nation (2005), 544 U.S. 197.

Smith, Sam B., and Harriet Chappell Owsley, eds. *The Papers of Andrew Jackson*. 17 vols. Knoxville: University of Tennessee Press, 1980.

Territorial Papers of the United States. Ed. Clarence Edwin Carter. 18 vols. Washington, D.C.: Government Printing Office, 1934–62.

Through Dakota Eyes: Narrative Accounts of the Minnesota Indian War of 1862. Ed. Gary Clayton Anderson and Alan R. Woolworth. St. Paul: Minnesota Historical Society Press, 1988.

Victor, Frances Fuller. *The Early Indian Wars of Oregon: Compiled from the Oregon Archives and Other Original Sources*. Salem: Frank C. Baker, 1894.

Walton, Joseph S. *Conrad Weiser and the Indian Policy of Colonial Pennsylvania*. Philadelphia: George W. Jacobs, n.d.

Wilson, James Grant, and John Fiske, eds. *Appleton's Cyclopaedia of American Biography*. 6 vols. New York: D. Appleton, 1888.

The Writings of Thomas Jefferson. Ed. Andrew A. Lipscomb. 20 vols. Washington, D.C.: Thomas Jefferson Memorial Association, 1903–1904.

Yoakum, Henderson. *History of Texas from the First Settlement in 1685 to Its Annexation to the United States in 1846*. 2 vols. New York: Redfield, 1855.

NEWSPAPERS

Dallas Herald, 1858–59

National Republican (Washington, D.C.), 1875

New Ulm Review (Minnesota), 1912

New York Times, 1875

New York World, 1874

Southern Intelligencer (Austin, Texas), 1858–59

SECONDARY SOURCES

Abel, Annie Heloise. *The American Indian under Reconstruction*. Cleveland: Arthur H. Clark: 1925; reprint Lincoln: University of Nebraska Press, 1993.

Abler, Thomas S. *Cornplanter: Chief Warrior of the Allegheny Senecas*. Syracuse: Syracuse University Press, 2007.

Ackerman, Robert K. *South Carolina Colonial Land Policies*. Columbia: University of South Carolina Press, 1977.

Alberts, Don E. *The Battle of Glorieta: Union Victory in the West*. College Station: Texas A&M University Press, 1998.

Almaráz, Félix D., Jr. *The San Antonio Missions and Their System of Land Tenure*. Austin: University of Texas Press, 1989.

Anderson, Fred. *Crucible of War: The Seven Years' War and the Fate of Empire in British North America, 1754–1766*. New York: Vintage Books, 2001.

———. *The Dominion of War: Empire and Liberty in North America, 1500–2000*. New York: Viking, 2005.

Anderson, Gary Clayton. *The Conquest of Texas: Ethnic Cleansing in the Promised Land*. Norman: University of Oklahoma Press, 2005.

———. *The Indian Southwest, 1580–1830: Ethnogenesis and Reinvention*. Norman: University of Oklahoma Press, 1999.

———. *Kinsmen of Another Kind: Dakota-White Relations in the Upper Mississippi Valley, 1650–1862*. Lincoln: University of Nebraska Press, 1984.

———. *Little Crow: Spokesman for the Sioux*. St. Paul: Minnesota Historical Society Press, 1986.

———. *Sitting Bull and the Paradox of Lakota Nationhood*. New York: Harper Collins, 1996; reprint Pearson/Longman, 2007.

Anderson, Virginia DeJohn. "King Philip's Herds: Indians, Colonists, and the Problem of Livestock in Early New England." *William and Mary Quarterly* 51 (October 1991): 601–24.

Andrews, K. R., N. P. Canny, and P. E. Hair. *The Westward Enterprise: English Activities in Ireland, the Atlantic, and America, 1480–1650*. Detroit: Wayne State University Press, 1979.

Aron, Stephen. *How the West Was Lost*. Baltimore: Johns Hopkins University Press, 1996.

Athearn, Robert F. *Forts of the Upper Missouri*. Englewood Cliffs, N.J.: Prentice-Hall, 1967.

———. *William Tecumseh Sherman and the Settlement of the West*. Norman: University of Oklahoma Press, 1956.

Atkison, Norman B. *Nez Perce Indian War and Original Stories*. Grangeville: Idaho County Free Press, 1966.

Bagley, Will. *Blood of the Prophets: Brigham Young and the Massacre at Mountain Meadows*. Norman: University of Oklahoma Press, 2002.

Bailyn, Bernard. *Atlantic History: Concept and Contours*. Cambridge, Mass.: Harvard University Press, 2005.

Baird, W. David, and Danney Goble. *Oklahoma: A History*. Norman: University of Oklahoma Press, 2008.

Bakeman, Mary H., and Antona M. Richardson, eds. *Trails of Tears: Minnesota's Dakota Indian Exile Begins*. Roseville, Minn.: Prairie Echoes, 2008.

Bakken, Gordon Morris, ed. *Law in the Western United States*. Norman: University of Oklahoma Press, 2000.

Banner, Stuart. *How the Indians Lost Their Land: Law and Power on the Frontier.* Cambridge, Mass.: Harvard University Press, 2005.

Bauer, William J. *We Were All Like Migrant Workers Here: Work, Community, and Memory on California's Round Valley Reservation, 1850–1941.* Chapel Hill: University of North Carolina Press, 2009.

Beal, Merrill D. *"I Will Fight No More Forever": Chief Joseph and the Nez Perce War.* Seattle: University of Washington Press, 1963.

Beckham, Stephen Dow, ed. *Oregon Indians: Voices from Two Centuries.* Corvallis: Oregon State University Press, 2006.

————. *Requiem for a People: The Rogue Indians and The Frontiersmen.* Norman: University of Oklahoma Press, 1971.

Belich, James. *Replenishing the Earth: The Settler Revolution and the Rise of the Anglo-world, 1783–1939.* New York: Oxford University Press, 2009.

————. "The Rise of the Angloworld: Settlement in North America and Australia, 1784–1918." In *Rediscovering the British World,* ed. Phillip Buckner and R. Douglas Francis, 39–57. Calgary: University of Calgary Press, 2005.

Bell-Fialkoff, Andrew. "A Brief History of Ethnic Cleansing." *Foreign Affairs* 72 (Summer 1993): 110–21.

Berry, John A., and Carol Pott Berry, eds. *Genocide in Rwanda: A Collective Memory.* Washington, D.C.: Howard University Press, 1999.

Berthrong, Donald J. *The Southern Cheyennes.* Norman: University of Oklahoma Press, 1963.

Blackhawk, Ned. *Violence over the Land: Indians and Empires in the American West.* Cambridge, Mass.: Harvard University Press, 2008.

Bolton, Herbert Eugene. *Coronado: Knight of Pueblos and Plains.* Albuquerque: University of New Mexico Press, 1949.

Bonvillain, Nancy. *Native Nations: Cultures and Histories of Native North Americans.* Upper Saddle River, N.J.: Prentice-Hall, 2001.

Boyd, Robert. *The Coming of the Spirit of Pestilence: Introduced Infectious Diseases and Population Decline among the Northwest Coast Indians, 1774–1874.* Seattle: University of Washington Press, 1999.

Bragdon, Kathleen J. *Native People of Southern New England, 1500–1650.* Norman: University of Oklahoma Press, 1996.

Bray, Kingsley. *Crazy Horse: A Lakota Life.* Norman: University of Oklahoma Press, 2006.

Brooks, James F. *Captives and Cousins: Slavery, Kinship, and Community in the Southwest Borderlands.* Chapel Hill: University of North Carolina Press, 2002.

Broome, Jeff. *Dog Soldier Justice: The Ordeal of Susanna Alderdice in the Kansas Indian War.* Lincoln: University of Nebraska Press, 2003.

Browning, Christopher R. *Ordinary Men: Reserve Police Battalion 101 and the Final Solution in Poland.* New York: Harper, 1992.

Buckley, Jay H. *William Clark: Indian Diplomat.* Norman: University of Oklahoma Press, 2008.

Buecker, Thomas R. *Fort Robinson and the American West, 1874–1899.* Norman: University of Oklahoma Press, 1999.

Burke, Thomas E., Jr. *Mohawk Frontier.* Albany: State University of New York Press, 1991.

Call, Charles T. *Building States to Build Peace.* London: Lynne Rienner, 2008.

Calloway, Colin G. *One Vast Winter Count: The Native American West before Lewis and Clark.* Lincoln: University of Nebraska Press, 2003.

————. *The Scratch of a Pen: 1763 and the Transformation of North America.* New York: Oxford University Press, 2006.

————. *White People, Indians, and Highlanders: Tribal Peoples and Colonial Encounters in Scotland and America.* New York: Oxford University Press, 2008.

Cantrell, Gregg. *Stephen F. Austin: Empresario of Texas.* New Haven: Yale University Press, 1999.

Carranco, Lynwood, and Estle Beard. *Genocide and Vendetta: The Round Valley Wars of Northern California.* Norman: University of Oklahoma Press, 1981.

Carrico, Richard L. "San Diego Indians and the Federal Government: Years of Neglect, 1850–1865." *San Diego Historical Quarterly* 26 (Summer 1980): 47–62.

Carriker, Robert. *Father Peter John De Smet: Jesuit in the West.* Norman: University of Oklahoma Press, 1998.

————. *Fort Supply, Indian Territory: Frontier Outpost on the Plains.* Norman: University of Oklahoma Press, 1970.

Carter, Kent. *The Dawes Commission and the Allotment of the Five Civilized Tribes, 1893–1914.* Oren, Utah: Ancestry.com, 1999.

Chalfant, William Y. *Cheyennes and Horse Soldiers: The 1857 Expedition and the Battle of Solomon's Fork.* Norman: University of Oklahoma Press, 1989.

————. *Cheyennes at Dark Water Creek: The Last Fight of the Red River War.* Norman: University of Oklahoma Press, 1997.

————. *Hancock's War: Conflict on the Southern Plains.* Norman: Arthur H. Clark, 2010.

Chamberlain, Kathleen. *Victorio: Apache Warrior and Chief.* Norman: University of Oklahoma Press, 2007.

Chevalier, François. *Land and Society in Colonial Mexico: The Great Hacienda.* Berkeley: University of California Press, 1963.

Chomsky, Carol. "The United States–Dakota War Trials: A Study in Military Justice." *Stanford Law Review* 43 (November 1990): 13–98.

Christensen, Scott R. *Sagwitch: Shoshone Chieftain, Morman Elder, 1822–1887.* Logan: Utah State University Press, 1999.

Churchill, Ward. *Kill the Indian, Save the Man: The Genocidal Impact of American Indian Schools.* San Francisco: City Lights, 2004.

————. *A Little Matter of Genocide: Holocaust and Denial in America.* San Francisco: City Lights, 1998.

————. *Struggle for the Land: Indigenous Resistance to Genocide, Ecocide, and Expropriation in Contemporary North America.* San Francisco: City Lights, 2002.

Clark, Blue. *Lone Wolf v. Hitchcock: Treaty Rights and Indian Law at the End of the Nineteenth Century.* Lincoln: University of Nebraska Press, 1994.

Coffer, William E. "Genocide among the California Indians." *Indian Historian* 10 (Spring 1977): 1–16.

Confederation of American Indians. *Indian Reservations: A State and Federal Handbook.* Jefferson, N.C.: McFarland, 1986.

Confer, Clarissa W. *The Cherokee Nation in the Civil War.* Norman: University of Oklahoma Press, 2007.

Cook, Sherburne F. *The Conflict between the California Indians and White Civilization.* Berkeley: University of California Press, 1976.

———. "The Epidemic of 1830–1833 in California and Oregon." *University of California Publications in American Archaeology and Ethnology* 43, no. 3 (1955): 303–25.

———. *The Population of the California Indians, 1769–1970.* Berkeley: University of California Press, 1976.

Corkran, David H. *The Cherokee Frontier: Conflict and Survival, 1740–1762.* Norman: University of Oklahoma Press, 1962.

———. *The Creek Frontier, 1540–1783.* Norman: University of Oklahoma Press, 1967.

Cotterill, R. S. *The Southern Indians: The Story of the Civilized Tribes before Removal.* Norman: University of Oklahoma Press, 1954.

Cozzens, Peter. *General John Pope: A Life for the Nation.* Urbana: University of Illinois Press, 2000.

Cronon, William. *Changes in the Land: Indians, Colonists, and the Ecology of New England.* New York: Hill and Wang, 1983.

Debo, Angie. *Geronimo: The Man, His Time, His Place.* Norman: University of Oklahoma Press, 1976.

———. "The Location of the Battle of Round Mountains." *Chronicles of Oklahoma* 41 (Spring 1963): 70–104.

De la Teja, Jesús F. *San Antonio de Béxar: A Community on New Spain's Northern Frontier.* Albuquerque: University of New Mexico Press, 1997.

De León, Arnoldo, and Kenneth L. Stewart. *Tejanos and the Numbers Game: A Socio-Historical Interpretation from the Federal Census, 1850–1900.* Albuquerque: University of New Mexico Press, 1989.

DeRosier, Arthur H., Jr. *The Removal of the Choctaw Indians.* Knoxville: University of Tennessee Press, 1970.

Dippie, Brian W. *The Vanishing American: Attitudes and U.S. Indian Policy.* Lawrence: University Press of Kansas, 1982.

Divine, Robert A., et al. *America, Past and Present.* New York: Longman, 2011.

Dobyns, Henry. *Their Numbers Become Thinned: Native American Population Dynamics in Eastern North America.* Knoxville: University of Tennessee Press, 1983.

Dowd, Gregory Evans. "'Insidious Friends': Gift Giving and the Cherokee–British Alliance in the Seven Years' War." In *Contact Points: American Frontiers from the Mohawk Valley to the Mississippi, 1750–1830,* ed. Andrew R. L. Cayton and Fredrika J. Teute, 114–50. Chapel Hill: University of North Carolina Press, 1998.

———. *War under Heaven: Pontiac, the Indian Nations, and the British.* Baltimore: Johns Hopkins University Press, 2002.

Downes, Randolph C. *Council Fires on the Upper Ohio: A Narrative of Indian Affairs in the Upper Ohio Valley until 1795.* Pittsburgh: University of Pittsburgh Press, 1940.

Dunbar-Ortiz, Roxanne. *Roots of Resistance: A History of Land Tenure in New Mexico.* Norman: University of Oklahoma Press, 2007.

Dunlay, Tom. *Kit Carson and the Indians.* Lincoln: University of Nebraska Press, 2000.

Duthu, N. Bruce. *American Indians and the Law.* New York: Viking, 2008.

DuVal Kathleen. *The Native Ground: Indians and Colonists in the Heart of the Continent.* Philadelphia: University of Pennsylvania Press, 2006.

Ebright, Malcolm. "New Mexican Land Grants: The Legal Background." In *Land, Water, and Culture: New Perspectives on Hispanic Land Grants,* ed. Charles L. Briggs and John R. Van Ness, 54–89. Albuquerque: University of New Mexico Press, 1987.

Eccles, W. J. *The Canadian Frontier, 1534–1760.* New York: Holt, Rinehart and Winston, 1969.

Edmunds, R. David. *The Potawatomis: Keepers of the Fire.* Norman: University of Oklahoma Press, 1978.

———. *The Shawnee Prophet.* Lincoln: University of Nebraska Press, 1983.

———. *Tecumseh and the Quest for Indian Leadership.* Boston: Little, Brown, 1984.

Edmunds, R. David, and Joseph L. Peyser. *The Fox Wars: The Mesquakie Challenge to New France.* Norman: University of Oklahoma Press, 1993.

Elliott, J. H. *Empires of the Atlantic World: Britain and Spain in America, 1492–1830.* New Haven: Yale University Press, 2006.

Ellis, Richard N. *General Pope and the U.S. Indian Policy.* Albuquerque: University of New Mexico Press, 1970.

Faiman-Silva, Sandra. *Choctaws at the Crossroads: The Political Economy of Class and Culture in the Oklahoma Timber Region.* Lincoln: University of Nebraska Press, 1997.

Faragher, John Mack. *Daniel Boone: The Life and Legend of an American Pioneer.* New York: Henry Holt, 1992.

Farmer, Jared. *On Zion's Mount: Mormons, Indians, and the American Landscape.* Cambridge, Mass.: Harvard University Press, 2008.

Fenn, Elizabeth A. "Biological Warfare in Eighteenth-Century America: Beyond Jeffrey Amherst." *Journal of American History* 86 (March 2000): 1552–80.

———. *Pox Americana: The Great Smallpox Epidemic of 1775–1782.* New York: Hill and Wang, 2001.

Fernández-Armesto, Felipe. *Amerigo: The Man Who Gave His Name to America.* London: Weidenfeld and Nicolson, 2006.

Fisher, Louis. *Military Tribunals and Presidential Power.* Lawrence: University Press of Kansas, 2005.

Fleisher, Kass. *The Bear River Massacre and the Making of History.* Albany: State University of New York Press, 2004.

Flores, Dan. "Bison Ecology and Bison Diplomacy: The Southern Plains from 1800 to 1850." *Journal of American History* 78 (September 1991): 465–85.

Folwell, William Watts. *A History of Minnesota.* 4 vols. St. Paul: Minnesota Historical Society Press, 1921–30.

Ford, Lisa. *Settler Sovereignty: Jurisdiction and Indigenous People in America and Australia, 1788–1836.* Cambridge, Mass.: Harvard University Press, 2010.

Foreman, Grant. *Indian Removal: The Emigration of the Five Civilized Tribes of Indians.* Rev. ed. Norman: University of Oklahoma Press, 1972.

Foster, Morris W. *Being Comanche: A Social History of an American Indian Community.* Tucson: University of Arizona Press, 1991.

Fox, Robin. *Kinship and Marriage: An Anthropological Perspective.* New York: Cambridge University Press, 1967.

Fritz, Henry. *The Movement for Indian Assimilation, 1860–1890.* Philadelphia: University of Pennsylvania Press, 1963.

Gallay, Alan. *The Indian Slave Trade: The Rise of the English Empire in the American South, 1670–1717.* New Haven: Yale University Press, 2002.

Gellately, Robert, and Ben Kiernan, eds. *The Specter of Genocide and Mass Murder in Historical Perspective.* New York: Cambridge University Press, 2003.

Gethyn-Jones, Eric. *George Thorpe and the Berkeley Company: A Gloucestershire Enterprise in Virginia.* London: Alan Sutton, 1982.

Gibson, Arrell Morgan. *The American Indian: Prehistory to the Present.* Lexington, Mass.: D. C. Heath, 1980.

———. *The Chickasaw.* Norman: University of Oklahoma Press, 1971.

Gilman, Rhoda. *Henry Hastings Sibley: Divided Heart.* St. Paul: Minnesota Historical Society Press, 2004.

Goldhagen, Daniel J. *Hitler's Willing Executioners: Ordinary Germans and the Holocaust.* New York: Knopf, 1996.

Gott, Richard. *Britain's Empire: Resistance, Repression, and Revolt.* New York: Verso, 2011.

Gray, John S. *Custer's Last Campaign: Mitch Boyer and the Little Bighorn Reconstructed.* Lincoln: University of Nebraska Press, 1991.

Greaser, Galen D., and Jesús de la Teja. "Quieting Title to Spanish and Mexican Land Grants in the Trans-Nueces: The Bourland and Miller Commission, 1850–1852." *Southwestern Historical Quarterly* 95 (April 1992): 445–64.

Green, Michael D. *The Politics of Indian Removal: Creek Government and Society in Crisis.* Lincoln: University of Nebraska Press, 1981.

Greene, Jack P. *The Quest For Power: The Lower Houses of Assembly in the Southern Royal Colonies, 1689–1776.* Chapel Hill: University of North Carolina Press, 1963.

Greene, Jerome A. *Beyond Bear's Paw: The Nez Perce Indians in Canada.* Norman: University of Oklahoma Press, 2010.

———. *Fort Randall on the Upper Missouri, 1856–1892.* Pierre: South Dakota State Historical Society, 2005.

———, ed. *Lakota and Cheyenne: Indian Views of the Great Sioux War, 1876–1877.* Norman: University of Oklahoma Press, 1994.

———. *Washita: The U.S. Army and the Southern Cheyennes, 1867–1869.* Norman: University of Oklahoma Press, 2004.

Greenwald, Emily. *Reconfiguring the Reservation: The Nez Perces, Jicarilla Apaches, and the Dawes Act.* Albuquerque: University of New Mexico Press, 2002.

Grenier, John. *The First Way of War: American War Making on the Frontier, 1607–1814.* New York: Cambridge University Press, 2005.

Grotius, Hugo. *The Rights of War and Peace: Including the Law of Nature and of Nations.* Trans. A. C. Campbell, with an intro. by David J. Hill. Washington, D.C.: Walter Dunne, Publisher, 1901; reprint Nabu Public Domain Reprint, n.d.

Grumet, Robert S. "The Selling of Lenapehoking." In *Proceedings of the 1992 People to People Conference: Selected Papers,* ed. Charles F. Hayes III, 19–24. Rochester, N.Y.: Rochester Museum and Science Center, 1994.

Gutiérrez, Ramón. *When Jesus Came, the Corn Mothers Went Away: Marriage, Sexuality, and Power in New Mexico, 1500–1846.* Stanford: Stanford University Press, 1991.

Hacket, Charles Wilson, ed., *Revolt of the Pueblo Indians and Otermín's Attempted Reconquest, 1680–1682.* Trans. Charmion Clair Shelby. Albuquerque: University of New Mexico Press, 1941.

Hagan, William T. *Taking Indian Lands: The Cherokee (Jerome) Commission.* Norman: University of Oklahoma Press, 2003.

———. *United States–Comanche Relations: The Reservation Years.* New Haven: Yale University Press, 1976.

Haley, James L. *The Buffalo War: The History of the Red River Indian Uprising of 1874.* Garden City, N.Y.: Doubleday, 1976.

———. *Sam Houston.* Norman: University of Oklahoma Press, 2002.

Hämäläinen, Pekka. *The Comanche Empire.* New Haven: Yale University Press, 2008.

Hanke, Lewis. *Aristotle and the American Indian: A Study in Race Prejudice in the Modern World.* Bloomington: Indiana University Press, 1959.

———. *The Spanish Struggle for Justice in the Conquest of America.* Boston: Little, Brown, 1965.

Hann, John H. *Apalachee: The Land between the Rivers.* Gainesville: University of Florida Press, 1988.

Hardin, Stephen L. *Texas Iliad: A Military History of the Texas Revolution.* Austin: University of Texas Press, 1994.

Hardorff, Richard G., ed. *Indian Views of the Custer Fight: A Source Book.* Norman: University of Oklahoma Press, 2005.

———. *Washita Memories: Eyewitness Views of Custer's Attack on Black Kettle's Village.* Norman: University of Oklahoma Press, 2006.

Harmon, Alexandra, ed. *The Power of Promises: Rethinking Indian Treaties in the Pacific Northwest.* Seattle: University of Washington Press, 2008.

Harper, Steven Craig. *Promised Land: Penn's Holy Experiment, the Walking Purchase, and the Dispossession of the Delawares, 1600–1763.* Bethlehem, Pa.: Lehigh University Press, 2006.

Hatch, Thom. *Black Kettle: The Cheyenne Chief Who Sought Peace but Found War.* New York: John Wiley, 2004.

Hatley, Thomas M. *The Dividing Paths: Cherokees and South Carolinians through the Era of Revolution.* New York: Oxford University Press, 1993.

Hauptman, Laurence M. *Between Two Fires: American Indians in the Civil War.* New York: Free Press, 1995.

————. "General John E. Wool in Cherokee Country, 1836–1837: A Reinterpretation." *Georgia Historical Quarterly* 85 (Spring 2001): 1–26.

Hauptman, Laurence M., and James D. Wherry, eds. *The Pequots in Southern New England: The Fall and Rise of an American Indian Nation.* Norman: University of Oklahoma Press, 1990.

Hayden, Robert M. "Schindler's Fate: Genocide, Ethnic Cleansing, and Population Transfer." *Slavic Review* 55 (Winter 1996): 732–43.

Hedren, Paul L. *After Custer: Loss and Transformation in Sioux Country.* Norman: University of Oklahoma Press, 2011.

————, ed. *The Great Sioux War, 1876–1877.* Helena: Montana Historical Association, 1991.

Heizer, Robert F., ed. *The Destruction of the California Indians: A Collection of Documents from the Period 1847 to 1865 in Which Are Described Some of the Things That Happened to Some of the Indians of California.* Santa Barbara: Peregrine Smith, 1972.

————. *The Eighteen Unratified Treaties of 1851–1852 between the California Indians and the United States Government.* Berkeley: University of California, Department of Anthropology, 1972.

————, ed. *George Gibb's Journal of Redick McKee's Expedition through Northwestern California in 1851.* Berkeley: University of California Press, 1972.

Henderson, Archibald. *The Conquest of the Old Southwest.* New York: Century, 1920.

Herzog, Tamar. *Defining Nations: Immigrants and Citizens in Early Modern Spain and Spanish America.* New Haven: Yale University Press, 2003.

Himmel, Kelley F. *The Conquest of the Karankawas and Tonkawas, 1821–1859.* College Station: Texas A&M University Press, 1999.

Hinton, Harwood E. "The Military Career of John Ellis Wool, 1812–1863." Ph.D. dissertation, University of Wisconsin, 1960.

Hoebel, E. Adamson. *The Cheyenne Indians of the Great Plains.* New York: Holt, Rinehart and Winston, 1960.

Hoig, Stan. *The Sand Creek Massacre.* Norman: University of Oklahoma Press, 1961.

Horsman, Reginald. *The Causes of the War of 1812.* New York: A. B. Barnes, 1962.

————. *Expansion and American Indian Policy, 1783–1812.* Norman: University of Oklahoma Press, 1992.

Hoxie, Frederick E. *A Final Promise: The Campaign to Assimilate the Indians, 1880–1920*. Lincoln: University of Nebraska Press, 1984.

Hoyle, Richard W., ed. *The Estates of the English Crown, 1558–1640*. Cambridge: Cambridge University Press, 1992.

Hurt, R. Douglas. *The Ohio Frontier: Crucible of the Old Northwest, 1720–1830*. Bloomington: Indiana University Press, 1996.

Hurtado, Albert. *Indian Survival on the California Frontier*. New Haven: Yale University Press, 1988.

———. *John Sutter: A Life on the North American Frontier*. Norman: University of Oklahoma Press, 2006.

Hutton, Paul, ed. *The Custer Reader*. Lincoln: University of Nebraska Press, 1991.

———. *Phil Sheridan and His Army*. Norman: University of Oklahoma Press, 1985.

Hyman, Colette A. "Survival at Crow Creek, 1863–1866." *Minnesota History* 61 (Winter 2009): 148–61.

Innis, Ben. *Bloody Knife: Custer's Favorite Scout*. Bismarck, N.D.: Smokey Water Press, n.d.

Ishay, Micheline R. *The History of Human Rights: From Ancient Times to the Globalization Era*. Berkeley: University of California Press, 2004.

Jackson, John C. *A Little War of Destiny: The First Regiment of Oregon Mounted Volunteers and the Yakima Indian War of 1855–1856*. Fairfield, Washington, D.C.: Ye Galleon Press, 1996.

Jackson, Robert H., and Edward Castillo. *Indians, Franciscans, and Spanish Colonization: The Impact of the Mission System on California Indians*. Albuquerque: University of New Mexico Press, 1995.

Jacoby, Karl. *Shadows at Dawn: A Borderlands Massacre and the Violence of History*. New York: Penguin, 2008.

Jennings, Francis. *The Ambiguous Iroquois Empire: The Covenant Chain of Indian Tribes within English Colonies from Its Beginnings to the Lancaster Treaty of 1744*. New York: W. W. Norton, 1984.

———. *Empire of Fortune: Crowns, Colonies and Tribes in the Seven Years War in America*. New York: W. W. Norton, 1988.

———. *The Invasion of America: Indians, Colonialism, and the Cant of Conquest*. New York: W. W. Norton, 1976.

Jones, Trevor. "In Defense of Sovereignty: Cherokee Soldiers, White Officers, and Discipline in the Third Home Guard." *Chronicles of Oklahoma* 82 (Winter 2004–2005): 412–27.

Jortner, Alvin M. *The Gods of Prophetstown: The Battle of Tippecanoe and the Holy War for the American Frontier*. New York: Oxford University Press, 2012.

Josephy, Alvin M. *The Nez Perce Indians and the Opening of the West*. New Haven: Yale University Press, 1965.

Jung, Patrick J. *The Black Hawk War of 1832*. Norman: University of Oklahoma Press, 2008.

Kades, Eric. "History and Interpretation of the Great Case of *Johnson v. M'Intosh*." *Law and History Review* 19 (March 2001): 67–116.

Kamen, Henry. *Empire: How Spain Became a World Power, 1492–1763.* New York: Harper/Collins, 2003.

Kellogg, Louise P. *Frontier Retreat on the Upper Ohio, 1779–1781.* Madison: Wisconsin Historical Society, 1917.

Kelton, Paul. *Epidemics and Enslavement: Biological Catastrophe in the Southeast, 1492–1715.* Lincoln: University of Nebraska Press, 2007.

Kennedy, Roger G. *Mr. Jefferson's Lost Cause: Land, Farmers, Slavery, and the Louisiana Purchase.* New York: Oxford University Press, 2003.

Kenny, Kevin. *Peaceable Kingdom Lost: The Paxton Boys and the Destruction of William Penn's Holy Experiment.* New York: Oxford University Press, 2009.

Kessell, John L. *Pueblos, Spaniards, and the Kingdom of New Mexico.* Norman: University of Oklahoma Press, 2008.

Kidwell, Clara Sue. *Choctaws and Missionaries in Mississippi, 1818–1918.* Norman: University of Oklahoma Press, 1995.

Kiernan, Benedict. *Blood and Soil: A World History of Genocide and Extermination from Sparta to Darfur.* New Haven: Yale University Press, 2007.

———. *The Pol Pot Regime: Race, Power, and Genocide under Khmer Rouge, 1975–1979.* New Haven: Yale University Press, 1996.

Kime, Wayne R. *Colonel Richard Irving Dodge: The Life and Times of a Career Army Officer.* Norman: University of Oklahoma Press, 2006.

Krech, Shepard, III. *The Ecological Indian: Myth and History.* New York: W. W. Norton, 1999.

Kroeber, Alfred. *Handbook of California Indians.* Washington, D.C.: Smithsonian Institution, 1925.

Kroeber, Theodora. *Ishi in Two Worlds: A Biography of the Last Wild Indian in North America.* Berkeley: University of California Press, 1962.

Lack, Paul D. *The Texas Revolutionary Experience: A Political and Social History, 1835–1836.* College Station: Texas A&M University Press, 1992.

Larson, Robert W. *Gall: Lakota War Chief.* Norman: University of Oklahoma Press, 2007.

Leach, Douglas Edward. *Flintlock and Tomahawk: New England in King Philip's War.* New York: W. W. Norton, 1958.

Lederer, Edith M. "US Supports War Crimes Tribunal for First Time." *Washington Post,* March 2, 2011.

Lepore, Jill. *King Philip's War and the Origins of American Identity.* New York: Knopf, 1998.

Levene, Mark. *Genocide in the Age of the Nation-State: Volume II, The Rise of the West and the Coming of Genocide.* New York: I. B. Tauris, 2005.

Lockhart, James. *Of Things of the Indies: Essays Old and New in Early Latin American History.* Stanford: Stanford University Press, 1999.

Lookingbill, Brad D. *War Dance at Fort Marion: Plains Indian War Prisoners.* Norman: University of Oklahoma Press, 2006.

Lubetkin, John M. *Jay Cooke's Gamble: The Northern Pacific Railroad, the Sioux, and the Panic of 1873.* Norman: University of Oklahoma Press, 2006.

Lustig, Mary Lou. *The Imperial Executive in America: Sir Edmund Andros, 1637–1714.* Madison: Fairleigh Dickinson University Press, 2002.

Madley, Benjamin. "California's Yuki Indians: Defining Genocide in Native American History." *Western Historical Quarterly* 34 (Autumn 2008): 303–32.

———. "Patterns of Frontier Genocide, 1803–1910: The Aboriginal Tasmanians, the Yuki of California, and the Herero of Namibia." *Journal of Genocide Research* 6 (June 2004): 167–92.

Madsen, Brigham D. *Glory Hunter: A Biography of Patrick Edward Connor.* Salt Lake City: University of Utah Press, 1990.

Mahon, John K. *History of the Second Seminole War, 1835–1842.* Gainesville: University of Florida Press, 1967.

Mann, Barbara Alice. *George Washington's War on Native America.* Lincoln: University of Nebraska Press, 2008.

Mardock, Robert Winston. *The Reformers and the American Indian.* Columbia: University of Missouri Press, 1971.

McChristian, Douglas C. *Fort Bowie, Arizona: Combat Post of the Southwest, 1858–1894.* Norman: University of Oklahoma Press, 2005.

———. *Fort Laramie: Military Bastion on the High Plains.* Norman: Arthur H. Clark, 2008.

McConnell, Michael N. *A Country Between: The Upper Ohio Valley and Its Peoples, 1724–1774.* Lincoln: University of Nebraska Press, 1992.

McCorkle, Thomas. "Intergroup Conflict." In *Handbook of North American Indians,* vol. 8, *California,* ed. William Sturtevant, 694–700. Washington, D.C.: Smithsonian Institution, 1978.

McDermott, John D. *Forlorn Hope: The Battle of White Bird Canyon and the Beginning of the Nez Perce War.* Boise: Idaho State Historical Society, 1978.

———. *Red Cloud's War: The Bozeman Trail, 1866–1868.* 2 vols. Norman: Arthur H. Clark, 2010.

McLoughlin, William G. *Cherokee Renascence in the New Republic.* Princeton: Princeton University Press, 1986.

Megehee, Mark K. "Creek Nativism since 1865." *Chronicles of Oklahoma* 56 (Fall 1978): 279–99.

Merrell, James H. *The Indians' New World: Catawbas and Their Neighbors from European Contact through the Era of Removal.* New York: W. W. Norton, 1989.

———. "Shamokin, 'the Very Seat of the Prince of Darkness': Unsettling the Early American Frontier." In *Contact Points: American Frontiers from the Mohawk Valley to the Mississippi, 1750–1830,* ed. Andrew R. L. Cayton and Fredrika J. Teute, 16–59. Chapel Hill: University of North Carolina Press, 1998.

Meyer, Melissa L. *The White Earth Tragedy: Ethnicity and Dispossession at a Minnesota Anishinaabe Reservation, 1889–1920.* Lincoln: University of Nebraska Press, 1994.

Miller, David Humphreys. *Custer's Fall: The Native American Side of the Story.* New York: Duell and Pearce, 1957; reprint New York: Meridian, 1992.

Miller, Mark E. *Hollow Victory: The White River Expedition of 1879 and the Battle of Milk Creek.* Boulder: University of Colorado Press, 1997.

Miller, Susan A. *Coacoochee's Bones: A Seminole Saga*. Lawrence: University Press of Kansas, 2003.

Milne, George Edward. "Picking Up the Pieces: Natchez Coalescence in the Shatter Zone." In *Mapping the Mississippian Shatter Zone: The Colonial Indian Slave Trade and Regional Instability in the American South,* ed. Robbie Ethridge and Sheri M. Shuck-Hall, 388–424. Lincoln: University of Nebraska Press, 2009.

Missall, John, and Mary Lou Missall. *The Seminole Wars: America's Longest Indian Conflict*. Gainesville: University Press of Florida, 2004.

Monjeau-Marz, Corinne L. *The Dakota Internment at Fort Snelling, 1862–1864*. St. Paul: Prairie Smoke Press, 2005.

Morgan, Edmund S. *American Slavery, American Freedom: The Ordeal of Colonial Virginia*. New York: W. W. Norton, 1975.

Morgan, Sharon. *Land Settlement in Early Tasmania: Creating an Antipodean England*. New York: Cambridge University Press, 1991.

Moses, A. Dirk, ed. *Genocide and Settler Society: Frontier Violence and Stolen Indigenous Children in Australian History*. New York: Berghahn Books, 2004.

Murray, Keith A. *The Modocs and Their War*. Norman: University of Oklahoma Press, 1959; reprint 1984.

Myers, Erika. "Conquering Peace: Military Commissions as a Lawforce Strategy in the Mexican War." *American Journal of Criminal Law* 35, no. 2 (2008): 201–40.

Naimark, Norman M. *Fires of Hatred: Ethnic Cleansing in Twentieth-Century Europe*. Cambridge, Mass.: Harvard University Press, 2001.

———. *Stalin's Genocide*. Princeton: Princeton University Press, 2010.

Nichols, Roger L. *Black Hawk and the Warrior's Path*. Arlington Heights, Ill.: Harlan Davidson, 1992.

Oatis, Steven J. *A Colonial Complex: South Carolina's Frontiers in the Era of the Yamasee War, 1680–1730*. Lincoln: University of Nebraska Press, 2004.

Oberg, Michael Leroy. *Uncas: First of the Mohegans*. Ithaca: Cornell University Press, 2003.

Olson, James C. *Red Cloud and the Sioux Problem*. Lincoln: University of Nebraska Press, 1965.

Ostler, Jeffrey. *The Lakota and the Black Hills*. New York: Viking, 2010.

———. *The Plains Sioux and U.S. Colonialism from Lewis and Clark to Wounded Knee*. New York: Cambridge University Press, 2004.

Otis, D. S. *The Dawes Act and the Allotment of Indian Lands*. Norman: University of Oklahoma Press, 1973.

Owens, Robert M. *Mr. Jefferson's Hammer: William Henry Harrison and the Origins of American Indian Policy*. Norman: University of Oklahoma Press, 2007.

Pagden, Anthony. *Lords of All the World: Ideologies of Empire in Spain, Britain, and France, c. 1500–c. 1800*. New Haven: Yale University Press, 1995.

Palmer, Frederick. *Clark of the Ohio: A Life of George Rogers Clark*. New York: Dodd and Mead, 1929.

Parker, Watson. *Gold in the Black Hills*. Norman: University of Oklahoma Press, 1966.

Paul, R. Eli. *Blue Water Creek and the First Sioux War, 1854–1856.* Norman: University of Oklahoma Press, 2004.

Pawlisch, Hans S. *Sir John Davies and the Conquest of Ireland: A Study in Legal Imperialism.* Cambridge: Cambridge University Press, 1985.

Pearce, Roy Harvey. *Savagism and Civilization: A Study of the Indian and the American Mind.* Baltimore: Johns Hopkins University Press, 1953.

Pearson, J. Diane. *The Nez Perces in the Indian Territory.* Norman: University of Oklahoma Press, 2008.

Peterson, Merrill D. *Thomas Jefferson and the New Nation: A Biography.* New York: Oxford University Press, 1970.

Phillips, George Harwood. *"Bring Them under Subjection": California's Tejon Reservation and Beyond, 1852–1864.* Lincoln: University of Nebraska Press, 2004.

———. *Indians and Indian Agents: The Origins of the Reservation System in California, 1849–1852.* Norman: University of Oklahoma Press, 1997.

Pope, Peter E. *The Many Landfalls of John Cabot.* Toronto: University of Toronto Press, 1997.

Potter, Steven R. "Early English Effects on Virginia Algonquian Exchange and Tribute in the Tidewater Potomac." In *Powhatan's Mantle: Indians in the Colonial Southeast,* ed. Gregory A. Waselkov, Peter H. Wood, and Tom Hatley, 215–42. Lincoln: University of Nebraska Press, 1989.

Power, Samantha. *"A Problem from Hell": America and the Age of Genocide.* New York: Basic Books, 2002.

Price, Catherine. *The Oglala People, 1841–1879: A Political History.* Lincoln: University of Nebraska Press, 1996.

Prucha, Francis Paul. *American Indian Policy in the Formative Years: The Indian Trade and Intercourse Acts, 1790–1834.* Cambridge, Mass.: Harvard University Press, 1962; reprint Lincoln: University of Nebraska Press, 1970, 46–53.

———. *The Great Father: The United States Government and the American Indians.* 2 vols. Lincoln: University of Nebraska Press, 1984.

———. *The Sword of the Republic: The United States Army on the Frontier, 1783–1846.* Bloomington: Indiana University Press, 1965.

Rand, Jacki Thompson. *Kiowa Humanity and the Invasion of the State.* Lincoln: University of Nebraska Press, 2008.

Rawls, James J. *Indians of California: The Changing Image.* Norman: University of Oklahoma Press, 1984.

Reid, John Philip. *A Better Kind of Hatchet: Law, Trade, and Diplomacy in the Cherokee Nation during the Early Years of European Contact.* University Park: Pennsylvania State University Press, 1976.

Remini, Robert V. *Andrew Jackson and His Indian Wars.* New York: Penguin Books, 2002.

Richards, Kent. *Isaac I. Stevens: Young Man in a Hurry.* Provo, Utah: Brigham Young University Press, 1979.

Richter, Daniel. *Facing East from Indian Country: A Native History of Early America.* Cambridge, Mass.: Harvard University Press, 2001.

Riddle, Jefferson C. Davis. *The Indian History of the Modoc War.* 1914; reprint Mechanicsburg, Pa.: Stockpole Books, 2004.

Robertson, Lindsay G. *Conquest by Law: How the Discovery of America Dispossessed Indigenous Peoples of Their Land.* New York: Oxford University Press, 2005.

Rohrbough, Malcolm J. *The Land Office Business: The Settlement and Administration of the American Public Lands, 1789–1837.* New York: Oxford University Press, 1968; reprint Belmont, Calif.: Wadsworth Publishing, 1990.

Roseberry, William. *Anthropologies and Histories: Essays in Culture, History, and Political Economy.* New Brunswick: Rutgers University Press, 1991.

Rosenheim, James M. *The Emergence of a Ruling Order: English Landed Society, 1650–1750.* London: Longman, 1998.

Ross, John R. *War on the Run: The Epic Story of Robert Rogers and the Conquest of America's First Frontier.* New York: Bantam Books, 2009.

Rountree, Helen C. *The Powhatan Indians of Virginia: Their Traditional Culture.* Norman: University of Oklahoma Press, 1989.

Royce, Charles C. *Indian Land Cessions in the United States.* Washington, D.C.: Government Printing Office, 1900.

Ruby, Robert H., and John A. Brown. *The Cayuse Indians: Imperial Tribesmen of Old Oregon.* Norman: University of Oklahoma Press, 1972.

———. *The Spokane Indians: Children of the Sun.* Norman: University of Oklahoma Press, 1970.

Rutman, Darrett B. *Winthrop's Boston: Portrait of a Puritan Town, 1630–1647.* New York: W. W. Norton, 1965.

Salinas, Martín. *Indians of the Rio Grande Delta: Their Role in the History of Southern Texas and Northeastern Mexico.* Austin: University of Texas Press, 1990.

Satz, Ronald. *American Indian Policy in the Jacksonian Era.* Lincoln: University of Nebraska Press, 1975.

Sauer, Carl. *Sixteenth Century North America: The Land and the People as Seen by the Europeans.* Berkeley: University of California Press, 1971.

Saunt, Claudio. *A New Order of Things: Property, Power, and the Transformation of the Creek Indians, 1733–1816.* New York: Cambridge University Press, 1999.

Scharnhorst, Gary. *Bret Harte: Opening the American Literary West.* Norman: University of Oklahoma Press, 2000.

Schiessl, Christoph. "An Element of Genocide: Rape, Total War, and International Law in the Twentieth Century." *Journal of Genocide Research* 4 (2002): 197–210.

Schlicke, Carl P. *General George Wright: Guardian of the Pacific Coast.* Norman: University of Oklahoma Press, 1988.

Schwartz, E. A. *The Rogue River Indian War and Its Aftermath, 1850–1980.* Norman: University of Oklahoma Press, 1997.

Service, Elman. *Primitive Social Organization: An Evolutionary Perspective.* New York: Random House, 1962.

Shannon, Timothy J. *Indians and Colonists at the Crossroads of Empire: The Albany Congress of 1754.* Ithaca: Cornell University Press, 2000.

Shapard, Bud. *Chief Loco: Apache Peacemaker.* Norman: University of Oklahoma Press, 2010.

Sheehan, Bernard W. *Seeds of Extinction: Jeffersonian Philanthropy and the American Indian.* Chapel Hill: University of North Carolina Press, 1973.

Sievers, Michael A. "Malfeasance or Indirection: Administration of the California Indian Superintendency's Business Affairs." *Southern California Quarterly* 53 (Fall 1974): 273–94.

Silbernagel, Robert. *Troubled Trails: The Meeker Affair and the Expulsion of the Utes from Colorado.* Salt Lake City: University of Utah Press, 2011.

Silver, Peter. *Our Savage Neighbors: How Indian War Transformed Early America.* New York: W. W. Norton, 2008.

Simmons, Marc. *The Last Conquistador: Juan de Oñate and the Settling of the Far Southwest.* Norman: University of Oklahoma Press, 1991.

Simmons, Virginia McConnell. *The Ute Indians of Utah, Colorado, and New Mexico.* Boulder: University Press of Colorado, 2000.

Smith, Shannon D. *Give Me Eighty Men: Women and the Myth of the Fetterman Fight.* Lincoln: University of Nebraska Press, 2008.

Snyder, Timothy. *Bloodlands: Europe between Hitler and Stalin.* New York: Basic Books, 2010.

Sprague, Marshall. *Massacre: The Tragedy at White River.* Boston: Little, Brown, 1957.

Stannard, David E. *American Holocaust: The Conquest of the New World.* New York: Oxford University Press, 1992.

Starling, Suzanne. *Land Is the Cry: Warren Angus Ferris, Pioneer Texas Surveyor and Founder of Dallas County.* Austin: Texas State Historical Association, 1998.

Strobridge, William F. *Regulars in the Redwoods: The U.S. Army in Northern California, 1852–1861.* Spokane, Wash.: Arthur H. Clark, 1994.

Sugden, John. *Blue Jacket: Warrior of the Shawnees.* Lincoln: University of Nebraska Press, 2000.

Sweeney, Edwin R. *Cochise, Chiricahua Apache Chief.* Norman: University of Oklahoma Press, 1991.

———. *From Cochise to Geronimo: The Chiricahua Apaches, 1874–1886.* Norman: University of Oklahoma Press, 2010.

Tanner, Helen Hornbeck. *Atlas of Great Lakes Indian History.* Norman: University of Oklahoma Press, 1987.

Tate, Michael L. *Indians and Emigrants: Encounters on the Overland Trails.* Norman: University of Oklahoma Press, 2006.

Taylor, Alan. *The Civil War of 1812: American Citizens, British Subjects, Irish Rebels, and Indian Allies.* New York: Vintage, 2011.

———. *The Divided Ground: Indians, Settlers, and the Northern Borderlands of the American Revolution.* New York: Alfred A. Knopf, 2006.

Taylor, John. *The Battle of Glorieta Pass: A Gettysburg in the West, March 26–28, 1862.* Albuquerque: University of New Mexico Press, 1998.

Thomas, David Hurst, ed. *Columbian Consequences: Volume 2, Archaeological and Historical Perspectives on the Spanish Borderlands East.* 2 vols. Washington, D.C.: Smithsonian Institution Press, 1990.

Thompson, Gerald. *Edward F. Beale and the American West.* Albuquerque: University of New Mexico Press, 1983.

Thornton, Russell. *American Indian Holocaust and Survival: A Population History since 1492.* Norman: University of Oklahoma Press, 1987.

Thrapp, Dan. *The Conquest of Apachería.* Norman: University of Oklahoma Press, 1975.

Tomlins, Christopher. *Freedom Bound: Law, Labor and Civil Identity in Colonizing English America, 1580–1865.* New York: Cambridge University Press, 2010.

Trafzer, Clifford E. *The Kit Carson Campaign: The Last Great Navajo War.* Norman: University of Oklahoma Press, 1982.

Trafzer, Clifford E., and Joel R. Hyer, eds. *Exterminate Them!: Written Accounts of the Murder, Rape, and Enslavement of Native Americans during the California Gold Rush.* East Lansing: Michigan State University Press, 2000.

Trennert, Robert A., Jr. *Alternative to Extinction: Federal Indian Policy and the Beginnings of the Reservation System, 1846–1851.* Philadelphia: Temple University Press, 1975.

Trigger, Bruce G. *Children of Aataentsic: A History of the Huron People to 1660.* 2 vols. Kingston, Canada: McGill–Queen's University Press, 1987.

———. "Early Native North American Responses to European Contact: Romantic versus Rationalistic Interpretations." *Journal of American History* 77 (March 1991): 1200–1204.

Trigger, Bruce G., and Wilcomb E. Washburn, eds. *The Cambridge History of the Native Peoples of the Americas.* 2 vols. New York: Cambridge University Press, 1996.

Unrau, William E. *The Kansas Indians: A History of the Wind People, 1673–1873.* Norman: University of Oklahoma Press, 1971.

Utley, Robert M. *Cavalier in Buckskin: George Armstrong Custer and the Western Military Frontier.* Norman: University of Oklahoma Press, 1988.

———. *Frontiersmen in Blue: The United States Army and the Indian, 1848–1865.* New York: Macmillan, 1967.

———. *The Indian Frontier of the American West, 1846–1890.* Albuquerque: University of New Mexico Press, 1984.

———. *The Lance and the Shield: The Life and Times of Sitting Bull.* New York: Henry Holt, 1993.

———. *The Last Days of the Sioux Nation.* New Haven: Yale University Press, 1963.

Vattel, Emer de. *The Law of Nations: Or, Principles of the Law of Nature, Applied to the Conduct and Affairs of Nations, and Sovereigns, with Three Early Essays on the Origin and Nature of Natural Law and on Luxury* (1758). Reprint: Bèla Kapossy and Richard Whatmore, eds. Indianapolis: Liberty Funds, 2008.

Veracini, Lorenzo. *Settler Colonialism: A Theoretical Overview.* New York: Palgrave Macmillan, 2010.

Wagner, David E. *Powder River Odyssey: Nelson Cole's Western Campaign of 1865: The Journals of Lyman G. Bennett and Other Eyewitness Accounts.* Norman: Arthur H. Clark, 2009.

Wallace, Anthony F. C. *The Death and Rebirth of the Seneca.* New York: Vintage Books, 1969.

————. *Jefferson and the Indians: The Tragic Fate of the First Americans.* Cambridge, Mass.: Harvard University Press, 1999.

Washburn, Wilcomb E. *The Assault on Indian Tribalism.* Philadelphia: Lippincott, 1975.

————, ed. *The Garland Library of Narratives of North American Indian Captives.* 103 vols. New York: Garland Publishing, 1975.

————. *The Governor and the Rebel: A History of Bacon's Rebellion in Virginia.* New York: W. W. Norton, 1957.

Watson, Blake. *Buying America from the Indians: Johnson v. McIntosh and the History of Native Land Rights.* Norman: University of Oklahoma Press, 2012.

Waziyatawin, Angela Wilson. *In the Footsteps of Our Ancestors: The Dakota Commemorative Marches of the 21st Century.* St. Paul, Minn.: Living Justice Press, 2006.

Weber, David. *The Spanish Frontier in North America.* New Haven: Yale University Press, 1992.

West, Elliott. *Contested Plains: Indians, Goldseekers, and the Rush to Colorado.* Lawrence: University Press of Kansas, 1998.

————. *The Last Indian War: The Nez Perce Story.* New York: Oxford University Press, 2009.

Whaley, Gray H. *Oregon and the Collapse of Illahee: U.S. Empire and the Transformation of an Indigenous World, 1792–1859.* Chapel Hill: University of North Carolina Press, 2010.

White, G. Edward. *The Marshall Court and Cultural Change, 1815–1835.* New York: Oxford University Press, 1991.

White, Richard. *The Middle Ground: Indians, Empires, and Republics in the Great Lakes Region, 1650–1815.* New York: Cambridge University Press, 1991.

————. *Railroads: The Transcontinentals and the Making of Modern America.* New York: W. W. Norton, 2011.

————. *The Roots of Dependency: Subsistence, Environment, and Social Change among the Choctaws, Pawnees, and Navajos.* Lincoln: University of Nebraska Press, 1983.

Wilkins, David E., and K. Tsianina Lomawaima, *Uneven Ground: American Indian Sovereignty and Federal Law.* Norman: University of Oklahoma Press, 2001.

Wilkins, Thurman. *Cherokee Tragedy: The Ridge Family and the Decimation of a People.* Norman: University of Oklahoma Press, 1970.

Wolfe, Patrick. "Settler Colonialism and the Elimination of the Native." *Journal of Genocide Research* 8 (December 2006): 387–409.

Woodward, Grace Steele. *The Cherokees.* Norman: University of Oklahoma Press, 1963.

Wray, Jacilee, ed. *Native Peoples of the Olympic Peninsula: Who We Are.* Norman: University of Oklahoma Press, 2002.

Wunder, John R. *"Retained by the People": A History of American Indians and the Bill of Rights.* New York: Oxford University Press, 1994.

WEB SOURCE

Rome Statute of the International Criminal Court (2002). Available at www .preventgenocide.org/law/icc/statute/part-a.htm.

INDEX